The Ethnicity Reader

Second Edition

The Ethnicity Reader

Nationalism, Multiculturalism and Migration

Second Edition

Edited by
Montserrat Guibernau
and John Rex

polity

First edition published in 1997 by Polity Press
This edition published in 2010 by Polity Press

Polity Press
65 Bridge Street
Cambridge CB2 1UR, UK

Polity Press
350 Main Street
Malden, MA 02148, USA

ISBN-13: 978-0-7456-4701-2 (hardback)
ISBN-13: 978-0-7456-4702-9 (paperback)

A catalogue record for this book is available from the British Library.

Typeset in 10 on 12 pt Sabon
by Toppan Best-set Premedia Limited
Printed and bound in Great Britain by MPG Books Group Limited, Bodmin, Cornwall

The publisher has used its best endeavours to ensure that the URLs for external
websites referred to in this book are correct and active at the time of going to press.
However, the publisher has no responsibility for the websites and can make no
guarantee that a site will remain live or that the content is or will remain appropriate.

Every effort has been made to trace all copyright holders, but if any have been
inadvertently overlooked the publisher will be pleased to include any necessary credits
in any subsequent reprint or edition.

For further information on Polity, visit our website: www.politybooks.com

Contents

Acknowledgements

The editors and publishers wish to thank the following for permission to reproduce copyright material:

The University of California Press for material from *Economics and Society*, 2 volumes, by Max Weber, edited and translated by Guenther Roth and Claus Wittich, copyright © 1978, the Regents of the University of California, published by the University of California (original German publication by J. C. B. Mohr (Paul Siebeck) Tübingen).

Blackwell Publishing Ltd for material from *The Ethnic Origin of Nations* by Anthony D. Smith copyright © 1986, reproduced with permission of Blackwell Publishing Ltd.

Pluto Press for material from *Ethnicity and Nationalism* by Thomas Hylland Eriksen copyright © 1993, Pluto Press.

Verso for material from *Imagined Communities* by Benedict Anderson copyright © 2006, Verso.

Blackwell Publishing Ltd and Cornell University Press for material from *Nations and Nationalism* by Ernest Gellner copyright © 1983 Ernest Gellner reproduced with permission of Blackwell Publishing Ltd and Cornell University Press.

Cambridge University Press and Eric J. Hobsbawm for material from *Nations and Nationalism since 1780* (Canto 1990, 1992) by E. J. Hobsbawm copyright © 1990, 1992 Cambridge University Press, reproduced with permission.

Princeton University Press for material from *Ethnic Conflict and International Security* edited by Michael E. Brown, 1993 copyright © the International Institute for Strategic Studies, London, England; Chapters 2–12 were first published in *Survival: The IISS Quarterly*, reprinted by permission of Princeton University Press.

Sage Publications Inc for material from Franke Wilmer, *The Indigenous Voice in World Politics* copyright © 1993, permission conveyed through Copyright Clearance Center.

Centre for Research in Ethnic Relations, University of Warwick for material from 'The concept of a multicultural society' by John Rex, published in *Occasional Papers in Ethnic Relations No. 3*, CRER, 1985, reproduced with permission from Professor Layton-Henry.

Dr J. Kuper for material from 'Plural societies' by Leo Kuper from *Pluralism in Africa*, University of California Press by L. Kuper and M. Smith 1969 copyright © Dr Jenny Kuper.

Oxford University Press for material from Will Kymlicka, *Multicultural Citizenship*, © Will Kymlicka 1995.

Professor Dr Frank-Olaf Radtke for material from *Ethnic Mobilization in a Multicultural Society* by F-O. Radtke edited by Rex and Drury, copyright © 1994 Professor Dr Frank-Olaf Radtke.

Population Council for material from 'Theories of international migration: a review and appraisal' (here 'Causes of migration') by Douglas S. Massey et al. in *Population and Development Review*, Vol. 19(3), September 1993 copyright © Population Council.

American Anthropological Association for material from 'Diasporas' by James Clifford from *Cultural Anthropology*, Vol. 9(3), pp. 302–38, 1994 reproduced by permission of the American Anthropological Association; not for sale or further reproduction.

Polity Press and Michel Wieviorka for material from *Racism, Modernity and Identity* by Michel Wieviorka edited by Rattansi and Westwood, copyright © 1994 Michel Wieviorka, reproduced with permission.

Beacon Press for material from *Turning Back* by Stephen Steinberg copyright © 1995, 2001 Stephen Steinberg, reprinted by permission of Beacon Press, Boston.

La Découverte for material from 'Class racism' in *Race, nation, classe, les identités ambiguës* by Étienne Balibar and Immanuel Wallerstein copyright © La Découverte, Paris, 1988.

Cambridge University Press and Rogers Brubaker for material from '1848 in 1998: the politics of commemoration in Hungary, Romania, and Slovakia' by Rogers Brubaker and Margrit Feischmidt, published in *Comparative Studies in Society and History*, 44(4): 700–44, 2002, originally titled 'Ethnicity without Groups', and published in *Archives européennes de sociologie XLIII*, 2 November 2002: 163–89 copyright © Cambridge University Press, reproduced with permission.

Lynne Reinner Publishers, Inc. for material from Toby Dodge from *Iraq: Preventing a New Generation of Conflict* edited by Markus E. Bouillon, David M. Malone and Ben Rowswell copyright © 2007 the International Peace Institute, used with permission by Lynne Reinner Publishers, Inc.

Russell Mellett for material from 'The importance of raising your own revenues' by Russell Mellett, *Scottish Affairs*, No. 67 (spring 2009), copyright © 2009, reproduced with permission of Institute of Governance, The University of Edinburgh.

University of Toronto Press, Inc. for material from *Federalism, Citizenship, and Quebec, Debating Multinationalism* by Alain G. Gagnon and Raffaele

Iacovino copyright © University of Toronto Press, 2006, reprinted with permission of the publisher.

Ramón Máiz for material from 'Breogan's nation', by Ramón Máiz.

Palgrave Macmillan for material from *Iran, Iraq, and the Legacies of War* by M. R. Izady edited by Lawrence G. Potter and Gary G. Sick copyright © 2004, reproduced with permission of Palgrave Macmillan.

Seminar Publications for material from *What is Multiculturalism?* by Bhikhu Parekh, adapted from http://www.india-seminar.com/1999/484/484%20 parekh.htm copyright © Seminar Publications.

Tariq Modood for material from 'Multiculturalism, citizenship and national identity' by Tariq Modood, copyright © 2007.

Center for Migration Studies for material from 'Rethinking assimilation theory for a new era of immigration' by Richard Alba and Victor Nee published in *International Migration Review*, Vol. 31, No. 4, *Special Issue: Immigrant Adaptation and Native-Born Responses in the Making of Americans*, winter 1997 copyright © Center for Migration Studies.

Taylor and Francis Ltd and Ma Rong for material from 'A new perspective in guiding ethnic relations in the twenty-first century: "de-politicization" of ethnicity in China' by Ma Rong, *Asian Ethnicity*, Vol. 8(3), October 2007, Routledge, reprinted by permission of the author and publisher (Taylor and Francis Ltd, http://www.informaworld.com).

Li Minghuan for material from 'Transnational migrant brokerage in China: functioning between the state and individual' by Li Minghuan, reproduced with permission.

In some instances we have been unable to trace the owners of copyright material and we would appreciate any information that would enable us to do so.

Introduction

The Growing Importance of the Concept of Ethnicity

The term ethnicity became increasingly crucial in the social sciences in the 1960s, a period marked by the consolidation of the process of decolonization in Africa and Asia as numerous new nation states were created. Anti-colonial and anti-racist arguments contributed to the generation of a new vocabulary in which the term 'ethnicity' was used by sociologists and others, as Spoonley has suggested, to acknowledge 'the *positive* feelings of belonging to a cultural group' (Spoonley [1988] 1993).

In more recent years, since the collapse of the Communist regimes, more negative aspects of ethnicity have come to the fore. The notion of 'ethnic cleansing' in the former Yugoslavia brought the very idea of ethnicity into political disrepute. However much a sense of shared ethnicity created positive feelings of belonging to an in-group, it seemed to imply total hostility and genocide towards neighbouring out-groups.

An additional reason for an increasing use of the term ethnicity was the coming to northern Europe of immigrants from post-colonial societies and from dependent economies. Their presence in the European Union was seen by many as constituting a political problem, a cultural problem and an identity problem. Moreover, since some of these immigrants would move on to North America, they were seen as constituting transnational communities with less than a complete commitment to the nation states in whose territory they had first settled. In North America, while many European immigrants had been assimilated over a period of more than a century, there now appeared two problems: that of assimilating new immigrants coming directly or indirectly from Asia, Africa and Latin America; and that of integrating black or African-American residents descended in part from a slave population and coming out of a semi-colonial plantation economy.

Whether it was viewed in positive or negative terms, however, one thing was clear. Ethnic bonding and ethnic identity were becoming more important for sociology and social psychology than mere biological descent or class. While gender differences were, it is true, given increasing prominence, their study always vied with the study of ethnicity.

In Part I of this collection we have included essays dealing with the relation between the concept of ethnicity and those of the nation, nationalism and the nation state. In Part II the essays deal with transnational migrant communities and the constitution of multicultural societies.

The Theory of Nationalism and the Concept of Ethnicity

The new emphasis upon ethnicity posed important problems for the theory of nations and nationalism. Theory in this area dealt with the nation in its eighteenth- and nineteenth-century European forms: the modern nation was seen in rational terms as part of the modernizing project of industrial societies. It was now increasingly recognized, however, that, far from resting solely on this rationalizing base, the nation state might be held together emotionally by bonds not unlike ethnic ones and would at the same time generate opposition and resistance by subordinated ethnic nations.

In attempting to grapple with this new intellectual situation sociologists could gain little from the classical sociological tradition. Marxism seemed to regard ethnicity as a form of false consciousness which would be replaced in due course by a consciousness of shared and opposed interests, while the tradition of Tönnies ([1887] 1963) and Durkheim (1933) was more concerned with the contrast between traditional and modern society, understanding the latter in terms of the concepts of 'Gesellschaft' and 'organic solidarity'.

The one classical theorist who did find space for a consideration of the ethnic concept was Max Weber, who sought, within the limitations of his own time, to conceptualize it in contrast to the notions of class, status and party. Weber called ethnic groups 'those human groups that entertain a subjective belief in their common descent because of similarities of physical type or of customs or of both, or because of memories of colonisation or migration' (Weber [1922] 1968: 389). This is an attempt at a comprehensive definition and it will be useful to draw attention to some of its implications.

In the first place it is clear that Weber distinguished ethnic groups from 'races' conceived in biological terms. It is not biological difference alone that constitutes an ethnic group, 'common customs' are also a factor. However, it is not simply having physical or cultural characteristics that is important but rather the subjective perception of these characteristics, both by those who share them and by those who react to them.

Secondly, Weber did not believe that shared ethnicity of itself leads to group formation. It only facilitates group formation, particularly in the political sphere. It is political community, however it is organized, which appeals to shared ethnicity and brings it into action. Yet, once ethnic groups have been constituted politically in this way, the belief in common ethnicity 'tends to persist even after the disintegration of the political community, unless drastic differences in the custom, physical type, or, above all, language exist among its members' (Weber

[1922] 1968: 389). Clearly, then, Weber saw united political action as central to the dynamic of ethnicity.

Thirdly, as a consequence, Weber had a strong sense of the role of history in shaping ethnic groups, which he perceived as having memories of a common past, attachment to a clearly demarcated territory and certain traditions or ways of life. All of these elements may survive for a long time in the collective consciousness of peoples who may have lost the political institutions which used to represent them, or may have migrated or been forced to migrate and become inhabitants and even citizens of nation states controlled by others. These are factors involved in the nationalisms of subordinate and minority groups which act as a counterweight to the incorporative rationalizing processes of the modern state.

Weber, it will be noted, did recognize the experience of migration in the history and consciousness of ethnic nations. Such a reference to the migration experience is at odds with the sense of belonging which the nation states in lands of present settlement may seek to encourage or impose. This is also a factor of central importance among immigrant communities in contemporary Europe and the US, and it is a theme to which we return in our discussion of 'multiculturalism' later in this introduction.

Fourthly, Weber recognized that ethnicity serves to delimit 'social circles' which are not identical with 'endogenous connubial groups'. What happens, however, is that some of the characteristics of such groups are attributed through myths and symbols to wider social circles. This, indeed, is the essence of the constitution of a so-called '*ethnie*'. Symbols are used to stand in for the presence of actual kin.

These issues are of some importance in such countries as contemporary Germany, where Germanness is thought to be based primarily upon the *jus sanguinis*. In these cases the subjective belief is that what unites Germans is not a shared culture but a unity of descent, a unity of blood. It matters little that this cannot really exist after centuries of intermarriage with those among whom they have settled. What is important is a myth through which the ethnic community has attributed to its sense of unity some of the characteristics of the small 'endogamous connubial group'.

One factor which must be taken into account in any discussion of ethnicity is the difference between the ethnicity claimed by the people themselves and that attributed to them by others. In either case the perception of ethnicity will rest not upon some scientific sociological truth but on subjective interpretation. Moreover, the subjective interpretations of the difference between groups may vary enormously in attitude to what group members think about themselves and how they are regarded by others. Those who classify them from the outside may do so in terms of particular aspects of physical appearance or culture, while different criteria may be applied in classifying themselves.

A point which is sometimes made is that the term 'ethnic group' may be used only to classify minorities and inferiors, whereas majority and dominant groups do not see themselves as ethnic at all. Thus, in Britain, the term 'ethnic minorities' is used to refer primarily to non-white immigrants, while in some other countries the term refers to such groups as the Australian Aborigines, the Sami in the Scandinavian countries, Roma or Gypsies, or the First Nations (Native Americans) of North America who seek to live outside the modern economy and polity, although sometimes seeking to develop their economic resources for their own advantage.

A further problem for the theory of ethnicity is posed by the use of the term 'ethnic identity'. Identity is both a psychological and a sociological term. It may provide 'a definition, an interpretation of the self that establishes what and where the person is in both social and psychological terms' (Guibernau 1996: 72). On the one hand it helps the individual to produce order in his or her own individual life. On the other it helps to place that individual within a group or involves 'identification' with a collectivity. Both of these forms of identity may be accomplished through the use of symbols. These two aspects of identity vary independently of each other. As Anthony Cohen put it, 'ethnicity has come to be regarded as a mode of action and of representation: it refers to a decision people make to depict themselves or others symbolically as the bearers of a certain cultural identity' (Cohen 1994: 119); but 'the apparently monolithic or generalised character of ethnicity at the collective level [...] does not preempt the continual reconstruction of ethnicity at a personal level' (Cohen 1994: 120). Others have pointed to the fact that acceptance of multiple identifications at a collective level does not mean a loss of identity at an individual and psychological level. It is simply a fact of human existence that human beings live within, and identify with, a multiplicity of groups according to occasion, without becoming individually psychologically disturbed; such disturbance, however, might occur among a minority.

The social dimensions of identity and identification may, as we have argued, be either chosen or imposed. Political communities of all shapes and sizes have sought to instil in their members a sentiment of belonging and a belief in a common destiny. Around the late eighteenth century and the early nineteenth, a process was initiated by which old loyalties to the lord or the monarch were replaced by loyalty to the nation. The nation thus became an emotionally charged object and nationalism emerged as an ideology centred upon the sentiment of belonging to a particular community and the subsequent desire to see it flourish and develop.[1] The nation state was created as a political institution with a territorial base which utilized the doctrine of nationalism in its foundational moment to generate a common culture and a sense of belonging among its members. Most of these nation states had a multinational character since they were established through dynastic unions and by conquest and annexations. Once the nation state was created, however, whether out of one nation or as a multinational or imperial entity, it actively promoted the cultural homogenization of its members and even appealed to a new common ethnicity which had to be constructed in a symbolic manner.

In the mid-nineteenth century the Romantic movement brought about the idea that cultural difference mainly expressed through linguistic diversity was valuable and had to be preserved. Such an assertion prompted the emergence of cultural movements (such as the Catalan *Renaixença*) to defend minority cultures struggling to survive within nation states; the latter were trying to expand an official culture and language which did not take account of – or sometimes actively pursued the eradication of – minority cultures and languages, perceived as a threat to the integrity of the state. Some of these initially cultural movements of resistance would turn into nationalist movements, vindicating the rights of nations once absorbed into nation states to exist and develop their own cultures and languages. They would then become nations without states claiming the right to decide about their political future.

The concepts of ethnicity and nationalism imply a certain commonality among members of a group, the ethnic group in one case, the nation in the other; these are constructed symbolically and presuppose the existence of boundaries which separate one group from another. In fact they both emphasize minimal differences between the members of certain groups. The nation predicates continuity with the past and common descent and this is how ethnicity is brought into nationalism.

The belief in the uniformity and the ancestral origins of a community which considers itself a natural grouping is not, however, a feature which defines all nationalisms. Greenfeld (1992) has made a useful distinction between 'ethnic' and 'civic' nationalism. Civic nationalism is identical with citizenship, and, in this case, 'nationality is at least in principle open and voluntaristic, it can sometimes be acquired'. Ethnic nationalism believes nationality 'to be inherent – one can neither acquire it if one does not have it, nor change it if one does; it has nothing to do with individual will, but constitutes a genetic characteristic' (Greenfeld 1992: 11). Common ethnicity is not a constant in all nationalisms; more than that, ethnicity is in no way conducive to nationality. According to Greenfeld, 'the population of the United States of America, the identity of which is unmistakably national and which undoubtedly possesses a well-developed sense of uniqueness, is a case in point: it has no "ethnic" characteristics because its population is not an "ethnic community"' (Greenfeld 1992: 13).

The appeal to common ethnicity in terms of a common cultural identity, which may or may not have a direct link with common descent, is often invoked by political leaders as a factor of social cohesion. In doing this, they reflect the force of the belief in a common ethnicity, or, in the case of nationalism, the power of the idea of belonging to the same nation. Ethnicity and nationalism may be latent for years and suddenly re-emerge with unexpected vigour, as has happened in the former Soviet Republics. In fact they are useful tools in periods of ideological vacuum. After the demise of communism, nationalism became a prominent alternative in a set of countries lacking a democratic tradition and unused to competing diverse political ideologies. At present nationalism is showing afresh its capacity to bring together people from different social and cultural backgrounds. Billig argues that 'nationalism, far from being an intermittent mood in established nations, is the endemic condition'. He uses the term 'banal nationalism' 'to cover the ideological habits which enable the established nations of the West to be reproduced' (Billig 1995: 6).

A shared ethnicity is sometimes made a condition of establishing membership of particular nations. In these cases nationalism adopts an ethnic character and, depending upon the political ideologies to which nationalism is attached, it might lead to violence and xenophobia. On the other hand, it might adopt what could be called a Durkheimian outlook, following the principle that nations may somehow become the vehicle of the human ideal, insofar as they assume that their main task is not to expand by extending their borders, but to improve the level of their members' morality (Giddens 1987: 201; Durkheim [1973]: 101). The connection between ethnicity and violence stems from the idea that those who do not belong should be treated as potential or actual enemies. Discrimination and the annihilation of the different follow from this assumption and are exemplified in nazism, fascism and other movements using 'ethnic cleansing' as a policy against selected strangers.

The meaning of ethnicity is not exhausted by its relation with violence. The appeal to a common ethnicity which emphasizes commonality of culture is actively defended by nationalist movements struggling for self-determination. This is the case in nations without states such as Catalonia, Quebec or Scotland: the larger states in which they are contained are usually reluctant to recognize their own multinational character. The plea for self-determination was also crucial in the Wilsonian dispensation of 1918 which was later involved in the process of decolonization of European empires in Asia and Africa. Nations without states continue to struggle for self-determination, their various political scenarios depending upon the political will of the state within which they are included.

In Part I we have sought to bring together extracts which deal with the relation of ethnicity to nationalism. This is important because much of the theorization of nations, the nation state and nationalism has been modernist in its emphasis and has underplayed not only the need of even the nation state to find a basis for emotional and moral attachment for its members but the fact that, in their modernizing projects, these nation states met ethnic resistance. We would hope that the extracts included here illustrate some of the complexity of the engagement of ethnicity with nationalism.

Ethnicity, Migration and Multiculturalism

Part II deals with the notion of multicultural societies and with the relation of transnational migrant communities to the nation state. To some extent this suggests that two separate problematics have developed, one concerned with ethnicity and nationalism, the other with ethnicity and migration. Another view is that these two problematics have a common root in a more general theory of ethnicity from which both may be thought to branch.

Some of these theoretical issues are covered in John Rex's discussion of 'The concept of a multicultural society'. Rex suggests that the theory of ethnicity has necessarily to address the problems raised by the notion of primordial ethnicity on the one hand and that of 'instrumental' or 'situational' ethnicity on the other. The notion of primordiality is a questionable one if it suggests inexplicable forms of bonding and social relationships. The task of social science may, indeed, be precisely to explain what appears inexplicable. A consideration of Geertz's attempt (Geertz 1963) to define primordiality shows that it can be deconstructed and shown to refer to a primary form of community or *Gemeinschaft*, as that term is used by Tönnies ([1887] 1963). Such a community is based upon kinship, neighbourhood, shared language and beliefs about the supernatural and some narrative or myth of the group's origin. It involves an intense feeling of belonging together, and, in the sense in which the term is used by Durkheim, of sacredness (Durkheim 1915).

Fredrik Barth, who is generally thought to be the proponent of the instrumental or situational theory of ethnicity, however, raises the important question of where the boundaries of such groups might lie. One of the problems of the primordial theory is that some of the component elements of a primary community stretch beyond the bounds of a small community. Barth therefore goes on to argue that the boundaries considered to constitute and define an ethnic group or community depend upon the purpose in hand. Who is and who is not a Pathan in the North-West Frontier Province of Pakistan depends upon what the particular group calling itself Pathan is doing.

If this holds even in relation to small-scale communities, it does so even more when an attempt is made to claim the features of intense belonging and sacredness for much larger groups, or, as they are sometimes called, *ethnies*. Much argument in the theory of ethnicity is about the constitution of such groups. We need not accept, as the theory of primordiality would suggest, that they are simply 'given'. Rather they must be seen as constituted to serve particular purposes, whether unconsciously by all the members of the *ethnie*, or by leaders who use the appeal to ethnicity to serve their own purposes.

One purpose which the *ethnie* may serve is to seek to assert its political control or sovereignty over a territory, and, when this occurs, the *ethnie* becomes an ethnic nation. It is not, however, the only possible purpose to which ethnic bonding might be applied. It might, for instance, refer to the formation of classes and status groups, or, of even greater importance for our purposes here, to the formation of transnational migrating communities (Rex 1991 and 1996).

One tendency in the theory of ethnicity has been to treat these communities as quasi-nations, or, emphasizing their spread across different territories, as 'diasporas' with an ideology of 'diasporic nationalism'. This, however, can be misleading if the term diaspora is taken, in its narrow sense, as referring to a group which has been dispersed from its historic home by some traumatic experience and wishes to return there. It is more acceptable if it is used more loosely to refer to any internationally dispersed ethnic group, whether or not it has nationalist aspirations.

The selection of papers in Part II is based upon the assumption that instead of using ethnicity as the basis of bonding in a group laying claim to a territory, it can be used in the process of migration to unite members of a group in their migration project. In order to clarify the nature of migrating groups it is necessary to place them within the framework of migration theory, which should be as important to the theory of ethnicity as the theory of nationalism and ethnic nationalism. Since, however, migration theory has been developed on an interdisciplinary basis by political economists, political theorists, anthropologists and sociologists, it becomes necessary to draw the threads together to show what such theories mean for the constitution of migrating groups.

One very important point which has to be understood in any theory of ethnicity, as mentioned above, is that ethnicity often has a dual nature. On the one hand there is the ethnicity which the members of a group claim and feel for themselves; on the other there is the ethnicity which is attributed to them by others. There is also the more complex possibility that the claimed or felt ethnicity of group members may be shaped by that which is attributed to them by others.

The others with whom a migrant ethnic group has to engage are often the agents of a nation state. Such a nation state may be of the modernizing kind as described in Gellner's theory (Gellner 1983), or it may be the agent of a dominant ethnic group. In either case it is very likely to be corrosive of subordinate ethnicity, as it is of class and other solidarities. Another possibility is that the nation state may define itself as 'multicultural' or 'multi-ethnic' and this is a possibility which must also be explored, especially in Europe and North America, where a number of societies have defined themselves in this way. There is, in fact, in most modern industrial and post-industrial societies, a conflict and tension between the principle of a unified nation and a multicultural one (Rex and Drury 1994; Rex 1996).

The notion of a multicultural society is sometimes confused with that of a plural one, but unfortunately the concept of the plural society has been developed to analyse the nature of colonial and post-colonial societies rather than those which are modern, industrial and democratic, though it is also true that something called 'pluralism' is a virtuous feature of these more democratic societies. The concept of multiculturalism may then be used to refer to features which are both democratic and egalitarian and those which are antidemocratic and hierarchical. It therefore becomes necessary to sort out the differences between malign and virtuous pluralism and malign and virtuous forms of multiculturalism as judged by the standards of modern democracy. For instance, in Britain and after 9/11, the Britishness of the 7th July 2005 London bombers, whose parents or grandparents had come to the country as immigrants, horrified not only the political class but also most of their fellow citizens. Since then questions have been raised about whether multiculturalism represents a viable option leading to a socially cohesive British society. Similar debates on multiculturalism are also taking place in the US and elsewhere in Europe.

Liberal society is generally built around the concept of individual human rights and it has had to extend itself to take account of group rights. This has been a very important theme in recent political philosophy, particularly in the work of such writers as Charles Taylor (Taylor 1992). Unfortunately in such writings, which are on a very abstract level, insufficient distinction is made between the problems of the nationality of subordinate nations, as in Quebec, and the problem of the treatment of immigrant minorities. What a sociology of ethnicity and nationalism therefore needs is a theory which takes account of both multinationality and of multiculturalism as a policy concerned with the position of minorities who have no aspiration to statehood in their land of settlement.

It should be added here that there is also a socialist or social democratic view of these problems: the modern state is seen not as simply following the logic of promoting human rights but as having emerged from a conflict of interests (largely class interests) which have been reconciled through the institutions of the welfare state. For social democrats the problem is that of the compatibility of the normal institutions of the welfare state and institutions set up especially for handling minority problems.

Much of the writing which exists on ethnicity concerns itself with the problem of minorities within nation states and it is quite right that this should be so. There is, however, an increasing concern in sociology with looking at all problems from an angle wider than that of the nation state. Thus Immanuel Wallerstein sought to transcend a narrow nation-based viewpoint by developing a theory of 'world systems' (Wallerstein 1974), and, much more commonly today, a new dominant approach is that of 'globalization'. These viewpoints probably overplay the notion that the nation state is no longer important; in our selection of essays we have sought to reflect both those which still concern themselves with the internal structures of the nation state and those based upon a world systems or globalization outlook. Arguably, moreover, our concern with transnational communities reflects our belief that the study of such communities represents a too much neglected part of the theory of globalization.

To return to the theme of attributed ethnicity, we have also thought it necessary to include studies which deal with what are generally referred to as 'racism' and 'xenophobia' or simply with ideologies of 'exclusion'. These all deal with an analysis of the reasons offered for treating ethnic minorities as inferiors.

Montserrat Guibernau
John Rex

Cambridge 30th July 2009

---

* Editors' note: Omissions from the material as originally published are indicated by ellipses within square brackets, thus: [. . .]. Where a paragraph or more has been excluded, there is a line space above and below such ellipses. All others are as in the original publication. Apart from minor amendments (e.g. capitalization and British rather than American spellings), the few editorial interventions necessitated by publishing these essays in a single volume also appear in square brackets.

Part I

Ethnicity and Nationalism

1

The Concept of Ethnicity

Max Weber emphasizes the subjective character of ethnicity and highlights the role of political community in fostering a sense of common ethnie and solidarity. Anthony D. Smith stresses the role of *ethnie* as precursor of nations and highlights the power of symbols, rituals, traditions and ways of life as key components in the construction of a shared identity among members of a particular group. In his view, the ethnic origins of nations can be traced back to antiquity, although modern concepts of nation and nationalism emerged in the late eighteenth century. Thomas H. Eriksen and Rogers Brubaker approach the study of ethnicity from a post-modern and deconstructionist perspective. Eriksen focuses on the study of identity and its relation with culture as key components of ethnicity. In turn, Brubaker criticizes the reification of concepts such as ethnicity, race, nation and class and argues that they are often treated as if they enjoyed a 'discrete existence, boundedness, coherence, identity interest and agency' when these attributes are in fact characteristics of organizations.

Ethnic groups, writes Max Weber, are 'those human groups that entertain a subjective belief in their common descent because of similarities of physical type or of customs or both, or because of memories of colonization and migration'. In his view, this belief is important for the propagation of group formation whether a blood relationship exists or not. The key idea in Weber's definition concerns the acknowledgement of the subjective character of ethnicity which he refers to as a 'presumed identity'.

For Weber, 'ethnic membership does not constitute a group; it only facilitates group formation of any kind, particularly in the political sphere'. He stresses that it is primarily the political community, no matter how artificially organized, that inspires the belief in common ethnicity. This would imply that the state has a capacity to create a 'presumed identity' among its citizens. Furthermore, Weber's assertion that the belief in common ethnicity 'tends to persist even after the disintegration of the political community, unless drastic differences in the custom, physical type, or, above all, language exist among its members', could be regarded as an explanation for the continuity of the belief in common ethnicity felt by the population of territories which had formed an independent political community in the past.

Weber offers a broad definition of ethnicity and stresses that 'if rationally regulated action is not widespread, almost any association, even the most rational one, creates the overarching communal consciousness; this takes the form of a brotherhood on the basis of the belief in common ethnicity'.

In particular, the political community can engender sentiments of likeness which will persist after its demise and will have an 'ethnic' connotation; but such an effect, Weber argues, is most directly created by the language group which is the bearer of a specific 'cultural possession of the masses' (*Massenkulturgut*) and makes mutual understanding (*Verstehen*) possible or easier.

The ethno-symbolist theory developed by Anthony D. Smith has offered fresh and illuminating insights into pre-modern forms of collective cultural identity such as those embodied in *ethnies*. Its contribution is located between stark modernist theories defending the recent, invented and constructed nature of nations and nationalism (Gellner 1983; Hobsbawm and Ranger 1983; Anderson 1983), and perennialist theories emphasizing the permanence of nations (van den Berghe 1978; Geertz 1973; Armstrong 1982).

The study of *ethnies*, 'named human populations with shared ancestry myths, histories and cultures, having an association with a specific territory, and a sense of solidarity' (Smith 1986: 32), is fundamental to the ethno-symbolist theory formulated by Anthony D. Smith. Its relevance stems from its status as the precursor of nations. Smith explores the origins of nations and national identity and finds them in ethnic identity as a pre-modern form of collective cultural identity. In his view, 'Collective cultural identity refers not to a uniformity of elements over generations but to a sense of continuity on the part of successive generations of a given cultural unit of population, to shared memories of earlier events and periods in the history of that unit and to notions entertained by each generation about the collective destiny of that unit and its culture' (Smith 1991: 25). Smith adds: 'there is a felt filiation, as well as a cultural affinity, with a remote past in which a community was formed, a community that despite all the changes it has undergone, is still in some sense recognized as the "same" community' (Smith 1991: 33).

Smith's work on the relevance of the ethnic origins of nations becomes central to his understanding of 'why and where particular nations are formed, and why nationalisms, though formally alike, possess such distinctive features and contents' (Smith 1998: 191). His research on the role of myths, memories, values, traditions and symbols, as powerful differentiators and reminders of the unique culture and fate of the ethnic community, is fundamental to his analysis of national identity. The ethno-symbolist perspective propounded by Anthony D. Smith endorses a middle way approach to the antiquity of national culture. He acknowledges the modernity of nations and nationalism (and those elements forming them, for instance national culture), while insisting on the ethnic origins of nations. He confers great relevance to the values, myths, symbols, holy places, memories and traditions embedded in the ethnic community, as a social formation which, in pre-modern times, did not normally act as the basis of alternative polity formation.[1]

Antiquity is employed as a source of legitimacy for a nation and its culture. It binds individuals to a past stretching over their own life span as well as those of their ancestors.

Rogers Brubaker challenges constructivist approaches in academic discussions of ethnicity and stands against what he regards as the tendency to reify groups as if they were internally homogeneous, externally bounded groups, even unitary collective actors with common purposes. He criticizes 'groupism' – the tendency to treat ethnic groups, nations and races as substantial entities to which interests and agency can be attributed.

He argues that 'ethnic conflict – or what might better be called ethnicized or ethnically framed conflict – need not, and should not, be understood as conflict *between ethnic groups*, just as racial or racially framed conflict need not be understood as conflict between *races*, or nationally framed conflict as conflict between nations'. Instead, ethnicity, race and nation should be conceptualized in relational, processual, dynamic, eventful and disaggregated terms. This implies that ethnicization, racialization and nationalization should be considered as political, cultural and psychological processes while 'groupness' is understood as a contextually fluctuating conceptual variable. Brubaker concludes that groupness should be treated as an 'event', as something that 'happens' rather than as a fixed and given phenomenon.

When examining current anthropological approaches, Thomas H. Eriksen signals a shift toward the study of identities rather than cultures, which places great emphasis upon conscious agency and reflexivity.[2] He defines ethnicity 'as an aspect of social relationship between agents who consider themselves as culturally distinctive from members of other groups with whom they have a minimum of regular interaction', adding that it can also be defined as 'a social identity characterized by metaphoric or fictive kinship'. In his view, ethnicity refers both to aspects of gain and loss in interaction, and to aspects of meaning in the creation of identity.

He signals that, in recent years, the main tendency has consisted of 'deconstructing instrumentalists' notions of authenticity and tradition, and showing not only that the internal variation within a group is much greater than one would expect but also that traditionalist ideologies are, paradoxically, direct results of modernization'.[3] Eriksen condemns reification and essentialism and insists on the existence of an infinite number of versions of each culture, none of which is more 'true' than the others.

The influence of 'post-modernist' thought and the deconstructionism associated with it denounces instrumentalists' approaches to culture and treats ethnicity and nationalism as 'political reifications or constructions of a particular authorized version of culture, freezing that which naturally flows, erecting artificial boundaries where they did not exist before, trimming and shaping the past to fit present needs, and inventing traditions where no organic traditions exist, or are not adequate, to ensure a sense of continuity with the past'.[4]

Notes

1 See Smith, Anthony D., *The Ethnic Origins of Nations* (Basil Blackwell: Oxford, 1986).

2 Eriksen, Thomas Hylland, 'Ethnic identity, national identity and intergroup conflict' in Ashmore, Richard D., Jussim, Lee and Wilder, David, *Social Identity, Intergroup Conflict, and Conflict Reduction* (Oxford University Press: Oxford, 2001), pp. 42–68, p. 45.
3 Eriksen, Thomas Hylland, 'Ethnic identity, national identity and intergroup conflict' in Ashmore, Richard D., Jussim, Lee and Wilder, David, *Social Identity, Intergroup Conflict, and Conflict Reduction* (Oxford University Press: Oxford, 2001), pp. 42–68, p. 45.
4 Eriksen, Thomas Hylland, 'Ethnic identity, national identity and intergroup conflict' in Ashmore, Richard D., Jussim, Lee and Wilder, David, *Social Identity, Intergroup Conflict, and Conflict Reduction* (Oxford University Press: Oxford, 2001), pp. 42–68, p. 46.

WHAT IS AN ETHNIC GROUP?

MAX WEBER

'Race' Membership

A [particularly] problematic source of social action [...] is 'race identity': common inherited and inheritable traits that actually derive from common descent. Of course, race creates a 'group' only when it is subjectively perceived as a common trait: this happens only when a neighbourhood or the mere proximity of racially different persons is the basis of joint (mostly political) action, or conversely, when some common experiences of members of the same race are linked to some antagonism against members of an *obviously* different group. The resulting social action is usually merely negative: those who are obviously different are avoided and despised or, conversely, viewed with superstitious awe. Persons who are externally different are simply despised irrespective of what they accomplish or what they are, or they are venerated superstitiously if they are too powerful in the long run. In this case antipathy is the primary and normal reaction. However, this antipathy is shared not just by persons with anthropological similarities, and its extent is by no means determined by the degree of anthropological relatedness; furthermore, this antipathy is linked not only to inherited traits but just as much to other visible differences.

If the degree of objective racial difference can be determined, among other things, purely physiologically by establishing whether hybrids reproduce themselves at approximately normal rates, the subjective aspects, the reciprocal racial attraction and repulsion, might be measured by finding out whether sexual relations are preferred or rare between two groups, and whether they are carried on permanently or temporarily and irregularly. In all groups with a developed 'ethnic' consciousness the existence or absence of intermarriage (*connubium*) would then be a normal consequence of racial attraction or segregation. Serious research on the sexual attraction and repulsion between different ethnic groups is only incipient, but there is not the slightest doubt that racial factors, that means, common descent, influence the incidence of sexual relations and of marriage, sometimes decisively. However, the existence of several million mulattos in the United States speaks clearly against the assumption of a 'natural' racial antipathy, even among quite different races. Apart from the laws against biracial marriages in the southern states, sexual relations between the two races are now abhorred by both sides, but this development began only with the Emancipation and resulted from the Negroes' demand for equal civil rights. Hence this abhorrence on the part of the Whites is socially determined by the previously sketched tendency toward the monopolization of social power and honour, a tendency which in this case happens to be linked to race.

The *connubium* itself, that means, the fact that the offspring from a permanent sexual relationship can share in the activities and advantages of the father's political, economic or status group, depends on many circumstances. Under undiminished patriarchal powers [...] the father was free to grant equal rights to his children from slaves. Moreover, the glorification of abduction by the hero made racial mixing a normal event within the ruling strata. However, patriarchal discretion was progressively curtailed with the monopolistic closure [...] of political, status or other groups and with the monopolization of marriage opportunities; these tendencies restricted the *connubium* to the offspring from a permanent sexual union within the given political, religious, economic and status group. This also produced a high incidence of inbreeding. The 'endogamy' of a group is probably everywhere a secondary product of such tendencies, if we define it not merely as the fact that a permanent sexual union occurs primarily on the basis of joint membership in some association, but as a process of social action in which only endogamous children are accepted as full members. (The term 'sib endogamy' should not be used: there is no such thing unless we want to refer to the levirate marriage and arrangements in which daughters have the right to succession, but these have secondary, religious and political origins.) 'Pure' anthropological types are often a secondary consequence of such closure; examples are sects (as in India) as well as pariah peoples, that means, groups that are socially despised yet wanted as neighbours because they have monopolized indispensable skills.

Reasons other than actual racial kinship influence the degree to which blood relationship is taken into account. In the United States the smallest admixture of Negro blood disqualifies a person unconditionally, whereas very considerable admixtures of Indian blood do not. Doubtlessly, it is important that Negroes appear aesthetically even more alien than Indians, but it remains very significant that Negroes were slaves and hence disqualified in the status hierarchy. The conventional *connubium* is far less impeded by anthropological differences than by status differences, that means, differences due to socialization and upbringing (*Bildung* in the widest sense of the word). Mere anthropological differences account for little, except in cases of extreme aesthetic antipathy.

The Belief In Common Ethnicity: Its Multiple Social Origins and Theoretical Ambiguities

The question of whether conspicuous 'racial' differences are based on biological heredity or on tradition is usually of no importance as far as their effect on mutual attraction or repulsion is concerned. This is true of the development of endogamous conjugal groups, and even more so of attraction and repulsion in other kinds of social intercourse, i.e., whether all sorts of friendly, companionable, or economic relationships between such groups are established easily and on the footing of mutual trust and respect, or whether such relationships are established with difficulty and with precautions that betray mistrust.

The more or less easy emergence of social circles in the broadest sense of the word (*soziale Verkehrsgemeinschaft*) may be linked to the most superficial features of historically accidental habits just as much as to inherited racial characteristics. That the different custom is not understood in its subjective meaning since the cultural key to it is lacking, is almost as decisive as the peculiarity of the custom as such. But [...] not all repulsion is attributable to the absence of a 'consensual group'. Differences in the styles of beard and hairdo, clothes, food and eating habits, division of labour between the sexes, and all kinds of other visible differences can, in a given case, give rise to repulsion and contempt, but the actual extent of these differences is irrelevant for the emotional impact, as is illustrated by primitive travel descriptions, the Histories of Herodotus or the older prescientific ethnography. Seen from their positive aspect, however, these differences may give rise to consciousness of kind, which may become as easily the bearer of group relationships as groups ranging from the household and neighbourhood to political and religious communities are usually the bearers of shared customs. All differences of customs can sustain a specific sense of honour or dignity in their practitioners. The original motives or reasons for the inception of different habits of life are forgotten and the contrasts are then perpetuated as conventions. In this manner, any group can create customs, and it can also effect, in certain circumstances very decisively, the selection of anthropological types. This it can do by providing favourable chances of survival and reproduction for certain hereditary qualities and traits. This holds both for internal assimilation and for external differentiation.

Any cultural trait, no matter how superficial, can serve as a starting point for the familiar tendency to monopolistic closure. However, the universal force of imitation has the general effect of only gradually changing the traditional customs and usages, just as anthropological types are changed only gradually by racial mixing. But if there are sharp boundaries between areas of observable styles of life, they are due to conscious monopolistic closure, which started from small differences that were then cultivated and intensified; or they are due to the peaceful or warlike migrations of groups that previously lived far from each other and had accommodated themselves to their heterogeneous conditions of existence. Similarly, strikingly different racial types, bred in isolation, may live in sharply segregated proximity to one another either because of monopolistic closure or because of migration. We can conclude then that similarity and contrast of physical type and custom, regardless of whether they are biologically inherited or culturally transmitted, are subject to the same conditions of group life, in origin as well as in effectiveness, and identical in their potential for group formation. The difference lies partly in the differential instability of type and custom, partly in the fixed (though often unknown) limit to engendering new hereditary qualities. Compared to this, the scope for assimilation of new customs is incomparably greater, although there are considerable variations in the transmissibility of traditions.

Almost any kind of similarity or contrast of physical type and of habits can induce the belief that affinity or disaffinity exists between groups that attract or repel each other. Not every belief in tribal affinity, however, is founded on the resemblance of customs or of physical type. But in spite of great variations in this area, such a belief can exist and can develop group-forming powers when it is buttressed by a memory of an actual migration, be it colonization or individual migration. The persistent effect of the old ways and of childhood reminiscences continues as a source of native-country sentiment (*Heimatsgefühl*) among emigrants even when they have become so thoroughly adjusted to the new country that return to their homeland would be intolerable (this being the case of most German-Americans, for example).

In colonies, the attachment to the colonists' homeland survives despite considerable mixing with the inhabitants of the colonial land and despite profound changes in tradition and hereditary type as well. In case of political colonization, the decisive factor is the need for political support. In general, the continuation of relationships created by marriage is important, and so are the market relationships, provided that the 'customs' remain unchanged. These market relationships between the homeland and the colony may be very close, as long as the consumer standards remain similar, and especially when colonies are in an almost absolutely alien environment and within an alien political territory.

The belief in group affinity, regardless of whether it has any objective foundation, can have important consequences especially for the formation of a political community. We shall call 'ethnic groups' those human groups that entertain a subjective belief in their common descent because of similarities of physical type or of customs or both, or because of memories of colonization and migration; this belief must be important for the propagation of group formation; conversely, it does not matter whether or not an objective blood relationship exists. Ethnic membership (*Gemeinsamkeit*) differs from the kinship group precisely by being a presumed identity, not a group with concrete social action, like the latter. In our sense, ethnic membership does not constitute a group; it only facilitates group formation of any kind, particularly in the political sphere. On the other hand, it is primarily the political community, no matter how artificially organized, that inspires the belief in common ethnicity. This belief tends to persist even after the disintegration of the political community, unless drastic differences in the custom, physical type, or, above all, language exist among its members.

This artificial origin of the belief in common ethnicity follows the [...] pattern [...] of rational association turning into personal relationships. If rationally regulated action is not widespread, almost any association, even the most rational one, creates an overarching communal consciousness; this takes the form of a brotherhood on the basis of the belief in common ethnicity. As late as the Greek city state, even the most arbitrary division of the polis became for the member an association with at least a common cult and often a common fictitious ancestor. The twelve tribes of Israel were subdivisions of a political community, and they alternated in performing certain functions on a monthly basis. The same holds for the Greek tribes (*phylai*) and their subdivisions: the latter, too, were regarded as units of common ethnic descent. It is true that the original division may have been induced by political or actual ethnic differences, but the effect was the same when such a division was made quite rationally and schematically, after the break-up of old groups and relinquishment of local cohesion, as it was done by Cleisthenes. It does not follow, therefore, that the Greek polis was actually or originally a tribal or lineage state, but that ethnic fictions were a sign of the rather low degree of rationalization of Greek political life. Conversely, it is a symptom of the greater rationalization of Rome that its old schematic subdivisions (*curiae*) took on religious importance, with a pretence to ethnic origin, to only a small degree.

The belief in common ethnicity often delimits 'social circles', which in turn are not always identical with endogamous connubial groups, for greatly varying numbers of persons may be encompassed by both. Their similarity rests on the belief in a specific 'honour' of their members, not shared by the outsiders, that is, the sense of 'ethnic honour' (a phenomenon closely related to status honour, which will be discussed later). These few remarks must suffice at this point. A specialized sociological study of ethnicity would have to make a finer distinction between these concepts. [...]

Groups, in turn, can engender sentiments of likeness which will persist even after their demise and will have an 'ethnic' connotation. The political community in particular can produce such an effect. But most directly, such an effect is created by the *language group*, which is the bearer of a specific 'cultural possession of the masses' (*Massenkulturgut*) and makes mutual understanding (*Verstehen*) possible or easier.

Wherever the memory of the origin of a community by peaceful secession or emigration ('colony', *ver sacrum*, and the like) from a mother community remains for some reason alive, there undoubtedly exists a very specific and often extremely powerful sense of ethnic identity, which is determined by several factors: shared political memories or, even more importantly in early times, persistent ties with the old cult, or the strengthening of kinship and other groups, both in the old and the new community, or other persistent relationships. Where these ties are lacking, or once they cease to exist, the sense of ethnic group membership is absent, regardless of how close the kinship may be.

Apart from the community of language, which may or may not coincide with objective, or subjectively believed, consanguinity, and apart from common religious belief, which is also independent of consanguinity, the ethnic differences that remain are, on the one hand, aesthetically conspicuous differences of the physical appearance (as mentioned before) and, on the other hand and of equal weight, the perceptible differences in the *conduct of everyday life*. Of special importance are precisely those items which may otherwise seem to be of small social relevance, since when ethnic differentiation is concerned it is always the conspicuous differences that come into play.

Common language and the ritual regulation of life, as determined by shared religious beliefs, everywhere are conducive to feelings of ethnic affinity, especially since the intelligibility of the behaviour of others is the most fundamental presupposition of group formation. But since we shall not consider these two elements in the present context, we ask: what is it that remains? It must be admitted that palpable differences in dialect and differences of religion in themselves do not exclude sentiments of common ethnicity. Next to pronounced differences in the economic way of life, the belief in ethnic affinity has at all times been affected by outward differences in clothes, in the style of housing, food and eating habits, the division of labour between the sexes and between the free and the unfree. That is to say, these things concern one's conception of what is correct and proper and, above all, of what affects the individual's sense of honour and dignity. All those things we shall find later on as objects of specific differences between status groups. The conviction of the excellence of one's own customs and the inferiority of alien ones, a conviction which sustains the sense of ethnic honour, is actually quite analogous to the sense of honour of distinctive status groups.

The sense of ethnic honour is a specific honour of the masses (*Massenehre*), for it is accessible to anybody who belongs to the subjectively believed community of descent. The 'poor white trash', i.e., the property-less and, in the absence of job opportunities, very often destitute white inhabitants of the southern states of the United States of America in the period of slavery, were the actual bearers of racial antipathy, which was quite foreign to the planters. This was so because the social honour of the 'poor whites' was dependent upon the social *déclassement* of the Negroes.

And behind all ethnic diversities there is somehow naturally the notion of the 'chosen people', which is merely a counterpart of status differentiation translated into the plane of horizontal co-existence. The idea of a chosen people derives its popularity from the fact that it can be claimed to an equal degree by any and every member of the mutually despising groups, in contrast to status differentiation which always rests on subordination. Consequently, ethnic repulsion may take hold of all conceivable differences among the notions of propriety and transform them into 'ethnic conventions'.

Besides the previously mentioned elements, which were still more or less closely related to the economic order, conventionalization [...] may take hold of such things as a hairdo or style of beard and the like. The differences thereof have an 'ethnically' repulsive effect, because they are thought of as symbols of ethnic membership. Of course, the repulsion is not always based merely on the 'symbolic' character of the distinguishing traits. The fact that the Scythian women oiled their hair with butter, which then gave off a rancid odour, while Greek women used perfumed oil to achieve the same purpose, thwarted – according to an ancient report – all attempts at social intercourse between the aristocratic ladies of these two groups. The smell of butter certainly had a more compelling effect than even the most prominent racial differences, or – as far as I could see – the 'Negro odour', of which so many fables are told. In general, racial qualities are effective only as limiting factors with regard to the belief in common ethnicity, such as in the case of an excessively heterogeneous and aesthetically unaccepted physical type; they are not positively group-forming.

Pronounced differences of custom, which play a role equal to that of inherited physical type in the creation of feelings of common ethnicity and notions of kinship, are usually caused, in addition to linguistic and religious differences, by the diverse economic and political conditions of various social groups. If we ignore cases of clear-cut linguistic boundaries and sharply demarcated political or religious communities as a basis of differences of custom – and these in fact are lacking in wide areas of the African and South American continents – then there are only gradual transitions of custom and no immutable ethnic frontiers, except those due to gross geographical differences. The sharp demarcations of areas wherein ethnically relevant customs predominate, which were not conditioned either by political or economic or religious factors, usually came into existence by way of migration or expansion, when groups of people that had previously lived in complete or partial isolation from each other and became accommodated to heterogeneous conditions of existence came to live side by side.

As a result, the obvious contrast usually evokes, on both sides, the idea of blood disaffinity (*Blutsfremdheit*), regardless of the objective state of affairs.

It is understandably difficult to determine in general – and even in a concrete individual case – what influence specific ethnic factors (i.e., the belief in a blood relationship, or its opposite, which rests on similarities, or differences, of a person's physical appearance and style of life) have on the formation of a group.

There is no difference between the ethnically relevant customs and customs in general, as far as their effect is concerned. The belief in common descent, in combination with a similarity of customs, is likely to promote the spread of the activities of one part of an ethnic group among the rest, since the awareness of ethnic identity furthers imitation. This is especially true of the propaganda of religious groups.

It is not feasible to go beyond these vague generalizations. The content of joint activities that are possible on an ethnic basis remains indefinite. There is a corresponding ambiguity of concepts denoting ethnically determined action, that means, determined by the belief in blood relationship. Such concepts are *Völkerschaft, Stamm* (tribe), *Volk* (people), each of which is ordinarily used in the sense of an ethnic subdivision of the following one (although the first two may be used in reversed order). Using such terms, one usually implies either the existence of a contemporary political community, no matter how loosely organized, or memories of an extinct political community, such as they are preserved in epic tales and legends; or the existence of a linguistic or dialect group; or, finally, of a religious group. In the past, cults in particular were the typical concomitant of a tribal or *Volk* consciousness. But in the absence of the political community, contemporary or past, the external delimitation of the group was usually indistinct. The cult communities of Germanic tribes, as late as the Burgundian period (sixth-century AD), were probably rudiments of political communities and therefore pretty well defined. By contrast, the Delphic oracle, the undoubted cultic symbol of Hellenism, also revealed information to the barbarians and accepted their veneration, and it was an organized cult only among some Greek segments, excluding the most powerful cities. The cult as an exponent of ethnic identity is thus generally either a remnant of a largely political community which once existed but was destroyed by disunion and colonization, or it is – as in the case of the Delphic Apollo – a product of a *Kulturgemeinschaft* brought about by other than purely ethnic conditions, but which in turn gives rise to the belief in blood relationship. All history shows how easily political action can give rise to the belief in blood relationship, unless gross differences of anthropological type impede it.

Tribe and Political Community: The Disutility of the Notion of 'Ethnic Group'

The tribe is clearly delimited when it is a subdivision of a polity, which, in fact, often establishes it. In this case, the artificial origin is revealed by the round numbers in which tribes usually appear, for example, the previously mentioned division of the people of Israel into twelve tribes, the three Doric *phylai* and the various *phylai* of the other Hellenes. When a political community was newly established or reorganized, the population was newly divided. Hence the tribe is here a political artefact, even though it soon adopts the whole symbolism of blood relationship and particularly a tribal cult. Even today it is not rare that political artefacts develop a sense of affinity akin to that of blood relationship. Very schematic constructs such as those states of the United States that were made into squares according to their latitude have a strong sense of identity; it is also not rare that families travel from New York to Richmond to make an expected child a 'Virginian'.

Such artificiality does not preclude the possibility that the Hellenic *phylai*, for example, were at one time independent and that the polis used them schematically when they were merged into a political association. However, tribes that existed before the polis were either identical with the corresponding political groups which were subsequently associated into a polis; and in this case they were called *ethnos*, not *phyle* or, as it probably happened many times, the politically unorganized tribe, as a presumed 'blood community', lived from the memory that it once engaged in joint political action, typically a single conquest or defence, and then such political memories constituted the tribe. Thus, the fact that tribal consciousness was primarily formed by common political experiences and not by common descent appears to have been a frequent source of the belief in common ethnicity.

Of course, this was not the only source: common customs may have diverse origins. Ultimately, they derive largely from adaptation to natural conditions and the imitation of neighbours. In practice, however, tribal consciousness usually has a political meaning: in case of military danger or opportunity, it easily provides the basis for joint political action on the part of tribal members or *Volksgenossen* who consider one another as blood relatives. The eruption of a drive to political action is thus one of the major potentialities inherent in the rather ambiguous notions of tribe and people. Such intermittent political action may easily develop into the moral duty of all members of tribe or people (*Volk*) to support one another in case of a military attack, even if there is no corresponding political association; violators of this solidarity may suffer the fate of the (Germanic, pro-Roman) sibs of Segestes and Inguiomer – expulsion from the tribal territory – even if the tribe has no organized government. If the tribe has reached this stage, it has indeed become a continuous political community, no matter how inactive in peacetime, and hence unstable, it may be. However, even under favourable conditions the transition from the habitual to the customary and therefore obligatory is very fluid. All in all, the notion of 'ethnically' determined social action subsumes phenomena that a rigorous sociological analysis – as [I] do not attempt it here – would have to distinguish carefully: the actual subjective effect of those customs conditioned by heredity and those determined by tradition; the differential impact of the varying content of custom; the influence of common language, religion and political action, past and present, upon the formation of customs; the extent to which such factors create attraction and repulsion, and especially the belief in affinity or disaffinity of blood; the consequences of this belief for social action in general, and specifically for action on the basis of shared custom or blood relationship, for diverse sexual relations, etc. – all of this would have to be studied in detail. It is certain that in this process the collective term 'ethnic' would be abandoned, for it is unsuitable for a really rigorous analysis. However, we do not pursue sociology for its own sake and therefore limit ourselves to showing briefly the diverse factors that are hidden behind this seemingly uniform phenomenon.

The concept of the 'ethnic' group, which dissolves if we define our terms exactly, corresponds in this regard to one of the most vexing, since emotionally charged concepts: the *nation*, as soon as we attempt a sociological definition.

Nationality and Cultural Prestige

The concept of 'nationality' shares with that of the 'people' (*Volk*) – in the 'ethnic' sense – the vague connotation that whatever is felt to be distinctively common must derive from common descent. In reality, of course, persons who consider themselves members of the same nationality are often much less related by common descent than are persons belonging to different and hostile nationalities. Differences of nationality may exist even among groups closely related by common descent, merely because they have different religious persuasions, as in the case of Serbs and Croats. The concrete reasons for the belief in joint nationality and for the resulting social action vary greatly.

Today, in the age of language conflicts, a shared common language is preeminently considered the normal basis of nationality. Whatever the 'nation' means beyond a mere 'language group' can be found in the specific objective of its social action, and this can only be the *autonomous polity*. Indeed, 'nation state' has become conceptually identical with 'state' based on common language. In reality, however, such modern nation states exist next to many others that comprise several language groups, even though these others usually have one official language. A common language is also insufficient in sustaining a sense of national identity (*Nationalgefühl*). [...] Aside from the examples of the Serbs and Croats, this is demonstrated by the Irish, the Swiss and the German-speaking Alsatians; these groups do not consider themselves as members, at least not as full members, of the 'nation' associated with their language. Conversely, language differences do not necessarily preclude a sense of joint nationality: the German-speaking Alsatians considered themselves – and most of them still do – as part of the French 'nation', even though not in the same sense as French-speaking nationals. Hence there are qualitative degrees of the belief in common nationality.

Many German-speaking Alsatians feel a sense of community with the French because they share certain customs and some of their 'sensual culture' (*Sinnenkultur*) [...] and also because of common political experiences. This can be understood by any visitor who walks through the museum in Colmar, which is rich in relics such as tricolors, *pompier* and military helmets, edicts by Louis Philippe and especially memorabilia from the French Revolution; these may appear trivial to the outsider, but they have sentimental value for the Alsatians. This sense of community came into being by virtue of common political and, indirectly, social experiences which are highly valued by the masses as symbols of the destruction of feudalism, and the story of these events takes the place of the heroic legends of primitive peoples. *La grande nation* was the liberator from feudal servitude, she was the bearer of civilization (*Kultur*), her language was *the* civilized language; German appeared as a dialect suitable for everyday communication. Hence the attachment to those who speak the language of civilization is an obvious parallel to the sense of community based on common language, but the two phenomena are not identical; rather, we deal here with an attitude that derives from a partial sharing of the same culture and from shared political experiences.

Until a short time ago most Poles in Upper Silesia had no strongly developed sense of Polish nationality that was antagonistic to the Prussian state, which is based essentially on the German language. The Poles were loyal if passive 'Prussians', but they were not 'Germans' interested in the existence of the *Reich*; the majority did not feel a conscious or a strong need to segregate themselves from German-speaking fellow-citizens. Hence, in this case there was no sense of nationality based on common language, and there was no *Kulturgemeinschaft* in view of the lack of cultural development.

Among the Baltic Germans we find neither much of a sense of nationality amounting to a high valuation of the language bonds with the Germans, nor a desire for political union with the *Reich*; in fact, most of them would abhor such a unification. However, they segregate themselves rigorously from the Slavic environment, and especially from the Russians, primarily because of status considerations and partly because both sides have different customs and cultural values which are mutually unintelligible and disdained. This segregation exists in spite of, and partly because of, the fact that the Baltic Germans are intensely loyal vassals of the Tsar and have been as interested as any 'national' Russian (*Nationalrusse*) in the predominance of the Imperial Russian system, which they provide with officials and which in turn maintains their descendants. Hence, here too we do not find any sense of nationality in the modern meaning of the term (oriented towards a common language and culture). The case is similar to that of the purely proletarian Poles: loyalty towards the state is combined with a sense of group identity that is limited to a common language group within this larger community and strongly modified by status factors. Of course, the Baltic Germans are no longer a cohesive status group, even though the differences are not as extreme as within the white population of the American South.

Finally, there are cases for which the term nationality does not seem to be quite fitting; witness the sense of identity shared by the Swiss and the Belgians or the inhabitants of Luxemburg and Liechtenstein. We hesitate to call them 'nations', not because of their relative smallness – the Dutch appear to us as a nation – but because these neutralized states have purposively forsaken power. The Swiss are not a nation if we take as criteria common language or common literature and art. Yet they have a strong sense of community despite some recent disintegrative tendencies. This sense of identity is not only sustained by loyalty towards the body politic but also by what are perceived to be common customs (irrespective of actual differences). These customs are largely shaped by the differences in social structure between Switzerland and Germany, but also all other big and hence militaristic powers. Because of the impact of bigness on the internal power structure, it appears to the Swiss that their customs can be preserved only by a separate political existence.

The loyalty of the French Canadians towards the English polity is today determined above all by the deep antipathy against the economic and social structure, and the way of life, of the neighbouring United States; hence membership in the Dominion of Canada appears as a guarantee of their own traditions.

This classification could easily be enlarged, as every rigorous sociological investigation would have to do. It turns out that feelings of identity subsumed under the term 'national' are not uniform but may derive from diverse sources: differences in the economic and social structure and in the internal power structure, with its impact on the customs, may play a role, but within the German *Reich* customs are very diverse; shared political memories, religion, language and finally, racial features may be sources of the sense of nationality. Racial factors often have a peculiar impact. From the viewpoint of the Whites in the United States, Negroes and Whites are not united by a common sense of nationality, but the Negroes have a sense of American nationality at least by claiming a right to it. On the other hand, the pride of the Swiss in their own distinctiveness, and their willingness to defend it vigorously, is neither qualitatively different nor less widespread than the same attitudes in any 'great' and powerful 'nation'. Time and again we find that the concept 'nation' directs us to political power. Hence, the concept seems to refer – if it refers at all to a uniform phenomenon – to a specific kind of pathos which is linked to the idea of a powerful political community of people who share a common language, or religion, or common customs, or political memories; such a state may already exist or it may be desired. The more power is emphasized, the closer appears to be the link between nation and state. This pathetic pride in the power of one's own community, or this longing for it, may be much more widespread in relatively small language groups such as the Hungarians, Czechs or Greeks than in a similar but much larger community such as the Germans 150 years ago, when they were essentially a language group without pretensions to national power.

STRUCTURE AND PERSISTENCE OF *ETHNIE*

ANTHONY D. SMITH

[…] *Ethnie* (ethnic communities) may […] be defined as named human populations with shared ancestry myths, histories and cultures, having an association with a specific territory and a sense of solidarity. I shall try to show that such communities have been widespread in all eras of history, at least since the onset of the Bronze Age in the Middle East and Aegean, when written records appear to recount communal exploits and chronicle ethnic vicissitudes, and that they still characterize many areas of the globe and are to be found even in the most modernized states of the industrialized world. I am not claiming that they have constituted the main mode of socio-cultural organization, let alone the sole one, even in pre-modern eras; only that they have been at least as important as other forms of organization and culture, and that we therefore neglect them at our peril. Even today they remain of significance in several culture-areas, notably Africa and parts of Asia, but also in the [former] Soviet Union, Europe and North America. Nor would I claim that ethnicity, let alone *ethnie*, have been continuous, even if invisible. That would smack of the 'perennialism', even 'primordialism', which has been rejected. Instead, I hope to show that *ethnie* (different ones, usually) have emerged and re-emerged at different periods in several continents and culture-areas right up to the modern era; and that ethnicity has remained as a socio-cultural 'model' for human organization and communication from the early third millennium BC until today, even if not every 'society' has followed this model of organization. In other words, while making no claims for its universality, I am arguing for the widespread and chronic, if intermittent, appearance and persistence of this phenomenon. The paradox of ethnicity is its mutability in persistence, and its persistence through change.

[...]

In identifying the 'bases' of ethnicity in the localism and nostalgia of a sedentary agrarian existence, in the organization and sectarianism of religious communities, and in the mobilization, myths and communal locations of interstate warfare, we do not mean to imply anything about the archaic origins of *ethnie*. While a combination of these factors might, in given cases, lie at the root of their formation, it cannot account for the initial cultural difference – of religion, customs, language, institutions, colour and the like – from which *ethnie* can emerge or be constructed. The origins of ethnic differentiation itself are shrouded in obscurity, even if the veil is lifted in a few cases, particularly in more recent times. But, then, the modern act of classifying populations as *ethnie* is itself modelled on the ubiqitous presence and longevity of other ethnic communities, which we nowadays take for granted. The original 'tower of Babel' which allowed and encouraged the formation of *ethnie* cannot be elucidated from our meagre records. At the point where written history begins, in the mid-third millennium BC, *ethnie* are already in evidence, and named culture-communities appear as historical actors.

What can be explained, through the factors outlined above – and no doubt others – is the extraordinary persistence and resilience of ethnic ties and sentiments, once formed, as well as the processes by which 'ethnic categories' become crystallized and integrated as genuine 'ethnic communities'. For the durability, or chronic recurrence, of these 'bases' of ethnic persistence ensures their continuous self-awareness, as well as their significance for the identities and loyalties of their members. What has not yet been ascertained is the optimal degree and combination of these and other bases and factors – optimal, that is, for the salience and survival of a given *ethnie* or for ethnicity in general. Perhaps, too, in different areas and periods, such combinations of factors will vary with the development of the particular ethnic community. Well-formed *ethnie*, for example, may no longer need the cement of peasant mores and territorial nostalgia, or the mobilizing effects of interstate warfare; commercially located diasporas or trading maritime city-state confederations can survive and flourish as selfconscious *ethnie* through their religious and literary cultures and arts, even in the absence of other bases, once their sense of community has become well crystallized. Alternatively, elements of organized religious culture and community may be subordinated to the needs of a warrior or knightly aristocratic *ethnie* engaged in the defence of its territorial space, and acting, as did the Hungarian knights, as the *antemurale* bulwark of a Christendom threatened by Mongol and Ottoman steppe nomads. Again, however, such 'recombinations' of bases and factors only operate in cases of well-formed ethnicity and where the typical format and structure of the *ethnie* has operated for a few generations.

But, what is this 'typical' format and structure of *ethnie*? An 'ideal-typical' picture of pre-modern ethnic communities (allowing for significant variations) would, I think, include the following elements:

1 A large mass of peasants and artisans in villages and small market towns, subject to various restrictions on their freedom (corvée labour, serfdom, ghettoization, caste) and wedded to local 'folk cultures' (vernaculars, legends, rural customs and rites, dress, dance and music, crafts) influenced loosely by the nearest Great Traditions;
2 A small urban stratum of competing elites in the main towns – rulers and their courts, bureaucrats, noble landowners, military leaders – monopolizing wealth and political power, and centred loosely on an administrative capital and core area, and patronizing specialist trading and artisan client strata;
3 A tiny stratum of priests/monks and scribes claiming a monopoly of the community's belief-system, ritual and educational services, and acting as transmitters and conduits of its symbolism between the various urban elites and between them and the peasants and rural artisans, thereby seeking to incorporate the various Little Traditions of the latter into the central Great Tradition of which they act as guardians and agents of socialization;
4 A fund of myths, memories, values and symbols, often encoded, which express and explain the community's perceptions of itself, its origins, development and destiny, and its place in the cosmic order; all of these being manifested in a round of ceremonies, rites, artefacts and laws which bind the community to its celestial pantheon and its homeland;
5 Processes of communication, transmission and socialization of the store of myths, memories, values and symbols among both urban elites and their specialist clients, and where necessary outwards and downwards to the dependent peasantry; using mainly temple ritual and worship, dissemination of the precepts and morals of sacred texts, the use of symbols in art, architecture and dress, the elaboration of oral traditions, ballads, epics and hymns, but also the promulgation of legal codes and edicts, some rudimentary rote learning in local schools for selected members of various strata, and the use of military service and public works labour forces.

In constructing such an 'ideal-type' *ethnie*, we leave open the question of the degree of penetration of ethnic myth and symbolism among non-urban strata. [...] For the present, it suffices that most of the urban strata are 'touched', in varying degrees by the forms and content of ethnic symbolic funds, and hence that they are open to one or more priestly monopolies of symbolic and mythic communication and transmission. [...] The role of priests and scribes is, in many ways, pivotal both as custodians of the ethnic fund and as transmission belts and conduits; indeed, in some instances, what we grasp as religious competition may equally well be understood as ethnic competition for the monopoly of symbolic domination and communication in a given population, whose 'ethnic' profile is as much *shaped* by priestly and scribal activities as it is reinforced. This is not to say that other agencies of ethnic socialization do not exist, and are of no importance. The role of polities themselves can, on occasion, be crucial, both in their civilian and military roles. Equally important is the family network, especially in ensuring the failure or success of ethnic socialization processes, something that ethnic leaders themselves fully comprehend; here the role of local aristocratic leaders and their families in spreading, by example and precept, the store of ethnic symbolism in the areas of their influence, is crucial.

There is, however, one important distinction that needs to be made in considering the structure and pervasiveness of ethnic communities in pre-modern eras, the distinction between ethnic polities and ethnic minorities which are incorporated into a wider polity. If the *ethnie* in question constitutes a majority of the population of the polity, if, for example, it constitutes a patrimonial kingdom or forms the core of a wider agrarian empire, then its ethnic myths and symbols will reflect the elements of political domination and kingship, and its conduits of ethnic communication will include officials, judges and officers alongside the priests and scribes which are common to all pre-modern ethnic communication. They will diffuse, along with other myths of origins and ancestry, myths of kingship and nobility, of royal lineage and political domination, as part of the ethnic fund, and the symbolism of the community will reflect the centrality of this political experience. Such was undoubtedly the case in ancient Egypt. The ruler became a god, his court, nobility and bureaucracy reflected Pharaonic patronage and glory, and royalty was placed at the apex of Memphite and Theban priestly mythologies. Despite some regionalism, the unique ecology of the Nile valley helped to diffuse the symbols of Pharaonic religion and royalty by a whole series of propaganda devices in artefacts and genres of painting, sculpture, pottery and jewellery, as well as royal and priestly inscriptions in the great temples and royal and noble tombs. During the more centralized periods of the three Kingdoms, Pharaoh and priests joined forces, with one brief exception, to expand their influence and incorporate every expression of rural regionalism and every peasant tradition from the Delta to Aswan; and the peculiar geography of the area enabled a greater degree of ethnic homogeneity to develop, despite internal breakdowns and external invasions (by Hyksos, Sea Peoples, Assyrians and Persians), than anywhere else in the ancient world, with the possible exception of the Jews. What characterized the content of both ethnic symbolism and ethnic social structure was exactly this identity between the ethnic community of Egyptians and the dynastic state.

In the case of incorporated *ethnie*, or ethnic 'minorities', on the other hand, no such identity was present. Here the ideal of a political kingdom and dynastic state is replaced by that of the ethnic homeland or territory of belonging. The Israelite tribes before their periods of unified monarchy, as well as afterwards; the Sumerian city states before their unification by the dynasty of Agade and the third dynasty of Ur; the Phoenician and Greek city states; the early Swiss cantons;

and, later, the various subjugated eastern European ethnic communities like the Serbs, Croats, Bulgarians, Greeks, Czechs and Slovaks; all relied for their sense of solidarity and continuity upon a real or alleged tie with an ancestral homeland and memories of a glorious past on its soil. Here, any burgeoning sense of ethnic unity expressed in political terms sprang, not from any pretensions of royalty or the impact of a conquest state and its dynastic rule, but from the pooling of more local loyalties in the face of common enemies and from a more or less vivid myth of common origins and common culture. Thus, in ancient Sumer and Akkad, the competing city states had their own *ensi* (lord), gods, temples and priesthoods; though there was a ceremonial centre at Nippur, it seems to have had no power to regulate inter-city conflicts and resist marauding tribes from the desert or marcher regions. There was no other political agent of unity until Sargon's conquests; but this did not impede a growing cultural unity, based on common language and religious myths and rituals, a common script and literature, common building styles and arts, and common irrigation techniques. It was just such a religio-linguistic-literary unity on which the Third Dynasty of Ur and later the Amorite dynasty of Babylon could capitalize in their quests for a measure of political unification, even when Akkadian replaced Sumerian as the language of commerce, diplomacy and literature, and even when the Babylonian Marduk became the chief god in the Mesopotamian pantheon.

[. . .] This difference between ethnic polities and divided and incorporated *ethnie* [left its] mark on the types of *mythomoteur* and modes of social penetration characteristic of the two types of *ethnie*. For the present, we need only note how both kinds of *ethnie* reveal otherwise similar structures and cultural features, and how frequently both are found in the historical record. For, whether politicized or not, whether as patrimonial kingdom or tribal confederation or city-state amphictyony, ethnic communities can be found playing active roles in human society and culture in most parts of the globe from at least the early Bronze Age, when writing first appears in the Near East, c.3000 BC. Whether, indeed, *ethnie* antedated this era is hard to say. Pottery styles in Mesopotamia and Egypt during the fifth and fourth millennia BC suggest a succession of cultures, like the Halaf and al-Ubaid on the lower Tigris, but, in the absence of written records or archaeological evidence, we have no means of ascertaining whether this stylistic succession expresses the presence of new ethnic migrations. Perhaps this period saw the formation of 'ethnic categories' with their separate myths of ancestry, memories, religions and languages, as successive waves of migrants settled in fertile riverine zones. But it was with the emergence of the first city states and patrimonial kingdoms in the early third millennium BC, and the first use of bronze weaponry in interstate warfare, that we find a growing sense of a more-than-local ethnic consciousness and sentiment, notably among the Egyptians and Sumerians.

Certainly, from the later third millennium BC, a succession of states based on a core ethnic community – Elamites, Amorites, Kushites, Canaanites, as well as Egyptians and Sumerians – appear in the historical records of the Near East, along with other communities whose political framework is far more tenuous, if it existed at all – peoples like the Guti or Lullubi, or the 'Harappans' – all of whom flourished in the period 2300–1700 BC. At this time, polities and *ethnie* do not often coincide; the more usual pattern is that of city states uniting temporarily because of common culture or religion in the face of a general threat, or of confederations of tribes seeking to expand their influence or dominate cities or districts, as it appears the Aryan tribes did in the early second millennium BC when they fanned out from Afghanistan and Central Asia into the Indus valley and the Punjab, and gradually subjugated the darker-skinned indigenous Dasa of the Harappan civilization. There is, at this stage, little ethnic cohesion or intense ethnic sentiments, except perhaps among the long-settled Egyptians and Sumerians.

By the later second millennium BC, more *ethnie* appear and evince greater self-awareness and cohesion. Apart from the Hittites and Mitannian Hurrians, Kassites, 'Minoans', Mycenaeans, Philistines, Arameans, Phoenicians, Assyrians and Canaanites are active for several centuries, some of them patrimonial king-doms (Hittites, Mitanni, Kassites, Assyrians) built usually over an excluded and conquered indigenous population, some peaceful or warring city kingdoms ('Minoans', Mycenaeans, Philistines, Phoenicians) and some tribal confederations (Arameans, Canaanites) who infiltrate and set up their own city kingdoms. The degree of ethnic unity or consciousness varies, but to judge by the biblical record of the Philistines and Syrian Arameans, it was greater than in earlier periods. We may surmise that the greater degree of interstate rivalry and communications during the Tell-el-Amarna period (fourteenth century BC), may have brought cultures and communities into more direct contact, and heightened their self-awareness through juxtaposition with neighbours and enemies.

Certainly, from this time until the great expansion of China and Rome in the late first millennium BC, ethnicity became of greater political importance and cultural salience. Both Hebraic and classical cultures reveal the growing role of *ethnie* in social life, as in the Books of Ruth and Jonah and the earlier Books of Kings, the histories of Herodotus and Xenophon and the *Persae* of Aeschylus. In Assyrian and Persian friezes, in Greek sculpture, as in later Egyptian art, there is a growing awareness of foreigners and their alien customs. In the Assyrian prac-tice of deportations of the ruling elites and whole cities of conquered states and peoples, there are the first signs of an awareness of the force of cultural and historic bonds in sustaining resistance to imperial rule.

Since this early period, *ethnie* have vied or colluded with other forms of com-munity – of city, class, religion, region – in providing a sense of identity among populations and in inspiring in them a nostalgia for their past and its traditions. In periods of grave crisis, it has even been able to arouse in them powerful senti-ments of anger and revenge for what were seen as attacks upon a traditional lifestyle and identity. For the most part, however, *ethnie* have provided foci of identification with ancestors and thereby a means of confronting death, especially violent death at the hands of enemies. By invoking a collective name, by the use of symbolic images of community, by the generation of stereotypes of the com-munity and its foes, by the ritual performance and rehearsal of ceremonies and feasts and sacrifices, by the communal recitation of past deeds and ancient heroes' exploits, men and women have been enabled to bury their sense of loneliness and insecurity in the face of natural disasters and human violence by feeling them-selves to partake of a collectivity and its historic fate which transcends their individual existences.

The evidence for the pervasiveness and ubiquity of ethnicity exists not only in the presence of such names, images, stereotypes, rituals and recitations, but in the very differences of styles in dress and coiffure, in crafts and furnishings, in tombs, temples and palaces, in the portrayal of the human figure, in characteristic use of metals and jewels, pottery and woodwork, in the depictions of activities and personages that have survived, as much as in the languages and scripts, laws and customs that differentiate human populations at all periods everywhere. All of these materials furnish rich evidence of ethnic differentiation and cultural identity, even if they cannot tell us how far a community felt itself to be unique and cohesive, and how deeply its fund of myths, memories, values and symbols had penetrated the social hierarchy. They may, however, by their durability, suggest something of the persistence of ethnicity, its ability to withstand change and absorb outside influences, particularly if they can be allied to more conventional written records. Though not all cultural differences reflect ethnic differentiation, much less ethnic community (*ethnie*), the persistence over centuries of separate styles attached to particular peoples in certain areas does point to the longevity and widespread incidence of *ethnie* in all periods. Along with polities, religious organizations and class, ethnicity provides one of the central axes of alignment and division in the pre-modern world, and one of the most durable.

ETHNICITY WITHOUT GROUPS[1]

ROGERS BRUBAKER

I. Common Sense Groupism

Few social science concepts would seem as basic, even indispensable, as that of group. In disciplinary terms, 'group' would appear to be a core concept for sociology, political science, anthropology, demography and social psychology. In substantive terms, it would seem to be fundamental to the study of political mobilization, cultural identity, economic interests, social class, status groups, collective action, kinship, gender, religion, ethnicity, race, multiculturalism, and minorities of every kind.

Yet despite this seeming centrality, the concept 'group' has remained curiously unscrutinized in recent years. There is, to be sure, a substantial social psychological literature addressing the concept (Hamilton et al. 1998, McGrath 1984), but this has had little resonance outside that sub-discipline. Elsewhere in the social sciences, the recent literature addressing the concept 'group' is sparse, especially by comparison with the immense literature on such concepts as class, identity, gender, ethnicity, or multiculturalism – topics in which the concept 'group' is implicated, yet seldom analysed on its own terms (Cooley 1962, Homans 1950 in sociology; Nadel 1957 in anthropology; Bentley 1908, Truman 1951 in political science; Olson 1965, Tilly 1978, and Hechter 1987). 'Group' functions as a seemingly unproblematic, taken-for-granted concept, apparently in no need of particular scrutiny or explication. As a result, we tend to take for granted not only the concept group', but also 'groups' – the putative things-in-the-world to which the concept refers.

My aim in this paper is not to enter into conceptual or definitional casuistry about the concept of group. It is rather to address one problematic consequence of this tendency to take groups for granted in the study of ethnicity, race and nationhood, and in the study of ethnic, racial and national conflict in particular. This is what I will call groupism: the tendency to take discrete, sharply differentiated, internally homogeneous and externally bounded groups as basic constituents of social life, chief protagonists of social conflicts, and fundamental units of social analysis.[2] In the domain of ethnicity, nationalism and race, I mean by 'groupism' the tendency to treat ethnic groups, nations and races as substantial entities to which interests and agency can be attributed. I mean the tendency to reify such groups, speaking of Serbs, Croats, Muslims and Albanians in the former Yugoslavia, of Catholics and Protestants in Northern Ireland, of Jews and Palestinians in Israel and the occupied territories, of Turks and Kurds in Turkey, or of Blacks, Whites, Asians, Hispanics and Native Americans in the US as if they were internally homogeneous, externally bounded groups, even unitary collective actors with common purposes. I mean the tendency to represent the social and cultural world as a multichrome mosaic of monochrome ethnic, racial or cultural blocs.

From the perspective of broader developments in social theory, the persisting strength of groupism in this sense is surprising. After all, several distinct traditions of social analysis have challenged the treatment of groups as real, substantial things-in-the-world. These include such sharply differing enterprises as ethnomethodology and conversation analysis, social network theory, cognitive theory, feminist theory, and individualist approaches such as rational choice and game theory. More generally, broadly structuralist approaches have yielded to a variety of more 'constructivist' theoretical stances, which tend – at the level of rhetoric, at least – to see groups as constructed, contingent, and fluctuating. And a diffuse postmodernist sensibility emphasizes the fragmentary, the ephemeral, and the erosion of fixed forms and clear boundaries. These developments are disparate, even contradictory in analytical style, methodological orientation and epistemological commitments. Network theory, with its methodological (and sometimes ontological) relationalism (Emirbayer and Goodwin 1994; Wellman 1988) is opposed to rational choice theory, with its methodological (and sometimes ontological) individualism; both are sharply and similarly opposed, in analytical style and epistemological commitments, to post-modernist approaches. Yet these and other developments have converged in problematizing groupness and undermining axioms of stable group being.

Challenges to 'groupism', however, have been uneven. They have been striking – to take just one example – in the study of class, especially in the study of the working class, a term that is hard to use today without quotation marks or some other distancing-device. Yet ethnic groups continue to be understood as entities and cast as actors. To be sure, constructivist approaches of one kind or another are now dominant in academic discussions of ethnicity. Yet everyday talk, policy analysis, media reports, and even much ostensibly constructivist academic writing routinely frame accounts of ethnic, racial and national conflict in groupist terms as the struggles 'of' ethnic groups, races, and nations (Allen and Seaton 1999, Seaton 1999). Somehow, when we talk about ethnicity, and even more so when we talk about ethnic conflict, we almost automatically find ourselves talking about ethnic groups.

Now it might be asked: 'What's wrong with this?' After all, it seems to be mere common sense to treat ethnic struggles as the struggles of ethnic groups, and ethnic conflict as conflict between such groups. I agree that this is the – or at least *a* – common-sense view of the matter. But we cannot rely on common sense here. Ethnic common sense – the tendency to partition the social world into putatively deeply constituted, quasi-natural intrinsic kinds (Hirschfeld 1996) – is a key part of what we want to explain, not what we want to explain things *with*; it belongs to our empirical data, not to our analytical toolkit.[3] Cognitive anthropologists and social psychologists have accumulated a good deal of evidence about common-sense ways of carving up the social world – about what Lawrence Hirschfeld (1996) has called 'folk sociologies'. The evidence suggests that some common sense social categories – and notably common-sense ethnic and racial categories – tend to be essentializing and naturalizing (Rothbart and Taylor 1992; Hirschfeld 1996; Gil-White 1999). They are the vehicles of what has been called a 'participants' primordialism' (Smith 1998: 158) or a 'psychological essentialism' (Medin 1989). We obviously cannot ignore such common-sense primordialism. But that does not mean we should simply replicate it in our scholarly analyses or policy assessments. As 'analysts *of* naturalizers', we need not be 'analytic naturalizers' (Gil-White 1999: 803).

Instead, we need to break with vernacular categories and common-sense understandings. We need to break, for example, with the seemingly obvious and uncontroversial point that ethnic conflict involves conflict between ethnic groups. I want to suggest that ethnic conflict – or what might better be called ethnicized or ethnically framed conflict – need not, and should not, be understood as conflict *between ethnic groups*, just as racial or racially framed conflict need not be understood as conflict between *races*, or nationally framed conflict as conflict between *nations*.

Participants, of course, regularly do represent ethnic, racial and national conflict in such groupist, even primordialist terms. They often cast ethnic groups, races or nations as the protagonists – the heroes and martyrs – of such struggles. But this is no warrant for analysts to do so. We must, of course, take vernacular categories and participants' understandings seriously, for they are partly constitutive of our objects of study. But we should not uncritically adopt *categories of ethnopolitical practice* as our *categories of social analysis*. Apart from the general unreliability of ethnic common sense as a guide for social analysis, we should remember that participants' accounts – especially those of specialists in ethnicity such as ethnopolitical entrepreneurs, who, unlike nonspecialists, may live 'off' as well as 'for' ethnicity – often have what Pierre Bourdieu has called a *performative* character. By *invoking* groups, they seek to *evoke* them, summon them, call them into being. Their categories are *for doing* – designed to stir, summon, justify, mobilize, kindle and energize. By reifying groups, by treating them as substantial things-in-the-world, ethnopolitical entrepreneurs may, as Bourdieu notes, 'contribute to producing what they apparently describe or designate' (1991a: 220; 1991b: 248–251).

Reification is a social process, not simply an intellectual bad habit. As a social process, it is central to the *practice of* politicized ethnicity. And appropriately so. To criticize ethnopolitical entrepreneurs for reifying ethnic groups would be a kind of category mistake. Reifying groups is precisely what ethnopolitical entrepreneurs are in the business of doing. When they are successful, the political fiction of the unified group can be momentarily yet powerfully realized in practice. As analysts, we should certainly try to *account* for the ways in which – and conditions under which – this practice of reification, this powerful crystallization of group feeling, can work. This may be one of the most important tasks of the theory of ethnic conflict. But we should avoid unintentionally *doubling* or *reinforcing* the reification of ethnic groups in ethnopolitical practice with a reification of such groups in social analysis.

II. Beyond Groupism

Rethinking ethnicity

We need to rethink not only ethnic conflict, but also what we mean by ethnicity itself. This is not a matter of seeking agreement on a definition. The intricate and ever-recommencing definitional casuistry in studies of ethnicity, race and nationalism has done little to advance the discussion, and indeed can be viewed as a symptom of the non-cumulative nature of research in the field. It is rather a matter of critically scrutinizing our conceptual tools. Ethnicity, race and nation should be conceptualized not as substances or things or entities or organisms or collective individuals – as the imagery of discrete, concrete, tangible, bounded and enduring 'groups' encourages us to do – but rather in relational, processual, dynamic, eventful and disaggregated terms. This means thinking of ethnicity, race and nation not in terms of substantial groups or entities but in terms of *practical categories, cultural idioms, cognitive schemas, discursive frames, organizational routines, institutional forms, political projects* and *contingent events*. It means thinking of *ethnicization, racialization* and *nationalization* as political, social cultural and psychological *processes*. And it means taking as a basic analytical category not the 'group' as an entity but *groupness* as a contextually fluctuating conceptual variable. Stated baldly in this fashion, these are of course mere slogans; I will try to fill them out a bit in what follows.

The reality of ethnicity

To rethink ethnicity, race and nationhood along these lines is in no way to dispute their reality, minimize their power or discount their significance; it is to construe their reality, power and significance in a different way. Understanding the reality of race, for example, does not require us to posit the existence of races. Racial idioms, ideologies, narratives, categories and systems of classification and racialized ways of seeing, thinking, talking and framing claims are real and consequential, especially when they are embedded in powerful organizations. But the reality of race – and even its overwhelming coercive power in some settings – does not depend on the existence of 'races'. Similarly, the reality of ethnicity and nationhood – and the overriding power of ethnic and national identifications in some settings – does not depend on the existence of ethnic groups or nations as substantial groups or entities.

Groupness as event

Shifting attention from groups to groupness and treating groupness as variable and contingent rather than fixed and given (Tilly 1978: 62*ff*, Hechter 1987: 8, Hamilton et al 1998), allows us to take account of – and, potentially, to account for – phases of extraordinary cohesion and moments of intensely felt collective solidarity, without implicitly treating high levels of groupness as constant, enduring or definitionally present. It allows us to treat groupness as an *event*, as something that 'happens', as E. P. Thompson famously said about class. At the same time, it keeps us analytically attuned to the possibility that groupness may *not* happen, that high levels of groupness may *fail* to crystallize, despite the group-making efforts of ethnopolitical entrepreneurs and even in situations of intense elite-level ethnopolitical conflict. Being analytically attuned to 'negative' instances in this way enlarges the domain of relevant cases and helps correct for the bias in the literature toward the study of striking instances of high groupness, successful mobilization or conspicuous violence – a bias that can engender an 'overethnicized' view of the social world, a distorted representation of whole world regions as 'seething cauldrons' of ethnic tension (Brubaker 1998) and an overestimation of the incidence of ethnic violence (Fearon and Laitin 1996). Sensitivity to such negative instances can also direct potentially fruitful analytical attention toward the problem of explaining failed efforts at ethnopolitical mobilization.

Groups and organizations

Although participants' rhetoric and common-sense accounts treat ethnic groups as the protagonists of ethnic conflict, in fact the chief protagonists of most ethnic conflict – and *a fortiori* of most ethnic violence – are not ethnic groups as such but various kinds of organizations, broadly understood and their empowered and authorized incumbents. These include states (or more broadly autonomous polities) and their organizational components such as particular ministries, offices, law enforcement agencies and armed forces units; they include terrorist groups, paramilitary organizations, armed bands and loosely structured gangs; and they include political parties, ethnic associations, social movement organizations, churches, newspapers, radio and television stations and so on. Some of these organizations may represent themselves, or may be seen by others, as organizations of and for particular ethnic groups.[4] But even when this is the case, organizations cannot be equated with ethnic groups. It is because and insofar as they are organizations and possess certain material and organizational resources, that they (or more precisely their incumbents) are capable of organized action and thereby of acting as more or less coherent protagonists in ethnic conflict.[5] Although common sense and participants' rhetoric attribute discrete existence, boundedness, coherence, identity, interest and agency to ethnic groups, these attributes are in fact characteristic of organizations. The IRA, KLA and PKK claim to speak and act in the name of the (Catholic) Irish, the Kosovo Albanians and the Kurds; but surely analysts must differentiate between such organizations and the putatively homogeneous and bounded groups in whose name they claim to act. The point applies not only to military, paramilitary and terrorist organizations, of course, but to all organizations that claim to speak and act in the name of ethnic, racial or national groups (Heisler 1991).

A fuller and more rounded treatment of this theme, to be sure, would require several qualifications that I can only gesture at here. Conflict and violence vary in the degree to which, as well as the manner in which, organizations are involved. What Donald Horowitz (zoos) has called the deadly ethnic riot, for example, differs sharply from organized ethnic insurgencies or terrorist campaigns. Although organizations (sometimes ephemeral ones) may play an important role in preparing, provoking and permitting such riots, much of the actual violence is committed by broader sets of participants acting in relatively spontaneous fashion and in starkly polarized situations characterized by high levels of groupness. Moreover, even where organizations are the core protagonists, they may depend on a penumbra of ancillary or supportive action on the part of sympathetic non-members. The 'representativeness' of organizations – the degree to which an organization can justifiably claim to represent the will, express the interests and enjoy the active or passive support of its constituents – is enormously variable, not only between organizations, but also over time and across domains. In addition, while organizations are ordinarily the *protagonists* of conflict and violence, they are not always the *objects* or *targets* of conflict and violence.

Entire population categories – or putative groups – can be the objects of organized action, much more easily than they can be the subjects or undertakers of such action. Finally, even apart from situations of violence, ethnic conflict may be at least partly amorphous, carried out not by organizations as such but spontaneously by individuals through such everyday actions as shunning, insults, demands for deference or conformity, or withholdings of routine interactional tokens of acknowledgement or respect (Bailey 1997). Still, despite these qualifications, it is clear that organizations, not ethnic groups as such, are the chief protagonists of ethnic conflict and ethnic violence and that the relationship between organizations and the groups they claim to represent is often deeply ambiguous.

Framing and coding[6]

If the protagonists of ethnic conflict cannot, in general, be considered ethnic groups, then what makes such conflict count as *ethnic* conflict? And what makes violence count as ethnic violence? Similar questions can be asked about racial and national conflict and violence. The answer cannot be found in the intrinsic properties of behaviour. The 'ethnic' quality of 'ethnic violence', for example, is not intrinsic to violent conduct itself; it is attributed to instances of violent behaviour. by perpetrators, victims, politicians, officials, journalists, researchers, relief workers or others. Such acts of framing and narrative encoding do not simply *interpret* the violence; they *constitute* it *as ethnic.*

Framing may be a key mechanism through which groupness is constructed. The metaphor of framing was popularized by Goffman (1974), drawing on Bateson 1985 [1955]. The notion has been elaborated chiefly in the social movement literature (Snow et al. 1986; Snow and Benford 1988; Gamson and Modigliani 1989; Gamson 1992; uniting rational choice and framing approaches, Esser 1999). When ethnic framing is successful, we may 'see' conflict and violence not only in ethnic, but in groupist terms. Although such imputed groupness is the product of prevailing interpretive frames, not necessarily a measure of the groupness felt and experienced by the participants in an event, a compelling *ex post* interpretive framing or encoding may exercise a powerful feedback effect, shaping subsequent experience and increasing levels of groupness. A great deal is at stake, then, in struggles over the interpretive framing and narrative encoding of conflict and violence.

Interpretive framing, of course, is often contested. Violence – and more generally, conflict – is regularly accompanied by social struggles to label, interpret and explain it. Such 'metaconflicts' or 'conflict[s] over the nature of the conflict', as Donald Horowitz has called them (1991:2), do not simply shadow conflicts from the outside, but are integral and consequential parts of the conflicts. To impose a label or prevailing interpretive frame – to cause an event to be seen as a 'pogrom' or a 'riot' or a 'rebellion' – is no mere matter of external interpretation, but a constitutive act of social definition that can have important consequences (Brass 1996b). Social struggles over the proper coding and interpretation of conflict and violence are therefore important subjects of study in their own right (Brass 1996a, 1997; Abelmann and Lie 1995).

Coding and framing practices are heavily influenced by prevailing interpretive frames. Today, ethnic and national frames are accessible and legitimate, suggesting themselves to actors and analysts alike. This generates a 'coding bias' in the ethnic direction. And this, in turn, may lead us to overestimate the incidence of ethnic conflict and violence by unjustifiably seeing ethnicity everywhere at work (Bowen 1996). Actors may take advantage of this coding bias and of the generalized legitimacy of ethnic and national frames, by strategically using ethnic framing to mask the pursuit of clan, clique or class interests. The point here is not to suggest that clans, cliques or classes are somehow more real than ethnic groups, but simply to note the existence of structural and cultural incentives for strategic framing.

Ethnicity as cognition[7]

These observations about the constitutive significance of coding and framing suggest a final point about the cognitive dimension of ethnicity. Ethnicity, race and nationhood exist only in and through our perceptions, interpretations, representations, categorizations and identifications. They are not things *in* the world, but perspectives *on* the world.[8] These include ethnicized ways of seeing (and ignoring), of construing (and misconstruing), of inferring (and misinferring), of remembering (and forgetting). They include ethnically oriented frames, schemas and narratives and the situational cues that activate them, such as the ubiquitous televised images that have played such an important role in the latest intifada. They include systems of classification, categorization and identification, formal and informal. And they include the tacit, taken-for-granted background knowledge, embodied in persons and embedded in institutionalized routines and practices, through which people recognize and experience objects, places, persons, actions or situations as ethnically, racially or nationally marked or meaningful.

Cognitive perspectives, broadly understood[9] can help advance constructivist research on ethnicity, race and nationhood, which has stalled in recent years as it has grown complacent with success. Instead of simply asserting *that* ethnicity, race and nationhood are constructed, they can help specify *how* they are constructed. They can help specify how – and when- people identify themselves, perceive others, experience the world and interpret their predicaments in racial, ethnic or national rather than other terms. They can help specify how 'groupness' can 'crystallize' in some situations while remaining latent and merely potential in others. And they can help link macro-level outcomes with micro-level processes.

III. Implications

At this point a critic might interject: 'What is the point of all this?' Even if we *can* study 'ethnicity without groups', why should we? Concepts invariably simplify the world; that the concept of discrete and bounded ethnic groups does so, suggesting something more substantial and clear-cut than really exists, cannot be held against it. The concept of ethnic group may be a blunt instrument, but it is good enough as a first approximation. This talk about groupness and framing and practical categories and cognitive schemas is all well and good, but meanwhile the killing goes on. Does the critique matter in the real world, or – if at all – only in the ivory tower? What practical difference does it make?

I believe the critique of groupism does have implications, albeit rather general ones, for the ways in which researchers, journalists, policymakers, NGOs and others come to terms, analytically and practically, with what we ordinarily – though perhaps too readily – call ethnic conflict and ethnic violence. Here I would like to enumerate five of these, before going on in the final section to discuss an empirical case.

First, sensitivity to framing dynamics, to the generalized coding bias in favour of ethnicity and to the sometimes strategic or even cynical use of ethnic framing to mask the pursuit of clan, clique or class interests can alert to the risk of over-ethnicized or overly groupist interpretations of (and interventions in) situations of conflict and violence (Bowen 1996). One need not subscribe to a reductionist 'elite manipulation' view of politicized ethnicity (Brubaker 1998) to acknowledge that the 'spin' put on conflicts by participants may conceal as much as it reveals and that the representation of conflicts as conflicts between ethnic or national groups may obscure the interests at stake and the dynamics involved. What is represented as ethnic conflict or ethnic war – such as the violence in the former Yugoslavia, may have as much or more to do with thuggery, warlordship, opportunistic looting and black-market profiteering than with ethnicity (Mueller 2000; *cf.* Collier 1999).

Second, recognition of the centrality of organizations in ethnic conflict and ethnic violence, of the often equivocal charif their leaders' claims to speak and act in the name of ethnic groups and of the performative nature of ethnopolitical rhetoric, enlisted in the service of group-making projects, can remin us not to mistake groupist rhetoric for real groupness, the putative groups of ethnopolitical rhetoric for substantial things-in-the-world.

Third, awareness of the interest that ethnic and nationalist leaders may have in living *off* politics, as well as *for* politics, to borrow the classic distinction of Max Weber (1946: 84), and awareness of the possible divergence between the interests of leaders and those of their putative constituents, can keep us from accepting at face value leaders' claims about the beliefs, desires and interests of their constituents.

Fourth, sensitivity to the variable and contingent, waxing and waning nature of groupness and to the fact that high levels of groupness may be more the result of conflict (especially violent conflict) than its underlying cause, can focus our analytical attention and policy interventions on the processes through which groupness tends to develop and crystallize and those through which it may subside. Some attention has been given recently to the former, including tipping and cascade mechanisms (Laitin 1995; Kuran 1998) and mechanisms governing the activation and diffusion of schemas and the 'epidemiology of representations' (Sperber 1985). But declining curves of groupness have not been studied systematically, although they are just as important, theoretically and practically. Once ratcheted up to a high level, groupness does not remain there out of inertia. If not sustained at high levels through specific social and cognitive mechanisms, it will tend to decline, as everyday interests reassert themselves, through a process of what Weber (in a different but apposite context [1968 (1922): 246–254]) called 'routinization' (*Veralltaeglichung*, literally 'towards everydayness').

Lastly, a disaggregating, non-groupist approach can bring into analytical and policy focus the critical importance of intra-ethnic mechanisms in generating and sustaining putatively interethnic conflict (Brubaker and Laitin 1998: 433). These include in-group 'policing,' monitoring, or sanctioning processes (Laitin 1995); the 'ethnic outbidding' throng which electoral competition can foster extreme ethnicization (Rothschild 1981; Horowitz 1985); the calculated instigation or provocation of conflict with outsiders by vulnerable incumbents seeking to deflect in-group challenges to their positions; and in-group processes bearing on the dynamics of recruitment into gangs, militias, terrorist groups or guerrilla armies, including honouring, shaming and shunning practices, rituals of manhood, intergenerational tensions and the promising and provision of material and symbolic rewards for martyrs.

Notes

1 Earlier versions of this paper were presented to the conference 'Facing Ethnic Conflicts', Center for Development Research, University of Bonn, December 54, 2000; the Working Group on Ethnicity and Nationalism, UCLA, January 13, 2001; the Anthropology Colloquium, University of Chicago, February 26, 2001; and the Central European University, Budapest, March 20, 2001. Thanks to participants in these events for their comments and criticisms, and to Margit Feischmidt, Jon Fox, Liana Grancea, David Laitin, Mara Loveman, Emanuel Schegloff, Peter Stamatov, Peter Waldmann, and Andreas Wimmer for helpful written comments.

2 In this very general sense, groupism extends well beyond the domain of ethnicity, race and nationalism to include accounts of putative groups based on gender, sexuality, age, class, abledness, religion, minority status and any kind of 'culture', as well as putative groups based on combinations of these categorical attributes. Yet while recognizing that it is a wider tendency in social analysis, I limit my discussion here to groupism in the study of ethnicity, race and nationalism.

3 This is perhaps too sharply put. To the extent that such intrinsic-kind categories are indeed constitutive of common-sense understandings of the social world, to the extent that such categories are used as a resource for participants, and are demonstrably deployed or oriented to by participants in interaction, they can also serve as a resource for analysts. But as Emanuel Schegloff notes in another context, with respect to the category 'interruption', the fact that this is a vernacular, common-sense category for participants 'does not make it a first-order category usable for professional analysis. Rather than being employed *in* professional analysis, it is better treated as a target category *for* professional analysis' (2000: 27). The same might well be said of common-sense ethnic categories.

4 One should remember, though, that organizations often compete with one another for the monopolization of the right to represent the same (putative) group.

5 In this respect the resource mobilization perspective on social movements, eclipsed in recent years by identity-oriented new social movement theory, has much to offer students of ethnicity. For an integrated statement, see McCarthy and Zald 1977.

6 These paragraphs draw on Brubaker and Laitin 1998.

7 These paragraphs draw on Brubaker et al. 2001.

8 As Emanuel Schegloff reminded me in a different context, this formulation is potentially misleading, since perspectives on the world – as every Sociology I student is taught – are themselves in the world and every bit as 'real' and consequential as other sorts of things.

9 Cognitive perspectives, in this broad sense, include not only those developed in cognitive psychology and cognitive anthropology but also those developed in the post- (and anti-) Parsonian 'cognitive turn' (DiMaggio and Powell 1991) in sociological and (more broadly) social theory, especially in response to the

influence of phenomenological and ethnomethodological work (Schutz 1962; Garfinkel 1967; Heritage 1984). Cognitive perspectives are central to the influential syntheses of Bourdieu and Giddens and – in a very different form – to the enterprise of conversation analysis.

References

Abelmann, Nancy and John Lie, 1995, *Blue Dreams: Korean Americans and the Los Angeles Riots* (Cambridge: Harvard University Press).

Allen, Tim and Jean Seaton (eds), 1999, *The Media of Conflict: War Reporting and Representations of Ethnic Violence* (London: Zed Books).

Bailey, Benjamin, 1997, Communication of Respect in Interethnic Service Encounters, *Language in Society 26*, 327–356.

Bateson, Gregory, 1985 [1955], A Theory of Play and Fantasy, in Robert E. Innis (ed.), *Semiotics: An Introductory Anthology*, 131–144.

Bentley, Arthur F., 1908, *The Process of Government: A Study of Social Pressures* (Chicago: University of Chicago Press).

Bourdieu, Pierre, 1991a, Identity and Representation: Elements for a Critical Reflection on the Idea of Region, *in* Pierre Bourdieu, *Language and Symbolic Power* (Cambridge: Harvard University Press), 220–228.

——, 1991b, Social Space and the Genesis of 'Classes', *in* Pierre Bourdieu, *Language and Symbolic Power* (Cambridge: Harvard University Press), 229–251.

Bowen, John R., 1996, The Myth of Global Ethnic Conflict, *Journal of Democracy 7*(4), 3–14.

Brass, Paul R. (ed.), 1996a, *Riots and Pogroms* (Washington Square: New York University Press).

——, 1996b, Introduction: Discourse of Ethnicity, Communalism and Violence, *in* Paul R. Brass (ed.), *Riots and Pogroms* (Washington Square: New York University Press), 1–55.

——, 1997, *Theft of an Idol: Text and Context in the Representation of Collective Violence* (Princeton: Princeton University Press).

Brubaker, Rogers, 1998, *Myths and Misconceptions in the Study of Nationalism*, in John Hall (ed.), *The State of the Nation: Ernest Gellner and the Theory of Nationalism* (New York: Cambridge University Press), 272–306.

Brubaker, Rogers and David D. Laitin, 1998, Ethnic and Nationalist Violence, *Annual Review of Sociology 24*, 423–452.

Brubaker, Rogers, Mara Loveman and Peter Stamatov, 2001, 'Beyond Social Construction: The Case for a Cognitive Approach to Race, Ethnicity and Nationalism'. Unpublished manuscript.

Collier, Paul, 1999, Doing Well Out of War. *http://www.worldbank.org/research/conflict/papers/econagenda.htm.*

Cooley, Charles H., 1962 (1909), *Social Organization* (New York: Schocken Books).

Dimaggio, Paul J. and Walter W. Powell, 1991, Introduction, *in* Walter W. Powell and Paul J. Dimaggio (eds), *The New Institutionalism in Organizational* (Chicago: University of Chicago Press), 1–38.

Emirbayer, Mustafa and Jeff Goodwin, 1994, Network Analysis, Culture and the Problem of Agency, *American Journal of Sociology* 99(6), 1411–1454.

Esser, Hartmut, 1999, Die Situationslogik ethnischer Konflikte: Auch eine Anmerkung zum Beitrag 'Ethnische Mobilisierung und die Logik von Identitätskämpfen' von Klaus Eder and Oliver Schmidtke, *Zeitschrift für Soziologie* 28(4), 245–262.

Fearon, James and David D. Laitin, 1996, Explaining Interethnic Cooperation, *American Political Science Review* 90(4), 715–735.

Gamson, William A., 1992, *Talking Politics* (New York: Cambridge University Press).

Gamson, William A. and Andre Modigliani, 1989, Media Discourse and Public Opinion on Nuclear Power: A Constructionist Approach, *American Journal of Sociology* 95, 1–37.

Garfinkel, Harold, 1967, *Studies in Ethnomethodology* (Englewood Cliffs, NJ: Prentice-Hall, Inc.)

Gil-White, Francisco, 1999, How Thick Is Blood? The Plot Thickens . . .: If Ethnic Actors Are Primordialists, What Remains of the Circumstantialist/Primordialist Controversy? *Ethnic and Racial Studies* 22(5), 789–820.

Goffman, Erving, 1974, *Frame Analysis* (San Francisco: Harper Colophon Books).

Hamilton, David L., Steven J. Sherman and Brian Lickel, 1998, Perceiving Social Groups: The Importance of the Entitativity Continuum, *in* Constantine Sedikides, John Schopler and Chester A. Insko (eds), *Intergroup Cognition and Intergroup Behavior* (Mahwah, NJ: Lawrence Erlbaum Associates), 47–74.

Hechter, Michael, 1987, *Principles of Group Solidarity* (Berkeley: University of California Press).

Heisler, Martin, 1991, Ethnicity and Ethnic Relations in the Modern West, *in* Joseph Montville (ed.), *Conflict and Peacemaking in Multiethnic* (Lexington: Lexington Books), 21–52.

Heritage, John, 1984, *Garfinkel and Ethnomethodology* (Cambridge: Polity Press).

Hirschfeld, Lawrence A., 1996, *Race in the Making: Cognition, Culture and the Child's Construction of Human Kinds* (Cambridge, MA: MIT Press).

Homans, George C., 1950, *The Human Group* (New York: Harcourt, Brace & World, Inc.).

Horowitz, Donald L., 1985, *Ethnic Groups in Conflict* (Berkeley, CA: University of California Press).

——, 1991, *A Democratic South Africa?: Constitutional Engineering in a Divided Society* (Berkeley: University of California Press).

——, 2001, *The Deadly Ethnic Riot* (Berkeley, CA: University of California Press).

Kuran, Timur, 1998, Ethnic Norms and their Transformation through Reputational Cascades, *Journal of Legal Studies* 27, 623–659.

Laitin, David D., 1995, National Revivals and Violence, *Archives européennes de sociologie* xxxvi, 3–43.

McCarthy, John D. and Mayer N. Zald, 1977, Resource Mobilization and Social Movements: A Partial Theory, *American Journal of Sociology* 82(6), 1212–1241.

McGrath, Joseph E., 1984, *Groups: Interaction and Performance* (New Jersey: Prentice-Hall).

Medin, Douglas L., 1989, Concepts and Conceptual Structure, *The American Psychologist* 44, 1469–1481.

Mueller, John, 2000, The Banality of 'Ethnic War', *International Security* 25, 42–70.

Nadel, S. F., 1957, *A Theory of Social Structure* (London: Cohen & West).

Olson, Mancur, 1965, *The Logic of Collective Action: Public Goods and the Theory of Groups* (Cambridge: Harvard University Press).

Rothbart, Myron and Marjorie Taylor, 1992, Category Labels and Social Reality: Do We View Social Categories As Natural Kinds? *in* Gün R. Semin and Klaus Fiedler (eds), *Language, Interaction and Social Cognition* (London: Sage Publications).

Rothschild, Joseph, 1981, *Ethnopolitics: A Conceptual Framework* (New York: Columbia University Press).

Schegloff, Emanuel A., 2000, Accounts of Conduct in Interaction: Interruption, Overlap and Turn-Taking, *in* J. H. Turner (ed.), *Handbook of Sociological Theory* (New York: Plenum).

Schutz, Alfred, 1962, *Collected Papers I: The Problem of Social Reality*, Maurice Natanson (ed.) (The Hague: Marinus Nijhofl).

Seaton, Jean, 1999, Why Do We Think the Serbs Do It? The New 'Ethnic' Wars and the Media, *Political Quarterly* 70(3), 254–270.

Smith, Anthony D., 1998, *Nationalism and Modernism: A Critical Survey of Recent Theories of Nations and Nationalism* (London: Routledge).

Snow, David A. and Robert D. Benford, 1988, Ideology, Frame Resonance and Participant Mobilization, *International Social Movement Research* 1, 197–217.

Snow, David A., E. B. Rochford Jr., Steven K. Worden and Robert D. Benford, 1986, Frame Alignment Processes, Micromobilization and Movement Participation, *American Sociological Review* 51, 464–481.

Sperber, Dan, 1985, Anthropology and Psychology: Towards an Epidemiology of Representations, *Man* 20, 73–89.

Tilly, Charles, 1978, *From Mobilization to Revolution* (Reading, Mass.: Addison-Wesley Publishing Company).

Truman, David B., 1951, *The Governmental Process: Political Interests and Public Opinion*. 2nd ed. (New York: Alfred A. Knopf).

Weber, Max, 1946, *From Max Weber. Essays in Sociology*, H. H. Gerth and Wright Mills (eds) (New York: Oxford University Press).

——, 1968 [1922], *Economy and Society*, Guenther Roth and Claus Wittich (eds) (Berkeley: University of California Press).

Wellman, Barry, 1988, Structural Analysis: From Method and Metaphor to Theory and Substance, in Barry Wellman and S. D. Berkowitz (eds), *Social Structures: A Network Approach* (Cambridge: Cambridge University Press), 19–61.

ETHNICITY, RACE AND NATION

THOMAS HYLLAND ERIKSEN

'Ethnicity seems to be a new term', state Nathan Glazer and Daniel Moynihan (1975: 1), who point to the fact that the word's earliest dictionary appearance is in the *Oxford English Dictionary* in 1972. Its first usage is attributed to the American sociologist David Riesman in 1953. The word 'ethnic', however, is much older. It is derived from the Greek *ethnos* (which in turn, derived from the word *ethnikos*), which originally meant heathen or pagan. It was used in this sense in English from the mid-fourteenth century until the mid-nineteenth century, when it gradually began to refer to 'racial' characteristics. In the United States, 'ethnics' came to be used around the Second World War as a polite term referring to Jews, Italians, Irish and other people considered inferior to the dominant group of largely British descent. None of the founding fathers of sociology and social anthropology – with the partial exception of Max Weber – granted ethnicity much attention.

Since the 1960s, ethnic groups and ethnicity have become household words in Anglophone social anthropology, although, as Ronald Cohen (1978) has remarked, few of those who use the terms bother to define them. I shall examine a number of approaches to ethnicity. Most of them are closely related, although they may serve different analytical purposes. All of the approaches agree that ethnicity has something to do with the *classification of people* and *group relationships*.

In everyday language the word ethnicity still has a ring of 'minority issues' and 'race relations', but in social anthropology it refers to aspects of relationships between groups which consider themselves, and are regarded by others, as being culturally distinctive. Although it is true that 'the discourse concerning ethnicity tends to concern itself with subnational units, or minorities of some kind or another' (Chapman et al., 1989: 17), majorities and dominant peoples are no less 'ethnic' than minorities.

[...]

Ethnicity, Race and Nation

A few words must be said initially about the relationship between ethnicity and 'race'. The term race has deliberately been placed within inverted commas in order to stress that it has dubious descriptive value. Whereas it was for some time common to divide humanity into four main races, modern genetics tends not to speak of races. There are two principal reasons for this. First, there has always been so much interbreeding between human populations that it would be meaningless to talk of fixed boundaries between races. Second, the distribution of hereditary physical traits does not follow clear boundaries. In other words, there is often greater variation within a 'racial' group than there is systematic variation between two groups.

Concepts of race can nevertheless be important to the extent that they inform people's actions; at this level, race exists as a cultural construct, whether it has a 'biological' reality or not. Racism, obviously, builds on the assumption that personality is somehow linked with hereditary characteristics which differ systematically between 'races', and in this way race may assume sociological importance even if it has no 'objective' existence. Social scientists who study race relations in Great Britain and the United States need not themselves believe in the existence of race, since their object of study is the social and cultural relevance of the *notion* that race exists. If influential people in a society had developed a similar theory about the hereditary personality traits of red-haired people, and if that theory gained social and cultural significance, 'redhead studies' would for similar reasons have become a field of academic research, even if the researchers themselves did not agree that redheads were different from others in a relevant way. In societies where ideas of race are important, they may therefore be studied as part of local discourses on ethnicity.

Should the study of race relations, in this meaning of the word, be distinguished from the study of ethnicity or ethnic relations? Pierre van den Berghe (1983) does not think so, but would rather regard 'race' relations as a special case of ethnicity. Others, among them Michael Banton (1967), have argued the need to distinguish between race and ethnicity. In Banton's view, race refers to the categorization of people, while ethnicity has to do with group identification. He argues that ethnicity is generally more concerned with the identification of 'us', while racism is more oriented to the categorization of 'them'. However, ethnicity can assume many forms, and since ethnic ideologies tend to stress common descent among their members, the distinction between race and ethnicity is a problematic one, even if Banton's distinction between groups and categories can be useful. I shall not, therefore, distinguish between race relations and ethnicity. Ideas of 'race' may or may not form part of ethnic ideologies, and their presence or absence does not seem to be a decisive factor in interethnic relations.

Discrimination on ethnic grounds is spoken of as 'racism' in Trinidad and as 'communalism' in Mauritius, but the forms of imputed discrimination referred to can be nearly identical. On the other hand, it is doubtless true that groups who 'look different' from majorities or dominating groups may be less liable to become assimilated into the majority than others, and that it can be difficult for them to escape from their ethnic identity if they wish to. However, this may also hold good for minority groups with, say, an inadequate command of the dominant language. In both cases, their ethnic identity becomes an imperative status, an ascribed aspect of their personhood from which they cannot escape entirely. Race or skin colour as such is not the decisive variable in every society.

The relationship between the terms ethnicity and nationality is nearly as complex as that between ethnicity and race. Like the words ethnic and race, the word nation has a long history, and has been used with a variety of different meanings in English. We shall refrain from discussing these meanings here, and will concentrate on the sense in which nation and nationalism are used analytically in academic discourse. Like ethnic ideologies, nationalism stresses the cultural similarity of its adherents and, by implication, it draws boundaries *vis-à-vis* others, who thereby become outsiders. The distinguishing mark of nationalism is by definition its relationship to the state. A nationalist holds that political boundaries should be coterminous with cultural boundaries, whereas many ethnic groups do not demand command over a state. When the political leaders of an ethnic movement make demands to this effect, the ethnic movement therefore by definition becomes a nationalist movement. Although nationalisms tend to be ethnic in character, this is not necessarily the case. [...]

Ethnicity and Class

The term ethnicity refers to relationships between groups whose members consider themselves distinctive, and these groups may be ranked hierarchically within a society. It is therefore necessary to distinguish clearly between ethnicity and social class.

In the literature of social science, there are two main definitions of classes. One derives from Karl Marx, the other from Max Weber. Sometimes elements from the two definitions are combined.

The Marxist view of social classes emphasizes economic aspects. A social class is defined according to its relationship to the productive process in society. In capitalist societies, according to Marx, there are three main classes. First, there is the capitalist class or bourgeoisie, whose members own the means of production (factories, tools and machinery and so on) and buy other people's labour-power (employ them). Second, there is the petit-bourgeoisie, whose members own means of production but do not employ others. Owners of small shops are typical examples. The third and most numerous class is the proletariat or working class, whose members depend upon selling their labour-power to a capitalist for their livelihood. There are also other classes, notably the aristocracy, whose members live by land interest, and the lumpenproletariat, which consists of unemployed and underemployed people – vagrants and the like.

Since Marx's time in the mid-nineteenth century, the theory of classes has been developed in several directions. Its adherents nevertheless still stress the relationship to property in their delineation of classes. A further central feature of this theory is the notion of class struggle. Marx and his followers held that oppressed classes would eventually rise against their oppressors, overthrow them through a revolution, and alter the political order and the social organization of labour. This, in Marx's view, was the chief way in which societies evolved.

The Weberian view of social classes, which has partly developed into theories of social stratification, combines several criteria in delineation of classes, including income, education and political influence. Unlike Marx, Weber did not regard classes as potential corporate groups; he did not believe that members of social classes necessarily would have shared political interests. Weber preferred to speak of 'status groups' rather than classes.

Theories of social class always refer to systems of social ranking and distribution of power. Ethnicity, on the contrary, does not necessarily refer to rank; ethnic relations may well be egalitarian in this regard. Still, many polyethnic societies are ranked according to ethnic membership. The criteria for such ranking are nevertheless different from class ranking: they refer to imputed cultural differences or 'races', not to property or achieved statuses.

There may be a high *correlation* between ethnicity and class, which means that there is a high likelihood that persons belonging to specific ethnic groups also belong to specific social classes. There can be a significant interrelationship between class and ethnicity, both class and ethnicity can be criteria for rank, and ethnic membership can be an important factor in class membership. Both class differences and ethnic differences can be pervasive features of societies, but they are not one and the same thing and must be distinguished from one another analytically.

[…]

From Tribe to Ethnic Group

There has been a shift in Anglophone social anthropological terminology concerning the nature of the social units we study. While one formerly spoke of 'tribes', the term 'ethnic group' is nowadays much more common. This switch in terminology implies more than a mere replacement of one word with another. Notably, the use of the term 'ethnic group' suggests contact and interrelationship. To speak of an ethnic group in total isolation is as absurd as to speak of the sound from one hand clapping. By definition, ethnic groups remain more or less discrete, but they are aware of – and in contact with – members of other ethnic groups. Moreover, these groups or categories are in a sense *created* through that very contact. Group identities must always be defined in relation to that which they are not – in other words, in relation to non-members of the group.

The terminological switch from 'tribe' to 'ethnic group' may also mitigate or even transcend an ethnocentric or Eurocentric bias which anthropologists have often been accused of promoting covertly. When we talk of tribes, we implicitly introduce a sharp, qualitative distinction between ourselves and the people we study; the distinction generally corresponds to the distinction between modern and traditional or so-called primitive societies. If we instead talk of ethnic groups or categories, such a sharp distinction becomes difficult to maintain. Virtually every human being belongs to an ethnic group, whether he or she lives in Europe, Melanesia or Central America. There are ethnic groups in English cities, in the Bolivian countryside and in the New Guinea highlands. Anthropologists themselves belong to ethnic groups or nations. Moreover, the concepts and models used in the study of ethnicity can often be applied to modern as well as non-modern contexts, to Western as well as non-Western societies. In this sense, the concept of ethnicity can be said to bridge two important gaps in social anthropology: it entails a focus on dynamics rather than statics, and it relativizes the boundaries between 'Us' and 'Them', between moderns and tribals.

What Is Ethnicity?

When we talk of ethnicity, we indicate that groups and identities have developed in mutual contact rather than in isolation. But what is the nature of such groups?

When A. L. Kroeber and Clyde Kluckhohn investigated the various meanings of 'culture' in the early 1950s they found about 300 different definitions. Although Ronald Cohen is correct in stating that most of those who write on ethnicity do not bother to define the term, the extant number of definitions is already high – and it is growing. Instead of going through the various definitions of ethnicity here, I will point out significant differences between theoretical viewpoints as we go along. As a starting-point, let us examine the recent development of the term as it is used by social anthropologists.

The term 'ethnic group' has come to mean something like 'a people'. But what is 'a people'? Does the population of Britain constitute a people, does it comprise several peoples (as Nairn, 1977, tends to argue), or does it rather form part of a Germanic, or an English-speaking, or a European people? All of these positions may have their defenders, and this very ambiguity in the designation of peoples has been taken on as a challenge by anthropologists. In a study of ethnic relations in Thailand, Michael Moerman (1965) asks himself: 'Who are the Lue?' The Lue were the ethnic group his research focused on, but when he tried to describe who they were – in which ways they were distinctive from other ethnic groups – he quickly ran into trouble. His problem, a very common one in contemporary social anthropology, concerned the boundaries of the group. After listing a number of criteria commonly used by anthropologists to demarcate cultural groups, such as language, political organization and territorial contiguity, he states: 'Since language, culture, political organization, etc., do not correlate completely, the units delimited by one criterion do not coincide with the units delimited by another' (Moerman, 1965:1215). When he asked individual Lue what were their typical characteristics, they would mention cultural traits which they in fact shared with other, neighbouring groups. They lived in close interaction with other groups in the area; they had no exclusive livelihood, no exclusive language, no exclusive customs, no exclusive religion. Why was it appropriate to describe them as an ethnic group? After posing these problems, Moerman was forced to conclude that '[s]omeone is Lue by virtue of believing and calling himself Lue and of acting in ways that validate his Lueness' (Moerman 1965: 1219). Being unable to argue that this 'Lueness' can be defined with reference to objective cultural features or clear-cut boundaries, Moerman defines it as an *emic category of ascription*.[1] This way of delineating ethnic groups has become very influential in social anthropology.

Does this imply that ethnic groups do not necessarily have a distinctive culture? Can two groups be culturally identical and yet constitute two different ethnic groups? [...] At this point we should note that, contrary to a widespread common-sense view, cultural difference between two groups is not the decisive feature of ethnicity. Two distinctive, endogamous groups, say, somewhere in New Guinea, may well have widely different languages, religious beliefs and even technologies, but that does not necessarily mean that there is an ethnic relationship between them. For ethnicity to come about, the groups must have a minimum of contact with each other, and they must entertain ideas of each other as being culturally different from themselves. If these conditions are not fulfilled, there is no ethnicity, for ethnicity is essentially an aspect of a relationship, not a property of a group. This is a key point. Conversely, some groups may seem culturally similar, yet there can be a socially highly relevant (and even volatile) interethnic relationship between them. This would be the case of the relationship between Serbs and Croats following the breakup of Yugoslavia, or of the tension between coastal Sami and Norwegians. There may also be considerable cultural variation within a group without ethnicity. Only insofar as cultural differences are perceived as being important, and are made socially relevant, do social relationships have an ethnic element.

Ethnicity is an aspect of social relationship between agents who consider themselves as culturally distinctive from members of other groups with whom they have a minimum of regular interaction. It can thus also be defined as a social identity (based on a contrast *vis-à-vis* others) characterized by metaphoric or fictive kinship. When cultural differences regularly make a difference in interaction between members of groups, the social relationship has an ethnic element. Ethnicity refers both to aspects of gain and loss in interaction, and to aspects of meaning in the creation of identity. In this way it has a political, organizational aspect as well as a symbolic one.

Ethnic groups tend to have myths of common origin and they nearly always have ideologies encouraging endogamy, which may nevertheless be of highly varying practical importance.

'Kinds' of Ethnic Relations?

This very general and tentative definition of ethnicity lumps together a great number of very different social phenomena. My relationship with my Pakistani greengrocer has an ethnic aspect; so, it could be argued, do the war in former Yugoslavia and 'race riots' in American cities. Do these phenomena have anything interesting in common, justifying their comparison within a single conceptual framework? The answer is both yes and no.

One of the contentions from anthropological studies of ethnicity is that there may be mechanisms of ethnic processes which are relatively uniform in every interethnic situation: to this effect, we can identify certain shared formal properties in all ethnic phenomena.

On the other hand, there can be no doubt that the substantial social contexts of ethnicity differ enormously, and indeed that ethnic identities and ethnic organizations themselves may have highly variable importance in different societies, for different individuals and in different situations. We should nevertheless keep in mind that the point of anthropological comparison is not necessarily to establish similarities between societies; it can also reveal important differences. In order to discover such differences, we must initially possess some kind of measuring stick, a constant or a conceptual bridgehead, which can be used as a basis of comparison. If we first know what we mean by ethnicity, we can then use the concept as a common denominator for societies and social contexts which are otherwise very different. The concept of ethnicity can in this way not only teach us something about similarity, but also about differences.

Although the concept of ethnicity should always have the same meaning lest it ceases to be useful in comparison, it is inevitable that we distinguish between the social contexts under scrutiny. Some interethnic contexts in different societies are very similar and may seem easily comparable, whereas others differ profoundly. In order to give an idea of the variation, I shall briefly describe some typical empirical foci of ethnic studies, some kinds of ethnic groups, so to speak. This list is not exhaustive.

1 Urban ethnic minorities. This category would include, among others, non-European immigrants in European cities and Hispanics in the United States, as well as migrants to industrial towns in Africa and elsewhere. Research on immigrants has focused on problems of adaptation, on ethnic discrimination from the host society, racism, and issues relating to identity management and cultural change. Anthropologists who have investigated urbanization in Africa have focused on change and continuity in political organization and social identity following migration to totally new settings. Although they have political interests, these ethnic groups rarely demand political independence or statehood, and they are as a rule integrated into a capitalist system of production and consumption.

2 Indigenous peoples. This word is a blanket term for aboriginal inhabitants of a territory, who are politically relatively powerless and who are only partly integrated into the dominant nation state. Indigenous peoples are associated with a non-industrial mode of production and a stateless political system. The Basques of the Bay of Biscay and the Welsh of Great Britain are not considered indigenous populations, although they are certainly as indigenous, technically speaking, as the Sami of northern Scandinavia or the Jivaro of the Amazon basin. The concept 'indigenous people' is thus not an accurate analytical one, but rather one drawing on broad family resemblances and contemporary political issues.

3 Proto-nations (so-called ethnonationalist movements). These groups, the most famous of ethnic groups in the news media of the 1990s, include Kurds, Sikhs, Palestinians and Sri Lankan Tamils, and their number is growing. By definition, these groups have political leaders who claim that they are entitled to their own nation state and should not be 'ruled by others'. These groups, short of having a nation state, may be said to have more substantial characteristics in common with nations than with either urban minorities or indigenous peoples. They are always territorially based; they are differentiated according to class and educational achievement, and they are large groups.

4 Ethnic groups in 'plural societies'. The term 'plural society' usually designates colonially created states with culturally heterogeneous populations (Furnivall 1948; M. G. Smith, 1965). Typical plural societies would be Kenya, Indonesia and Jamaica. The groups that make up the plural society, although they are compelled to participate in uniform political and economic systems, are regarded as (and regard themselves as) highly distinctive in other matters. In plural societies, secessionism is usually not an option and ethnicity tends to be articulated as group competition. [...]

The definition of ethnicity proposed earlier would include all of these 'kinds' of group, no matter how different they are in other respects. Surely, there are aspects of politics (gain and loss in interaction) as well as meaning (social identity and belonging) in the ethnic relations reproduced by urban minorities, indigenous peoples, proto-nations and the component groups of plural societies alike. Despite the great variations between the problems and substantial characteristics represented by the respective kinds of group, the term ethnicity may, in other words, meaningfully be used as a common denominator for them.

Note

1 In the anthropological literature, the term *emic* refers to 'the native's point of view'. It is contrasted with *etic*, which refers to the analyst's concepts, descriptions and analyses. The terms are derived from phonemics and phonetics.

References

Banton, Michael (1967), *Race Relations*. London: Tavistock.

Berghe, Pierre L. van den (1983), 'Class, race and ethnicity in Africa'. *Ethnic and Racial Studies*, vol. 6(2), pp. 221–36.

Chapman, Malcolm, Maryon McDonald and Elizabeth Tonkin (1989), 'Introduction: History and social anthropology' in Elizabeth Tonkin, Maryon McDonald and Malcolm Chapman (eds) *History and Ethnicity*, pp. 1–21. London: Routledge.

Cohen, Ronald (1978), 'Ethnicity: Problem and focus in anthropology'. *Annual Review of Anthropology*, vol. 7, pp. 379–404.

Furnivall, J. S. (1948), *Colonial Policy and Practice: A Comparative Study of Burma and Netherlands India*. Cambridge: Cambridge University Press.

Glazer, Nathan and Daniel P. Moynihan (eds) (1975), *Ethnicity: Theory and Experience*. Cambridge, Mass.: Harvard University Press.

Kroeber, A. L. and Clyde Kluckhohn (1952), *Culture: A Critical Review of Concepts and Definitions*. Cambridge, Mass.: Harvard University Press.

Moerman, Michael (1965), 'Who are the Lue?: Ethnic identification in a complex civilization'. *American Anthropologist*, vol. 67, pp. 1215–29.

Nairn, Tom (1977), *The Break-up of Britain*. London: New Left Books.

Smith, M.G (1965), *The Plural Society of the British West Indies*. London: Sangster's.

2

Ethnicity and Nationalism

Benedict Anderson defines the nation as an 'imagined community', limited, sovereign and worthy of sacrifices. He writes: 'nationalism has to be understood by aligning it, not with self-consciously held political ideologies, but with large cultural systems that preceded it, out of which – as well as against which – it came into being'. Anderson points to the importance of the development of the printed word as the basis for the mergence of national consciousnesses.[1]

Anderson argues that print-languages laid the basis for national consciousness in three ways: they created unified fields of exchange and communication below Latin and above the spoken vernaculars; they gave a new fixity to language, helping to build an image of antiquity, central to the subjective idea of the nation; and they created languages of power which differed from the older administrative vernaculars (1983: 47).

The crucial factor in this process was that, for the first time, the language in which the people of a discrete area spoke and thought was the same as that in which the ruling strata, the intellectuals and the clergy wrote and read. This was a revolutionary event, since it progressively erased the need to learn Latin if one sought to take the first step into the world of literature or science, have access to the Scriptures, or enter the realms of administration and trade.

Ernest Gellner considers nationalism in terms of modernization. Gellner offers the most sophisticated account of nationalism within this framework. Gellner holds that the nation and nationalism are modern phenomena closely connected to the emergence of industrial society and correctly observes the enormous paradox that nations can be defined only in terms of the age of nationalism, rather than, as one might expect, the other way round: 'Admittedly, nationalism uses the pre-existing, historically inherited proliferation of cultures or cultural wealth, though it uses them very selectively, and it most often transforms them radically' (1983: 55).

In his view, the economies of industrialized states depend upon a homogenizing high culture, mass literacy and an educational system controlled by the state. 'Industrial man' writes Gellner, 'can be compared with an artificially produced or bred species which can no longer breathe effectively in the nature-given atmosphere, but can only function effectively and survive in a new, specially blended and artificially sustained air or medium…It requires a specialized plant. The name for this plant is a national educational and communications system. Its only effective keeper and protector is the state.'[2]

The modern state has the power to control two elements that, through their role in reproducing and modifying culture, become crucial in the homogenization of the state's population: the media and education. Gellner stresses the unprecedented importance of communication and culture in industrial societies – both key features in his theory of nationalism.

Eric Hobsbawm also offers a modernist approach to the study of nationalism. He stresses the recent origin and invented nature of most traditions presented as rooted in ancient times as implying a continuity that is largely factitious. In so doing he does not deny the significance of old traditions adapting to meet new needs, nor does he deny that traditions have been 'invented' in previous times, rather he emphasizes the rapid change of modernity and the constant need to 'invent' traditions in order to: foster social cohesion and group membership; legitimize institutions, status or power-relations; and, inculcate beliefs, value systems and conventions (Smith: 1998, 119).

Hobsbawm argues that the liberal criteria of nation-making employed in the nineteenth century and in the early twentieth century assumed that only what were considered as culturally and economically 'viable' nations could enjoy the right to self-determination. To this extent, he notes, 'Mazzini's and Mill's idea of national self-determination was fundamentally different from President Wilson's'.[3] Real great nations should survive, small and backward ones were doomed to disappear and with them their specific cultures and languages. Hobsbawm argues that this position did not arise from chauvinistic motives but described the general attitude: 'it did not imply any hostility to the languages and culture of such collective victims to the laws of progress (as they would certainly have been called then). On the contrary, where the supremacy of the state-nationality and the state-language were not an issue, the major nation could cherish and foster the dialects and lesser languages within it: the historic and folkloric traditions of the lesser communities it contained, if only as proof of the range of colours on its macro-national palette' (1990: 35). Hobsbawm contended that the main objective of nationalism – a political programme – is the construction of a nation state.

Notes

1 Anderson, B., *Imagined Communities* (Verso, London: 1983).
2 Gellner, E., *Nations and Nationalism* (Basil Blackwell, Oxford: 1983).
3 Hobsbawm, E., *Nations and Nationalism since 1780* (Cambridge University Press: Cambridge: 1992 [1990]).

THE NATION AND THE ORIGINS OF NATIONAL CONSCIOUSNESS

BENEDICT ANDERSON

Nationality, or, as one might prefer to put it in view of that word's multiple significations, nation-ness, as well as nationalism, are cultural artefacts of a particular kind. To understand them properly we need to consider carefully how they have come into historical being, in what ways their meanings have changed over time, and why, today, they command such profound emotional legitimacy. I will be trying to argue that the creation of these artefacts towards the end of the eighteenth century was the spontaneous distillation of a complex 'crossing' of discrete historical forces; but that, once created, they became 'modular', capable of being transplanted, with varying degrees of self-consciousness, to a great variety of social terrains, to merge and be merged with a correspondingly wide variety of political and ideological constellations. I will also attempt to show why these particular cultural artefacts have aroused such deep attachments.

Concepts and Definitions

Before addressing the questions raised above, it seems advisable to consider briefly the concept of 'nation' and offer a workable definition. Theorists of nationalism have often been perplexed, not to say irritated, by these three paradoxes:

1 The objective modernity of nations to the historian's eye vs. their subjective antiquity in the eyes of nationalists;
2 The formal universality of nationality as a socio-cultural concept - in the modern world everyone can, should, will 'have' a nationality, as he or she 'has' a gender - vs. the irremediable particularity of its concrete manifestations, such that, by definition, 'Greek' nationality is *sui generis*;
3 The 'political' power of nationalisms vs. their philosophical poverty and even incoherence.

In other words, unlike most other -isms, nationalism has never produced its own grand thinkers: no Hobbeses, Tocquevilles, Marxes or Webers. This 'emptiness' easily gives rise, among cosmopolitan and polylingual intellectuals, to a certain condescension. Like Gertrude Stein in the face of Oakland, one can rather quickly conclude that there is 'no there there'. It is characteristic that even so sympathetic a student of nationalism as Tom Nairn can nonetheless write that: ' "Nationalism" is the pathology of modern developmental history, as inescapable as "neurosis" in the individual, with much the same essential ambiguity attaching to it, a similar built-in capacity for descent into dementia, rooted in the dilemmas of helplessness thrust upon most of the world (the equivalent of infantilism for societies) and largely incurable' (Nairn 1977: 359).

Part of the difficulty is that one tends unconsciously to hypostasize the existence of Nationalism-with-a-big-N – rather as one might Age-with-a-capital-A – and then to classify 'it' as an ideology. (Note that if everyone has an age, Age is merely an analytical expression.) It would, I think, make things easier if one treated it as if it belonged with 'kinship' and 'religion' rather than with 'liberalism' or 'fascism'.

In an anthropological spirit, then, I propose the following definition of the nation: it is an imagined political community – and imagined as both inherently limited and sovereign.

It is *imagined* because the members of even the smallest nation will never know most of their fellow-members, meet them, or even hear of them, yet in the minds of each lives the image of their communion. Renan referred to this imagining in his suavely back-handed way when he wrote that 'Or l'essence d'une nation est que tous les individus aient beaucoup de choses en commun, et aussi que tous aient oublié bien des choses' (Renan 1947: 892). With a certain ferocity Gellner makes a comparable point when he rules that 'Nationalism is not the awakening of nations to selfconsciousness: it invents nations where they do not exist' (Gellner 1964: 169). The drawback to this formulation, however, is that Gellner is so anxious to show that nationalism masquerades under false pretences that he assimilates 'invention' to 'fabrication' and 'falsity' rather than to 'imagining' and 'creation'. In this way he implies that 'true' communities exist which can be advantageously juxtaposed to nations. In fact, all communities larger than primordial villages of face-to-face contact (and perhaps even these) are imagined. Communities are to be distinguished, not by their falsity/genuineness, but by the style in which they are imagined. Javanese villagers have always known that they are connected to people they have never seen, but these ties were once imagined particularistically – as indefinitely stretchable nets of kinship and clientship. Until quite recently, the Javanese language had no word meaning the abstraction 'society'. We may today think of the French aristocracy of the *ancien régime* as a class; but surely it was imagined this way only very late. To the question 'Who is the Comte de X?' the normal answer would have been not 'a member of the aristocracy' but 'the lord of X', 'the uncle of the Baronne de Y' or 'a client of the Duc de Z'.

The nation is imagined as *limited* because even the largest of them, encompassing perhaps a billion living human beings, has finite, if elastic, boundaries, beyond which lie other nations. No nation imagines itself coterminous with mankind. The most messianic nationalists do not dream of a day when all the members of the human race will join their nation in the way that it was possible, in certain epochs, for, say, Christians to dream of a wholly Christian planet.

It is imagined as *sovereign* because the concept was born in an age in which Enlightenment and Revolution were destroying the legitimacy of the divinely ordained, hierarchical dynastic realm. Coming to maturity at a stage of human history when even the most devout adherents of any universal religion were inescapably confronted with the living *pluralism* of such religions, and the allomorphism between each faith's ontological claims and territorial stretch, nations dream of being free, and, if under God, directly so. The gage and emblem of this freedom is the sovereign state.

Finally, it is imagined as a *community* because, regardless of the actual inequality and exploitation that may prevail in each, the nation is always conceived as a deep, horizontal comradeship. Ultimately it is this fraternity that makes it possible, over the past two centuries, for so many millions of people, not so much to kill, as willingly to die for such limited imaginings.

These deaths bring us abruptly face to face with the central problem posed by nationalism: what makes the shrunken imaginings of recent history (scarcely more than two centuries) generate such colossal sacrifices? I believe that the beginnings of an answer lie in the cultural roots of nationalism.

The Origins of National Consciousness

If the development of print-as-commodity is the key to the generation of wholly new ideas of simultaneity, still, we are simply at the point where communities of the type 'horizontal-secular, transverse-time' become possible. Why, within that type, did the nation become so popular? The factors involved are obviously complex and various. But a strong case can be made for the primacy of capitalism.

At least 20 million books had already been printed by 1500, signalling the onset of Benjamin's 'age of mechanical reproduction'. If manuscript knowledge was scarce and arcane lore, print knowledge lived by reproducibility and dissemination. If, as Febvre and Martin believe, possibly as many as 200 million volumes had been manufactured by 1600, it is no wonder that Francis Bacon believed that print had changed 'the appearance and state of the world'.

One of the earlier forms of capitalist enterprise, book publishing felt all of capitalism's restless search for markets. The early printers established branches all over Europe: 'in this way a veritable "international" of publishing houses, which ignored national [sic] frontiers, was created' (Febvre and Martin 1976: 122). And since the years 1500–1550 were a period of exceptional European prosperity, publishing shared in the general boom. More than at any other time it was a great industry under the control of wealthy capitalists. Naturally, booksellers were primarily concerned to make a profit and to sell their products, and consequently they sought out first and foremost those works which were of interest to the largest possible number of their contemporaries.

The initial market was literate Europe, a wide but thin stratum of Latin-readers. Saturation of this market took about 150 years. The determinative fact about Latin – aside from its sacrality – was that it was a language of bilinguals. Relatively few were born to speak it and even fewer, one imagines, dreamed in it. In the sixteenth century the proportion of bilinguals within the total population of Europe was quite small; very likely no larger than the proportion in the world's population today, and – proletarian internationalism notwithstanding – in the centuries to come. Then and now the vast bulk of mankind is monoglot. The logic of capitalism thus meant that once the elite Latin market was saturated, the potentially huge markets represented by the monoglot masses would beckon. To be sure, the Counter-Reformation encouraged a temporary resurgence of Latin publishing, but by the mid-seventeenth century the movement was in decay, and fervently Catholic libraries replete. Meanwhile, a Europe-wide shortage of money made printers think more and more of peddling cheap editions in the vernaculars.

The revolutionary vernacularizing thrust of capitalism was given further impetus by three extraneous factors, two of which contributed directly to the rise of national consciousness. The first, and ultimately the least important, was a change in the character of Latin itself. Thanks to the labours of the Humanists in reviving the broad literature of pre-Christian antiquity and spreading it through the print market, a new appreciation of the sophisticated stylistic achievements of the ancients was apparent among the trans-European intelligentsia. The Latin they now aspired to write became more and more Ciceronian, and, by the same token, increasingly removed from ecclesiastical and everyday life. In this way it acquired an esoteric quality quite different from that of Church Latin in medieval times. For the older Latin was not arcane because of its subject-matter or style, but simply because it was written at all, i.e. because of its status as text. Now it became arcane because of what was written, because of the language-in-itself.

Second was the impact of the Reformation, which, at the same time, owed much of its success to print capitalism. Before the age of print, Rome easily won every war against heresy in western Europe because it always had better internal lines of communication than its challengers. But when in 1517 Martin Luther nailed his theses to the chapel door in Wittenberg, they were printed up in German translation, and within fifteen days [had been] seen in every part of the country. In the two decades 1520–40 three times as many books were published in German as in the period 1500–1520, an astonishing transformation to which Luther was absolutely central. His works represented no less than one third of all German-language books sold between 1518 and 1525. Between 1522 and 1546, a total of 430 editions (whole or partial) of his biblical translations appeared. [...] In effect, Luther became the first best-selling author so known. Or, to put it another way, the first writer who could 'sell' his new books on the basis of his name.

Where Luther led, others quickly followed, opening the colossal religious pro-paganda war that raged across Europe for the next century. In this titanic 'battle for men's minds', Protestantism was always fundamentally on the offensive, precisely because it knew how to make use of the expanding vernacular print market being created by capitalism, while the Counter-Reformation defended the citadel of Latin. The emblem for this is the Vatican's *Index Librorum Prohibitorum* – to which there was no Protestant counterpart – a novel catalogue made necessary by the sheer volume of printed subversion. Nothing gives a better sense of this siege mentality than François I's panicked 1535 ban on the printing of any books in his realm – on pain of death by hanging! The reason for both the ban and its unenforceability was that by then his realm's eastern borders were ringed with Protestant states and cities producing a massive stream of smugglable print. To take Calvin's Geneva alone: between 1533 and 1540 only forty-two editions were published there, but the numbers swelled to 527 between 1550 and 1564, by which latter date no fewer than forty separate printing presses were working overtime.

The coalition between Protestantism and print capitalism, exploiting cheap popular editions, quickly created large new reading publics – not least among merchants and women, who typically knew little or no Latin – and simultaneously mobilized them for politico-religious purposes. Inevitably, it was not merely the Church that was shaken to its core. The same earthquake produced Europe's first important non-dynastic, non-city states in the Dutch Republic and the Commonwealth of the Puritans. (François I's panic was as much political as religious.)

Third was the slow, geographically uneven, spread of particular vernaculars as instruments of administrative centralization by certain well-positioned would-be absolutist monarchs. Here it is useful to remember that the universality of Latin in medieval western Europe never corresponded to a universal political system. The contrast with Imperial China, where the reach of the mandarinal bureaucracy and of painted characters largely coincided, is instructive. In effect, the political fragmentation of western Europe after the collapse of the Western Empire meant that no sovereign could monopolize Latin and make it his-and-only-his language-of-state, and thus Latin's religious authority never had a true political analogue.

The birth of administrative vernaculars pre-dated both print and the religious upheaval of the sixteenth century, and must therefore be regarded (at least initially) as an independent factor in the erosion of the sacred imagined community. At the same time, nothing suggests that any deep-seated ideological, let alone proto-national, impulses underlay this vernacularization where it occurred. The case of 'England' – on the north-western periphery of Latin Europe – is here especially enlightening. Prior to the Norman Conquest, the language of the court, literary and administrative, was Anglo-Saxon. For the next century and a half virtually all royal documents were composed in Latin. Between about 1200 and 1350 this 'state' Latin was superseded by Norman French. In the meantime, a slow fusion between this language of a foreign ruling class and the Anglo-Saxon of the subject population produced Early English. The fusion made it possible for the new language to take its turn, after 1362, as the language of the courts – and for the opening of parliament. Wycliffe's vernacular manuscript Bible followed in 1382. It is essential to bear in mind that this sequence was a series of 'state', not 'national', languages; and that the state concerned covered at various times not only today's England and Wales, but also portions of Ireland, Scotland and France. Obviously, huge elements of the subject populations knew little or nothing of Latin, Norman French, or Early English. Not until almost a century after Early English's political enthronement was London's power swept out of 'France'.

On the Seine, a similar movement took place, if at a slower pace. As Bloch wrily puts it, 'French, that is to say a language which, since it was regarded as merely a corrupt form of Latin, took several centuries to raise itself to literary dignity' (Bloch 1961: 98), only became the official language of the courts of justice in 1539, when François I issued the Edict of Villers-Cotterêts (Sewn-Watson 1977:48). In other dynastic realms Latin survived much longer – under the Habsburgs well into the nineteenth century. In still others, 'foreign' vernaculars took over: in the eighteenth century the languages of the Romanov court were French and German.

In every instance, the 'choice' of language appears as a gradual, unselfconscious, pragmatic, not to say haphazard development. As such, it was utterly different from the selfconscious language policies pursued by nineteenth-century dynasts confronted with the rise of hostile popular linguistic-nationalisms. One clear sign of the difference is that the old administrative languages were just that: languages used by and for officialdoms for their own inner convenience. There was no idea of systematically imposing the language on the dynasts' various subject populations. Nonetheless, the elevation of these vernaculars to the status of languages-of-power, where, in one sense, they were competitors with Latin (French in Paris, [Early] English in London), made its own contribution to the decline of the imagined community of Christendom.

At bottom, it is likely that the esotericization of Latin, the Reformation, and the haphazard development of administrative vernaculars are significant, in the present context, primarily in a negative sense – in their contributions to the dethronement of Latin and the erosion of the sacred community of Christendom. It is quite possible to conceive of the emergence of the new imagined national communities without any one, perhaps all, of them being present. What, in a positive sense, made the new communities imaginable was a half-fortuitous, but explosive, interaction between a system of production and productive relations (capitalism), a technology of communications (print), and the fatality of human linguistic diversity.

The element of fatality is essential. For whatever superhuman feats capitalism was capable of, it found in death and languages two tenacious adversaries. Particular languages can die or be wiped out, but there was and is no possibility of man's general linguistic unification. Yet this mutual incomprehensibility was historically of only slight importance until capitalism and print created monoglot mass reading publics.

While it is essential to keep in mind an idea of fatality, in the sense of a general condition of irremediable linguistic diversity, it would be a mistake to equate this fatality with that common element in nationalist ideologies which stresses the primordial fatality of particular languages and their association with particular territorial units. The essential thing is the interplay between fatality, technology and capitalism. In pre-print Europe, and, of course, elsewhere in the world, the diversity of spoken languages, those languages that for their speakers were (and are) the warp and woof of their lives, was immense; so immense, indeed, that had print capitalism sought to exploit each potential oral vernacular market, it would have remained a capitalism of petty proportions. But these varied idiolects were capable of being assembled, within definite limits, into print-languages far fewer in number. The very arbitrariness of any system of signs for sounds facilitated the assembling process. (At the same time, the more ideographic the signs, the vaster the potential assembling zone. One can detect a sort of descending hierarchy here from algebra through Chinese and English, to the regular syllabaries of French or Indonesian.) Nothing served to 'assemble' related vernaculars more than capitalism, which, within the limits imposed by grammars and syntaxes, created mechanically reproduced print-languages, capable of dissemination through the market.

These print-languages laid the bases for national consciousnesses in three distinct ways. First and foremost, they created unified fields of exchange and communications below Latin and above the spoken vernaculars. Speakers of the huge variety of Frenches, Englishes or Spanishes, who might find it difficult or even impossible to understand one another in conversation, became capable of comprehending one another via print and paper. In the process, they gradually became aware of the hundreds of thousands, even millions, of people in their particular language-field, and at the same time that only those hundreds of thousands, or millions, so belonged. These fellow-readers, to whom they were connected through print, formed, in their secular, particular, visible invisibility, the embryo of the nationally imagined community.

Second, print capitalism gave a new fixity to language, which in the long run helped to build that image of antiquity so central to the subjective idea of the nation. As Febvre and Martin remind us, the printed book kept a permanent form, capable of virtually infinite reproduction, temporally and spatially. It was no longer subject to the individualizing and 'unconsciously modernizing' habits of monastic scribes. Thus, while twelfth-century French differed markedly from that written by Villon in the fifteenth, the rate of change slowed decisively in the sixteenth. 'By the 17th century languages in Europe had generally assumed their modern forms' (Febvre and Martin 1976: 319). To put it another way, for now three centuries these stabilized print-languages have been gathering a darkening varnish; the words of our seventeenth-century forebears are accessible to us in a way that his twelfth-century ancestors were not to Villon.

Third, print capitalism created languages-of-power of a kind different from the older administrative vernaculars. Certain dialects inevitably were 'closer' to each print-language and dominated their final forms. Their disadvantaged cousins, still assimilable to the emerging print-language, lost caste, above all because they were unsuccessful (or only relatively successful) in insisting on their own print form. 'North-western German' became Platt Deutsch, a largely spoken, thus substandard German, because it was assimilable to print-German in a way that Bohemian spoken Czech was not. High German, the King's English, and, later, Central Thai, were correspondingly elevated to a new politico-cultural eminence. (Hence the struggles in late twentieth-century Europe for certain 'sub-'nationalities to change their subordinate status by breaking firmly into print – and radio.)

It remains only to emphasize that in their origins, the fixing of print-languages and the differentiation of status between them were largely unselfconscious processes resulting from the explosive interaction between capitalism, technology and human linguistic diversity. But as with so much else in the history of nationalism, once 'there', they could become formal models to be imitated, and, where expedient, consciously exploited in a Machiavellian spirit. Today, the Thai government actively discourages attempts by foreign missionaries to provide its hill-tribe minorities with their own transcription-systems and to develop publications in their own languages: the same government is largely indifferent to what these minorities *speak*. The fate of the Turkic-speaking peoples in the zones incorporated into today's Turkey, Iran, Iraq and the [former] USSR is especially exemplary. A family of spoken languages, once everywhere assemblable, thus comprehensible, within an Arabic orthography, has lost that unity as a result of conscious manipulations. To heighten Turkish-Turkey's national consciousness at the expense of any wider Islamic identification, Atatürk imposed compulsory romanization. The Soviet authorities followed suit, first with an anti-Islamic, anti-Persian compulsory romanization, then, in Stalin's 1930s, with a Russifying compulsory Cyrillicization.

We can summarize the conclusions to be drawn from the argument thus far by saying that the convergence of capitalism and print technology on the fatal diversity of human language created the possibility of a new form of imagined community, which in its basic morphology set the stage for the modern nation. The potential stretch of these communities was inherently limited, and, at the same time, bore none but the most fortuitous relationship to existing political boundaries (which were, on the whole, the highwater marks of dynastic expansionisms).

Yet it is obvious that while today almost all modern self-conceived nations – and also nation states – have 'national print-languages', many of them have these languages in common, and in others only a tiny fraction of the population 'uses' the national language in conversation or on paper. The nation states of Spanish America or those of the 'Anglo-Saxon family' are conspicuous examples of the first outcome; many ex-colonial states, particularly in Africa, of the second. In other words, the concrete formation of contemporary nation states is by no means isomorphic with the determinate reach of particular print-languages. To account for the discontinuity-in-connectedness between print-languages, national consciousnesses and nation states, it is necessary to turn to the large cluster of new political entities that sprang up in the Western hemisphere between 1776 and 1838, all of which selfconsciously defined themselves as nations, and, with the interesting exception of Brazil, as (non-dynastic) republics. For not only were they historically the first such states to emerge on the world stage, and therefore inevitably provided the first real models of what such states should 'look like', but their numbers and contemporary births offer fruitful ground for comparative enquiry.

References

Bloch, Marc (1961), *Feudal Society*. Chicago: University of Chicago Press (2 vols, translated by I. A. Manyon).

Febvre, Lucien, and Henri-Jean Martin (1976), *The Coming of the Book. The Impact of Printing, 1450–1800*. London: New Left Books (translation of L'Apparition du livre. Paris: Albin Michel. 1958).

Gellner, Ernest (1964), *Thought and Change*. London: Weidenfeld and Nicholson.

Nairn, Tom (1977), *The Break-up of Britain*. London: New Left Books.

Renan, Ernest (1947–61), 'Qu'est-ce qu'une nation?' In *Oeuvres Completes*. Paris: Calmann-Lévy, vol. I, pp. 887–906.

Seton-Watson, Hugh (1977), *Nations and States. An Enquiry into the Origins of Nations and the Politics of Nationalism*. Boulder, Colo.: Westview Press.

NATIONALISM AS A PRODUCT OF INDUSTRIAL SOCIETY

ERNEST GELLNER

Nationalism is primarily a political principle, which holds that the political and the national unit should be congruent.

Nationalism as a sentiment, or as a movement, can best be defined in terms of this principle. Nationalist *sentiment* is the feeling of anger aroused by the violation of the principle, or the feeling of satisfaction aroused by its fulfilment. A nationalist *movement* is one actuated by a sentiment of this kind.

There is a variety of ways in which the nationalist principle can be violated. The political boundary of a given state can fail to include all the members of the appropriate nation; or it can include them all but also include some foreigners; or it can fail in both these ways at once, not incorporating all the nationals and yet also including some non-nationals. Or again, a nation may live, unmixed with foreigners, in a multiplicity of states, so that no single state can claim to be *the* national one.

But there is one particular form of the violation of the nationalist principle to which nationalist sentiment is quite particularly sensitive: if the rulers of the political unit belong to a nation other than that of the majority of the ruled, this, for nationalists, constitutes a quite outstandingly intolerable breech of political propriety. This can occur either through the incorporation of the national territory in a larger empire, or by the local domination of an alien group.

In brief, nationalism is a theory of political legitimacy, which requires that ethnic boundaries should not cut across political ones, and, in particular, that ethnic boundaries within a given state – a contingency already formally excluded by the principle in its general formulation – should not separate the power-holders from the rest.

The nationalist principle can be asserted in an ethical, 'universalistic' spirit. There could be, and on occasion there have been, nationalists-in-the-abstract, unbiased in favour of any special nationality of their own, and generously preaching the doctrine for all nations alike: let all nations have their own political roofs, and let all of them also refrain from including non-nationals under it. There is no formal contradiction in asserting such non-egoistic nationalism. As a doctrine it can be supported by some good arguments, such as the desirability of preserving cultural diversity, of a pluralistic international political system, and of the diminution of internal strains within states.

In fact, however, nationalism has often not been so sweetly reasonable, nor so rationally symmetrical. It may be that, as Immanuel Kant believed, partiality, the tendency to make exceptions on one's own behalf or one's own case, is *the* central human weakness from which all others flow; and that it infects national sentiment as it does all else, engendering what the Italians under Mussolini called the *sacro egoismo* of nationalism. It may also be that the political effectiveness of national sentiment would be much impaired if nationalists had as fine a sensibility to the wrongs committed by their nation as they have to those committed against it.

But over and above these considerations there are others, tied to the specific nature of the world we happen to live in, which militate against any impartial, general, sweetly reasonable nationalism. To put it in the simplest possible terms: there is a very large number of potential nations on earth. Our planet also contains room for a certain number of independent or autonomous political units. On any reasonable calculation, the former number (of potential nations) is probably much, *much* larger than that of possible viable states. If this argument or calculation is correct, not all nationalisms can be satisfied, at any rate at the same time. The satisfaction of some spells the frustration of others. This argument is further and immeasurably strengthened by the fact that very many of the potential nations of this world live, or until recently have lived, not in compact territorial units but intermixed with each other in complex patterns. It follows that a territorial political unit can only become ethnically homogeneous, in such cases, if it either kills, or expels, or assimilates all non-nationals. Their unwillingness to suffer such fates may make the peaceful implementation of the nationalist principle difficult.

These definitions must, of course, like most definitions, be applied with common sense. The nationalist principle, as defined, is not violated by the presence of *small* numbers of resident foreigners, or even by the presence of the occasional foreigner in, say, a national ruling family. Just how many resident foreigners or foreign members of the ruling class there must be before the principle is effectively violated cannot be stated with precision. There is no sacred percentage figure, below which the foreigner can be benignly tolerated, and above which he becomes offensive and his safety and life are at peril. No doubt the figure will vary with circumstances. The impossibility of providing a generally applicable and precise figure, however, does not undermine the usefulness of the definition.

State and Nation

Our definition of nationalism was parasitic on two as yet undefined terms: state and nation.

Discussion of the state may begin with Max Weber's celebrated definition of it, as that agency within society which possesses the monopoly of legitimate violence. The idea behind this is simple and seductive: in well-ordered societies, such as most of us live in or aspire to live in, private or sectional violence is illegitimate. Conflict as such is not illegitimate, but it cannot rightfully be resolved by private or sectional violence. Violence may be applied only by the central political authority, and those to whom it delegates this right. Among the various sanctions of the maintenance of order, the ultimate one – force – may be applied only by one special, clearly identified, and well-centralized, disciplined agency within society. That agency or group of agencies *is* the state.

The idea enshrined in this definition corresponds fairly well with the moral intuitions of many, probably most, members of modern societies. Nevertheless, it is not entirely satisfactory. There are 'states' – or, at any rate, institutions which we would normally be inclined to call by that name – which do not monopolize legitimate violence within the territory which they more or less effectively control. A feudal state does not necessarily object to private wars between its fief-holders, provided they also fulfil their obligations to their overlord; or again, a state counting tribal populations among its subjects does not necessarily object to the institution of the feud, as long as those who indulge in it refrain from endangering neutrals on the public highway or in the market. The Iraqi state, under British tutelage after the First World War, tolerated tribal raids, provided the raiders dutifully reported at the nearest police station before and after the expedition, leaving an orderly bureaucratic record of slain and booty. In brief, there are states which lack either the will or the means to enforce their monopoly of legitimate violence, and which, nonetheless remain, in many respects, recognizable 'states'.

Weber's underlying principle does, however, seem valid *now*, however strangely ethnocentric it may be as a general definition, with its tacit assumption of the well-centralized Western state. The state constitutes one highly distinctive and important elaboration of the social division of labour. Where there is no division of labour, one cannot even begin to speak of the state. But not any or every specialism makes a state: the state is the specialization and concentration of order maintenance. The 'state' is that institution or set of institutions specifically concerned with the enforcement of order (whatever else they may also be concerned with). The state exists where specialized order-enforcing agencies, such as police forces and courts, have separated out from the rest of social life. They *are* the state.

Not all societies are state-endowed. It immediately follows that the problem of nationalism does not arise for stateless societies. If there is no state, one obviously cannot ask whether or not its boundaries are congruent with the limits of nations. If there are no rulers, there being no state, one cannot ask whether they are of the same nation as the ruled. When neither state nor rulers exist, one cannot resent their failure to conform to the requirements of the principle of nationalism. One may perhaps deplore statelessness, but that is another matter. Nationalists have generally fulminated against the distribution of political power and the nature of political boundaries, but they have seldom if ever had occasion to deplore the absence of power and of boundaries altogether. The circumstances in which nationalism has generally arisen have not normally been those in which the state itself, as such, was lacking, or when its reality was in any serious doubt. The state was only too conspicuously present. It was its boundaries and/or the distribution of power, and possibly of other advantages, within it which were resented.

This in itself is highly significant. Not only is our definition of nationalism parasitic on a prior and assumed definition of the state: it also seems to be the case that nationalism emerges only in milieux in which the existence of the state is already very much taken for granted. The existence of politically centralized units, and of a moral-political climate in which such centralized units are taken for granted and are treated as normative, is a necessary though by no means a sufficient condition of nationalism.

By way of anticipation, some general historical observations should be made about the state. Mankind has passed through three fundamental stages in its history: the pre-agrarian, the agrarian, and the industrial. Hunting and gathering bands were and are too small to allow the kind of political division of labour which constitutes the state; and so, for them, the question of the state, of a stable specialized order-enforcing institution, does not really arise. By contrast, most, but by no means all, agrarian societies have been state-endowed. Some of these states have been strong and some weak, some have been despotic and others law-abiding. They differ a very great deal in their form. The agrarian phase of human history is the period during which, so to speak, the very existence of the state is an option. Moreover, the form of the state is highly variable. During the hunting-gathering stage, the option was not available.

By contrast, in the post-agrarian, industrial age there is, once again, no option; but now the *presence*, not the absence of the state is inescapable. Paraphrasing Hegel, once none had the state, then some had it, and finally all have it. The form it takes, of course, still remains variable. There are some traditions of social thought – anarchism, Marxism – which hold that even, or especially, in an industrial order the state is dispensable, at least under favourable conditions or under conditions due to be realized in the fullness of time. There are obvious and powerful reasons for doubting this: industrial societies are enormously large, and depend for the standard of living to which they have become accustomed (or to which they ardently wish to become accustomed) on an unbelievably intricate general division of labour and co-operation. Some of this co-operation might under favourable conditions be spontaneous and need no central sanctions. The idea that all of it could perpetually work in this way, that it could exist without any enforcement and control, puts an intolerable strain on one's credulity.

So the problem of nationalism does not arise when there is no state. It does not follow that the problem of nationalism arises for each and every state. On the contrary, it arises only for *some* states. It remains to be seen which ones do face this problem.

The Nation

The definition of the nation presents difficulties graver than those attendant on the definition of the state. Although modern man tends to take the centralized state (and, more specifically, the centralized national state) for granted, nevertheless he is capable, with relatively little effort, of seeing its contingency, and of imagining a social situation in which the state is absent. He is quite adept at visualizing the 'state of nature'. An anthropologist can explain to him that the tribe is not necessarily a state writ small, and that forms of tribal organization exist which can be described as stateless. By contrast, the idea of a man without a nation seems to impose a far greater strain on the modern imagination. Chamisso, an *emigré* Frenchman in Germany during the Napoleonic period, wrote a powerful proto-Kafkaesque novel about a man who lost his shadow: though no doubt part of the effectiveness of this novel hinges on the intended ambiguity of the parable, it is difficult not to suspect that, for the author, the Man without a Shadow was the Man without a Nation. When his followers and acquaintances detect his aberrant shadowlessness they shun the otherwise well-endowed Peter Schlemiehl. A man without a nation defies the recognized categories and provokes revulsion.

Chamisso's perception – if indeed this is what he intended to convey – was valid enough, but valid only for one kind of human condition, and not for the human condition as such anywhere at any time. A man must have a nationality as he must have a nose and two ears; a deficiency in any of these particulars is not inconceivable and does from time to time occur, but only as a result of some disaster, and it is itself a disaster of a kind. All this seems obvious, though, alas, it is not true. But that it should have come to *seem* so very obviously true is indeed an aspect, or perhaps the very core, of the problem of nationalism. Having a nation is not an inherent attribute of humanity, but it has now come to appear as such.

In fact, nations, like states, are a contingency, and not a universal necessity. Neither nations nor states exist at all times and in all circumstances. Moreover, nations and states are not the *same* contingency. Nationalism holds that they were destined for each other; that either without the other is incomplete, and constitutes a tragedy. But before they could become intended for each other, each of them had to emerge, and their emergence was independent and contingent. The state has certainly emerged without the help of the nation. Some nations have certainly emerged without the blessings of their own state. It is more debatable whether the normative idea of the nation, in its modern sense, did not presuppose the prior existence of the state.

What then is this contingent, but in our age seemingly universal and normative, idea of the nation? Discussion of two very makeshift, temporary definitions will help to pinpoint this elusive concept.

1 Two men are of the same nation if and only if they share the same culture, where culture in turn means a system of ideas and signs and associations and ways of behaving and communicating.

2 Two men are of the same nation if and only if they *recognize* each other as belonging to the same nation. In other words, *nations maketh man*; nations are the artefacts of men's convictions and loyalties and solidarities. A mere category of persons (say, occupants of a given territory, or speakers of a given language, for example) becomes a nation if and when the members of the category firmly recognize certain mutual rights and duties to each other in virtue of their shared membership of it. It is their recognition of each other as fellows of this kind which turns them into a nation, and not the other shared attributes, whatever they might be, which separate that category from nonmembers.

Each of these provisional definitions, the cultural and the voluntaristic, has some merit. Each of them singles out an element which is of real importance in the understanding of nationalism. But neither is adequate. Definitions of culture, presupposed by the first definition, in the anthropological rather than the normative sense, are notoriously difficult and unsatisfactory. It is probably best to approach this problem by using this term without attempting too much in the way of formal definition, and looking at what culture *does*.

[...]

Nationalism and Industrialization

If cognitive growth presupposes that no element is indissolubly linked *a priori* to any other, and that everything is open to rethinking, then economic and productive growth requires exactly the same of human activities and hence of human roles. Roles become optional and instrumental. The old stability of the social role structure is simply incompatible with growth and innovation. Innovation means doing new things, the boundaries of which cannot be the same as those of the activities they replace. No doubt most societies can cope with an occasional redrawing of job specifications and guild boundaries, just as a football team can experimentally switch from one formation to another, and yet maintain continuity. One change does not make progress. But what happens when such changes themselves are constant and continuous, when the persistence of occupational change itself becomes the one permanent feature of a social order?

When this question is answered, the main part of the problem of nationalism is thereby solved. Nationalism is rooted in *a certain kind* of division of labour, one which is complex and persistently, cumulatively changing.

High productivity, as Adam Smith insisted so much, requires a complex and refined division of labour. Perpetually growing productivity requires that this division be not merely complex, but also perpetually, and often rapidly, changing. This rapid and continuous change both of the economic role system itself and of the occupancy of places within it, has certain immediate and profoundly important consequences. Men located within it cannot generally rest in the same niches all their lives; and they can only seldom rest in them, so to speak, over generations. Positions are seldom (for this and other reasons) transmitted from father to son. Adam Smith noted the precariousness of bourgeois fortunes, though he erroneously attributed stability of social station to pastoralists, mistaking their genealogical myths for reality.

The immediate consequence of this new kind of mobility is a certain kind of egalitarianism. Modern society is not mobile because it is egalitarian; it is egalitarian because it is mobile. Moreover, it has to be mobile whether it wishes to be so or not, because this is required by the satisfaction of its terrible and overwhelming thirst for economic growth.

A society which is destined to a permanent game of musical chairs cannot erect deep barriers of rank, of caste or estate, between the various sets of chairs which it possesses. That would hamper the mobility, and, given the mobility, would indeed lead to intolerable tensions. Men can tolerate terrible inequalities, if they are stable and hallowed by custom. But in a hectically mobile society, custom has no time to hallow anything. A rolling stone gathers no aura, and a mobile population does not allow any aura to attach to its stratification. Stratification and inequality do exist, and sometimes in extreme form; nevertheless they have a muted and discreet quality, attenuated by a kind of gradualness of the distinctions of wealth and standing, a lack of social distance and a convergence of lifestyles, a kind of statistical or probabilistic quality of the differences (as opposed to the rigid, absolutized, chasm-like differences typical of agrarian society), and by the illusion or reality of social mobility.

That illusion is essential, and it cannot persist without at least a measure of reality. Just how much reality there is in this appearance of upward and downward mobility varies and is subject to learned dispute, but there can be no reasonable doubt that it does have a good deal of reality: when the system of roles itself is changing so much, the occupants of positions within it cannot be, as some left-wing sociologists claim, tied to a rigid stratificational system. Compared with agrarian society, this society is mobile and egalitarian.

But there is more than all this to the egalitarianism and mobility engendered by the distinctively industrial, growth-oriented economy. There are some additional subtler traits of the new division of labour, which can perhaps best be approached by considering the difference between the division of labour in an industrial society and that of a particularly complex, well-developed agrarian one. The *obvious* difference between the two is that one is more stable and the other is more mobile. In fact, one of them generally wills itself to be stable, and the other wills itself to be mobile; and one of them pretends to be more stable than social reality permits, while the other often claims more mobility, in the interest of pretending to satisfy its egalitarian ideal, than its real constraints actually permit. Nevertheless, though both systems tend to exaggerate their own central features, they do indeed markedly possess the trait they claim as their own when contrasted with each other: one is rigid, the other mobile. But if that is the obvious contrast, what are the subtler features which accompany it?

Compare in detail the division of labour in a highly advanced agrarian society with that of an average industrial one. Every kind of function, for instance, now has at least one kind of specialist associated with it. Car mechanics are becoming specialized in terms of the make of car they service. The industrial society will have a larger population, and probably, by most natural ways of counting, a larger number of different jobs. In *that* sense, the division of labour has been pushed much further within it.

But by some criteria, it may well be that a fully developed agrarian society actually has the more complex division of labour. The specialisms within it are more distant from each other than are the possibly more numerous specialisms of an industrial society, which tend to have what can only be described as a mutual affinity of style. Some of the specialisms of a mature agrarian society will be extreme: they will be the fruits of lifelong, very prolonged and totally dedicated training, which may have commenced in early youth and required an almost complete renunciation of other concerns. The achievements of craft and art production in these societies are extremely labour- and skill-intensive, and often reach levels of intricacy and perfection never remotely equalled by anything later attained by industrial societies, whose domestic arts and decorations, gastronomy, tools and adornments are notoriously shoddy.

Notwithstanding their aridity and sterility, the scholastic and ritual complexity mastered by the schoolmen of a developed agrarian society is often such as to strain the very limits of the human mind. In brief, although the peasants, who form the great majority of an agrarian society, are more or less mutually interchangeable when it comes to the performance of the social tasks which are normally assigned to them, the important minority of specialists within such societies are outstandingly complementary to each other; each one of them, or each group of them, is dependent on the others and, when sticking to its last, its specialism, quite incapable of self-sufficiency.

It is curious that, by contrast, in industrial society, notwithstanding its larger number of specialisms, the distance between specialists is far less great. Their mysteries are far closer to mutual intelligibility, their manuals have idioms which overlap to a much greater extent, and retraining, though sometimes difficult, is not generally an awesome task.

So, quite apart from the presence of mobility in the one case and stability in the other, there is a subtle but profound and important qualitative difference in the division of labour itself. Durkheim was in error when he in effect classed advanced pre-industrial civilizations and industrial society together under the single heading of 'organic solidarity', and when he failed to introduce properly this further distinction within the wider category of organic solidarity or of complementary division of labour. The difference is this: the major part of training in industrial society is *generic* training, not specifically connected with the highly specialized professional activity of the person in question, and *preceding* it. Industrial society may by most criteria be the most highly specialized society ever; but its educational system is unquestionably the least specialized, the most universally standardized, that has ever existed. The same kind of training or education is given to all or most children and adolescents up to an astonishingly late age. Specialized schools have prestige only at the end of the educational process, if they constitute a kind of completion of a prolonged previous unspecialized education; specialized schools intended for a younger, earlier intake have negative prestige.

Is this a paradox, or perhaps one of those illogical survivals from an earlier age? Those who notice the 'gentlemanly' or leisure-class elements in higher education have sometimes supposed so. But, although some of the frills and affectations attached to higher education may indeed be irrelevancies and survivals, the central fact – the pervasiveness and importance of generic, unspecialized training – is conjoined to highly specialized industrial society not as a paradox, but as something altogether fitting and necessary. The kind of specialization found in industrial society rests precisely on a common foundation of unspecialized and standardized training.

A modern army subjects its recruits first to a shared generic training, in the course of which they are meant to acquire and internalize the basic idiom, ritual and skills common to the army as a whole; and only subsequently are the recruits given more specialized training. It is assumed or hoped that every properly trained recruit can be retrained from one specialism to another without too much loss of time, with the exception of a relatively small number of very highly trained specialists. A modern society is, in this respect, like a modern army, only more so. It provides a very prolonged and fairly thorough training for all its recruits, insisting on certain shared qualifications: literacy, numeracy, basic work habits and social skills, familiarity with basic technical and social skills. For the large majority of the population the distinctive skills involved in working life are superimposed on the basic training, either on the job or as part of a much less prolonged supplementary training; and the assumption is that anyone who has completed the generic training common to the entire population can be retrained for most other jobs without too much difficulty. Generally speaking, the additional skills required consist of a few techniques that can be learned fairly quickly, plus 'experience', a kind of familiarity with a milieu, its personnel and its manner of operation. This may take a little time to acquire, and it is sometimes reinforced by a little protective mystique, but seldom really amounts to very much. There is also a minority of genuine specialists, people whose effective occupancy of their posts really depends on very prolonged additional training, and who are not easily or at all replaceable by anyone not sharing their own particular educational background and talent.

The ideal of universal literacy and the right to education is a well-known part of the pantheon of modern values. It is spoken of with respect by statesmen and politicians, and enshrined in declarations of rights, constitutions, party programmes and so forth. So far, nothing unusual. The same is true of representative and accountable government, free elections, an independent judiciary, freedom of speech and assembly, and so on. Many or most of these admirable values are often and systematically ignored in many parts of the world, without anyone batting an eyelid. Very often, it is safe to consider these phrases as simple verbiage. Most constitutions guaranteeing free speech and elections are as informative about the societies they allegedly define as a man saying 'Good morning' is about the weather. All this is well known. What is so very curious, and highly significant, about the principle of universal and centrally guaranteed education, is that it is an ideal more honoured in the observance than in the breach. In this it is virtually unique among modern ideals; and this calls for an explanation. Professor Ronald Dore has powerfully criticized this tendency, particularly among developing societies, of overrating formal 'paper' qualifications, and no doubt it has harmful side effects. But I wonder whether he fully appreciates the deep roots of what he castigates as the Diploma Disease. We live in a world in which we can no longer respect the informal, intimate transmission of skills, for the social structures within which such transmission could occur are dissolving. Hence the only kind of knowledge we can respect is that authenticated by reasonably impartial centres of learning, which issue certificates on the basis of honest, impartially administered examinations. Hence we are doomed to suffer the Diploma Disease.

All this suggests that the kind of education described – universal, standardized, and generic – *really* plays some essential part in the effective working of a modern society, and is not merely part of its verbiage or self-advertisement. This is in fact so. To understand what that role is, we must, to borrow a phrase from Marx (though not perhaps in the sense in which he used it), consider not merely the mode of production of modern society, but above all its mode of *reproduction*.

Social Genetics

The reproduction of social individuals and groups can be carried out either on the one-to-one or on-the-job principle, or by what may be called the centralized method. There are, of course, many mixed and intermediate ways of doing this job, but their consideration can best be postponed until after the discussion of these two extreme, as it were polar, possibilities.

The one-to-one, on-the-job method is practised when a family, kin unit, village, tribal segment or similar fairly small unit takes the individual infants born into it, and by allowing and obliging them to share in the communal life, plus a few more specific methods such as training, exercises, precepts, *rites de passage* and so forth, eventually turns these infants into adults reasonably similar to those of the preceding generation; and in this manner the society and its culture perpetuate themselves.

The centralized method of reproduction is one in which the local method is significantly complemented (or in extreme cases, wholly replaced) by an educational or training agency which is distinct from the local community, and which takes over the preparation of the young human beings in question, and eventually hands them back to the wider society to fulfil their roles in it, when the process of training is completed. An extreme version of this system developed a high degree of perfection and effectiveness in the Ottoman empire, when under the *devshirme* and janissary systems, young boys, either secured as a tax obligation from conquered populations, or purchased as slaves, were systematically trained for war and administration and, ideally, wholly weaned and separated from their families and communities of origin. A less total version of this system was and in part still is practised by the British upper class, with its reliance on boarding schools from an early age. Variants of this system can on occasion be found even in relatively simple, preliterate agrarian societies.

Societies consisting of sub-communities can be divided into those in which the sub-communities can, if necessary, reproduce themselves without help from the rest of society, and those in which mutual complementarity and interdependence are such that they cannot do this. Generally speaking, the segments and rural communities of agrarian society *can* reproduce themselves independently. The anthropological concept of a segmentary society contains precisely this idea: the 'segment' is simply a smaller variant of the larger society of which it is a part, and can do on a smaller scale everything done by the larger unit.

Furthermore, one must distinguish between economic and educational self-sufficiency, in the sense of capacity for self-reproduction. The ruling strata of an agrarian society are, of course, dependent on a surplus drawn from the rest of society, but they may nevertheless be educationally quite self-sufficient. Various other kinds of non-self-sufficiency can also be engendered by social rules, such as those which make communities dependent on external ritual specialists, or on the supply of brides from outside. Here we are concerned with educational, not economic capacity for group self-reproduction. There are numerous complex, mixed and intermediate forms of group reproduction. When feudal lords send their sons as half-trainees, half-hostages to the local court, when masters accept apprentices who are not their sons, and so forth, we are obviously in the presence of such mixed systems.

Generally speaking, the situation in agrarian society seems to be this: the great majority of the population belongs to self-reproducing units, such as in effect educate their young on the job, in their stride, as part and parcel of the general business of living, without relying much or at all on any kind of educational specialist. A minority of the population receives specialized training. The society will contain one or more strata of full-time educators, who both reproduce themselves by taking on apprentices, and perform part-time services for the rest of the community: ritual, therapeutic, admonitory, secretarial, and so on. It may be useful to distinguish between one-to-one, intra-community training, and call it acculturation, and specialized *exo-training* (on the analogy of exogamy), which calls for skills outside the community, and call that education proper.

A very important stratum in literate agrarian society are the clerks, those who can read and transmit literacy, and who thus form one of the classes of specialists in that society. They may or may not form a guild or be incorporated in an organization. As, generally speaking, writing soon transcends its purely technical use in record-keeping, and acquires moral and theological significance, the clerks or clerics are almost invariably far more than mere grapho-technicians. It is not just writing, but what is written that counts, and, in agrarian society, the ratio of the sacred to the profane, within the realm of the written, tends to be heavily weighted in favour of the first. So the writers and readers are specialists and yet more than specialists; they are both part of a society, and claim to be the voice of the whole of it. Their specialism *says* something, something special, more so perhaps than that of the woodcarvers and other designers, and much more than that of the tinkers.

Specialists are often feared and despised in this kind of society. The clerics may be viewed ambivalently, but in the main their standing is rather high. They are both specialists and a part of society among others, and yet also, as stated, claim to be the voice of the totality. They are in an inherently paradoxical situation. Logicians possess, in their armoury of allegedly deep and significant puzzles, the Problem of the Barber: in a village, all men can be divided into those who shave themselves, and those who are shaved by the barber. But what of the barber himself? Is he a self-shaver, or one of the barber-shaved? In this form, let us leave it to the logicians. But the clerics are somewhat in the barber's situation. They reproduce their own guild by training entrants, but they also give a bit of training or provide services for the rest of society. Do they or do they not shave themselves? The tension and its problems (and they are not just logical) are with them, and they are not easily resolved.

In the end, modern society resolves this conundrum by turning *everyone* into a cleric, by turning this potentially universal class into an effectively universal one, by ensuring that everyone without exception is taught by it, that exo-education becomes the universal norm, and that no-one, culturally speaking, shaves himself. Modern society is one in which no sub-community, below the size of one capable of sustaining an independent educational system, can any longer reproduce itself. The reproduction of fully socialized individuals itself becomes part of the division of labour, and is no longer performed by sub-communities for themselves.

That is what developed modern societies are like. But why *must* this be so? What fate impels them in this direction? Why, to repeat the earlier question, is this one ideal, that of universal literacy and education, taken with this most unusual, untypical seriousness?

Part of the answer has already been given, in connection with the stress on occupational mobility, on an unstable, rapidly changing division of labour. A society whose entire political system, and indeed whose cosmology and moral order, is based in the last analysis on economic growth, on the universal incremental Danegeld and the hope of a perpetual augmentation of satisfactions, whose legitimacy hinges on its capacity to sustain and satisfy this expectation, is thereby committed to the need for innovation and hence to a changing occupational structure. From this it follows that certainly between generations, and very often within single lifespans, men must be ready for reallocation to new tasks. Hence, in part, the importance of the generic training, and the fact that the little bit extra of training, such as is attached to most jobs, doesn't amount to too much, and is moreover contained in manuals intelligible to all possessors of the society's generic training. (While the little bit extra seldom amounts to much, the shared and truly essential generic core is supplied at a rather high level, not perhaps when compared with the intellectual *peaks* of agrarian society, but certainly when placed alongside its erstwhile customary average.)

But it is not only mobility and retraining which engender this imperative. It is also the *content* of most professional activities. Work, in industrial society, does not mean moving matter. The paradigm of work is no longer ploughing, reaping, thrashing. Work, in the main, is no longer the manipulation of things, but of meanings. It generally involves exchanging communications with other people, or manipulating the controls of a machine. The proportion of people at the coal-face of nature, directly applying human physical force to natural objects, is constantly diminishing. Most jobs, if not actually involving work 'with people', involve the control of buttons or switches or levers which need to be *understood,* and are explicable, once again, in some standard idiom intelligible to all comers.

For the first time in human history, explicit and reasonably precise communication becomes generally, pervasively used and important. In the closed local communities of the agrarian or tribal worlds, when it came to communication, context, tone, gesture, personality and situation were everything. Communication, such as it was, took place without the benefit of precise formulation, for which the locals had neither taste nor aptitude. Explicitness and the niceties of precise, rule-bound formulation were left to lawyers, theologians or ritual specialists, and were parts of their mysteries. Among intimates of a close community, explicitness would have been pedantic and offensive, and is scarcely imaginable or intelligible.

Human language must have been used for countless generations in such intimate, closed, context-bound communities, whereas it has only been used by schoolmen and jurists, and all kinds of context-evading conceptual puritans, for a very small number of generations. It is a very puzzling fact that an institution, namely human language, should have this potential for being used as an 'elaborate code', in Basil Bernstein's phrase, as a formal and fairly context-free instrument, given that it had evolved in a milieu which in no way called for this development, and did not selectively favour it if it manifested itself. This puzzle is on a par with problems such as that posed by the existence of skills (for example, mathematical ability) which throughout most of the period of the existence of humanity had no survival value, and thus could not have been in any direct way produced by natural selection. The existence of language suitable for such formal, context-liberated use is such a puzzle; but it is also, clearly, a fact. This potentiality, whatever its origin and explanation, happened to be there.

Eventually a kind of society emerged – and it is now becoming global – in which this potentiality really comes into its own, and within which it becomes indispensable and dominant.

To sum up this argument: a society has emerged based on a high-powered technology and the expectancy of sustained growth, which requires both a mobile division of labour, and sustained, frequent and precise communication between strangers involving a sharing of explicit meaning, transmitted in a standard idiom and in writing when required. For a number of converging reasons, this society must be thoroughly exo-educational: each individual is trained by specialists, not just by his own local group, if indeed he has one. Its segments and units – and this society is in any case large, fluid, and in comparison with traditional, agrarian societies very short of internal structures – simply do not possess the capacity or the resources to reproduce their own personnel. The level of literacy and technical competence, in a standardized medium, a common conceptual currency, which is required of members of this society if they are to be properly employable and enjoy full and effective moral citizenship, is so high that it simply *cannot* be provided by the kin or local units, such as they are. It can only be provided by something resembling a modern 'national' educational system, a pyramid at whose base there are primary schools, staffed by teachers trained at secondary schools, staffed by university-trained teachers, led by the products of advanced graduate schools. Such a pyramid provides the criterion for the minimum size for a viable political unit. No unit too small to accommodate the pyramid can function properly. Units cannot be *smaller* than this. Constraints also operate which prevent them being too large, in various circumstances; but that is another issue.

The fact that sub-units of society are no longer capable of self-reproduction, that centralized exo-education is the obligatory norm, that such education complements (though it does not wholly replace) localized acculturation, is of the very first importance for the political sociology of the modern world; and its implications have, strangely enough, been seldom understood or appreciated or even examined. At the base of the modern social order stands not the executioner but the professor. Not the guillotine, but the (aptly named) *doctorat d'état* is the main tool and symbol of state power. The monopoly of legitimate education is now more important, more central than is the monopoly of legitimate violence. When this is understood, then the imperative of nationalism, its roots, not in human nature as such, but in a certain kind of now pervasive social order, can also be understood.

Contrary to popular and even scholarly belief, nationalism does not have any very deep roots in the human psyche. The human psyche can be assumed to have persisted unchanged through the many, many millennia of the existence of the human race, and not to have become either better or worse during the relatively brief and very recent age of nationalism. One may not invoke a *general* substrate to explain a *specific* phenomenon. The substrate generates many surface possibilities. Nationalism, the organization of human groups into large, centrally educated, culturally homogeneous units, is but one of these, and a very rare one at that. What is crucial for its genuine explanation is to identify its specific roots. It is these specific roots which alone can properly explain it. In this way, specific factors are superimposed on to a shared universal human substrate.

The roots of nationalism in the distinctive structural requirements of industrial society are very deep indeed. This movement is the fruit neither of ideological aberration, nor of emotional excess. Although those who participate in it generally, indeed almost without exception, fail to understand what it is that they do, the movement is nonetheless the external manifestation of a deep adjustment in the relationship between polity and culture which is quite unavoidable.

The Age of Universal High Culture

Let us recapitulate the general and central features of industrial society. Universal literacy and a high level of numerical, technical and general sophistication are among its functional prerequisites. Its members are and must be mobile, and ready to shift from one activity to another, and must possess that generic training which enables them to follow the manuals and instructions of a new activity or occupation. In the course of their work they must constantly communicate with a large number of other men, with whom they frequently have no previous association, and with whom communication must consequently be explicit, rather than relying on context. They must also be able to communicate by means of written, impersonal, context-free, to-whom-it-may-concern type messages. Hence these communications must be in the same shared and standardized linguistic medium and script. The educational system which guarantees this social achievement becomes large and is indispensable, but at the same time it no longer possesses monopoly of access to the written word: its clientele is co-extensive with the society at large, and the replaceability of individuals within the system by others applies to the educational machine at least as much as to any other segment of society, and perhaps more so. Some very great teachers and researchers may perhaps be unique and irreplaceable, but the average professor and schoolmaster can be replaced from outside the teaching profession with the greatest of ease and often with little, if any, loss.

What are the implications of all this for the society and for its members? The employability, dignity, security and self-respect of individuals, typically, and for the majority of men now hinges on their *education*; and the limits of the culture within which they were educated are also the limits of the world within which they can, morally and professionally, breathe. A man's education is by far his most precious investment, and in effect confers his identity on him. Modern man is not loyal to a monarch or a land or a faith, whatever he may say, but to a culture. And he is, generally speaking, gelded. The Mamluk condition has become universal. No important links bind him to a kin group; nor do they stand between him and a wide, anonymous community of culture.

The obverse of the fact that a school-transmitted culture, not a folk-transmitted one, alone confers his usability and dignity and self-respect on industrial man, is the fact that nothing else can do it for him to any comparable extent. It would be idle to pretend that ancestry, wealth or connections are unimportant in modern society, and that they are not on occasion even sources of pride to their beneficiaries; all the same, advantages secured in these ways are often explained away and are viewed at best ambivalently. It is interesting to ask whether the pervasive work ethic has helped to produce this state of affairs, or whether, on the contrary, it is a reflection of it. Drones and rentiers persist, of course, but they are not very conspicuous, and this in itself is highly significant. It is an important fact that such privilege and idleness as survive are now discreet, tending to prefer obscurity to display, and needing to be uncovered by eager researchers bent on unmasking the inequality which lurks underneath the surface.

It was not so in the past, when idle privilege was proud and brazen, as it persists in being in some surviving agrarian societies, or in societies which continue to uphold the ethos of pre-industrial life. Curiously enough, the notion of conspicuous waste was coined by a work-oriented member of a work-addicted society, Thorsten Veblen, scandalized by what he saw as the survivals from a pre-industrial, predatory age. The egalitarian, work- and career-oriented surface of industrial society is as significant as its inegalitarian hidden depths. Life, after all, is lived largely on the surface, even if important decisions are on occasion made deep down.

The teacher class is now in a sense more important – it is indispensable – and in another sense much less so, having lost its monopoly of access to the cultural wisdom enshrined in scripture. In a society in which everyone is gelded by identification with his professional post and his training, and hardly anyone derives much or any security and support from whatever kin links he may have, the teaching clerics no longer possess any privileged access to administrative posts. When everyone has become a Mamluk, no special mamluk class predominates in the bureaucracy. At long last the bureaucracy can recruit from the population at large, without needing to fear the arrival of dozens of cousins as unwanted attachments of each single new entrant.

Exo-socialization, education proper, is now the virtually universal norm. Men acquire the skills and sensibilities which make them acceptable to their fellows, which fit them to assume places in society, and which make them 'what they are', by being handed over by their kin groups (normally nowadays, of course, their nuclear family) to an educational machine which alone is capable of providing the wide range of training required for the generic cultural base. This educational infrastructure is large, indispensable and expensive. Its maintenance seems to be quite beyond the financial powers of even the biggest and richest organizations within society, such as the big industrial corporations. These often provide their personnel with housing, sports and leisure clubs, and so forth; they do not, except marginally and in special circumstances, provide schooling. (They may subsidize school bills, but that is another matter.) The organization man works and plays with his organization, but his children still go to state or independent schools.

So, on the one hand, this educational infrastructure is too large and costly for any organization other than the biggest one of all, the state. But at the same time, though only the state can sustain so large a burden, only the state is also strong enough to control so important and crucial a function. Culture is no longer merely the adornment, confirmation and legitimation of a social order which was also sustained by harsher and coercive constraints; culture is now the necessary shared medium, the life-blood or perhaps rather the minimal shared atmosphere, within which alone the members of the society can breathe and survive and produce. For a given society, it must be one in which they can *all* breathe and speak and produce; so it must be the *same* culture. Moreover, it must now be a great or high (literate, training-sustained) culture, and it can no longer be a diversified, locality-tied, illiterate little culture or tradition.

But some organism must ensure that this literate and unified culture is indeed being effectively produced, that the educational product is not shoddy and sub-standard. Only the state can do this, and, even in countries in which important parts of the educational machine are in private hands or those of religious orga-nizations, the state does take over quality control in this most important of industries, the manufacture of viable and usable human beings. That shadow state dating back to the time when European states were not merely fragmented but socially weak – the centralized Church – did put up a fight for the control of education, but it was in the end ineffectual, unless the Church fought on behalf of an inclusive high culture and thereby indirectly on behalf of a new nationalist state.

Time was when education was a cottage industry, when men could be made by a village or clan. That time has now gone, and gone forever. (In education, small can now be beautiful only if it is covertly parasitic on the big.) Exo-social-ization, the production and reproduction of men outside the local intimate unit, is now the norm, and must be so. The imperative of exo-socialization is the main clue to why state and culture *must* now be linked, whereas in the past their con-nection was thin, fortuitous, varied, loose, and often minimal. Now it is unavoid-able. That is what nationalism is about, and why we live in an age of nationalism.

References

Dore, R. (1976), *The Diploma Disease*, London: Allen & Unwin.
Goody, J., ed. (1968), *Literacy in Traditional Societies*, Cambridge: Cambridge University Press.

AN ANTI-NATIONALIST ACCOUNT OF NATIONALISM SINCE 1989

ERIC HOBSBAWM

Since [...] early 1990 more new nation states have been formed, or are in the process of formation, than at any time in this century. The break-up of the USSR and Yugoslavia have so far added sixteen to the number of internationally rec-ognized sovereign entities, and there is no immediately foreseeable limit to the further advance of national separatism. All states are today officially 'nations', all political agitations are apt to be against foreigners, whom practically all states harry and seek to keep out. It may therefore seem wilful blindness to [include here] some reflections on the *decline* of nationalism as a vector of historical change, compared with its role in the century from the 1830s to the end of the Second World War.

It would indeed be absurd to deny that the collapse of the Soviet Union and the regional and international system of which, as one superpower, it was a pillar for some forty years marks a profound, and probably permanent, historical change, whose implications are, at the time of writing [1992], entirely obscure. However, they introduce *new* elements into the history of nationalism only insofar as the break-up of the USSR in 1991 went far beyond the (temporary) break-up of Tsarist Russia in 1918–20, which was largely confined to its European and transcaucasian regions. For, basically, the 'national questions' of 1989–92 are not new. They belong overwhelmingly to the traditional home of national causes, Europe. There is so far no sign of serious political separatism in the Americas, at least south of the US–Canadian border. There is little sign that the Islamic world, or at least the rising fundamentalist movements within it, are concerned with multiplying state frontiers. They want to return to the true faith of the founders. In fact, it is hard to see how separatism could interest them as such. Separatist agitations (largely terrorist) are clearly shaking corners of the South Asian sub-continent, but so far (except for the secession of Bangladesh) the successor states have held together. In fact, the post-colonial national regimes not only in this region still overwhelmingly accept the nineteenth-century traditions of nationalism, both liberal and revolutionary-democratic. Gandhi and the Nehrus, Mandela and Mugabe, the late Zulfikhar Bhutto and Bandaranaike, and, I would wager, the imprisoned leader of Burma (Myanmar), Ms Aung-San Su Xi, were or are not nationalists in the sense of Landsbergis and Tudjman. They are or were on exactly the same wavelength as Massimo d'Azeglio: nation-builders not nation-splitters.

Many more post-colonial African states may collapse into chaos and disorder, as has recently happened to some; including – though one hopes not – South Africa. Yet it is to stretch the sense of words to see the collapse of Somalia or Ethiopia as being brought about by the inalienable right of peoples to form independent sovereign nation states. Friction between ethnic groups and conflicts, often bloody ones, between them, are older than the political programme of nationalism, and will survive it.

In Europe the outburst of separatist nationalism has even more specific historical roots in the twentieth century. The eggs of Versailles and Brest Litowsk are still hatching. Essentially the permanent collapse of the Habsburg and Turkish empires and the short-lived collapse of the Tsarist Russian empire produced the same set of national successor-states with the same sort of problems, insoluble in the long run, except by mass murder or forced mass migration. The explosive issues of 1988–92 were those created in 1918–21. Czechs were then yoked to Slovaks for the first time, and Slovenes (formerly Austrian) with Croats (once the military frontier against the Turks) and, across a millennium of divergent history, with the Serbs who belonged to Orthodoxy and the Ottoman empire. The doubling of Romania's size produced friction between its component nationalities. The victorious Germans set up three small Baltic nation states for which there was no historical precedent at all, and – at least in Estonia and Latvia – no noticeable national demand. They were maintained in being by the Allies as part of the 'quarantine belt' against Bolshevist Russia. At the moment of Russia's greatest weakness, German influence encouraged the setting up of an independent Georgian and Armenian state, and the British the autonomy of oil-rich Azerbaijan. Transcaucasian nationalism (if such a term is not too strong for the grassroots anti-Armenian resentment of the Azeri Turks) had not been a serious political issue before 1917: the Armenians were, for obvious reasons, worried about Turkey rather than Moscow, the Georgians supported a nominally Marxist all-Russian party (the Mensheviks) as their national party. However, unlike the Habsburgs and the Ottoman empire, the multinational Russian empire survived for another three generations, thanks to the October Revolution and Hitler. Victory in the Civil War eliminated the possibility of Ukrainian separatism, and the recovery of Transcaucasia eliminated local nationalisms, though – since it was achieved partly through negotiations with Kemalist Turkey – it left a few sensitive issues for future nationalist resentment, notably the problem of the Armenian enclave of Mountain Karabakh in Azerbaijan. In 1939–40 the USSR in practice recovered all that Tsarist Russia had lost, except for Finland (which had been allowed to secede peacefully by Lenin) and former Russian Poland.

The simplest way to describe the apparent explosion of separatism in 1988–92 is thus as 'unfinished business of 1918–21'. Conversely, ancient and deep-seated national questions which actually seemed dangerous to European chanceries *before* 1914, have not proved explosive. It was not 'the Macedonian Question', well known to scholars as leading to battles between rival experts in a half-dozen fields at international congresses, which provoked the collapse of Yugoslavia. On the contrary, the Macedonian People's Republic did its best to stay out of the Serb-Croat imbroglio, until Yugoslavia was actually collapsing, and all its components, in sheer self-defence, had to look after themselves. (Characteristically enough, its official recognition has been hitherto sabotaged by Greece, which had annexed large parts of Macedonian territory in 1913.) Similarly, the only part of Tsarist Russia which contained a genuine national movement before 1917, though not a separatist one, was Ukraine. Yet Ukraine remained relatively quiet while Baltic and Caucasian republics demanded secession, remained under the control of the local Communist Party leadership, and did not resign itself to separation until after the failed coup of August 1991 destroyed the USSR.

Moreover, the definition of 'the nation' and its aspirations which, paradoxically, Lenin shared with Woodrow Wilson, automatically created the fracture lines along which multinational units constructed by communist states were to break, just as the colonial frontiers of 1880–1950 were to form the state frontiers of post-colonial states, there being no others available. (Most of their inhabitants did not know what frontiers were, or took no notice of them.) In the Soviet Union we can go further: it was the communist regime which deliberately set out to *create* ethno-linguistic territorial 'national administrative units', i.e. 'nations' in the modern sense, where none had previously existed or been thought of, as among the Asian Muslim peoples – or, for that matter, the Bielorussians. The idea of Soviet Republics based on Kazakh, Kirghiz, Uzbek, Tajik and Turkmen 'nations' was a theoretical construct of Soviet intellectuals rather than a primordial aspiration of any of those Central Asian peoples (G. Smith 1990: 215, 230, 262).

The idea that these peoples, whether because of 'national oppression' or Islamic consciousness, were putting the Soviet system under the intolerable strain which led to its collapse seems to be merely another expression for some Western observers' justified horror of the Soviet system and their belief that it could not last long. In fact, Central Asia remained politically inert until the collapse of the Union, except for some pogroms of the national minorities whom Stalin had tended to banish into those remote regions. Such nationalism as is developing in those republics is a post-Soviet phenomenon.

The changes in and after 1989 were thus essentially not due to national tensions, which remained under effective control even where they genuinely existed, as in Poland and among the Yugoslav peoples, so long as central party operated, but primarily to the decision of the Soviet regime to reform itself, and in doing so (a) to withdraw military support from its satellite regimes, (b) to undermine the central command and authority structure which allowed it to operate, and consequently also (c) to undermine the foundations of even the independent communist regimes in Balkan Europe. Nationalism was the beneficiary of these developments but not, in any serious sense, an important factor in bringing them about. Hence, indeed, the universal amazement at the sudden collapse of the eastern regimes, which had been entirely unexpected, even in Poland, where a deeply unpopular regime had shown that it could keep a massively organized opposition movement under control for almost a decade.

One has only to compare the German unifications of 1871 and 1990 to note the differences. The first was seen as the long-awaited achievement of an objective which, in one way or another, was the central concern of everyone interested in politics in the German lands, even those who wanted to resist it. [...] But until the autumn of 1989 none of the major parties in the Federal Republic had paid more than lip-service to the creation of a single German state for many years. This was not only because it was obviously not practicable until Gorbachev made it so, but because nationalist organizations and agitations were politically marginal. Nor did the desire for German unity motivate the political opposition in the DDR, or the ordinary East Germans, whose mass exodus precipitated the collapse of the regime. No doubt, among all their doubts and uncertainties about the future, most Germans welcome the unification of the two Germanies, but its very suddenness, and the patent lack of serious preparation for it, demonstrate that, whatever the public rhetoric, it was the by-product of unexpected events outside Germany.

As for the USSR, it collapsed not, as some Sovietologists had predicted, under its internal national tensions (Carrère d'Encausse 1978 and 1990), undeniable as these were, but under its economic difficulties. *Glasnost*, which the reform-communist leadership of the country regarded as a necessary condition of *perestroika*, reintroduced freedom of debate and agitation and also weakened the centralized command system on which both regime and society rested. The failure of *perestroika*, i.e. the growing deterioration of living conditions for ordinary citizens, undermined faith in the all-Union government made responsible for it, and indeed encouraged or even imposed regional and local solutions to problems.

It is safe to say that before Gorbachev no Soviet republic envisaged secession from the USSR except the Baltic states, and even there independence was then obviously a dream. Nor can it be argued that only fear and coercion kept the USSR together, though it undoubtedly helped to stop ethnic and communal tensions in mixed regions from degenerating into mutual violence, as they have subsequently done. Indeed, in the long Brezhnev era local and regional autonomy was by no means illusory. Moreover, as the Russians never ceased to complain, most of the other republics were rather better off than the inhabitants of the RSFSR. The national disintegration of the USSR, and incidentally of its constituent republics, almost all effectively multinational, is plainly more the consequence of events in Moscow than their cause.

Paradoxically, the case for nationalist movements with the power to undermine existing regimes is rather stronger in the West, where such agitations disrupt some of the most ancient nation states: the United Kingdom, Spain, France, even in a more modest way Switzerland, not to mention Canada. Whether complete secession of Quebec, Scotland or some other region will actually take place is at present (1992) a matter for speculation. Outside the former Euro-Soviet red belt, successful secessions since the Second World War are extremely rare, and peaceful separations virtually unknown. Nevertheless, the possible secession of Scotland or Quebec can today be discussed as a realistic possibility, which it was not twenty-five years ago.

[...]

The anguish and disorientation which finds expression in this hunger to belong, and hence in the 'politics of identity' – not necessarily national identity – is no more a moving force of history than the hunger for 'law and order' which is an equally understandable response to another aspect of social disorganization. Both are symptoms of sickness rather than diagnoses, let alone therapy. Nevertheless, they create the illusion of nations and nationalism as an irresistibly rising force ready for the third millennium. This force is further exaggerated by the semantic illusion which today turns all states officially into 'nations' (and members of the United Nations), even when they are patently not. Consequently, all movements seeking territorial autonomy tend to think of themselves as establishing 'nations' even when this is plainly not the case; and all movements for regional, local or even sectional interests against central power and state bureaucracy will, if they possibly can, put on the national costume, preferably in its ethnic-linguistic styles. Nations and nationalism therefore appear more influential and omnipresent than they are. Aruba plans to break away from the rest of the Netherlands West Indies, because it does not like to be yoked to Curaçao. Does that make it a nation? Or Curaçao, or Surinam, which is already a member of the United Nations? The Cornish are fortunate to be able to paint their regional discontents in the attractive colours of Celtic tradition, which makes them so much more viable, even though it leads some of them to reinvent a language not spoken for 200 years, and even though the only popular public tradition with genuine roots in the county is Wesleyan Methodism. They are luckier than, say, Merseyside, which can mobilize in defence of the equally or more hard-hit local interests only the memory of the Beatles, of generations of Scouse comedians, and the proud tradition of its rival football teams, while taking care to keep away from anything that reminds its inhabitants too obviously of the divisive colours Orange and Green. Merseyside cannot blow a national trumpet. Cornwall can. But are the situations which produce discontent in one area substantially different from those which do so in the other?

In fact, the rise of separatist and ethnic agitations is partly due to the fact that, contrary to common belief, the principle of state-creation since the Second World War, unlike that after the First, had nothing to do with Wilsonian national self-determination. It reflected three forces: decolonization, revolution and, of course, the intervention of outside powers.

Decolonization meant that, by and large, independent states were created out of existing areas of colonial administration, within their colonial frontiers. These had, obviously, been drawn without any reference to, or sometimes even without the knowledge of, their inhabitants and therefore had no national or even proto-national significance for their populations; except for colonial-educated and Westernized native minorities of varying, but generally exiguous, size. Alternatively, where such territories were too small and scattered, as in many colonized archipelagos, they were combined or broken up according to convenience or local politics. Hence the constant, and eventually often vain, calls of the leaders of such new states to surmount 'tribalism', 'communalism', or whatever forces were made responsible for the failure of the new inhabitants of the Republic of X to feel themselves to be primarily patriotic citizens of X rather than members of some other collectivity.

In short, the appeal of most such 'nations' and 'national movements' was the opposite of the nationalism which seeks to bond together those deemed to have common ethnicity, language, culture, historical past, and the rest. In effect it was *internationalist*. The internationalism of the leaders and cadres of national liberation movements in the Third World is more obvious where such movements played a leading part in the liberation of their countries than where countries were decolonized from above, for the post-independence breakdown of what previously operated, or seemed to operate, as a united movement of 'the people' is more dramatic. Sometimes, as in India, the unity of the movement has already cracked before independence.

More commonly, soon after independence tensions develop between the component parts of the independence movement (e.g. in Algeria, Arabs and Berbers), between peoples actively involved in it and those not, or between the emancipated non-sectional secularism of the leaders and the feelings of the masses. However, while the cases where multi-ethnic and multi-communal states have fractured, or are close to breaking, naturally attract most attention – the partition of the Indian sub-continent in 1947, the splitting of Pakistan, the demands for Tamil separatism in Sri Lanka – it should never be forgotten that these are special cases in a world where multi-ethnic and multi-communal states are the norm. What was written almost thirty years ago remains substantially true: 'Countries including many language and culture groups, like most African and Asian ones, have not split up, and those taking in only part of a single language group, like the Arab ones and North Africa, have...not united' (Kautsky 1962: 35).

The intervention of outside powers, finally, has obviously been non-nationalist in both motivation and effect, except by pure accident. This is so evident that it does not require illustration. However, so also has been the impact of social revolution, though rather less effectively. Social revolutionaries have been keenly aware of the force of nationalism, as well as ideologically committed to national autonomy, even when it is not actually wanted, as among the Lusatian Slavs, whose language is slowly retreating, in spite of the admirable efforts of the German Democratic Republic during its period of independent existence to foster it. The *only* form of constitutional arrangements which socialist states have taken seriously since 1917 are formulas for national federation and autonomy. While other constitutional texts, where they existed at all, have for long periods been purely national, national autonomy has never ceased to have a certain operational reality. However, inasmuch as such regimes do not, at least in theory, identify with any of their constituent nationalities and regard the interests of each of them as secondary to a higher common purpose, they are non-national.

Hence, as we can now see in melancholy retrospect, it was the great achievement of the communist regimes in multinational countries to limit the disastrous effects of nationalism within them. The Yugoslav revolution succeeded in preventing the nationalities within its state frontiers from massacring each other almost certainly for longer than ever before in their history, though this achievement has now unfortunately crumbled. The USSR's potential for national disruption, so long kept in check (except during the Second World War), is now patent. In fact, the 'discrimination' or even 'oppression' against which champions of various Soviet nationalities abroad used to protest, was far less than the consequences of the withdrawal of Soviet power. Official Soviet anti-semitism, which has undoubtedly been observable since the foundation of the state of Israel in 1948, must be measured against the rise of popular anti-semitism since political mobilization (including that of reactionaries) became permitted again, not to mention the massacre of Jews on a considerable scale *by local elements* in the Baltic states and Ukraine as the Germans marched in but *before the systematic German killing of Jews began.* Indeed, it may be argued that the current wave of ethnic or mini-ethnic agitations is a response to the overwhelmingly non-ethnic and non-nationalist principles of state formation in the greater part of the twentieth-century world. However, this does not mean that such ethnic reactions provide in any sense an alternative principle for the political restructuring of the world in the twenty-first century.

A third observation confirms this. 'The nation' today is visibly in the process of losing an important part of its old functions, namely that of constituting a territorially bounded 'national economy' which formed a building-block in the larger 'world economy', at least in the developed regions of the globe. Since the Second World War, but especially since the 1960s, the role of 'national economies' has been undermined or even brought into question by the major transformations in the international division of labour, whose basic units are transnational or multinational enterprises of all sizes, and by the corresponding development of international centres and networks of economic transactions which are, for practical purposes, outside the control of state governments. The number of *intergovernmental* international organizations grew from 123 in 1951 through 280 in 1972 to 365 in 1984; the number of international *nongovernmental* organizations from 832 through 2173 in 1972, more than doubling to 4615 in the next twelve years (Held 1988: 15). Probably the only functioning 'national economy' of the late twentieth century is the Japanese.

Nor have the old (developed) 'national economies' been replaced as the major building-blocks of the world system only by larger associations or federations of 'nation states' such as the European Economic Community, and collectively controlled international entities like the International Monetary Fund, even though the emergence of these is also a symptom of the retreat of the world of 'national economies'. Important parts of the system of international transactions, such as the Eurodollar market, are outside any control whatever.

All this has, of course, been made possible both by technological revolutions in transport and communication, and by the lengthy period of free movements of the factors of production over a vast area of the globe which has developed since the Second World War. This has also led to the massive wave of international and intercontinental migration, the largest since the decades before 1914, which has, incidentally, both aggravated inter-communal frictions, notably in the form of racism, and made a world of national territories 'belonging' exclusively to the natives who keep strangers in their place, even less of a realistic option for the twenty-first century than it was for the twentieth. At present we are living through a curious combination of the technology of the late twentieth century, the free trade of the nineteenth, and the rebirth of the sort of interstitial centres characteristic of world trade in the Middle Ages. City states like Hong Kong and Singapore revive, extraterritorial 'industrial zones' multiply inside technically sovereign nation states like Hanseatic Steelyards, and so do offshore tax-havens in otherwise valueless islands whose only function is, precisely, to remove economic transactions from the control of nation states. The ideology of nations and nationalism is irrelevant to any of these developments.

This does not mean that the economic functions of states have been diminished or are likely to fade away. On the contrary, in both capitalist and non-capitalist states they have grown, in spite of a tendency in both camps to encourage private or other non-state enterprise in the 1980s. Quite apart from the continued importance of state direction, planning and management even in countries dedicated in theory to neo-liberalism, the sheer weight of what public revenue and expenditure represent in the economies of states, but above all their growing role as agents of substantial redistributions of the social income by means of fiscal and welfare mechanisms, have probably made the national state a more central factor in the lives of the world's inhabitants than before. National economies, however, undermined by the transnational economy, coexist and intertwine with it. However, except for the most self-sealed at one end – and how many of these are left after even Burma appears to consider reentering the world? – and perhaps Japan at the other extreme, the old 'national economy' is not what it was. Even the USA, which in the 1980s still seemed sufficiently vast and dominant to deal with its economic problems without taking any notice of anyone else, at the end of that decade became aware that it 'had ceded considerable control over its economy to foreign investors...[who] now hold the power to help keep the US economy growing, or to help plunge it into recession' (*Wall Street Journal*, 5 December 1988: 1). As for all small and practically all medium-sized states their economies had plainly ceased to be autonomous, insofar as they had once been so.

Another observation also suggests itself. The basic political conflicts which are likely to decide the fate of the world today have little to do with nation states, because for half a century there has not existed an international state system of the nineteenth-century European type.

Politically the post-1945 world was bi-polar, organized round two superpowers which may just be describable as jumbo-sized nations, but certainly not as parts of an international state system of the nineteenth-century or pre-1939 type. At most, third-party states, whether aligned with a superpower or nonaligned, could act as a brake on superpower action, though there is no strong evidence that they did so to much effect. Moreover, as far as the USA was concerned – but vestigially this was probably also true of the USSR before the Gorbachev era – the basic conflict was ideological, the triumph of the 'right' ideology being equated with the supremacy of the appropriate superpower. Post-1945 world politics were basically the politics of revolution and counterrevolution, with national issues intervening only to underline or disturb, the main theme. Admittedly this pattern broke down in 1989 when the USSR ceased to be a superpower; and indeed the model of a world divided by the October Revolution had ceased to have much relation to the realities of the late twentieth century for some time before then. The immediate result was to leave the world without any international system or principle of order, even though the remaining superpower attempted to impose itself singlehanded as the global policeman, a role probably beyond its, or any other single state's, economic and military power.

There is thus at present no system at all. That ethnic-linguistic separation provides no sort of basis for a stable, in the short run even for a roughly predictable, ordering of the globe is evident in 1992 from the merest glance at the large region situated between Vienna and Trieste in the west, and Vladivostock in the east. All maps for one fifth of the world's surface are uncertain and provisional. And the only thing clear even about its cartographic future is that it will depend on a handful of major players outside the region, except for Russia (which is likely to remain a political entity of some substance). They are major players precisely because they have not so far been disrupted by separatist agitations: Germany, Turkey, Iran, China, Japan and – at one remove – the USA.

For a new 'Europe of nations', and still more a 'world of nations', would not even create an ensemble of independent and sovereign states. In military terms the independence of small states depends on an international order, whatever its nature, which protects them against rapacious stronger neighbours, as the Middle East immediately demonstrated after the ending of the superpower balance. Until a new international system emerges at least a third of the existing states – those with populations of two and a half million or less – have no effective guarantees of independence. The establishment of several additional small states would merely increase the number of insecure political entities. And when such a new international system emerges, the small and the weak will have as little real role in it as Oldenburg or Mecklenburg-Schwerin had over the politics of the German Federation in the nineteenth century. Economically, as we have seen, even much more powerful states depend on a global economy over which they have no control and which determines their internal affairs. A Latvian or Basque 'national' economy separate from some larger entity of which it forms a part is as meaning-less a concept as a Parisian economy considered in separation from France.

The most that could be claimed is that small states are today economically no less viable than larger states, given the decline of the 'national economy' before the transnational one. It may also be argued that 'regions' constitute more rational sub-units of large economic entities like the European Community than the historic states which are its official members. Both observations are correct, in my view, but they are logically unconnected. West European separatist nation-alisms like the Scottish, Welsh, Basque or Catalan are today in favour of bypass-ing their national governments by appealing directly to Brussels as 'regions'. However, there is no reason to suppose that a smaller state *ipso facto* forms more of an economic region than a larger one (say Scotland than England) and con-versely there is no reason why an economic region should *ipso facto* coincide with a potential political unit constituted according to ethnic-linguistic or historic criteria. Moreover, when separatist small-nation movements see their best hope in establishing themselves as sub-units of a larger politico-economic entity (in this case the European Community) they are in practice abandoning the classical aim of such movements, which is to establish independent and sovereign nation states.

However, the case against *Kleinstaaterei* today, at least in its ethnic-linguistic form, is not only that it provides no solution for the actual problems of our day, but that, insofar as it has the power to carry out its policies, it makes these problems more difficult. Cultural freedom and pluralism at present are almost certainly better safeguarded in large states which know themselves to be plurinational and pluricultural than in small ones pursuing the ideal of ethnic-linguistic and cultural homogeneity.

[...]

As I have suggested, 'nation' and 'nationalism' are no longer adequate terms to describe, let alone to analyse, the political entities described as such, or even the sentiments once described by these words. It is not impossible that national-ism will decline with the decline of the nation state, without which being English or Irish or Jewish, or a combination of all these, is only one way in which people describe their identity among the many others which they use for this purpose, as occasion demands. It would be absurd to claim that this day is already near. However, I hope it can at least be envisaged. After all, the very fact that historians are at least beginning to make some progress in the study and analysis of nations and nationalism suggests that, as so often, the phenomenon is past its peak. The owl of Minerva which brings wisdom, said Hegel, flies out at dusk. It is a good sign that it is now circling round nations and nationalism.

References

Carrère d'Encausse, H. (1978), *L'Empire éclaté*, Paris: Flammarion.

Carrère d'Encausse, H. (1990), *La Gloire des nations, ou La Fin de l'empire sovietique*, Paris: Fayard; translated (1993) as *The End of the Soviet Empire: The Triumph of the Nations*, New York: Basic Books.

Held, David (1988), 'Farewell nation state', *Marxism Today*, December, p. 15.

Kautsky, John H. (1962), 'An essay in the politics of development' in *Political Change in Underdeveloped Countries: Nationalism and Communism,* ed. John. H. Kautsky, New York and London: Wiley.

Smith, Graham, ed. (1990), *The Nationalities Question in the Soviet Union,* London and New York: Longman.

3

Ethnicity and Violence

Michael Brown examines the causes and implications of ethnic conflict, understood as a dispute about important political, economic, social, cultural or territorial issues between two or more ethnic communities. Such conflicts may involve full-scale military hostilities as seen in Angola, Bosnia, the Caucasus and elsewhere; however in other cases ethnic conflict may involve little or no violence. Ongoing struggles for political recognition in Quebec, Catalonia, Flanders and Scotland are cases in point. Among the various causes of ethnic conflict, Brown singles out: systemic, domestic and perceptual explanations.

Systemic explanations concentrate on the nature of the security systems in which ethnic groups operate and the security concerns of these groups. Domestic explanations refer to factors such as the effectiveness of states in addressing the concerns of their constituents, the impact of nationalism on inter-ethnic relations, and the consequences of democratization upon inter-ethnic relations. Perceptual explanations focus on the false histories that many ethnic groups have of themselves and others. Brown also considers the international dimension of ethnic conflicts and examines the consequences of ethnic separation and ethnic war. Brown's theoretical piece is followed by two case-studies, Iraq and Somaliland.

Toby Dodge highlights the profound security vacuum created in Iraq since the arrival of US troops on 9 April 2003. He rejects the primordial template describing Iraq as a divided society constituted by three mutually hostile communities; instead he emphasizes the fluid, historically discontinuous, and contingent role that ethnic and religious identities play in political mobilization.

In his view, undoubtedly religious and ethnic divisions are to play a key role in any analytical judgement of how Iraq's population will mobilize in the near future but this must be done in historical perspective. Recent opinion polls signal the dominance of Islam as a marker or identity, a feature that runs in tandem with strong support across Iraqi society for democracy, but not necessarily on a European or US model. In addition, polling data indicate a popular shared sense of national identity and a widespread wish for a strong unitary state centred on Baghdad. Obviously the commitment to a new Iraqi state varies across different sections of society and it is at this point that Dodge emphasizes the need for the emergence of a subnational elite, ethnic or otherwise, able to provide leadership and supply a degree of stability and certainty. He writes: 'Ultimately, however, the sustainability of state capacity is anchored in the extent to which its actions are judged to be legitimate in the eyes of its citizens. This is not primarily an issue of ethnic identity; the evolution of state power is intimately linked to the ability of state institutions to penetrate society in a regularized fashion and become central to the population's ongoing and daily "strategies of survival".'

Mark Bradbury focuses on the state-building process initiated in Somaliland after the declaration of independence from Somalia in May 1991 and the establishment of Somaliland's first government. He mentions the widespread devastation uncovered by the SNM *mujahideen* and civilian refugees as they returned to the northern cities as a factor deepening Isaaq grievances against the south. The Isaaq were afraid of maintaining a relationship with Mogadishu which would probably result in further persecution.

The potential for a new relationship with Ethiopia – also undergoing 'regime change'– and the declining relevance of the Somali state may also have been an impetus for secession. In addition, pressure from armed movements, a reduction in foreign aid and the impact of structural adjustment programmes had greatly weakened the state's control over the economy. There is a sharp contrast between the process leading to the consolidation of Somaliland and peace processes in other parts of the world. The transformation of a rebel movement into a government proved difficult and, initially, the international response to Somaliland's declaration of independence was viewed as a regressive step that threatened to break up a sovereign state.

Somaliland was on the edge of a civil war in 1992. In Bradbury's view, Somaliland did not follow the pattern of the south due to a strong sense of political community that could be traced back to its particular colonial history, the experience of north-west Somalia within the Somali Republic, and the experience of the Isaaq people within the Somali state and during the war.

Somaliland stands up as an original example of the strength and influence of traditional and indigenous systems of governance in local peace processes. It also supports the case for locally financed and managed peace processes, which in the case of Somaliland proved to be more effective than externally sponsored 'national' conferences in Somalia.

CAUSES AND IMPLICATIONS OF ETHNIC CONFLICT

MICHAEL E. BROWN

Expectations were too high. The Cold War generated great tension, but also exceptional stability – at least as far as Europe was concerned. When the Cold War ended, many people assumed that international tensions would be reduced, but that stability would be retained – perhaps even extended to previously troubled parts of the world. Learned commentators spoke of 'the end of history'. Presidents suggested that the great powers would work together to create a 'New World Order'. Many people expected, inferring too much from the international community's response to the Iraqi invasion of Kuwait, that effective international action would be taken in the future to prevent conflicts from breaking out and to resolve those that did. Many people seemed to think that the end of the Cold War marked the advent of the millennium.

These great expectations – which could only have been generated by wilfully ignoring the many ethnic conflicts around the world that have raged for years, even decades – have been dashed. People have been stunned by both the breadth and depth of the ethnic conflicts that are now taking place in many regions. The war in Bosnia-Herzegovina has received the most attention in the West because of the intense coverage it has received from the Western media, but equally if not more horrific conflicts are under way in Afghanistan, Angola, Armenia, Azerbaijan, Burma, Georgia, India, Indonesia, Liberia, Sri Lanka, Sudan and Tajikistan. Other trouble spots abound – Bangladesh, Belgium, Bhutan, Burundi, Estonia, Ethiopia, Guatemala, Iraq, Latvia, Lebanon, Mali, Moldova, Niger, Northern Ireland, Pakistan, the Philippines, Romania, Rwanda, South Africa, Spain and Turkey, for example – and the prospects for ethnic conflict in Russia and China cannot be dismissed.

Expectations about the willingness and ability of outside powers to prevent and resolve ethnic conflicts have also been dampened. European and American leaders have agonized over the conflict in Bosnia, trying to decide if genocidal acts and threats to outside interests have created either moral or strategic imperatives for intervention. Except for providing some small measure of humanitarian assistance, no action was taken as cities were bombed and civilians slaughtered. The possibility that Western powers will intervene in other ethnic conflicts, where their interests are even less engaged and where media attention is less intense, is remote.

This [essay examines] the causes and implications of ethnic conflict, as well as the recommendations that have been put forward to minimize the potential for instability and violence. [...] It begins with a brief discussion of some basic definitional issues, in an effort to sharpen an understanding of the parameters of the term 'ethnic conflict'. Second, it examines alternative explanations of the causes of ethnic conflict, focusing in turn on systemic, domestic and perceptual explanations. Third, it analyses the regional and international implications of ethnic conflicts, arguing that one must distinguish among the effects of three basic kinds of conflict outcomes: peaceful reconciliation, peaceful separation, and ethnic war. This last, it is argued, can affect the strategic interests and moral calculations of the outside world in seven important ways. This essay concludes with a discussion of recommendations that have been developed to prevent or dampen ethnic conflicts, focusing in particular on steps outside powers and the international community could take in this regard.

Definitions

The term 'ethnic conflict' is often used loosely, to describe a wide range of intra-state conflicts that are not, in fact, ethnic in character. The conflicts in Somalia, for example, is occasionally referred to as an ethnic conflict even though Somalia is the most ethnically homogenous country in Africa. The conflict in Somalia is not between rival ethnic groups, but between rival gangs, clans and warlords, all of whom belong to the same ethnic group.

This inquiry consequently begins with some definitions. According to Anthony Smith, an 'ethnic community' is 'a named human population with a myth of common ancestry, shared memories, and cultural elements; a link with a historic territory or homeland; and a measure of solidarity' (A. D. Smith, in Brown 1993: 28–9). Six criteria must be met, therefore, before a group can be called an ethnic community. First, the group must have a name for itself. This is not trivial; a lack of a name reflects an insufficiently developed collective identity. Second, the people in the group must believe in a common ancestry. This is more important than genetic ties, which may exist, but are not essential. Third, the members of the group must share historical memories, often myths or legends passed from generation to generation by word of mouth. Fourth, the group must have a shared culture, generally based on a combination of language, religion, laws, customs, institutions, dress, music, crafts, architecture, even food. Fifth, the group must feel an attachment to a specific piece of territory, which it may or may not actually inhabit. Sixth and last, the people in a group have to think of themselves as a group in order to constitute an ethnic community; that is, they must have a sense of their common ethnicity. The group must be self-aware.

At the risk of stating the obvious, an 'ethnic conflict' is a dispute about important political, economic, social, cultural or territorial issues between two or more ethnic communities. Some ethnic conflicts involve little or no violence. The struggle of French Canadians within Quebec to win more autonomy from the Canadian government is a case in point; Czechoslovakia's 'velvet divorce' is another. Tragically, other ethnic conflicts involve full-scale military hostilities and unspeakable levels of savagery, as seen in Angola, Bosnia, the Caucasus and elsewhere.

Two points should be kept in mind about these definitions. First, although Smith's conception of ethnic communities is a broad one – it would include many groups defined in terms of religious and tribal distinctions – many domestic disputes and civil wars are not ethnic in character. The war between the Sendero Luminoso and the Peruvian government, for example, is primarily political and ideological in nature, as is the continuing struggle between the Khmer Rouge and other factions in Cambodia; Cambodian persecution of ethnic Vietnamese is another matter, however. The problems in Georgia with South Ossetian and Abkhazian separatists are ethnic in nature; the struggle for power in Tblisi among various Georgian factions is not. The Burmese military's repression of Karen, Kachin, Naga and Rohingya insurgents is an ethnic conflict; its suppression of the democracy movement in the country as a whole has other political motivations.

Second, many ethnic conflicts start out as domestic disputes, but become inter-state conflicts when outside powers become involved. In some cases, trouble spills over into neighbouring countries. In others, neighbouring powers intervene in domestic disputes to protect the interests of their ethnic brethren. Disinterested powers may intervene in ethnic wars, which often involve attacks on civilian populations, for humanitarian reasons. For these and other reasons that will be discussed in more detail below, ethnic conflicts often become internationalized.

Causes

The conventional wisdom among journalists and policy-makers is that ethnic conflicts have sprung up in eastern Europe, the former Soviet Union, and else-where because the collapse of authoritarian rule has made such conflicts possible. The 'lid' on ancient rivalries, it is said, has been taken off, and long-suppressed grievances are now being settled. Scholars generally agree that this conventional wisdom offers an inadequate explanation of the causes of ethnic conflict. It fails to explain why conflicts have broken out in some places, but not others, and it fails to explain why some ethnic disputes are more violent than others. In short, this single-factor explanation cannot account for significant variation in the incidence and intensity of ethnic conflict.

Serious academic studies of the causes of ethnic conflict develop explanations at three main levels of analysis: the systemic level, the domestic level, and the perceptual level.

Systemic explanations

Systemic explanations of ethnic conflict focus on the nature of the security systems in which ethnic groups operate and the security concerns of these groups. The first and most obvious systemic prerequisite for ethnic conflict is that two or more ethnic groups must reside in close proximity. This condition is met in many parts of the world. As David Welsh observes, 'Of the approximately 180 states that exist today, fewer than 20 are ethnically homogenous, in the sense that minorities account for less than 5 percent of the population.'

The second systemic prerequisite for ethnic conflict is that national, regional, and international authorities must be too weak to keep groups from fighting and too weak to ensure the security of individual groups. As Barry Posen explains, in systems where there is no sovereign – that is, where anarchy prevails –

individual groups have to provide for their own defence. They have to worry about whether neighbouring groups pose security threats and whether threats will grow or diminish over time. The problem groups face is that, in taking steps to defend themselves – mobilizing armies and deploying military forces – they often threaten the security of others. This, in turn, can lead neighbouring groups to take actions that will diminish the security of the first group. This is the security dilemma. Groups are often unaware of, or insensitive to, the impact their actions will have on others. In other cases, they are aware of this problem, but act anyway because they feel compelled to address what they see as imminent security threats. This, of course, is the situation in eastern Europe and the former Soviet Union today. Imperial 'sovereigns' have disappeared, and individual groups have to provide for their own defence.

According to Posen, instabilities develop when either of two conditions hold. First, when offensive and defensive military forces are hard to distinguish, groups cannot signal their defensive intentions by the kinds of military force they deploy. Forces deployed for defensive purposes will have offensive capabilities and will therefore be seen as threatening by others. Second, if offensive military operations are more effective than defensive operations, due to the nature of military technology or the kinds of capability that are available, groups will adopt offensive military postures, and they will have powerful incentives to launch pre-emptive attacks in political crises.

Posen argues that these conditions are often generated when empires collapse and ethnic groups suddenly have to provide for their own security. First, under these circumstances, offensive and defensive forces are generally hard to distinguish. The military hardware available to newly independent ethnic groups is often unsophisticated from a technological standpoint, so defences are based on infantry. Whether or not these forces are effective is essentially a function of the number, cohesiveness and motivation of the troops in the field. Not surprisingly, newly independent ethnic groups often have large numbers of highly motivated, like-minded volunteers on which to draw. Cohesive, well-motivated infantries have inherent offensive capabilities against similarly configured forces, however, so they will inevitably be seen as threatening by other newly independent ethnic groups. This, in turn, will serve as a stimulus to military mobilization elsewhere.

Second, Posen argues that when empires break up, ethnic geography frequently creates situations that favour the offence over the defence. In some cases, ethnic groups will effectively surround 'islands' of people from other groups. Defending these islands in the event of hostilities is generally quite difficult: all are vulnerable to blockades and sieges, and some are simply indefensible. Often, groups will try to expel pockets of minorities from their territory. The offence has tremendous tactical advantages in these 'ethnic cleansing' operations; even small, lightly armed forces can generate tremendous amounts of terror in attacks on civilians. Posen is careful to note that ethnic geography is a variable, not a constant: some ethnic islands are large, economically autonomous, and militarily defensible; others could be reinforced by nearby brethren. In short, ethnic geography can be stabilizing or destabilizing. In some cases, groups will be able to defend themselves and their brethren. In many cases, however, the offence will have the upper hand, and stability will be tenuous.

Posen identifies two other factors that have to be taken into account in analyses of the prospects for ethnic stability. First, windows of opportunity and vulnerability will be created because newly independent groups will develop state structures at different rates. Groups that are further along in developing states and deploying military forces will have powerful incentives to go on the offensive – expelling minorities, rescuing islands of brethren, launching preventive attacks against potential adversaries – before rival groups are able to defend themselves or launch offensives of their own. Second, the presence of nuclear weapons will affect stability in important ways: nuclear weapons make infantries less important, they make defence easier, and they can prevent windows of vulnerability from opening up. In the hands of a *status quo* power, nuclear weapons could enhance stability.

Domestic explanations

Other explanations of ethnic conflict focus on factors that operate primarily at the domestic level: the effectiveness of states in addressing the concerns of their constituents, the impact of nationalism on interethnic relations, and the impact of democratization on interethnic relations.

Jack Snyder argues that people look to states to provide security and promote economic prosperity. Nationalism, he maintains, reflects the need to establish states capable of achieving these goals. Thus, it is not surprising that nationalism has flared up in parts of eastern Europe and the former Soviet Union, where state structures have weakened or collapsed altogether. New state structures have been, or are in the process of being, established, but in many cases they are not yet able to provide for the security and well-being of their constituents. In some cases, ethnic minorities feel persecuted by the new states in which they find themselves. More generally, many in eastern Europe and the former Soviet Union feel that they are not being adequately protected from unregulated markets. Inflation and unemployment are high, and economic prospects are often grim. Ethnic minorities frequently find themselves being blamed for these economic difficulties.

These problems are compounded by the fact that, when state structures are weak, nationalism is likely to be based on ethnic distinctions, rather than the idea that everyone who lives in a country is entitled to the same rights and privileges. As Snyder explains: 'By its nature, nationalism based on equal and universal citizenship rights within a territory depends on a framework of laws to guarantee those rights, as well as effective institutions to allow citizens to give voice to their views. Ethnic nationalism, in contrast, depends not on institutions, but on culture.' It is not surprising, therefore, that there are strong currents of ethnic nationalism in eastern Europe and the former Soviet Union, where state structures and political institutions have diminished capacities, and in those parts of the developing world where state structures and political institutions are inherently fragile.

The emergence of ethnic nationalism makes some form of ethnic conflict almost inevitable. The rise of ethnic nationalism in one group will be seen as threatening by others and will lead to the development of similar sentiments elsewhere. This will sharpen distinctions between groups, make it more likely that minority groups will be persecuted and more likely that ethnic minorities will demand states of their own. Secessionist crusades might be launched – and opposed. Ethnic nationalism will also make it easier for groups to field large, highly motivated armies. This will lead others to be more vigilant and to build up their own military forces. This, in turn, can make pre-emptive attacks or preventive war between neighbouring groups more likely.

Other scholars – such as Donald Horowitz (1985), Arend Lijphart (1990), Renée de Nevers and David Welsh (both in Brown 1993) – have examined the impact that democratization and other domestic political factors have on the prospects for ethnic conflict. Democratization, scholars agree, is particularly problematic in multi-ethnic societies. It often exacerbates existing ethnic problems.

Much depends on the level of ethnic tension when the democratization process begins, according to de Nevers (in Brown 1993). If the old regime was an extension of a minority ethnic group that suppressed demographically larger groups, then ethnic problems will complicate negotiations over new political arrangements from the very beginning. If the old regime exacerbated ethnic problems by engaging in forced assimilation, forced relocation, ethnic expulsion or extermination campaigns, then the democratization process is likely to be both highly problematic and emotionally charged; many ethnic problems will be on the agenda. If, on the other hand, the old regime drew from all major ethnic groups in a fairly representative way and pursued comparatively benign policies towards the ethnic groups under its sway, ethnic issues will probably play a less prominent role in negotiations over new arrangements. These negotiations, in turn, will be more likely to resolve those ethnic problems that do exist.

A second factor in the equation, de Nevers argues, is the relative size of the ethnic groups in the country. If one group is substantially larger than the others, then it is more likely that the majority group will be able to dominate discussions about new political arrangements and that minority interests will be neglected. If negotiations are between two or more groups of roughly equal size, however, it is more likely that all groups' core concerns will be addressed. Third, if the opposition to the old regime was led by only one or two groups and if the old regime itself was an extension of another, the country's political system could easily fragment along ethnic lines as the democratization process unfolds. Ethnic tensions would intensify correspondingly. If, on the other hand, the opposition to the old regime emanated from all major ethnic groups in that society, these groups will have a co-operative foundation on which to build when they begin their discussions on new political arrangements. Fourth, if the military is loyal to a single ethnic group, rather than the state, then the prospects for managing ethnic conflict are not good. If the military is loyal to the state, however, the prospects are substantially better.

Finally, de Nevers points out that different kinds of democratization processes pose different problems for the management of ethnic conflict. If the fall of the old regime comes about suddenly, negotiations on new political arrangements will be conducted in great haste. Ethnic problems are more likely to be ignored, and power struggles, perhaps along ethnic lines, are more likely to take place. The euphoria experienced as the old regime passes from the scene might produce a moment of national unity, but this moment will not endure if underlying problems are neglected. If the demise of the old regime takes place over a period of months or even years, opposition leaders will have more time to address ethnic problems when they go about devising new political institutions and processes. They will also have more of an opportunity to develop a broad-based political alliance, and ethnic leaders will have a stronger co-operative foundation on which to build. One of the keys to minimizing ethnic conflict during democratic transitions, de Nevers maintains, is addressing ethnic problems early in the transition process. If ethnic grievances can be anticipated and dealt with early, ethnic conflicts are more likely to be prevented or at least mitigated.

A number of other domestic factors also affect the prospects for ethnic conflict. One problem, as Horowitz and Welsh point out, is the tendency in multi-ethnic societies for political parties to be organized along ethnic lines. When this happens, party affiliations are a reflection of ethnic identity rather than political conviction. Political systems organized along these lines contain few independent voters, individuals who might cast votes for different parties in different elections. Under these circumstances, elections are mere censuses, and minority parties have no chance of winning power. In countries where parties are organized along ethnic lines and where winner-take-all elections are conducted – not uncommon in many parts of the world – democratic forms might be observed, but minorities remain essentially powerless, victims of a 'tyranny of the majority'.

A related problem is the tendency in multi-ethnic societies for opportunistic politicians to appeal to communal, ethnic and nationalistic impulses. This is often an effective way of mobilizing support and winning elections. Along the way, ethnic minorities are often blamed for many of society's ills; ethnic bashing and scapegoating are common features of electoral politics in many parts of the world. In many multi-ethnic societies, especially those coming out from under years or decades of authoritarian rule, political accommodation and compromise are alien principles. This, along with a lack of familiarity with and interest in coalition-building, undermines the prospects for ethnic rapprochement and the development of broad-based political communities. The mass media are often used for partisan and propagandistic purposes in ways that further damage interethnic relations.

Finally, many countries have inadequate constitutional safeguards for minority rights. Even in places where minority rights guarantees exist on paper, they are often inadequately enforced. In short, constitutional and political reforms are needed in many places to address important ethnic grievances.

Perceptual explanations

Some explanations of ethnic conflict focus on the false histories that many ethnic groups have of themselves and others. As Posen and Snyder point out (both in Brown 1993), these histories are not subjected to dispassionate, scholarly scrutiny because they are usually passed from generation to generation by word of mouth.

These stories become part of a group's lore. They tend to be highly selective in their coverage of events and not unbiased in their interpretation of these events. Distorted and exaggerated with time, these histories present one's own group as heroic, while other groups are demonized. Grievances are enshrined, and other groups are portrayed as inherently vicious and aggressive. Group members typically treat these ethnic myths as received wisdom.

It is not surprising, therefore, that the oral histories of groups involved in an intense rivalry tend to be mirror images of each other. Serbs, for example, see themselves as heroic defenders of Europe and they see Croats as belligerent thugs; Croats see themselves as valiant victims of oppression and Serbs as congenital aggressors. Under such circumstances, the slightest provocation on either side simply confirms deeply held systems of belief and provides the justification for a retaliatory response. Incendiary perceptions such as these, especially when they are held by both parties in a rivalry – which is generally the case – make conflict hard to avoid and even harder to limit. These kinds of belief and perception create tremendous escalatory pressures. The fact that opportunistic politicians use, propagate and embellish these myths compounds the problem.

These problems are particularly pronounced in countries that have experienced long stretches of authoritarian rule. Authoritarian regimes invariably suppress ethnic histories and, in an effort to create their own political myths, manipulate historical facts to suit their own purposes. Furthermore, authoritarian regimes fail to promote objective historical inquiry or scholarly standards of evidence in political discourse. Therefore, it is no surprise that the pernicious effects of ethnic mythology are especially pronounced today in eastern Europe and the former Soviet Union.

Explaining the causes of ethnic conflict

If political science was as advanced as the physical sciences, it might be possible to integrate these systemic, domestic and perceptual factors in an overarching theory of the causes of ethnic conflict. Sadly, that is not possible. It is not yet clear what conditions are necessary and sufficient for the initiation of ethnic hostilities, nor is there a rigorous understanding of why some conflicts are more intense than others. Perhaps this is because, as Albert Einstein once remarked, politics is like physics, only harder.

However, it is possible to delineate some systemic conditions that are necessary for ethnic conflict to occur. First, two or more ethnic groups must reside in close proximity. Second, national, regional and international authorities must be too weak to keep groups from fighting and too weak to ensure the security of individual groups. It is far from clear, however, that the presence of these and other systemic factors by themselves will be sufficient for ethnic conflict to break out. It seems more likely that systemic conditions will make conflict possible – and some of the systemic factors analysed by Posen might even make it highly probable – but in most cases factors operating at the domestic and perceptual levels will have to be taken into account as well. More effort needs to be put into integrating explanations across these levels of analysis, as Posen and Snyder have begun to do. Equally important, more effort needs to be put into developing testable propositions about the incidence and intensity of ethnic conflict, as Posen, Snyder, Welsh, de Nevers and others have done.

Implications

What are the implications of ethnic conflicts for outside powers and the international community in general? The answer to this question depends on the type of conflict and its course. Three broad types of ethnic conflict outcomes can be identified: peaceful reconciliation, peaceful separation, and war. In other words, groups might agree to live together, agree to live apart, or fight for control of the situation.

Ethnic reconciliation

In some cases, the ethnic groups involved in a dispute may stay associated with each other under some sort of overarching political and legal framework, although they may devise new constitutional arrangements to address specific concerns and grievances. Often, more local autonomy and more explicit minority rights guarantees will be incorporated into new schemas. Austria, Belgium and Switzerland operate under federal arrangements of various kinds that have been altered in various ways without recourse to violence. The onset of democratization provided the occasion for negotiations on more autonomy for Catalans, Galicians and Basques in Spain. Disputes between the Indian government, on the one hand, and Naga, Mizo and Gharo separatists, on the other, were resolved when internal statehood was granted to the latter. Negotiations between Quebec and the other Canadian provinces about Quebec's constitutional status have been continuing for years; whether new, mutually acceptable constitutional arrangements can be devised remains an unresolved issue, however.

When ethnic groups are able to resolve their differences peacefully, ethnic conflicts pose comparatively few problems for outside powers because the international *status quo* is, by and large, maintained. In cases in which negotiations are the main conduit for conflict resolution, the international community may be able to help mediate disputes, devise minority rights guarantees, and suggest possible constitutional changes. When these internal negotiations are completed, outside powers may have to devise new trading arrangements with newly autonomous regional actors, but little else would change as far as the outside world is concerned.

Ethnic separation

In other cases, groups may be unable to devise new constitutional arrangements that are satisfactory to all concerned. They may consequently decide to dissolve existing legal ties. In some cases – the break-up of the Soviet Union and the separation of Czechoslovakia into separate, independent republics – this process might involve comparatively little bloodshed. Velvet divorces are likely to be rare, however, because ethnic geography is generally complicated and because many groups will see fragmentation as a threat to their identity, their regional influence, and their place in world affairs.

Be that as it may, cases such as these pose several problems for the international community. Specifically, cases such as these disrupt the international *status quo* in at least six respects. First, what were previously internal borders will have to be accepted and respected as international borders. Second, outside powers will have to decide if and when to extend diplomatic recognition to the new political entities. If diplomatic recognition is extended, outside powers will have to decide how to go about establishing and exchanging diplomatic missions with the new states. Third, outside powers will have to decide if and when to extend member-ship in regional and international organizations – such as the Conference on Security and Cooperation in Europe (CSCE), the Organization of African Unity (OAU), the Council of Europe (COE), the European Community (EC), the Inter-national Monetary Fund (IMF), the General Agreement on Tariffs and Trade (GATT) and the United Nations (UN).

Fourth, international treaties signed by the defunct state will have to be refor-mulated. For example, the first Strategic Arms Reduction Treaty (START I), signed by the United States and the Soviet Union in July 1991, had to be revised in 1992 to take into account the demise of the Soviet Union; Soviet strategic nuclear weapons were deployed in four republics – Russia, Ukraine, Kazakhstan, and Belarus – each of which had to be made a party to the agreement. In general, outside powers will want to receive assurances from new states that they will uphold the treaties and commitments undertaken by the defunct state, with rea-sonable allowances for the political and economic circumstances in which the new states find themselves. Fifth, new commercial and financial relationships will have to be developed with the new states. Decisions will have to be made about granting most favoured nation trading status to new states and about providing economic, financial and technical assistance to these states. Sixth, outside powers will have to assess the implications of these developments for regional stability and the international balance of power. These implications could be momentous indeed, as they were in the case of the break-up of the Soviet Union. At a practi-cal level, outside powers will have to decide how these developments will affect their defence postures and alliance commitments, and how they will respond to requests from new states for security guarantees and membership in existing military alliances. Several eastern European states and several republics of the former Soviet Union have expressed an interest in joining the North Atlantic Treaty Organization (NATO), for example.

Many of these issues will come up before negotiations between the disputing groups have been completed. Outside powers, therefore, will be under great pressure to make the right decisions at the right time. If they fail to do so, they may find that they have disrupted the negotiating process and made war more likely.

The break-up of the Russian Federation, a possibility that cannot be ruled out, would present special problems for the international community. Although

Russia's future is particularly murky, it is at least conceivable that economic collapse and ethnically based secessionist movements could lead to the disintegration of the Russian Federation. Bashkortostan, Chechnia, Kalmyk, Tatarstan, Tyumen and Yakutsia (now Sakha) have been lobbying for – and some have already received – substantial amounts of autonomy from Moscow. Should this process lead to the fragmentation of Russia and the collapse of the Russian military, effective control of Russia's 25,000 strategic and tactical nuclear weapons and 40,000 agent tons of chemical weapons could be lost, along with control of Russia's extensive nuclear weapons establishment. Should this occur, international efforts to control the transfer of assembled nuclear weapons, nuclear weapon components, nuclear weapon technology, fissile material, technical expertise and chemical weapon stockpiles would suffer a cataclysmic setback. National and international security policies would have to be radically overhauled as a result.

Ethnic war

In many cases, antagonistic ethnic groups will not be able to agree on new constitutional arrangements or a peaceful separation. Many ethnic disputes consequently become violent, some escalating into all-out interethnic wars. The objectives of the combatants will of course vary from case to case. A minority group might insist on seceding and establishing an independent state of its own; it might demand an independent state within a confederation of states; it might insist on an independent political entity within a new federal structure; it might want more political, economic, cultural or administrative autonomy within existing institutional arrangements; or it might be satisfied with democratic reforms aimed at the implementation of a consociational democracy, ethnic power-sharing or simply more equitable representation. Groups of roughly equal size and power might fight about similar issues or control of the state. Majority groups might fight to retain or extend their influence and position in the rest of the country.

In some cases, those seeking more autonomy are defeated, and central authorities are successful in imposing their own conception of order on the vanquished, as in the case of Tibet. Cases such as these have few direct effects on the international community because the international *status quo* is unchanged. The issue that is added to the international agenda is whether or not outside powers want to exert pressure on the winner to respect the rights of the loser. In other cases, secessionist groups are successful in breaking away and establishing states of their own, as in Bangladesh, Eritrea and Slovenia, for example. Once this process is completed, the implications for the international community are similar to those for peaceful separation, with the added complication that outside assistance will probably be needed to help the combatants recover from the effects of war. In still other cases, neither party is able to win on the battlefield, and the conflict degenerates into a stalemate. This is the situation today in Angola, Cyprus, Kashmir, Lebanon and Sri Lanka, for example, where neither political nor military solutions are in sight. It is not yet clear how other conflicts – in Afghanistan,

Bosnia, the Caucasus, Liberia and Tajikistan, for example – will eventually play out.

Why should outside powers care about ethnic wars? Why should they even think about intervening in these potential quagmires? The short answer to these questions is that some ethnic conflicts create moral imperatives for intervention, and some threaten the strategic interests of outside powers and the international community as a whole. Specifically, ethnic wars can affect the outside world in seven respects.

Ethnic wars and civilian slaughter

Ethnic wars almost always involve deliberate, systematic attacks on civilians. Why is this so? First, ethnic conflicts are rarely high-technology affairs. They are usually fought by recently formed or recently augmented militias composed of ordinary citizens. A group's civilian population, therefore, is the well spring of its military power; it is the group's main source of military manpower and an essential source of economic and logistical support. Civilian populations are attacked to weaken the military resources on which adversaries can draw. Second, militarily weak groups will have strong incentives to conduct guerrilla campaigns and launch terrorist attacks against soft, high-value targets – cities, towns and villages – in an attempt to force powerful adversaries into acquiescence. Third, the civilian populations of warring groups are often intermingled. When battle lines exist, they often cut through cities, towns, even neighbourhoods. Civilians are inevitably killed under such circumstances. Fourth, ethnic conflicts are often fought for control of particular pieces of territory. To secure complete territorial control, militias seek to drive out civilians from other groups: intimidating, threatening, evicting, assassinating, raping, massacring and commiting genocide along the way. Many ethnic conflicts involve forced expulsions and systematic slaughter of civilians, now known as ethnic cleansing.

Why should outside powers care about civilian slaughter in distant lands? One reason is that it poses a direct challenge to important international norms of behaviour, the maintenance and promotion of which is in the interest of the international community as a whole. The international community has tried to distinguish between combatants and noncombatants in formulating rules and laws about the conduct of war; it will find its distinctions and norms hard to sustain in the long run if it allows them to be trampled in ethnic conflicts, in which civilians are attacked not just indiscriminately, but deliberately and systematically. Another reason for caring about – and taking action against – civilian slaughter is that tolerating it is morally diminishing. The savagery in Bosnia, it could be argued, has been proscribed by the Genocide Convention. If so, the international community has a moral obligation – as well as a legal right – to intervene.

Ethnic wars and refugees

Ethnic conflicts often generate staggering numbers of refugees, precisely because they typically involve systematic attacks on civilian populations. It has been estimated, for example, that 100,000 Hindus have fled their homes because of the war in Kashmir, and an equal number of South Ossetians have become refugees as a result of their conflict with Georgia. The war between Armenia and Azerbaijan has generated an estimated 500,000 refugees, and 600,000 people – roughly one-quarter of the total population – have been displaced by the war in Liberia. Conflict in the former Yugoslavia has uprooted an estimated 3 million people, 600,000 of whom have fled the Balkans altogether. In addition, huge numbers of refugees have been generated by the ethnic conflicts in Bhutan, Burma, Cambodia, Ethiopia, Iraq, Sri Lanka, Sudan and Tajikistan.

Refugee problems, especially of this magnitude, affect the outside world in several ways. First, offering sanctuary to refugees can invite military reprisal, thereby drawing the host country into the conflict. Often, fighters mingle with refugee populations, using refugee camps for rest, recuperation and recruitment. Second, if refugees flee to neighbouring countries where large numbers of their ethnic brethren live, their plight can lead their compatriots to become more involved in the original conflict, thereby widening the war. Third, refugees impose tremendous economic costs on host states. Large numbers of impoverished people have to be housed and fed for long and sometimes indefinite periods of time. Fourth, refugees can be seen as potential threats to the cultural identity of host states, especially when refugee communities are large and when they establish their own schools, newspapers, cultural organizations and places of worship. Fifth, refugees can become political forces in host countries, particularly regarding foreign policy issues relating to their homeland. Some host governments worry that refugee communities will turn against them if they pursue uncongenial policies. Sixth and last, when refugee problems pose threats to 'international peace and security', as they often do, the United Nations has a right, if not an obligation, to consider intervening in the crisis.

Ethnic wars and weapons of mass destruction

The proliferation of nuclear weapons and other weapons of mass destruction has added a new dimension to ethnic conflicts: the possibility, however remote, that these weapons could be used in interstate or intrastate ethnic wars. Both India and Pakistan have nuclear and chemical weapon capabilities, and tensions between the two have risen to high levels on more than one occasion in recent years. One of the main sources of tension between the two is India's claim that Pakistan is supporting Kashmiri separatists and Pakistan's claim that India is supporting Sindh insurgents. India and Pakistan are also involved in a prolonged, bitter battle over the Siachen Glacier and their northern border. Russia and Ukraine both have nuclear weapons stationed on their territory, although the latter does not yet have operational control of the weapons on its soil. Although military hostilities between the two are unlikely at present, they cannot be ruled out for the future.

Another possibility is that central authorities could use weapons of mass destruction against would-be secessionists in desperate attempts to maintain the integrity of their states. China has both nuclear and chemical weapon capabilities, and the current regime in Beijing would presumably use every means at its disposal to prevent Tibet, Xinxiang or Inner Mongolia from seceding, which many in these nominally autonomous regions would like to do. Iran has chemical weapon capabilities and is trying to develop or acquire nuclear weapon capabilities. One suspects that Tehran would not rule out using harsh measures to keep Azeris in north-western Iran from seceding, should they become inclined to push this course of action. It is not inconceivable that Russian, Indian and Pakistani leaders could be persuaded to take similar steps in the face of national collapse.

Use of nuclear or chemical weapons in any of these situations would undermine international taboos about the use of weapons of mass destruction and, thus, would be detrimental to international non-proliferation efforts, as well as international security in general. Although the possibility that a state would use weapons of mass destruction against its citizens might appear remote, it cannot be dismissed altogether: the Iraqi government used chemical weapons in attacks on Kurdish civilians in the 1980s.

Ethnic wars and chain reaction effects

Ethnic conflicts can spread in a number of ways. If a multi-ethnic state begins to fragment and allows some ethnic groups to secede, other groups will inevitably press for more autonomy, if not total independence. This is happening in the former Soviet Union, where fourteen republics successfully broke away from Moscow. Now, other groups want to redefine their relationships with the Russian Federation; as noted earlier, Bashkortostan, Chechnia, Kalmyk, Tatarstan, Tyumen and Yakutsia (now Sakha) have been lobbying for – and some have already received – substantial amounts of autonomy from Moscow. India is fighting tenaciously to retain control of Kashmir because it fears that Kashmiri secession would be the first step in a process that would lead to disintegration of perhaps the most heterogenous state in the world. The view in Delhi, a view not unsupported by logic and history, is that fragmentation is easier to prevent than control.

Other problems are created when state A fragments, allowing B to secede and form its own state. A minority group in B might attempt to secede from B. If it has ethnic ties to A, it might prefer to be associated with its brethren in A. When Croatia seceded from Yugoslavia, for example, Serbs in Croatia attempted to secede from Croatia to maintain ties with Serbs in what was left of Yugoslavia. Similarly, when Georgia seceded from the Soviet Union, South Ossetians attempted to secede from Georgia and pressed for union with their Ossetian brethren in Russia. Other problems are created when the minority group in question has a distinct ethnic identity. It might want its own state, C, either because it fears persecution or simply because establishing an independent state appears to be within the realm of the possible. When Moldova seceded from the Soviet Union, for example, the Gagauz attempted to secede from Moldova and form their own state.

Many of these chain reactions have been accompanied by extremely high levels of violence. This has important international implications and not just because fragmentation and violence can combine to create chaos. The more worrisome prospect, at least from the West's viewpoint, is that fragmentation, violence and chaos in and around Russia could provide a useful pretext for hard-liners in

Moscow to seize power. A hard-line regime might then deploy large numbers of troops in unstable parts of Russia. This, in turn, might lead Moscow to attempt to reassert control over unstable neighbouring states. This would inevitably lead to interstate war, and it would constitute a breach of Moscow's pledge not to use military force to resolve international disputes. Developments of this kind, were they to take place, would have profound implications for Moscow's relations with the West and for international security in general, for all the obvious reasons.

Another kind of chain reaction effect is more indirect: successful secessions in one part of the world could inspire secessionist movements in others. The growth of international telecommunications capabilities and international media networks makes these 'demonstration effects' increasingly potent.

Ethnic wars and neighbouring powers

Neighbouring powers can become involved in ethnic wars in a variety of ways. First, if state A fragments, allowing B to secede and form its own state, a minority group in B might attempt to secede from B and join with its brethren in C. When Azerbaijan seceded from the Soviet Union, for example, Armenians in Nagorno-Karabakh pushed forward with their demand to secede from Azerbaijan and join Armenia.

Second, when minority groups are persecuted, their brethren in neighbouring states might come to their defence. If Serbia took steps to drive ethnic Albanians from Kosovo, for example, Albania might try to defend them. The war in the Balkans could consequently spread. Many in Moscow argue that Russia should come to the aid of ethnic Russians who are being denied their political and economic rights in Estonia and Latvia. In many cases, of course, those who come to the defence of their brethren have ulterior motives in mind – absorption and expansion. Many believe that Belgrade's assistance to Serbs in Croatia and Bosnia, for example, is part of a blatant campaign to create a 'Greater Serbia'. Similarly, Delhi believes that Pakistani support for Kashmiri insurgents in India reflects Islamabad's desire to control more of Kashmir.

Third, the establishment of new, ethnically defined states might create pressures in neighbouring states for more autonomy or outright independence. As John Chipman points out (in Brown 1993), the creation of an independent Azerbaijani state has worried Iran, which has a large Azeri population. Similarly, the creation of an independent Kazakhstan has troubled China: China fears that Kazakhs in China's Xinxiang Province might try to develop ties with their newly independent brethren or agitate for more autonomy. Similarly, India feared that a federal solution to the conflict in Sri Lanka would give more autonomy to Tamils there than India was willing to grant to Tamils living in the Indian state of Tamil Nadu.

Fourth, if an ethnic group spread over two (or more) states is persecuted in one, the group as a whole could become more nationalistic and militant. This, in turn, could lead to trouble with central authorities in other states. Iraqi persecution of its Kurdish population, for example, has intensified Kurdish sensitivities and, along with the creation of large numbers of Kurdish refugees, has led to increased agitation in Turkey.

Finally, in some cases, states might take advantage of ethnic troubles in neighbouring states to further their own strategic and political ends. Indian support for Sindh separatists in Pakistan, for example, is at least in part motivated by a desire to weaken a regional rival and create another lever in Indian-Pakistani relations.

Ethnic wars and distant interests

In some cases, the interests of distant powers will be affected by ethnic conflicts. In 1990, for example, the United States sent military forces into Liberia to rescue US citizens trapped and endangered by the conflict there. France and Belgium sent forces into Rwanda in 1990 for the same reason. In other cases, states intervene to protect or promote broader strategic and political interests. Saudi Arabia, for example, has tried to contain Iranian influence by opposing Shi'a factions and the Persian-speaking Tajiks in the Afghan civil war; it has thrown its weight behind fundamentalist Pashtuns instead. Although unlikely at the moment, it is possible that intensified ethnic warfare in Iraq in the future could lead Western powers to intervene in an effort to safeguard the Kirkuk oil fields in the north, on Kurdish lands, and the Rumaila oil fields in the south, where large numbers of Shi'a live.

Ethnic wars and international organizations

Finally, ethnic wars affect outside powers because they can undermine the credibility of regional and international security organizations. Among its functions, the CSCE is supposed to help European powers anticipate, prevent and resolve European conflicts. One of the reasons for preserving NATO, it is often said, is that it helps to maintain stability in Europe. Neither of these organizations has played an effective role in the Yugoslav crisis, which can only diminish their viability and long-term prospects. Similarly, Bosnian Serb defiance of UN Security Council resolutions and UN humanitarian initiatives, a prominent feature of the Yugoslav crisis, will inevitably impede the development of the United Nations' peacemaking and peacekeeping capabilities. This, in turn, will have an impact on the prospect for ethnic violence and international conflict in general: just as effective intervention would bolster the credibility of international action and possibly have a deterrent effect elsewhere, ineffective intervention has a demonstration effect of its own.

More generally, casual defiance of international norms of behaviour – with respect to minority rights and the use of force, for example – will undercut principles that the international community would do well to maintain and extend. In short, ethnic wars can undermine the long-term ability of outside powers to preserve international order.

Recommendations

What, if anything, can outside powers do to minimize the potential for ethnic violence? The conventional wisdom among many journalists and policy-makers is that there is little outsiders can do because these conflicts are driven by implacable ancient hatred. Their implicit policy recommendation, as Snyder points out, is to steer clear and let conflicts play themselves out. In fact, the causes of ethnic conflict are complex. A number of variables affect the probability and intensity of ethnic conflict, and some of these variables are manipulable; that is, they can be influenced by outside powers.

Jenonne Walker (in Brown 1993) argues persuasively that the best course of action is to address ethnic problems early, before concrete disputes materialize and violence erupts. If ethnic conflicts are easier to prevent than resolve, then the first question to be considered should be: what can outside powers usefully do to ease tensions between and among potentially hostile ethnic groups?

At the systemic level, as Posen argues, groups worry about immediate, imminent and potential security threats. One of the keys to dampening the potential for ethnic violence, therefore, is to address these security concerns. This will not be easy, however. Providing arms to a group, thus enhancing its ability to protect itself, will often increase its offensive military capacities. This, in turn, will be seen as threatening by others. Providing arms to several rival groups in an attempt to establish a balance of power will be problematic as well. Vague security commitments from outsiders who do not have much at stake will not be particularly credible. Security commitments will be more credible – and, therefore, more effective – if an ethnic war would have important security implications for powerful outside actors.

At the domestic level, three main avenues are open. First, as Snyder suggests, outside powers should help groups develop effective states. This will dampen nationalism in general and ethnic nationalism in particular. Therefore, international economic initiatives should be framed with these overriding political objectives in mind; imposing harsh economic medicine on groups already in turmoil could weaken fragile state structures and trigger a nationalistic backlash. Similarly, outside powers should be careful not to bully groups in turmoil, as this could also weaken already fragile states.

Second, outside powers can help groups develop more representative political institutions. Welsh explains: 'No salient group should be prohibited from a share of effective power. Political institutions should be designed to ensure that minorities are proportionately represented in parliaments and bureaucracies and that their interests – political, cultural and economic – are heeded.' Ideally, governments would be based on broad coalitions. To achieve this, winner-take-all elections should be proscribed. In addition to playing an advisory role, outside powers can help shape political institutions and processes in troubled countries by withholding diplomatic recognition and economic assistance from those who retain or advance unrepresentative schemas.

Third, outside powers should insist that cultural diversity be respected, even nourished, in multi-ethnic states. At a minimum, outside powers should insist that discrimination against minorities be prohibited. All ethnic groups should be equal before the law. All should have the same political and economic rights and opportunities. All should be entitled to worship as they see fit. As far as possible, ethnic groups should be allowed to use their own languages in schools, bureaucracies, parliaments and courts. Legal mechanisms for redress of grievances should be established if they do not already exist.

In December 1992 the UN General Assembly passed a Declaration on the Rights of Persons Belonging to National or Ethnic, Religious and Linguistic Minorities that outlined the international community's views on these issues. However, as Kathleen Newland points out (in Brown 1993), this declaration, like other UN human rights instruments, contains no implementation or enforcement provisions. On the whole, Newland maintains the UN human rights regime is weak. To improve the situation, outside powers and the United Nations should do more to help states draft effective minority rights safeguards. They should develop more effective capabilities to detect minority rights violations and be more aggressive in deploying monitors in potentially troubled areas. Indeed, deploying monitors might help deter violations in the first place. In addition, outside powers should withhold diplomatic recognition, economic assistance, and membership in regional and international organizations from new states until they develop effective minority rights safeguards. Trial memberships in regional and international institutions should be granted in cases in which the prospects for minorities are uncertain. Finally, outside powers should impose sanctions – diplomatic, economic, even military – on states that fail to grant and protect these rights. In short, outside powers should do more to help develop and enforce minority rights standards and utilize more effectively the considerable leverage they all too often squander.

At the perceptual level, outside powers should try to help ethnic groups develop better histories of each other. Posen suggests that oral histories should be openly discussed with other groups and assessed by disinterested parties. Where possible, competing versions of events should be reconciled. This process should involve outsiders, including academics and representatives from non-governmental organizations. Obviously, as Posen points out, a few conferences will not undo 'generations of hateful politicized history, bolstered by reams of more recent propaganda'. However, these exercises would cost little and, therefore, should be tried.

What should outside powers do if preventive measures fail, violence erupts and an ethnic war breaks out? Under what conditions should outside powers intervene in such a war? Drawing on the arguments developed by Robert Cooper and Mats Berdal (in Brown 1993), five conditions should be met before action is taken. First, there should be either a strategic or moral imperative for action. Second, those contemplating intervention should have clear political objectives. If military forces are to be used, political objectives must be translatable into clear military objectives. Third, one must have options – diplomatic, political, economic, military – that will lead to the attainment of one's objectives. Fourth, one must be willing and able to persevere in the face of adversity. Ethnic wars tend to be both long-lasting and intense: warring groups are highly motivated because, in many cases, they believe their existence is on the line. If outsiders are to impose their will on such combatants, they will have to be determined. Multinational or international efforts, therefore, must be based on a strong, sustainable political consensus; legitimization in the form of strong backing from the UN Security Council is extremely important in this regard. Fifth, before one intervenes in an ethnic war, one should identify the circumstances that would lead one to withdraw. These are general guidelines, to be sure, but policy-makers need to keep such considerations in mind when they contemplate intervening in ethnic wars. Discrete decisions should be made one way or the other; otherwise, leaders run the risk of gradually becoming involved in conflicts about which they care little and can do less.

In contemplating intervention in ethnic wars, it is important to note that diplomatic efforts are unlikely to be successful unless they are backed by the threat of economic and military sanctions. It is also important to note that military operations will be more effective at keeping combatants apart than bringing people together. Military interventions, by themselves, will not resolve the underlying strategic, political and perceptual problems that propel ethnic conflicts. The key to true conflict resolution is the development of civil societies in genuine political communities. That, however, is something about which the international community still has much to learn – and not just in conjunction with ethnic conflict.

References

Brown, Michael E., ed. (1993), *Ethnic Conflict and International Security*, Princeton University Press, Princeton.

Horowitz, Donald (1985), *Ethnic Groups in Conflict*, University of California Press, Berkeley.

Lijphart, Arend (1990), 'The Power-Sharing Approach', in *Conflict and Peacemaking in Multiethnic Societies*, Lexington Books, Lexington, Mass., pp. 491–509.

Smith, A. D. (1986), *The Ethnic Origins of Nations*, Basil Blackwell, Oxford.

STATE COLLAPSE AND THE RISE OF IDENTITY POLITICS IN IRAQ

TOBY DODGE

Ever since US troops arrived in Baghdad on April 9, 2003, Iraqi society has been dominated by a profound security vacuum. The opportunities provided by the collapse of the state and the disbanding of the Iraqi army were seized upon by a myriad of groups deploying violence for their own ends. Organized crime continues to be the dominant source of insecurity in the everyday lives of ordinary Iraqis.[1] For coalition and Iraqi security forces, the diffuse groups fighting the insurgency in the name of Iraqi nationalism, increasingly fused with a militant Islamism, have caused the highest loss of life. But the destruction of the al-Askariya Mosque in Samarra on February 22, 2006, and its violent aftermath, may prove to be a watershed moment because it brought to the fore the spectre of sectarian violence, a communalist civil war.

It is sectarian violence that now has the greatest potential to destabilize post-Saddam Iraq beyond the point of no return, derailing attempts at state building and driving US forces from the country. This dynamic was heralded in August 2003 by the massive explosion outside the Imam Ali Mosque in Najaf (one of the holiest shrines of Shia Islam) that killed over one hundred people, including Ayatollah Mohammad Baqir al-Hakim, the leader of the Supreme Council for the Islamic Revolution in Iraq (SCIRI). In February 2004, the tactic was extended to the area controlled by the Kurdish Regional Government (KRG), when two suicide bombers killed 101 people, including the deputy prime minister of the KRG, Sami Abdul-Rahman, at the offices of the main Kurdish parties, the Kurdistan Democratic Party (KDP) and the Patriotic Union of Kurdistan (PUK) in Erbil. Attacks in March 2004 targeted the large crowds that had gathered to commemorate the Shia festival of Ashura in Baghdad and Karbala, in a clear attempt to trigger a civil war between Iraq's different communities. This assumption was strengthened by the discovery in Baghdad of a letter allegedly written by the senior jihadi figure, the Jordanian Abu Musab al-Zarqawi. The letter asserted that the only way to 'prolong the duration of the fight between the infidels and us' was by 'dragging them into a sectarian war, this will awaken the sleepy Sunnis who are fearful of destruction and death at the hands of the Shi'a'. (For discussion see Filkins 2004 and Huggler 2004.)

Estimates of those civilians killed in the immediate aftermath of February's destruction of the al-Askariya Mosque vary from 220 to 550 (O'Hanlon and Kamp 2006). US military sources judge that Baghdad's homicide rate tripled from eleven to thirty-three deaths a day (Gettleman 2006). Of even greater concern is the displacement of the population triggered by intimidation and the threat of sectarian violence. The Iraqi government has estimated this to be as high as sixty-five thousand people, with the majority coming from in and around Baghdad (North 2006). The influential 'Correlates of War' project has developed an operational definition of civil war that has become dominant in the social-science literature: 'sustained military combat, primarily internal, resulting in at least 1,000 battle-deaths per year, pitting central government forces against an insurgent force capable of effective resistance, determined by the latter's ability to inflict upon government forces at least 5 percent of the fatalities that the insurgents suffer'. (See Henderson and Singer 2000; Cole 2006.)

There are no definitive statistics for civilian casualties but rough-and-ready estimates range from 350 to 600 a month to former prime minister Ayad Allawi's claim of fifty a day (Diamond 2006 and Cole 2006). Figures released by the Iraqi government at the beginning of 2007 estimated that 13,896 Iraqis, civilians, police officers, and soldiers died during 2006. The United Nations in Baghdad, which also collates casualty figures, has put a much higher number on the death toll for 2006. In mid-January 2007, it calculated that 34,452 civilians had been killed in 2006 (Cave and O'Neil 2007; Associated Press 2007). A team from Johns Hopkins Bloomberg School of Public Health writing in *The Lancet* estimated that as of July 2006, 654,965 more Iraqis had been killed than if the invasion had not taken place (Burnham et al 2006).

Against this statistical background, Iraq is clearly in the midst of an increasingly bloody civil war. Arguments to the contrary are primarily driven not by facts on the ground but by the political ramifications in both Baghdad and Washington of admitting the obvious.

Seeking to Understand Violence in Iraq

The dominant approach used to explain Iraq's descent into civil war and to draft policy proposals to end the violence is simply to impose a primordial template onto the political and societal complexities of the situation. This argument starts with an *a priori* assertion of a deeply divided society. David Phillips, for example, claims: 'Iraqis lack a sense of national identity. They are deeply divided along ethnic and sectarian lines (Phillips 2005: 337).' Leslie Gelb and Peter Galbraith have become the chief promoters of this approach. For them Iraq has 'three distinct and sectarian communities', Sunni, Shia, and Kurd (Gelb 2004; Galbraith 2004). These communities, it is claimed, are largely geographically homogeneous and mutually hostile. They have been locked in an artificial, Sunni-dominated state for eighty-five years. This analysis leads its promoters to view the post-Saddam civil war as tragic but largely unavoidable. This approach asserts that Iraqi politics has always been and will continue to be animated by deeply held communal antipathies; the civil war is simply an outcome of this. From this perspective, there can be only one policy option: the situation will be stabilized by dividing the country into three smaller, ethnically purer and more manageable units. There is a possibility that this could be done through a form of drastic decentralization, as proposed by US senator Joseph R. Biden and Leslie Gelb. But the primordialization of Iraq has led Gelb and others to argue consistently for its complete division into separate states (Biden and Gelb 2006; Gelb 2004).

From an academic, as well as a policy point of view, the primordial approach, although increasingly influential, is far from satisfactory. Those studying the social and political evolution of Iraq as a whole and over a broad sweep of its modern history since 1920 (as opposed to a specific focus on the Kurdish region during the 1990s), have long stressed that to describe it as divided into three mutually hostile communities is a static caricature that does great damage to a complex, historically grounded, reality (Visser 2006; Dodge 2005).

Comprehensive and comparative academic explanations of the role that ethnic and religious identities play in political mobilization stress their fluid, historically discontinuous, and contingent roles (Kasfir 1986; Laitin 1998; Rothchild 1981). The political utility of communal identity is defined by and reacts to the changing nature of society and crucially how a state seeks to interact with and control its population. With this in mind, it is clear that Iraqis, like people everywhere, have several different aspects to their individual and collective societal identities: familial, professional, and geographic, as well as ethnic and religious. These are clearly not static but change over time and react to the politics of any given historical moment. A political situation and its history will determine which social identity will be most important to the individuals involved. Clearly on certain occasions, ethnic or religiously based identities may come to dominate political mobilization. But an accurate assessment of a given situation needs to explain why communalist affiliation, as opposed to other identities, becomes the dominant vehicle for political mobilization.

Crucial to the success of political mobilization is the institutional capacity of those groups and organizations seeking to mobilize support and the ideological resources at their disposal. At base, one has to explain how individuals perceive their position within their immediate social groupings and beyond that the role they and these collectives have in the wider society, in this case Iraq. To continue to select one aspect of an individual's identity above all others, in this case ethnic and religious identity, or to insist that this identity will be deployed adversarially, leading to violence or civil war, is overly deterministic, if not racist. An analytical judgment of how Iraq's population will mobilize over the coming months and years will certainly focus on its religious and ethnic divisions. But it must do this in historical perspective, seeking to identify the sources of political identity and trends that either run counter to religion and ethnicity or support them. An accurate conflict assessment focused on contemporary Iraq needs to look at three aspects of the present violence: it should first judge the institutional capacity of the state and then compare this to the capabilities of different organizations seeking to mobilize the population and deploy violence for political advantage. Finally, it needs to be aware of the political discourses available to individuals and subnational and national groups to understand their present situation and to shape their future.

To explain the evolution of violence in Iraq today, the collapse of the state in April 2003 is of equal if not greater significance to the supposedly transhistorical existence of communal antipathies. The collapse of a state's institutional capacity means the loss of national authority but also of the central focus for identity formation. In the aftermath of state failure, authoritative institutions, societal and political, quickly lose their capacity and legitimacy (Zartman 1995: 6). The geographic boundaries, within which national politics and economics are enacted, simultaneously expand and contract. On one level, because the state has lost its administrative and coercive capacity, the country's borders become increasingly meaningless, and decision-making power leaks out to neighbouring capitals, as regional and international actors are drawn into the conflict. More damagingly, however, power devolves into what is left of society, away from the state capital and down to a lower level, where organizational capacity begins to be reasserted. Politics becomes both international and also highly local (Zartman 1995: 5). In the aftermath of state collapse, public goods, services, economic subsistence, and ultimately physical survival are to be found through *ad hoc* and informal channels: 'When state authority crumbles, individuals not only lose their protection normally supplied by public offices, but are also freed from institutional restraints. In response, they often seek safety, profit, or both. Their motives become more complex than when they could depend on the state (Kasfir 2004: 55).' Once state capacity is removed, civil society's ability positively to influence events quickly disappears (Posner in Rotberg 2004: 237, 240). People will look to whatever grouping, militia, or identity offers them the best chance of survival in times of profound uncertainty (Talentino 2004: 569). The result is certainly a fracturing of the polity. But path dependencies built up before the collapse of the state help structure what emerges, which local, substate, and ethnic identities provide the immediate basis for political organization (Laitin 1998: 16). For communalistic identities to triumph as an organizing principle in this fluid and unpredictable situation, there needs to be a certain type of subnational elite. These entrepreneurs, ethnic or otherwise, have to supply what the wider community desperately needs, a degree of stability and certainty. They can then legitimize their role in terms of communalistic identity and the competition for scarce resources (Rothchild 1981: 29). However, once this process has been set in motion, when ethnic entrepreneurs, in the face of state failure, have mobilized a significant section of the population on the basis of communalistic identity, the process quickly solidifies (Wimmer 2003–2004: 120). Previously 'fuzzy' or secondary identity traits become politicized and 'enumerated' (Kaviraj 1994: 21–32). The struggle to survive, to gain a degree of predictability for yourself and your family, then becomes obtainable primarily through the increasingly militant deployment of ethnic or sectarian identity. There is nothing inevitable about the unfolding of this process; the primary causal factor in its evolution is the collapse of the state and the subsequent security vacuum, not the communalistic conflict that emerges in its wake.

Complexity Beyond Sectarianism: Societal Atomization, Nationalism, and Islamism

The whole process of stabilizing Iraq, of building administrative, coercive, and political capacity in the aftermath of regime change, has been greatly complicated by the legacy of thirty-five years of Baathist rule. The Baathist regime, built by Hassan al-Bakr beginning in 1968 and consolidated under Saddam after 1979, created a powerful set of state institutions through the 1970s and 1980s. These deliberately reshaped Iraqi society, breaking organized resistance to Baathist rule and effectively atomizing the population. During the 1980s and 1990s, however, both the Iraqi state and its relations with society were transformed. The eight-year war with Iran, the 1990–1991 Gulf War, and finally the imposition of sanctions, changed the Iraqi state, and with it Saddam's strategy of rule. From their application in 1990 until 1997, when UN-supervised oil revenues arrived, sanctions proved to be extremely efficient. They restricted the government's access to large-scale funding, which meant that economic policy was largely reactive, dominated by the short-term goal of staying in power. From 1991 until 2003, the effects of the sanctions regime combined with government policy in southern and central Iraq led to hyperinflation, widespread poverty, and malnutrition. The historically generous state welfare provision that had been central to the regime's governing strategy disappeared, and the government was forced to cut back on the resources it could devote to the armed forces and the police. The large and well-educated middle class that formed the bedrock of Iraqi society became impoverished and Iraq's once complex and all-pervasive bureaucracy was hollowed out. Bribery became commonplace, as civil servants' official wages rapidly devalued. State employees, teachers, and medical staff had to manage as best they could, extracting resources from the impoverished people who depended upon their services. Many professionals left public service, took their chances in the private sector, or fled into exile. Put simply, there was no functioning civil society in southern and central Iraq before regime change in 2003 (Jabar 2003: 89). The Baathist regime's attack on the organizing capacity of society meant that personal ties to family and extended family, town, city, or neighbourhood, as well as to province and religion, were the only ones to survive (ICG 2003).

In the aftermath of regime change, as meaningful research in southern and central Iraq became possible, a complex picture of the Iraqi polity has emerged. Opinion polling in a country that has recently emerged from dictatorship and is racked with profound uncertainty and violence is bound to be an inexact science. Results from several polls from 2003 to 2005 have been somewhat contradictory, but offer an indication of developments in public opinion (O' Neill 2004; Zogby 2003). During the 1990s, as sanctions devastated Iraqi society, there was a retreat into the certainties of religion. This trend was encouraged by the regime's *al-hamla al-imaniyya*, or faith campaign, which relaxed the rules governing religious observance and channelled state resources into mosque building (Hashim 2003: 10). This has left its mark on Iraqi society, particularly in the south and centre. In an April 2004 poll, 67 per cent identified religion as the most important expression of their identity.[2] Counter to some orientalist descriptions of contemporary Iraq, only 1 per cent of those questioned gave their tribe as the most important expression of identity. Interestingly, across the country as a whole, only 12 per cent cited their ethnicity, with the figure rising to 66 per cent in the area controlled by the Kurdish Regional Government. The dominance of Islam as a marker of identity runs in tandem with strong support across Iraqi society for democracy, but not necessarily on a European or US model. Of three thousand Iraqis polled in May 2004, three-quarters said that they 'want to live in a moderate Islamic democracy, rather than a secular liberal one (www.bridgesconsortium.org)'.

More surprisingly, Iraqi nationalism and even remnants of Baathist ideology appear to have resonance within the population, with the majority supporting a strong interventionist state. The Iraqi Centre for Research and Strategic Studies found that 64.7 per cent favoured "a politically centralized, unitary state as opposed to a federation," with 67 per cent saying that they wanted both fiscal and administrative centralization. The Oxford Research International polls of February, March, and June 2004 and November 2005 found broadly similar views. In February and November, the question "Which structure should Iraq have in the future?" was answered by 79 per cent of respondents; 70 per cent agreed with the statement "one unified Iraq with a central government in Baghdad." Although the figures differed according to the geographic location of those questioned, only 12 per cent of those in areas controlled by the Kurdish Regional Government, and 3.8 per cent of all those surveyed in 2004, called for Iraq to be broken up into separate states, with the figure rising to 20 per cent – and 9 per cent overall – in November 2005.

What these figures clearly indicate is that Iraqi public opinion is far more complicated than the caricature of three clearly delineated and mutually hostile communities divided by religion and ethnicity. The polling data indicate a popular sense of national identity and a widespread wish for a strong unitary state centred on Baghdad. Obviously this commitment to a new Iraqi state varies across different sections of society and in different areas of the country. Pundits have been correct in stressing a widely held suspicion about renewed, Baghdad-based, state capacity among those in areas controlled by the KRG. However, opinion across the country is clearly fluid, as are political identities and the basis for political mobilization. Having long been the target of state oppression, the Kurdish populations in the north of Iraq will need to be convinced that new state structures will not be used to oppress them, but these fears about the uses of the state are neither transhistorical nor insurmountable. Against this background of both historically grounded suspicion but also ahistorical primordial understandings of Iraq it is essential that care should be taken as the nascent state institutions set about interacting with the population. If done incorrectly or on the basis of widely held misperceptions about Iraqi society, the state could continue to exacerbate sectarian and religious tensions. If, however, the state encourages a civic nationalism based on equal citizenship for all in a legal, rational, democratic state, then Iraqi politics could stabilize and the state could evolve into a legitimate and sustainable organization.

The Organizations Driving Conflict in Iraq

The main driving force behind violence in Iraq is the absence of state institutions. The Iraqi state on the eve of the invasion was on the verge of collapse. It had survived three wars in twenty years and thirteen years of harsh international sanctions. The combination of war, sanctions fatigue, and rampant criminality led to a complete state breakdown. The three weeks of looting that greeted the arrival of US troops in Baghdad was estimated to have cost $12 billion, with seventeen of the Iraqi government's twenty-three ministry buildings destroyed (Packer 2005: 139; Phillips 2005: 135). In the aftermath of regime change, the Iraqi state ceased to exist in any meaningful form and has yet to be reconstituted.

The resultant security vacuum has given birth to or empowered three distinct sets of groups deploying violence and ultimately driving Iraq toward civil war. The first are the "industrial strength" criminal gangs who are still the most potent source of violence and instability. These groups were born in the mid-1990s when Saddam Hussein's regime was at its weakest. Encouraged by the regime's decision to empty the jails before the invasion, criminal gangs were quick to reconstitute in the aftermath of regime change. Although there is clear overlap between simple criminality and politically motivated violence, especially where kidnapping is concerned, the continuing crime wave is the most glaring example of state incapacity. The persistent reports that crime is as big a problem for the citizens of Basra as Baghdad indicate that the state's inability to impose and guarantee order is a general problem across large swathes of southern and central Iraq. The high levels of criminal activity across the majority of Iraqi territory indicate that violence is driven primarily by state weakness, not the antipathy of competing groups within Iraqi society. Crime is obviously instrumentally driven and primarily noncommunal and the key factor delegitimizing the state. Going well beyond the government's ability to increase electrical output or stimulate the job market, the continued ability of criminal gangs to operate is indicative of a failed state.

The second set of groups that have capitalized on the inability of occupation forces and the Iraqi government to impose order is the plethora of independent militias, estimated to hold between 60,000 and 102,000 fighters in their ranks (Bremer and McConnell 2006: 274; Diamond 2005: 222). These militias have overtly organized and legitimized themselves by reference to sectarian ideology. Although they may not enjoy widespread popular support, their existence is testament to the inability of the Iraqi government to guarantee the personal safety of Iraqis on the basis of equal citizenship, not sectarian identity. The militias themselves can be divided into three broad groups, depending on their organizational coherence and relation to national politics. The first group is made up of the two Kurdish militias of the KDP and PUK. These two separate forces number, in total, between 50,000 and 75,000 fighters. On the one hand, the Kurdish militias are the most organized, institutionalized, and comparatively disciplined in the country. With a long history of fighting against the central government in Baghdad, the KDP and PUK quickly set about imposing order on their respective fighting forces once the United Nations had given their enclave protection in the aftermath of the 1991 Kurdish uprising. However, their fractured political loyalties were highlighted by the damaging civil war that broke out between the two parties in the 1990s over control of the profits from oil smuggling. This had a highly detrimental effect on the governing structures of Iraqi Kurdistan. The two militias remain separate and represent little more than the political and personal ambitions of their two leaders.

Another distinct set of militias are those that were organized in exile and brought back to Iraq in the wake of Saddam's fall. The most powerful of these is the Badr Corps, the military arm of SCIRI. The Badr Corps, along with SCIRI itself, was set up as a foreign policy vehicle for the Iranian government. Indeed, the Badr Corps was trained and officered by the Iranian Revolutionary Guard, at least until their return to Iraq. It is the integration of Badr Corps into the security forces, especially the police and paramilitary units associated with the Ministry of Interior, which has done so much to delegitimize the state-controlled forces of law and order. The use of the police and National Guard units for electioneering in January 2005 by both the Shia list in the south and Allawi's coalition in and around Baghdad gave an indication of the blatant politicization of the nascent security services so early on in the life of the new state.[3] Along with SCIRI, the majority of the formerly exiled parties likewise set up militias to provide security for their leaders and to exert coercive influence beyond the newly created democratic structures of government.

The third group of militias includes those that have been set up at local village or town levels across southern and central Iraq. These are a direct response to the lawlessness that followed regime change. They vary in size, organization, and discipline, from a few thugs with guns to militias capable of running whole towns. In combination with the insurgency itself, the militia fighters are a key factor in the civil war. Although they were formed as an instrumental response to the security vacuum they have attempted to legitimize themselves by the deployment of hybrid ideologies – sectarian and religious but also nationalistic.

The most powerful and well-organized indigenous militia in southern and central Iraq is Muqtada al-Sadr's Mandi Army. Capitalizing on a large charitable network set up before regime change by his late father, Sadr has used radical anti-US rhetoric to rally disaffected Iraqis to his organization. As the occupation failed to deliver significant improvements to people's lives, Sadr's popularity increased. During the first weeks of April and again in August 2004 Sadr, faced with an arrest warrant for murder, launched a rebellion across the south of the country. The resulting revolts in the key towns of Basra, Amara, Kut, Nassiriya, Najaf, Kufa, and Karbala, as well as Baghdad, showed that Sadr's organization had been preparing for just such a confrontation from regime change onward.[4] More worryingly, the geographic spread of the uprisings indicated that smaller militias were using Sadr's confrontation to assert autonomy against the nascent state.

Sadr cannot simply be written off as a rabble-rouser deploying sectarianism to mobilize cannon fodder. The constituency that Sadr aspires to represent, the economically disadvantaged and politically alienated, has, if anything, increased since the revolts of 2004. Sadr successfully utilized nationalist and radical Islamic trends amongst sections of the Shia population. His use of radical anti-US rhetoric has extended his support into the lower ranks of the religious establishment, where he has found significant backing from young clerics, attracted by his youth, his lack of a religious education (younger clerics face long and arduous training), and the promise of a shortcut to moral and political influence (ICG 2003a: 8; Jabar 2003: 26). Finally, within Najaf, Sadr has capitalized on tensions between the large number of returning exiles and those who feel threatened by their arrival (ICG 2003c: 18).

Finally, other organizations fuelling the spiral of increasing violence are those of the insurgency. Those organizations fighting the occupation and the new Iraqi government are frequently described as 'the Sunni insurgency' (Packer 2005: 132). But this blanket term runs the risk of giving too much organizational and ideological coherence to those who are fighting. It is important to remember that several key individuals on the Bush administration's 'most wanted' list of insurgent leaders are actually Shia.

In the aftermath of regime change, the insurgency was born in a reactive and highly localized fashion as the US military's inability to control Iraq became apparent. This process saw the creation of a number of small, autonomous fighting groups built around dyadic ties of trust, cemented by family, locality, or friendship. Since the summer of 2003, it has been estimated that between fifty and seventy-four such groups have been fighting to rid the country of US forces.[5] With between twenty thousand and fifty thousand fighters in their ranks, it is this force that has to date proved to be the most destructive.[6] Over the past three years, they have been able to innovate both in the technology they deploy and the tactics they use (Dodge 2005: chapter 2). US troops initially formed the main target, especially where they were at their most vulnerable, along supply lines and during troop transportation. But as US troops were redeployed to decrease their vulnerability and political visibility, the insurgents increased their targeting of Iraqis who were serving with fledgling state institutions. In addition, international institutions, specifically foreign embassies, the United Nations, and the Red Cross, have been targeted, signaling the high costs of any attempt to multilateralize postwar state building. Finally, a growing radical Sunni jihadist section of the insurgency has sought to encourage civil war by murdering high-profile

Shia and Kurdish political figures and deploying suicide bombers in mass casualty attacks on specific sections of the community.

The year 2005 saw a degree of organizational consolidation around four or five main groups. These include Al-Jaysh al-Islami fi'l-'Iraq (the Islamic Army in Iraq), Jaysh Ansar al-Sunna (the Partisans of the Sunna Army), Jaysh al-Mujahidin (the Mujahidin's Army), Jaysh Muhammad (Muhammad's Army), Harakat al-Muqawama al-Islamiya fi'l-'Iraq (the Islamic Resistance Movement in Iraq), and Al-Jabha al-Islamiyya li'1-Muqawama al-'Iraqiya (the Islamic Front of the Iraqi Resistance). In terms of numbers, the role played by Arabs from neighbouring countries, and behind them the organizing capacity of Al-Qaida in Mesopotamia (Tandhim al-Qa'ida fi Bilad al-Rafidayn), appears to be comparatively low, estimated by the US Army to be around 10 per cent of the total. But they have played a disproportionately large role in the insurgency's increased ideological coherence, fusing the powerful appeal to Iraqi nationalism with an austere and extreme Sunni Salafism. It is Al-Qaida in Mesopotamia that has claimed responsibility or has been blamed for most of the violence that increased sectarian tensions in the country. However, the organizations behind the sectarian attacks are much more likely to be a hybrid, with elements of the old regime acting in alliance with indigenous Islamic radicals and a small number of foreign fighters. This has allowed midranking members of the old regime to deploy their training and weapons stockpiles. They have sought to ally themselves with a new brand of Islamic nationalism, seeking to mobilize Sunni fears of Shia and Kurdish domination and a widespread resentment at foreign occupation.

Over the last year, widespread political violence has increasingly been justified in sectarian terms and this instability has certainly been a major causal factor behind the growth of communalistic identity. However, explanations of this phenomenon that focus solely on the deeply divided nature of Iraqi society run the risk of mistaking effect for cause. It is the criminality and violence that dominated post-regime-change Iraq that have driven the rise in sectarian identity politics: faced with state collapse and profound insecurity, the population in southern and central Iraq has been placed at the mercy of those groups that could quickly build coercive capacity. Organized initially on a street, neighbourhood, and town level, the resultant informal militias have been *ad hoc* coalitions thrown together by those with weapons and military training. The result has been an implicit deal between populations and those with coercive capacity in their neighbourhoods: recognition for protection, which has then been partially legitimized through the guise of sectarian identity politics. At a regional and national level, this process was somewhat different. Muqtada al-Sadr gained an organizational and ideological head start because of the mantle he inherited from his late father, Ayatollah Muhammad Sadiq al-Sadr. Initially Sadr's political message was less sectarian, merging a militant Iraqi nationalism with a commitment to Islamic radicalism. The personnel of the SCIRI, Badr, and Al-Dawa groups were primarily exiles who returned to a post-Saddam Iraq. They found it difficult to mobilize a population suspicious of those who had spent many years outside the country and had come back under the auspices of the US military. For them, a specifically sectarian ideology was deployed to break this suspicion and rally a significant section of the population to vote for them in the two elections of 2005. Against this background, the primary cause of Iraq's civil war is not the deeply divided nature of the population, but the political dynamics of a foreign occupation trying to reconstitute a state in the midst of profound violence.

State Building as the Only Solution

The Gelb and Galbraith thesis of simply dividing Iraq into three ethnically purer states misses the main cause of the violence: the lack of institutional and coercive state capacity across the whole of central and southern Iraq. The radical decentralization of political power runs the distinct danger of devolving the violent struggle for supremacy. This could localize the conflict between SCIRI and Sadr's Mahdi Army or reignite the conflict between the KDP and PUK. Those arguing for decentralization would be hard pressed to explain how their policy recommendations would reduce the violence that erupted in Basra in April and May 2006, forcing the new prime minister, Nuri al-Maliki, to declare martial law. The city has a very small Sunni population. The militias that were responsible for the deaths of 174 Iraqis in April and May 2006 were made up of Iraqi Shias. They were not fighting over religion or even ideology, but money (Tavernise and Mizher 2006; Lasseter 2006). Basra is the centre of Iraq's oil exports and the conflict was primarily concerned with the division of the spoils (Karouny 2006). What Iraq desperately needs is one coherent and functioning state, not three. Its governing institutions, bureaucratic, military, and political, must be rebuilt from the ground up across the territorial extent of the country.

Crucial to the state's ability to perform these tasks is the veracity of its claim to 'binding authority' over its citizenship and ultimately 'over all actions taking place in the area of its jurisdiction' (Weber 1978: 56). Its capacity is ultimately grounded in the extent to which its 'administrative staff successfully upholds the claim to the monopoly of the legitimate use of physical force in the enforcement of its order' (Weber 1978: 54). The degree to which a state has reached this ideal-typical level can be judged by the ability of its institutions to impose and guarantee the rule of law, to penetrate society, mobilize the population, and extract resources (Migdal 1988).

Iraq is a very long way from this standard. The speed with which the United States rebuilt the Iraqi army and police force means most of its personnel are ill-trained and ill-equipped. If the Iraqi military is still very much a work in progress, then the police force poses an even graver cause for concern. As with the new army, police training has been extremely hurried. There is clear evidence in Basra and Baghdad that the loyalty of the police is not to the state but to various local militias. Across Iraq, but particularly in the south of the country, there is strong evidence to suggest that the political militias have targeted the police force, infiltrating their members into its ranks and placing their own senior commanders in regional management positions. Against this background, the recruitment, training, and management of the security services will have to be revisited for state building to stand any chance of gaining momentum. International assistance should focus on increasing the capacity of security-force management, both to impose law and order and to resist the massive pressures to use the police and army as tools of the political parties.

Ultimately, however, the sustainability of state capacity is anchored in the extent to which its actions are judged to be legitimate in the eyes of its citizens (Talentino 2004: 571). This is not primarily an issue of ethnic identity; the evolution of state power is intimately linked to the ability of state institutions to penetrate society in a regularized fashion and become central to the population's ongoing and daily 'strategies of survival (Migdal 1988)'. Both Joel Migdal and Michael Mann argue that the success of this process, the positive relevance of the state to the everyday lives of its citizens, is the key to society tolerating state institutions and ultimately to the growth of state legitimacy (Mann 1988). The record of the three Iraqi governments that have held power since the handover of sovereignty in June 2004 is very poor. One of the key reasons for this is that constitutionally real political power is vested in the political parties, not in the office of prime minister or president. Electoral success is rewarded by dividing up the spoils of government – cabinet portfolios and the jobs and resources they bring with them. The result has been highly variable governance, with some ministers managing their institutions fairly efficiently. A sizable minority, if not majority, of others, however, set about carving out fiefdoms for personal or factional benefit. Large swathes of the government have disengaged from the pressing need to build state capacity and extend this across the geographical extent of the country. To make inroads in such a situation both international diplomacy and donor assistance need to be highly coordinated. The United Nations, the European Union, and the United States need to present Iraqi ministers with the same specific demands for good governance and reduction of the scope for corruption, patronage, and abuse in return for further aid and assistance.

The growth of stable state institutions, with a meaningful presence in people's lives, forms the framework within which the longer-term goal of successful state building, the reconstruction of an Iraqi nation, can be achieved. The successful creation of state capacity would re-establish a framework within which a civic identity based on a shared vision of the future could be built (Talentino 2004: 558). Civil society could then become the vehicle for building a national, collective sense of identity that can rival or even replace substate, centrifugal political mobilization. A collective appreciation of administrative capacity and a loyalty toward the state would bind individuals together and to the government (Meierhenrich 2004: 154–162). Indeed, successful sustainable state building 'entails much more than merely forming a state, which may be achieved, say, by granting independence to a previous colony. It entails in addition forming a community where none previously existed, or shoring up one that was not firmly or properly constructed (Etzioni 2004: 3).' It is this process of imposing order – building institutionalized administrative capacity and developing a civic identity – that could slow Iraq's slide deeper into civil war.

However, if this process continues to fail and international policy coordination cannot improve the quantity and quality of state building, then public goods, services, economic subsistence, and ultimately physical survival will be obtained through *ad hoc* and informal channels (Rotberg 2004: 9). In Iraq, this process has fuelled the rapid growth in sectarian identity. People have sought out whatever local group, militia, and identity that can provide a modicum of pre-dictability and security in times of profound uncertainty. The result is a fracturing of the polity, with local, substate, and ethnic identities providing the immediate basis for political organization (Talentino 2004: 569). If this process continues, then the fracturing of the polity will likewise continue. Given the collapse of the state and the legacy of Saddam's totalitarianism it is extremely unlikely that this process will end in the dominance of one faction or militia over all others. Instead, this war of all against all will solidify not in state building but warlordism. Militias will carve out small islands of domination from a sea of violence. Groups may triumph on a local scale, receiving help from neighbouring states or their own institutional capacity. However, the Iraqi civil war, if left unchecked by the international community, will result in numerous unstable statelets or fiefdoms. This would be highly destabilizing for the region and the international community beyond.

Notes

1 In 2004, the US military estimated that 80 per cent of all violence in Iraq is 'criminal in nature.' There is no reason to think this situation has radically changed (Schmitt and Shanker 2003).
2 The poll was commissioned by *USA Today* and CNN. It questioned 3,444 people across Iraq between March 22 and April 2, 2004. The confessional breakdown was: Shia – 73 per cent, Sunni – 76 per cent, and Kurd – 33 per cent.
3 For examples, see "Iraqi Police Drawn into Poll Contest as Gloves Come Off," *Financial Times*, 19 January 2005.
4 This is based on interviews carried out in Baghdad in the aftermath of the fall of the regime.
5 The International Crisis Group, from studying Web traffic, estimates fifty groups, whereas the figure of seventy-four comes from coalition intelligence sources.
6 See the interview given by General Muhammad Abdullah Shahwani, Iraq's intelligence chief, to *Asharq al Awsat*, 4 January 2005.

References

Associated Press, 'Iraq Sets Toll of Civilians at 12,000 for 2006' *New York Times* 3 January 2007.

Biden, Joseph and Leslie Gelb, 'Unity Through Autonomy in Iraq' *New York Times* 1 May 2006.

Bremer III, L. Paul with Malcolm McConnell, *My Year in Iraq: The Struggle to Build a Future of Hope* (New York: Simon and Schuster, 2006).

Burham, Gilbert, Riyadh Lafta, Shannon Doocy and Les Roberts, 'Mortality After the 2003 Invasion of Iraq: A Cross-Sectional Cluster Sample Survey' *Lancet On-Line* 11 October 2006.

Cave, Damien and John O' Neil, 'UN Puts '06 Iraq Toll of Civilians at 34,000' *International Herald Tribune* 17 January 2007.

Cole, Juan, 'Civil War? What Civil War? Desperate to Convince Voters We're Winning, Bush is Denying That Iraq is Having a Civil War. But the Facts Contradict Him.' *Salon* March 23 2006 www.salon.com/opinion/feature/2006/03/23/civil_war/print.html

Diamond, Larry, *Squandered Victory: The American Occupation and the Bungled Effort to Bring Democracy to Iraq* (New York: Times Books, 2005).

——'What Civil War Looks Like. Slide Rules' *New Republic* March 13 2006, 11.

Dodge, Toby, *Iraq's Future: The Aftermath of Regime Change* (London: Routledge, 2005)

Engles, Dagmar and Shula Marks, *Contesting Colonial Hegemony: State and Society in Africa and India* (London: British Academic Press, 1994).

Etzioni, Amitai, 'A Self-Restrained Approach to Nation-Building by Foreign Powers' *International Affairs* 80, no.1 (2004).

Filkins, Dexter, 'Memo Urges al-Qa'ida to Wage War in Iraq' *International Herald Tribune*, 10 February 2004.

Galbraith, Peter W., 'How to Get Out of Iraq' *New York Review of Books* 13 May 2004.

Gelb, Leslie H., 'Divide Iraq into Three States' *International Herald Tribune* 26 November 2004.

Gettleman, Jeffrey, 'Iraqis Bound, Blindfolded, and Dead' *New York Times*, 2 April 2006.

Hashim, Ahmed S., 'The Sunni Insurgency' *Middle East Institute Perspective*, August 15 2003.

Henderson, Errol A. and J. David Singer, 'Civil War in the Post-Colonial World, 1946–92' *Journal of Peace Research* 37, no.3 (May 2000).

Huggler, Justin, 'Is This Man the Mastermind of the Massacres?' *Independent on Sunday*, 7 March 2004.

International Crisis Group (ICG) 2003a, *Governing Iraq* (Baghdad, Washington, DC, Brussels: ICG, August 2003).

—— 2003b *Shi'ism: Varied Social Settings, Rival Centre of Power, and Conflicting Visions* (Baghdad, Washington, DC, and Brussels, 2003).

—— 2003c *Iraq's Shiites Under Occupation* (Baghdad and Brussels, 2003).

Jabar, Faleh A., 'Sheikhs and Ideologues: Deconstruction and Reconstruction of Tribes Under Patrimonial Totalitarianism in Iraq, 1968–1998' in Jabar and Dawod 2003.

—— *The Shi'ite Movement in Iraq* (London: Saqi, 2003).

Jabar, Faleh. A and Hosham Dawod, *Tribes and Power: Nationalism and Ethnicity in the Middle East* (London: Saqi, 2003).

Karouny, Mariam, 'Shi-ite Faction Menaces Iraq's Basra Oil Exports' *Reuters*, 26 May 2006.

Kasfir, Nelson, 'Explaining Ethnic Political Participation,' in *The State and Development in the Third World*, ed. Atol Kholi (Princeton, NJ: Princeton Univ. Press, 1986).

—— 'Domestic Anarchy, Security Dilemmas, and Violent Predation' in Rotberg 2004.

Laitin, David D., *The Russian-Speaking Populations in the Near Abroad* (Ithaca, NY: Cornell Univ. Press, 1998).

Kaviraj, Sudipta, 'On the Construction of Colonial Power, Structure, Discourse, Hegemony' in Engles and Marks 1994.

Lasseter, Tom, 'Iranian-backed Militia Groups Take Control of Much of Southern Iraq' *Knight Ridder Newspapers*, 26 May 2006.

Mann, Michael, 'The Autonomous Power of the State: Its Origins, Mechanisms, and Results' in *States, War and Capitalism: Studies in Political Sociology* ed. Michael Mann (Oxford: Blackwell, 1988).

Meierhenrich, Jens, 'Forming States After Failure' in Rotberg 2004.

Migdal, Joel S., *Strong Societies and Weak States: State-Society Relations and State Capabilities in the Third World* (Princeton, NJ: Princeton Univ. Press, 1988).

North, Andrew, *Iraq Unrest Forces 65,000 to Flee* 14 April 2006 newsvote.bbc.co.uk/mpsppd/pagetools/print/news.bbc.co.uk/1/hi/world/middle_east

O'Hanlan, Michael E. and Nina Kamp, *Iraq Index* (Washington, DC: Brookings Institution, April 27, 2006).

O'Neill, Brendan, 'Another Dodgy Dossier' *Guardian*, 25 March 2004.

Packer, George, *Assassin's Gate: America in Iraq* (New York: Farrar, Straus and Giroux, 2005).

Phillips, David L., *Losing Iraq: Inside the Post-War Reconstruction Fiasco* (Boulder, CO: Westview, 2005).

Posner, Daniel N., 'Civil Society and the Reconstruction of Failed States' in Rotberg 2004.

Rotberg, Robert I ed., *When States Fail: Causes and Consequences* (Princeton, NJ: Princeton Univ Press, 2004).

Rothchild, Joseph, *Ethnopolitics: A Conceptual Framework* (New York: Columbia Univ. Press, 1981).

Schmitt, Eric and Thom Shanker, 'Estimates by US See More Rebels with Funds,' *Guardian*, 23 October 2004.

Talentino, Andrea Kathyrn, 'The Two Faces of Nation-Building: Developing Function and Identity' *Cambridge Review of International Affairs* 17, no. 3 (October 2004).

Tavernie, Sabrina and Qais Mizher, 'Iraq's Premier Seeks to Control a City in Chaos' *Washington Post*, 31 May 2006.

Visser, Reidar, 'Centralism and Unitary State Logic in Iraq from Midhat Pasha to Jawad al-Maliki: A Continuous Trend?' April 22 2006, historiae.org

Weber, Max, *Economy and Society* vol.1 (Berkeley: Univ. of California Press, 1978).

Wimmer, Andreas, 'Democracy and Ethno-religious Conflict in Iraq' *Survival* 45, no.4 (Winter 2003–2004).

Zartman, I. William, 'Posing the Problem of State Collapse' in *Collapsed States: The Disintegration and Restoration of Legitimate Authority* ed. I. William Zartman (Boulder, CO: Lynne Rienner, 1995).

Zogby, James, 'Bend It Like Cheney' *Guardian*, 20 October 2003.

ETHNICITY AND THE EMERGENCE OF SOMALILAND

MARK BRADBURY

Post-war recovery and the process of state-building in Somaliland began with a formal cessation of hostilities among northern clans in the port town of Berbera in February 1991, followed by the declaration of independence in May and the establishment of Somaliland's first government. The Somali National Movement's policy of peaceful coexistence among the northern clans and the decision to break with Somalia created an environment that was relatively stable: peaceful economic activity could begin, and international relief organizations could return after an absence of two years.

But Somaliland's immediate prospects were not promising. Public rejection of the union with Somalia should not have been entirely unexpected, given their experience of the previous ten years, yet the SNM leadership had made no preparations for the eventuality, anticipating instead that they would form a united government with the United Somali Congress (USC) and the Somali Patriotic Movement (SPM). The SNM interim government inherited a territory devastated by a decade of insurgency and war. It had no revenue, no financial institutions, no social services and no direct international support. The infrastructure was shattered, the country and towns were littered with landmines, and half of the population was displaced or living in refugee camps.

Post-war reconstruction and state-building was to bring many challenges: internal conflicts; the disruption of the livestock trade after Gulf states placed embargoes on Somali livestock; lack of diplomatic recognition; meagre levels of foreign assistance; limited human resources in government; a fragile infrastructure; and an environment under strain from sedentarization and urban migration. But gradually since 1991 a modest state structure has been established that fulfils most international criteria of statehood. Why did a 'national movement' decide to break away from Somalia? How did a rebel movement, bereft of resources, set about rebuilding a government and a state? How and by what processes were security and law and order established?

The political and economic recovery and development of the new Somaliland state can be traced through four periods, coinciding with four different government administrations. The first, 1991–1993, covers the SNM post-war government. This period witnessed the spontaneous return of tens of thousands of refugees, the arrival of others displaced by war in the south and a destabilizing conflict between political factions. Civil war was averted by a series of peace conferences, during which a framework for security and a power-sharing, clan-based system of governance were agreed and the political architecture of Somaliland began to take shape. The second period, 1993–1997, began with the installation of a new government under the presidency of Mohamed Ibrahim Egal. Between 1994 and 1996 progress towards a viable state was nearly derailed by civil war, which was formally ended in 1996 by another national conference.

A third period, 1997–2002, covers the second administration of Mohamed Ibrahim Egal and ends with his death and the peaceful transfer of power to his successor Dahir Riyale Kahin. During this period, government bureaucracy expanded, the country enjoyed considerable economic development and a constitution was finalized and publicly approved. The fourth period, 2002–2005, covers the administration of President Kahin and the transition to a constitutional form of government and a multi-party democracy.

The Cessation of Hostilities

The SNM took no active part in the battle for Mogadishu and the final overthrow of Siyad Barre on 27 January 1991, or the bloody civil war that ensued. Regime change in north-west Somalia was of a very different nature. The SNM captured Berbera on 29 January and within a week had control of Hargeysa, Burco, Borama and Erigavo. The SNM's takeover was not entirely peaceful. Some government soldiers were subjected to summary trials and executions for alleged 'war crimes' (ICG 2003). The town of Dilla west of Hargeysa was destroyed in clashes with Gadabursi militia; an SNM force attacked the Warsengeli settlement of Hadaftimo in eastern Sanaag; and Dhulbahante families also evacuated Aynabo in Togdheer region. Fearing reprisals from the SNM, 125,000 people (105,170 Gadabursi and 19,362 'Iisa [Brons 2001: 202]), mostly from the Gadabursi, 'Iise and Darod clans, fled to Ethiopia, where they were settled in separate refugee camps.[1] In February SNM forces clashed with troops from Siyad Barre's army and fighters from the 'Iise-based United Somali Front when they tried to annex Zeyla to Djibouti (Drysdale 1992: 32). However, the military clashes were short-lived; most ex-soldiers were allowed to return to their regions of origin unharmed; and the SNM made no attempt to enforce its authority over the Harti regions in Sool and eastern Sanaag.

Instead of projecting the SNM's authority through force, which might have ignited a new war, the SNM leadership consented to a reconciliation process initiated by elders. In mid-February, less than two weeks after Barre was toppled, delegations from the Isaaq, 'Iise, Gadabursi, Dhulbahante and Warsengeli met in Berbera and agreed a formal cessation of hostilities and a date for a regional conference. A separate meeting also took place to reconcile the Isaaq and Gadabursi following the fighting in Dilla. According to Drysdale (1992: 24), no mention was made in Berbera of secession, although talk of revising the 1960 act of union may have alluded to a future federal constitution.

The Grand Conference of the Northern Peoples

In May 1991, the senior elders of the Isaaq, Harti and Dir clans and the leadership of the SNM converged on the town of Burco for the 'Grand Conference of the Northern Peoples' (*Shirweynaha Beelaha Waqooyi*), and a meeting of the SNM central committee. They were joined by intellectuals, artists, militia commanders, religious leaders, delegates from the diaspora and business people who financed the event. The purpose of the conference was to consolidate the cessation of hostilities agreed at Berbera and to discuss the future of the north. Secession was not on the agenda of the SNM central committee. At the time, the SNM leadership had little interest in severing links with the south, believing such a decision would not secure international support (Drysdale 1992). Despite the formation of an interim government in Mogadishu by a faction of the USC in early February, the SNM leadership maintained its support for a unitary state with a devolved form of government. Shortly before the Burco conference, an SNM delegation to Mogadishu had stated its preference for a federal system with an Executive Prime Minister and a more equitable sharing of resources. Among the public, however, agitation to sever ties with Mogadishu was growing. Various factors contributed to this.

The widespread devastation uncovered by the SNM *mujahideen* and civilian refugees as they returned to the northern cities deepened Isaaq grievances against the south. The pre-emptive move by a faction of the USC to form an interim government in Mogadishu without consulting the SNM caused many Isaaq to fear that maintaining a relationship with Mogadishu would lead to a repeat of the persecution they had suffered under the military government. Stories told by people fleeing the violence in Mogadishu reinforced this fear.

The decision to secede has also been interpreted in terms of lineage politics. The unification of the Somali territories in 1960 had been predicated on nationalist aspirations to unite the Somali 'nation' within a 'Greater Somalia'. Subsequent events and the experience of alienation felt by many Isaaq meant that a united nation was no longer seen as an attractive or advantageous option.

The potential for a new relationship with Ethiopia, which was also undergoing 'regime change', may also have influenced the secessionist mood. Defeat in the Ogaden war had ended the dream of re-establishing access to the Haud grazing lands through a united Somalia. Years of conducting a guerrilla campaign from within Ethiopia, and the presence of Isaaq in refugee camps in the Haud in 1988, had healed relations with Ethiopia, and may have persuaded northerners that unhindered access to the Haud for pastoralists could better be achieved through cooperation with Ethiopia rather than through unity with the south.[2]

The declining relevance of the Somali state may also have been an impetus for secession. Pressure from armed movements, a reduction in foreign aid and the impact of structural adjustment programmes had greatly weakened state authority and its control over the economy. As the significance of the informal economy increased, the incentive for northern business people and the political elite to engage with the state of Somalia diminished. With the USC takeover of Mogadishu, opportunities to participate in the economy were unlikely to materialize. Potentially, independence could offer northern businessmen greater control or even monopoly over regional trade and economic assets. Some also believed that by restoring security in the north they could attract much-needed international aid.

By the time of the Burco conference a consensus was emerging among elders of the northern clans that the union with the south should be reviewed (Gilkes 1993: 8; ICG 2003: 9). On 15 May, an agitated crowd, including SNM fighters,

surrounded the building where the SNM Congress was meeting after hearing
from Radio Mogadishu that the SNM had agreed to hold negotiations with
southern political leaders in Cairo. Witnesses describe how with chants of 'no
more Mogadishu' they demanded the SNM central committee declare the 1960
Act of Union null and void (Drysdale 1992: 139–42). Lack of external sponsor-
ship in the 1980s had obliged the SNM to develop a popular support base among
the Isaaq. This now dictated the direction the SNM should take. With some
reluctance, the SNM central committee acceded to popular demand and included
in the conference conclusions a resolution establishing the Republic of Somaliland
(see Box 3.1) (WSP 2005: 14). The name given to the new entity was chosen in
preference to the 'State of Somaliland', as it had been known in 1960, and 'Puntland',[3] a name later adopted by the people in north-east Somalia, On 18 May
1991, having informed the USC in Mogadishu, the SNM chairman duly proclaimed the creation of the independent Republic of Somaliland and raised its
flag for the first time.

A provisional National Charter was hastily drafted, its first article proclaiming
that the state formerly known as Somaliland was being 'reconstituted as a full
Independent and Sovereign State' (ICG 2003: 9). The SNM was mandated to
govern the country as the sole political party for two years, with its chairman
Abdirahman Ahmed Ali 'Tuur' appointed as Somaliland's first interim
President.

The Burco Declaration was agreed to by all the delegates assembled in Burco
(Gilkes 1992), and in June 1992 a meeting of Dhulbahante elders reaffirmed their
support for Somaliland (Gilkes 1993: 43). It is unclear, however, whether there
was a common understanding among those assembled in Burco that what was
being created was a new and fully independent state. Several representatives of
the Dhulbahante, Warsengeli, Gadabursi and 'Iise who accepted the decision in
Burco later retracted their support for Somaliland, as did several Isaaq leaders.[4]
What is clear is that the Declaration was a response to a particular set of events
and to public pressure, without benefit of planning or careful consideration of
the possible consequences. Only after the fact did the Somaliland authorities
develop their legal arguments in support of independence. This has two aspects:
the existence of Somaliland as a geopolitical entity from 1897, when the
British Protectorate was established, to 1960; and international recognition of
Somaliland as an independent sovereign state between 26 June and 1 July 1960,

---

Box 3.1 Resolutions of Burco Grand Conference of the Northern Peoples

- Reconciliation of the warring parties to the conflict.
- Declaration of the creation of the Republic of Somaliland.
- The establishment of an SNM government for two years and the accom-
  modation of the non-Isaaq communities in the government.
- Initiation of a separate reconciliation process for Sanaag Region.

when Somaliland gained independence from Britain and before it united with Italian Somalia to form the Somali Republic. According to Shinn, during these five days thirty-five governments recognized Somaliland, including the US (ICG 2003: 4fn9). The Somaliland authorities have asserted that the decision in Burco was not an act of secession *per se*, but a 'voluntary dissolution between sovereign states' based on the perception by one of the parties that the union had failed (Somaliland Ministry of Foreign Affairs 2002: 9).[5] The option of political association with Somalia in some form at some future date has never been ruled out totally. But successive Somaliland administrations have made recognition of Somaliland's independence status a precondition for their participation in Somalia-wide peace conferences.

The Burco conference did not end all hostilities, as will be seen, and it was followed by numerous local reconciliation conferences. Nevertheless, the immediate consequences of the decision to break with Somalia meant that Somaliland avoided being drawn into the protracted conflict in the south and could get on with rebuilding the shattered country.

The SNM administration 1991–3

In 1991 the SNM was the only organization in Somaliland with sufficient authority to establish law and order and to oversee a process of recovery. Responsibility fell on Abdirahman 'Tuur' as the appointed President of the new republic to form the first interim administration. Its tasks were daunting: establishing security; accommodating non-Isaaq communities within the government; building institutions; drafting a constitution as a basis for the first democratic elections; reviving the economy; and restoring basic services. All this it had to accomplish within a brief two-year tenure. It was hardly surprising, given the condition of the territory and people, and the limited resources available, that this first administration failed to deliver on this.

A decade-long insurgency had devastated the country. Half of the population had been forcibly displaced to refugee camps in neighbouring countries, the south or further abroad. Mass graves in Hargeysa and Berbera were a testament to the criminal violence of the war. Between 70 and 90 per cent of buildings in Hargeysa and Burco had been damaged or destroyed by military bombardment and the looting of public and private buildings (Coultan et al., 1991: 52)

Other settlements had suffered similar fates. Water supplies had been contaminated or destroyed, along with sanitation and electricity systems, and the country was littered with upwards of two million landmines and unexploded ordinance (de Waal 1993). A handful of Somali and international agencies provided limited emergency health services, but there were no functioning schools. There was neither public administration nor public employment; commercial activity was limited; agricultural production was almost non-existent; road traffic was minimal; there was no commercial air traffic; and the main form of long-distance communication was via private VHF radios. Internationally Somaliland's declaration of independence was viewed initially as a regressive step that threatened to break up a sovereign state and with the Gulf War, the Balkans and southern

Somalia consuming media and diplomatic attention there were no immediate promises of support. In 1991 only the ICRC and two other international relief organizations were operating in Somaliland.

Somaliland's first administration, formed on 4 June 1991, featured nineteen ministries, a civil service, a high court, security services and a central bank. A carefully chosen broad-based cabinet allocated six seats to non-Isaaq clans (Drysdale 1992: 8).[6] Police and custodial services were established in several towns and restrictions were placed on the carrying of weapons. But the transformation of a rebel movement into a government proved difficult. In contrast to the Eritrean People's Liberation Front in Eritrea, the SNM had not developed strong organizational structures that could be transferred to a new government and the leadership had no ready-made plan for a post-war administration. The SNM's organizational structure was therefore simply adopted by the provisional government, with the Chairman and Vice-Chairman transformed into President and Vice-President. The option of having a constitutional President and Prime Minister instead of an executive presidential system was discussed but rejected by the central committee (ibid.: 26). The intention was to transform the SNM central committee into a parliamentary-style national council, with the *Guurti* having a mediating and adjudicating function in the Upper House of a bicameral Parliament. But the administration proved to be little more than a chimera. Bereft of a revenue base, President Tuur failed to establish an authoritative administration capable of addressing the country's needs. The central committee was legally bound to meet every six months but, due to disagreements over the clan allocation of seats, a lack of resources and concerns about a coup, it did not meet at all in 1992 (Gilkes 1993). This paralyzed the government, because legislation could not be drafted or government appointments approved. Financial support for the SNM from the diaspora dried up. The unity that had existed in the face of a common enemy dissipated and the schisms that had existed within the SNM re-emerged. At this critical juncture the government and the central committee were both found lacking in leadership to steer the country forward.

The Stabilization of Somaliland

In 1992 Somaliland was teetering on the edge of civil war. There are various reasons why Somaliland did not disintegrate into the protracted conflict and famine experienced in the south. Those alluded to so far include the sense of political community that existed in Somaliland as a consequence of its particular colonial history, the experience of north-west Somalia within the Somali Republic, and the experience of the Isaaq people within the Somali state and during the war. Other reasons include the particular political, social and economic conditions that existed in Somaliland in 1991, the particular form of international political and humanitarian engagement in Somalia in the 1990s, the ambitions of Somaliland's political and business classes, and the capacity of indigenous social institutions.

[...]

Models of Peace Building

In the 1990s the institutions and mechanisms that had been designed to maintain international peace and security between states during the Cold War were challenged by a proliferation of civil wars, such as the one in Somalia. Alternative policy instruments were developed in response to these wars 'within' states. The concept of 'peace building' proposed in the United Nations publication *An Agenda for Peace* (Boutros-Ghali 1992), for example, signalled a shift from classic peacekeeping to multiple and multi-level forms of foreign intervention to end wars. The inability of many states (or their lack of interest) in mediating social conflict also generated an interest in indigenous non-state approaches to conflict resolution, and a proliferation of non-state actors taking on tasks of conflict management.

The efficacy of indigenous processes of conflict resolution and the role of non-governmental organizations in conflict resolution have generated considerable debate.[7] Two conclusions can be drawn from the local peace processes in Somaliland that are relevant to these discussions. First, despite the efforts of the Barre regime and previous civilian governments to exorcize the clan system and 'modernize' Somali society, the traditional and indigenous system of governance remained strong. In the absence of effective government people placed their faith in their customary institutions to resolve and manage conflict. Second, the locally financed and managed peace processes in Somaliland proved to be more effective than externally sponsored 'national' conferences in Somalia.

The 1993 Borama conference was not only a defining political event in Somaliland, but also an example of an indigenous popular peacemaking process that has few parallels in contemporary Africa.[8] At the time it offered an alternative model to the formal peacemaking and state-building processes that were being supported by the international bodies in Somalia, such as the March 1993 National Reconciliation Conference in Addis Ababa (Bradbury 1994a). Some similarities existed between the Borama model and the process that led to the formation of the short-lived Digil-Mirifle Supreme Governing Council for Bay and Bakool regions in 1994, and the series of locally sponsored conferences of clan elders in north-east Somalia that led to the creation of the state of Puntland in 1998 (WSP 2001). In both these cases, however, the international community gave some support.

Since the beginning of the civil war in Somalia two schools of thought have tended to dominate approaches to conflict resolution and state-building there. One has supported formal mediation between Somalia's *de facto* political leaders – the warlords or faction leaders – to secure a ceasefire and a power-sharing deal. The other, so-called 'bottom-up' or 'grassroots' approach has advocated support for local reconciliation and peacemaking to build cross-clan cooperative relations, which would marginalize and disempower the warlords. In the early 1990s, United Nations Operation in Somalia (UNOSOM) pursued two 'tracks'[9] in southern Somalia. It engaged with the warlords and their factions through internationally brokered peace conferences, while simultaneously opening dialogue with what was intended to be a broader, grassroots constituency through the formation of district councils. Both approaches proved to be problematic. UNOSOM was a bureaucratic, state-centric body constituted by governments, with a mandate to re-establish a central government, albeit one with some decentralized structures. International diplomacy did nothing to rein in the predatory forces which unleashed the violence. On the contrary, the internationally sponsored peace conferences shored up the authority of the faction leaders, who were paid to attend, and prevented alternative leaders from surfacing. There was little incentive for these leaders and their militias, who were profiting from plunder and extortion, to implement any peace accord. And as long as the peace conferences were held outside Somalia there was little social pressure on the factional leaders to adhere to the agreements. On the other 'track', the formation of district councils was poorly managed and implemented.[10] In places they legitimized the capture of territory by clans and exacerbated violent competition. Elsewhere they did provide a vehicle for improved inter-clan relations, but their impact was highly localized (Bradbury 1994a; Human Rights Watch 1995).

The contrast with Somaliland was very striking. In Somaliland there was a synergy between the Somaliland-wide peace conferences and the local peacemaking processes, which succeeded in containing violence while crafting a political consensus and power-sharing arrangement that provided the foundations for new state structures. Again, to understand the different functions of local and Somaliland-wide peace conferences, the distinction between 'constitutional' and 'civil' issues is helpful. In Somaliland the defeat of Barre's forces effectively resolved the constitutional conflict by leaving the SNM as the only real power in the north-west. This enabled local and regional peace processes, like that in Sanaag, to focus on civil issues. These included the restoration of cooperative relations to facilitate commerce; the opening of roads and access to grazing lands; the restoration of stolen property; the reduction of livestock raiding; and the attraction of investment, including support from international aid agencies. When these local processes tried to deal with 'constitutional issues', they usually proved detrimental. This was apparent at a peace meeting between the Warsengeli and Habar Yunis in Sanaag Region in November 1992. The Warsengeli refused to recognize the presence of SNM representatives in the Habar Yunis delegation. The only way they were able to proceed with peace negotiations was as clans (Bradbury 1994b). By removing the state as a primary object of conflict, social relations could be addressed through customary institutions.

Key differences between the peace processes in Somaliland and the external peacemaking efforts in Somalia were that the former were locally designed, managed and financed; that they generally involved the participation of locally selected leadership; that they accepted the need for a long time-frame; and that they involved broad public participation. Critically, they were also rooted in a popular desire for peace and stability that was linked to the aspiration for international recognition of an independent Somaliland. This did not exist among the warlords and 'spoilers' in Somalia, who had interests in perpetuating state collapse (Menkhaus 2004). Moreover, in Somalia the peace meetings were designed to meet external agendas, were externally financed, and were primarily oriented to re-establishing central government.

In Somalia, over time, the need to restore cooperative and predictable community relations to ensure livelihoods, facilitate trade and economic recovery has generated a variety of localized governance structures, including municipal administrations, business consortiums, committees of elders, religious communities – and, since the mid-1990s, Islamic courts. These have brought modest levels of security and lawfulness to some places. The internationally sponsored Somalia national peace talks in Djibouti in 2000 and Kenya in 2002–4 sought to apply some lessons from past experiences, taking a longer-term, more holistic approach to conflict resolution, and engaging both political leaders and civic actors. To call them peace conferences or 'peace processes', however, is perhaps a misnomer. They were exercises in politics and power, in which political elites manoeuvred for a share of government and its anticipated spoils. Thus, to date, external efforts to reconstitute a state have served to exacerbate armed conflict (ibid. 2004). In Somaliland the series of peace conferences in the early 1990s were critical events in the formation of a new state, but it was the absence of effective government that allowed these local processes to succeed. Whereas externally funded processes in Somalia came to nothing, the Somaliland conferences created a system of government that lasted for a decade and provided the basis for a state that, at the time of writing, has endured for sixteen years – a third of the territory's eventful journey since it first gained independence in 1960.

Notes

1 The camps included Arabi, Teferiber and Darwanaje east of Jigjiga, and Kabari Byah and Aisha north-east of Diredawa. The Darod included former refugees from the camps in the north, and were associated with the Siyad Barre regime.
2 Interestingly the previous 'Grand Conference' of the northern clans occurred in 1954, when the British ceded the Haud to Ethiopia.
3 Interview, Rashid Sheikh Abdillahi Ahmed, May 2003.
4 Dr Ali Khalif Galayd, for example, who was part of the Dhulbahante delegation in Burco, was to become the first Prime Minister of the Transitional Federal Government in 2000 which claimed sovereignty over all Somalia including Somaliland.
5 For a detailed rehearsal of the historical and legal arguments for recognition see, for example, Rajagopal and Carroll 1992. For counter-arguments see Samatar and Samatar 2003.
6 Dhulbahaate 2, Gadabursi 2, Warsengeli 1, 'Iise 1.
7 For example, see the papers of the All-Africa Conference on African Principles of Conflict Resolution and Reconciliation, held in Addis Ababa, November 1999. For Somalia see, for example, Farah and Lewis 1993; Helander 1995.
8 Another example of grassroots peacemaking in Africa is the 1999 Wunlit Peace Conference in South Sudan and the wider people-to-people peace process (New Sudan Council of Churches 2002; Bradbury et al: 2006).
9 In diplomatic parlance these two approaches are also referred to as Track I and Track II diplomacy.

10 The UN insisted on token women representatives, and officials were helicoptered into villages for meetings and to approve councils.

References

African Rights (1994) *Grass and the Roots of Peace*. London: unpublished.

Boutros-Ghali, B. (1992) *An Agenda for Peace*. New York: United Nations.

Bradbury, M. (1994a) *The Somali Conflict*. Oxfam Research Paper No. 9. Oxford: Oxfam UK/I.

—— (1994b) *The Politics of Vulnerability, Development and Conflict*. MSc dissertation, University of Birmingham, UK.

Bradbury, M., Ryle, J., Medley, M. & Sansculotte-Greenidge, K. (2006) *Local Peace Processes in Sudan*. London: Rift Valley Institute.

Brons, M. H. (2001) *Society, Security, Sovereignty and the State in Somalia*. Utrecht: International Books.

de Waal, A. (1993) *Violent Deeds Live On*. London: African Rights and Mines Advisory Group.

Drysdale, J. (1992) *Somaliland*. Brighton: Global Stats Ltd.

Farah, Ahmed Y. & Lewis, I. M. (1993) *Somalia*. London: ActionAid.

Gilkes, P. (1992) *Ethnic and Political Movements in Ethiopia and Somalia*. London: Save the Children Fund (UK).

—— (1993) *Two Wasted Years*. London: Save the Children Fund (UK).

Helander, B. (1995 August) *Some Problems in African Conflict Resolution*. Internet edition: NomadNet.

Human Rights Watch / Africa (1995) *Somalia Faces the Future*, Vol. 7, No. 2. New York, Washington & London.

International Crisis Group (2003) *Somaliland*. Africa Report No. 66. Nairobi/Brussels.

—— (2006) *Somaliland*. Africa Report No. 110. Nairobi/Brussels.

Menkhaus, K. (1999) 'Traditional Conflict Management in Contemporary African Crises', in William Zartman (ed.), *Traditional Cures for Modern Conflicts*. Boulder, CO: Lynne Rienner, pp. 183–199.

—— (2004) *Somalia*. London: International Institute for Strategic Studies.

New Sudan Council of Churches (2002) *Inside Sudan*. Nairobi.

Rajagopal, B. & Carroll, A. (1992) *The Case for the Independent Statehood of Somaliland*. Mimeographed report. Washington DC.

Samatar, Abdi I. & Samatar Ahmed I. (2003) *International Crisis Group Report on Somaliland*. Mimeo. University of Minnesota & Macalester College.

Somaliland Ministry of Foreign Affairs (2002) *The Case for Somaliland's International Recognition as an Independent State*. Briefing Paper. Hargeisa: Somaliland Government 2002.

WSP International (2001) *Rebuilding Somalia*. London: HAAN Associates.

4

Ethnicity and Self-Determination

In the last twenty years or so we have witnessed a dynamic re-emergence of some old nations which currently lack a state of their own but possessed an independent status in a more or less remote past. This section concentrates upon the relationship between ethnicity and self-determination in Europe, North America and the Middle East by focusing on the cases of Catalonia, Scotland, Galicia, Quebec, First Nations in the USA, and the Kurds in Iraq and Iran.

All these nations have ethnic origins that can be traced back to an era previous to the rise of the nation state. Most of them are evolving within industrialized societies endowed with democratic institutions that grant them varying degrees of autonomy and recognition. Thriving nationalist movements exist in all these 'nations without states', that is, nations which maintain a separate sense of national identity generally based upon a common culture, history, attachment to a particular territory and the explicit wish to rule themselves.[1] Self-determination is sometimes understood as political autonomy, in other cases it stops short of independence and often involves the right to secede.

Montserrat Guibernau's paper provides a theoretical framework for the study of the relationship between intellectuals and nationalism in Western nations without states. In particular, it focuses on the role of intellectuals in the re-emergence of Catalan nationalism during Franco's dictatorship (1939–75). First, it sets up a theoretical framework which includes a definition of the concepts of nation, state and nationalism and also introduces the concept of nations without states. Second, it analyses the relationship between intellectuals and nationalism in the work of Elie Kedourie, Tom Nairn, John Breuilly and Anthony D. Smith. Third, it studies the role of Catalan intellectuals in protecting the Catalan language and culture during Franco's dictatorship together with the processes which, in the 1960s and 1970s, turned Catalan nationalism from an elite into a mass movement. Particular attention is given to the cultural resistance activities carried out by Catalan intellectuals during this period, the reasons why some intellectuals may feel attracted to nationalism, and the rational and emotional arguments employed by intellectuals as mobilizing agents.

One of the most controversial issues regarding devolution concerns the financial arrangement between the state and the devolved institutions. Russell Mellett argues that 'a permanent transfer of revenue raising capacity from the UK government to each of Scotland, Wales and Northern Ireland would enhance the direct accountability of these governments to their citizens'. Mellett highlights the asymmetric character of the Devolved Administrations which differ as to actual circumstances, and differ in respect to the political power. Mellett makes a strong argument in favour of the Devolved Administrations being able to raise a substantial portion of their own revenue so that, their own borrowing could enhance responsive and responsible government for Scotland, Wales and Northern Ireland.

Yet, while Catalonia and Scotland have maintained a strong sense of national identity throughout time, and played a key role in the development of the industrial revolution both in Spain and the United Kingdom, other nations such as Galicia – in north-western Spain – suffered economic backwardness and a late de-ruralization that could be located in the 1960s. Ramón Máiz points at the historical imposition of Castilian (Spanish) as the official language, first during the seventeenth-century absolute monarchy and again under the liberal Spanish state in the nineteenth-century. In spite of that, the language was maintained as a key marker of a Galician identity extending to mores, private law, customs, family structures and productive strategies and became crucial in the emergence of a Galician cultural renaissance in the nineteenth century and the rise of nationalism in the twentieth century. Máiz offers a succinct account of the nature and evolution of Galician nationalism during the Spanish transition to democracy while comparing it with that of both Catalonia and the Basque Country.

The case of Quebec is somehow different from those already considered here due to its colonial origin. The European first came to North America in the sixteenth century; at that time Iroquois, Cree, Algonquin, Huron and Montagnais were the main Indian nations living at the site of present-day Quebec. It was not until 1608 that a permanent French settlement was duly established in Quebec City by Samuel de Champlain. By the Treaty of Paris (1763) Quebec became a British colony and was ruled under the terms of a Royal Proclamation. A history of domination and discrimination defined the life of Quebec society until the 1960s when Quebecois nationalism emerged. Alain Gagnon and Raffaele Iacovino paint a precise picture of the political development of Quebec up to the present time and focus on Quebec's current position within the Canadian federation. In so doing, Gagnon and Iacovino establish a distinction between what they refer to as 'visions of decentralization' and 'centralizing visions' within Canada. Their analysis concerns coexisting views on federalism within Canada which have the ability to radically transform the relationship between the federal government and its provinces.

Franke Wilmer explores the circumstances which brought native peoples in North America to their current situation. It stands as a good example of indigenous groups which progressively became marginalized within the territory they had inhabited for centuries when white settlers from Europe began to expand and dominate their lands. It is a story about two civilizations which confronted one another and, as had happened before in many periods and in many places, the newcomers alienated the native peoples and founded their own states, kingdoms or dominions upon lands once alien to them. The original inhabitants lost their sovereignty and became minorities within their own land. Wilmer examines the initial trade relationship between native peoples and European settlers and the different policies of the US government towards the Indians including: their relocation, internment and guardianship, assimilation, reform and termination.

The land the Kurds claim as their own stretches across five nation-states: Iraq, Turkey, Syria, Iran and Armenia. After the First World War and the consequent dismantling of the Ottoman empire, the Kurds were promised a state (Treaty of Sèvres, 1920); however, the influence of Woodrow Wilson's principle of the self-determination of peoples was to be forgotten when the Treaty of Lausanne (1923) determining the new borders of Turkey was ratified. The Kurds have always been regarded as a threat to the modern Turkish state founded by Kemal Atatürk.[2] M. R. Izady focuses on the study of the Kurds in Iraq and Iran. The Kurds were regarded as a tribal and backward people by the modernizing nationalism of the Shah of Iran. Their condition as Sunni Muslims, while most Iranians were Shias, contributed to a marginalization which acquired an even darker side after the fundamentalist revolution of the Ayatollahs in 1979. The history of Kurdish repression in Iraq since the 1970s, when Saddam Hussein came to power, is a long, violent and complicated one in which internal Kurdish differences were exploited by both the Iraqi and the Turkish governments. Izady examines the status and political relationship of the Kurds with the governments of Iran and Iraq, as well as internal differences emerging within the Kurdish people. He also offers a detailed account of political events leading to the creation of the enclave of Kurdistan in 1991.

Notes

1 Guibernau, M., *Nations without States: Political Communities in the Global Age* (Polity: Cambridge, 1998), p. 16.
2 Ignatieff, M., *Blood and Belonging* (BBC Books: London, 1993), p. 65.

CATALONIA: NATIONALISM AND INTELLECTUALS IN NATIONS WITHOUT STATES

MONTSERRAT GUIBERNAU

I. Introduction: What are Nations Without States?

A basic conceptual distinction between nation, state and nationalism has to be made. By 'state', taking Weber's definition, I refer to 'a human community that (successfully) claims the *monopoly of the legitimate use of physical force* within a given territory' (Weber 1991, p. 78), although not all states have successfully accomplished this, and some of them have not even aspired to accomplish it. By 'nation' I refer to a human group conscious of forming a community, sharing a common culture, attached to a clearly demarcated territory, having a common past and a common project for the future and claiming the right to rule itself. Thus, in my view, the 'nation' includes five dimensions: psychological (consciousness of forming a group), cultural, territorial, political and historical. By offering this definition, I distinguish the term nation from both the state and the nation-state, and I shall be using this distinction later when considering what I call 'nations without states'. By 'nationalism' I mean the sentiment of belonging to a community whose members identify with a set of symbols, beliefs and ways of life, and have the will to decide upon their common political destiny.

But still another term needs to be defined and distinguished from the ones I have just mentioned: the nation state. The nation state is a modern phenomenon which emerged around the French Revolution in the late eighteenth century. It is characterized by the formation of a kind of state which has the monopoly of what it claims to be the legitimate use of force within a demarcated territory and seeks to unite the people subjected to its rule by means of homogenization, creating a common culture, symbols, values, reviving traditions and myths of origin, and sometimes inventing them.

The distinctive character of this paper derives from its aim to provide a theoretical framework for the study of the relationship between intellectuals and nationalism in 'nations without states'. By 'nations without states' I refer to nations which, in spite of having their territories included within the boundaries of one or more states maintain a separate sense of national identity generally based upon a common culture, history, attachment to a particular territory and the explicit wish to rule themselves (Guibernau 1999). At present, most thriving nationalist movements in Western nations without states emerge within nations which once enjoyed a separate political and/or cultural identity which is now being invoked, revitalized and adapted to the new socio-political circumstances in which the nation lives and evolves.

Self-determination is sometimes understood as political autonomy, in other cases it stops short of independence and often involves the right to secede. Catalonia, Quebec, Scotland, the Basque Country and Flanders represent but a few nations without states currently demanding further autonomy. It could be argued that some of these nations already have some kind of state of their own since a substantial number of powers have been devolved to their regional parliaments. But political autonomy or even federation differ substantially from independence since they tend to exclude foreign and economic policy, defence and constitutional matters, and this is why it continues to make sense to refer to them as 'nations without states'.

I argue that a specific distinction between 'state nationalism' and nationalism in 'nations without states' is necessary in order to understand some of the key specific features of nationalism in both cases. It should be stressed that what distinguishes both types of nationalism has nothing to do with issuing a value judgement and claiming that one type of nationalism is 'good' while the other is 'bad', one is 'ethnic' and the other 'civic'. Rather the two fundamental differences between 'state nationalism' and nationalism in 'nations without states' concern their different access to power and resources, and the fact that while the former seeks to consolidate and strengthen the state, the latter challenges its legitimacy and often, but not always, seeks to construct a new state.

When considering the relationship between intellectuals and nationalism, I shall be following Smith's definition of intellectuals as those who create artistic works and produce ideas. In so doing I distinguish them from the 'wider intelligentsia or professionals who transmit and disseminate those ideas and creations and form a still wider educated public that "consumes" ideas and works of art' (Smith 1991, p. 93), although in practice, the same individual may fulfill all these different roles.

Before turning to the specific study of the task of intellectuals in nations without states, this paper reviews the theories of Kedourie, Nairn, Breuilly and Smith since they all have devoted some sections of their work to the analysis of the relationship between nationalism and intellectuals. But it should be stressed that their theories do not address the specific role of intellectuals in nations without states. On the contrary, they neglect the need to establish a clear-cut distinction between those intellectuals operating within the nation state and contributing to create 'state nationalism', and those evolving within nations lacking a state of their own. An exception to this is represented by Kedourie's analysis of intellectuals in colonial societies.

II. Intellectuals and Nationalism

Elie Kedourie: On 'marginal men'
'...I began to rebel against the glory I could not be associated with.'
(Quoted by Kedourie in *Nationalism in Asia and Africa*, p. 88).

Kedourie sustains an hostile attitude towards nationalism and defines it as a sort of politics which is not concerned with reality, rather 'its solitary object is an inner world and its end is the abolition of all politics' (Kedourie 1986, p. 85). He sees nationalism as a disease which originated in the West and then spread to other parts of the world. In his view, intellectuals are to be blamed for the generation of a doctrine based on the assumption that nations are obvious and natural divisions of the human race as history, anthropology and linguistics prove.

According to Kedourie, alienated and restless intellectuals marginalized from politics under the impact of Enlightenment rationalism turned to Romanticism and generated nationalism as a doctrine that would have the capacity to grant them a major role within society.[1] He is extremely critical of Romantic intellectuals such as Herder or Fichte and fully identifies nationalism with Romanticism.

Kedourie focuses on the role of intellectuals in colonial societies. He describes how some Western educated indigenous people became completely alienated from their traditional societies and identified with the culture and manners of the colonizers only to discover that indigenous elites were excluded from positions of honour and responsibility reserved for the white colonizers. He writes,

> an Indian could be admitted to the civil service only if he had become so completely Europeanized as to be really and practically on the footing and imbued with the character of an English highly educated gentleman. But it did not prove to be the case that an Indian who had become 'imbued' with such a character would be easily or automatically treated like an English gentleman (Kedourie 1971, p. 84).

In fact, what Kedourie writes about indigenous elites in colonial societies is highly relevant to the analysis of some indigenous elites in nations without states, specially where some specific regional affiliation acts as a barrier for promotion within the state's socio-political and economic structure.

One of the main objections to Kedourie's theory is that it fails to account for the nationalism defended and generated by 'official' intellectuals who already have secured honour and status within the state. In doing so he ignores the nationalism espoused by the colonizers which included their own intellectuals and political leaders. It could be argued that the colonizers' nationalism was to be blamed for the exclusion experienced by indigenous elites who, in spite of being culturally homogenized and integrated, were never viewed as 'belonging' to the colonizer's nation.

Kedourie's theory presumes a wide gap between active intellectual elites and inert and disoriented masses. In his view, the only way to persuade the people to support the nationalist movement is through propaganda and control over education. To mobilize the people, elites must 'appeal to the indigenous beliefs and practices, invoke the dark gods and their rites, and transform purely religious motifs and figures into political and national symbols and heroes – which is all part of the "ethnicization" and nationalization of previously universal and transhistorical religions' (Smith 1998, p. 113).

Kedourie concedes that an elite of intellectuals captures the main injustices endured by the mass of the population and constructs a nationalist doctrine whose aim is to eliminate the unjust situation shared by all those belonging to the same nation, thus uniting elites and masses under a single banner. But, for him, the objective of these fanatical intellectuals goes well beyond the wish to end the unjust situation that their fellow countrymen and women are enduring. The intellectuals' objective is to gain power in society and halt their alienation and exclusion from positions of honour and privilege.

Tom Nairn: The people's mobilizers
'The new middle-class intelligentsia of nationalism had to invite the masses into history; and the invitation-card had to be written in a language they understood.'
(*The Break-Up of Britain*, p. 340).

Nairn approaches the study of nationalism from a Marxist perspective. He considers nationalism as a bourgeois phenomenon which can be derived from the class consequences of the uneven diffusion of capitalism (Nairn 1977, pp. 98–99). Nationalism generates and, at the same time, requires the exploitation of peripheries whose deprived elites have no alternative but to turn to the masses and engage them in the nationalist project. In this context, nationalism's main objective is to fight against a concrete form of 'progress' promoted by the colonial capitalist while at the same time embracing a distinctive idea of progress generated by the intellectuals capable of leading their struggle against capitalist oppression (Nairn 1977, p. 339).

Nairn explains the emergence of nationalism in deprived areas as a reaction against the uneven spread of capitalism. But he also acknowledges the existence of some exceptions to the connection he establishes between nationalism, backwardness and periphery.

To mobilize the masses and gain their support for the nationalist cause, the new intellectual elites have to work towards the construction of a 'militant interclass community' sharing a common identity even if, as Nairn stresses, they only share this identity in a mythical way.

Nairn, as well as Hroch and Peter Worsley, envisages a chronological progression in the spread of nationalism from elite into mass involvement.

In Nairn's theory, the support of the masses is crucial if a nationalist movement is to succeed. But, what are the implications of turning to the people? He points at three main implications: (1) speaking their language; (2) taking a more kind view of their general 'culture' which had been relegated by the Enlightenment and (3) coming to terms with the enormous and still irreconcilable diversity of popular and peasant life (Nairn 1977, p. 101).

John Breuilly: The creators of ideology

'Nationalist ideology has its roots in intellectual responses to the modern problem
  of the relationship between state and society.'

(*Nationalism and the State*, p. 349).

Breuilly understands nationalism as a form of politics, principally opposition politics. In his view, 'the term "nationalism" is used to refer to political movements seeking or exercising state power and justifying such actions with nationalist arguments' (Breuilly 1982, p. 3).

Breuilly, in line with Kedourie and Nairn, stresses the ability of nationalism to attain mass support and confers a pre-eminent role on intellectuals and members of the professions as key figures in the construction of nationalist ideologies. But, according to him 'nationalism cannot be seen as the politics of any particular social class...[and] neither can it be regarded as the politics of intellectuals', although most nationalist leaders are drawn from the professions (Breuilly 1982, p. 332).

In his view, the idea that 'nationalism should be seen primarily as the search for identity and power on the part of displaced intellectuals is a gross exaggeration, even if that is what it means to many intellectuals in nationalist movements' (Breuilly 1982, p. 332). Breuilly admits, however, that the exclusion from expected positions suffered by some intellectuals and members of the professions may contribute to their support for nationalism as an ideology able to provide a new identity containing 'images of an ideal state and an ideal society' in which they will have a secure, respected and leading position (Breuilly 1982, p. 329).

Breuilly points at two sets of arguments to explain the intellectuals' attraction to nationalism. First, although he portrays nationalist intellectuals as unsuccessful professionals, he argues that their failure is relative, since it involves both failing to obtain certain positions, and not getting the financial and social status expected from the position attained. Here the argument echoes that of Kedourie's theory about indigenous intellectuals being excluded from top positions in colonial societies and how this made them turn to nationalism. Second, he argues that the excessive number of intellectuals produced by some societies and the inability to 'absorb' them, may also contribute to explain why some intellectuals turn to nationalism.

He perceives nationalist politics as elite politics in politically fragile states, or as a form of politics which can arouse mass support without having to tie itself too closely to the specific concerns of that support. The compelling character of the nationalist ideology stems from the connection between the intellectuals' portrayal of the nation and the common beliefs and often widespread political grievances shared by large sectors of the population.

He argues that symbols and ceremonies award nationalist ideas a definite shape and force in two major ways: they project certain images of the nation, and enable people to come together expressing some type of national solidarity.

Anthony D. Smith: 'In search of identity'
'There is, in fact, an "elective affinity" between the adapted model of a civic, territorial nation and the status, needs and interests of the professionals (and to a lesser extent of the commercial bourgeoisie).'

(*National Identity*, p. 121).

In his early work Smith confers pre-eminence to political and religious, rather than social and cultural factors in the emergence of what he refers to as ethnic nationalism. He argues that the modern era is characterized by the rise of what he calls the 'scientific state', that is, 'a state whose efficacy depends on its ability to harness science and technology for collective purposes' (Smith 1998, p. 189). In his view, the emergence of the 'scientific state' challenges the legitimacy of religious explanations and favours situations of 'dual legitimation', in which rival grounds of authority dispute for the allegiance of humanity. Intellectuals, as the equivalent of pre-modern priests, are particularly affected by this dispute.

According to Smith, the rise of a secular intelligentsia within the framework of the 'scientific state' has encountered several obstacles, among them: the overproduction of highly qualified personnel, the opposition on the part of entrenched hierarchical bureaucrats to the critical rationalism of the intelligentsia, and the use of ethnic or other cultural grounds for discrimination in admitting sections of the intelligentsia to public high-status positions.

Smith emphasizes the crucial role of intellectuals as generators of ideology and leaders of the nationalist movement in its early stages, although he is more sceptical about their function once the nationalist movement develops. He rejects those who define intellectuals as fanatical power-seeking individuals, though he accepts that, in some instances, it is possible to point at some excluded and resentful intellectuals especially in colonial societies.

Smith concludes that the beneficiaries of nationalism are the members of the mobilized *ethnie* at large, since nationalism favours both the activation of the masses and the end of their role as passive objects of external domination, and the elevation of popular culture into literary 'high' culture performed by intellectuals. Against those who stress the invented nature of nations and nationalism (Hobsbawm and Ranger, 1983), Smith highlights the 'ethnic origins' of most of the cultural elements selected by intellectuals in the construction of modern nationalism.

To explain the attraction that many intellectuals in different parts of the world have felt for nationalism and their influential imprint on the ideology and language of nationalism, Smith invokes the 'identity crisis' experienced by people in general and the intellectuals in particular stemming from the challenges posed to traditional religion and society by the 'scientific state'. He argues that the 'nationalist solution' allows individuals to draw their own identity from the collective identity of the nation. In so doing, 'she or he becomes a citizen, which is, a recognized and rightful member of a political community that is, simultaneously a cultural "community of history and destiny"' (Smith 1991, p. 97). Here Smith stresses the relation between national identity and citizenship thus emphasizing the cultural and political aspects of nationalism.

The writings of Kedourie, Nairn, Breuilly and Smith firmly place intellectuals as the generators of nationalism. In so doing, these scholars coincide in defining nationalism as a modern political ideology which, to be successful, requires the support of the masses; however, they regard the relationship between intellectuals and the masses in very different ways.

Kedourie underlines the wide gap between intellectual elites and the masses. In contrast, Nairn accents the need to create an inter-class community united by a common objective and Breuilly describes what we could refer to as an 'interactive' relationship between intellectual elites and the masses. Smith highlights the shared character of national identity among members of the same nation.

Kedourie, Nairn, Breuilly and Smith agree on the significance of mass support if a nationalist movement is to succeed. They also emphasize the power of culture, language, symbols and ceremonials as key constituents of nationalism. What is lacking from their analysis is a specific theory considering whether the task of intellectuals in nations without states is different, and if so, to what extent, from the task of intellectuals in nation-states. Apart from Kedourie who studies the relationship between intellectuals and nationalism in colonial societies, neither Nairn, Breuilly or Smith specify the context within which the intellectuals they analyse live and develop their theories.

There is considerable literature on the role of intellectuals in oppositional nationalisms; however, most of it concerns the study of underdeveloped countries (Hobsbawm, Gouldner, Kautsky). An exception to the considerable literature devoted to the study of nationalism and intellectuals in colonial societies is exemplified by the work of Pinard and Hamilton who study the participation of intellectuals in Quebec nationalism (Pinard and Hamilton, 1984). But their work has a primarily empirical focus and fails to provide a theoretical framework for the study of the relationship between intellectuals and nationalism in stateless nations. In what follows, I address this particular task.

III. The Case of Catalonia: Intellectuals in Nations without States

The third part of this paper offers a theoretical analysis of the socio-political context within which intellectuals operate in nations without states. In particular, it focuses on the role of intellectuals in the maintenance of the Catalan language and culture during Franco's dictatorship (1939–1975). First, I offer a brief account of the cultural resistance activities carried out by Catalan intellectuals. Second, I analyse the processes that saw Catalan nationalism transformed from an elite into a mass movement. In conclusion, the paper examines a number of the rational and emotional arguments that intellectuals invoke as they pursue their role as mobilizing agents in contemporary Catalan nationalism.

I am aware of the existence of substantial differences between the role of intel-lectuals at the birth and the re-emergence of a nationalist movement that has been dismantled. I am justified, I believe, in selecting the re-emergence of Catalan nationalism during Franco's dictatorship because of its devastating effects on Catalan language and culture (Benet, 1973). In that context, only small circles of intellectuals and clandestine political activists engaged in the maintenance of key components of Catalan identity and primarily devoted their efforts to the cultivation of Catalan high culture. To begin with, I turn to the issue of the discussion of the specific context within which intellectuals develop their activities in nations without states.

The socio-political context

I argue that the study of nationalism in nations without states requires a specific approach which should take into account two key factors. First, that sub-state nationalism emerges within already established nation-states and second, the need for an 'alternative elite' ready to challenge the state, construct a nationalist ideology and lead the nationalist movement.

(1) The nationalism of nations without states emerges within already established nation-states endowed with their own national education system, a specific media system, a constituted power elite and a set of institutions forming the state and defining its territorial, political, social and economic framework. Nation-states embody a cluster of institutions which both define and govern the country while stateless nations may or may not enjoy some kind of cul-tural or political autonomy, as a result of the state's decision.

Often, more than one nation live under the umbrella of a single state. Almost invariably, one nation prevails above the others and plays a leading role in the governance of the country and also in defining its identity through the promotion of a specific culture and language, which generally involves the marginalization of minority cultures and languages. In Spain, Castile turned to be the dominant nation to the detriment of Catalonia, the Basque Country, Galicia and other regions.

The mere existence of a community which considers itself to be a nation other than the one the state seeks to promote poses a threat to and questions the legitimacy of the state wherever it is defined as a unitary political institution. Democratic states recognize internal diversity; however, they are often reluctant to employ the term 'nation' when referring to their national minorities since the political consequences which this may entail, for instance the recognition of a nation's right to self-determination, are usually quite problematic. For this reason, the state tends to regard minority nationalisms as dangerous, or at least, as an uncomfortable phenomenon to deal with.

The ways in which the state responds to the demands of the national minorities included within its territory depend upon the state's own nature, the specific character of the nationalist movement, and the international support this is able to secure.

(2) The emergence of a nationalist movement in a nation without a state requires the existence of some intellectuals prepared to build up a nationalist discourse different from, and often opposed to, that of the state.

In contrast, intellectuals indigenous to the nation state develop their work within already established frameworks created and supported by the state. As the nation-state was in the process of being created, intellectual discourse was structured by the culture and language employed in the homogenization of its citizenry and the simultaneous marginalization of regional languages and cultures. As a result, such intellectuals are often critical and even dismissive of regional nationalist movements.

The 'potential elite'

Crucial to the development of nationalism in nations without states is the existence and position occupied by the 'potential elite'. By this I refer to those educated individuals who, if the nationalist movement succeeds, are likely to become its leaders. The potential elite includes:

(a) Individuals who feel dissatisfied with the state's treatment of their community. The degree and strength of their dissatisfaction may vary. In some cases, it is connected to the intensity of the state's repressive and discriminatory measures which may range from cultural and socio-political measures to the use of force. Catalan intellectuals who engaged in resistance activities against Franco's regime are a case in point.
(b) Individuals who have been excluded from the state's 'official' elite because of their regional origin. In such cases, individuals are unable to develop their work within the state's circles of power and influence, and have to

circumscribe their activities to their region. This could be exemplified by the widespread Castilian adverse attitude towards Catalans which lead to their exclusion from influential positions in the Spanish economic and political power structure during the nineteenth and most of the twentieth century.

(c) Individuals who decide to prioritize their allegiance to the nation without a state instead of aspiring to be integrated within the state's official elite. This involves their commitment to the advancement of a national cause opposed to that of the state, which often translates itself into their automatic exclusion from the state's selected elite. In these cases, it is the individual's choice rather than the state's systematic exclusion of some people because of their regional origin which leads to the inclusion of these individuals in the category of potential elite. In contemporary democratic Spain, the choice of some Catalan intellectuals to develop their work exclusively in Catalan automatically excludes them from Spanish speaking intellectual circles, unless their work is translated into Spanish. It has been argued that this is a strategy by means of which some educated people who would otherwise be unlikely to achieve a prominent position within the state's elite – because of fierce competition – would easily obtain a prominent position within a nation which is smaller and where competition is bound to be less intense. This argument emphasizes the self-interest of some individuals in promoting regional forms of nationalism in order to gain access to privileged positions.

In my view, although self-interest may in some cases play a substantial part in explaining why some intellectuals support sub-state forms of nationalism, it is misleading to explain all nationalist allegiances through economic motivation and the desire for power. A genuine love for the nation and a desire for its flourishing inspires many nationalists in nations without states, especially in those cases where the nation feels culturally, politically or economically oppressed by the state. Devoting one's life to the defence and enhancement of the specific character of one's own nation may act as a potent force. It provides meaning to the individual's life whilst setting a concrete and clear-cut objective to his or her actions. Because individuals usually embark upon nationalist projects as part of a group, they are bound to experience some kind of moral support and solidarity as members of a movement with a common goal. The sense of belonging to a nation can somehow be lived through the experience of comradeship arising within the nationalist movement or party.

In spite of this, differences amongst nationalist leaders are not to be ignored since fierce confrontation between them is a common phenomenon. Jealousy and competition amongst intellectuals are also commonplace. They struggle to become more influential, obtain more recognition or be offered a better job.

Intellectuals and nationalism in Catalonia

During Franco's regime, the Catalan intellectual elite was divided between those who supported Francoism and those who stood against it and took upon themselves the task of maintaining the vernacular language and culture. Yet, while some of the former were incorporated into mainstream Spanish elite, the latter were automatically excluded and often persecuted by the regime. When considering the initiatives to preserve Catalan culture and language which rose during that period we should distinguish between: initiatives rising from particular individuals and groups, and those emerging from some sectors of two powerful institutions: the Catholic Church and the University.

Individual and collective initiatives

The Institute for Catalan Studies (*Institut d'Estudis Catalans*), dismantled in 1939, was reorganized in 1942 by Josep Puig i Cadafalch and Ramon Aramon. Their clandestine activities involved the publication of books and articles on medicine, science and other subjects in Catalan. *Omnium Cultural*, a semi-clandestine institution from 1964, was legally recognized in 1967 and then saw a dramatic increase in membership (from 639 in 1968 to 11,000 in 1971). Among the activities of *Omnium Cultural* were the teaching of Catalan and the sponsoring of the Prize of Honour of the Catalan Letters (*Premi d'honor de les lletres catalanes*) (Vilar 1989, p. 358). The organization of cultural clandestine groups such as *Amics de la Poesia*, *Estudi* or *Miramar*, together with the holding of Literary competitions such as the *Nit de Santa Llúcia* (St. Lucy's evening) and the *Cantonigrós*, and the publication of journals in Catalan (Fabré, Huertas and Ribas 1978, pp. 156 ff), were some of the major activities organized by intellectual elites (Casassas 1999).

The Catholic Church

Further to the activities of private individuals, the Catholic Church and the University contributed to sustain Catalan culture. The position of the Catalan Church was not homogeneous. Thus, while some sectors supported the Francoist regime, others were reluctant to adopt an attitude that could undermine the strong relationship between religion and Catalan culture sustained since the Middle Ages. Some sectors of the Catholic Church assumed a crucial role by preaching and teaching religion in Catalan and employing it as an instrument of culture and communication. In 1942, the first book legally published in Catalan after the Civil War appeared. It was a religious book produced under the auspices of the Catholic Church.

Amid other activities, the Abbey of Montserrat played a remarkable part in continuing to publish in Catalan. They created and promoted, among others, some children's publications (*L'Infantil, Tretzevents*) and some cultural and religious journals (*Serra d'Or, Qüestions de vida cristiana*). In 1958, the Abbey founded the *Estela* Press to promote religious books in Catalan (Masot i Muntaner, 1986) and in 1971 the PAM Press (Publications of the Montserrat Abbey) became official (Faulí 1999, pp. 35–39). The Abbey was also active in supporting and providing shelter to intellectuals and clandestine political activists from a wide political spectrum.

The university

The official organization of student life centred around the University Students Union (*Sindicato de Estudiantes Universitarios* or SEU) under the control of pro-regime individuals; however, constant resistance activities developed within the university. The University Front of Catalonia (*Front Universitari de Catalunya* or FUC) combined people from different backgrounds. It advocated the reconstruction of Catalonia and produced a critical account of pre-war Catalan politics.

Other university organizations included the National Front of Catalonia (*Front Nacional de Catalunya* or FNC), and the National Federation of Students of Catalonia (*Federació Nacional d'Estudiants de Catalunya* or FNEC) which represented an attempt to unify efforts in fighting the SEU. The university movement received new strength in the mid and late 1950s when new associations emerged. Three major campaigns were launched by the students between 1960 and 1961: the demand for the creation of Catalan culture and language Departments; a campaign against the increasing influence of Opus Dei; and the demand of amnesty for political prisoners and those in exile.

In the late sixties and early seventies, the influence of the 1968 student uprisings in France and the 'Prague Spring' favoured the proliferation of radical organizations within the university, and nationalist claims came to be perceived as bourgeois. Nationalist groups disappeared from the university arena to return only after Franco's death.

From elite into mass movement

Three main phenomena marked the transition of Catalan nationalism from an elite into a mass movement; these are: the *Nova Cançó*, the Assembly of Catalonia and the proliferation of 'solidarity actions'.

The long years of repression endured by Catalans resulted in a widening gap between intellectual elites and the masses and such a gap posed a serious threat to the survival of the Catalan language and culture. The *Nova Cançó* (New Folk Song) movement of the sixties played a key role in the regeneration of the public sphere in Catalonia. The movement was founded by a small middle-class intellectual group of amateur singers and soon developed into an entirely popular phenomenon. The more Catalan singers were banned from the media and their concerts prohibited, the more popular they became. The *Nova Cançó* contributed to 'give people – especially young people – all over the *Països Catalans*, or Catalan-speaking territories, a sense of community till then never felt nor expressed so intensely' (Giner 1998, pp. 71–76).

The Assembly of Catalonia (*Assemblea de Catalunya*, 1971) brought together three hundred people from diverse social backgrounds and political allegiances. It was the most important clandestine unitary movement in Catalonia since the Civil War and had no equivalent in any other part of Spain. The Assembly presented a common platform based upon four demands: (1) a general amnesty for political prisoners and exiles; (2) the upholding of human rights; (3) the provisional re-establishment of the 1932 Catalan Statute of Autonomy; (4) and the coordination of all peninsular peoples in fighting for democracy (Batista and Playà Maset 1991, pp. 301–302). The Assembly continued its unitary mobilizing activities until the first Spanish democratic elections (15 June 1977). From that moment onwards, the recently legalized political parties took over leadership and concentrated on emphasizing difference between them in order to obtain good results in regional and national elections. Intellectual unity was definitely broken and differing nationalist discourses emerged.

While remaining a dictatorship wedded to conservative ideology, the Francoist regime went through different stages as a number of its policies were certainly modified over time. These modifications were a response to pressures to become more acceptable to Western democracies and were reinforced by deepening technocratic influences upon the regime during the late 1950s and early 1960s. In addition, free market ideals fundamentally transformed the structure of the Spanish economy with unintended consequences on Spanish society and social structure.

In the late 1960s and 1970s, the resistance movement took advantage of all possible breaches to actively protest against the regime. For instance, the early 1970s saw an increase in the number of 'solidarity actions'. By 'solidarity action' I mean an action that is usually instilled by a small elite but whose aim is to attain mass mobilization. The objective of a 'solidarity action' is to show the opposition's strength by focusing upon a particular demand and presenting it as undeniable due to the massive support it receives (Guibernau 1996, p. 105). A 'solidarity action' which exemplifies the moment in which Catalan nationalism had definitely shifted from an elite into a mass movement concerns the one million strong mass demonstration in Barcelona on 11 September 1977 demanding a statute of autonomy for Catalonia. Franco had died in 1975 and the Political Reform Programme presented by the then Prime Minister, Adolfo Suárez, had been ratified by an overwhelming majority. In spite of that, the status that Catalonia might achieve within the new democratic Spanish state had not been decided yet. The Constitution that would define Spain as a democratic state and confer autonomy to Catalonia was to be ratified in 1978.

Rational and emotional arguments as mobilizing agents

Rational and emotional arguments become intertwined when intellectuals seek to awaken the nation and generate a mass nationalist movement. Rationality stems from the objective reasons invoked by nationalists when defending their case. Independence or greater autonomy may mean: a better economy by encouraging regional development and the right to retain regionally generated wealth; a higher quality of life; freedom from a series of constraints imposed by the state; and even a deepening of democracy by favouring decentralization and self-determination.

Emotions are aroused when the nation is presented as a community which transcends the limited lives of particular individuals while providing them with a collective sense of identity. Belonging to a nation, which is real in the minds of its members, confers on them a sense of continuity grounded upon the sentiment of being part of a group portrayed as an extended family. Individuals are born into particular families in the same way as they are placed within specific nations which act as major socializing agents. Individuals are brought up within particular cultures which define the way in which they relate to themselves, others and nature. The use of a particular language increases the sentiment of belonging to a community sharing a common history and a common set of values and practices. As in a family, membership of the nation implies a certain solidarity, in this case, with fellow nationals. It also demands sacrifices and generates sentiments of love and affection which generally become more prominent when the well-being of the group is under threat.

Rational arguments in contemporary Catalan nationalism

Rational and emotional arguments have a strong presence in Catalan nationalism which is currently split between a majority movement for greater political autonomy within Spain, and a minority, but growing, movement for Catalan independence. During Franco's regime, the key objective was to restore democracy and with it the right of Catalonia to develop its language and culture, and recover its autonomous political institutions. These were rational demands capable of arousing intense emotional reactions.

Among the main arguments currently being invoked by Catalan nationalists, including intellectuals as well as political leaders, to legitimize their demands for greater political autonomy for Catalonia are a fiscal regime balancing out regional inequalities and is recognized as a nation within Spain with the means to develop fully its distinct identity. Certain Catalan nationalists argue that only through independence can Catalonia thrive culturally and economically and thereby find itself considered a fully fledged political actor in the international arena.

I distinguish three main rational arguments destined to convince not only those who share a strong sense of national identity but also those who are solely interested in supporting Catalan nationalism insofar as it proves capable of improving their quality of life, deepening democracy and/or dynamizing civil society.

First, the argument that Catalonia's contribution to the Spanish coffers heavily outweighs the income it receives from the central government: such imbalance is currently generating an annual fiscal deficit of 9.8 per cent of the GDP of Catalonia.[2] This is presented as an unjust situation which, if reversed, would automatically increase the Generalitat's spending power and improve the Catalans' quality of life.

Second, the argument that political decentralization tends to strengthen democracy inasmuch as it brings decision-making processes closer to the people. Problems are identified, analysed and resolved where they emerge. Regional politicians usually have greater awareness of the needs and aspirations of their electorates; thus the argument follows, greater devolved powers for Catalonia would strengthen Spanish democracy and encourage greater democratic participation within the region.

Third, the devolution of powers to regional institutions requires the reallocation of resources to facilitate discrete policies and regional budget planning. These processes, in turn, contribute to revitalize civil society, encouraging local and regional initiatives which include cultural, economic and social projects. The demand for greater autonomy is connected with the wish to increase Catalonia's ability and efficiency to govern itself and be recognized as a distinct political actor within the European Union and other international institutions.

Emotional arguments in contemporary Catalan nationalism

In Catalan nationalism, emotional arguments emphasize the sentiment of belonging to a cultural and territorial community which has suffered and rejoiced together throughout time. Emotional arguments evolve around three major clusters: history, territory and art.

First, a considerable number of people who suffered under Francoism still hold live images of either their own or their loved one's experiences which may include: torture, imprisonment, exile, proscription, and lack of freedom to cultivate their vernacular language and culture. Memories of oppression under Franco are connected with a long list of grievances, most of them concerned with repeated Spanish attempts to eradicate Catalan language, culture and political institutions. Key historical events, invested with particular meaning and capable of arousing an emotional response when Catalans 'tell their history' include: The Revolt of the Reapers (*Revolta dels Segadors*) in 1640, when Catalans united against the harsh treatment they were receiving from Castile (Elliott, 1963) and the abolition of Catalan rights and liberties in 1714 when on 11 September (turned into Catalonia's national day), after a massive Franco-Spanish attack, Barcelona surrendered. Philip V (*Felipe V*) ordered the dissolution of Catalan political institutions and Catalonia was subject to a regime of occupation; its language was forbidden and Castilian (Spanish) was proclaimed official (Balcells 1996, pp. 12–17). More recent historical memories include the suppression of the administrative government of the Catalan Mancomunitat (1913–1923) after the *coup d'état* of Miguel Primo de Rivera.

Second, references to the territory of Catalonia are contested. A substantial number of people refers to the so-called *Països Catalans* (Catalan Countries) including Catalonia, Valencia, the Balearic Islands and territories across the Pyrenees on the French side of the border. They justify their claim by stressing that these territories which, in medieval times were included in the dominion of the Count of Barcelona, share a common linguistic and cultural background. Dialects of Catalan are currently spoken in Valencia, the Balearic Islands and the area around Perpignan (France).

Particular landscapes are emotionally charged and portrayed as embodying Catalan traditions, history and culture. The monasteries of Ripoll, Montserrat and Cuixà (France); mountains such as the Canigó (France), or urban landscapes such as the Fossar de les Moreres (Barcelona) are among them.

Third, selected works of art and artists turned into symbols of Catalan identity are often portrayed as part of a corpus of Catalan high culture which has received international recognition. The work of Joan Miró, Salvador Dalí, Antoni Gaudí, Antoni Tàpies, Pau Casals and Jordi Savall, among others, stands side by side with fine examples of Romanesque (Taüll) and Gothic art (Barcelona's gothic area). The rich Catalan folklore including the *sardana* (Catalan national dance) should be added to the list of symbols of Catalan identity.

A further and powerful symbol of Catalan identity which somehow escapes the above typology concerns sport, football in particular. During Francoism, the Barcelona Football Club (*Barça*) was portrayed as a representative of the Catalan nation and exemplified resistance against the dictatorship. In Catalonia, the Barça's victories were celebrated as Catalan victories and whenever Barcelona

F. C. and Real Madrid played each other the significance of the match went well beyond sport. Emotions were and are still aroused at the *Nou Camp* (Barça's stadium). At present, Catalan nationalists have launched a campaign demanding the central government the right for Catalonia to create its own Catalan Football Team able to compete in international contests. This movement has galvanized a very large section of the population and is putting pressure on Madrid to reverse its initial negative response.

The way in which people identify with and relate to history, territory and art as part of a common shared heritage which contributes to define the community they belong to is not homogeneous. It is important to emphasize that symbols are effective because they are imprecise. Symbols transform difference into the appearance of similarity, thus allowing people to invest the 'community' with ideological integrity. This, in my view, accounts for the ability of nationalism to bind together people from different cultural levels and social backgrounds.

The power of emotional arguments stems from their capacity to appeal to individuals who share the same culture, feel attached to a concrete land, have the experience of a common past and a project for the future. Intellectuals and political leaders (in some cases religious leaders should also be included) select and promote the key elements which conform to national identity, and they also re-create and generate occasions in which all that unites those belonging to the nation is emphasized. In these moments, individuals forget about themselves, and the sentiment of belonging to the group occupies the prime position. The collective life of the community stands above that of the individual. Through symbolism and ritual, individuals are able to feel an emotion of unusual intensity that springs from their identification with an entity – the nation – which transcends them, and of which they actively feel a part.

Concluding remarks

Intellectuals play a double role. On the one hand, they act as architects of the nationalist movement by providing cultural, historical, political and economic arguments to sustain the distinctive character of the nation and to legitimize its will to decide upon its political future.

On the other hand, as we have already mentioned, intellectuals are subversive and construct a discourse which undermines the legitimacy of the current order of things. They denounce the nation's present situation within the state and offer an alternative to it by promoting the conditions and processes of conflict. Intellectuals are to be considered as formulators of the nationalist ideology; however, their task does not end here, since many of them do also act as agitators and mobilizers of the nationalist movement. Valentí Almirall (1841–1904), Enric Prat de la Riba (1870–1917), Jordi Pujol (1930), and Pasqual Maragall (1941) represent but a few examples of key ideologists of Catalan nationalism who have turned into extremely influential political leaders.

I have argued that two main factors define the socio-political context within which intellectuals operate in nations without states. First, sub-state nationalism emerges within already established nation-states with their own elites, culture, education and media systems and international recognition as political institutions. Second, to be successful, sub-state nationalism requires the existence of an alternative elite able to construct a discourse critical of the current *status quo*, and ready to formulate an alternative nationalist ideology.

Notes

1 See also: Hodgkin, 1964; Trevor-Roper, 1962; Kohn, 1944.
2 *El País*, 11 May 2008.

References

Balcells, A. (1996) *Catalan Nationalism*, London: Macmillan.

Batista, A. and Playà Maset, J. (1991) *La Gran Conspiració: crónica de l'Assemblea de Catalunya*, Barcelona: Empúries.

Benet, J. (1973) *Catalunya sota el régim franquista*, Paris: Edicions Catalanes de Paris.

Breuilly, J. (1982) *Nationalism and the State*, Manchester: Manchester University Press.

Casassas, J. (ed) (1999) *Els intellectuals i el poder a Catalunya (1808–1975,* Barcelona: Pòrtic.

Elliott, J. H. (1963) *The Revolt of the Catalans*, Cambridge: Cambridge University Press.

Fabré, J. Huertas, J.M. and Ribas, A. (1978) *Vint anys de resistència catalana (1939–1959)*, Barcelona: La Magrana.

Faulí, J. 'Un segle d'edicions montserratines', *Serra d'Or*, 478, 35–39.

Giner, S. (1998) *La Societat Catalana*, Barcelona: ICE.

Gouldner, A. (1979) *The future of intellectuals and the rise of the New Class*, London: Macmillan.

Guibernau, M. (1996) *Nationalisms*, Cambridge: Polity Press.

Guibernau, M. (1999) *Nations without States*, Cambridge: Polity Press.

Guibernau, M. (2007) *The Identity of Nations*, Cambridge: Polity Press.

Hobsbawm, E. and Ranger, T. (eds) (1983) *The Invention of Tradition*, Cambridge: Cambridge University Press.

Hodgkin, T. (1956) *Nationalism in Colonial Africa*, London: Muller.

Hroch, M. (1985) *Social Preconditions of national revival in Europe*, Cambridge: Cambridge University Press.

Kautsky, J. H. (1976) *Political change in underdeveloped countries: Nationalism and Communism*, New York: Robert E. Krieger Publishing Company.

Kedourie, E. (1960) *Nationalism*, London: Hutchinson.

Kedourie, E. (1971) *Nationalism in Asia and Africa*, London: Weidenfeld and Nicolson.

Kohn, H. (1967) *The Idea of Nationalism*, New York: Collier-Macmillan.

Masot i Muntaner, J. 'Cristianisme i Catalanisme' in Termes, J. et al. (eds) *Catalanisme: història, política i cultura*, Barcelona: L'Avenç.

Nairn, T. (1977) *The Break-Up of Britain*, London: NLB.

Pinard, M. and Hamilton, R. (1984) 'The class bases of the Quebec independence movement: conjecture and evidence', *Ethnic and Racial Studies*, 7 (1), 17–54.

Smith, A. D. (1991) *National Identity*, London: Penguin Books.

Smith, A. D. (1998) *Nationalism and Modernism*, London: Routledge.

Trevor-Roper, H. (1962) *Jewish and Other Nationalisms*, London: Weidenfeld and Nicolson.

Vilar, P. (ed) (1989) *Història de Catalunya*, vol. 2 by De Riquer, B. and Culla, J.B. Barcelona: Edicions 62.

Weber, M. (1991) [1948] 'Politics as a Vocation' in Gerth, H. H. and Wright Mills, C. (eds) *From Marx Weber: essays in sociology*, London: Routledge.

Worsley, P. (1964) *The Third World*, London: Weidenfeld and Nicolson.

SCOTLAND: THE IMPORTANCE OF RAISING YOUR OWN REVENUES

RUSSELL MELLETT

A permanent transfer of revenue raising capacity from the UK government to each of Scotland, Wales and Northern Ireland would enhance the direct accountability of these governments to their citizens, and, together with changes in borrowing practices, provide reasonable fiscal and governance flexibility. Raising part of their own revenues and insuring their own borrowing could enhance responsive and responsible government for Scotland, Wales and Northern Ireland.

Context

The Devolved Administrations, the regional governments of Scotland, Wales and Northern Ireland, do not raise their own revenues nor do they have the ability to raise revenues by borrowing on financial markets. Instead, each Devolved Administration relies on a transfer of funds from the United Kingdom government, the unconditional block grant whose changes are determined by the Barnett formula. Data, as explained and elaborated in the Statistical Annex, indicate:

- for the Scottish Government: 91% of total managed expenditure was financed via the block grant over the period 2002–03 to 2007–08;
- for the National Assembly for Wales: net operating costs from 1999–00 to 2006–07 were financed almost exclusively by the block grant; and
- for the Northern Ireland Executive: about 91.5% of the spending managed by the executive over the period 2003–04 to 2007–08 was financed by the block grant.

Despite the reliance on external financing, the Devolved Administrations are responsible for providing significant kinds and levels of public services within their own jurisdictions. According to public expenditure data, detailed in the statistical annex[1] for the period 2003–04 to 2005–06:

- For Scotland: identifiable spending by the Scottish Executive and local authorities combined was 68% of total government expenditure. The Scottish Executive was directly responsible for 38% of the total.
- For Wales: identifiable spending by the National Assembly government and local authorities combined was 62% of total government expenditure. The National Assembly was directly responsible for 33% of the total.
- For Northern Ireland: identifiable spending by the Northern Ireland Executive and local authorities combined was 85% of total government expenditure. The Northern Ireland Executive was directly responsible for 81% of the total.

On international comparison, the UK follows a unique approach to devolution financing. Essentially, one order of government (UK) taxes while the other order of government (Devolved Administration) spends. There is complete spending autonomy within an externally determined spending envelope, but little control over the size of the envelope itself. The exception here is Scotland's ability to vary the basic rate of income tax up or down by three pence in the pound. This small power to vary on the margin would not yield substantial revenues[2] and there is little incentive for Scotland to bear the political cost of imposing the Tartan tax provided that the Barnett transfer is generous enough.

This unique financing set-up is the legacy of fiscal arrangements that were in place for UK departments at the time of devolution. Specifically, the manner of financing the Scotland. Wales and Northern Ireland offices was carried over to finance the Devolved Administrations.

If current fiscal arrangements 'work', for the governments involved, and they promise to if the ongoing transfer from the centre to each devolved administration is large enough, why ask questions – let alone propose change? From a governance policy perspective there are a number of outstanding issues that touch on Devolved Administration inability to borrow, and their inability or unwillingness to raise their own revenues. There is also an important governance question regarding the seeming non-conditionality of the current block grant system. All is not well.

Own Revenues

The problem

The inability or unwillingness of the Devolved Administrations to raise own revenues leads to a limited capacity to govern. These regional governments cannot offer their electorate increased levels of public spending at increased tax rates, nor decreased levels of public spend at decreased tax rates should they choose to do so, or should their electorates demand this policy mix. As to whether or not regional government ought to have such power, fiscal arrangements are part of the overall governance arrangement, reflecting what the sub-national government is intended to do. Here it may be handy to think about sub-national governments as carrying out an agency function on behalf of the central government or as having choice over the public services that they offer at a given tax price. The alternative is to have the ability to substantially determine the size of their budgetary expenditures, rather than being restricted to how an externally determined budget envelope is spent. Overall, there should be coherence between the intended governance capability of the Devolved Administrations and how these governments are financed.

Efficiency in public spending may be enhanced if marginal increases (decreases) in public spend were reflected in marginal increases (decreases) in taxation. More expansively, fairness and fiscal efficiency suggest that the citizens that benefit from increased levels of public service should pay the incremental cost of provision. Similarly, should citizens wish incrementally lower levels of public services, these same citizens should benefit from marginally lower taxes. The fact that Devolved Administrations have limited or no ability to tax may prevent fiscal efficiency on the margin.

More generally, there is no direct fiscal accountability from Devolved Administrations to their own electorate as they do not raise a significant part of their own revenue requirements. It is politically costly to impose taxes, particularly taxes that are perceptible to the tax-paying electorate. There is a growing literature which suggests that 'the more government income is earned the more likely are state-society relations to be characterized by accountability, responsiveness and democracy',[3] where earning income requires states to put forward fiscal effort, and provide reciprocal services to citizens in exchange for taxes paid. Applied to the Devolved Administrations there is a question of not only having the ability to raise taxes on the margin, but actually expending substantial fiscal effort, incurring the related political cost and thereby putting in place a means of direct fiscal accountability between governments and taxpayers.[4] Most importantly, government finance is key to defining state-society relations in a polity; consequently, a slogan for UK devolution could be 'no representation without taxation'.[5]

The current block funded system is far from transparent to both the electorate and the Devolved Administrations. HM Treasury controls both the Barnett calculation and the extent to which adjustments are made to the block grant 'outside' of this calculation (the extent to which the formula is bypassed). Details about the 'inner workings' of the formula and all of the data on which it is based remain a mystery to the Devolved Administrations, let alone the general public.[6] To the extent that Devolved Administrations raise their own revenues or engage in their own borrowing, and that the relevant facts are reported in the public accounts of each of these regional governments, transparency would improve. More generally, public finance transparency would be enhanced to the extent that Barnett or its successor is determined by a formula and underpinned by principles, with the details and results of formula calculations made publicly available.[7]

Regarding current fiscal arrangements, it is important to note that the block grant from the UK is unconditional: that the UK government does not explicitly indicate what Devolved Administrations are to do with the monies received. Nevertheless, there may be some implicit direction or pressures. Annual funding increments calculated using the Barnett formula are directly tied to UK (English) policy decisions, and there is some evidence that Devolved Administration incremental policy decisions have been influenced by this funding practice.[8] The Barnett calculation also assumes that all Devolved Administrations will deliver the same basket of public goods, thereby leading to pressure to have similar rosters of publicly and privately delivered goods (which is not the case now as

Scottish Water is public, while water utilities in England are privately run). Overall, the Barnett calculation together with little or no revenue powers may skew Devolved Administration choices over their public/private goods mix and restrict alternate means of financing these.[9]

HM Treasury dictates the annual spending envelope of the Devolved Administrations by controlling the Barnett formula and access to borrowing. There is risk when another jurisdiction controls your revenues; this fact and an accompanying lack of transparency make the Devolved Administrations open to 'moral suasion' by the UK government which is a concern whether it occurs or only appears to occur.[10]

[...]

Own Borrowing

The problem

Revenue volatility for Devolved Administrations may occur due to underlying economic change, and spending plans may have to be multi-year to accommodate, for example, capital spending. Borrowing is key to matching spending plans to available revenues over time: own borrowing would allow Devolved Administrations to responsibly plan their spending over time, provide greater funding flexibility and aid year over year stability in total revenues.

Policy discussion

The ability to raise revenues, whether through own taxation or own borrowing, should be seen as linked. Moreover, if the Devolved Administrations are to borrow then their own revenue-raising capacity together with transfers from the UK government provide them with a means to 'extinguish' any debt incurred. There is a question as to whether lenders would 'look more kindly' on own revenue raising rather than UK transfers as a source of funds to guarantee debt, the first revenue source being within the control of the Devolved Administration, the second dependent on central government decision-making.[11]

Irrespective of how lenders may view Devolved Administration capacity to repay based on their sources of funds, for policy purposes it may be best to follow the dictum of Alexander Hamilton that 'the creation of debt should always be accompanied by the means of extinguishment'.[12] Simply put: governments that have the ability to issue debt should have autonomy over the tax base that backs it up.

There may be a concern that unrestricted access to borrowing by the Devolved Administrations could lead to payment default and a subsequent bailout by the UK government. More expansively, if borrowing is restricted only by the financial markets and the 'political market' faced by each of Scotland, Wales or Northern Ireland, then the UK government may find it difficult or impossible to avoid a bailout of these regional governments – even if the debt originally incurred was not issued or guaranteed by the UK, and despite the fact that a financial bailout may mean a take-over of the finances of Scotland, Wales or Northern Ireland with resultant loss of *de facto* sovereignty for these governments. It is important to point out that the above may be a concern, particularly for the central government, not that there is any evidence to suggest that the regional governments would be incapable of paying back monies borrowed or that Westminster would be more frugal.

[...]

Own Revenues and Transfers

This article is not advocating that the Devolved Administrations raise all of their own revenue from their own sources. Indeed there are questions as to whether this is actually feasible, if on a UK wide basis governments wish to provide 'reasonably comparable levels of public services at reasonably comparable levels of taxation'.[13] As the expenditure requirements and the revenue means will vary between the nations that make up the UK, some sort of equalization transfer from the central government to each Devolved Administration would seem to be required in order to enable fiscal equity – and this may or may not be a modified Barnett formula or its successor. What this article is advocating is a mixed system of own revenue raising and intergovernmental transfers within a comprehensive and common taxation and transfer system.

Incremental change?

It could be argued that any transfer of fiscal capacity to UK regional governments or any changes in borrowing rules should be part of a complete overhaul of devolution financing in the UK. Such a policy direction could focus on changes to the Barnett formula; specifically, whether or not Barnett should be based on explicit measurements of the expenditure needs of each of Scotland, Wales and Northern Ireland. An exploration of possible changes to the Barnett formula lie well beyond the scope of this article.[14] In any event, the opportunity to realize substantial changes to Barnett may never emerge. Practically, officials, both elected and unelected, seem to prefer incremental change. The immediate question is whether the smaller steps of transferring fiscal capacity from the UK government to the governments of Scotland, Wales and Northern Ireland would aid the direct accountability of those governments to their citizens and, together with changes in borrowing rules, provide reasonable fiscal and governance flexibility.

Asymmetry

The Devolved Administrations of Scotland, Wales, and Northern Ireland differ as to actual circumstances, and differ with respect to political power (e.g. Wales having relatively little legislative power). Nevertheless, all of these administrations could and should raise a substantial portion of their own revenue requirements for the reasons discussed above. At a minimum, these governments could simply follow the tax rate policies of the UK government and not borrow, leading to no change in the tax effort within their jurisdiction but leading to their own revenue generation all the same. So political asymmetry does not suggest asymmetry in own revenue generation.

Conclusion

Are changes, such as those suggested above, to UK devolution financing desirable, wanted, or demanded? This takes us back to the idea of the purpose of the Scottish, Welsh, and Northern Irish governments. To what extent does governance extend to raising part of your own revenue – no representation without taxation? And to what extent should Devolved Administrations have the ability to vary the overall level of public services provided to and taxation borne by their own citizens? To what extent should the Devolved Administrations be directly fiscally responsible to their own citizens or taxpayers? These are ultimately political questions, and there is no ideal or correct fiscal recipe. Nevertheless, this article concludes that raising part of your own revenues, and insuring your own borrowing, could enhance responsive and responsible government for Scotland, Wales and Northern Ireland. Moreover, these changes can be made independently of a more through-going review of the Barnett formula, which, as it implies addressing the thorny issue of relative spending needs, may never occur.

Statistical Annex: Overview

The Annex makes three sets of comparisons:

- Comparing the expenditures of each Devolved Administration with the revenues of each Devolved Administration (see context section of the article and below).
- Comparing identifiable spending across each Devolved Administration (see context section of the article and below).
- Comparing income tax data for each of Scotland, Wales and Northern Ireland with the spending of each Devolved Administration (see 'Own Revenues' section of the article and below).

In comparing the expenditures of each Devolved Administration with the revenues of each Devolved Administration what are needed are public accounts data. What have been constructed for this article and presented in this Annex is a consistent set of time series data for each Devolved Administration based on their own data. A choice was made to be internally consistent between the expenditure and revenue data for each Devolved Administration as the goal was to determine the dependence of each Devolved Administration on Barnett block grant funding. Importantly, a common, consistent set of public accounts data spanning both revenues and expenditures of the Devolved Administrations does not exist. Moreover, there is no simple fix to this problem across Devolved Administrations. What is available is Public Expenditure Statistical Analysis (PESA), which covers only the spending side and is inconsistent in its coverage over time.

Indeed the construction of a common set of public expenditure accounts is a major challenge faced by the UK in terms of the future development of fiscal arrangements. In Canada, for example, each province produces their own public accounts, while Statistics Canada produces a common set of accounts based on standard statistical definitions. This represents a significant effort on an annual basis by Statistics Canada. Something similar needs to be done in the UK, but this is far beyond the scope of this article.

The second comparison is identifiable spending across Devolved Administrations. Here the paper uses PESA. These are the only data available. Also the paper uses these data to illustrate the fact that, when examining spending, the most comparable aggregate across regions is (Devolved Administration+ local government) as each Devolved Administration gives their local government a different set of responsibilities. Note, again, the difference in purpose in this case compared with comparing the expenditures and revenue of each Devolved Administration; and hence the requirement to use different data.

The income tax data for each of Scotland, Wales and Northern Ireland was compared with the spending of each devolved administration as reported by them, to gauge the possible contribution to total Devolved Administration spending of transferring the income tax to each Devolved Administration. This spending data was chosen to maintain internal consistency between the spending and revenue aggregates for each Devolved Administration.

Statistical Annex: Total Identifiable Expenditure

	Identifiable Expenditure					
Millions of GBP	*2005–06*	*x/TIE*	*2004–05*	*x/TIE*	*2003–04*	*x/TIE*
Scotland						
Tot I Exp	41,671	1.00	38,578	1.00	37,152	1.00
Scot Exec	15,956	0.38	14,625	0.38	14,281	0.38
Loc Auth	12,239	0.29	11,188	0.29	10,505	0.28
(SE+LA)	28,195	0.68	25,813	0.67	24,786	0.67
Wales						
Tot I Exp	23,028	1.00	21,398	1.00	20,277	1.00
NAW	7,555	0.33	6,915	0.32	6,555	0.32
Loc Auth	6,662	0.29	6,174	0.29	5,701	0.28
(NAW+LA)	14,217	0.62	13,089	0.61	12,256	0.60
NIreland						
Tot I Exp	15,024	1.00	14,052	1.00	13,527	1.00
NI Exec	12,223	0.81	11,516	0.82	11,054	0.82
Loc Auth	486	0.03	396	0.03	364	0.03
(NIE+LA)	12,709	0.85	11,912	0.85	11,418	0.84

Notes:
Identifiable spending is actual expenditure by each order of government. Identifiable spending differs conceptually from the spending as reported by Scottish, Welsh and NI governments. For example, transfer payments to local government may be reported by regional governments as own spending, but included as local government identifiable expenditures by PESA. The implication is that own spending reported by regional governments may be greater than their identifiable spending according to PESA.
More generally, identifiable spending reported by PESA and own spending as reported by Scottish, Welsh and NI government are not comparable.
Regarding data from Public Expenditure Statistical Analysis (PESA): over time, data classifications and coverage change; so time series from this source (PESA) are suspect.
Source: HM Treasury Public Expenditure Statistical Analysis (2007, 2006, 2005).

Statistical Annex: Scotland

| | Scottish Executive Government | | | |
| | Thousands of GBP | | | |
Year	Total Managed Expenditure	Transfer from UK govt	Non-Domestic Rates	European Funding
2002–03	21,478,685	19,545,603	1,503,508	429,574
2003–04	23,643,581	21,515,641	1,655,049	472,871
2004–05	25,520,071	23,223,265	1,786,405	510,401
2005–06	27,389,916	24,924,824	1,917,294	547,798
2006–07	29,748,127	27,070,796	2,082,369	594,963
2007–08	31,283,577	28,468,055	2,189,850	625,672

Notes:
Total Managed Expenditure (TME) is composed of the Departmental Expenditure Limit (DEL) and Annual Managed Expenditure (AME). DEL is ongoing and funded via the Barnett Formula, whereas AME is set each year.
The 2007 Scottish Government draft budget indicates that about 86% of TME is DEL, about 14% is AME.
The 2007 Scottish government draft budget and subsequent correspondence with the Scottish Executive indicated that between 2002–03 and 2007–08, 91% of TME funding came from HM Treasury as a block fund (mostly Barnett-determined), 7% came from non-domestic (business property) tax rates, and 2% from European funding, and that these percentages varied little between the years. Consequently, these percentages have been used to generate the corresponding numbers in this table.
TME are actual budgetary data from 2002–03 to 2006–07.
TME data for 2007–08 are plans.
Source: The Scottish Government Draft Budget, http://www.scotland.gov.uk/ Publications/2006/09/05/31713/2 p. 185.

Statistical Annex: Wales

| | National Assembly for Wales Government | | | | |
| | Thousands of GBP | | | | |
Year	Net Operating Cost	Transfer from Cons Fund	(transfer/ NOP)	Cash Requirement	(transfer/ cashreq)
2006–07	11,865,267	11,676,200	0.98	na	
2005–06	11,295,884	10,884,421	0.96	na	
2004–05	10,229,990	9,873,565	0.97	na	
2003–04	9,820,303	9,606,147	0.98	9,639,115	1.00
2002–03	9,534,762	9,011,340	0.95	8,966,913	1.00
2001–02	8,482,487	7,694,552	0.91	8,112,282	0.95
2000–01	7,551,554	7,117,727	0.94	7,491,828	0.95
1999–00	5,400,748	5,037,907	0.93	4,519,295	1.11

Notes:
Total managed expenditure by the NAW is not available. The closest concept is net operating cost.
Sources of Finance are (almost exclusively) transfers from the Consolidated Revenue Fund via the Wales Office, and (occasionally) European Funding.
Correspondence with NAW confirmed that the transfers from the consolidated revenue fund are the (Barnett) block transfer; or that operating costs are almost entirely backed by the block transfer. Data reporting between 1999–00 and 2003–04 showed a total cash requirement number (resource accounts).
Data reporting between 2004–05 and 2006–07 do not indicate a total cash requirement number (consolidated resource accounts).
Sources: National Assembly for Wales, Resource Accounts, Consolidated Resource Accounts, http://new.wales.gov.uk/about/finance/nationalassemblyforwalesaccounts/ nawaccountsindex/?lang=en

Statistical Annex: Northern Ireland

	Northern Ireland Executive Budgetary Expenditures			
	millions of GBP			
year	2004–05	2005–06	2006–07	2007–08
DELcurrent	6,905.40	7,469.30	7,826.70	8,205.00
DELcapital	972.40	1,133.20	1,304.50	1,338.50
DELtotal	7,877.80	8,602.50	9,131.20	9,543.50
AME	6,005.20	6,832.90	7,008.50	7,286.70
TMEcurrent	12,910.60	14,302.20	14,835.20	15,491.70
TMEcapital	972.40	1,133.20	1,304.50	1,338.50
TMEtotal	13,883.00	15,435.40	16,139.70	16,830.20

Notes:
The functions to be included within Annual Managed Expenditure (AME) are determined by HM Treasury with the amounts allocated to each spending area within Northern Ireland based on forecasts provided by NI Executive Departments. The NI Executive determines how Departmental Expenditure Limits (DEL) are allocated through the NI Budget process.
Total Managed Expenditure (TME) is the sum of Departmental Expenditure Limits (DEL) and Annual Managed Expenditure (AME).
Sources: Priorities and Budget 2006–08 Secretary of State for Northern Ireland http:// www.pfgbudgetni.gov.uk/index/priorities-documents/budget-documents.htm and through correspondence with NI Executive.

Statistical Annex: Northern Ireland

	Source of NI DEL funding from 2003–2008				
£000's	2003–04	2004–05	2005–06	2006–07	2007–08
Assigned DEL	91.50%	91.20%	91.10%	91.30%	91.60%
EU Peace	0.70%	0.80%	1.00%	0.80%	0.40%
Rates	5.10%	5.40%	5.50%	5.70%	5.80%
Borrowing	2.70%	2.60%	2.40%	2.20%	2.10%
	100.00%	100.00%	100.00%	100.00%	100.00%

Notes:
AME is funded with UK government receipts as with UK public expenditure in general. Assigned DEL is funded by the block grant transferred to the NI Executive by the NI office. Changes to the block grant are determined by the Barnett formula.
Sources: Priorities and Budget 2006–08 Secretary of State for Northern Ireland http:// www.pfgbudgetni.gov.uk/index/priorities-documents/budget-documents.htm and through correspondence with NI Executive.

Statistical Annex: Income Tax

2004-05

| | Total Income | | | Total Income Tax | | | | |
	Number of Individuals	Mean	Median	Number of individuals	Mean	Median	Amount	Amount/Tot Spend
UK	30300	22800	16400	30300	4060	2100	123000	
England	25400	23300	16600	25400	4210	2140	107000	
Eng/UK	0.838284	1.0219	1.0122	0.838284	1.037	1.019	0.869919	
Wales	1410	19100	15000	1410	2920	1800	4110	0.40176
Wales/UK	0.046535	0.8377	0.9146	0.046535	0.719	0.8571	0.033415	
Scotland	2570	20900	16000	2570	3440	2030	8840	0.346395
Scot/UK	0.084818	0.9167	0.9756	0.084818	0.847	0.9667	0.07187	
N Ireland	746	19600	15400	746	3120	1940	2330	0.29576
NI/UK	0.02462	0.8596	0.939	0.02462	0.768	0.9238	0.018943	

Units:
Number of Individuals = thousands
Amount = millions of GBP
Mean = GBP
Median = GBP
Notes:
Wales Tot Spend = net operating cost = 10,229.990 million GBP
Scotland Tot Spend = Total Managed Expenditure = 25,520.071 million GBP
N Ireland Tot Spend = Departmental Expenditure Limit = 7,877.80 million GBP
Sources: Personal Incomes by Tax Year, HM Revenue and Customs
http://www.hmrc.gov.uk/stats/Income_distribution/menu-by-year.htm#313 tables 3.13, 3.11.

Statistical Annex: Income Tax

| | Total Income | | | 2003–04 Total Income Tax | | | | |
	Number of Individuals	Mean	Median	Number of Individuals	Mean	Median	Amount	Amount/Tot Spend
UK	28500	21900	16000	28500	3880	2050	111000	
England	23800	22400	16200	23800	4030	2090	96100	
% of UK	0.835088	1.0228	1.0125	0.835088	1.039	1.0195	0.865766	0.379837
Wales	1340	18300	14600	1340	2790	1750	3730	
% of UK	0.047018	0.8356	0.9125	0.047018	0.719	0.8537	0.033604	
Scotland	2470	20000	15500	2470	3250	1970	8050	0.340467
% of UK	0.086667	0.9132	0.9688	0.086667	0.838	0.961	0.072523	
N Ireland	701	18900	14700	701	3000	1810	2100	
% of UK	0.024596	0.863	0.9188	0.024596	0.773	0.8829	0.018919	

Units:
Number of Individuals = thousands
Amount = millions of GBP
Mean = GBP
Median = GBP
Notes:
Wales Tot Spend = net operating cost = 9,820.303 million GBP
Scotland Tot Spend = Total Managed Expenditure = 23,643.561 million GBP
N Ireland Executive data not available for 2003–04
Sources: Personal Incomes by Tax Year, HM Revenue and Customs
http://www.hmrc.gov.uk/stats/income_distribution/menu-by-year.htm#313
tables 3.13, 3.11.

Notes

1 It should be pointed out that the comparable spending aggregate across regions would be the Devolved Administrations plus the relevant local government, as each Devolved Administration assigns different responsibilities to local government and transfers monies to their local government to carry out these responsibilities.

2 Heald and Macleod (2003) report that full application of the Scottish tax varying power, three pence in the pound, was estimated by HM Treasury to be worth about 450 million pounds, or about 2.8% of an estimated 16 billion pound budget in Scotland in 1997.

3 Mick Moore (1998, p. 95); although this literature refers largely to developing nations, the general argument remains valid as these are countries where, as in the UK, most sub-sovereign governments are heavily, if not almost exclusively, dependent on revenue transfers from the central government to fund their activities.

4 It may be that accountability, and the efficient use of public funds, are greatest when a substantial proportion of total outlays are funded from own-sources since taxpayers are more likely to pay attention when they know that a significant amount of the taxes they pay go to sub-national governments, rather than just a small slice at the margin.

5 *The Economist* (3 November 2007), 'Tax and Mend', p. 16, uses this slogan as a heading for an article on taxation by the Scottish Government. Interestingly, a draft of this essay including the slogan was written prior to *The Economist* article.

6 See Gallagher and Hinze 2005, Heald and Macleod 2005.

7 There may be issues of statistical confidences over how much detail can be released publicly; nevertheless, available information should allow all governments and the interested public to engage in an informed policy debate.

8 See Gallagher and Hinze (2005) pp. 6–7 comparison of Scottish and English spending plans for the NHS.

9 See Gallagher and Hinze (2005), in particular, p. 10 and footnote 20.

10 See Heald and Macleod (2005) pp. 512–513.

11 It should be made clear that own revenue raising means the capacity of the Devolved Administration to raise taxes, and not tax assignment from the UK over which the Devolved Administration would exert no control. Tax assignment, in effect, would be a transfer from the UK government to the Devolved Administration.

12 As quoted in Jonathan Rodden (2004, p. 1). Also see related discussion following this quote in Rodden.

13 This is the characterization of the fiscal equity principle as stated in the 1982 Constitution Act of Canada, section 36(2).

14 I have argued elsewhere (Mellett 2009) that the Barnett formula should be re-formulated, guided by the following principles: fiscal equity, accountabil-

ity, transparency, and flexibility. Moreover, the block grant design should be flexible enough to accommodate changes in expenditure and revenue assignments between the UK government and the devolved governments, and to accommodate asymmetries in fiscal powers and practices between devolved governments.

References

Australian Commonwealth Government (2006), 'Australian Loan Council Arrangements', Budget 2005–06, Budget Paper number 3. http://www.budget.gov.au/2005-O6/bp3/htm1/bp3_main-l4.htm

Bell, David and Alex Christie (2002), 'A New Fiscal Settlement for Scotland', Scottish Affairs, no. 41, pp. 121–140.

British Columbia Municipal Financing Authority website http://www.mfa.bc.ca

The Economist (November 3, 2007), 'Tax and Mend', p. 16.

Gallagher, James and Daniel Hinze (2005), 'Financing Options for Devolved Government in the UK', University of Glasgow, Department of Economics, discussion paper 2005–24.

Goudie, Andrew (2002), GERS and Fiscal Autonomy, Scottish Affairs, no. 41, pp. 56–85.

Heald, David and Alasdair Macleod (2002), 'Fiscal Autonomy Under Devolution: Introduction to Symposium', Scottish Affairs no. 41, pp. 5–25.

Heald, David and Alasdair Macleod (2003), 'Revenue-raising by UK Devolved Administrations in the Context of an Expenditure-based Financing System', Regional and Federal Studies, Vol. 13, number 4, Winter 2003, pp. 67–90.

Heald, David and Alasdair Macleod (2005), 'Embeddedness of UK Devolution Finance within the Public Expenditure System', Regional Studies Vol. 39.4, June 2005, pp. 495–518.

MacLean, Ian and Allistair McMillan (2002), 'The Fiscal Crisis of the United Kingdom', Nuffield College Working Papers in Politics, 2002 W10.

Mellett, Russell (2009), 'A Principles-based Approach to the Barnett Formula', The Political Quarterly, vol. 80, no. 1 (Jan–Mar), 2009.

Moore, Mick (1998), 'Death Without Taxes' in *The Democratic Developmental State,* Mark Robinson and Gordon White eds, Oxford University Press, Oxford UK, 1998.

Rodden, Jonathon (2004), 'Achieving Fiscal Discipline in Federations: Germany and the EMU', paper presented for *Fiscal Policy in the EMU: new issues and challenges,* workshop organized by European Commission, Brussels, 12 November 2004.

QUEBEC AND CANADA: UNDERSTANDING THE FEDERAL PRINCIPLE

ALAIN-G GAGNON & RAFFAELE IACOVINO

Pre-Confederation: The Seeds of a Federal State

The British conquest of New France coincided with the Treaty of Paris, ending the Seven Years' War and severing France's association with its American colonies. This culminated in the Royal Proclamation of 1763, which gave the French-speaking inhabitants of Quebec their first civil constitution under the British crown. In this early post-conquest period, inhabitants were not consciously aware of their rights as a collective unit – indeed, their identity was largely predicated on their ties to absolutist France – and they were expected to assimilate as but another trading unit in the British Empire. Their fate was largely dictated by external events over which they had little control: the American Revolution and the persistence of Anglo-French international conflict constituted the main concerns of London. While most accounts of Canadian federalism begin with Confederation, or in some cases, with the Act of Union in 1840, this period is nevertheless pertinent to the extent that the British authorities were faced with inhabitants who, collectively, were not loyal to the crown, had to face the knowledge that they were formally cut off from France, and were made aware of public declarations by British governors that assimilation was the preferred policy course. Although the Conquest did not result in an indigenous nationalist movement, the early French-speaking *Canadiens* nevertheless feared the loss of their culture and traditions (perhaps most importantly, at the time, their Catholic faith), their institutions, and their laws. The early foundation of a distinct cultural collective sense of belonging was paradoxically the result of a conquest by a foreign military power. Perhaps of utmost importance is that the British authorities themselves defined the new subjects as a 'separate race' and tailored the Royal Proclamation to address this particular sociological reality.

The Royal Proclamation formally instituted British law. The *Canadiens* had no political rights – indeed, they could not hold official positions or be publicly employed unless they denounced Catholicism – and the English made it clear that a bishop would no longer be appointed by the pope. A House of Assembly was proposed, yet it was exclusive to English merchants. The proclamation also sought to replace civil law with English common law and to disband the seigneurial system. The intentions of the British authorities were to assimilate these adopted inhabitants as soon as possible. Yet the reality on the ground was interpreted much differently by the colony's first governor, General Murray, who learned soon after the Royal Proclamation came into effect in August 1764 that this group of subjects would not be easily assimilated, and did not enforce many of the act's provisions. He allowed the *Canadiens* to serve on the King's Bench and as lawyers in the lower courts. Moreover, he believed that a House of Assembly with no representation for the overwhelming majority of inhabitants would be an unworkable arrangement, so it was never actually adopted. Murray also reinstituted the seigneurial system and allowed the *Canadiens* to continue practising the Catholic faith, going as far as to endorse the first bishop under British rule, Jean-Olivier Briand.[1]

In 1774, the Quebec Act was adopted to redress the failed policy of assimilation of the Royal Proclamation. Indeed, many of the provisions in this policy shift by the British authorities simply formalized what Governor Murray had already practised. Murray's disdain for the crumbling of the *ancien régime* in the American colonies is well documented, and his vision of a distinct social and political order for the *Canadiens* was inherently conservative, preferring to restore the quasi-feudal privileges of the church and seigneurs. The Quebec Act thus opted for a legislative council, to be appointed by London, as opposed to a House of Assembly. According to A. L. Burt, the seigneurial system had already been re-established as early as 1771, and the act simply formalized this fact in law.[2] The act also acknowledged the legitimacy of the Catholic Church, yet Bishop Briand had been installed as early as 1766, along with the tithe. Moreover, Murray had already allowed for the application of French laws in lower courts, the use of French when litigants were French-speaking, and permitted *Canadien* lawyers and juries. The act essentially affirmed the pre-eminent status of aristocracy and clergy, denied popular government, and restored the body of civil law that had been in use prior to the Royal Proclamation, although clear demarcation lines between the application of common and civil law remains a debate among historians.[3]

For Alain-G. Gagnon and Luc Turgeon, the primary significance of the act is that it constituted the first imperial statute to establish a constitution for a British colony,[4] which institutionalized Quebec's distinctiveness and responded to the demands of the French elite regardless of whether it was motivated by events surrounding the American Revolution or by altruistic considerations.[5] Even under the force of imperial dictates, sociological variables could not be undone in the colony. Whether or not one ascribes the birth of a national consciousness to this event is not the salient issue. Civil society was allowed some continuity; the customs and habits of a minority group were permitted to persist. Historian Maurice Séguin explains:

> Whether they were seigneurs or men of the legal profession, the repeal of the Royal Proclamation and later the Quebec Act of 1774 provided Canadian leaders with a Constitutional text, a 'grand charter' that they later exploited to the benefit of the French-Canadian collectivity. The Quebec Act legalized survival. It encouraged those Canadians to continue to consider themselves as a people of the colony.[6]

Indeed, James Tully contends that this nascent constitution was part of a broader normative philosophy of the Whigs that rested on the continuity associated with the ancient constitution, in which fundamental laws that were custom-based could not simply be wiped away by a conquering force without negating the liberty of the people.[7]

Brian Young disputes the tendency of historians to view the act as the founding moment of a French-Canadian national identity: its recognition, affirmation, and legitimacy. Indeed, Young notes that mainstream history in Canada has tended to appropriate the act as an early indication of a tolerant pan-Canadian nation. For Young, the Quebec Act institutionalized an early variant of pluralism which sanctioned the co-existence of distinct social and legal traditions, not the reimposition of an organic order that can be somehow conceptualized by employing secular Jacobin conceptions about national belonging and equality.[8] Indeed, according to Jean-Pierre Wallot, the Quebec Act did not constitute a radical shift in approaches by Great Britain.[9] Rather, it stemmed from aristocratic conceptions that were well anchored in British tradition. Wallot even claims that the British would have probably preferred to institute such constitutions in its other North American colonies if it was possible. For this historian, the contemporary idea that the act was the first to recognize the distinct status of Quebec is misleading, since it was not based on recognition of distinct status as though it was an earned moral imperative. Rather, Quebec was distinct because it was the only colony where circumstances allowed the British to reimpose the much preferred order of the *ancien régime*. Wallot gives the final word to Hilda Neatby:

> If...the Act is to be taken with all its accompanying instructions, it cannot possibly be called 'liberal' from any modern viewpoint. If the instructions are forgotten and the Act stands alone, it is a Charter for French-Canadians...If the instructions are emphasized, then the concessions to Canadians become a simple protection to property and custom, and in no sense a recognition of...'nation'...In short, if the Act and all the instructions are read together and thought of as equally expressing the policy of the ministry, that policy can be seen only as one of gentle but steady and determined Anglicization.[10]

Whatever dualism existed after 1774 was purely cultural and inherently conservative, and without significant political repercussions that can be appropriated for proof of early signs of contemporary notions of national political recognition. This was not a national movement but a rejection of the burgeoning idea of the nation altogether.

It was the Constitution Act of 1791 that formally connected the cultural duality of the colony with territorially-based quasi-representative institutions. At the request of some 10,000 British colonists who sought to separate from 150,000 *Canadiens*, as well as Liberal professionals who had begun to assert themselves as leaders among the *Canadiens*, London divided the colony into Upper and Lower Canada, consisting of two parliaments but one appointed governor. The implication of the act, according to historian George Stanley, was 'to give renewed vigour to the idea of French Canadian separateness. It provided the French fact with a geographical as well as a political buttress.'[11] By the early 1800s a full-fledged nationalist movement developed among French Canadians. Many liberal professionals demanded an end to the political pre-eminence of

Anglo-dominated executive bodies. This movement sought a shift of power to Lower Canada's representative institutions and, generally, greater autonomy from London. Similar uprisings in Upper Canada were quite distinct,[12] and by the time armed rebellion erupted in 1837, they functioned separately, under two different leaders, Louis-Joseph Papineau and William Lyon Mackenzie. Cultural dualism, coupled with distinct territory and institutions, was beginning to take shape in the colony.

The defeat of the rebellions resulted in a concession that, a decade later, granted responsible government, along with the recommendation that the two colonies be merged into a United Canada. Lord Durham, asked to provide an assessment of the unrest in the colonies, believed the ultimate resolution to the conflict was to rid the colony of cultural dualism and to assimilate French Canadians. Flowing from liberal traditions at the time, Durham believed that 'undoing the backwardness' of the French Canadians was necessary for their own good. In order to accomplish this, he argued that a legislative union with an ever-increasing majority of English colonists, loyal to the crown, would eventually coerce French Canadians into abandoning any notion of a separate nationality.[13] The Act of Union of 1840 united Upper and Lower Canada, renaming the territories Canada West and Canada East. The language of the new legislature was to be exclusively English, and both provinces were allotted an equal number of seats, ensuring that the English majority would prevail. While the intention was to assimilate the French, the new arrangement paradoxically allowed French blocs in the legislature to protect their interests in the face of the split English majority, with English Reformers[14] from Canada West often aligned with the bloc from Canada East. Conventions thus began to develop around a 'double majority,' in which any proposal that affected one language group could not be adopted without the majority consent of that bloc.

[...]

Competing Federal Visions

The founding moments of the Canadian federal system have not been interpreted with unanimity. Beyond the rough guide provided by the division of powers, the intentions of the framers continue to inform debates about the principles upon which federalism was adopted. Moreover, subsequent developments have continued to exhibit an uneasy sense of ambiguity about the grand ideas that legitimate Canadian federalism, as evident in the ongoing tensions between identity claimants. In the end, federalism is impossible to evaluate outside of specific political contexts. In the United States and Germany, for example, federalism was adopted to limit the excesses of executive power, as a device that was to promote the liberty of citizens, not as a means by which to accommodate diversity. Franz Neumann went as far as to conclude that evaluating federal systems in general is futile: federalism could be good, bad or indifferent depending on particular circumstances and the positions of key participants.[15] Several interpretations of federalism have emerged in the course of Canada's history.[16]

[...]

Visions of decentralization I: the compact theory

This view flows from a classical theory of federalism and in its basic formulation establishes that Canada is a creation of the provinces. Theoretically, it implied that each member state was sovereign in its area of jurisdiction. The very existence of a federal regime was deemed to be the result of a contract between pre-existing states. This conception of federalism defines allegiance along provincial lines – that is, the first order of representation for citizens are provincial governments.

[...]

Visions of decentralization II: intrastate federalism

Those seeking to accommodate the diversity of provincial interests without defining Canadian federalism as a compact between two founding peoples, or as a political community marked by intergovernmental bargaining espoused a vision that would reform central institutions. In effect, calls for intrastate federalism, particularly in force in the 1970s, were meant to represent more adequately provincial concerns at the federal level without conceiving of the polity as a loose confederation of provincial governments at the expense of a national community. Constant federal-provincial conflict, in this view, would be resolved if provincial governments were equally represented at the centre, in a permanent institutional framework that would allow provincial concerns to be expressed without recourse to executive-level bargaining between the orders of government. Territorial interests would not have to be invested solely in provincial governments.

[...]

The dualist vision of Canada has largely been driven by Quebec. Aboriginals, however, have made the basic claim that binationalism in Canada is sociologically inaccurate and has detracted attention away from the notion that they possess an inherent right to self-government. In what would constitute a third order of government in Canada, the asymmetry sought by Aboriginals challenges the very conception that Canadian federalism is based solely on a division of powers between the federal Parliament and the provincial legislatures. As such, the discourse of federalism that has provided the framework for conceptions of binationalism must be revisited to accommodate new institutions, a new sharing of powers, and a corresponding fiscal formula. Although the details of future relations remain unclear, since the present constitution merely makes reference to the inherent right of self-government for First Nations, the salient starting point for Aboriginal groups is clear: the federal government must terminate its paternalistic relationship with Aboriginal peoples and begin the long road to accommodation on a nation-to-nation basis. Such groups seek a partnership that would, at a minimum, recognize that they possess sovereignty over the territories and resources upon which they depend.[17]

[...]

Centralizing visions I: the nationalizing conception of the founders

[...] According to Roger Gibbins, the recurring theme in the construction of Canada's founding principles as seen from the perspective of the central government is articulating the need for a single political community, one that is more than instrumental, through the institution of federalism. Institutionalist scholars fail to see the paradox of such an approach – and indeed, the centralizing visions of Canadian federalism have in many ways reflected a desire for national integration as opposed to federalism in its classic sense. For Gibbins, the compact theory of premiers and the dualist approach of Quebec make it difficult to even talk of a Canadian community or nation, much less base the country's self-understanding on such principles.[18] The common element of the decentralized visions for Canadian federalism outlined above is, in many respects, that they are reactions to a competing vision of federalism that seeks to craft a larger political identity in a nationalizing project. Interpretations of such intentions for the future of the Canadian political community also date back to its founding debates.
  [...]

Centralizing visions II: the Trudeau era, individual rights, and national unity

Upon assuming leadership of the Liberal party in 1968, Pierre Elliott Trudeau sought to settle the question of splintered loyalties in Canada once and for all by introducing a model of national integration that sought to transcend local allegiances as the basis for citizenship. Trudeau's vision of federalism stemmed in part from his political philosophy, which rejected what he perceived as a closed and inward-looking nationalism in Quebec in favour of a uniform liberal conception of the state resting on his notion of a 'just society,' where citizenship implied equal rights across Canada, provincial equality and institutional bilingualism. Indeed, Trudeau's ascendance in Ottawa reflected a desire to settle the mounting state-led nationalism in Quebec, which culminated in the election of the secessionist Parti Québécois in 1976. By far the most powerful centralist vision ever articulated in Canada, Trudeau's mark on federalism remains embedded to this day. While Trudeau's political philosophy favoured universalism over particularism and reason over what he termed 'emotive' sentiments of belonging, he nevertheless recognized the power of state-led pan-Canadian nationalism in offsetting what he considered to be backward and retrograde nationalist movement for secession in Quebec.
  [...]
Trudeau's vision has been somewhat consolidated in a view of Canada that emphasizes the primacy of individual rights. Canadian federalism today contains elements of non-territorial political identity that is the direct result of Trudeau's centralizing initiatives. This represents a watershed in Canadian federalism, with the polity increasingly characterized by groups and individuals making rights-claims to a central institution, in direct contrast to the traditional dualist and provincialist visions outlined above and seen to constitute the basic foundations

of the original compromise. The legacy of the Charter is that the future reshaping of Canadian federalism must contend with the entrenched notion that any provision threatening 'equal rights' across Canada is an affront to its self-understanding as a political community. An amending formula that alienates Quebec, the drafting of the Meech Lake and Charlottetown accords because of perceived injustices associated with special status for Quebec, the drafting of the Calgary Declaration which emphasized an equality of provinces doctrine, the signing of the SUFA without blinking an eye at Quebec's refusal to consent, and the popular imposition of the Clarity Act among Canadians outside Quebec, all indicate the continuing force of Trudeau's vision in Canada.

Notes

1 For a useful analysis of the role of General Murray in consolidating the distinct collective consciousness of the *Canadiens,* see Christian Dufour, *A Canadian Challenge* (Lantzville and Halifax: Oolichan Books and the Institute for Research on Public Policy, 1990).

2 Alfred LeRoy Burt, *The Old Province of Quebec* (Toronto: Ryerson Press, 1933), p. 186.

3 See John Bierley, 'The Co-existence of Legal Systems in Quebec: "Free and Common Socage" in Canada's pays de droit civil,' *Cahiers de droit* 20 (1979), p. 280.

4 See Alain-G. Gagnon and Luc Turgeon, 'Managing Diversity in Eighteenth and Nineteenth Century Canada: Quebec's Constitutional Development in Light of the Scottish Experience,' *Journal of Commonwealth and Comparative Politics* 41, no. 1 (March 2003), pp. 1–23.

5 For an exposition of this debate, see Philip Lawson, *The Imperial Challenge: Quebec and Britain in the Age of the American Revolution* (Montreal and Kingston: McGill-Queen's University Press, 1999).

6 Maurice Séguin, *Une Histoire du Québec* (Montreal: Guérin, 1995), p. 36.

7 James Tully, *Strange Multiplicity: Constitutionalism in an Age of Diversity* (Cambridge: Cambridge University Press, 1994), pp. 145–51. For more on the Whig philosophy of the ancient constitution, see John Pocock, *The Ancient Constitution and the Feudal Law: A Study of English Historical Thought in the Seventeenth Century* (Cambridge: Cambridge University Press, 1987).

8 Brian Young, 'Everyman's Trope: The Quebec Act of 1774,' in *Cahiers du PEQ,* no. 21, December 2001 (Quebec Studies Program, McGill University).

9 Jean-Pierre Wallot, 'L'Acte de Québec, ses causes, sa nature et l'Ancien Régime,' in ibid.

10 Hilda Neatby, *Quebec: The Revolutionary Age, 1760–1791* (Toronto: McClelland and Stewart, 1966), quoted in Wallot, 'L'Acte de Québec,' p. 7.

11 George F.C. Stanley, 'Act or Pact: Another Look at Confederation'; Proceedings of the Canadian Historical Association, 1956, p. 5; quoted in Kenneth

McRoberts, *Misconceiving Canada: The Struggle for National Unity* (Don Mills: Oxford University Press, 1997), p. 5.

12 McRoberts, ibid.

13 See William Ormsby, *The Emergence of the Federal Concept in Canada, 1839–1845* (Toronto: University of Toronto Press, 1969). For more on Lord Durham's justification for a legislative union, see Ged Martin, *Britain and the Origins of Canadian Confederation, 1837–67* (Vancouver: University of British Columbia Press, 1995).

14 Led by Robert Baldwin, the Reformers defected from a cohesive English bloc over the issue of responsible government, which would be eventually inaugurated in 1849.

15 Franz Neumann, 'On the Theory of the Federal State,' in *The Democratic and the Authoritarian State* (Glencoe: Free Press, 1957).

16 For earlier assessments of distinct visions of the federal principle in Canada, particularly in the period preceding patriation in 1982, see Mallory, 'The Five Faces of Canadian Federalism'; Black, *Divided Loyalties;* and Garth Stevenson; *Unfulfilled Union: Canadian Federalism and National Unity,* rev. ed. (Toronto: Gage, 1982).

17 For an excellent overview of Aboriginal peoples' relationship to the federal system, see Frances Abele and Michael J. Prince, 'Aboriginal Governance and Canadian Federalism: A To-Do List for Canada,' in Rocher and Smith, eds., *New Trends in Canadian Federalism*, pp. 135–61.

18 Gibbins, 'The Interplay of Political Institutions and Political Communities,' in David P. Shugarman and Reg Whitaker, eds., *Federalism and Political Community* (Peterborough: Broadview Press, 1989), pp. 423–38.

GALICIA: ECONOMIC BACKWARDNESS AND NATIONALIST REVIVAL[1]

RAMÓN MÁIZ

'Far and wide our giant voice proclaims the redemption of the beautiful nation of Breogán.'

Galician National Anthem (1890)

I. The Roots of a Political Deficit: Ethnic and Social Pre-conditions

From an ethno-cultural perspective, Galicia is a relatively homogeneous, differentiated territory that coincides in general terms with the area of a specific language, Galician. This language is spoken and understood by almost the entire population, 90% and 96%, respectively, much higher figures than for other Spanish nationalities, the Basque language in the Basque Country or even Catalonian in Catalonia (although the latter has a higher number of people that can read and write the vernacular: 49% of the population in Catalonia versus 35% in Galicia)[2]. Historical imposition of Castilian as the official language, first during the 17th century Absolute Monarchy and again under the liberal Spanish State in the 19th century, reduced Galician to the status of a lower-class colloquial language. This was reinforced by the historical difficulties of the nation-building process in Spain, the economic backwardness of Galicia and its late de-ruralization. In spite of all this, the language has maintained very high levels of usage among the non-urban majority and recently among the urbanized Galician population.

This linguistic ethnic distinctiveness is additionally strengthened by the cultural distinctiveness of Galicia, which extends to mores, private law, customs, family structures and productive strategies[3]. In any case this ethnic and cultural difference always was compatible with an overlapping Spanish/Galician collective identity, slightly different from the Catalonia case and strongly different from the Basque country case (see table 2). Historical backwardness along with late modernization and urbanization processes meant that an agrarian society persisted until recently, with over 70% of the active population working in the primary sector until the mid-20th century (specifically the 1960s); it has now decreased to 35%. This ethnic distinctiveness gave rise to a solid differential base within Spain, but at the same time had to face a peculiar *political-institutional deficit*. In stark contrast with the Basque Country and Catalonia, the early historical inclusion of Galicia in centralized territorial monarchies – the Kingdom of Leon (10th–13th century) and the Crown of Castile (13th–16th century), and the centralist Spanish State of the 19th century – deprived Galicia ethno-culturally of any residual institutions harkening back to a prior autonomy or independence and a historical memory of self-government that might be activated to serve as the basis for a symbolic remembrance of Loss and internal community solidarity. In the absence of anything like the Basque *fueros* or the Catalonian *Generalitat*, with their decisive symbolic capital and institutionally generated political interests, Manuel Murguía rather unconvincingly proposed as a Galician institution for self-government the example of the *Junta* of the Kingdom of Galicia, a 'representative' assembly from the times of the urban oligarchies during the *ancien régime*. This gave way to consideration of the Roman province of *Gallaecia*, as well as the 6th century Suevi 'kingdom', as material for spinning a mythical discourse of Galician nationalism in the 19th century, even though these myths were already politically de-activated due to their distance in time and their territorial disparity[4].

Yet it is in the *social pre-conditions* for Galician nationalism that a matrix of potential political deficits arise. It is of primary interest to note not only the eminently rural character of the Galician population due to late modernization, but also a series of additional elements in the process of nation building. Foremost were the *foros*, the land ownership regime that preserved a pre-capitalist land rent system until 1926. In conjunction with the socio-political hegemony of the agrarian aristocrats (*fidalguía*), this fostered stagnation in agricultural production, deficient incorporation into the markets and the continuance of a peasant subsistence economy[5]. *Minifundismo*, the dividing of arable land into ever smaller, individually inherited plots, led to a dispersion of the population into small, isolated nuclei. Finally, an early crisis affected one of the potentially modernizing elements of the Galician economy: the domestically-based proto-industry of textile agriculture[6]. Slow incorporation into the market, a scattered population, a self-consumption economy and other factors reinforced chronic external and even internal communication deficiencies, isolating parishes and generally de-structuring the territory. This created strong localism, a closed world of tiny, isolated villages centred on the ecclesiastical institution and subsistence farming, along with a very low index of social mobility and communication. The virtual absence of networks of contact beyond the local sphere[7] hindered the construction of any global collective identity. This localism is manifest, for example, in the historical lack of a traditional collective myth or any religious symbol shared by all Galicians as a marker of community identity or meaning.

During the entire 19th century and much of the 20th century, there was no clear hegemonic centre of urban development and exchange centralization. The scant weight of urban centres reinforced territorial de-structuring and localist confrontations; it also facilitated church control at the parish level and an endemic form of political clientelism known as '*caciquismo*'. In contrast with Catalonia and the Basque Country, during the social formation of Spanish capitalism in the 19th century Galicia received no immigrant influx, which is a decisive factor in creating identities by exploiting differences based on confrontational 'us-them' stereotypes. Instead, due to its weak economic development, Galicia suffered very high rates of emigration throughout the 19th and much of the 20th century. Between 1860 and 1960 Galicia lost over one million inhabitants[8]. The qualitative dimension of the phenomenon is as significant as the quantitative, as it resulted in the loss of the youngest and most active components of the population, a fostering of fatalism and individualist behaviour, and a free-rider mentality regarding internal collective mobilization.

The deepest, most substantive and lasting contributions to the construction of an ideological space – at first cultural but ultimately political and nationalist – took place in the literary field. A fact that is commonly agreed upon by those who study nationalism is that the intelligentsia, through the mythical-aesthetic founding of national distinctiveness, can provide the initial definition of the meaning of the national code. In Galicia a common identity of origin and basic communitarian solidarity were established through 're-discovering' the bases of the 'us-them' distinction: the language, literature, folklore and customs of the land[9]. The 'recovery' of the Galician language in written form in conjunction with an over-emphasis on *Galego* as the central distinguishing feature transformed it into the essential symbol of the Galician homeland. The prominent literary figures of Rosalía de Castro and Eduardo Pondal during the *rexurdimento*, the Galician renaissance, took the language to new heights. It provided the maximum mythical-symbolical effect and aesthetically framed social evidence of a Galician nation. Pondal penned the poem that became the Galician anthem while Rosalía stigmatized Castile as the 'other', the antithesis of Galicia, and rhetorically identified the peasantry as the immortal guardian of the essences of the homeland, distilled in the Galician language[10].

The evolution of literary jousting, known as the 'Floral Games', demonstrated the growing political relevance of Galicianist literary discourse. After the Games of 1871, and especially after those of 1884 in Pontevedra, the expressive potential of the Galician language became patent as a marker of a historically intact national identity. This link between Galicianist culture and politics, highlighted particularly in the Games of 1891, involved important figures such as Alfredo Brañas and Manuel Murguía, who used the Irish case ('Like in Ireland, like in Ireland') as a model to openly address the defence of Galicia as an 'oppressed nationality' in political terms. As a result, any attempt at gallego literary expression outside the political-discursive conditions of emergent Galicianism became completely futile.

Murguía, one of the leaders of the *regionalist* movement that developed in Galicia between 1886 and 1907, formulated the central interpretative frame for Galician nationalism and established the founding myths of the national community. In various publications that began in 1865 with the first volume of his monumental *Historia de Galicia*, this author carried out a detailed discursive construction of Galicia as a *Nation* through an original synthesis of historical and organic elements (race, language, history...) in conjunction with liberal voluntarist concepts rooted explicitly in the works of Mancini. This liberal political position was in peculiar contrast with the formulations of the other peripheral nationalisms in 19th century Spain. In the Basque Country, Sabino Arana y Goiri built upon traditionalist, xenophobic and anti-democratic elements that entirely eliminated any liberal perspective. In Catalonia, a lesser degree of emphasis on ethnicity still ultimately eroded the liberal perspective of Enric Prat de la Riba.

2. The Break with the XIX Century Tradition and Radical Anti-colonialism: Galician Nationalism under the Franco Dictatorship (1939–1975)

The Franco era created a radical break in the incipient social support for Galician nationalism of the Republican period and in the attempts to consolidate a stable, territorially-based organization. Traumatically, it also disrupted in its initial phases the settling of a balanced interpretative frame for inclusion and intensity. Unlike Catalonia and the Basque Country, any substantive resistance of the nationalist movement was undermined by the interrelated absence of any Galicianist political sub-culture, what Scott referred to as a hidden transcript, intertwined into the family or ecclesiastical spheres. In Galicia a dramatic generational fracture was created: historical memory and the organizational and ideological tradition of the movement were lost, relegated to marginal circles of the cultural realm.

Francoist repression was purposefully selective: it respected the conservative *Dereita Galeguista* leaders and was even supported by its most extreme voice, Vicente Risco; many other voices simply kept silent regarding the dictatorship.

In contrast, progressive leaders were persecuted: several were murdered in 1936 and the rest fled into exile. Nationalism then disappeared within Galicia and was reduced to groups of political refugees with limited activity in South America; the *Consello de Galiza* was established in Argentina in 1944 as a coordinating organism for the scattered Galicianist members. In 1946, the prominent nationalist leader Castelao was appointed to the Spanish Republican government in exile, led by Giral. But by 1950 nationalism in exile had become quite disconnected from the Spanish and Galician reality, the political events in Spain, and even from the Republican government in exile. It gradually adopted maximalist positions based on out-of-touch analyses, creating an unspoken break with the nationalists in Galicia, a break that later became obvious[11].

Nationalists in Galicia abandoned the sphere of politics, dissolved the *Partido Galeguista* (PG) and, under the guidance of Ramon Piñeiro, pragmatically focused on the cultural sphere in order to recover historical memory and transmit the Galicianist ideological capital to the next generations. They founded the Galaxia publishing house in 1950, bringing together the Republican generation (Pedrayo, Cuevillas, Cabanillas) with that of the Civil War (Piñeiro, Blázquez, del Riego). Difficulties avoiding censorship were constant until the end of the 1950s, when a certain degree of openness made possible the launching of the *Revista de Economía de Galicia* (1958) and *Grial* (1962). Addressing cultural, economic, social and historical matters, these periodicals recovered the use of written Galician, in an uphill effort to make the historical memory of Galicianism contemporary and involve the next generation of intellectuals and university students in the cause of nationalism. The cultural effort was seen as a substitute, not a supplement, for any sort of political re-organization of Galician nationalism. The idea of building a nationalist party was abandoned along with self-identification as a 'nationalism'. By weakening the political-organizational dimension of the movement, they sought to 'galicianize' society in such a way that eventually all political parties would assume a common Galicianist heritage, seen through their various particular ideological approaches.

From the 1960s on, deep transformations slowly but irreversibly took place in Galician economy and society, due to fundamental changes in the Spanish economy that altered the traditional social conditions in which Galician nationalism would develop. Two processes are very relevant: the increasing industrialization of the Atlantic coast of Galicia accompanied by the emergence of a substantive working class, and the massive increase in migration, particularly towards Europe, which in turn meant the aging of the peasant population. After 1960 Galicia joined the market economy fully, with a strong increase in naval construction in Vigo and Ferrol that went from 50,000 metric tons gross register weight in 1960 to 868,000 in 1975, with more than 25,000 stable jobs in the sector. In addition, various companies entered Galicia seeking to develop key industries for procuring raw materials, maritime access and diverse productive facilities involving aluminium, automobiles, refineries, etc. However, some of them completed the productive cycles outside Galicia, and did not generate enough jobs to counter-balance migration, which between 1951 and 1970 totalled 500,000 persons[12]. After 1960 Galician agriculture experienced an accelerated process of mercantilization, gradually losing its subsistence nature. Even so, in 1973 agriculture continued to occupy 52% of the active population, while 26% worked in services and only 21% in industry.

3. From Anti-Spanish Radicalism to a Centre-left 'Common Project': Galician Nationalism during the Political Transition and Consolidation of Democracy (1978–2005)

Galicia in the 1970s was characterized by decisive economic and social changes, a new constitutional and regional autonomy framework and discontinuity with the Galicianist tradition, which during the final Franco years defined Galician nationalism in radical and extreme left terms. Against this backdrop, Galician nationalism entered an entirely new scenario of democracy, with attempts to extend political evidence of a Galician nation throughout the population. The initial electoral results (see graph) revealed a Galician political arena with the following basic features, which were particularly evident in the critical general elections of 1982[13]:

• weak political participation, seen in the high levels of non-voting; the provinces of Lugo and Ourense had the lowest electoral participation in all of Spain.
• moderate pluralism and little ideological distance between the most important parties, along with a clear conservative slant in the electorate, as seen in the patent, stable and permanent electoral hegemony of the centre right (UCD, AP, PP); the political weight of the main, centre-right state-wide parties was much higher in Galicia than in Catalonia and the Basque Country.
• weak impact of nationalist segmentation with a very weak electoral presence of Galician nationalism in an arena dominated by state-wide parties.

The Galician political panorama demonstrated clear differences with the Catalonian and Basque situations, and even with the Spanish political arena: a) the socialist party PSOE did not become the main political force; b) the *Unión del Centro Democrático* party (UCD) did not lose as much support as in other parts of Spain; c) nationalists' results did not improve as they had in Catalonia and the Basque Country; d) in spite of the increase in participation, non-voting continued to characterize the Galician panorama; and e) the conservative *Alianza Popular* (AP) became the clear leading political force.

Between 1977 and 1984, the small sphere of nationalist electoral representation (see table 1) was characterized by: a) a diverse and broad nationalist offer; b) constant crisis and re-articulation of the nationalist parties; c) hegemonic presence of the extreme left position against autonomy; d) disaggregation and erosion of nationalist party members into Spanish state-wide parties; and e) intense organizational effort and strong activism that did not translate into electoral results, in spite of a growing political presence in areas of culture, communications and social conflicts.

Table 1 Galicia Regional Elections 1981–2005

Parties	1981		1985		1989		1993		1997		2001		2005	
	% Votes	Seats	% Votes	Seats	% Votes	Seats	% Votes	Seats	% Votes	Seats	% Votes	Seats	% Votes	Seats
AP/CD/PP	30.52	26	41.14	34	44.20	38	52.62	43	52.88	42	52.51	41	45.20	37
PSG-PSOE	19.62	16	28.84	22	32.81	28	23.89	19	19.72	15	22.20	17	33.20	25
BNG			4.30	1	8.01	5	18.55	13	25.11	18	22.97	17	18.70	13

Source: Author's Own.

Deep social and political changes, the late re-organization of the *Partido Gale-guista* (PG) after 1977, the hegemony of the *Unión do Pobo Galego* (UPG) over all nationalist discourse, and chronically weak social support for a centre-right nationalism made it impossible to capitalize on historical memory and the symbolic legitimacy of the earlier Republican period. It was not even possible to amalgamate in the mid-1970s the political personalities who had represented that lost tradition. The dis-articulation of the Galicianist elite and the culturalist strategy led several Galicianist political and cultural figures into the *Partido Socialista Obrero Español* (PSOE).

The PG was unable to present itself in the democratic elections of 1977, but managed to join a coalition (*Unidade Galega*) for the 1979 elections, which gave it the brief illusion of presence. The 1981 PG Convention demonstrated the party's incapacity to incorporate historic Galicianist elites and produced definitive public clashes between some of its most representative figures, ultimately undermining its future as a political force. Appearing again as a single party in the 1981 elections, the PG met with serious failure (3.2% of the votes), becoming the only major Galician party with no parliamentary presence. This led to internal crisis, with defecting members and de-mobilization, to the point that it could not enter the general elections of 1982. From then on, the PG would be composed of a miniscule group of nationalists with very little presence in the Galician political scenario. As the PG disappeared from the political arena, some of its members joined a new political project, *Coalición Galega*. This moderately nationalist centre-right party, composed also of ex-members of the Galician branch of the UCD, focused on working the existing clientelistic voting networks, particularly in rural areas.

The eminently centrist Galician electorate with a very solid Spanish/Galician overlapping collective identity (see table 2), faced a radical nationalism (leftist and anti-Spain) very far from its moderate positions. The interpretative frame for nationalism now ran along far-left lines and opposed autonomy; it was de-aligned with the voters and had a marginal presence for several years. This was exacerbated by constant changes in party compositions and re-structuring of nationalist political forces, which were plagued by schisms and expulsions due to intense, sectarian, vanguardist and exclusivist perspectives within organizations dominated by 'democratic centralism'. Of the nationalist political parties, only the UPG was present at all electoral moments, incorporating other parties under broader and varying labels such as the *Bloque Nacional Popular Galego* (composed of UPG and ANPG) and the *Bloque Nacionalista Galego* (BNG).

In the general elections of 1996, the nationalist political sphere consolidated around the BNG, which presented itself to the electorate as the only truly nationalist force. Its sole competitor was the smaller and weaker *Esquerda Unida-Esquerda Galega*. This time, however, there was continuity from the prior period, both in the electoral results and in the substantive changes that had already taken place in the autonomic elections of 1993 (see table 1), the true turning point.

A new framing strategy was particularly evident in the moderate BNG programme and discourse during the 1996 electoral campaign. There were no demands for self-determination or sovereignty and no criticism of regional autonomy or the Spanish Constitution, as there had been in the old interpretative frame of Galician nationalist versus Spanish minded politicians (and people). Instead, the regional autonomy was accepted as 'reasonable' and a catch-all message sought votes from a broad spectrum of the population, spanning traditional radical nationalism to centre nationalists who lacked a political party and even PSOE voters that felt disconnected from their party. This had to do with the political baggage of years of PSOE government, with internal PSOE crises and especially with the lack of an autonomous programme designed by the *Partido Socialista de Galcia-PSOE*. Under the new 'common project' framing strategy, the BNG programme was adapted to the Galicia/Spanish overlapping identities (see table 2) and focused on a generic 'defence of Galicia's productive sectors', the 'deepening of the Galician self government' and acting as the 'voice of Galicia in Madrid'. The electoral outcome of these strategic changes of discourse, pro-

Table 2 National Identities in Comparative Perspective

Catalonia

	2001	*2002*	*2003*	*2004*	*2005*
Only Spanish	10.5	11.5	8.5	12.6	8.0
More Spanish than Catalan	11.4	7.8	4.1	6.1	9.0
As Spanish as Catalan	44.4	42.2	40.9	38.3	40.0
More Catalan than Spanish	18.7	22.9	27.2	25.8	25.0
Only Catalan	13.5	13.1	16.4	14.7	12.0
NK/NA	1.4	2.6	2.8	2.6	7.0
Total (n)	1600	1200	1200	1200	1200

Basque Country

	2001	*2002*	*2003*	*2004*	*2005*
Only Spanish	3.6	4.7	5.5	5.8	2.8
More Spanish than Basque	6.3	6.4	5.7	5.8	5.6
As Spanish as Basque	36.8	36.0	34.5	32.4	32.5
More Basque than Spanish	27.4	19.3	23.4	18.7	22.3
Only Basque	19.8	25.2	27.1	33.4	32.2
NK/NA	6.1	8.4	3.8	3.9	4.7
Total (n)	1200	1200	1200	1200	1200

Galicia

	2001	*2002*	*2003*	*2004*	*2005*
Only Spanish	4.9	3.8	3.2	3.9	3.8
More Spanish than Galician	4.5	5.8	6.3	4.3	3.3
As Spanish as Galician	59.7	58.0	57.6	64.6	65.8
More Galician than Spanish	20.5	23.4	27.1	22.2	20.9
Only Galician	6.5	6.9	4.8	3.8	5.3
NK/NA	3.9	2.2	1.0	1.2	0.8
Total (n)	2400	1200	1200	1200	1200

Source: Barómetro Político Gallego and Opa 2006.

gramme, allies and repertoire of mobilization was very positive: a substantive increase in votes (22% in 2001 and 19% in 2005 regional elections, see table 1) and a clear consolidation of the central position in the Galician party system that the BNG had gained from 1993 onwards[14]. Moreover, after the 2005 regional elections the BNG finally reached the autonomous government through a coalition with the Socialist party (PSdG-PSOE), once previously and successfully experimented at the local level in Galician councils. A very long road from the marginal opposition to the political responsibilities at the Xunta de Galicia was so accomplished.

In sum, the current resolution of the traditional political deficit of Galician nationalism and the hegemony of the BNG are explained by several factors:

- A set of collective Galician interests, that were differentiated from the EU and the Spanish state (Madrid), and became evident due to economic and social changes, uneven modernization and urbanization, along with crises in the industrial, agricultural and fishing sectors due to the EU, re-structuring, etc.
- Favourable modification of the political opportunity structure – the federalization of the Spanish state of the autonomies – with its formal opening and access possibilities, and a process of institutional nationalization in the political, economic and cultural spheres due to political autonomy (regional government and parliament).
- Newly de-aligned electoral segments that were distanced from their former political loyalties (PSOE, PP). New allies in the Spanish party system: the coalition GALEUSCAT with PNV (Basque country) and CiU (Catalonia) afforded the BNG increased visibility and a increasing image of moderation and centrism.
- Successful mobilization of organizational (the flexible and plural format of the movement) and interpretative resources (a radical change in discourse strategies, cantering the message now far away from the Marxist-Leninist vocabulary and radical nationalism of the seventies). The progressive electoral coordination of constituencies (and militancy) of the previous fragmented nationalist parties.
- A profound transformation of the framing strategy to become more inclusive and less sectarian ('common project', 'alternative of government', 'centring the country' etc.)

Notes

1 This study is part of a broader research project on *Dimensions of Collective Identity in Galicia*, directed by the author and financed by the *Ramon Piñeiro Research Centre* through an agreement with the University of Santiago de Compostela.

2 See Garcia Ferrando, López Aranguren and M. Beltrán: *La conciencia nacional y regional en la España de las autonomías*, Madrid, 1994, pp. 35 and ff. Regarding the evolution of Galician overlapping identities the key texts are: Rivera, J. M. & Lagares, N. *Barómetro político gallego* (1998–2008) USC: Santiago de Compostela; *Observatorio Político Autonómico* (2001–2008) ICPS: Barcelona.

3 On this matter, see Lisón Tolosana; *Antropología cultural de Galicia*, Madrid, 1981; R. Iturra: *Antropología económica de la Galicia rural*, Santiago, 1988.

4 M. Artaza, *A Xunta do reino de Galicia no final do antigo réxime*, La Coruña, 1993.

5 R. Villares, *La propiedad de la tierra en Galicia, 1500–1936*, Madrid, 1982.

6 J. Carmona, *El atraso industrial de Galicia, 1750–1900*, Barcelona, 1990, and Alonso Alvarez, *Industrialización y conflictos sociales en la Galicia del Antiguo Régimen*, Madrid, 1976.

7 Regarding the permanence of these traditional features in Galicia during the 1970s, see W. Ettema, *Spanish Galicia: A Case Study in Peripheral Integration*, Amsterdam, 1980.

8 See M. X. Rodríguez Galdo, *O fluxo migratorio galego dos séculos XVII ó XX*, Santiago, 1995, and bibliography.

9 For a detailed account of the political development of the Galician nationalism during the XIX century, see Máiz, R. (1994) *O Rexionalismo Galego. Organización e ideología* O Castro: Coruña.

10 The most complete history of Galician nationalism available is Beramendi, J. (2007) *De Provincia a Nación. Historia do galeguismo político* Vigo: Xerais.

11 X. M. Núñez, 'La supervivencia del nacionalismo gallego en la emigración americana, 1939–1960', in J. Tusell, *La oposición al régimen de Franco*, Vol.1, Madrid, 1990, pp. 312–322.

12 X. López Facal and C. Nogueira, *O poder industrial en Galicia*, Vigo, 1980, and X. Leiceaga, *Capital extranxeiro e industrialización en Galicia*, Vigo, 1993.

13 See R. Blanco, R. Máiz and J. Portero, *Las elecciones en Galicia 1. El Parlamento Gallego*, La Coruña, 1982, and *Las elecciones generales de 1982 en Galicia*, Santiago, 1983.

14 Regarding the new framing strategies and the rising electoral coordination by the BNG see Máiz, R. (2003) 'Making Opportunities: contemporary Evolution of Galician Nationalism in Spain' *Studies in Ethnicity and Nationalism* vol. 3, 2. 20–34; and Máiz, R. & Lago, I. (2004) 'Le nationalisme galicien: mobilisation politique et coordination électorale' *Pôle Sud* 20, 25–46.

FIRST NATIONS IN THE USA

FRANKE WILMER

The Moral Dilemma – Savage Peoples and Civilized Nations

By the late sixteenth century several European states had made contact with the indigenous peoples of the Americas. The Spanish invasion in the southern hemisphere opened up a debate among theologian advisers to the Spanish crown regarding the existence and extent to which the European doctrine of natural rights extended to the indigenous peoples of the region. Further north, the Dutch, English and French were dealing with the native peoples on the basis of international treaty relationships. Agreements between the European states and Indian nations addressed issues of peace, trade, territory and free passage. International norms compelled the Europeans to approach the indigenous political communities as international equals. During the colonial era, individuals were appointed (Benjamin Franklin, among others) to serve in an official capacity as diplomatic envoys to certain Indian societies. The British joined with the Iroquois in a security alliance known as the Covenant Chain (Jennings 1975).

Although treaties, diplomatic ties and security alliances attest to the international character of the relationship as between equals, there was also an element of moral arrogance in the attitude of the Europeans towards the 'savage natives' (Sheehan 1973). Therefore, although from the international level relations were conducted more or less on a basis of mutuality, on a cultural level the moral boundaries, from the viewpoint of the Europeans, were clearly marked. It should also be kept in mind that war as an instrument of foreign policy, and one by which territory could be acquired and dominance over the local population by the victorious conqueror could be established, was quite acceptable and unregulated in the eighteenth century.

[...]

International law, much weaker then than now, compelled the European powers and their colonial offspring to take into consideration the international legal norms that might pertain to the settler–native relationship. However, international law, as designed by the Europeans primarily to regulate relations among themselves, was understood as a system governing relations between 'civilized nations' (Lindley [1926] 1969). The natives, in the judgement of the European mind, did not belong to the class of 'civilized nations'. Still, they often functioned as politically distinct communities in a manner recognizable to the Europeans as organized and orderly (Lindley [1926] 1969). So, was extending the civilities of international law to the indigenous population a gratuitous act on the part of the Europeans? Could it be rescinded unilaterally? This was the first moral dilemma of the colonizers.

In part, favouring a civil approach to relations with the indigenous population was probably as much a function of economic and political expedience as a sense of moral obligation. Initially, the Europeans did not know the extent of the indigenous population nor their capacity to organize in resistance. Competition among several European powers and their tendency to involve the indigenous population in their alliances further complicated matters. Finally, the Europeans had established trade relations, and the indigenous communities simply had the appropriate knowledge and skills needed by the Europeans in order to exploit local resources. It was in the material interest of the colonizing Europeans to attempt to maintain good relations with the indigenous population as long as these factors remained influential.

Does the idea of an ambiguous but evolving moral boundary explain contradictions that were already developing in the colonial policy towards the Indians? I think it is significant at this point to note that the moral necessities flowing from international relations indicated a respect on the basis of sovereign equality among political communities more or less recognizable as states. Now understandable, at the time the Europeans may not have been certain about whether or not, or to what extent in each case, the indigenous nations they encountered resembled the European image of a state as a political community. Coupled with unknown variables – the size, ability to mobilize, and effectiveness of combat technologies on the part of the native population – there were good reasons to approach the indigenous nations on the basis of international equality.

But there are other indications that the moral community might help to explain the growing conflict between the equality required by international norms and the exclusion that would follow from marking off moral boundaries as the new European immigrant political community solidified.

[...]

Dissimilarity was clearly the dominant influence and became the basis for labelling the indigenous peoples as subhuman or savage – a strong antecedent for rationalizing moral exclusion. In fact, although there were numerous cultural differences among Indian tribes as well as among the Europeans, the metacultural distinction between European and indigenous peoples can be traced to this period. That is, the Europeans did not, for the most part, see many different cultures but rather only Indians; and the indigenous peoples as well saw only Europeans. Pan-European and pan-Indian selfconsciousness have since become important sources of identity in the larger global context. And in light of the association of moral superiority with the concept of civilization relative to the inferior status of the so-called savage, these also served as markers circumscribing the boundaries of a moral community dominated by Europeans and their descendants.

Conflict between the settler and native population progressively worsened, creating even more pressure on policy-makers to articulate moral justification for either public or private violence, or both, against the Indians. Perhaps the Indians' superior knowledge of the terrain and resources, along with the fact that during this time the Europeans were unsure of the extent of the indigenous population, only served to delay the process of moral exclusion. The following passages from official policy documents between 1785 and 1789 illustrate the growing tension between the moral imperatives of justice and the pressure to expand, giving rise to increased conflict:

> That the Indians may have full confidence in the justice of the United States, respecting their interests, they shall have the right to send a deputy of their choice, whenever they think fit, to Congress (Article 13, Treaty of Hopewell with the Cherokees, 28 November 1788; see Prucha 1975: 6).

> The utmost good faith shall always be observed toward the Indians, their lands and property shall never be taken from them without their consent; and in their property, rights and liberty, they never shall be invaded or disturbed, unless in just and lawful wars authorised by Congress (Northwest Ordinance, 13 July 1787; see Prucha 1975: 9).

> An avaricious disposition in some of our people to acquire large tracts of land and often by unfair means, appears to be the principal source of difficulties with the Indians. There can be no doubt that settlements are made by our people on the lands

secured by the Cherokees, by the late treaty between them and the United States (Committee Report on the Southern Department, 3 August 1787; see Prucha 1975: 10).

[...]

Relocation

The practice of relocating whole communities of indigenous peoples so that industrializing societies might gain access to certain resources began during the early colonial era, and continues into the present time.

[...]

First of all, it is perhaps not entirely accurate to characterize the post-colonial white society as dominant in every respect to the Indian population. In terms of numbers, and the extent of occupied territory, it clearly was not. But the white society was deliberately expanding, especially during the era of manifest destiny between 1850 and 1860 (Trennert 1975). The frontier of expansion changed rapidly and dramatically, and with it the front line of private violence and encroachment into Indian territory also moved.

Second, the American government during the 1820s and 1830s developed a policy of separation between the Indians and whites primarily as a means of controlling the conflict, evincing Washington's view that 'the country is big enough for us all'. This policy was embodied in the Indian Trade and Intercourse Acts of 1789, 1819 and 1834 and in the creation of an Indian Affairs Bureau administered by the War Department. The acts placed restrictions on whites, not Indians, reflecting the fact that the government did not consider the Indians to be proper subjects of US law. Accordingly, American citizens were required to obtain a licence from the American government before trading with the Indians, prohibited from trapping and hunting in Indian territory, and prohibited from settling or inhabiting any land that had been guaranteed to the Indians. Furthermore, the government promised to forcibly remove anyone (non-Indians) violating the settlement prohibition.

In 1819 a second policy track also emerged that would ultimately combine with removal during the reservation era beginning roughly around 1851. The second track emphasized the civilization of the Indians and was initiated by the Civilization Fund Act of 1819. Civilizing the Indian was believed to be both a humanitarian act and a peaceful, least-cost solution to the so-called Indian problem. The fund was created 'for the purpose of providing against the further decline and final extinction of the Indian tribes, adjoining the frontier settlements of the United States' (Prucha 1975: 33).

Another factor complicating relations between whites and Indians during the first few decades of the nineteenth century was the growing conflict between the federal and state governments over their respective reserved and shared powers. This became particularly evident in the court cases involving conflicts between Indian, state and federal sovereignty, for example, *Fletcher* v. *Peck* (1819), *Johnson* v. *MacIntosh* (1823), *Cherokee* v. *Georgia* (1831) and *Worcester* v. *Georgia* (1832). Talk of a removal policy began in earnest in 1825, and, although initially conceived of as voluntary, the so-called removal treaties with the south-eastern tribes thinly disguised the coercive nature of the policy, as evidenced by the use of the military to implement its terms (Trennert 1975). The Mississippi River would provide an Indian barrier, necessary to their protection against the press of white expansion until such time as they could be readied for assimilation. It was believed, however naively, that

> the land to the west was so vast that white encroachment would not be significant for a long time. By then it was hoped, the Indians would be ready to integrate into American society without disturbance (Trennert 1975: 10).

There are two reasons for questioning the sincerity of the desire to reculturize the Indians satisfactorily as a prerequisite to their enjoyment of peaceful co-existence with the whites. First, the very tribes first subjected to the harsh reality of removal were precisely those which had already demonstrated a remarkable ability to adapt by forming a European-style government, passing 'fixed laws' and a constitution in 1827. They were then and are now called the Five Civilized Tribes for this reason. The government took the following initial position on the morality of removal:

> [Removal] should be voluntary, for it would be as cruel as unjust to compel the aborigines to abandon the graves of their fathers and seek a home in a distant land (President Jackson, 8 December 1829; see Prucha 1975: 47).

These were a settled people, living peacefully in the Smokey Mountain region until the discovery of gold in their territory led to the rapid infiltration of miners and an ensuing perpetual conflict with the Cherokee. Suddenly, efforts to civilize them were pronounced a failure and removal was espoused as the only hope for their survival. Six years after renouncing the immorality of forced removal, President Jackson, known as Sharp Knife to the Cherokee, had altered his view:

> The plan of removing the aboriginal people who yet remain within the settled por-tions of the United States to the country west of the Mississippi River approaches its consummation.... All preceding experiments for the improvement of the Indians have failed. It seems now to be an established fact that they cannot live in contact with a civilized community and prosper.
>
> ...Such are the arrangements for the physical comfort and for the moral improve-ment of the Indians. The necessary measures for their political advancement and for their separation from our citizens have not been neglected. The pledge of the United States has been given by Congress that the country destined for the residence of this people shall be forever secured and guaranteed to them (President Jackson, 7 Decem-ber 1835; see Prucha 1975: 71–2).

Anyone who doubts the cruelty of implementing this policy might consider this confession of a white American soldier in his diary on his eightieth birthday. It is a powerful testament to the moral dilemma of Indian-white ethnohistory in the United States. For this reason, it is worth quoting at length. Private John G. Burnett wrote:

> The removal of the Cherokee Indians from their life long homes in the year of 1838 found me a young man in the prime of life and a Private soldier in the American Army. Being acquainted with many of the Indians and able to fluently speak their language, I was sent as interpreter into the Smokey Mountain Country in May, 1838, and witnessed the execution of the most brutal order in the History of American Warfare. I saw the helpless Cherokees arrested and dragged from their homes, and driven at bayonet point into the stockades. And in the chill of a drizzling rain on an October morning I saw them loaded like cattle or sheep in six hundred and forty-five wagons and started toward the west.
>
> …The trail of the exiles was a trail of death. They had to sleep in the wagons and on the ground without fire. And I have known as many as twenty-two of them to die in one night of pneumonia due to ill treatment, cold and exposure.
>
> …The long painful journey to the west ended March 26th, 1839, with four-thousand silent graves reaching from the foothills of the Smokey Mountains to what is known as Indian territory in the West. And covetousness on the part of the white race was the cause of all that the Cherokees had to suffer.
>
> Future generations will read and condemn the act and I do hope posterity will remember soldiers like myself, and like the four Cherokees who were forced by General Scott, to shoot an Indian chief and his children had to execute the orders of our superiors.
>
> …However murder is murder, whether committed by the villain skulking in the dark or by uniformed men stepping to the strains of martial music.
>
> Murder is murder and somebody must answer, somebody must explain the streams of blood that flowed in the Indian country in the summer of 1838. Somebody must explain the four thousand silent graves that mark the trail of the Cherokees to their exile. I wish I could forget it all, but the picture of six-hundred and forty-five wagons lumbering over the frozen ground with their Cargo of suffering humanity still lingers in my memory, (Burnett [1890] 1956: 21–7).

One young volunteer from Georgia summed up his feelings this way: 'I fought through the Civil War, and have seen men shot to pieces and slaughtered by thousands, but the Cherokee removal was the cruellest work I ever knew' (quoted in Price 1950: 16).

Internment and Guardianship

[…]

Geographic separation as the final solution to the Indian problem was hopelessly unrealistic. Expansion fuelled by manifest destiny and the discovery of gold in California in 1848 brought Mormons, miners, lumberjacks, farmers and cattle ranchers into the territory of Indian country from the Mississippi along the Oregon Trail to the Pacific Northwest. Reporting on a study completed in 1939, one author writes that owing largely to the gold discoveries the whites disrupted the Indians of the Pacific areas before they descended on those of the plains. In Oregon and California from the eighteen forties to the eighteen seventies miners and settlers displayed a brutality, and the United States Government a neglect, which were all the more scandalous because they extended into allegedly civilized times. In Oregon, the legislature, politicians, subordinate Indian agents and even Methodist clergy participated in massacres which were embellished but not disguised by the title of Indian wars. In California the whites killed Indians as 'a sport to enliven Sundays and holidays'. In 1871 the kindly Kingsley wrote that he had to use his 38 calibre revolver to shoot children as his 56 calibre rifle 'tore them up so bad.'

> ...Those who escaped slaughter or enslavement were ruthlessly pushed up and down the country. Women were raped and enslaved in a sudden and brutal race-miscegenation that created many mixed bloods (Price *1950:* 16–17).

[...]

Viewed as a 'contest of civilization with barbarism' that had been going on 'since the commencement of time' (Prucha 1975: 77), the Indians were blamed for their own demise, marked for extinction by a Christian God or by nature in the form of evolution. In this way, the policy of colonizing the Indians – which would be rapidly transformed into an official reservation policy – came to be thought of as an act of ultimate benevolence in light of the Indians' otherwise inevitable fate: extinction (Trennert 1975).

Thus began a new era in the white society's Indian policy. The whites could not be restrained because, as a superior race, they believed themselves to be ordained to take command of the territory and resources of North America. If the Indians continued to roam freely while the whites advanced and settled west of the Mississippi, the Indians would all surely die. To save them, they had to be segregated and civilized, by force if necessary, for their own good. Ironically, the legal justification for such a policy can be traced to the same majority decision written by Chief Justice Marshall in 1831, *Cherokee* v. *Georgia,* that has for over 150 years attested to the existence of Indian nationhood and land rights extinguishable only by voluntary cession, to their sovereign status before European contact, and their residual sovereignty after contact (Wilkinson 1987; Price and Clinton 1983). Drawing specifically on international law, Marshall wrote that the Indians 'are in a state of pupilage. Their relation to the United States resembles that of a ward to his guardian' (Prucha 1975: 59).

In this spirit, the 'great work of regenerating the Indian race' (Trennert 1975: 56) began by 'forcing the Indians to cease their wandering ways' (Prucha 1975: 92). Responsibility for Indian affairs was transferred from the War Department to the newly created Department of Interior in 1849. The 'limited efforts to domesticate and civilize' the Indians by 1858 was attributed to

> three serious, and, to the Indians, fatal errors.... [T]heir removal from place to place as our [white] population advanced; the assignment to them of too great an extent of country, to be held in common; and the allowance of large sums of money, as annuities, for the lands ceded by them (Prucha 1975: 92).

A reservation policy was also proposed as the solution to the constant 'threat' of intertribal wars (Prucha 1975: 92). The trust relationship, in combination with the creation of reservations, was outlined in 1856 by Commissioner Manypenny.

[...]

Understandably, white as well as Indian writers recalling this period have concluded that the so-called Indian wars of the second half of the nineteenth century were caused by the US government policy by the military, and the use of the military to prevent them from leaving the reservations (Brown 1971; Price and Clinton 1983). These wars were never declared, and, in fact, responsibility for Indian affairs remained within the Interior Department. Until 1871 the government continued to deal with the Indian tribes in treaties and referred to many of them as nations. However, by 1868 it had also become the official policy of the United States to consider any Indian violation of treaties – in particular, breaches of the peace between Indians and whites – as grounds for extinguishing such recognition. A tribe failing to maintain good faith would 'no longer be regarded as a nation with which to treat, but as a dependent uncivilized people, to be cared for, fed when necessary, and governed' (Prucha 1975: 117).

[...]

Americanizing the Indian

Although the Civilization Fund had first been established in 1819, and the involvement of various private missionary and reform groups in efforts to civilize the Indians had long been encouraged by official policy, it was not until the 1870s that the focus shifted entirely to the goal of assimilation. Such a policy, of course, presumed that the individual may be separated from his or her culture with no net loss to the individual. In fact, in the case of the 'uncivilized' Indians, they would be better off without it. The Indian culture was perceived to be the only prohibition to the progress of the Indian, awaiting the reculturized individual at the moment of enlightenment upon achieving the so-called civilized state (Sheehan 1973).

Assimilation policy proceeded in several stages. These included replacing the traditional communal economic base with a system of private property; intensified education, primarily through boarding schools; the regulation of every aspect of Indian social life, including marriage, dispute settlement and religious practice; the granting of citizenship, thus further eroding any claim of a relationship between tribal membership and political affiliation; and finally, allowing the Indian tribes to become self-governing by adopting constitutions ultimately subject to the approval of the US government. The transition from communal to private property was accomplished through the passage of the Dawes Allotment Act in 1887, which not only allotted lands to individual Indians but opened up 'surplus' lands to white homesteaders. By all estimates, the net loss of land held by Indians as a result of this policy was staggering, somewhere around 86 million acres (Wilkinson 1987). The law required that land allotted be held in trust for twenty-five years, and that before achieving sole ownership an Indian title holder must be proven to be competent. Much of the loss was due to scheming land-grabbers who swindled the very old, very young or descendants of original title holders. Yet the allotment policy was supported by both friends and enemies of the Indians. Friends saw it was the only means of Indian adaptation to white economic and political institutions, which in turn was the only way to prevent their complete extermination, 'as many people in the West and certain officers of the army desired' (Deloria and Cadwalader 1984: 5).

The practice of issuing certificates of competency continued until the early years of the twentieth century. Exemptions were allowed for 'able-bodied adult Indians of less than one-half Indian blood' (Prucha 1975: 212). The allotment programme also left Indian country in what is widely characterized today as a chequerboard pattern of 'tribal land, allotted trust land held by individual Indians, fee land held by non-Indians, federal public land, state and county land' (Wilkinson 1987: 9).

Boarding schools not only instructed students in the English language, and punished them for using their native tongue, but were also used to inculcate patriotism. By 1901 some sixteen thousand pupils, five to twenty-one years old, were attending 113 boarding schools. Here, students were prepared for citizenship and self-support:

> It is freely admitted that education is essential. But it must be remembered that there is a vital difference between white and Indian education. When a white youth goes away to school or college his moral character and habits are already formed and well defined.
>
> ...With the Indian youth it is quite different. Born a savage and raised in an atmosphere of superstition and ignorance, he lacks at the outset those advantages which are inherited by his white brother and enjoyed from the cradle. His moral character has yet to be formed. If he is to rise from his low estate the germs of a nobler existence must be implanted in him and cultivated. He must be taught to lay aside his savage customs like a garment and take upon himself the habits of civilized life.
>
> ...In a word, the primary object of a white school is to educate the mind; the primary essential of Indian education is to enlighten the soul.
>
> ...That being done, he should be thrown entirely upon his own resources to become a useful member of the community in which he lives....He must be made to realize that in the sweat of his face he shall eat his bread.
>
> ...In pursuance of the policy of the Department to cut off rations from all Indians except those who are incapacitated in some way...and to inaugurate, wherever it is possible, the policy of giving rations only in return for labour performed (Prucha 1975: 201–2).

Through a series of congressional actions, executive orders and favourable decisions in the Supreme Court upholding the plenary powers of the US government in Indian affairs, few areas of Indian life remained untouched by the 'civilization' programme. At the end of the twenty-five year trust, an allottee could apply for a certificate of competency and, if granted, would be issued a patent in fee to the allotted land as well as citizenship in the United States. Because the allotment act had originally excluded the Five Civilized Tribes in the Indian territory, these were dealt with in separate legislation and granted citizenship in 1901. Two more acts of Congress in 1919 and 1924 granted citizenship to veterans of the First World War and all other Indians not yet citizens, respectively.

Reform and Reparation

The period from 1933 to 1945 is often called the era of reform in federal Indian policy, or the 'Indian New Deal'. It was strongly supported by President Roosevelt. It was embodied in the Indian Reorganization or Wheeler-Howard Act, or IRA, of 1934. It was brought on by the combination of three forces: the political activism of social reformer and Indian Commissioner John Collier, who held that position for this entire period; the legal advocacy of Felix Cohen during the 1930s and 1940s; and the publication of the Meriam report for Congress in 1928.

For many, the most significant feature of the IRA, as the act is known, was that it would bring an end to the allotment and assimilation programmes and even make it possible to begin a process of land recovery by the tribes and their members. It was widely believed that without radical reform, the Indians' days were numbered. The Indian population had declined by 82 per cent from the time of contact in the sixteenth century until the 1930s. In 1917 one Bureau of Indian Affairs staff member conveyed to Congress the opinion that 'since the Indians were by policy being liquidated' there was no need for a continued concern for the conservation of their resources which were being held by the US government in 'trust' for the tribes. The transcontinental railroad and successful white homesteading had resulted in a secure annexation of the western lands; allotment destroyed reservations, now a chequerboard of titles held by individual whites, individual Indians, the tribes and the US government. The destruction of reservations meant the destruction of tribal life. In 1890 the last battle in the war on Indian culture was won by the US government when troops left an estimated three hundred Sioux men, women and children dead after attempting to hold a ghost dance ceremony in celebration of the Indian Messiah ghost dance religion. From a pre-European contact population of between 10 and 20 million native people in the area now occupied by the United States, there were only about 290,000 Indians left by 1890 (Prucha 1984).

In 1928 the Meriam report concluded that neither the reservation nor the allotment and citizenship policies had benefited the Indians and were failures in accomplishing any official policy objectives as well. In fact, the report suggested, the net effect had been to serve only the interest of white land-grabbers who swindled the Indians both directly as well as by applying political pressure to Congress and the Bureau of Indian Affairs. [...]

In addition to ending the allotment of Indian land and authorizing the Secretary of Interior to purchase land for tribes and individual Indians, the IRA had two other objectives: to strengthen tribal self-government and to promote economic development by helping tribes incorporate for business purposes and to make available 10 million dollars for development loans. The act also provided funds for tuition at colleges and vocation schools as well as funds to help tribes establish constitutions and draw up by-laws and charters for incorporation (Philp 1986).

The act was, and still is, very controversial because it was supposed to give tribes self-government; many of them never believed that they had lost it. The tribal elections held to approve of the act were surrounded by charges of fraud and misrepresentation. Tribal governments would derive legitimacy from the American government, whose approval of their constitutions was required; the government derived its legitimacy in the matter from the fact that the act was accepted by the tribes through referenda. After a century of undeclared war, forced relocation and assimilation, and reservation internment, it was an attempt to re-establish a consent relationship between the US government and the Indian tribes.

[...] In August 1946, a year after Collier left office, the Indian Claims Commission Act was approved (Philp 1986). The act allowed suit for monetary compensation for lands taken by Congress by executive order or by treaty when taken without compensation, as a result of 'unconscionable dealings' or with inadequate compensation due to the inclusion of 'gratuitous offsets' (Prucha 1975: 341). All claims were to be filed between 1946 and 1951. Attorneys' fees were limited to a maximum of 10 per cent; many settlements have been between 10 and 12 million dollars. Approximately 800 million dollars have been awarded under the act. The five-judge commission was disbanded in 1978 and its cases transferred to the Court of Claims. Long delays are said to be common.

Termination – Ending Federal Responsibility for and Obligation to the Indians

The establishment of the Claims Commission was supported by many in Congress as a necessary step towards reparation between the federal government and the aboriginal inhabitants of the country. It was necessary, they said, as a prerequisite for terminating the special status of the tribes. By providing monetary compensation, although not allowing recovery of actual land, the settlement of claims would quiet aboriginal title while at the same time provide funds for economic development and eventually, therefore, self-sufficiency. It was viewed as a part of the termination process. Termination would also encourage Indians to leave the reservations and 'join the rest of American society' (Fixico 1986). The policy of termination was rife with the paternalistic rhetoric that had always characterized federal Indian policy. By ending the trust relationship, unsupervised Indians would be free and self-supporting; the government would solve the 'Indian problem' for once and for all (Fixico 1986). The policy consisted of four parts: wiping the slate of Indian-white relations clean through the payment of reparative compensation through the Claims Commission; a determination of readiness for termination, made by the Bureau of Indian Affairs on a tribe-by-tribe basis; a unilateral declaration to terminate the historic relationship with tribes determined to be ready; and a relocation programme to assist Indians in making a new life in the American mainstream, mostly in cities.

[...]

The Modern Era – Red Power, Activism, and Fighting Back

Termination was not only not the end of the story but in some ways, along with the creation of the Claims Commission and earlier developments related to the IRA, it fostered the kind of mobilization on the part of Indians leading to the present national and international activism. Even though many Indian lawyers were preoccupied with suits brought before the Claims Commission when, their critics say, they should have been working to prevent termination actions, Indians nevertheless fought and won hard legal and political battles against the termination policy (Wilkinson 1987; Philp 1986).

Ironically, the first signs of modern Indian activism surfaced even as the new termination policy was being outlined in Washington and the post-war world order was being negotiated by the European states. A group of intellectual Indian youth in 1944 organized the first meeting of the National Congress of American Indians, representing approximately one hundred Indian groups and called informally the United Nations of Tribes. This historic meeting provided the first step towards the development of intertribal consensus and pan-Indian political dialogue.

A second important meeting during the termination era took place in Santa Fe in 1954. This time the concern was over the direction and impact of Indian education, particularly at university level. The conferees sought strategies to bridge the cultural gap between reservation and traditional Indians, on the one hand, and the growing number of college-educated off-reservation youths who had no desire to abandon their traditional identity. The most important outcome of the meeting was the formation of the Southwestern Regional Youth Conference, which, meeting in the early spring of 1960, brought together representatives from fifty-seven tribes. Here they began to discuss the idea of Indian nationalism as a goal of Indian activism.

A third historic conference took place in Chicago in 1960 and was organized by anthropologist Sol Tax in order to engage Indian leaders in developing policy guidelines for the new administration. The conference produced a final 'declaration of Indian purpose' which affirmed Indian

> self government, sovereignty, and nationalism, [and] made it clear that Indian people wanted complete autonomy to protect their land base from expropriation and to make their own plans and decisions in building an economic system to rid themselves of poverty while reasserting traditional cultural values (Day 1972: 512).

Also as a result of this conference a new organization was formed by a group of young Indian college students who, impatient with the 'routine rhetoric of the official Indian leaders', had created their own 'Youth Caucus' at the Chicago meeting (Day 1972). Some had chaired groups at the Chicago meeting. They later formed the National Indian Youth Council (NIYC) and were the first to articulate the Indian viewpoint on a policy of self-determination and self-help. They have gained widespread support among reservation elders and traditionalists as well as many of the more mainstream Indian leaders. The NIYC was probably the first contemporary pan-Indian organization to emphasize Indian sovereignty, and it now has the status of an official and nongovernmental organization with the United Nations. The council has expanded its communications and monitoring role to include Indians in other countries.

During the 1960s activism became increasingly apparent in the courts, largely due to the fact that Congress acted in 1966 to strengthen the statutory footing of 'any Indian tribe or land with a governing body duly recognized by the Secretary of Interior' (Price and Clinton 1983) by allowing them to bring suit in federal district court regarding controversies arising under the US Constitution, laws of Congress and treaties. Tribes expanded their land rights in the north-east, hunting and fishing rights in the Pacific Northwest and Great Lakes region, and water rights in the west as a result of cases filed following the 1966 action. By 1968, the year Congress passed the Indian Civil Rights Act, President Johnson announced 'a new goal for our Indian programs: A goal that ends the old debate about 'termination' of Indian programs and stresses self-determination; a goal that erases old attitudes of paternalism and promotes partnership and self-help' (Prucha 1975: 248).

A report on the state of Indian education, begun under the chairmanship of Robert Kennedy and completed by his brother Ted, said:

> We are shocked at what we discovered.
>
> Others before us were shocked. They recommended and made changes. Others after us will likely be shocked, too – despite our recommendations and efforts at reform. For there is much to do – wrongs to right, omissions to fill, untruths to correct – that our own recommendations, concerned as they are with education alone, need supplementation across the whole board of Indian life. We have developed page after page of statistics. These cold figures mark a stain on our national conscience, a stain which has spread slowly for hundreds of years.
>
> ...One theme running through all our recommendations is increased Indian participation, and control of their own education programs. For far too long, the Nation has paid only token heed to the notion that Indians should have a strong voice in their own destiny. We have made a number of recommendations to correct this historic, anomalous paternalism (Prucha 1975: 254–5).

In 1970 President Nixon called for an Indian policy of 'Self-Determination without Termination'. In the opening statement of his Special Message on Indian Affairs, he said:

> The first Americans – the Indians – are the most deprived and most isolated minority group in our nation. On virtually every scale of measurement – employment, income, education, health – the conditions of the Indian people rank at the bottom.
>
> This condition is the heritage of centuries of injustice. From the time of their first contact with European settlers, the American Indians have been oppressed and brutalized, deprived of their ancestral lands and denied the opportunity to control their own destiny (quoted in Prucha 1975: 256).

In 1970, after sixty-four years of struggling to regain lands sacred to the Pueblo Indians' religious ceremonies that had been taken by President Roosevelt for a national park, President Nixon signed a bill returning the lands to the Indians (Prucha 1975: 258). President Nixon also proclaimed the termination policy both immoral and illegal in light of the reciprocal nature of treaties between the US government and Indian tribes. The federal obligation to Indians, President Nixon suggested, was not based on a paternalistic trust relationship with its implicit assignment of Indian moral incompetence. Rather the obligation flowed from the agreement of the US government through treaties to guarantee the well-being of the tribes in consideration of their having ceded large tracts of territory. The obligation of the US government towards the Indian tribes was contractual. In 1973 the restoration of terminated tribes began.

In 1974, in the aftermath of the scathing report on Indian education, the Indian Self-Determination and Educational Assistance Act was passed by Congress. The Indian Child Welfare Act was passed in 1978 in order to maximize tribal jurisdiction in child custody and adoption cases. Before 1978, in states with larger Indian populations, as many as 25 to 35 per cent of the Indian children were placed in foster care homes – a rate which is 660 to 2240 per cent higher than for non-Indian children (McShane 1987).

The Indian activists of the 1960s formed an alliance, for a while, with the broader movement for the civil rights of American minorities but never abandoned their claim to a special status based on aboriginal identity. The IRA had provided support for the development of business savvy. Many tribal councils now retained legal counsel. A number of Indians attended colleges and law schools by using funds provided through educational assistance initiated by the IRA. They had gained experience in suits brought before the Claims Commission, not to mention recognition of their legal standing to sue, which had previously been denied. Ironically, the urbanization of American Indians, deliberately promoted by relocation programmes, was also an important factor in the emergence of a new pan-Indian activism.

In asserting a right to cultural integrity, they were and are supported by the resurgence of ethnic minorities throughout the modernized Western world. They had become survivors of a colonial experience. Thus they are also linked to indigenous peoples worldwide as well as, less directly, to the populations in the Third World struggling to retain, rediscover, or redesign their own identities in a system of world order brought on largely by developments arising out of the Western experience.

References

Brown, Dee (1971) *Bury my heart at Wounded Knee: An Indian history of the American West*. New York: Holt, Rinehart & Winston.

Burnett, John (1890) 'Removal of the Cherokees 1838–39', in *Cherokee legends and the trail of tears*, ed. Thomas Bryan Underwood, 1956, pp. 21–7. Knoxville, TN: McLemore Printing Co.

Day, Robert C. (1972) 'The emergence of activism as a social Movement', in *Native Americans today*, ed. Howard M. Bahr, Bruce A. Chadwick and Robert C. Day, pp. 506–31. New York: Harper & Row.

Deloria, Vine, Jr., and Sandra Cadwalader (1984) *The aggressions of civilization: American Indian policy since the 1880s.* Philadelphia: Temple University Press.

Fixico, Donald Lee (1986) *Termination and relocation: Federal Indian policy, 1945–1960.* Albuquerque: University of New Mexico Press.

Jennings, Francis (1975) *The invasion of the Americas.* Chapel Hill: University of North Carolina Press.

Lindley, M.F. ([1926] 1969) *The acquisition and government of backward territory in international law: Being a treatise on the law and practice relating to colonial expansion.* Reprint. New York: Negro Universities Press.

McShane, Damian (1987) 'Mental health and North American Indian/native communities: Cultural transactions, education and recognition'. *American Journal of Community Psychology* 15(1): 95–116.

Philp, Kenneth R. (1986) *Indian self-rule: First hand accounts of Indian-White relations from Roosevelt to Reagan.* Salt Lake City, UT: Howe Brothers.

Price, Grenfell (1950) *White settlers and native peoples.* Cambridge: Cambridge University Press.

Price, Monroe E., and Robert N. Clinton (1983) *Law and the American Indian: Readings, notes and cases.* Charlottesville, VA: Michie.

Prucha, Francis Paul (1975) *Documents of United States Indian policy.* Lincoln: University of Nebraska Press.

Prucha, Francis Paul (1984) *The great father: The United States government and the American Indian.* Lincoln: University of Nebraska Press.

Sheehan, Bernard W. (1973) *Seeds of extinction: Jeffersonian philanthropy and the American Indian.* Chapel Hill: University of North Carolina Press.

Trennert, Robert A., Jr. (1975) *Alternative to extinction: federal Indian policy and the beginnings of the reservation system.* Philadelphia: Temple University Press.

Wilkinson, Charles F. (1987) *American Indians, time and the law: Native societies in a modern constitutional democracy.* New Haven, CT: Yale University Press.

THE KURDS IN IRAQ AND IRAN

M. R. IZADY

Kurdish Geopolitics

The geopolitics of Kurdistan has effectively precluded the formation of an independent Kurdish state in the last century. Currently stretching over seven international boundaries (with detached pockets in two more states), Kurdistan resembles an arching shield of highlands, which until 1991 separated the Middle East from the militaries of the Soviet Union in the Caucasus. With the dissolution of the Soviet Union, and the receding power of Russia, an unclear future looms on the northern horizons of the Middle East, where Kurdistan continues to serve as a buffer zone.

The Kurds have the dubious distinction of being the only ethnic group in the world with indigenous representatives in four contending world geopolitical power formations: the Arab world (in Iraq and Syria), NATO (in Turkey), the former Warsaw Pact and the Soviet bloc (in Armenia, Azerbaijan, and Georgia), and the South Asian–Central Asian bloc (in Iran and Soviet Turkmenistan). The Kurdish question and their fate in the twentieth century must be understood within the context of power politics among these world blocs and their shifting interests.

For world powers to help the Iranian Kurds meant to indirectly but seriously press Turkey's eastern flank with the USSR, with clear ramifications for NATO's security. To help the Iraqi Kurds is to assist Iran and Syria indirectly in their longstanding antagonism toward Baghdad, and again worry Turkey. The Arab bloc, for its part, has found it unacceptable to have non-Arab minorities in Iraq or Syria wooed by outside forces. For the West, not to help the Kurds at all left them with the option of seeking aid from the Soviet Union, or pushed them toward terrorism as the only other alternative for furthering their cause. The demise of the Soviet Union has removed this northern card from the Kurdish leaders' deck, but the present fluid situation can easily lead to terrorism, as it already has with some Iraqi Kurds in the form of the small but lethal Islamic terror group, Ansar al-Islam.[1]

Kurdistan as the primary watershed in an otherwise parched Middle East is of critical importance to the states that now administer it. Further, nearly all the Syrian and Turkish petroleum deposits are in Kurdistan, while the old Kirkuk fields in Iraq constitute about one-third of that state's total petroleum reserves. In fact economic concerns likely were the principal reason Britain chose to short-circuit the process set in motion by the Treaty of Sèvres for an independent Kurdistan after World War I. Because of the importance of the oil-bearing territories of central Kurdistan, Britain incorporated them in its Mandate of Iraq, allowing the rest to be annexed by Turkey in return.

Let us examine the political and sociopsychological events of the twentieth century to better understand the Kurdish predicament today, and the role they have played and will continue to play as pawns in the geopolitical game between Iran and Iraq.

Kurds in Iraq and Iran

Kurds in Iraq

Almost from the moment of Iraq's formation as a British mandate, the British had to deal with Kurdish unrest in the north. However, the Kurds there were never a match for the technologically and numerically superior imperial troops. In fact, the Iraqi Kurds became one of history's first civilian targets of bomber aircraft, when the British Royal Air Force in Iraq routinely bombed villagers in central Kurdistan.[2]

In Iraqi Kurdistan an independent Kurdish kingdom was proclaimed in 1922 by Sheikh Mahmoud, under the banner of the 'Free Kurdistan Movement'. Although he had no connection with the old Kurdish princely houses, Mahmoud sprang from an illustrious Qadiri Sufi religious order, that of Barzinja (Barzanja). He thus enjoyed supreme religious status when he sought political station as well. His power base was in the Sorani-speaking, less tribal and more urbane, southern portion of Iraqi Kurdistan, where he was a precursor of Jalal Talabani and his political party, the Patriotic Union of Kurdistan (PUK).

Mahmoud was originally chosen by the British authorities to help them in administering the Kurdish regions of their newly acquired Mandate of Iraq. He soon proved to have other ideas and priorities, the least of which being to hand over his homeland to a European potentate. He was quickly arrested and sent to exile in India, only to be brought back a year later. True to the problem facing every Kurdish leader in the twentieth century, throughout his 12-year struggle Mahmoud had to fight as much against Kurdish tribal chiefs and political aspirants as the British forces, and could claim real authority only in his home district of Sulaymania. He was a representative of the old society, and aroused considerable animosity among the modernist Kurdish intellectuals, who blamed the Kurdish predicament on just those values that Mahmoud and traditionalists like him stood for and promoted. Meanwhile, the local tribal chieftains for their part did not see much difference between giving up their semi-independence to Mahmoud or to London and Baghdad. Mahmoud's strong and specific religious background could not have helped his cause among those Kurds who were not Sunni Muslims of the Qadiri Sufi order. Yet despite all these handicaps, Mahmoud and his aspirations for an independent Kurdish state remained popular.[3]

In 1926, the League of Nations Commission, citing the cruel treatment of both the Assyrian Christians and the Kurds at the hands of Turkish troops, awarded the former Ottoman province of Mosul (the Mosul Velayet) to Iraq. The League required Iraq to allow cultural and social autonomy in the Kurdish regions.

Having hoped to receive central Kurdistan as his independent kingdom from the League of Nations, the disappointed Mahmoud went into action again. First he moved his headquarters across the border into Iran to commence a new round of struggle from relative safety. There, Mahmoud staged a revolt in the town of Marivan, hoping to wrest the territory from Persia and use it as a staging ground against the British in Iraqi Kurdistan. Beaten back by Persian forces sent by the new Pahlavi monarch, Reza Shah, he moved once again across the border to Sulaymania, where he was suppressed one more time by the British in the spring of 1930.

As early as 1927, the Kurmanji-speaking[4] northern section of Iraqi Kurdistan was the scene of another, rather peculiar, uprising led by the charismatic religious leader of the Barzani clan, Sheikh Ahmad. He was the elder brother of the well-known Kurdish political leader, General Mustafa Barzani, and a leader of the influential Naqshbandi Sufi order. Ahmad took on the British, Turks, and Arabs, as well as fellow Kurds (the rival Baradost clan). As if that were not enough,

Ahmad also challenged traditional Islam by instituting a new religion, which was to bring together Christianity, Judaism, and Islam in one. Possibly hoping to unite the religiously fragmented Kurds, he also included elements of Yazdanism by declaring himself the new avatar of the Divine Spirit.[5]

Ahmad's forces were put down by British and Iraqi troops after several years of fighting. They were supported by Royal Air Force bombers, whose appearance stunned the Kurdish villagers more than the destruction their bombs wrought on their lives and property.[6] Defeated, Sheikh Ahmad escaped to Turkey, but later was arrested and sent into exile in southern Iraq. His legacy within the Barzani clan was passed on to his brother Mustafa, who raised the spectre of Kurdish home rule (as early as 1940, but mainly in the course of the 1960s), which stretches to this day.

An unfortunate result of Mahmoud's and Ahmad's fierce and long struggles against the British in central Kurdistan was that it weakened British resolve to grant local Kurdish autonomy, as called for in the League of Nations' articles of incorporation of central Kurdistan into the State of Iraq. The Anglo-Iraqi Treaty of 1930, which provided for the independence of Iraq in 1932, did not include any specific rights of autonomy, or in fact rights of any other kind, for the Kurds.

Protesting against the terms of the treaty of Iraqi independence, the seemingly unsinkable Mahmoud rose one last time in 1931. Having finally scaled down his expectations following a dozen years of fruitless struggle, Mahmoud this time asked for only an autonomous Kurdistan. The British refused, and by December 1931, Mahmoud had been broken for good. But his tenacity and dogged struggle for the rights and aspirations of his people bore fruit nonetheless in an unexpected manner. The Iraqi independence treaty of 1932 provided for the teaching of Kurdish in the schools and for the election of local Kurdish officials in Iraqi Kurdistan. After 1932 a relative calm descended upon the ravaged countryside of central Kurdistan, for the first time since 1914. But now the game was being played with increasing ferocity in Turkey and soon in Iran as well.

Kurds in Iran

As an independent state, Iraq did not exist before its invention by the British following their takeover of the region in 1918. Therefore, Kurds have been part of Iraq since 1926 and the inclusion of the Kurdish-inhabited Ottoman Velayet of Mosul in the British Mandate. In contrast, there are no clear beginnings in Iran – Persia until 1935 – an ancient state that finds its name mentioned even in the Old Testament. There have been myriad dynasties representing scores of ethnic groups that have ruled Persia, Kurds included. On occasion, Persia/Iran has been divided into many independent states, while at other times, it has been unified and brought under a powerful central government that expanded its borders into Asia, Africa, and Europe.

One may place the beginning of the modern state of Iran/Persia to AD 1501 and the emergence of the Safavid dynasty. Henceforth, the state we recognize today as Iran came to be a permanent and a primary political actor of the Middle

East. The Safavid dynasty itself was a hybrid of Kurdish and Turcoman blood-lines, with the root being fully and completely Kurdish.[7] On another occasion, a hybrid of Kurd and Lur elements ruled Persia under the Zand dynasty, A.D. 1750–94. Despite this, at all times until relatively recently a number of ancient Kurdish dynasties ruled autonomously (and occasionally, independently) over Kurdish lands and paid the scantiest fealty to the imperial government of Persia. Not until 1867 did the writ of Tehran run directly in Kurdistan via governors appointed from the capital.

The last of the Kurdish autonomous principalities, the ancient house of Ardalan, was overthrown in 1867 by the central government of Persia, ruled at the time by the (Turcoman) Qajar dynasty. Smaller Kurdish chiefdoms, meanwhile, lasted until the late 1920s. Then came the unique phenomenon of a short-lived Kurdish republic.

By the autumn of 1940 and as a result of the Allied invasion of Iran, the Iranian Kurds initiated an independence movement. Having suffered from a lack of security, the interference of Soviet forces in the local economy, and the resulting famines, in 1945 Iranian Kurds established an independent Kurdish republic in Mahabad. Republican forces quickly expanded their domain south toward Sanandaj and Kirmanshah. Beaten back at the battle of Divandara, they retreated to a tiny enclave behind the Soviet defence lines in the zone they occupied in Iran. Democratic elections held with an admirable absence of ballot fraud resulted in the formation of a national parliament and state ministries, election of a president (Ghazi Muhammad) and a cabinet. Technically, the Republic lasted for one year (from December 1945 to December 1946), during which time Kurdish state apparatuses and ministries were formed and functioned, until their destruction at the hands of the Iranian forces. The memory of the Republic is held supreme in Kurdish national consciousness.

The Republic of Kurdistan (or the Mahabad Republic, as it is often known to Western writers) was, nonetheless, a by-product of the Soviet occupation of north-west Iran (the Soviets also helped with the creation of a neighbouring Azerbaijan Democratic Republic centred on Tabriz). The Republic would have had no chance of emerging, had the central Iranian government not been evicted from the area by Soviet forces. Both the Kurdish and Azerbaijan republics unquestionably were marked by the Russians for incorporation into the Soviet Union when World War II ended. This was so, although the historical records of the time and the recently opened Soviet archives prove that the Kurds' republic was not a Soviet creation.[8]

It is rather naive, however, to believe there would have been any chance of survival for this brave Kurdish experiment with a democratic independent state, once the Soviet Union withdrew its supportive military umbrella. Iranian troops took Mahabad with ease, and the Republic's government surrendered without resistance. President Ghazi Muhammad refused to abandon ship when the day of reckoning for his people had arrived. The president and many of his cabinet members remained, and were hanged by Iranian forces in the city's main public square at the site where they had taken their oath of office nearly two years earlier.[9] The Kurdish republic was disbanded, one week short of its first anniversary.[10]

Postwar Developments

Kurds in Iraq

The relative calm that descended upon Iraqi Kurdistan due to the progressive articles included in the Iraqi Constitution, which guaranteed the rights of the religious and ethnic minorities, was to last until the fall of the monarchy in Iraq in 1958. Kurds viewed this new, republican period with much hope. In fact, the military regime of 'Abd al-Karim Qasim between 1959 and 1963 placed the Kurdish sun disc (a yellow disc surrounded by seven red rays) as the central emblem on the Iraqi state flag. Qasim is believed to have been an assimilated, Arabized Kurd himself, even though his adversarial policies toward the Kurdish leadership did not endear him or his government to them, resulting in a few, rather minor, insurgencies. After toppling Qasim's military junta in Baghdad, the Baath party leaders who replaced him reached a comprehensive settlement with the Kurds. The Kurdish sun disc was, however, now dropped from the Iraqi state flag.

On March 11, 1970, Saddam Hussein (then vice-chairman of the Revolutionary Command Council, the second most powerful man in the regime) negotiated a deal with General Mulla Mustafa Barzani, the Iraqi Kurdish Democratic Party (KDP) leader.[11] The agreement explicitly declared, 'The people of Iraq are made up of two principal nationalities, the Arab and the Kurdish.' The Iraqi flag, meanwhile, carried three stars as its centrepiece: one for the Shi'i, the other for the Sunni Arabs, and the third for the Kurds, representing the three largest groups of the ethno-religiously diverse country. Kurdish was to be accorded the status of the second national language alongside Arabic, and an autonomous Kurdish Region was to be established within four years of the signing of the treaty. Only Kurdish-speaking government officials would be appointed to serve within the autonomous region. A Kurd was actually appointed the vice-president of the Iraqi Republic. But the agreement was not destined to stand.

Each side seemed to think it could have got a better deal, and that it had been tricked by the other party. Both sides, the following events showed, were just buying time. General Barzani escaped an assassination attempt on September 29, 1971, less than a year after signing the agreement. This event did not diminish his misgivings as to the intentions of Baghdad, and of Saddam Hussein, whom he suspected as the mastermind of the attempt.

By the beginning of 1973 the KDP's publications were already bitterly dismissing the agreement and sincerity of Baghdad. They complained of the continued Arabization programme, the arming of the KDP's rival Kurdish groups, and attempts against the lives of its leadership. [...]

Barzani repudiated the agreement later in 1973. He quickly established ever more cordial relations, overt and covert, with the three archenemies of Iraq – Iran, Israel, and the United States.

In 1974, at the end of the four-year interim period, Baghdad published the details of the law that would govern the Kurdish autonomous area. While it provided for Kurdish executive and legislative local councils, real power over the internal affairs of the autonomous region was held in Baghdad.[12] The restrictive law conformed with neither the word nor the spirit of the 1970 agreement.

Both sides were itching to show their military muscle, and this provided them with ample excuse. Kurdish forces, under Iraqi KDP direction, within a few weeks commenced massive guerrilla attacks on government forces and installations. Their alliance with Iran became more and more conspicuous, as cash and arms from the shah were augmented by US and Israeli intelligence and funding. Seeking regional supremacy and an upper hand in his territorial dispute with Iraq, the shah found the Iraqi Kurds a suitable thorn to press in the side of Baghdad. He did not, however, want an outright Kurdish victory, as he would then need to deal with the heightened aspirations of his own Kurdish minority. The shah shrewdly profited from the Iraqi Kurdish uprising, increasing aid to the Kurds when they were in trouble, and decreasing it when they were gaining ground. Barzani, meanwhile, appeared oblivious to this.

Armed with these 'allies,' Barzani appeared to have the Iraqi government at a disadvantage. He then committed a strategic mistake by ordering a switch from guerrilla to conventional warfare against the central forces. The Kurdish *pesh-merga* guerrillas, adept at elusive warfare in the mountains since at least the time of the Medes and the conquest of Assyria, were no match in a conventional war against the clearly superior Iraqi forces, and were soon cut to pieces. By 1975, the Kurdish forces had been chased to within a few miles of the Iranian border and then over it.

Realizing the fast-approaching defeat of Barzani's forces, and that the war gave him the opportunity to press Baghdad into a treaty on terms favourable to Iran, the shah correctly concluded that the Iraqi Kurds' day in the sun had passed. He agreed in Algiers (March 6, 1975) on the terms of a treaty of friendship with Iraq, and, for turning his back on the Kurds, received all the land and sea concessions he had wanted. Saddam Hussein signed for Iraq. Mustafa Barzani ended up in exile in Tehran on a meager Iranian government stipend.[13]

Triumphant, Baghdad embarked on a systematic programme of reducing the influence of Kurdish political parties in its domain, while pouring financial and human resources into rebuilding the devastated Kurdish countryside. It hoped to co-opt the Kurdish citizens by giving them a fairly reasonable 'piece of the pie.' A small 'Kurdish Autonomous Region' was created in Iraqi Kurdistan under Baghdad's strict supervision and control. It included about half of the Kurdish-populated lands in Iraq. Meanwhile, a government-sponsored programme of Arabization of certain Kurdish regions gained momentum. This last programme, however, appears in retrospect to have been in vain, despite many population transfers, deportations, and the enticement of Arab immigrants from as far afield as Sudan and Mauritania to settle the Kurdish highlands.

Kurds during the Iran–Iraq War

The start of the war between Iraq and Iran, and the open siding of the Iraqi KDP with Iran, did not help the Kurdish case in the eyes of average Iraqis. This was to have been expected, however, since the KDP had its headquarters in Iran and had derived a good deal of its budget from Iranian sources since Barzani's 1975 flight from Iraq. While the war was going well for Iraq, Baghdad cared little what the Iraqi KDP was doing in Iran. After the reversal of its fortunes and the invasion of Iraqi territories by Iranian forces in the summer of 1982, it began to care much more. Failing to co-opt the KDP with a number of peace offerings, in 1984 Baghdad struck a deal with the other Kurdish political party, the PUK, led by Jalal Talabani.

As the war with Iran went ever more awry, Baghdad was forced to site for a settlement with the Kurds, at almost any price. Talabani succeeded in extracting from the desperate Saddam Hussein concessions that were much more generous than in the original 1970 agreement with Mustafa Barzani. The Autonomous Region was to expand to include all of the disputed areas, and Kirkuk. The degree of local autonomy was to be strengthened, to include free elections for local councils. The region was also to be allocated 25–30 per cent of the overall Iraqi state budget. Nonetheless, since the agreement was made by Saddam under duress, it is doubtful that, had it been signed and ratified, Baghdad would have adhered to it without major alterations after the ceasefire of 1988. As *The Economist* observed,

> The break [in Talabani-Baghdad negotiations] came when Turkey's foreign minister arrived in Baghdad to assert that the Kurdish autonomous area with the proposed expanded powers was too autonomous for Turkey's liking, and that the agreement, at that point awaiting signature, should not be implemented. Dependent on the pipelines through Turkey for its oil exports, Iraq complied with its big neighbor's wish and dropped the Kurdish deal. It also, the same year, granted Turkey the right of hot pursuit of dissident Turkish Kurds across the frontier.[14]

Fighting between Kurdish and Iraqi troops resumed, lasting for another four years, but now with a sinister dimension. The Iraqi military had used chemical weapons with caution on the Kurdish fighters and then on civilians since 1985. Having been encouraged by the silence of the international community and the United Nations while using them regularly on Iranian forces, in March 1988 the Kurdish town of Halabja became the site of the first extensive use of chemical weapons on civilians since they were outlawed after the horrors of World War I. Up to 5,000 people were reported to have perished in Halabja. Between March and August 1988, Baghdad finally put down the insurrection by the use of chemical weapons on civilians and guerrilla fighters alike.

On August 20, 1988, a ceasefire took effect between Iran and Iraq, ending their eight years of war. Free to act against Kurdish rebels, Baghdad resorted to much more extensive use of chemicals. In the same month, an area to the north of Mosul was victimized. The affected region is a triangle located on the Iraqi borders with Syria and Turkey. The Kurdish towns of Zakho, Duhok, and Amadiya mark the corners of this triangle. Through this region pass the Iraqi–Turkish oil pipelines to the Mediterranean and the highway connecting Iraq to Europe via Turkey. By any measure this area is of extreme economic importance to Baghdad. Gas canisters dropped from planes and helicopters on villages, hamlets, and farms in the region were apparently meant to flush out or kill every inhabitant. Approximately 65,000 Kurdish civilians lost their lives.[15]

To enforce better control over the Kurdish populace and deny civilian logistical support to the Kurdish guerrillas, after 1988 Baghdad embarked on a scorched earth policy reminiscent of the Persian policy of the sixteenth and seventeenth centuries. An astonishing amount of work was dedicated to the destruction of hundreds of villages and infrastructure supporting life in central Kurdistan. Buildings were first blown up and then bulldozed. Cement was poured neatly into wells and irrigation works to choke them. Power transmission towers were pulled down and burned, if of wood, or dynamited if of concrete. Witnessing such an admirably efficient, and costly, effort in even the far corners of Iraqi Kurdistan, one cannot help remark on the irony. The Kurdish countryside was long in want of just such attention, and such meticulous feats of engineering, as the Iraqis were lavishing on it – but it was needed for construction, not, as it was now receiving, for destruction.

Kurds versus the Iranian government

In Iran, the relative calm that had taken effect after the fall of the Kurdish Republic and the heavy-handed repression by Iranian military and security forces broke down with the country-wide disturbances and bloodshed that followed the 'White Revolution' of Shah Mohammad Reza Pahlavi starting in 1962. Benefiting from the diversion of attention of Tehran from Kurdistan to more dangerous hot spots around the country, Kurds took up arms again. But now, and for the first time, they had the United States to answer to.

[…]

Following the fall of the Iranian monarchy in February 1979 and until the Islamic government could tighten its grip on the country, the grievances of several ethnic groups were transformed into armed uprisings. In Kurdistan, long-suppressed political organizations such as the Kurdish Democratic Party of Iran (KDP-I) and the Komala, a Marxist organization founded during the time of the Kurdish Republic,[16] quickly moved to secure a form of local autonomy while Tehran was still weak and willing to compromise. As the Iranian government regained strength, it used Kurdish demands for extensive autonomy as 'proof' of the Kurdish goal of dismembering the state. It declared all-out war on the Kurds.

[…]

By 1983, the uprising had diminished to just a minor headache for Tehran, which, except for some remote mountain hideouts, had the Kurdish territories firmly under its control. Faced with these reverses, and following the end of the war with Iraq, the general secretary of the KDP-I, Abdul Rahman Ghassemlou, sued for peace talks with the Iranian government in 1989. However, after arriving in Vienna to meet with an Iranian delegation, he and his colleagues were machine-gunned on July 13 by the 'peace negotiators' at the appointed hotel. His successor, Dr. Sadeq Sharafkandi, sought a new round of peace negotiations and made conciliatory gestures. His eloquence and urbanity, however, did not awaken honour and decency in his enemies in Tehran or across the border in Iraq. Dr. Sharafkandi was gunned down by assassins in Berlin in 1993.

The transition this time did not go as smoothly as before. The new KDP-I leader, Mustafa Hijri (Hedjri) demanded revenge on the government forces in Kurdistan. This was a desperate move out of sheer anger, as the KDP-I forces were no match for their enemies. The new leadership of the KDP-I – in fact all those party members who had returned to Iranian Kurdistan during Sharafkandi's conciliatory term of office – were hunted down by government troops and the dreaded Revolutionary Guards (the *Pasdaran*). [...]

Kurdish 'democracy' in Iraq

In August 1990, Iraq invaded its small, but rich neighbour, Kuwait, prompting an international military coalition to expel the Iraqi forces seven months later. In March 1991, less than a week after the announcement of the Allied powers' ceasefire, the Kurds staged a general uprising in Iraqi Kurdistan. While the elite Iraqi Republican Guards were battling a Shi'i revolt in the south, the Kurdish forces, which had gathered under a coalition of all major Kurdish political parties in Iraq, took over all Kurdish-inhabited areas of Iraq, and more. On March 20, Kirkuk, the jewel in the crown of their 'victory,' was won. This proved to be, however, an empty victory and a cruel illusion.

After putting down the Shi'is in the south, the battle-hardened, dreaded Republican Guards advanced into Kurdistan. A massive flight ensued. Nearly half of all Iraqi Kurds fled to the borders of Turkey and Iran, as a horrific drama of mass starvation, freezing, epidemics, and harassment by Iraqi and Turkish troops unfolded. Nearly 1.5 million Kurds passed into Iran. Another 500,000 massed on the Turkish border, with only about 200,000 being allowed in by the Turks, who closed their borders after two days.

Allied forces (mainly British and American) were sent into northern Iraq to protect the Kurds. They also declared the area north of the 36th parallel off limits to the Iraqi air force. This was a little strange. The ethnic line separating Kurds from Arabs in Iraq runs almost north–south. The area thus included a large Arab population, and the multiethnic Mosul, the second largest city in Iraq. Although the designated area also included Arbil and a score of smaller towns, it left out over two-thirds of Iraqi Kurdistan, including Sulaymania, Kirkuk, Kifri, Khanaqin, and Badra. Allied forces also occupied a 'Security Zone', a sliver of land north of Mosul that included the Kurdish towns of Zakho, Amadiya, and Duhok – exactly the same area that had been extensively gassed by Baghdad in August 1988. The creation of the Security Zone was designed to entice Kurdish refugees to return to Iraq and the area was later handed over to Kurdish forces.

Iraqi government functionaries were eventually chased out of the area by the Kurds, prompting a quarantine of all Kurdish-occupied areas by Baghdad. As of the end of 1991, this Security Zone had grown to include almost half of Iraqi Kurdistan, and to stretch from the Syrian borders, along the Turkish and Iranian borders to the Diyala River.

The Iraqi Kurds then ushered in what appeared to be democratic rule for their liberated region, complete with general elections, a parliament, and a government. Elections were held in the summer of 1992, in which the two main Iraqi

Kurdish parties, the KDP and PUK, were joined by a dozen other smaller ones to solicit Kurdish votes. After the primary, a suspiciously equal 48 per cent of the votes were reported to have been cast for each of the two major parties. Surprisingly, no runoff followed. A runoff would of course have allowed for a winner, and then a government to be formed by the winner – all at the expense of the losing parties. But neither the KDP nor the PUK was prepared to be the loser, no matter what democracy's dictum. They muzzled any call for a runoff.

A parliament was, however, formed in Arbil, and a cabinet divided up conveniently between the candidates of these two main parties (plus a token few from the others) was seated. This was as much for the benefit of Western governments and human rights groups – those who were providing protection and doling out money to the Kurdish regional government and political leaders – as for the average Kurd.

Struggle between the KDP and PUK

As one ethnic region after another declared its independence, from Slovakia to Tajikistan, and was greeted with open arms by the international community, blind luck had also delivered Iraqi Kurdistan from its tormentors in Baghdad. Georgia, Armenia, and Azerbaijan – regions that actually border on Kurdistan – declared their independence and were admitted immediately into the United Nations. However, the Iraqi Kurdish leaders missed this historic alignment of local and international factors conducive to their independence.[17] The facade of cooperation between Barzani and Talabani was soon to shatter, as their differences led beyond verbal disagreement and into bloodshed.

Iraqi Kurdish 'democracy,' trumpeted with much fanfare in 1992, was as dead as it was unreal from the beginning. Domestic affairs in Iraqi Kurdish territories were abominably mishandled by the autonomous Kurdish 'government.' The continuing feud between the two warlords-turned-politicians, Massoud Barzani of KDP and Jalal Talabani of PUK, had by 1995 increased from low-intensity assassinations and murders to open warfare. The main cause was money. Having been deprived of a cut in the lucrative smuggling and sanction-busting business taking place across the border between Turkey and Iraq, Talabani put his close relationship with Iran to good use. By the beginning of 1995, PUK forces had pushed the KDP out of the autonomous capital at Arbil and in fact all the way up against the Turkish border.

Realizing the gravity of the situation, Barzani played the only card left in his deck: he appealed for help to President Saddam Hussein and his military – the same man and force who had poisoned Kurdish children at Halabja and in the Northern Triangle in 1988. President Hussein now issued a general amnesty to all Iraqi Kurds, inviting them back. In return, he declared there would be free movement of Kurds in the 'autonomous region' (that which was recognized by Baghdad in 1975, not the one established by force in 1992). He also promised to lift the economic embargo (which was an empty gesture, realizing it was Kurdistan that was smuggling its ample surpluses into Iraq and not the reverse), and begin communication and exchange with the 'rulers of the autonomous area'.

The invasion of the 'safe' autonomous zone of Kurdistan by Baghdad's forces in 1996, even if by the personal invitation of one of the Kurdish leaders, offended and baffled the United States, leading to cruise missile attacks on Baghdad and a stiff warning to withdraw. Iraqi forces did so after having reinstalled Mr. Barzani, but they remained clandestinely to help Barzani regain his fief and incur more favours to Baghdad. It was now his turn to corner Talabani between a rock and a hard place – the Iranian border.

Notes

1 The Ansar al-Islam is a terrorist organization founded around the towns of Penjwin and Khurmal on the Iranian border by one 'Shaikh Krakar', who was imprisoned in October 2002 in Norway for his violent activities. The Ansar have already killed many Kurds and a number of American personnel in the area.

2 Sir Arnold Wilson, the British Civil Commissioner in Mesopotamia, verifies this by stating: 'In Southern Kurdistan, four out of five people support Sheikh Mahmoud's plans for independent Kurdistan.' See his book, *Mesopotamia, 1917–1920: A Clash of Loyalties; a Personal and Historical Record* (London: Oxford University Press, 1931), p. 137.

3 Kurmanji is one of the four main dialects of Kurdish, the others being Sorani, Gurani, and Dimili/Zazaki.

4 Yazdanism was the pre-Islamic, native religion of most Kurds. It survives today mainly in its denominations of Alevism, Yezidism, and Yarisanism/ Ahl-i Haqq. For more on the religion of the Kurds, see Mehrdad R. Izady, *The Kurds: A Concise Handbook* (Washington: Taylor & Francis, 1992), chapter 5.

5 The use of air power against Kurdish civilian and military targets was only to expand from these landmark beginnings. Both Iranian and Turkish governments used their tiny air force against the Kurds. Turkish use of air strikes was initiated in 1931–32 at Mt. Ararat, but with negligible results. It was put to more effective use from March 1937 to October 1938 against the Kurdish district of Dersim, where the Turkish aircraft were fitted with chemical and incendiary weapons. An untold number of civilians lost their lives when they were gassed in their villages or set alight by aerial bombardment in the Dersim forests. World War II brought some initial bombardment by the British and Soviet air forces on Iranian military targets located in Kurdistan, which caused some 'collateral' casualty among civilian Kurds. These attacks, however, soon ceased.

6 The putative ancestor of the dynasty, Shaikh Safi al-Din Ardabili, was of pure Kurdish descent (Ibn Bazzaz Ardabili, *Safivat al-Safa,* trans. and ed. Ahmad Kasravi (Tehran, 1927)).

7 See Olga Jigalina, 'The Lessons of Mahabad,' in *The International Journal of Kurdish Studies*, vol. 11, nos. 1–2 (1997).

8 For a refreshingly intimate and candid review of the Republic by current Kurdish political leaders, see 'The Republic of Kurdistan: Fifty Years Later,' Special Issue of *The International Journal of Kurdish Studies*, vol. 11, nos. 1–2 (1997).

9 True to his race, half a century after these tragic events, the new leader of the Iranian Kurdish movement, Dr. Sadeq Sharafkandi, was also to misjudge his foe. And like his illustrious predecessor, President Ghazi Muhammad, Sharafkandi paid with his life for his trust in the decency of his enemy.

10 Following the lead of the Iranian Kurds and their Republic, in 1941 the Iraqi Kurds established a branch of the Kurdish Democratic Party (KDP) – one of the two primary political parties of the Republic of Kurdistan – in Iraqi Kurdistan. After the demise of the Republic, the Iraqi Kurds made their own KDP independent of the Iranian main body, which continues as such to the present day.

11 Edmund Ghareeb, *The Kurdish Question in Iraq* (Syracuse: Syracuse University Press, 1981), pp. 156–70.

12 He died of cancer while receiving treatment in Virginia in 1978.

13 *The Economist*, April 27, 1991, 46.

14 U.S. Senate Foreign Relations Committee Report, 1988.

15 The Komala's main area of operation is the city of Sanandaj and surrounding districts. It has been a rival to the KDP of Iran ever since.

16 When questioned by this author in New York in August of 1992 about their reason for refusing to deliver independence and salvation to the beleaguered Iraqi Kurds, Messrs. Barzani and Talabani announced before a group of reporters that 'the international conditions were not right'. Barzani added it was out of deference to the foreign allies, while Talabani pointed to the fear of neighbouring armies marching into their territories.

Part II

Multiculturalism, Migration and Racism

5

Multicultural and Plural Societies

Migration is not a recent phenomenon; the movement of people across the globe has been a constant in world history. What is fundamentally new about migration in late modernity concerns the relative ease with which people are able to travel around the globe due to the radical transformations experienced by the transport industry. The media play a key role by disseminating images, accurate or not, of what some potential immigrants may expect to find in what they often perceive as a land of opportunity which could improve their economic situation or act as a safe haven for those fleeing war and persecution.

The diversity of migrants is greater than ever before. Wherever they settle, migrants act as carriers of distinct cultures and languages which, while in some cases are similar to those of the host society, in others are completely alien to it. Not all immigrants are regarded as 'the same' by the host society; thus perceptions and attitudes toward them frequently depend on physical appearance, culture, traditions, religion, language, and behaviour. The number of migrants concentrating in any single area is also a significant issue, since only a 'noticeable' presence of migrants tends to raise fears about a potential threat to the country's national identity and culture, and also about the labour market impact of their presence.

The terms 'ethnic community', 'ethnic group' and 'ethnic minority' are employed to refer to different groups of people. For instance, they refer to communities of migrant origin who settle in urban environments, non-European migrants in European cities and Hispanos in the USA are cases in point. They also apply to indigenous peoples such as First Nations in the United States and Canada, Maori in New Zealand and Sami in Finland. Furthermore, the term 'ethnic minority' also refers to distinctive cultural communities within colonial and post-colonial societies, that is 'plural societies' according to Furnivall (1948) and M. G. Smith (1965).

Multiculturalism 'implies that immigrants should be granted equal rights in all spheres of society, without being expected to give up their diversity, although usually within an expectation of conformity to certain key values'.[1] A distinction should be made between 'laissez-faire' multiculturalism as practised in the USA, where ethnic communities are accepted but the state does not take upon itself the task to ensure social justice or to support ethnic diversity, and multicultural-ism understood as a government policy, as in Canada, Australia and Sweden. The latter involves the acceptance of cultural diversity and the state's willingness to guarantee equal rights for minorities.

In what follows we examine the position of John Rex, as a pioneer in the study of ethnic relations in the United Kingdom and one of the main advocates of multiculturalism; Leo Kuper and his classic definition of plural societies; Bhikhu Parekh offering an innovative approach to classical definitions of multicultural-ism; and Tariq Modood's analysis of the relationship between multiculturalism and liberal citizenship after 9/11 in Britain.

John Rex in his seminal work in the field of ethnic relations defines multicul-turalism as 'a society which is unitary in the public domain but which encourages diversity in what are thought of as private or communal matters'.[2] In his view, 'the crucial point about our multiculturalism ideal is that it should not be con-fused with…a society which might allow diversity and differential rights for groups in the public domain and also encourage or insist upon diversity of cul-tural practice by different groups'.

This, in Rex's view, is often the case 'under all forms of colonialism and was represented above all by the South African apartheid system'. Also writing on South Africa, John Stone points out that migration 'can never be viewed in a political vacuum, for it has inevitable structural consequences for the society as a whole and affects the delicately poised internal balance of power'.[3]

Leo Kuper establishes a clear-cut distinction between the concept of plural societies in the work of Furnivall and M. G. Smith. The 'conflict' model of the plural society according to Furnivall is one of colonial domination, the social basis of which is a medley of peoples living side by side, but separately, within the same political unit. In this context, integration is not voluntary, but imposed by the colonial power and the force of economic circumstances.

M. G. Smith further elaborates on the 'conflict' model of the plural society characterized by cultural diversity, social cleavage and dissensus where domina-tion is in the hands of a cultural minority. The originality of his view rests on the assumption that cultural diversity is implicit, as a theoretical necessity, in the concept of the plural society: it is the necessary and sufficient condition of plural-ism. Yet, while Furnivall is primarily concerned with colonial societies under the impact of Western domination, in contrast, Smith includes societies originating in conquest and consolidation or by migration, attributable to a wide range of sources beyond those of colonialism.

Bhikhu Parekh stresses that, from a multiculturalist perspective, 'no political doctrine or ideology can represent the full truth of human life. Each of them…is necessarily narrow and partial…the good society cherishes the diversity of and encourages a creative dialogue between its different cultures and their moral visions'.[4]

Significantly, he adds that a multicultural society 'cannot be stable and last long without developing a common sense of belonging among its citizens'[5] and that this sense of belonging should not be ethnic but political.

For multiculturalism to work, it is vital for culture not to be regarded as sacred and as a set of values and traditions which must be imposed by the state. Bhikhu

Parekh[6] and Rainer Forst[7] argue that not all ethno-cultural groups share the liberal conception of autonomy and culture; in fact, some value norms of authority and deference. This highlights the hardly universal value of autonomy and raises questions about the foundations of a theory of multicultural citizenship grounded on a single cultural tradition.[8]

Critics of multiculturalism such as Arthur Schlesinger[9] and Neil Bissoondath[10] share the view that it promotes a 'cult of ethnicity' which 'intensifies resentments and antagonisms, and drives even deeper the awful wedges between races and nationalities. The end-game is self-pity and self-ghettoization.'[11]

Tariq Modood considers the relationship between multiculturalism, liberal citizenship and national identity after 9/11 and points at a 'crisis of multiculturalism' connected to the size or activities of the Muslim population in specific countries. He carefully examines the tension between multiculturalism and some classical liberal ideas and concludes that 'Liberal citizenship is not interested in group identities and shuns identitarian politics; its interest in "race" is confined to anti-discrimination and simply as an aspect of the legal equality of citizens. Strictly speaking, race is of interest to liberal citizenship only because no one can choose their race.' It is his concern that, controversially for some: 'Marginalized and other religious groups, most notably Muslims, are now...making a claim that religious identity, just like gay identity, and just like certain forms of racial identity, should not just be privatized or tolerated, but should be part of the public space.' Modood rejects the view that equality as recognition (uniquely) does not apply to oppressed religious communities. In so doing, he defends multiculturalism as a better basis for integration than its two current rivals, namely, 'social cohesion' and 'multiculture'.

Notes

1 Castles, Stephen and Miller, Mark J., *The Age of Migration* (Macmillan Press Ltd: London, 1998 [1993]), p. 248.
2 Rex, John, 'The Concept of Multicultural Society' in Guibernau, M. and Rex, J. (eds) *The Ethnicity Reader: Nationalism, Multiculturalism and Migration* (Polity: Cambridge, 1997), pp. 205–20, p. 208.
3 Stone, John, 'The "migrant factor" in a plural society: a South African case study', *International Migration Review*, vol. 9, no. 1 (spring, 1975), pp. 15–28.
4 Parekh, Bhikhu, 'What is multiculturalism?', December 1999. http://www.india-seminar.com pp. 1–8, p. 3.
5 Parekh, Bhikhu, 'What is multiculturalism?', December 1999. http://www.india-seminar.com pp. 1–8, p. 4.
6 Parekh, Bhikhu, 'Dilemmas of a theory of multicultural citizenship', *Constellations*, 4/1, pp. 54–62.
7 Forst, Rainer, 'Foundations of a theory of multicultural justice', *Constellations*, 4/1, pp. 63–71.
8 Parekh, Bhikhu, 'Dilemmas of a theory of multicultural citizenship', *Constellations*, 4/1, p. 59.

9 Schleshinger, Arthur, *The Disuniting of America* (Norton: New York, 1992).
10 Bissoondath, Neil, *Selling Illusions: The Cult of Multiculturalism in Canada* (Penguin: Toronto, 1994).
11 Bissoondath, Neil, *Selling Illusions: The Cult of Multiculturalism in Canada* (Penguin: Toronto, 1994), p. 111.

THE CONCEPT OF
A MULTICULTURAL SOCIETY

JOHN REX

Most researchers in the field of ethnic relations feel that they should perform more than a technical role, gathering facts which might be useful to government in the pursuit of undisclosed policy objectives. If the *ends of* such policies are subject to criticism, however, some way has to be found of distinguishing the value standards used by researchers from those of political partisans.

Value Orientations in Social Science

These problems were discussed in 1939 by the great Swedish social scientist Gunnar Myrdal when he was invited to make a definitive study of race relations in the United States (Myrdal 1944). The fundamental principles governing his research were as follows:

1 Social science always involves something more than the mere description of facts.
2 It claims not merely that such-and-such is the case but that it is necessarily the case. That is to say, it not merely describes but explains.
3 The concept of something being necessarily the case, however, has a special meaning in sociology. What is necessary from the point of view of one value standpoint is not necessary from another. What is necessary from the point of view of one interest is not necessary from the point of view of another.
4 Sociology cannot of itself declare one value standpoint to be morally preferable to another. All it can do and what it certainly should do is to make its value standpoint or the state of affairs which it is taking desirable, clear and explicit.

In studying American race relations, Myrdal chose to ask the question, 'what structures, institutions and policies are necessary to achieve the ends set out in the American constitution, as interpreted?'

The key to any honest approach to policy-oriented research is to be found in Myrdal's fourth principle. If asked what conditions are necessary for the successful implementation of policy, the researcher should ask for a clear and explicit declaration of policy goals. Unfortunately, all too often, when policy questions are posed there is no such explicitness or clarity. The honest researcher must therefore begin with a critical review of policy goals, focusing on what states of affairs are being held to be desirable and claiming 'necessity' for any policy, institution or structure only relative to the stated goals.

What I am going to suggest in this essay is that a new goal has become widely accepted in British race relations, namely that of the multicultural society, but that the meaning of this term remains remarkably obscure. One of the first and central tasks of a Centre for Research in Ethnic Relations must be to clarify its meaning, because it is in relation to the meaning given to the concept that our various specific researches fall into place.

Multiculturalism is a new goal for British race relations. It was not discussed much before 1968 and even today much research is directed by another and quite different value standpoint, namely that which emphasizes equality of individual opportunity. In theory, if not in practice, this other ideal is shared across a wide political spectrum and is certainly the basis of much discourse in the social service departments about social policy.

Much ethnic relations research in Britain has concentrated very largely on the study of inequality and racial discrimination in the spheres of housing, employment, education and urban planning. Most of this work has served to confirm in special institutional contexts the conclusion reached in successive analyses of national samples carried out by the Policy Studies Institute: that in all these spheres immigrant minorities from Asia, Africa and the West Indies have suffered disadvantage due to racial discrimination (Daniel 1968; D. Smith 1977).

There is, of course, a need to continue such studies and to locate and publicize the origins of and responsibility for discrimination. But more and more of the problems posed to us are not about equality and how it can be promoted, but about the multicultural society, which *prima facie* at least, must mean a society in which people are not equally but differently treated. If in fact we pretend that multiculturalism and equality are the same goal under different names we are creating precisely that kind of fuzziness which Myrdalian principles would suggest we should avoid.

The issues which arise here originally crystallized for me when I participated in the UNESCO experts meeting on the nature of racism and race prejudice in 1967 (Montague 1972). The main theme of the statement which we drew up was about racial discrimination and inequality and how they could be overcome. Some black Americans on the committee then argued that the statement should begin with an affirmation of 'the right to be different'. We eventually decided to exclude such a reference because, as one member of the Steering Committee put it, 'every racially oppressive and segregationist government would seize on the statement as a justification of inequality'.

It was surprising perhaps that the desire to include a reference to difference came from black Americans. After all, the whole history of the civil rights movement had turned upon a rejection of the Plessey versus Ferguson decision of 1896 that facilities which were separate and segregated could nonetheless be equal. What was evident now, however, was that black politics included another theme. Assimilation was rejected as a sign of equality. The goal of the black movement was to attain *equality of respect* for a separate black culture.

In Britain today there are many egalitarians who take a similar view. They believe that anti-racism and the goal of equality requires that all minority cultures should enjoy equal respect. The unfortunate thing, however, is that because of the fuzziness of the ideal of multiculturalism, they gain apparent support from those who aim to ensure that minorities should receive something different and inferior, the very reverse of equality. This is particularly true in the sphere of education.

Plural and Multicultural Societies

One good way of clarifying these issues is to look at the theories which sociologists and anthropologists have developed in studying plural, multicultural and multiracial societies. It can be seen from these studies that the definition of an ideal varies widely, and it must therefore be in some very special sense that we speak of such an ideal in contemporary conditions.

Most sociological theory had dealt with unitary societies or with conflict within society. Furnivall broke new ground, however, with his study of the plural society in Indonesia (Furnivall 1939). There he found different ethnic groups living side by side but interacting with each other only in the market place. The result of this was that, while the separate ethnic communities were governed by the morality and the religion and the kinship order, the market place was subject to no kind of moral control. While European capitalism had grown slowly out of the past and was constrained by some kind of common will, capitalism in Indonesia involved a market place in which one group simply oppressed or resisted another. The plural society was plural in two senses. One was that each ethnic community existed separately and had its own communal morality. The other was that the private and communal world was separated from that of the market place. The question which this raises for us is whether a multicultural society will encourage tight-knit communal morality within groups or a world of total exploitation between groups.

M. G. Smith argues along similar lines (M. G. Smith 1965 and 1974). As he sees it, unitary social systems have a single and complete set of institutions covering the spheres of domestic life, religion, law, politics, economics, education and so on, whereas plural societies in the British West Indies characteristically have no such overall institutional set but a number of ethnic segments each of which has its own nearly complete institutional set. These segments would in fact be separate societies were they not bound together by the political institution, i.e. the state. In other words, such societies are held together only because one group dominates the others. The various groups are differentially incorporated, if not *de jure*, at least *de facto*. Here again it would seem the plural society model is a model of racial domination.

If we are to maintain the model of the multicultural society it must clearly be distinguished from that suggested by Furnivall and Smith. This can best be done by drawing a distinction between the public and the private domain. There appear then to be four possibilities:

1 One might envisage a society which is unitary in the public domain but which encourages diversity in what are thought of as private or communal matters.
2 A society might be unitary in the public domain and also enforce or at least encourage unity of cultural practice in private or communal matters.
3 A society might allow diversity and differential rights for groups in the public domain and also encourage or insist upon diversity of cultural practice by different groups.

4 A society might have diversity and differential rights in the public domain even though there is considerable unity of cultural practice between groups.

The ideal of multiculturalism, in which multiculturalism is held to be compatible with equality of opportunity, is represented by the first possibility. The second might be represented by the French ideal of assimilation of minority groups. The third is common under all forms of colonialism and was represented above all by the South African apartheid system, while the fourth is the state of affairs which existed in the Deep South of the United States before the civil rights programme took effect. The crucial point about our multicultural ideal is that it should not be confused with (3). All too often it is, and those who support that possibility are likely to accept the slogan of multiculturalism and bend it in that direction.

Let us now be more precise about what we mean by the public and private domain.

The notion of the two domains seems at first to be at odds with mainstream sociological theory, as most sociologists see all institutions as being interconnected with one another in a single system. This seems to me to be equally true of the functionalist paradigm as developed by Malinowski (1962) and Radcliffe Brown (1952), of the structural functionalism of Talcott Parsons (Parsons 1952; Parsons, Shils and Bales 1953) and the structuralism of French Marxism (Althusser 1969). In all of these the private domain is not an optional extra but plays a part in socializing individuals for participation in the public sphere. On the other hand the public domain is seen as shaped by the morality which is inculcated in the family and through religious institutions.

The actual history of European social institutions, however, belies functionalist theory. The polity, the economy and the legal system have been liberated from control by traditional values and have been based upon new values of an abstract kind. Yet it has seemed possible to permit the continuance of folk values and folk religions as long as these do not interfere with the functioning of the main political, economic and legal institutions of society.

A great deal of classical sociological theory deals principally with the evolution of the new abstract value systems which a large-scale society requires. Ferdinand Tönnies ([1887] 1963) saw that folk community must give way historically to association and society, the first being based upon the natural or real will, the second upon the deliberate artificial and rational will. Durkheim wrote about 'organic solidarity' based upon the division of labour, which would replace the 'mechanical solidarity' of small-scale community based upon kinship (1933), and, even more radically of an 'egoistic society' ([1897] 1952) in which values were located in the minds of separate individuals. Finally Weber saw in Calvinist religion and the Protestant ethic the end-point of an increasingly rationalistic trend in religion and, together with that, the development of political leadership based upon rational legal authority (Weber [1965] 1930).

Moral and legal systems of an abstract character thus were seen by all these authors as governing the social evolution of the modern state and of a formally rational capitalist economy. This is how what Parsons calls the Hobbesian problem of order (i.e. of how to avoid a war of all against all) was solved. This too is the significance of Furnivall's observation that the common will which characterized European capitalism was absent in Indonesia. It is under colonialism that we find what Marx called 'the callous cash nexus'. Economic and political institutions in Europe were embodied in what one might call 'the civic culture'.

The development of this 'civic culture' (e.g. the abstract public morality, law and religion) by no means implied the disappearance of folk morality, folk culture and folk religion. These now came to fulfil new functions. On the one hand they bound men together into separate communities into which individuals were socialized and within which they achieved their social identities. On the other they provided for what Parsons called 'pattern maintenance and tension management'. Living in a larger world with abstract moral principles was, so Parsons believed, psychologically possible only if individuals could retreat somewhere conducive to intimate relations and letting their hair down.

The ideal of the multicultural society which I have outlined above really presupposes the evolution of the modern type of society, of which Weber and Durkheim especially wrote. In simple societies morality and kinship structures had to govern the whole range of human activity. In an abstract and impersonal society a new more abstract form of law and morality had to be developed to govern large-scale political and economic organizations, while the old folk culture and morality helped the individual to retain some sort of psychological stability through more immediate social interdependence. Thus multiculturalism in the modern world involves on the one hand the acceptance of a single culture and a single set of individual rights governing the public domain and a variety of folk cultures in the private domestic and communal domains.

How does the above discussion relate to Marxist sociology and political thought? I think that the latter contains a certain duality. On the one hand the liberation of the market from traditional restraints represents for Marx the creation of precisely that type of society without a common will to which Furnivall refers. On the other Marx may be seen as envisaging the emergence through class struggle of a new rational socialist economic order. To the extent that he does one may see Marx too as envisaging the possibility of a new civic culture.

The Institutions of the Public Domain

We must now consider more closely the institution of the public and the private domain and in each case look more closely at the ways in which they are likely to intrude on one another. As we shall see education intrudes into both spheres and the communal ideologies which bind people together in the private sphere may have implications for their integration or non-integration into public life.

The main institutions which constitute the public domain are those of law, politics and the economy.

Law determines the rights of any individual and the way in which he or she is incorporated into society. The very mark of the plural society is that different groups and categories of people are differentially incorporated. In our ideal multicultural society, however, we are positing that all individuals are equally incorporated and that they have equality before the law. The ideals of the multicultural society and of its civic culture are not realized insofar as any individual or category of individuals is harassed or under-protected by the police or are denied access to the protection of the courts.

In the sphere of politics again, in the plural society different groups have differing degrees of political power. In the ideal multicultural society each individual and group is deemed to have the same right to exercise political power through the vote or by other means. This by no means excludes the notion of conflict but no individual or group should find the rules governing such conflict disadvantageous. Participation in such a political system is a part of the multicultural ideal.

The economy refers in the first place to the institution of the market. This involves the processes of bargaining and competition and the sole sanction which one individual may use against the other is the threat to go to another supplier. The market should exclude the use of force and fraud. But while it is a rule-governed institution it excludes by definition the concept of 'charity', a concept which belongs to the world of community and folk morality. What is involved in market behaviour is the more abstract morality of sticking to the rules of peaceful market bargaining. The maintenance of such a system is another and quite central part of the civic culture and the multicultural ideal.

This is not to say that a market economy cannot be replaced by another type or allocation system or what is sometimes called the command economy. Here certain abstract goals are made explicit and organizations are set up to advance them. But the best that such a system can achieve is formal justice. Here as in the market economy there is no principle of charity, which is again assigned to the folk community.

To say that these are the macro-institutions which are required in the civic culture of a multicultural society is not to say that such a society will always be totally harmonious and peaceful. The pursuit of directly political goals involves conflict and markets breaking down and giving way to collective bargaining and political conflict. All that I wish to claim is that it is to be assumed in a multicultural society that no individual has more or less rights than another or a greater or lesser capacity to operate in this world of conflict because of his or her ethnic category.

Any suggestion that individuals or groups should receive differential treatment in the public domain is a move away from the multicultural ideal towards the plural society of colonialism. It would mean that groups were differentially incorporated *de facto* if not *de jure*. And this is true even in an atmosphere of paternalism. This would be the case, for example, if, while other groups had their needs provided by separate functional departments, all the needs of the minority were provided by a single Department of Minority affairs.

It may perhaps be suggested here that the efflorescence of race relations programmes at local level reflects not a genuine multiculturalism but this trend towards different and separate provision. It is moreover a process which it is very difficult to stop once it is in train because a considerable number of individuals from minority groups may be rewarded for staffing it.

The Boundaries of the Public Domain

So far I have discussed the institutions of law, politics and the economy as institutions of the public domain, and I have suggested that matters relating to the family, to morality and religion belong in the private sphere. It is now necessary to note, however, that the public domain is often extended through bureaucratic state activity in matters of the family and morality, particularly in the welfare state.

Two kinds of barrier are breached in the modern state: the state may intervene in the economic sphere through ownership, through control and through subsidies to ensure efficient production; but it also intervenes in what are essentially family and community matters. It directs the economy towards full employment so that all bread-winners may have jobs. It permits as well as directs trade union activity to ensure job security. It makes provision through social insurance to ensure that individuals without employment have an income. It may build homes for letting or subsidize the building of houses for private ownership. It may provide education for children and for adults and it may provide social work services to help in resolving personal and family problems. All of these activities involve breaches in the barrier between public and private domains. When the state provides, moreover, its provision is universally oriented. It cannot easily make its provision multicultural; if it does, it may provide unequally and unfairly for different groups.

T. Marshall (1950) has suggested that it is the mark of the modern state that it provides, in addition to legal and political rights, a substantial body of social rights and that this has led workers to feel a greater sense of loyalty to the state and nation than they do to class. In terms of my argument, however, there is an even more fundamental point: much of the feeling of identification which individuals once had with the private domain and the local community is transferred to the state.

Undoubtedly functions have been lost by the family and community to the state, although there is an argument that state intervention actually supports the family and enables it to perform its primary tasks of consumption and primary socialization more effectively (Fletcher 1966). What seems to be the case is that there is inevitably a degree of state socialist provision for family welfare in the modern world and that this is an area of collaboration between public and private domains. When the state intervenes in education, however, more difficult problems arise.

Education and the Public and Private Domains

A modern educational system has three clear functions. *It selects individuals* on the basis of their achievement for training for various occupational roles. *It transmits important skills* necessary for survival and for work in industry. And *it also transmits moral values*. It is this third function which brings it into conflict with the private domain, for clearly one part of the socialization process consists precisely in the transmission of moral values.

Clearly no ethnic minority will object to the selection mechanism being part of the public domain. What is important is simply that this mechanism should give equal opportunity to all. Again, if the minority is committed to living by employment in the industrial system, it will itself wish to take advantage of any skill training which is available. Moral training, however, involves other issues. Insofar as such training at school level is concerned simply with the transmission of what we might call civic morality and culture, the problems arising will be small. True, there will be doubts about the desirability of encouraging competitive and individualist values, because, taken out of context, these conflict with the principles of charity and mutual aid underlying local communities and the private domain. But this is an inherent tension in industrial society and one with which industrial man has learned to live. Moreover there are parts of civic morality which are of value and importance to minorities, especially in relation to the notion of equality of opportunity. Much more important than any objection to this aspect of the school's moral role is the objection to its interference in matters considered to be private or to involve individual choice. This is true of all matters relating to sex, marriage, the family and religion.

It is arguable that schools ought not to intervene in these matters at all or to do so only on the most general and basic level. Such an argument hinges on showing that these practices do not prevent the proper functioning of the state and may positively assist it. The counter-argument is that it is of concern to the state how family matters are arranged, both because the state is concerned with the law of inheritance, and because it has to uphold individual rights even against the family.

On family matters, however, there are considerable tensions between minority communities and the school in contemporary Britain. Among Asians, for example, there is a great emphasis upon arranged marriage and the relative exclusion and modesty of females. Neither the official curriculum of British schools nor the peer group culture in which minority children inevitably participate fosters the relevant values. Sometimes schools may be unnecessarily provocative, for example when girls are required to take part in mixed swimming classes, but more generally the whole ethos of the school, based as it is on the encouragement of individual choice and free competition, strikes at the root of any tight-knit marriage and family system.

There is often a fundamental clash of values on these matters in any modern society. The notion of equality of opportunity appears to point to the rights not merely of families but to those of individuals, male and female, against the constraints imposed by families. Feminism has made the issues here especially sharp. It is unacceptable in terms of feminist values that a woman should be forced into a marriage or that girls should be denied the maximum degree of education because of some preconceived notion of the female role.

Such emphases in the argument are, however, quite misleading from the point of view of Asian parents. They fail to acknowledge the fact that an arranged marriage reflects the care which the family shows towards its daughters: the guaranteed dowry is likely to be far more substantial than anything a European girl might get from her parents to initiate married life. Indeed it can be said that the whole system gives the bride more rights than does the notion of marriage based upon random selection and romantic love. Furthermore, the assertion of freedom in the sexual sphere is bound up with a whole set of values about the marketability of sex as reflected in the media and in sex shops. The feminist demand for greater freedom is therefore seen as part of this larger package which offends against all Asian concepts of modesty and love.

This clash of values cannot be examined here. It is simply important to note that it exists and that in a society which seeks to achieve *both* equality of opportunity *and* the toleration of cultural diversity, institutional arrangements will evolve to deal with this tension. Parents may seek to limit the role of equality of opportunity offered at certain schools by withdrawing their children from certain kinds of activity; they may also seek to provide supplementary moral education outside the school.

Another potential source of discord is religion. Here, however, the way has been prepared in a Christian society for dealing with potential conflicts. Because the various Christian sects and denominations have engaged in conflicts, even in international and civil wars, which have threatened the unity of the state, most nominally Christian societies have already downgraded religion to a matter of minor importance towards which there was no danger in exercising toleration. Once Roman Catholics had been given the right to teach their own religion in schools, there was no barrier in principle to allowing Islam or Sikhism or Hinduism to be taught in a similar way. Difficulties seemed to arise only with quasi-religious movements, for example Rastafarianism, because of their strong political associations.

Wider than the religious question was that of instruction in minority cultures, thought by many to be the key issue in any programme of multicultural education. Such innovations, however, are often far from popular with minority communities, who see them as diverting energies from subjects more important to examination success, and, in any case as caricatures of their culture. The strong preference of minority people is that, unless such teaching can be carried out by minority teachers in schools, it is best done outside school hours. What may perhaps be important is that while minority children learn about majority culture, provision should also be made for majority children to learn about minority culture, since this will foster equality by encouraging equal respect for other cultures.

The question of language creates greater dilemmas. Teaching *in* mother tongues and teaching *of* mother tongues have both been seen to be important in a wide variety of minority communities. Teaching *in* mother tongue is important at the outset for those who do not speak the main school language. If children are simply confronted by another language on entering school, their education is likely to be seriously retarded. What is required therefore is initial teaching in the mother tongue with the main language of the school gradually introduced until it replaces the mother tongue as a medium of instruction. Paradoxically, the importance of using mother tongue as an initial medium of instruction is that it can facilitate assimilation. Much more important, however, is the fact that it promotes equality of opportunity.

The teaching *of* mother tongue is of separate importance. Systematic provision for such teaching is beyond the means of most minority communities, and, if it were literally left to mother, the mother tongue would simply become a restricted ghetto language. What minority people want is to have financial support so that it can be used to enlarge the cultural experiences of the group. In the kind of society under consideration here it cannot ever attain anything like equality with the main language in some sort of bilingual state. But there is no reason why minority people should not be able to express themselves and communicate with each other about their experiences in their own language.

What I am suggesting here is that, once the inherent tensions of the educational system are recognized, it is possible to envisage a balance of control because education belongs to both the public and private domains. The school should be concerned as the agent of the public domain with selection, with the transmission of skills and with civic morality. The community should control education in all matters concerning language, religion and family affairs, for which the state should provide financial support in a multicultural society.

The other alternative is to take education out of the public domain and make it an intra-communal matter. This is what has been done in England in the case of Roman Catholic schools and, in principle, no new ground is opened up if, say, Muslim or Hindu schools receive similar recognition. Obviously there would be a danger in such schools that the task fulfilled by the mainstream schools would be subordinated to the inculcation of communal values, but it is also possible that a balance could be struck here in which the controllers of minority schools themselves recognized the instrumental value of education in a modern society along with education in its own culture. If this were recognized it might be more possible to achieve the right balance in a school controlled by the minority than in normal majority schools which find themselves in tension with minority cultures.

The Problem of Ethnic Social Work

Clearly education is a sphere in which the distinction between that which is necessary from the point of view of maintaining the culture of minorities and that which is necessary from the point of view of a large-scale society is difficult to draw. Another even more difficult area is that which arises in connection with social welfare and social work. Social workers have sometimes claimed that what is necessary in dealing with minorities is a special kind of multicultural social work. If, however, the problems of minority people are so different would it not be possible for the community to be subsidized so that it could take care of its own? Alternatively, is the problem not that of *combining* professional standards with sensitivity to community values? In that case would not the answer be to train social workers from the minority communities so that they could add professionalism to their existing sensitivity? The problem of trying to train majority social workers in sensitivity is much more difficult than that of training already sensitive minority people in professional standards.

The Structures of the Private Domain

The nature of the sociological problem with which we have to deal is this. For a member of the majority as a society, the world of the family and the primary community is an integrated structural part of the whole network of social relations which constitutes his or her society. It is also a functional subsystem of the whole and its culture is continuous with that of the main society. Among ethnic minorities the situation is wholly different. For such minorities the family and community are part of another social system and another culture. Quite possibly in that society the extended kinship group carried much more weight than it does in industrial society and in some cases provided the whole of the social structure.

The most important function of the immigrant minority kinship group is, of course, primary socialization. In the case of the majority this function is performed by the family, which exists in relative isolation from any larger community or network. In the case of the minority communities, however, the family is part of a wider network of communal and associational ties, the socializing community is larger and more people are involved in the child's socialization. The extended family is not solely a socializing agency but also provides a unit for economic mobilization; this function may even be performed when members are separated from one another by migration. The family and kin group has an estate to which members may be expected to contribute either in terms of property or in terms of skills and qualifications. An event like marriage is not, therefore, and cannot be solely a matter of individual choice. It involves the transfer of capital from one group to another and, as a result, the linking of two groups. At the same time the new family constituted by marriage starts with a carefully husbanded inheritance of material and social capital.

Because extended kinship is seriously damaged by the fact of migration, the networks within which family life occurs come to depend more on artificial structures which are thought of as associations, but which are actually structures through which the wider community life is expressed. In my study of Sparkbrook (Rex 1973) I suggested that these associations had four functions. They helped individuals to overcome social isolation; they did pastoral work among their members and helped them to deal with moral and social problems; they served as a kind of trade union defending the interests of the group; and it was through them that values and beliefs were affirmed and religious and political ideologies perpetuated.

Of particular importance is the role of the association in the affirmation of values and beliefs. Included in this is that individuals can be offered beliefs about themselves, that is to say identity options or ideas about who he or she is. Naturally it is not the case that individuals automatically accept these options, but the associations are flexible instruments through which new identities appropriate to the new situation are suggested as possible.

Values and beliefs, however, cohere around the more systematic teachings of minority religions. Such religions have belief systems which go far beyond the present situation in explaining mankind's relation to nature and to our fellows. As such they can never be simply functional in a modern society. Nevertheless, whatever their particular content, these religions provide a metaphysical underpinning for beliefs of all kinds and therefore help to provide the psychological security which the whole community structure gives.

To a very large extent the kinship structures, the associations and the religions of the minorities may be seen as acting together to perform a function for the larger society. It is the function of what Parsons calls 'pattern maintenance and tension management' (Parsons 1952). We may say that they provide individuals with a concept of who they are as they embark on action in the outside world and also give them moral and material support in coping with that world. To the extent that they perform these functions, communal structures and belief systems become a functioning part of the larger society, whatever the particular form of the social structure and whatever the content of its culture.

Minority communities and minority cultures do not threaten the unity of society. Nor do they imply inequality between groups. They can have their place within a society which is committed in its main structures to equality of opportunity. What I have tried to suggest is that a multicultural society must find a place for both diversity and equality of opportunity. Emphasis upon the first without allowing for the second could lead to segregationism, inequality and differential incorporation. Emphasis upon the second at the expense of the first could lead to an authoritarian form of assimilationism. Both of these are at odds with the ideal of the multicultural society.

Conflict and Compromise in the Multicultural Society

Finally, to qualify what I have said about the functionality of minority structures, I believe that we would do an injustice to the religious, cultural and political ideas of minority groups if we saw them as fitting easily and snugly into the social *status quo*. Sometimes their ideas and their institutions may be revolutionary or secessionist. Sometimes they are not addressed to the problems of the society of settlement at all, but to those of the original homeland. Should this mean that they are dangerous and should be repressed?

I think not. After all, British culture is by no means unitary. It can be and I think should be interpreted in terms of class struggle. The working classes nationally and regionally have developed definite forms of organization and revolutionary notions of social solidarity which challenge the social order and the culture of the ruling classes. The result of all this, however, is that what I have called civic culture includes the notion of conflict. The social order which we have is the resultant of social conflict. I see no reason why there should not be a similar process as that between majority and minority groups. Ours is a society which has produced institutions to deal with the injustices of capitalism. Surely it is not impossible to envisage a similar outcome to the struggle initiated by Rastafarianism which seeks to set right the injustices of the past 400 years. The only belief system which must be outlawed in the multicultural society is that which seeks to impose inequality of opportunity on individuals or groups. That is why the multicultural society must be an anti-racist society.

Summary: The Essentials of a Multicultural Society

1 The multicultural ideal is to be distinguished from the notion of a plural society.

2 In a multicultural society we should distinguish between the public domain in which there is a single culture based upon the notion of equality between individuals and the private domain, which permits diversity between groups.
3 The public domain includes the world of law, politics and economics. It also includes education insofar as this is concerned with selection, the transmission of skills and the perpetuation of civic culture.
4 Moral education, primary socialization and the inculcation of religious belief belong to the private domain.
5 The structure of the private domain among immigrant minority communities includes kinship that extends back into a homeland, a network of associations and a system of religious organization and belief. This structure provides a valuable means in an impersonal society of providing a home and a source of identity for individuals.
6 Nonetheless minority communities at any one time may conflict with and challenge the existing order as have communities based upon social class in the past. The new social order of the multicultural society is an emergent one which will result from the dialogue and the conflict between cultures.

Is a society of this kind likely to come into being in Britain? I think not. The concept of a multicultural society which is now in vogue is too confused for that. It might lead much more readily to 'differential incorporation'. Moreover there are still many to whom the very idea of multiculturalism is anathema and they would oppose the emphasis upon diversity which I have advocated. But it never was the task of a sociologist to provide happy endings. All I can do is to clarify my value standpoint and indicate what institutional arrangements are necessary for its realization.

References

Althusser, L. (1969) *For Marx*, Allen Lane: London.
Daniel, W. (1968) *Racial Discrimination in Britain*, Penguin: Harmondsworth.
Durkheim, E. (1933) *The Division of Labor in Society*, Free Press: Glencoe, Illinois.
Durkheim, E. ([1897] 1952) *Suicide*, Routledge and Kegan Paul: London.
Fletcher, R. (1966) *The Family and Marriage in Britain*, Penguin: Harmondsworth.
Furnivall, J. S. (1939) *Netherlands India*, Cambridge University Press: Cambridge.
Malinowski, B. (1962) *A Scientific Theory of Culture*, University of North Carolina Press: Chapel Hill.
Marshall, T. (1950) *Citizenship and Social Class*, Cambridge University Press: Cambridge.
Montague, A. (1972) *Statements on Race*, Oxford University Press: London.
Myrdal, G. (1944) *The American Dilemma: The Negro Problem and Modern Democracy*, Harper and Row: New York.
Parsons, T. (1952) *The Social System*, Tavistock: London.

Parsons, T., Shils, E. and Bales, R. (1953) *Working Papers in the Theory of Actions*, Free Press: New York.

Radcliffe-Brown, A. (1952) *Structure and Function in Primitive Society*, Cohen and West: London.

Rex, J. (1973) *Race, Colonialism and the City*, Routledge and Kegan Paul: London.

Smith, D. (1977) *Racial Disadvantage in Britain*, Penguin: Harmondsworth.

Smith, M. G. (1965) *The Plural Society in the British West Indies*, University of California Press: Berkeley and Los Angeles.

Smith, M. G. (1974) *Corporations and Society*, Duckworth: London.

Tönnies, F. ([1887] 1963) *Community and Association*, translated by C.P. Loomis, Routledge and Kegan Paul: London.

Weber, M. ([1905] 1930) *The Protestant Ethic and the Spirit of Capitalism*, Allen and Unwin: London.

Weber, M. ([1922] 1968) *Economy and Society*, Vol. 1, Bedminster Press: New York.

PLURAL SOCIETIES

LEO KUPER

[...] There are two quite antithetical traditions in regard to the nature of societies characterized by pluralism. The first tradition, which I am following, is relatively recent. It is expressed in the theory of the plural society. In this tradition, the stability of plural societies is seen as precarious and threatened by sharp cleavages between different plural sections, whose relations to each other are generally characterized by inequality. The second tradition is much older, and offers a conception (or ideal type) of the pluralistic society, in which the pluralism of the varied constituent groups and interests is integrated in a balanced adjustment, which provides conditions favourable to stable democratic government. The second tradition is well established in the United States, and I refer below to some contemporary examples of this tradition. The adoption of, or affinity for, one tradition or the other is no doubt shaped by different experiences of social life, in the colonies or in the United States, but it seems also to derive from the opposition between two basic social philosophies expressed in the antithesis between equilibrium models of society (particularly consensual) and conflict models of society. The difficulties that arise in the attempted synthesis of these models also affect attempts to relate the different conceptions of the plural society and the pluralistic society in a broader framework.

'Equilibrium' Model of Pluralism

The 'equilibrium' model tends to associate democracy with pluralism (Kornhauser 1960; Shils 1956; Aron 1950). Shils indeed emphasizes his view that pluralism is consistent with diverse political positions – conservatism and liberalism, laissez-faire and socialism, traditionalism and rationalism, hierarchy and egalitarianism. But he does not regard these differences in political position as crucial; he argues instead that the really crucial dividing line in politics lies between pluralistic moderation and monomaniac extremism (Shils 1956); and much of his discussion of pluralistic society concerns liberal democracy, which presumably exemplifies for him the ideal realization of the principles of pluralism. Kornhauser also finds in pluralism a basis for liberal democracy. He writes that a pluralist society supports liberal democracy; that liberty and democracy tend to be strong where social pluralism is strong; and that where the introduction of democracy is not based on a pluralist society, democracy may readily lose out to new forms of autocracy (Kornhauser 1960).

The political structure of the society, in the 'equilibrium' model, is itself plural. A system of constitutional checks and balances is designed to effect a separation of powers among the legislature, the executive, the administrative sector, and the judiciary, and in this way to ensure pluralism in the structure of authority. The struggle for power by political parties and leaders is seen as the plural political counterpart of the social pluralism, of competing interest groups, and as the basis for democratic rule (in the sense of popular choice among competing candidates). If analysis of political process is directed to the role of elites, then political pluralism is represented by a divided elite.

As the preceding references indicate, the social basis for political pluralism is to be found in social pluralism. This may be conceived as a balance, and a relative autonomy, between institutional spheres. Shils, in his discussion of the pluralistic society, describes this aspect:

> Every society is constructed of a set of spheres and systems: the domestic and kinship system, the political system, the economic system, the religious *sphere,* the cultural sphere, and the like. Different types of societies are characterized by the preponderance of one of the systems or spheres over the others.... *The* system of individualistic democracy or liberalism is characterized by an approximate balance among the spheres. Liberalism is a system of pluralism (Shils 1956: 153–4).

In addition to the separation of spheres, Kornhauser emphasizes the presence of a strong structure of stable and independent groups, intermediate between the individual and the state. This provides the basis for a system of social checks and balances, a dispersion of power contributing to the maintenance of political pluralism.

Integration is seen as effected in part by a system of crosscutting loyalties or multiple affiliations. Thus Kornhauser argues that a multiplicity of associations is not in itself a sufficient basis for the pluralist society. The different associations, such as ethnic associations, may be highly inclusive, encompassing many aspects of their members' lives, and thus encouraging social cleavage, divisive loyalties, and submission to authoritarian control. Hence Kornhauser insists on multiple affiliation as a further condition of pluralism. This extends the concept of pluralism to the level of individual pluralism, in the sense of individual participation in a variety of plural structures. The pluralist dispersion of the individual's different roles is expected to foster diversity of interests, to restrain exclusive loyalties, and to link the plural structures together by innumerable ties of personal relationship. It may also be expected to contribute to integration by promoting the diffusion of common values.

The commitment to common values is, of course, the main basis for integration in the consensual form of the 'equilibrium' model. Shils, in his discussion of pluralistic societies, refers to some of these common values – sentiments of communal affinity among the elites, respect for the rule of law and belief in its sanctity, moderation in political involvement, commitment to gradual change, and recognition of the dignity of other values and activities within the society. But the 'equilibrium' model of the pluralistic society does not necessarily postulate consensus. Kornhauser describes it as exhibiting a fluidity and diversity of value standards which make difficult the achievement of consensus; and he finds the basis for integration in the competitive balance of independent groups and in the multiple affiliation of their members.

The model of the society is thus one of political pluralism, with a corresponding social pluralism in which the units are bound together by crosscutting loyalties and by common values or a competitive balance of power. It is a model that appeals to an optimistic view of society and of the relationships between social groups. The wide acceptance in the United States of models of this type as fairly descriptive of the society is encouraged by the experience in the acculturation and absorption of white immigrants from many different nations (Simpson and Yinger 1953; Berry 1951). From this point of view, optimism is easy to understand. It is more difficult to understand in the context of the relationship between American whites and American Negroes. Here there is much that recalls the more pessimistic view of the plural society of conflict theory.

'Conflict' Model of Plural Societies

The 'conflict' model of the plural society derives from Furnivall, who applied the concept to tropical societies. For Furnivall, the political form of the plural society is one of colonial domination, which imposes a Western superstructure of business and administration on the native world, and a forced union on the different sections of the population (Furnivall 1939 and 1945).

The social basis is a medley of peoples living side by side, but separately, within the same political unit. It is in the strictest sense a medley of peoples, 'for they mix but do not combine. Each group holds by its own religion, its own culture and language, its own ideas and ways. As individuals they meet, but only in the market place, in buying and selling' (Furnivall 1945: 304–7). Economic symbiosis and mutual avoidance, cultural diversity and social cleavage, characterize the social basis of the plural society.

In the functioning of the society, there is a primacy of economic forces, relatively freed from social restraint. Furnivall argues that the plural society, arising where economic forces are exempt from control by social will, is a specifically modern invention, because only in modern times have economic forces been set free to remould the social order; and he quotes with approval, as applicable to plural societies, the following description of colonial Java by Dr Boeke:

> There is materialism, rationalism, individualism, and a concentration on economic ends far more complete and absolute than in homogeneous western lands; a total absorption in the exchange and market; a capitalist structure with the business concern as subject, far more typical of capitalism than one can imagine in the so-called 'capitalist' countries, which have grown up slowly out of the past and are still bound to it by a hundred roots (Furnivall 1945: 312).

The economic forces act as determinants, creating and maintaining the plural society in situations of cultural and social diversity under colonial domination.

Integration is not voluntary, but imposed by the colonial power and the force of economic circumstances. Furnivall emphasizes the prevalence of dissensus: there is a failure of the common or social will not only in the plural society as a whole, but also within each of the plural sections, which are atomized from communities with corporate life to crowds of aggregated individuals. Lacking a common social life, men in a plural society become decivilized, and share in common only those wants that they share with animal creation. Even the worship of Mammon, the sole common deity, does not create consensus, for the typical plural society is a business partnership in which bankruptcy signifies, for many partners, release *rather* than disaster. At many points, economic forces tend to create friction, and the plural society is in fact held together only by pressure exerted from outside by the colonial power; 'it has no common will' (Hinden 1945:168). The failure of the common will is a crucial element in Furnivall's discussion of the plural society; and the institutions he discusses under the heading 'Resolutions of Plural Economy', namely, caste, the rule of law, nationalism and federalism (Furnivall 1939; Rex 1959), may each be viewed as a possible mechanism for attaining some measure of consensus.

The most extensive analysis of the 'conflict' model of the plural society is given by M. G. Smith (1960). In the tradition of Furnivall, he sees plural societies as characterized by cultural diversity, social cleavage and dissensus, but he organizes these characteristics within a different theoretical framework.

The political form of the plural society, in Smith's concept, is domination by one of the units, or more precisely, domination by a unit that is a cultural minority. This is in part a matter of definition. Smith argues that if the different units of the plural society were to carry on their different institutional practices, including the political, they would constitute separate societies. Since *they* are bound together within a single polity, however, it must follow that the formal political institutions of subordinate sections have been repressed as a condition of the political unity of the total society under control of the dominant group: 'plurality of form in political institutions cannot obtain.' The further specification of the form of government as domination by a cultural minority is again a matter of definition, suggested perhaps by the observation that in these circumstances pluralism attains its most characteristic expression. Smith writes that when the dominant section is also a minority, the structural implications of cultural pluralism have their most extreme expression, and the dependence on regulation by force is greatest. Pluralism under a dominant minority corresponds to an extreme type.

The specification of domination by one section as characteristic of plural societies is not, however, simply a matter of definition. The necessity for it arises also from theoretical consideration of the nature and consequences of cultural pluralism. Smith defines cultural pluralism as the practice of different forms of compulsory institutions, such as kinship, education, religion and economy, these different forms being incompatible in the sense that roles are not interchangeable. Since institutions combine social and cultural aspects, the culturally differentiated sections will also differ in their internal social organization. There is therefore a social pluralism corresponding to the cultural pluralism, but the boundaries of the culturally differentiated units and the structurally differentiated units may not fully coincide, since there may be a marginal association between adherents of different cultural traditions, and conversely there may be social division between adherents of the same cultural tradition.

Cultural pluralism is the major determinant of the structure of the plural society. It plays much the same role of primacy as economic forces in Furnivall's analysis. It is cultural pluralism that imposes the necessity for domination by a cultural section. Smith writes that 'where culturally divergent groups together form a common society, the structural imperative for maintenance of this inclusive unit involves a type of political order in which one of these cultural sections is subordinated to the other. Such a condition derives from the structural requisites of society on the one hand, and the condition of wide cultural differences within some populations on the other' (1965a: p. 62). Elsewhere, he describes the monopoly of power by one cultural section as the essential precondition for maintenance of the total society in its current form (1965a: p. 86).

Other factors are secondary to cultural pluralism. Thus racial differences derive social significance from cultural diversity. They are stressed in contexts of social and cultural pluralism. Culturally distinct groups of the same racial stock may even express their cultural differences in racial terms. In culturally homogeneous units, on the other hand, racial differences lack social significance (1965a: p. 84). Hierarchic race relations in a society reflect conditions of cultural heterogeneity and tend to lapse or lose their hierarchic character as cultural uniformity increases.

Plural societies are held together by regulation and not by integration. Smith appears to restrict the term 'integration' to a social cohesion which derives from consensus. He writes that 'social quiescence and cohesion differ sharply, and so do regulation and integration' (1965a: p. 90). There is no predominance of common values and of common motivations in the plural society, and in consequence the society must be held together by regulation. This regulation consists in the rigid and hierarchical ordering of the relations between the different sections. Since the various sections are culturally differentiated, consensus is a remote possibility. Further, the subordinate sections are unlikely to accord equal value and legitimacy to the preservation of the hierarchic pattern. Thus authority, power and regulation are of crucial significance in maintaining, controlling and co-ordinating the plural society. Changes in the social structure presuppose political changes, and these usually take a violent form (1 965a: p. 91).

Comparing the approaches of Furnivall and Smith, there is basic agreement on domination by a cultural minority as characteristic of the plural society. This is a matter of historical fact for Furnivall, and a matter of definition and theoretical necessity for Smith. Again, both writers emphasize social cleavage and cultural diversity as qualities of the plural society. For Furnivall, this cultural diversity is again historical fact, tropical colonial societies having brought into contact two contrary principles of social life: a tropical system resting on religion, personal custom, and duties, and a Western system resting on reason, impersonal law, and rights (Hinden 1945: 162). For Smith, cultural diversity is implicit, as a theoretical necessity, in the concept of the plural society: it is the necessary and sufficient condition of pluralism.

Major differences between the two models are first in the range of societies conceived as plural. Furnivall is primarily concerned with colonial tropical societies under the impact of Western economic expansion. Smith includes societies other than colonial pluralities, whether originating in conquest and consolidation or by migration, and whether attributable to Western economic activity or to other forces. They differ also in the approach to causal factors. Furnivall stresses the role of colonial capitalism in the formation of the plural society; cultural diversity is the context within which the primacy of economic forces disintegrates the common will and transforms groups into mass aggregates. Smith, on the other hand, imputes causal significance to cultural incompatibility or wide cultural differences, regardless of the specific content of the cultural differences.

The model proposed by Smith has the advantage of extending the perceptions of Furnivall within a general theoretical framework. But it has serious social implications and a number of critical questions must be raised. Smith distinguishes two basic mechanisms, one of integration and the other of regulation, by which groups may be held together within the same society. Integration rests on common values and common motivations at the individual level, and on the functional relations of common institutions at the societal level. It presupposes cultural homogeneity (or cultural heterogeneity, but only in the form of variations around a common basic institutional system). Cultural diversity or pluralism automatically imposes the structural necessity for domination by one of the cultural sections. It excludes the possibility of consensus, or of institutional integration, or of structural balance between the different sections, and necessitates non-democratic regulation of group relationships.

This implies a distinction between two basic types of society, integrated societies characterized by consensus and cultural homogeneity (or cultural heterogeneity, as described above), and regulated societies characterized by dissensus and cultural pluralism. It implies that cultural homogeneity (or heterogeneity) is a requisite for democratic forms of government; and it suggests the prediction, in concrete terms, that many of the newly independent states may either dissolve into separate cultural sections, or maintain their identity, but only under conditions of domination and subordination in the relationships between groups.

Since cultural diversity is assigned a crucial role in political structure, it becomes necessary to define the nature and extent of the diversity, which necessitates political domination. Smith recognizes that there are differences in the degree of cultural pluralism, and presumably also in the degree of incompatibility between institutions. While it is no doubt true, as he remarks, that these differences do not affect the analytical status of the social phenomena as expressions of cultural pluralism, they may be highly relevant for the political consequences. This relevance seems also to be accepted by Smith in his reference to 'wide cultural differences' as imposing the need for domination. No doubt a certain measure of cultural pluralism may be entirely consistent with democratic participation in government by the different sections.

There are also distinctions to be made in the texture or patterns of cultural pluralism. Thus cultural pluralism between sections may be expected to vary in different institutional contexts. There may be a greater incompatibility in familial institutions, for example, than in religious ones; and presumably some institutions have greater salience for the political constitution of a society. Thus in many plural societies which seek to unify their peoples through a uniform system of law, institutional diversity in family law is nevertheless often given explicit recognition, the customary regulation of family relationships in the different sections being accorded legal status. This cultural pluralism in family institutions may have little relevance for political structure; or it may have political significance under certain social conditions, but not others. In order to assess the political consequences of cultural pluralism, it is therefore necessary to distinguish different patterns of cultural pluralism and to relate them to the varied social conditions under which they appear.

The problem is further complicated by the inevitable co-existence of common institutions and plural institutions. The model of cultural pluralism represents an extreme type which would be most nearly approximated immediately after the establishment of a plural society by conquest. Even then, certain shared activities are likely to have preceded conquest. Once the plural society is constituted, some growth of common institutions, in addition to common governmental institutions, and some association between members of different cultural groups, are inevitable. Intersectional association and common institutions may be expected to modify the political consequences of cultural pluralism, and the relationship between what is common and shared and what is divisive and incompatible must therefore be analysed as part of the social context of cultural pluralism, affecting its political expression.

Social conditions may also influence the perception of cultural pluralism. To some extent, objective measures of cultural pluralism can be devised without regard to particular social contexts or the perceptions of members of the society. Thus it is possible to make paired comparisons between different family institutions, and to assert that one set of differences exceeds the other. But there is also a relative and subjective element in the measurement of cultural pluralism. Cultural differences may be magnified or minimized. Members of the society may seek out and emphasize elements of cultural similarity as a basis of association, or they may stress cultural differences as absolute impediments to association. The political significance of pluralism is likely to fluctuate with the changing conditions of domination. Rather than accord primacy to cultural pluralism, it may contribute to understanding to analyse its significance in a plural society as in part a derivative of domination. Smith sees racist ideology as derivative, as symbolizing and legitimizing intersectional relations (1965a: p. 90). In much the same way it may be argued that cultural pluralism is, in some measure, an ideology of domination or of conflict in a struggle for power between different groups, the significance that the parties attach to cultural difference varying with changes in the structure of their relationships, and more particularly, with changes in relative power.

Cultural pluralism may also be seen as relative to the systems of government in the plural societies and to their dominant legal and political philosophies. Some systems of government may be more tolerant of cultural differences than others. Political philosophies influence the extent to which cultural sections are the basis of administration, as in systems of indirect rule, or are denied recognition and replaced by other categories of administration. In a paper dealing with 'The Sociological Framework of Law' (Smith 1965b; Kuper and Kuper 1965), Smith assigns a significant role to the theory of law of the dominant power. He argues that the common law tradition in the British system and the acceptance of the ruler's discretion as a legitimate source of law in Islam contributed to a flexible recognition of African traditional systems of authority and law, whereas the French emphasis on the imperium of the French state as the source of law impeded the administrative and legal acceptance of African cultural pluralism. If there is validity to these comments, then cultural pluralism may be seen not only as a cause but also as a consequence of political domination.

References

Aron, R. (1950), 'Social Structure and the Ruling Class', *British Journal of Sociology*, Vol. I (March 1950), London.

Berry, B. (1951), *Race Relations*, Houghton Mifflin, New York.

Furnivall, J. S. (1939), *Netherlands India*, Cambridge University Press, Cambridge.

Furnivall, J. S. (1945), 'Some Problems of Tropical Economy', in *Fabian Colonial Essay*, ed. R. Hinden, Allen and Unwin, London.

Furnivall, J. S. (1948), *Colonial Policy and Practice*, Cambridge University Press, Cambridge.

Hinden, R., ed. (1945), *Fabian Colonial Essays*, Allen and Unwin, London.

Kornhauser, W. (1960), *The Politics of Mass Society*, Routledge and Kegan Paul, London.

Kuper, L. and Kuper, H., eds (1965), *African Law: Adaptation and Development*, University of California Press, Berkeley and Los Angeles.

Rex, J. (1959), 'The Plural Society in Sociological Theory', *British Journal of Sociology*, Vol. 10 (June 1959), London.

Shils, E. (1956), *The Torment of Secrecy*, Heinemann, London.

Simpson, G. F. and Yinger, M. (1953), *Racial and Cultural Minorities*, Harper, New York.

Smith, M. G. (1960), 'Social and Cultural Pluralism', *Annals of the New York Academy of Sciences* (January 1960), pp. 761–916.

Smith, M. G. (1965a), *The Plural Society in the British West Indies*, University of California Press, Berkeley and Los Angeles.

Smith, M. G. (1965b), 'The Sociological Framework of Law', in *African Law: Adaptation and Development*, University of California Press, Berkeley and Los Angeles, pp. 24–48.

WHAT IS MULTICULTURALISM?

BHIKHU PAREKH

The early 1970s marked the emergence of the multicultural movement at first in Canada and Australia and then in the USA, UK, Germany and elsewhere. It has now begun to dominate the political agenda of even France, the strongest bastion of the nation state, which takes no official note of its citizens' ethnicity, culture and religion and does not record these in its decennial census. Since the multicultural movement sprang up unplanned in many different political contexts, attracted a diverse cluster of groups, and has so far failed to throw up a coherent philosophical statement of its central principles, it lacks a clear focus and identity. I would therefore like to begin by clarifying what it means and stands for, and then briefly highlight some of the problems facing a multicultural society.

Multiculturalism is best understood neither as a political doctrine with a programmatic content nor a philosophical school with a distinct theory of man's place in the world but as a perspective on or a way of viewing human life. Its central insights are three, each of which is sometimes misinterpreted by its advocates and needs to be carefully reformulated if it is to carry conviction. First, human beings are culturally embedded in the sense that they grow up and live within a culturally structured world and organize their lives and social relations in terms of a culturally derived system of meaning and significance.

This does not mean that they are determined by their culture in the sense of being unable to rise above its categories of thought and critically evaluate its values and system of meaning, but rather that they are deeply shaped by it, can overcome some but not all of its influences, and necessarily view the world from within a culture, be it the one they have inherited and uncritically accepted or reflectively revised or, in rare cases, one they have consciously adopted.

Second, different cultures represent different systems of meaning and visions of the good life. Since each realises a limited range of human capacities and emotions and grasps only a part of the totality of human existence, it needs other cultures to help it understand itself better, expand its intellectual and moral horizon, stretch its imagination, save it from narcissism to guard it against the obvious temptation to absolutize itself, and so on. This does not mean that one cannot lead a good life within one's own culture, but rather that, other things being equal, one's way of life is likely to be richer if one also enjoys access to others, and that a culturally self-contained life is virtually impossible for most human beings in the modern, mobile and interdependent world.

Nor does it mean that all cultures are equally rich and deserve equal respect, that each of them is good for its members, or that they cannot be compared and critically assessed. All it means is that no culture is wholly worthless, that it deserves at least some respect because of what it means to its members and the creative energy it displays, that no culture is perfect and has a right to impose itself on others, and that cultures are best changed from within.

Third, every culture is internally plural and reflects a continuing conversation between its different traditions and strands of thought. This does not mean that it is devoid of coherence and identity, but that its identity is plural, fluid and open. Cultures grow out of conscious and unconscious interactions with each other, define their identity in terms of what they take to be their significant other, and are at least partially multicultural in their origins and constitution. Each carries bits of the other within itself and is never wholly *sui generis*. This does not mean that it has no powers of self-determination and inner impulses, but rather that it is porous and subject to external influences which it assimilates in its now autonomous ways.

A culture's relation to itself shapes and is in turn shaped by its relation to others, and their internal and external pluralities presuppose and reinforce each other. A culture cannot appreciate the value of others unless it appreciates the plurality within it; the converse is just as true. Closed cultures cannot and do not wish or need to talk to each other. Since each defines its identity in terms of its differences from others or what it is not, it feels threatened by them and seeks to safeguard its integrity by resisting their influences and even avoiding all contacts with them. A culture cannot be at ease with differences outside it unless it is at ease with its own internal differences. A dialogue between cultures requires that each should be willing to open itself up to the influence of and learn from others, and this presupposes that it is self-critical and willing and able to engage in a dialogue with itself.

What I might call a multiculturalist perspective is composed of the creative interplay of these three important and complementary insights – namely the cultural embeddedness of human beings, the inescapability and desirability of cultural plurality, and the plural and multicultural constitution of each culture. When we view the world from its vantage point, our attitudes to ourselves and others undergo profound changes. All claims that a particular institution or way of thinking or living is perfect, the best, or necessitated by human nature itself appear incoherent and even bizarre, for it goes against our well-considered conviction that all ways of thought and life are inherently limited and cannot embody the full range of the richness, complexity and grandeur of human existence.

We instinctively suspect attempts to homogenize a culture and impose a single identity on it, for we are acutely aware that every culture is internally plural and differentiated. And we remain equally sceptical of all attempts to present it as one whose origins lie within itself, as self-generating and *sui generis,* for we feel persuaded that all cultures are born out of interaction with and absorb the influences of others and are shaped by wider economic, political and other forces. This undercuts the very basis of Afrocentrism, Eurocentrism, Indocentrism, Sinocentrism, and other kinds of centrisms, all of which isolate the history of the culture concerned from that of others and credit its achievements to its own genius.

From a multiculturalist perspective, no political doctrine or ideology can represent the full truth of human life. Each of them – be it liberalism, conservatism, socialism or nationalism – is embedded in a particular culture, represents a particular vision of the good life, and is necessarily narrow and partial. Liberalism, for example, is an inspiring political doctrine stressing such great values as human dignity, autonomy, liberty, critical thought and equality. However, they can be defined in several different ways, of which the liberal is only one and not always the most coherent.

And it also ignores or marginalizes such other great values as human solidarity, community, a sense of rootedness, selflessness, deep and self-effacing humility and contentment. Since it grasps only some aspects of the immensely complex human existence and misses out too much of what gives value to life, liberalism, socialism or for that matter any other political doctrine cannot provide the sole basis of the good society. Political doctrines are ways of structuring political life and do not offer a comprehensive philosophy of life. And even so far as political life is concerned, they need to be interpreted and defined in the light of the wider culture and the unique history and political circumstances of the community concerned.

From a multiculturalist perspective the good society cherishes the diversity of and encourages a creative dialogue between its different cultures and their moral visions. Such a society not only respects its members' rights to their culture and increases their range of choices but also cultivates their powers of self-criticism, self-determination, imagination, intellectual and moral sympathy, and contributes to their development and well-being.

If some groups in it wish to lead self-contained lives and avoid interaction with others, it should respect their choices so long as they meet the consensually derived basic conditions of the good life. A multicultural society should not repeat the mistake of its monocultural counterpart by requiring that all its communities should become multicultural. Indeed, it is precisely because it cherishes cultural plurality that it accommodates those that do not share its dominant cultural ethos.

A multicultural society cannot be stable and last long without developing a common sense of belonging among its citizens. The sense of belonging cannot be ethnic and based on shared cultural, ethnic and other characteristics, for a multicultural society is too diverse for that, but must be political and based on a shared commitment to the political community. Its members do not directly belong to each other as in an ethnic group but through their mediating membership of a shared community, and they are committed to each other because they are all in their own different ways committed to a common historical community. They do and should matter to each other because they are bonded together by the ties of common interest and attachment. This is why, although they might personally loathe some of their fellow-members or find their lifestyles, views and values unacceptable, their mutual commitment and concern as members of a shared community remain unaffected.

The commitment to a political community is highly complex in nature and easily misunderstood. It does not involve commitment to common goals, for members of a community might deeply disagree about these, nor to a common view of its history which they may read very differently, nor to its form of government about which they might entertain very different views, nor to its dominant cultural ethos which some might strongly disapprove of. The commitment to the political community involves commitment to its continuing existence and well-being, and implies that one cares enough for it not to harm its interests and undermine its integrity. It is a matter of degree and could take such forms as a quiet concern for its well-being, deep attachment, affection, and intense love.

While different citizens would develop different emotions towards their community, what is necessary to sustain it and can legitimately be expected of them is a basic commitment to its integrity and well-being, what one might call patriotism or political loyalty. Guided by such loyalty, they might criticize their form of government, institutions, policies, values, ethos and dominant self-understanding in the strongest possible terms if they think that these harm its survival and well-being. Their criticisms need not arouse unease or provoke charges of disloyalty so long as their basic commitment to the community is not in doubt. Patriotism is not the monopoly of the conservatives, and the socialists, the radicals and the communists can be loyal to their community just as much as and even more than they are.

Commitment or belonging is reciprocal in nature. A citizen cannot be committed to her political community unless it is also committed to her, and she cannot belong to it unless it accepts her as one of it. The political community therefore cannot expect its members to develop a sense of belonging to it unless it in turn belongs to them. It must, therefore, value and cherish them all equally and reflect this in its structure, policies, conduct of public affairs, self-understanding and self-definition. This involves granting them equal rights of citizenship, a decent standard of living, and the opportunity to develop themselves and participate in and make their respective contributions to its collective life.

In a multicultural society different communities have different needs, and some might be structurally disadvantaged or lack the skill and the confidence to participate in the mainstream society and avail of its opportunities. Both justice and the need to foster a common sense of belonging then require such measures as group-differentiated rights, culturally differentiated applications of laws and policies, state support for minority institutions, and a judicious programme of affirmative action.

Although equal citizenship is essential to fostering a common sense of belonging, it is not enough. Citizenship is about status and rights; belonging is about acceptance, feeling welcome, a sense of identification. The two do not necessarily coincide. One might enjoy all the rights of citizenship but feel that one does not quite belong to the community and is a relative outsider, as do some groups of African-Americans in the United States, Afro-Caribbeans and Asians in Britain, Arabs in France and Israel, and Muslims and, until recently, Sikhs in India.

This feeling of being fully a citizen and yet an outsider is difficult to analyse and explain, but it can be deep and real and seriously damage the quality of one's citizenship as well as one's sense of commitment to the political community. It is caused by, among other things, the manner in which the wider society defines itself, the demeaning ways in which the rest of its members talk about these groups, and the dismissive or patronizing ways in which they treat them. Although members of these groups are in principle free to participate in its public life, they often stay away for fear of rejection and ridicule or out of a deep sense of alienation.

When the dominant culture defines the minorities in a demeaning way and systematically reinforces it by all the institutional and other means at its disposal, they consciously or unconsciously internalize the negative self-image, lack self-esteem, and feel alienated from the mainstream society. As Charles Taylor correctly observes, social recognition is central to the individual's identity and self-worth and misrecognition can gravely damage both. This raises the question as to how the demeaned minorities can secure recognition, and here Taylor's analysis falters. He seems to take the rather naive liberal view that the dominant group can be rationally persuaded to change its view of them by intellectual arguments and moral appeals. This is to misunderstand the dynamics of the process of recognition.

Misrecognition has both a cultural and a material basis. The American Whites, for example, take a demeaning view of Blacks partly under the influence of the racist culture, partly because this helps them justify the prevailing system of domination, and partly because the deeply disadvantaged Blacks do sometimes exhibit some of the features that confirm White stereotypes. Misrecognition, therefore, can only be countered by undertaking a rigorous critique of the dominant culture and radically restructuring the prevailing inequalities of economic and political power.

Since the dominant group generally welcomes neither, recognition is not given willingly as a gift or an act of grace. It needs to be fought for and involves a cultural and political contestation and sometimes even violence as Hegel stressed in his analysis of the dialectic of recognition and which Taylor's sanitized version of it ignores. The Muslim protests in Britain in the aftermath of the publication of Salman Rushdie's *The Satanic Verses* were a good example of this. The increasingly Hindu orientation of India's political culture and national self-understanding, with its consequent marginalization of the minority communities, has understandably led the latter in recent years to mobilize themselves and press for their adequate political recognition. The wisdom of a multicultural society consists in its ability to anticipate, minimize and manage such demands.

Multicultural societies in their current form are new to our age and throw up theoretical and political problems that have no parallel in history. The political theories, institutions, vocabulary, virtues and skill that we have developed in the course of consolidating and conducting the affairs of a culturally homogeneous state during the past three centuries are of limited help, and sometimes even a positive handicap, in dealing with multicultural societies. The latter need to find ways of reconciling the legitimate demands of unity and diversity, of achieving political unity without cultural uniformity, and cultivating among its citizens both a common sense of belonging and a willingness to respect and cherish deep cultural differences.

This is a formidable theoretical and political task and no multicultural society has so far succeeded in tackling it. The erstwhile Soviet Union and Yugoslavia lacked the requisite imagination and wisdom and met their doom. Even such affluent, stable and politically mature democracies as the USA and the UK and France have so far had only a limited success, and show signs of strong moral and emotional disorientation in the face of increasing minority demands for recognition and equality. Thanks to the wisdom of its founding fathers, and the judicious balance between unity and diversity embodied in the Indian Constitution, India has managed to persist for five decades as a territorially intact and moderately successful polity.

The political context in which the Constitution was drafted has however altered considerably. The Constitution presupposed a much higher rate of economic growth and a much greater degree of equitable distribution of resources among the diverse communities than has proved to be the case. It took full account of religious and a rather limited account of cultural diversity, but none of ethnic self assertion. Assuming, paradoxically, that India had minorities but not a majority, it sought to nurture the former's cultural self-expression but not the latter's and allowed the minorities to act as collective agents while ignoring the real and fraught possibility of the majority becoming integrated and acting as a collective subject.

It also assumed a culturally neutral and socially transcendental state, able to ensure political impartiality, and did not anticipate that a determined majority might culturally monopolize the state and use it to enforce a narrow vision of India. Now that these and other possibilities have materialized, we need to undertake a radical reconsideration of some of the constitutive principles of the Indian state, and find a historically more sensitive and realistic way of evolving political unity out of the newly emergent forms of diversity. There is little sign that we have even begun to grasp the enormity of the problem facing us, let alone explore ways of tackling it.

MULTICULTURALISM, LIBERAL CITIZENSHIP AND NATIONAL IDENTITY: ON BRITISH MUSLIMS[1]

TARIQ MODOOD

A Crisis of Multiculturalism

A central feature of the political discourses in contemporary western Europe is a critique of multiculturalism that focuses on Muslims. It pre-dates the terrorist attacks of 9/11 and their aftermath, though in Britain, at least, 2001 is a pivotal year (in relation to other countries, see Modood, 2007, pp. 12–14). The late spring of that year saw urban disturbances in a number of northern English towns and cities in which young Muslim, mainly Pakistani, men played a central role. The dominant political response was that the riots were due to a one-sided multiculturalism having facilitated, even encouraged, segregated communities which shunned each other. All subsequent events seem to point in the same direction. For example, Gilles Keppel observed that the 7/7 bombers 'were the children of Britain's own multicultural society' and that the bombings have 'smashed' the implicit social consensus that produced multiculturalism 'to smithereens' (Keppel, 2005). While not all commentators are so gleeful in their reading of these events, it is nevertheless true that virtually throughout the western world there is disaffection against multiculturalism, even amongst its erstwhile supporters. Indeed, it would be no exaggeration to speak of a 'crisis of multiculturalism' and to note that its prevalence is linked to the size or activities of the Muslim population in specific countries (Kymlicka 2007, p. 55; for qualifications see Jedwab 2005).

I would like to respond to this state of affairs by restating a conception of multiculturalism which, while not within certain narrow forms of liberalism, places it squarely within an understanding of democratic citizenship and nation-building and so offers a prospect of winning back the lost support for multicultural politics.

Difference and Equality

Multiculturalism gives political importance to a respect for identities that are important to people, as identified in minority assertiveness, arguing that they should not be disregarded in the name of integration or citizenship (Young 1990; Parekh 1991; Taylor 1994).

Sociologically we have to begin with the fact of negative 'difference', with alien-ness, inferiorization, stigmatization, stereotyping, exclusion, discrimination, racism etc.; but also the senses of identity that groups so perceived have of themselves. The two together are the key datum for multiculturalism. The differences at issue are those perceived both by outsiders or group members to constitute not just some form of distinctness but a form of alien-ness or inferiority that diminishes or makes difficult equal membership in the wider society or polity. There is a sense of groupness in play, a mode of being, but also subordination or marginality, a mode of oppression, and the two interact in creating an unequal 'us–them' relationship.[2] The differences in question are in the fields of race, ethnicity, cultural heritage or religious community; typically, differences that overlap between these categories, not least because these categories do not have singular, fixed meanings.

Multiculturalism refers to the struggle, the political mobilization but also the policy and institutional outcomes, to the forms of accommodation in which 'differences' are not eliminated or washed away but to some extent 'recognized'. Through both these ways, group assertiveness and mobilization, and through institutional and policy reforms to address the claims of the newly settled, marginalized groups, the character of 'difference' is addressed. Ideally, a negative difference is turned into a positive difference, though in most contemporary situations something of each is likely to be simultaneously present.

It should be clear from the above that the concept of equality has to be applied to groups and not just individuals (e.g., Parekh 2000). Different theorists have offered different formulations on this question. Charles Taylor (1994), for example, argues that when we talk about equality in the context of race and ethnicity, we are appealing to two different albeit related concepts: *equal dignity* and *equal respect*. Equal dignity appeals to people's humanity or to some specific membership like citizenship and applies to all members in a relatively uniform way. A good example is Martin Luther King Jr.'s demand for civil rights. He said black Americans want to make a claim upon the American dream; they wanted American citizenship in the way that the constitution theoretically is supposed to give to everybody, but in practice failed to do so. We appeal to this universalist idea in relation to anti-discrimination policies where we appeal to the principle that everybody should be treated the same.

On the other hand, Taylor, and other theorists in differing ways, also posit the idea of *equal respect*. If equal dignity focuses on what people have in common, and so is gender-blind, colour-blind and so on, equal respect is based on an understanding that difference is also important in conceptualizing and institutionalizing equal relations between individuals. This is because individuals have group identities and these may be the ground of existing and long-standing inequalities such as racism, for example, and the ways that some people have conceived and treated others as inferior, less rational and culturally backward. While those conceptions persist they will affect the dignity of non-white people, above all where they share imaginative and social life with white people. The negative conceptions will lead to direct and indirect acts of discrimination; they will eat away at the possibilities of equal dignity. They will affect the self-understanding of those who breathe in and seek to be equal participants in a culture in which ideas of their inferiority, or even just of their absence, their invisibility, is pervasive. They will stand in need of self-respect and the respect of others, especially of the dominant group; the latter will be crucial for it is the source of their damaged self-respect and it is where the power for change lies (Du Bois 1903).

Hence we must not lose sight of the fact that *both* equal dignity and equal respect are essential to multiculturalism; while the latter marks out multiculturalism from classical liberalism it does not make multiculturalism normatively particularistic or relativist.

3 + 1 Implications for Liberal Citizenship

Multiculturalism arises within contemporary liberal egalitarianism but it is at the same time in tension with, and a critique of, some classical liberal ideas. Specifically, it has four major implications for liberal citizenship. First, it is clearly a collective project and concerns collectivities and not just individuals. Second, it is not colour/gender/sexual orientation 'blind' and so breaches the liberal public–private identity distinction which prohibits the recognition of particular group identities in order that no citizens are treated in a more or less privileged way or divided from each other. These two implications are obvious from the discussion so far but the next two implications are less obvious and more controversial. The first of these is that multiculturalism takes race, sex and sexuality beyond being merely ascriptive sources of identity, merely categories. Liberal citizenship is not interested in group identities and shuns identarian politics; its interest in 'race' is confined to anti-discrimination and simply as an aspect of the legal equality of citizens. Strictly speaking, race is of interest to liberal citizenship only because no one can choose their race: it is either a biological fact about them or, more accurately, is a way of being categorized by the society around them by reference to some real or perceived biological features, and so one should not be discriminated against on something over which one has no control. But if, as I have argued, equality is also about celebrating previously demeaned identities (e.g., taking pride in one's blackness rather than accepting it as a merely 'private' matter), then what is being addressed in anti-discrimination, or promoted as a public identity, is a chosen response to one's ascription, namely pride, identity renewal, the challenging of hegemonic norms and asserting of marginalized identities and so on. Of course this is not peculiar to race/ethnicity. Exactly the same applies to sex and sexuality. We may not choose our sex or sexual orientation but we choose how to politically live with it. Do we keep it private or do we make it the basis of a social movement and seek public resources and representation for it? In many countries the initial liberal – and social democratic and socialist – response that the assertions of race, political femininity, gay pride politics and so on were divisive and deviations from the only political identity that mattered (citizenship; and/or class, in the case of socialists) soon gave way to an understanding that these positions were a genuine and significant part of a plural, centre-left egalitarian movement.

Marginalized and other religious groups, most notably Muslims, are now utilizing the same kind of argument and making a claim that religious identity, just like gay identity, and just like certain forms of racial identity, should not just be privatized or tolerated, but should be part of the public space. In their case, however, they come into conflict with an additional fourth dimension of liberal citizenship. This additional conflict with liberal citizenship is best understood as a '3 + 1' rather than merely a fourth difficulty because while it is not clear that it actually raises a new difficulty, for many on the centre-left this one, unlike the previous three, is seen as a demand that should not be conceded. One would think that if a new group was pressing a claim which had already been granted to others then what would be at issue would be a practical adjustment, not fundamental principle. But as a matter of fact, the demand by Muslims for not just toleration and religious freedom but for public recognition is indeed taken to be philosophically very different to the same demand made by black people, women and gays. It is seen as an attack on the principle of secularism, the view that religion is a feature, perhaps uniquely, of private and not public identity.

Hence it is commonly found in the op-ed pages of the broadsheets, that Muslims (and other religious groups) are simply not on a par with the groups with which I have aligned them. It is argued that woman, black and gay are ascribed, involuntary identities while being a Muslim is about chosen beliefs, and that Muslims therefore need or ought to have less legal protection than the other kinds of identities. I think this is sociologically naïve (and a political con). The position of Muslims today in countries like Britain is similar to the other identities of 'difference' as Muslims catch up with and engage with the contemporary concept of equality. No one chooses to be or not to be born into a Muslim family. Similarly, no one chooses to be born into a society where to look like a Muslim or to be a Muslim creates suspicion, hostility, or failure to get the job you applied for. Of course how Muslims respond to these circumstances will vary. Some will organize resistance, while others will try to stop looking like Muslims (the equivalent of 'passing' for white); some will build an ideology out of their subordination, others will not, just as a woman can choose to be a feminist or not. Again, some Muslims may define their Islam in terms of piety rather than politics; just as some women may see no politics in their gender, while for others their gender will be at the centre of their politics.

I reject, therefore, the contention that equality as recognition (uniquely) does not apply to oppressed religious communities. Of course many people's objections may be based on what they (sometimes correctly) understand as conservative, even intolerant and inegalitarian views held by some Muslims in relation to issues of personal sexual freedom. My concern is with the argument that a commitment to a reasonable secularism rules out extending multicultural equality to Muslims and other religious groups.

I proceed on the basis of two assumptions: first that a religious group's view on matters of gender and sexuality, which of course will not be uniform, are open to debate and change; and second, that conservative views cannot be a bar to multicultural recognition.[3] Those who see the current Muslim assertiveness as an unwanted and illegitimate child of multiculturalism have only two choices if they wish to be consistent. They can repudiate the idea of equality as identity recognition and return to the 1950s liberal idea of equality as colour/sex/religion etc. blindness (Barry 2001). Or they must appreciate that a programme of racial and multicultural equality is not possible today without a discussion of the merits and limits of secularism.

Muslims and Identity

British Muslim identity politics was virtually created by the *Satanic Verses* Affair of the late 1980s and beyond (Modood, 1992). Muslims began to make demands for recognition and civic inclusion into a polity which had up to that point misrecognized them (as black or Asian) or had kept them invisible and voiceless; a polity which was struggling to recognize gender, race and ethnicity within the terms of citizenship but was not even aware that any form of civic recognition was due to marginalized religious groups. The conflict that erupted led many to think of themselves for the first time as Muslims in a public way, to think that it was important in their relation to other Muslims and to the rest of British and related societies. This is, for example, movingly described by the author, Rana Kabbani, whose *Letter to Christendom* begins with a description of herself as 'a woman who had been a sort of underground Muslim before she was forced into the open by the Salman Rushdie affair' (Kabbani, 1989, p. ix).

This sense of feeling that one must speak up as a Muslim is of course nothing necessarily to do with religiosity. Like all forms of difference it comes into being as a result of pressures from 'outside' a group as well as from the 'inside'. In this particular case, both the 'inside' and the 'outside' have a powerful geo-political dimension. The emergence of British Muslim identity and activism has been propelled by a strong concern for the plight of Muslims elsewhere in the world, especially (but not only) where this plight is seen in terms of anti-imperialist emancipation and where the UK government is perceived to be part of the problem – tolerant of, if not complicit in or actively engaged in the destruction of, Muslim hopes and lives, usually civilian. That British, American and Australian (perhaps to some extent most western) Muslims are having to develop a sense of national citizenship, to integrate into a polity, which has a confrontational posture against many Muslim countries and is at war or occupying some of them in what is perceived by all sides to be a long-term project is an extremely daunting task and I suppose one has to say that success cannot be taken for granted. Moreover, domestic terrorism, as well as political opposition, has unfortunately become part of the context. The danger of 'blowback' from overseas military activity is, as events have shown, considerable and capable of destroying the movement towards multicultural citizenship.

One of the reasons why I do not think we should simply give up and pursue a less attractive political goal is that I am impressed by how many British Muslims have and are responding to the crisis, namely, with a concern to stand up for their community through civic engagement; with a refusal to give up neither on their Muslim identity nor being part of democratic citizenship. Despite this dependency on overseas circumstances outside their control and so where one might anticipate passivity and a self-pitying introspection, many British Muslims exhibit a dynamism and a confidence that they must rise to the challenge of dual loyalties and not give up on either set of commitments. Ideological and violent extremism is indeed undermining the conditions and hopes for multiculturalism, but, contrary to the multiculturalism blamers I began with, this extremism has nothing to do with the promotion of multiculturalism but is coming into the domestic arena from the international.

National Identity and Being British

Multiculturalism has been broadly right and does not deserve the desertion of support from the centre-left, let alone the blame for the present crisis. It offers a better basis for integration than its two current rivals, namely, 'social cohesion' and 'multiculture' (Meer and Modood, forthcoming). For while the latter is appreciative of a diversity of interacting lifestyles and the emergence of new, hybridic cultures in an atmosphere of 'conviviality', it is at a loss as to how to sympathetically deal with the claims of newly settled ethno-religious groups, especially Muslims, who are too readily stereotyped as 'fundamentalists' (Modood, 1998). Some advocacy of multiculturalism has, however, perhaps overlooked or at least underemphasized the other side of the coin, which is not just equally necessary but is integral to multiculturalism. For one cannot just talk about difference. Difference has to be related to things we have in common. The commonality that most multiculturalists emphasize is citizenship. I have argued that this citizenship has to be seen in a plural, dispersed and dialogical way and not reduced to legal rights, passports and the franchise (important though these are). I would now like to go further in suggesting that a good basis for or accompaniment to a multicultural citizenship is a national identity.

We in Europe have overlooked that where multiculturalism has been accepted and worked as a state project or as a national project – Canada, Australia and Malaysia, for example – it has not just been coincidental with but integral to a nation-building project, to creating Canadians, Aussies and Malaysians etc. Even in the US, where the federal state has had a much lesser role in the multicultural project, the incorporation of ethno-religious diversity and hyphenated Americans has been about country-making, civic inclusion and making a claim upon the national identity. This is important because some multiculturalists, or at least advocates of pluralism and multiculture (the vocabulary of multiculturalism is not always used)[4] – even where they have other fundamental disagreements with each other – argue as if the logic of the national and the multicultural are incompatible. Partly as a result, many Europeans think of multiculturalism as antithetical to, rather than as a reformer of, national identity.

Moreover, it does not make sense to encourage strong multicultural or minority identities and weak common or national identities; strong multicultural identities are a good thing – they are not intrinsically divisive, reactionary or fifth columns – but they need a framework of vibrant, dynamic, national narratives and the ceremonies and rituals which give expression to a national identity. It is clear that minority identities are capable of having an emotional pull for the individuals for whom they are important. Multicultural citizenship requires, therefore, if it is to be equally attractive to the same individuals, a comparable counter-balancing emotional pull. Many Britons, for example, say they are worried about disaffection amongst some Muslim young men and more generally a lack of identification with Britain amongst many Muslims in Britain. As a matter of fact, surveys over many years have shown Muslims have been reaching out for an identification with Britain. For example, in a Channel 4 NOP survey done in Spring 2006, 82% of a national sample of Muslims said they very strongly (45%) or fairly strongly (37%) felt they belonged to Britain.[5] Of course there is a lot of anger and fear around these issues, especially in relation to the aggressive US–UK foreign policies and terrorism. While I do not feel that we are at all close to undoing the mess we have got into with these policies, to not build on the clear support there is for a sense of national belonging is to fail to offer an obvious counterweight to the ideological calls for a jihad against fellow Britons.

Notes

1 This is a version of the web essay at <http://www.opendemocracy.net/faith-europe_islam/multiculturalism_4627.jsp>. The full argument is presented in my *Multiculturalism: A Civic Idea*, Cambridge, UK; Malden, MA, USA: Polity Press, 2007.

2 In Modood (2007) I clarify that I do not mean terms such as 'groupness', 'mode of being', 'subordination', 'identity' and so on to denote univocal,

internally undifferentiated concepts (see my discussion of Wittgenstein's concept of 'family resemblance' in chapter 5).

3 It is clear that 'moderate' Muslim public figures in Britain are divided on homosexuality (Modood and Ahmad 2007) in just the way that all religions seem to be divided today.

4 For a discussion of the differences and tensions between communitarian multiculturalism and 'multiculture', see Modood (1998) and Meer and Modood (forthcoming).

5 Full survey at http://www.channel4.com/news/microsites/D/dispatches2006/muslim_survey/index.html.

References

Barry, B. (2001) *Culture Equality* (Cambridge: Polity Press).

Du Bois, W. E. B. (1999 [1903]) *The Souls of Black Folk Centenary Edition.* H. L. Gates Jr and H.Oliver (Eds) (London: Norton Critical Edition).

Jedwab, J. (2005) Muslims and multicultural futures in western democracies: is Kymlicka's pessimism warranted?, *Canadian Diversity*, 4(3), pp. 92–96.

Kabbani, R. (1989) *A Letter to Christendom* (London: Virago Press).

Keppel, G. (2005) Europe's answer to Londonistan, *openDemocracy*, **23-08-05** http://www.opendemocracy.net/conflict-terrorism/londonistan_2775.jsp.

Kymlicka, W. (2007) The new debate on minority rights (and postscript), in: A. S. Laden and D. Owen (eds) *Multiculturalism and Political Theory* (Cambridge: Cambridge University Press).

Meer, N. and Modood, T. (forthcoming) The Multicultural State We're In: Muslims, 'Multiculture' and the 'Civic Rebalancing' of British Multiculturalism, *Political Studies*.

Modood, T. (1992) *Not Easy Being British: Colour, Culture and Citizenship* (London: Runnymede Trust/Trentham Books).

Modood, T. (1998) Anti-essentialism, multiculturalism and the 'recognition' of religious minorities, *Journal of Political Philosophy*, 6(4), pp. 378–399; reproduced in W. Kymlicka and W. Norman (eds) *Citizenship in Diverse Societies* (Oxford: Oxford University Press).

Modood, T. (2007) *Multiculturalism: A Civic Idea* (Cambridge: Polity Press).

Modood, T. and Ahmad, F. (2007) 'British Muslim Perspectives on Multiculturalism' in *Theory, Culture and Society*, Special Issue on Global Islam guest edited by Volpi, F. and Turner, 24(1), 187–214.

Parekh, B. (1991) 'British citizenship and cultural difference' in Andrews, G (ed.) *Citizenship* London: Lawrence & Wishart.

Parekh, B. (2000) *Rethinking Multiculturalism: Cultural Diversity and Political Theory* (Basingstoke: Macmillan).

Taylor, C. (1994) Multiculturalism and 'the politics of recognition', in: A. Gutmann (ed.) *Multiculturalism and 'The Politics of Recognition'* (Princeton: Princeton University Press).

Young, I. M. (1990) *Justice and the Politics of Difference* (Princeton: Princeton University Press).

6

Citizenship, Assimilation and Multiculturalism

The nation-state's aim was to build a homogeneous nation out of a diverse population while simultaneously constructing a distinct national identity destined to foster sentiments of belonging and solidarity among its members. This proves that the nation state is not ethno-culturally free and that nation-building is ethnically charged. This assertion contradicts the position defended by scholars of liberalism, such as Michael Walzer[1], who argue that the liberal state is 'neutral' with regard to the ethnic make-up of its citizens.

Kymlicka disagrees with him and argues that, from a liberal position, it makes sense to defend minority rights precisely because the liberal state is not blind to ethnic difference. In his view, minority rights are consistent with liberal culturalism if they protect the freedom of individuals within the group and promote relations of equality (non-dominance) between groups.

Notwithstanding, while national identity refers to the sentiment of belonging to the nation, citizenship refers to the political bond, which defines membership of the state. Yet, while members of a single nation state share the same citizenship they may not share the same national identity. For instance, citizens of Wales, Scotland and England are all British citizens, but they still retain specific Welsh, Scottish and English national identities. In a similar manner, British citizens include, among others, members of the Pakistani and the Indian communities as well as people of Afro-Caribbean and Chinese origin who may, in turn, feel that they belong to various nations, some of which may not even be included in the United Kingdom.

Will Kymlicka argues that, from a liberal position, it makes sense to defend minority rights precisely because the liberal state is not blind to ethnic difference. In his view, minority rights are consistent with liberal culturalism if they protect the freedom of individuals within the group and promote relations of equality (non-dominance) between groups.

Kymlicka establishes a distinction between immigrant multiculturalism and minority nationalism. He stands firmly in favour of multiculturalism and argues that it has to be regarded as one of the policies – not the only or even the primary one – regulating the integration of immigrants. In his view, multiculturalism 'is just one modest component in a larger package' and that 'many aspects of public policy affect [immigrant] groups, including policies relating to naturalization, education, job training and professional accreditation, human rights and anti-discrimination law, civil service employment, health and safety, even national defence. It is these other policies, which are the major engines of integration. They all encourage, pressure, even legally force immigrants to take steps towards integrating into society.'[2]

In contrast, national minorities have only a limited range of options when confronted with these sort of nation-building policies. He argues that 'the historical experience of the Québécois suggests that a minority can only sustain its societal culture if it has substantial powers regarding language, education, government employment, and immigration. If the minority can be outvoted on any of these issues, their hope of sustaining their societal culture would be seriously jeopardized. But they can only exercise these powers if they have some forum of collective decision-making. That is, there must be some political body or political unit that they substantially control.'[3] The main difference between immigrant multiculturalism and minority nationalism regarding their objectives is that while the former is not engaged in nation-building processes or, at least, there is no evidence from any of the major Western immigration countries that immigrants are seeking to form themselves into national minorities, or to adopt a nationalist political agenda the latter, in order to survive, must use the same nation-building tools employed by the majority nation and this often results in the formulation of a separatist agenda.

Samuel Huntington's main objective is to analyse the main factors contributing to, what he perceives as, a weakening of American identity. Among them, he mentions: a much more relaxed approach towards assimilation into the country's mainstream culture; the impact of Hispanic immigration and the linguistic and cultural challenges it poses to American identity; as well as the consequences of multiculturalism and cosmopolitanism – as ideas contributing to a widening gap between elites and the masses in the USA.

In Huntington's view: 'Throughout American history, people who were not white Anglo-Saxon Protestants have become Americans by adopting America's Anglo-Protestant culture and political values. This benefited them and the country...Millions of immigrants and their children achieved wealth, power and status in American society precisely because they assimilated themselves into the prevailing American culture.'[4]

Huntington is particularly concerned by large and steady migration of Mexicans to the USA since no other immigrant group in American history has asserted or has been able to assert a historical claim to American territory. Mexicans and Mexican-Americans can and do make that claim since almost all of Texas, New Mexico, Arizona, California, Nevada, and Utah were part of Mexico until 1835–6, when Mexico lost them in the War of Independence fought against the United States of America.

For Richard Alba and Victor Nee assimilation occupies a central place in the American experience. It is their concern that assimilation crucially contributed to the Americanization of earlier waves of immigrants, most of them from European origin. A recent study of new immigration to the USA argues that it will be hard for contemporary immigrants to move up in the social ladder, since the majority of jobs available to them tend to be unskilled and badly paid. As a result, most immigrants have fewer possibilities to acquire a good education able to contribute to their social mobility, as it was the case with previous waves of immigration. They even raise the issue of whether second generation immigrants may experience no, or even downward, mobility unless the American economy becomes more dynamic; an issue that points at the role of economic opportunities as a major incentive for cultural and linguistic assimilation. They also highlight the ability of well-established ethnic sub-economies, such as those of Cubans in Miami or Chinese and Japanese urban enclaves, to draw on ethnic solidarity and resources.

Frank-Olaf Radtke discusses the problems of grafting a multicultural apparatus on to the institutions of what he calls 'the social democratic welfare state'. Radtke writes with the case of Frankfurt particularly in mind. He argues that the religious community of ethics is situated in the private sphere and that political pluralism will work only if the different spheres – private and public – are separated and their ruling maxims are not confused.

In the former Federal Republic of Germany social welfare was placed in the hands of private social welfare organizations which promoted differences of language and religion among immigrants. The Catholic *Caritas* supported Catholic migrants from Italy, Spain, Portugal and Croatia, the Protestant *Diakonie* supported non-Catholic but Christian migrants from Greece; and the *Arbeiterwohlfahrt* was close to trade unions and supported non-Christian immigrants from Turkey and the Maghreb. Radtke argues that the German model involves dealing with immigrants according to their ethnic and religious ascription rather than according to their social roles. As a result, minorities in Germany are kept away from the public sphere and invited by the legal system to form apolitical communities in the private sphere instead of interest groups.

Ma Rong refers to 'culturalization' as a tradition of thousands of years in China. It refers to a process by means of which 'relatively less advanced minority 'barbarians', including nomads in grasslands and people living in mountainous areas in the south were acculturated by the more 'advanced' Chinese civilization-led Han Chinese. Such a distinction between 'advanced' and 'less advanced' peoples, according to Confucianism, does not refer to apparent differences in physical features or language. Rather, it is mainly shown in cultural differences with values and norms of behaviour as the distinguishing characteristics.

Until the late *Qing* dynasty, tradition resulted in a united–pluralistic polity with a huge population brought together by cultural assimilation and a prosperous economy. Under the new historical conditions of the twentieth century, however, China adopted the policies of the former USSR. From the 1950s, China conferred greater political emphasis to its ethnic minorities in a process commonly referred to as 'politicization' of ethnic minorities. Ma Rong argues that, in the twenty-first century, China should learn both from its own historical heritage and from the lessons of the USA, the former USSR and other nations, and redirect its policy from 'politicization' to 'culturalization' of ethnic issues in order to strengthen national identity among its ethnic minorities.

Notes

1 Walzer, Michael, 'Comment' in Gutman, Amy (ed.) *Multiculturalism and the 'Politics of Recognition'* (Princeton University Press: Princeton, 1992), pp. 99–103.
2 Kymlicka, Will, *Politics in the Vernacular: Nationalism, Multiculturalism and Citizenship* (Oxford University Press: Oxford, 2001) p. 155.
3 Kymlicka, Will, *Politics in the Vernacular: Nationalism, Multiculturalism and Citizenship* (Oxford University Press: Oxford, 2001), p. 158.
4 Huntington, Samuel P., *Who Are We? America's Great Debate* (Free Press, Simon and Shuster: London, 2004), p. 61.

ETHNICITY AND LIBERALISM IN THE USA

WILL KYMLICKA

Rethinking the Liberal Tradition

[...] Few contemporary theorists have explicitly discussed the rights of ethnic and national minorities, or developed any principles for evaluating claims to language rights, for example, or federal autonomy. It was not always this way. For most of the nineteenth century and the first half of the twentieth, the rights of national minorities were continually discussed and debated by the great liberal statesmen and theorists of the age. As I will show, they disagreed about how best to respond to multinational states, but they all took it for granted that liberalism needed some or other theory of the status of national minorities.

Contemporary liberals, by contrast, have been surprisingly silent about these issues. There are very few discussions of the differences between nation states and polyethnic or multinational states, or of the demands associated with each form of ethnic or national diversity. And when contemporary liberals have addressed these issues – often in brief pronouncements or parenthetical asides – they have tended to recite simplistic formulas about 'non-discrimination' or 'benign neglect', formulas that cannot do justice to the complexities involved.

In this [essay], I will trace the origin of contemporary liberal attitudes towards minority rights. I will first explore some of the historical debates about national minorities, then consider some of the reasons why this issue virtually disappeared from view after the Second World War [...].

In the process, I hope to correct some common mistakes about the liberal tradition. It is widely believed that liberals have always opposed the political recognition and support of ethnicity and nationality, and that demands for group-differentiated rights for cultural groups are a recent and illiberal deviation from long-established liberal practice (Kymlicka 1989).

This is simply not true. Minority rights were an important part of liberal theory and practice in the nineteenth century and between the world wars. If anything, it is the idea of 'benign neglect' which is a recent arrival in the liberal tradition. Moreover, its emergence can be traced to a series of contingent factors, including ethnocentric denigration of non-European cultures, fears about international peace and security, and the influence of racial desegregation decisions in the United States. These factors have had a profound but often distorting effect on liberal thinking. Issues and arguments that were relevant in one set of circumstances have been mistakenly generalized to other cases where they do not apply. Once we sort out these confusions, it should become clear that minority rights are a legitimate component of the liberal tradition.

The History of Liberal Views on National Minorities

The liberal tradition contains a striking diversity of views on the rights of minority cultures. At one end of the spectrum, there have been strong proponents of minority rights. Indeed, there have been times in the last two centuries when endorsement of minority rights was considered a clear sign of one's liberal credentials.

For example, it was a common tenet of nineteenth-century liberalism that national minorities were treated unjustly by the multinational empires of Europe, such as the Habsburg, Ottoman and Tsarist empires. The injustice was not simply the fact that the minorities were denied individual civil and political liberties, since that was true of the members of the dominant nation in each empire as well. The injustice was rather the denial of their national rights to self-government, which were seen as an essential complement to individual rights, since 'the cause of liberty finds its basis, and secures its roots, in the autonomy of a national group' (Barker 1948: 248; cf. Mazzini 1907: 51–2, 176–7; Humboldt [1836] 1988: 21, 41–3, 153). The promotion of national autonomy 'offers a realization of the ideal of an "area of liberty", or in other words, of a free society for free men' (Hoernlé 1939: 181).

The precise connection between individual freedom and nationality is not always clear in these theorists. In some cases, it was simply the assumption that multinational states were inherently unstable, and so liable to authoritarianism (I discuss this claim below). But in other theorists, such as Wilhelm von Humboldt and Giuseppe Mazzini, the claim is that the promotion of individuality and the development of human personality is intimately tied up with membership in one's national group, in part because of the role of language and culture in enabling choice.

This liberal commitment to some form of national self-government was so common that George Bernard Shaw once quipped that 'A Liberal is a man who has three duties: a duty to Ireland, a duty to Finland, and a duty to Macedonia' (Zimmern 1918). (All three nations were incorporated into multinational empires at the time.) Notice that the liberal aim was not to grant individual rights to all citizens of these multinational empires, but rather to grant political powers to the constituent nations within each empire. Liberals predicted (accurately) that these empires would fall apart because of their reluctance to grant 'any system of autonomy under which the various nations could have enjoyed the position of quasi-States' (Barker 1948: 254).

It may seem odd that a liberal could ever have been defined (even in jest) by a commitment to national rights rather than individual rights. But we find the same linkage between liberalism and support for the rights of national minorities between the world wars. Leonard Hobhouse, for example, said that 'the more liberal statesmanship' of his day had recognized the necessity of minority rights to ensure 'cultural equality' (Hobhouse 1966: 297, 299). There is more than one way to meet the legitimate demands of national minorities, he thought, but 'clearly it is not achieved by equality of franchise. The smaller nationality does not merely want equal rights with others. It stands out for a certain life of its own' (Hobhouse 1928: 146–7). One manifestation of this liberal commitment was the minority protection scheme set up under the League of Nations for various European national minorities, which provided both universal individual rights and certain group-specific rights regarding education, local autonomy, and language.

Again, the precise connection between equality and minority rights was rarely spelled out. But the general idea was clear enough. A multinational state which accords universal individual rights to all its citizens, regardless of group membership, may appear to be 'neutral' between the various national groups. But in fact it can (and often does) systematically privilege the majority nation in certain fundamental ways – for example, the drawing of internal boundaries; the language of schools, courts and government services; the choice of public holidays; and the division of legislative power between central and local governments. All of these decisions can dramatically reduce the political power and cultural viability of a national minority, while enhancing that of the majority culture. Group-specific rights regarding education, local autonomy and language help ensure that national minorities are not disadvantaged in these decisions, thereby enabling the minority, like the majority, to sustain 'a life of its own'.

We have here the two major claims which, I believe, underlie a liberal defence of minority rights: that individual freedom is tied in some important way to membership in one's national group; and that group-specific rights can promote equality between the minority and majority. [...]

These two claims were widely accepted by many nineteenth- and early twentieth-century liberals. To be sure, some liberals opposed various demands for minority rights. But not because of a commitment to the principle of 'benign neglect'. Rather, they believed, with John Stuart Mill, that free institutions are 'next to impossible' in a multination state:

> Among a people without fellow-feelings, especially if they read and speak different languages, the united public opinion necessary to the workings of representative institutions cannot exist. . . [It] is in general a necessary condition of free institutions that the boundaries of governments should coincide in the main with those of nationalities (Mill 1972: 230, 233).

For liberals like Mill, democracy is government 'by the people', but self-rule is only possible if 'the people' are 'a people' – a nation. The members of a democracy must share a sense of political allegiance, and common nationality was said to be a precondition of that allegiance. Thus T. H. Green argued that liberal democracy is possible only if people feel bound to the state by 'ties derived from a common dwelling place with its associations, from common memories, traditions and customs, and from the common ways of feeling and thinking which a common language and still more a common literature embodies' (Green 1941: 130–1; cf. Rich 1987: 155). According to this stream of liberal thought, since a free state must be a nation state, national minorities must be dealt with by coercive assimilation or the redrawing of boundaries, not by minority rights.

The alleged need for a common national identity is an important issue which, as we will see, has been raised again and again throughout the liberal tradition. Some liberals support the need for a common national identity, others deny its necessity. Moreover, some liberals deny that a multinational state even has the capacity to promote a common national identity which will displace or take precedence over the existing identity of a national minority. [...]

However, in the nineteenth century, the call for a common national identity was often tied to an ethnocentric denigration of smaller national groups. It was commonplace in nineteenth-century thought to distinguish the 'great nations', such as France, Italy, Poland, Germany, Hungary, Spain, England and Russia, from smaller 'nationalities', such as the Czechs, Slovaks, Croats, Basques, Welsh, Scots, Serbians, Bulgarians, Romanians and Slovenes. The great nations were seen as civilized, and as the carriers of historical development. The smaller nationalities were primitive and stagnant, and incapable of social or cultural development. So some nineteenth-century liberals endorsed national independence for great nations, but coercive assimilation for smaller nationalities.

Thus Mill insisted that it was undeniably better for a Scottish Highlander to be part of Great Britain, or for a Basque to be part of France, 'than to sulk on his own rocks, the half-savage relic of past times, revolving in his own little mental orbit, without participation or interest in the general movement of the world' (Mill 1972: 363–4). Mill was hardly alone in this view. As I discuss later in this chapter, nineteenth-century socialists shared this ethnocentric view, which was also invoked to justify the coerced assimilation of indigenous peoples throughout the British Empire.

Other liberals argued the opposite position, that true liberty was possible only in a multinational state. For example, Lord Acton argued, against Mill, that the divisions between national groups and their desire for an internal life of their own serves as a check against the aggrandisement and abuse of state power (Acton 1922: 285–90). This debate was revisited by British liberals during and after the First World War. For example, Alfred Zimmern defended Acton's claim that a multinational state checks the abuse of state power (Zimmern 1918), while Ernest Barker defended Mill's belief that a nation state can best sustain free institutions (Barker 1948). Here again very different views about the status of national minorities were defended, yet each side claimed that it represented the truly liberal view.

So there is a considerable range of views on minority rights within the liberal tradition. Notice also that none of these earlier positions endorses the idea – championed by many contemporary liberals – that the state should treat cultural membership as a purely private matter. On the contrary, liberals either endorsed the legal recognition of minority cultures, or rejected minority rights not because they rejected the idea of an official culture, but precisely because they believed there should only be *one* official culture.

This is just a quick sketch of the way many earlier liberals viewed nationality. A fuller account would probably reveal an even greater range of views, since it was a prominent theme in most major liberal writings of the era. What explains this remarkable level of interest and debate in one era, and its subsequent virtual disappearance in post-war liberal thought? It is partly related to the rise and fall of the British Empire. From the early 1800s to the beginning of decolonization after the Second World War, English liberals were constantly confronted with the issue of how to export liberal institutions to their colonies. The desire to transplant liberal institutions was fuelled by a somewhat contradictory combination of old-fashioned imperialism (expanding England's domain by setting up little Englands overseas), and a universalistic liberal faith in the 'rights of man', which viewed liberal institutions in the colonies as the first step towards their freedom and independence from English power.

But whatever the motives, English liberals were constantly confronted with the fact that liberal institutions which worked in England did not work in multinational states. It quickly became clear that many English liberal institutions were as much English as liberal – that is, they were appropriate for only a (relatively) ethnically and racially homogeneous society such as England. As Lord Balfour put it, while 'constitutions are easily copied', the successful working of English institutions 'may be difficult or impossible' if national divisions in the colonies are 'either too numerous or too profound'. English institutions presupposed 'a people so fundamentally at one that they can afford to bicker' (Hancock 1937: 429).

According to Hancock, who studied national conflicts within the Empire, British colonial policy was at first shaped by 'abstract universalizers of liberal doctrine' who possessed 'an irresistible propensity to generalize the Englishman's "principles" at large, without realizing that in so doing they [were] taking for granted the whole rich and stable background of English history'. They tried to 'assert their 'principles' in the Empire without realizing that what they [were] really seeking [was] to impose their own national forms, regardless of the historic life and culture and needs of some quite different community'. In short, they 'thought it sufficient to transplant, where the need was to translate' (Hancock 1937: 496).

As a result, liberals who went to administer or study British colonies found that the liberalism they learned in England simply did not address some of the issues of cultural diversity they faced. An early example of this was Lord Durham, one of John Stuart Mill's circle, who was sent to Canada to head an inquiry into the causes of the Rebellions of 1837. On the surface, the rebellions in English and French Canada were about demands for more responsible and democratic government (like the American Revolution), and this was how British liberals initially interpreted them. But, as Durham put it in his report, 'I expected to find a contest between a government and a people: I found two nations warring in the bosom of a single state.' He also found that existing liberal theory was not much help in resolving this sort of dispute. His solution, endorsed by J. S. Mill and adopted by the British government, was the more or less forcible assimilation of the French, so as to create a homogeneous English nation state. He had no sympathy for the 'vain endeavour' of the French Canadians to maintain their 'backward' culture (Craig 1963: 146–50).

However, Durham's policy was a complete failure, as French-Canadian resistance to assimilation led to a paralysis in colonial government. Most subsequent liberals, therefore, proposed accommodating national divisions in the colonies. Indeed, many liberals believed that developing a theory of national rights was the greatest challenge facing English liberalism if its appeal was to move beyond the boundaries of its (culturally homogeneous) homeland (e.g. Hoernlé 1939: 123–5, 136–8; Hobhouse 1928: 146; Hancock 1937: 429–31, 495–6; Clarke 1934: 7–8).

My guess is that the same story was repeated a hundred times throughout the British Empire, from the early 1800s to the beginning of decolonization. There must have been generations of English thinkers who learned the essentials of liberal theory at universities in England, and who went overseas with the hope of transplanting those principles, but who were then faced with a set of issues regarding minority rights that they were unprepared to deal with. It would be interesting to have a proper study of the ways English liberals adapted their principles to deal with the existence of minority cultures in their various colonies. Problems of nationality arose throughout the Commonwealth – from Canada and the Caribbean to Africa, Palestine and India – and the colonial experience led to a wealth of experimentation regarding communal representation, language rights, treaties and other historical agreements between national groups, federalism, land rights and immigration policy. With the decline of the Empire, however, liberals stopped thinking about these issues, and little of this experience was fed back into British liberal theory.

The issue of minority rights was raised not only in the colonies, but also by events on the Continent. Nationalist conflicts in Europe were a constant threat to international peace before the Second World War, and this too encouraged liberals to attend to the rights of national minorities. Yet this factor also disappeared after the Second World War, as nationalist conflicts in Europe were replaced by Cold War conflicts over ideology.

So the ushering in of the post-war era relieved British liberals of the two major reasons for thinking about national minorities – governing overseas colonies, and responding to nationalist conflicts on the Continent. Perhaps as a result, many theorists have reverted to being 'abstract liberal universalizers' who cannot distinguish the core principles of liberalism from its particular institutional manifestations in uninational states like England.

American liberals during the nineteenth and early twentieth centuries were less involved in this debate. They did not have to deal with the existence of colonies, and they were some distance from Europe. As a result, they were not forced to develop a more generalized or comparative view about the application of liberal principles to multinational states. Two American liberals who did talk about minority rights were Randolph Bourne and Horace Kallen (Bourne 1964; Kallen 1924). But they were almost exclusively concerned with the status of white immigrant groups in the USA, and ignored the claims of territorially concentrated and historically settled national minorities, of the sort we find in Europe, Quebec and the Third World.

Post-war American liberalism exhibits the same neglect of national minorities. As I discuss later, virtually all American political theorists treat the United States as a polyethnic nation state, rather than a truly multinational state. Perhaps this is because national minorities in the United States are relatively small and isolated (e.g. Puerto Ricans, American Indians, native Hawaiians, Alaskan Eskimos). These groups are virtually invisible in American political theory. If they are mentioned at all, it is usually as an afterthought. This has had a profound effect on liberal thought around the world, since American theorists have become the dominant interpreters of liberal principles since the Second World War.

These factors – the fall of the British Empire, the rise of Cold War conflict and the prominence of American theorists within post-war liberalism – help explain why the heated debate about national minorities amongst pre-war liberals has given way to a virtual silence. But these factors do not explain why contemporary liberals in practice have become so hostile to minority rights. Why, even in the absence of theoretical discussions, have liberals not intuitively supported minority rights – as many did before the war – and seen them as promoting liberal values of individual freedom and social equality? Why have they instead adopted the idea of 'benign neglect'?

I believe this is the result of the convergence of a number of post-war political changes. Three features of the post-war world have conspired to lead liberals to adopt a misplaced antagonism towards the recognition of national rights: (1) disillusionment with the minority rights scheme of the League of Nations; (2) the American racial desegregation movement; and (3) the 'ethnic revival' among immigrant groups in the United States. I will discuss each of these in turn, to see how they have helped shape the new liberal distrust of minority rights.

The Failure of the Minority Treaties

The first important change in liberal views came with the failure of the League of Nations's minority protection scheme, and its role in the outbreak of the Second Word War. The scheme gave international recognition to the German-speaking minorities in Czechoslovakia and Poland, and the Nazis encouraged them to make demands and lodge complaints against their governments. When the Polish and Czech governments were unwilling or unable to meet the escalating demands of their German minorities, the Nazis used this as a pretext for aggression. This Nazi manipulation of the League scheme, and the cooperation of the German minorities in it, created 'a strong reaction against the concept of international protection of [national minorities]...the hard fact was that statesmen, generally backed by a public opinion which was deeply impressed by the perfidy of irredentist and disloyal minorities, were disposed to curtail, rather than to expand, the rights of minorities' (Claude 1955: 57, 69). This curtailing of minority rights was done, not in the interest of justice, but by people 'within whose frame of reference the interests of the national state ranked as supreme values...[The majority nationality] has an interest in making the national state secure, and its institutions stable, even at the cost of obliterating minority cultures and imposing enforced homogeneity upon the population' (Claude 1955: 80–1).

This 'frame of reference' is similar to the earlier liberal view that freedom requires cultural homogeneity, although it differs in emphasis. Whereas Mill and Green were concerned with domestic stability, post-war statesmen were primarily concerned with international peace. But the effect was the same – questions about the fairness of minority rights were subordinated to the higher demands of stability. There was an explicit desire to leave the issue of minority rights off the United Nations agenda, and the UN has only recently agreed to reconsider the legitimacy of minority rights claims (Sohn 1981; Thornberry 1980; 1991). The fear that national minorities will be disloyal (or simply apathetic) continues to inhibit discussion of the justice of these claims, both internationally and in the domestic politics of many countries.

Recent events in the former Yugoslavia show that the threat to international peace from irredentist minorities is still a very real one. The likelihood of violence is dramatically increased when a minority is seen (or sees itself) as belonging to an adjacent 'mother country' which proclaims itself as the legitimate protector of the minority. The government of Hungary has declared itself the protector of ethnic Hungarians in Slovakia and Romania; leaders in Russia and Serbia have made similar declarations about ethnic Russians in the Baltics and ethnic Serbs in Bosnia and Croatia. Protecting the rights of a national minority in these circumstances can become a pretext for territorial aggression by the self-proclaimed protector state. This shows the necessity of developing truly international mechanisms for protecting national minorities that do not rely on the destabilizing threat of intervention by kin states.

The problem of irredentism is much greater in Europe than in North America. Indigenous peoples in North America have no protector state to appeal to, and it has been over 100 years since anyone has viewed France as the protector of the Québécois in Canada. It has been almost as long since anyone viewed Spain as the protector of the Puerto Ricans. In these contexts, while minority rights may affect domestic stability, they pose little threat to international peace.

Racial Desegregation in the United States

The modern liberal rejection of minority rights began with worries about political stability, but it acquired the mantle of justice when it was linked to racial desegregation. In *Brown* v. *Board of Education*, the American Supreme Court struck down the system of segregated educational facilities for black and white children in the South. This decision, and the civil rights movement generally, had an enormous influence on American views of racial equality. The new model of racial justice was 'colour-blind laws', replacing 'separate but equal treatment', which was now seen as the paradigm of racial injustice.

But the influence of *Brown* was soon felt in areas other than race relations, for it seemed to lay down a principle which was equally applicable to relations between ethnic and national groups. According to this principle, injustice is a matter of arbitrary exclusion from the dominant institutions of society, and equality is a matter of non-discrimination and equal opportunity to participate. Viewed in this light, legislation providing separate institutions for national minorities seems no different from the segregation of blacks. The natural extension of *Brown*, therefore, was to remove the separate status of minority cultures, and encourage their equal participation in mainstream society.

This reasoning underlay the Canadian government's 1969 proposal to remove the special constitutional status of Indians. Drawing on the language of *Brown*, the government said that `separate but equal services do not provide truly equal treatment', and that 'the ultimate aim of removing the specific references to Indians from the constitution...is a goal to be kept constantly in view' (Bowles et al. 1972). Similarly, the Canadian Supreme Court invoked *Brown* when striking down a law which gave group-specific status to Indians.

Brown's formula for racial justice has also been invoked against the rights of American Indians, native Hawaiians, and the rights of national minorities in international law. Under the influence of *Brown*, these national groups have been treated as a 'racial minority', and their autonomous institutions have been struck down as forms of 'racial segregation' or 'racial discrimination'.

But the actual judgement in *Brown* does not support this application of the colour-blind formula to the rights of national minorities. The Court was simply not addressing the issue of national rights, like the right of a culture to the autonomous institutions needed to be able to develop itself freely within a multinational state. Segregationists were not claiming that whites and blacks formed different cultures, with different languages and literatures. On the contrary, the whole burden of their case was that the education received by blacks in their segregated facilities was *identical* with that of whites. The question was whether racial groups could be given separate facilities, so long as the facilities were identical. And the Court ruled that, *in those circumstances*, segregation was inherently unequal, since it would be seen as a 'badge of inferiority', as a sign of racism.

Nothing in the judgement warrants the claim that national rights are incompatible with liberal equality. Indeed, the judgement, examined more closely, may argue *for* the recognition of national rights. Consider the situation of American Indians, whose separate institutions came under attack after *Brown*. As Michael Gross notes:

> Where blacks have been forcibly *excluded* (segregated) from white society by law, Indians–aboriginal peoples with their own cultures, languages, religions and territories – have been forcibly *included* (integrated) into that society by law. That is what [is] meant by coercive assimilation – the practice of compelling, through submersion, an ethnic, cultural and linguistic minority to shed its uniqueness and identity and mingle with the rest of society (Gross 1973: 244).

Integrated education for the Indians, like segregated education for the blacks, is a 'badge of inferiority' for it fails 'to recognize the importance and validity of the Indian community'. In fact, the integration of Indian children in white-dominated schools had the same negative educational and emotional effects which segregation was held to have in *Brown*. Hence the 'underlying principle' which struck down the segregation of blacks – namely, that racial classifications harmful to a minority are prohibited – should also strike down legislated integration of Indians (Gross 1973: 242–8).

The point is not that Indians do not need protection against racism. But whereas racism against blacks comes from the denial by whites that blacks are full members of the community, racism against Indians comes primarily from the denial by whites that Indians are distinct peoples with their own cultures and communities. Unfortunately, the centrality of the civil rights movement for African-Americans has prevented people from seeing the distinctive issues raised by the existence of national minorities.

In one sense, it is paradoxical that *Brown* has been taken as a model for all ethnic and national groups. [...] The historical situation and present circumstances of African-Americans are virtually unique in the world, and there is no reason to think that policies which are appropriate for them would be appropriate for either national minorities or voluntary immigrants (or vice versa). But in another sense, this extension of *Brown* is understandable. The history of slavery and segregation represents one of the greatest evils of modern times, and its legacy is a society with very deep racial divisions. It is not surprising that the American government and courts, and public opinion generally, should wish to eliminate anything which even remotely resembles racial segregation. While separate and self-governing institutions for Indians or native Hawaiians have only a superficial resemblance to racial segregation, this has been enough to expose them to legal assault. While understandable, this over-generalization of *Brown* is unfortunate, and unjust. There is no reason why justice for African-Americans should come at the price of injustice for indigenous peoples and other national minorities.

Polyethnicity and the American Ethnic Revival

The belief that minority rights are unfair and divisive was confirmed, for many liberals, by the ethnic revival which rocked the United States and elsewhere in the 1960s and 1970s. [...] This revival began with the claim that it was legitimate (not 'unamerican') for ethnic groups to express their distinctive characteristics (as opposed to the 'Anglo-conformity' model of immigration). But it soon moved on to new demands. For example, one result of the more open expression of ethnic identity was that ethnic groups became more conscious of their status as a group. It became common to measure the distribution of income or occupations among ethnic groups, and some of those groups which were faring less well demanded group-based ameliorative action, such as quotas in education and employment. They also wanted their heritage recognized in the school curriculum and government symbols.

American liberals have had an ambiguous relationship to this ethnic revival. Most liberals accepted the initial demand by ethnic groups for the abandonment of the Anglo-conformity model. But as demands escalated, liberal support diminished. In fact, the increasing politicization of immigrant groups profoundly unsettled American liberals, for it affected the most basic assumptions and self-conceptions of American political culture. And this anxiety has had important repercussions for their attitude towards national minorities.

As I noted earlier, most American political theorists think of the United States as an immigrant country. Indeed, it is the original immigrant country. The idea of building a country through polyethnic immigration was quite unique in history, and many people thought it untenable. There were no historical precedents to show that an ethnically mixed country of immigrants would be stable. What would bind people together when they came from such different backgrounds, including every conceivable race, religion, language group, sharing virtually nothing in common?

The answer, of course, was that immigrants would have to integrate into the existing Anglophone society, rather than forming separate and distinct nations with their own homelands inside the United States. There was no hope for the long-term survival of the country if the Germans, Swedes, Dutch, Greeks, Italians, Poles and so on each viewed themselves as separate and self-governing peoples, rather than as members of a single (polyethnic) American people. As John Higham put it, the English settlers conceived of themselves as 'the formative population' of the American colonies/states, and 'theirs was the polity, the language, the pattern of work and settlements, and many of the mental habits to which the immigrants would have to adjust' (Higham 1976: 6; cf. Steinberg 1981: 7).

Immigrants would not only have the right to integrate into the mainstream Anglophone society (and so would be protected against discrimination and prejudice); they also had the obligation to integrate (and so would be required to learn English in schools, and English would be the language of public life). The commitment to integrating immigrants was not just evidence of intolerance or ethnocentrism on the part of WASPs (although it was that in part), it was also an understandable response to the uncertainty about whether a country built through polyethnic immigration would be viable.

It was fundamental, then, that immigrants view themselves as ethnic groups, not as national minorities. For a long time, immigrants seemed content with this arrangement. But the ethnic revival challenged this traditional model. As the ethnic revival escalated, some immigrant associations in the United States adopted the language and attitudes of colonized 'nations' or 'peoples' (Glazer 1983: 110–11). They labelled social pressures for integration as 'oppression', and demanded their right to 'self-determination', including state recognition of their mother tongue, and state support for separate ethnic institutions.

As I discuss below, these sorts of demands represented only a minor element among American immigrant groups. However, they caused serious anxiety among liberals. Most liberals viewed the adoption of nationalist rhetoric by immigrant groups not only as a threat to social unity, but also as morally unjustified. Liberals argued that immigrants had no legitimate basis to claim such national rights. After all, they had come voluntarily, knowing that integration was expected of them. When they chose to leave their culture and come to America, they voluntarily relinquished their national membership, and the national rights which go with it.

This attitude towards the ethnic revival is clearly expressed in the writings of Michael Walzer, a leading American political theorist (and editor of the left-liberal journal *Dissent*), and Nathan Glazer, a leading American sociologist (and editor of the right-liberal journal *Public Interest*). According to Glazer, immigrants

> had come to this country not to maintain a foreign language and culture but with the intention...to become Americanized as fast as possible, and this meant English language and American culture. They sought the induction to a new language and culture that the public schools provided – as do many present-day immigrants, too – and while they often found, as time went on, that they regretted what they and their children had lost, this was *their* choice, rather than an imposed choice (Glazer 1983: 149).

Similarly, Walzer argues that because the immigrants 'had come voluntarily', the 'call for self-determination' had no basis here. Nor was there any basis or reason for rejecting English as the public language (Walzer 1982: 6–7, 10; 1983b: 224).

Both Glazer and Walzer emphasize how the process of integrating voluntary immigrants differs from the assimilation of conquered or colonized national minorities in the multinational states of Europe. In the latter case, it is wrong to deprive 'intact and rooted communities' that 'were established on lands they had occupied for many centuries' of mother-tongue education or local autonomy. Under these conditions, integration is an 'imposed choice' which national minorities typically (and justifiably) have resisted. The integration of immigrants, by contrast, 'was aimed at peoples far more susceptible to cultural change, for they were not only uprooted; they had uprooted themselves. Whatever the pressures that had driven them to the New World, they had chosen to come, while others like themselves, in their own families, had chosen to remain' (Walzer 1982: 9; cf. Glazer 1983: 227, 283). Demands for national rights by immigrant groups are not only unjustified. They are also divisive, since each group will resent any special rights given to other groups, and impracticable, since American ethnic groups are too 'dispersed, mixed, assimilated and integrated' to exercise collective autonomy. Indeed, any attempt to turn ethnic groups into the 'compact, self-conscious, culture-maintaining entities' necessary for collective autonomy would require coercion, since many immigrants prefer to integrate into the mainstream society, both culturally and geographically. Implementing the extensive new demands of the ethnic revival would, therefore, be unjust, impracticable, divisive and coercive (Glazer 1983: 124, 227).

I think that Glazer and Walzer are right to emphasize the difference between immigrants and national minorities, and to focus on the fact that (in most cases) the decision to emigrate was voluntary. This fact does, I believe, affect the legitimacy of their claims [...]; while voluntary immigrants can legitimately assert certain polyethnic rights, they have no claim of justice to national self-government.

Given the centrality of immigration to American society, it is not surprising that liberals have been so hostile to any signs of latent nationalism among immigrant groups. In a country built primarily on immigration, with immigrants from virtually every linguistic and cultural group around the world, any serious attempt to redefine ethnic groups as national minorities would undermine the very fabric of society.

What is perhaps more surprising is that liberals have been so hostile to self-government claims by the few national minorities which do exist in the United States. Having emphasized the difference between immigrants and national minorities, one might have expected Walzer and Glazer to endorse the self-government demands of American Indians, Puerto Ricans, native Hawaiians, etc. These groups, after all, really are conquered and colonized peoples, like the national minorities in Europe.

Glazer recognizes that these groups 'possess much more in the way of national characteristics' (1983: 283–4), and that they are demanding national rights on just the grounds that he emphasizes are inapplicable to immigrant groups:

Both blacks and the Spanish-speaking point to a distinctive political situation: the blacks were brought as slaves, and the Mexicans and Puerto Ricans were conquered. The American Indians were also conquered. The white ethnic groups, however, came as free immigrants. Thus the blacks, the Spanish-speaking groups, the American Indians, and perhaps some other groups can make stronger claims for public support of their distinctive cultures than can European groups (Glazer 1983: 118).

Glazer accepts that 'there is a good deal of weight' in their demands for national rights (Glazer 1983: 119). Similarly, the logic of Walzer's argument suggests these national minorities should not be forced to accept an approach which is 'not primarily the product of their experience', but rather 'adapted to the needs of immigrant communities' (Walzer 1982: 6, 27).

Yet liberals in the United States have not endorsed the rights of national minorities. Some liberals simply ignore the existence of such groups. While Glazer and Walzer recognize their existence, they none the less insist that 'benign neglect' is appropriate for them as well as immigrants. Thus Glazer expresses his hope that 'these groups, with proper public policies to stamp out discrimination and inferior status and to encourage acculturation and assimilation, will become not very different from the European and Asian ethnic groups, the ghost nations, bound by nostalgia and sentiment and only occasionally coalescing around distinct interests' (Glazer 1983: 284). Similarly, Walzer hopes that the policies which have worked for immigrants can 'successfully be extended to the racial minorities now asserting their own group claims' (Walzer 1982: 27; cf. Ogbu 1988: 164–5).

Why do Glazer and Walzer reject the implications of their own argument? At one point, Walzer suggests that Indians do not really want national rights: 'Racism is the great barrier to a fully developed pluralism and as long as it exists American Indians and blacks, and perhaps Mexican Americans as well, will be tempted' by national rights. These national rights claims would not be tempting if national minorities had the 'same opportunities for group organization and cultural expression' available to immigrant groups (Walzer 1982: 27).

But there is no evidence that Indians, for example, desire national rights only because they have been prevented from becoming an ethnic group. Indeed, this is completely at odds with the history of Indian tribes in America or Canada. Indians have often been pressured to become 'just another ethnic group', but they have resisted that pressure and fought to protect their distinct status. As I noted earlier, Indians are indeed subject to racism, but the racism they are most concerned with is the racist denial that they are distinct peoples with their own cultures and communities.

In the end, the main reason why Glazer and Walzer reject self-government claims for national minorities is that these claims are, in effect, 'un-american'. According to Glazer, there

is such a thing as a state ideology, a national consensus, that shapes and determines what attitude immigrant and minority groups will take toward the alternative possibilities of group maintenance and group rights on the one hand, or individual integration and individual rights on the other...The United States, whatever the realities of discrimination and segregation, had as a national ideal a unitary and new ethnic identity, that of American (Glazer 1978: 100).

Although minority rights are not inherently unfair, they are none the less incompatible with America's 'national consensus' and 'state ideology'.

Similarly, Walzer says that the question of national rights within a multinational state 'must itself be worked out politically, and its precise character will depend upon understandings shared among the citizens about the value of cultural diversity, local autonomy, and so on. It is to these understandings that we must appeal when we make our arguments' (Walter 1983a: 29). And in America, the larger political community sees national rights as 'inconsistent with our historical traditions and shared understandings – inconsistent, too, with contemporary living patterns, deeply and bitterly divisive' (Walzer 1983a: 151).

This appeal to a 'state ideology' or 'shared understandings' is puzzling. For one thing, their description of the alleged consensus is biased. Walzer and Glazer say the state must either give political recognition to both ethnic and national groups, or deny political recognition to both sorts of group. But why can the national consensus not emphasize what they themselves emphasize – the difference between the coerced assimilation of minority nations and the voluntary assimilation of immigrants? Why can the national consensus not recognize that national minorities have legitimate claims which voluntary immigrants do not?

Indeed, this is the actual practice in both the USA and Canada. Indians, Inuit, French Canadians, native Hawaiians and Puerto Ricans all have a special political status that ethnic groups do not have. This has been a long-standing arrangement, and it is not clear why both countries could not continue to support self-government for national minorities but not for ethnic groups.

Walzer and Glazer apparently think that this arrangement is unstable. After asserting that the 'proper' policy is to assimilate national minorities, Glazer goes on to note 'a final complication':

> If the public policy gets turned around to the point where, rather than trying to suppress or ignore the existence of the ethnic group as a distinctive element in American society and polity, it acknowledges a distinctive status for some groups and begins to attach rights in public law to membership in them, will that not react on the others, halfway toward assimilation, and will they not begin to reassert themselves so that they will not be placed at a disadvantage? (1983: 284).

Here is the crux of the matter for Glazer. National minorities who desire recognition of their national rights may have both justice and established practice on their side, but

> Our problem is that we are not a federation of peoples (like Canada or the Soviet Union) but of states, and our ethnic groups are already too dispersed, mixed, assimilated, integrated to permit without confusion a policy that separates out some for special treatment. But if we try, then many other groups will join the queue, or try to, and the hope of a larger fraternity of all Americans will have to be abandoned … In a multiethnic society, such a policy can only encourage one group after another to raise claims to special treatment for its protection … The demand for special

treatment will lead to animus against other groups that already have it, by those who think they should have it and don't (Glazer 1983: 227–9).

In other words, recognizing the legitimate demands of Indians or Puerto Ricans would make European and Asian ethnic groups demand illegitimate and divisive benefits, and thereby jeopardize the 'larger fraternity of all Americans'.

This is yet another version of Mill's argument about the need for a common identity to ensure stability in a democracy. But it adds a new twist to that argument. Unlike Mill, Glazer is not concerned about the destabilizing impact of the national minorities themselves on domestic stability. In the United States, these groups are too small and geographically isolated to jeopardize the overall stability of the country. And, unlike post-war statesmen, Glazer is not concerned about the potential for national minorities to create international conflict. National minorities in the United States are not irredentist.

Instead, Glazer is concerned about the ripple effect of national minorities on immigrant groups. He is worried that according self-government rights to national minorities will encourage immigrant groups to make similar claims. Is this a realistic fear? I think not. The idea that immigrant groups are looking to establish themselves as national minorities is, I believe, based on a misreading of the 'ethnic revival'. The ethnic revival is not a repudiation of integration into the mainstream society. Even the most politicized ethnic groups are not interested in reconstituting themselves as distinct societies or self-governing nations alongside the mainstream society.

On the contrary, the ethnic revival is essentially a matter of self-identity and self-expression, disconnected from claims for the revival or creation of a separate institutional life. People want to identify themselves in public as members of an ethnic group, and to see others with the same identity in prominent positions of respect or authority (e.g. in politics and the media, or in textbooks and government documents). They are demanding increased recognition and visibility within the mainstream society. The ethnic revival, in other words involves a revision in the terms of integration, not a rejection of integration [...].

Where then did Walzer and Glazer get the idea that ethnic groups were demanding national rights? In retrospect, it may simply be the fact that the ethnic revival among American immigrants arose at the same time as nationalist movements resurfaced in Europe and Quebec. But as John Stone notes, this 'coincidence in time' does not mean that the two developments 'were part of the same political process' (Stone 1985: 101).

Some commentators point to demands for affirmative action programmes as evidence of a desire to be treated as a national minority. But that is a mistake. Demands for affirmative action within the mainstream economy are evidence of a desire to integrate into the institutions of the larger society, not a desire for separate and self-governing institutions. And there is no reason to think that accommodating the legitimate demands of national minorities will change this aspiration of immigrants.

In any event, it is worth pointing out how, here again, justice is being sacrificed to stability. Neither Glazer nor Walzer suggests there is anything unfair or illiberal about self-government for national minorities. On the contrary, both give good arguments why national minorities should, in principle, have special political status. Moreover, they admit that the 'national consensus' which rejects such rights was defined by settler groups to suit their own distinctive circumstances, and that national minorities do not share its aims. Like Mill and post-war statesmen, however, they feel that rights for national minorities are inconsistent with political unity, and that the latter takes precedence over the former.

This concludes my overview of the history of minority rights within the liberal tradition. I have noted the striking diversity of views about such rights within the tradition, from strong support to deep anxiety. But what is equally striking is that few if any liberals, until very recently, have supposed that such rights are inherently illiberal. Even those liberals who objected to minority rights did so on grounds of stability, not freedom or justice, and indeed they have often conceded that they are purchasing stability at the price of injustice.

Yet somehow many contemporary liberals have acquired the belief that minority rights are inherently in conflict with liberal principles. Liberals today insist that the liberal commitment to individual liberty precludes the acceptance of collective rights, and that the liberal commitment to universal (colour-blind) rights precludes the acceptance of group-specific rights. But these bald statements are no part of the liberal tradition. Few if any liberals, until very recently, supposed that liberal principles allowed only universal individual rights. What contemporary liberals take to be well-established liberal principles are in fact novel additions to the liberal canon.

Moreover, these new 'principles' are primarily the result of confusions and over-generalizations. I have looked at three factors in the development of the post-war liberal consensus against group-differentiated rights for ethnic and national groups: a *realpolitik* fear about international peace, a commitment to racial equality, and a worry about the escalating demands of immigrant groups. Underlying each is legitimate concern. But each has also been over-generalized. Certain arguments against the demands of particular groups, based on localized factors (irredentism, racial segregation, voluntary immigration), have been mistakenly generalized to all cases of cultural pluralism. And the combined effect of all three has been a distortion of liberal thinking on minority rights. Out of this mixture has arisen the belief that minority rights are inherently unjust, a betrayal of liberal equality. But these influences, examined more closely, argue the opposite – the first concedes the fairness of minority rights, and the second and third argue against separate political institutions for racial and immigrant groups on grounds that are consistent with, and indeed support, the legitimacy of national rights.

In fact, none of these factors challenges the two basic claims which, I suggested earlier, underlie a liberal defence of minority rights: namely, that individual freedom is tied to membership in one's national group; and that group-specific rights can promote equality between the minority and majority.

References

Acton, Lord (1922), 'Nationalism', in *The History of Freedom and Other Essays*, ed. J. Figgis and R. Laurence, Macmillan, London.

Barker, E. (1948), *National Character and Factors in its Formation*, Methuen, London.

Bourne, R. S. (1964), 'Transnational America', in *War and the Intellectual: Essays by Randolph S. Bourne 1915–1919*, ed. C. Resek, Harper and Row, New York.

Bowles, S. et al., eds (1972), *The Indian: Assimilation, Integration or Separation?*, Prentice Hall, Scarborough.

Clarke, F. (1934), *Quebec and South Africa: A Study in Cultural Adjustment*, Oxford University Press, London.

Claude, I. (1955), *National Minorities: An International Problem*, Harvard University Press, Cambridge, Mass.

Craig, G. (1963), *Lord Durham's Report: An Abridgement of Report on the Affairs of British North America*, McLelland and Stewart, Toronto.

Glazer, N. (1975), *Affirmative Discrimination: Ethnic Inequality and Public Policy*, Basic Books, New York.

Glazer, N. (1978), 'Individual Rights against Group Rights', in *Human Rights*, ed. A. Tay and E. Kamenka, Edward Arnold, London.

Glazer, N. (1983), *Ethnic Dilemmas: 1964–1982*, Harvard University Press, Cambridge, Mass.

Green, T. (1941), *Lectures on the Principles of Political Obligation*, Longman, Green and Co., London.

Gross, M. (1973), 'Indian Control for Quality Indian Education', *North Dakota Law Review*, 49/2.

Hancock, W. (1937), *Survey of British Commonwealth Affairs, 1: Problems of Nationality 1900–1936*, Oxford University Press, London.

Higham, J. (1976), *Send These to Me*, Atheneum, New York.

Hobhouse, L. T. (1928), *Social Evolution and Political Theory*, Columbia University Press, New York.

Hobhouse, L. T. (1966), *Social Development: Its Nature and Conditions*, George Allen & Unwin, London.

Hobsbawm, E. (1990), *Nations and Nationalism since 1780: Programme, Myth and Reality*, University of California Press, Berkeley.

Hoernlé, R. (1939), *South African Native Policy and the Liberal Spirit*, Lovedae Press, Cape Town.

Humboldt, W. von. ([1836], 1988), *On Language: The Diversity of Human Language-Structure and its Influence on the Mental Development of Mankind*, translated by Peter Heath, Cambridge University Press, Cambridge.

Kallen, H. (1924), *Culture and Diversity in the United States*, Boni and Liveright, New York.

Kymlicka, W. (1989), *Liberalism, Community and Culture*, Oxford University Press, Oxford.

Mazzini, J. (1907), *The Duties of Man and Other Essays*, J. M. Dent, London.

Mill, J. (1972), *Considerations on Representative Government*, in *Utilitarianism, Liberty and Representative Government*, ed. H. Acton, J. M. Dent, London.

Ogbu, J. (1988), 'Diversity and Equality in Public Education: Community, Forces and Minority School Adjustment and Performance', in *Policies for America's*

Public Schools: Teachers, Equity and Indicators, ed. R. Haskins and D. MacRae, Ablex Publishers, Norwood, New Jersey.

Rich, P. (1987), 'T. H. Green, Lord Scarman and the Issue of Ethnic Minority Rights in English Liberal Thought', *Ethnic and Racial Studies*, 10, pp. 149–68.

Sohn, L. (1981), 'The Rights of Minorities', in *The International Bill of Rights: The Covenant on Civil and Political Rights*, Columbia University Press, New York.

Steinberg, S. (1981), *The Ethnic Myth: Race, Ethnicity and Class in America*, Atheneum, New York.

Stone, J. (1976), 'Black Nationalism and Apartheid: Two Variations on a Separatist Theme', *Social Dynamics*, 2/1, pp. 19–30.

Stone, J. (1985), *Racial Conflict in Contemporary Society*, Harvard University Press, Cambridge, Mass.

Thornberry, P. (1980), 'Is there a Phoenix in the Ashes? International Law and Minority Rights', *Texas International Law journal*, 15, pp. 421–58.

Thornberry, P. (1991), *International Law and the Rights of Minorities*, Oxford University Press, Oxford.

Walzer, M. (1982), *The Politics of Ethnicity*, Harvard University Press, Cambridge, Mass.

Walzer, M. (1983a), *Spheres of Justice: A Defence of Pluralism and Equality*, Blackwell, Oxford.

Walzer, M. (1983b), 'States and Minorites', in *Minorities: Community and Identity*, ed. C. Fried, Springer-Verlag, Berlin, pp. 219–27.

Zimmern, A. (1918), *Nationality and Government*, Chatto and Windus, London.

THE 'HISPANIC' CHALLENGE TO AMERICAN IDENTITY

SAMUEL HUNTINGTON

The Mexican/Hispanic Challenge

By the mid-twentieth century, America had become a multiethnic, multiracial society with an Anglo-Protestant mainstream culture encompassing many subcultures and with a common political creed rooted in that mainstream culture. In the late twentieth century, developments occurred that, if continued, could change America into a culturally bifurcated Anglo-Hispanic society with two national languages. This trend was in part the result of the popularity of the doctrines of multiculturalism and diversity among intellectual and political elites, and the government policies on bilingual education and affirmative action that those doctrines promoted and sanctioned. The driving force behind the trend toward cultural bifurcation, however, has been immigration from Latin America and especially from Mexico.

Mexican immigration is leading toward the demographic *reconquista* of areas Americans took from Mexico by force in the 1830s and 1840s, Mexicanizing them in a manner comparable to, although different from, the Cubanization that has occurred in southern Florida. It is also blurring the border between Mexico and America, introducing a very different culture, while also promoting the emergence, in some areas, of a blended society and culture, half-American and half-Mexican. Along with immigration from other Latin American countries, it is advancing Hispanization throughout America and social, linguistic, and economic practices appropriate for an Anglo-Hispanic society.

Mexican immigration has these effects because of the characteristics that differentiate it from past and present immigration from other countries and because of the extent to which Mexican immigrants and their progeny have not assimilated into American society as other immigrants did in the past and as many other immigrants are doing now.

Why Mexican Immigration Differs

Contemporary Mexican immigration is unprecedented in American history. The experience and lessons of past immigration have little relevance to understanding its dynamics and consequences. Mexican immigration differs from past immigration and most other contemporary immigration due to a combination of six factors.

Contiguity. Americans have thought of immigration as symbolized by the Statue of Liberty, Ellis Island, and more recently perhaps Kennedy Airport. Immigrants arrived in the United States after crossing several thousand miles of ocean. American attitudes toward immigrants and American immigration policies have been and, in considerable measure, still are shaped by this image. These assumptions and policies, however, have little or no relevance for Mexican immigration. America is now confronted by a massive influx of people from a poor, contiguous country with more than one third the population of the United States, who come across a two-thousand-mile border marked historically simply by a line in the ground and a shallow river.

This situation is unique for the United States and unique in the world. No other First World country has a land frontier with a Third World country, much less one of two thousand miles. Japan, Australia, New Zealand are islands; Canada is bordered only by the United States; the closest western European countries come to Third World countries are the Strait of Gibraltar between Spain and Morocco and the Straits of Otranto between Italy and Albania. The significance of the long Mexican-American border is enhanced by the economic differences between the two countries. 'The income gap between the United States and Mexico,' Stanford historian David Kennedy points out, 'is the largest between any two contiguous countries in the world.'[1] The consequences of migrants crossing two thousand miles of relatively open border rather than two thousand miles of open ocean are immense for policing and controlling immigration, for the blurring of the border with the rise of trans-border communities, for the society, people, culture, and economy of the American Southwest, and for America as a whole.

Numbers. The causes of Mexican, as well as other, immigration are found in the demographic, economic, and political dynamics of the sending country and the economic, political, and social attractions of the United States. Contiguity, however, obviously encourages immigration. The costs, challenges, and risks of immigration for Mexicans are much less than for others. They can easily go back and forth to Mexico and maintain contact with family and friends there. Aided by these factors, Mexican immigration increased steadily after 1965. About 640,000 Mexicans legally migrated to the United States in the 1970s, 1,656,000 in the 1980s, and 2,249,000 in the in 1990s. In these three decades, Mexicans accounted for 14 per cent, 23 per cent, and 25 per cent of total legal immigration. These percentages do not equal the percentages of immigrants who came from Ireland between 1820 and 1860 or from Germany in the 1850s and 1860s.[2] Yet they are high compared to the very dispersed sources of immigrants before World War I and compared to other contemporary immigrants. And to them must be added the large numbers of Mexicans who each year enter the United States illegally.

In 1960 the foreign-born people from the five principal countries of origin were relatively dispersed:

Italy	1,257,000
Germany	990,000
Canada	953,000
United Kingdom	833,000
Poland	748,000

In 2000 the foreign-born of the top five countries were distributed very differently:

Mexico	7,841,000
China	1,391,000
Philippines	1,222,000
India	1,007,000
Cuba	952,000

In the course of four decades, the numbers of foreign-born expanded immensely, Asians and Latin Americans replaced Europeans and Canadians, and diversity of source dramatically gave way to the dominance of one source: Mexico. Mexican immigrants constituted 27.6 per cent of the total foreign-born population in 2000. The next largest contingents, Chinese and Filipinos, amounted to only 4.9 per cent and 4.3 per cent of the foreign-born.[3]

In the 1990s, Mexicans also were over one half of the Latin American immigrants to the United States, and Latin American immigrants were about one half the total immigrants to the continental United States between 1970 and 2000. Hispanics, twelve per cent of the total US population in 2000 (two-thirds of Mexican origin), increased by almost 10 per cent from 2000 to 2002 and became more numerous than blacks. It is estimated they will constitute up to 25 per cent of the population by 2040. These changes are driven not just by immigration but also by fertility. In 2002, total fertility rates were estimated at 1.8 for non-Hispanic whites, 2.1 for blacks, and 3.0 for Hispanics. 'This is the characteristic shape of developing countries,' the *Economist* commented. 'As the bulge of Latinos enters peak child-bearing age in a decade or two, the Latinos' share of America's population will soar.'[4]

In the mid-nineteenth century, immigration was dominated by English speakers from the British Isles. The pre–World War I immigration was highly diversified linguistically, including many speakers of Italian, Polish, Russian, Yiddish, English, German, and Swedish, as well as others. The post-1965 immigration differs from both these previous waves because now almost half speak a single non-English language. 'The Hispanic domination of the immigrant flow,' as Mark Krikorian observes, 'has no precedent in our history.'[5]

Illegality. Substantial illegal entry into the United States is a post-1965 and Mexican phenomenon. For almost a century after the Constitution was adopted, illegal immigration was virtually impossible: no national laws restricted or prohibited immigration, and only a few states imposed modest limits. During the following ninety years, illegal immigration was minimal: control of immigrants coming by ship was fairly easy, and a good proportion of those arriving at Ellis Island were denied entry. The 1965 immigration law, the increased availability of transportation, and the intensified forces promoting Mexican emigration drastically changed this situation. Apprehensions by the US Border Patrol rose from 1.6 million in the 1960s to 11.9 million in the 1980s, and 12.9 million in the 1990s. Estimates of the Mexicans who successfully enter illegally each year range from 105,000 by a binational Mexican-American commission up to 350,000 per year by the INS for the 1990s. Roughly two thirds of post-1975 Mexican immigrants, it has been estimated, entered the United States illegally.[6]

The 1986 Immigration Reform and Control Act contained provisions to legalize the status of existing illegal immigrants and to reduce future illegal immigration through employer sanctions and other means. The former goal was achieved: some 3.1 million illegal immigrants, about 90 per cent from Mexico, became legal 'green card' residents of the United States. The latter goal was not achieved. Estimates of the total number of illegal immigrants in the United States rose from four million in 1995 to six million in 1998 and eight to ten million by 2003. Mexicans accounted for 58 per cent of the total illegal population in the United States in 1990; by 2000, an estimated 4.8 million illegal Mexicans were 69 per cent of that population.[7] In 2003 illegal Mexicans in the United States were twenty-five times as numerous as the next largest contingent, from El Salvador. Illegal immigration is, overwhelmingly, Mexican immigration. [...]

Regional Concentration. As we have seen, the Founding Fathers thought dispersion essential to assimilation, and historically that has been the pattern and continues to be for most contemporary non-Hispanic immigrants. Hispanics, however, have tended to concentrate regionally: Mexicans in Southern California, Cubans in Miami, Dominicans and Puerto Ricans, the last of whom are not technically immigrants, in New York City. In the 1990s, the proportions of Hispanics continued to grow in these regions of heaviest concentration. At the same time, Mexicans and other Hispanics were also establishing beachheads elsewhere. While the absolute numbers often are small, the states with the largest percentage increases in Spanish speakers between 1990 and 2000 were, in decreasing order: North Carolina (449 per cent increase), Arkansas, Georgia, Tennessee, South Carolina, Nevada, and Alabama (222 per cent increase). Hispanics have also established concentrated presences in individual cities and towns in various parts of the country. In 2003 more than 40 per cent of the population of Hartford, Connecticut, was Hispanic (primarily Puerto Rican), 'the largest concentration among major cities outside California, Texas, Colorado and Florida,' outnumbering the city's 38 per cent black population. Hartford, its first Hispanic mayor proclaimed, 'has become a Latin city, so to speak. It's a sign of things to come,' with Spanish increasingly the language of commerce and government.[8]

[...]

Persistence. Previous waves of immigration, we have seen, subsided and the proportions coming from individual countries fluctuated greatly. At the moment, however, the current wave shows no sign of ebbing and the conditions creating the large Mexican component of that wave are likely to endure for some while, absent a major war or recession. In the long term, Mexican immigration could decline when the economic well-being of Mexico approximates that of the United States. As of 2000, American per capita GDP was nine to ten times that of Mexico. If that difference were reduced to three to one, the economic incentives for migration might also drop substantially. To reach that ratio in any meaningful future, however, would require extremely rapid economic growth in Mexico, at a rate greatly exceeding that of the United States. Even if this occurred, economic development in itself need not reduce the impulse to emigrate. During the nineteenth century, when Europe was rapidly industrializing and per capita incomes rising significantly, 50 million Europeans emigrated to the Americas, Asia, and Africa. On the other hand economic development and urbanization may also lead to a decline in birth rates and thus reduce the numbers of people likely to move north. The Mexican birth rate has been declining. In 1970–1975 the total fertility rate was 6.5 per cent; by 1995–2000, it had been more than halved to 2.8. Yet in 2001 the Mexican government's National Population Council predicted that these developments would not have any significant immediate impact and that total immigration was likely to average 400,000 to 515,000 a year until 2030.[9] By then, more than a half graphic profile of the United States and the demographic relation between Mexico and the United States.

[...]

Historical Presence. No other immigrant group in American history has asserted or has been able to assert a historical claim to American territory. Mexicans and Mexican-Americans can and do make that claim. Almost all of Texas, New Mexico, Arizona, California, Nevada, and War of Independence in 1835–1836 and the Mexican-American War of 1846–1848. Mexico is the only country that the United States has invaded, occupied its capital, placing the Marines in the 'halls of Montezuma,' and then annexed half its territory. Mexicans do not forget these events. Quite understandably, they feel that they have special rights in these territories. 'Unlike other immigrants,' Peter Skerry notes, 'Mexicans arrive here from a neighboring nation that has suffered military defeat at the hands of the United States; and they settle predominantly in a region that was once part of their homeland...Mexican Americans enjoy a sense of being on their own turf that is not shared by other immigrants.'[10] That 'turf' takes human form in the some twenty-five Mexican communities that have existed continuously since before the American conquest. Concentrated in the Mexican 'homelands' of northern New Mexico and along the Rio Grande, their populations are more than 90 per cent Hispanic with over 90 percent of the Hispanics speaking Spanish at home. One hundred and fifty years after these communities became part of the United States, 'Hispanic cultural and demographic dominance of society and space has been maintained and Hispanic assimilation is weak.'[11]

[…]

How Mexican Assimilation Lags

The criteria that can be used to gauge assimilation of an individual, a group, or a generation include language, education, occupation and income, citizenship, intermarriage, and identity. With respect to almost all of these indices, Mexican assimilation lags behind that of non-Mexican immigrants and that of immigrants in the previous waves.

Language. Language assimilation historically has tended to follow a common pattern. The large majority of first-generation immigrants do not, unless they come from English-speaking countries, achieve fluency in English. The second generation, who either arrive as very young children with their parents or are born in the United States, have relatively high degrees of fluency in both English and their parents' language. The third generation is completely fluent in English and has little or no knowledge of their family's ancestral language, which creates a problem for communication with their grandparents, but is also often accompanied by a nostalgic interest in and expressed desire to learn the language of their ancestors.[12]

At the beginning of the twenty-first century, whether language assimilation by Mexicans would follow this pattern was unclear. The recency of this wave meant there was only a relatively small third generation. The evidence on English acquisition and Spanish retention also was limited and ambiguous. In 2000, over 26 million people spoke Spanish at home (10.5 per cent of people over age five), and almost 13.7 million of these spoke English less than 'very well,' an increase of 65.5 per cent over 1990. According to a Census Bureau survey, in 1990 about 95 per cent of Mexican-born immigrants spoke Spanish at home; 73.6 per cent of these did not speak English very well; and 43 per cent of the Mexican foreign-born were 'linguistically isolated.'[13] For the second generation, born in the United States, the results were quite different. Only 11.6 per cent spoke only Spanish or more Spanish than English, while 25 per cent spoke both languages equally, 32.7 per cent more English than Spanish, and 30.1 per cent only English. Over 90 per cent of the U.S.-born people of Mexican origin spoke English fluently.[14]

[…]

Education. The education of Mexican-origin people differs significantly from the American norm. In 2000, 86.6 per cent of native-born adults had graduated from high school. The rates for the foreign-born in the United States varied from

81.3 per cent for Europeans, 83.8 per cent for Asians, and 94.9 per cent for Africans, down to 49.6 per cent for all Latin Americans and only 33.8 per cent for Mexicans. In 1990, the Mexican rate of high school graduation was half the rate for the entire foreign-born population.[15]

[...]

Occupation and Income. The economic position of Mexican immigrants parallels, as one would expect, their educational attainment. In 2000, 30.9 per cent of employed native-born Americans held professional and managerial positions. The extent to which immigrants from different countries approximated this norm varied greatly.

Canada	46.3%
Asia	38.7
Europe	38.1
Africa	36.5
Latin America	12.1
Mexico	6.3

[...]

Overall, Mexican immigrants are the bottom of the economic ladder. Do the next generations stay there? The evidence is spotty. The regional concentration of Mexican-Americans, which retards other forms of assimilation, may help their economic progress by fostering a relatively large enclave economy with a variety of businesses, occupations, and opportunities for upward economic mobility within that enclave. The argument has, however, been made that pre–World War I economic success of Jewish immigrants and their offspring, along with that of Japanese, other Asian immigrants and Florida Cubans, reflects economic success in their birth countries.[16] Few Mexican immigrants have been economically successful in the United States. In addition, any significant improvement of their educational level, and the ongoing influx of poorly educated people from Mexico makes that difficult. Joel Perlmann and Roger Waldinger are pessimistic about the economic prospects of second-generation Mexican-Americans.

[...]

The Hispanization of Miami

Miami is the most Hispanic large city in the fifty states. In the course of thirty years, Spanish speakers, overwhelmingly Cuban, established their dominance in virtually every aspect of the city's life and fundamentally changed its ethnic composition, its culture, its politics, and its language. The Hispanization of Miami is without precedent in the history of major American cities.

This process began in the early 1960s with the arrival of middle- and upper-class Cubans who did not want to live under the Castro regime. In the dozen years following Castro's victory, 260,000 Cubans fled the country, mostly to South Florida, which historically had always been the refuge for Cuban political exiles, including two Cuban presidents buried there. Cuban immigrants to the United States numbered 265,000 in the 1970s, 140,000 in the 1980s, and 170,000 in the

1990s. The US government classified them as refugees and provided them special benefits, which aroused the resentment of other immigrant groups. In 1980, the Castro regime permitted and even encouraged the migration of 125,000 Cubans through the port of Mariél to Florida. These Marielitos were generally poorer, less well-educated, younger, and more likely to be black than the earlier migrants. They had grown up under the Castro regime and their culture was the product of that regime. Castro also included some criminals and mentally retarded people.[17]

Meanwhile, the economic growth of Miami, led by the early Cuban immigrants, made it a magnet for migrants from other Latin American and Caribbean countries. By 2000, 96 per cent of the foreign-born population of Miami was from Latin America and the Caribbean, almost all of whom were Spanish speakers except for the Haitians and Jamaicans. Two-thirds of Miami's people were Hispanic, and more than half of them were Cuban or of Cuban descent. In 2000, 75.2 per cent of Miami city residents spoke at home a language other than English, compared to 55.7 per cent of the residents of Los Angeles and 47.6 per cent of New Yorkers. Of Miamians speaking a non-English language at home, 89.3 per cent spoke Spanish. In 2000, 59.5 per cent of the residents of Miami were foreign-born, compared to 40.9 per cent in Los Angeles, 36.8 per cent in San Francisco, and 35.9 per cent in New York. In most other major cities less than 20 per cent of the population was foreign-born. In 2000, 31.1 per cent of adult Miami residents said they spoke English very well, compared to 39.0 per cent in Los Angeles, 42.5 per cent in San Francisco, and 46.5 per cent in New York.[18]

The Cuban influx and takeover had major consequences for Miami. Traditionally Miami had been a somewhat somnolent place dependent on retirees and modest tourism. In the 1960s, the elite and entrepreneurial refugees from Castro started dramatic economic development. Unable to send money home, the Cubans invested in Miami. Personal income growth in Miami averaged 11.5 per cent a year in the 1970s and 7.7 per cent a year in the 1980s. Payrolls in Miami-Dade County tripled between 1970 and 1995. The Cuban economic drive made Miami an international economic dynamo, with expanding international trade and investment. The Cubans promoted international tourism, which, by the 1990s, exceeded domestic tourism and made Miami a leading centre of the cruise ship industry. Major American corporations in manufacturing, communications, and consumer products moved their Latin American headquarters to Miami from other American and Latin American cities. A vigorous Spanish artistic and entertainment community emerged. The Cubans can legitimately claim that, in the words of Professor Damian Fernandez, 'We built modern Miami,' and made its economy larger than those of most Latin American countries.[19]

A key part of this development was the expansion of Miami's economic ties with Latin America. Brazilians, Argentines, Chileans, Colombians, and Venezuelans flooded into Miami, bringing their money with them. By 1993, some $25 billion from foreign countries, mostly Latin American, had been deposited in Miami banks.'[20] Throughout the hemisphere, Latin Americans concerned with investment, trade, culture, entertainment, holidays, drug smuggling, increasingly turned to Miami. It truly had become, in an oft-repeated phrase, 'the capital of Latin America'.

Achieving this eminence involved, of course, the transformation of Miami from a normal American city into a Cuban-led Hispanic city. By 2000 Spanish was not just the language spoken in most homes; it was also the principal language of commerce, business and politics. The media and communications generally became increasingly Hispanic. In 1988, a Spanish language television station became the number one station watched by Miamians, the first time a foreign language station achieved that rating in a major American city. The changing linguistic and ethnic make-up of Miami was reflected in the troubled history in the1980s and 1990s of the *Miami Herald*, one of the most respected papers in the United States and winner of numerous Pulitzer Prizes. The owners of the *Herald* first attempted to maintain its traditional 'Anglo focus', while appealing to Hispanic readers and advertisers with a Spanish supplement. This attempt to reach both Hispanics and Anglos failed. In 1960 the *Herald* was read in 80 per cent of Miami households. In 1989, it was read in 40 per cent. The paper antagonized the leaders of the Cuban community, who retaliated vigorously. Eventually the *Herald* had to set up a separate Spanish paper, *El Nuevo Herald*.'[21]

The Cubans did not, in the traditional pattern, create an enclave immigrant neighbourhood in Miami. They brought into existence an enclave city with its own cultural community and economy, in which assimilation and Americanization were unnecessary and in some measure undesired. By the late 1980s, 'the Cubans had created in Miami their own banks, businesses, and voting blocs,' which dominated the economy and politics and from which non-Hispanics were excluded. 'They're outsiders,' as one successful Hispanic put it. 'Here we are members of the power structure,' another boasted.[22] Miami Hispanics had little or no incentive to assimilate into American mainstream culture.

[...]

The Cuban and Hispanic dominance of Miami left Anglos, as well as blacks, outside minorities that could often be ignored. Unable to communicate with government bureaucrats and discriminated against by store clerks, the Anglos came to realize, as one of them put it, 'My God, this is what it like to be the minority.' The Anglos had three choices. They could accept their subordinate and 'outsider' position. They could attempt to adopt the manners, customs, and language of the Hispanics and assimilate into the Hispanic community, 'acculturation in reverse,' as the scholars Alejandro Portes and Alex Stepick labelled it. Or, third, they could leave Miami, and between 1983 and 1993 about 140,000 did due to 'the city's growing Hispanic character,' their exodus reflected in a widely prevalent bumper sticker, 'Will the last American to leave, please haul down the flag.'[23]

Notes

1 David M. Kennedy, 'Can We Still Afford to Be a Nation of Immigrants?' *Atlantic Monthly*, 278 (November 1996), p. 67.

2 Roger Daniels, *Coming to America* (New York: Harper and Collins, 1990), pp. 129–146.

3 Campbell J. Gibson and Emily Lennon, 'Historical Census Statistics on the Foreign-Born Population of the United States, 1850–1990' (population Division Working Paper 29, U.S. Census Bureau, February 1999) Table 3; U.S. Census Bureau, March 2000 Current Population Survey, Profile of the

Foreign-Born Population in the United States 2000 (PPL-145, 2001), Tables 1.1, 3.1, 3.2, 3.3 and 3.4.

4 *Economist*, 24 August 2002, pp. 21–22; U.S. Department of Homeland Security, Office of Immigration Statistics, 2002 *Yearbook of Immigration Statistics* (Washington 2003), Table 2; *New York Times*, 19 June 2003, p. A22.

5 Mark Krikorian, 'Will Americanization Work in America?' *Freedom Review*, 28 (Fall 1997), pp. 48–49.

6 Barry Edmonston and Jeffrey S. Passel, 'Ethnic Demography: U.S. Immigration and Ethnic Variations,' in Edmonston and Pasell, eds., *Immigration and Ethnicity* (Washington D.C.: Urban Institute Press, 1994), p. 8.

7 *Economist*, 20 May 1995, p. 29; *New York Times*, 3 January 1995, p. B2; Immigration and Naturalization Service study, reported in *New York Times*, 8 February 1997, p. 9; INS study, reported in *Boston Globe*, 1 February 2003, p. A8; Census Bureau figure reported in *Washington Post*, 25 October 2001, p. A24; 2002 *Yearbook of Immigration Statistics*, p. 213.

8 Michael Fix and Wendy Zimmerman, 'After Arrival: An Overview of Federal Immigrant Policy in the United States,' in Edmonston and Passell, eds., pp. 257–258; Frank D. Bean et al., 'Educational and Sociodemographic Incorporation Among Hispanic Immigrants to the United States,' in Edmonston and Passell, eds., pp. 80–82; George J. Borjas, *Heaven's Door* (Princeton: Princeton University Press, 1999), p. 118; 'U.S. Survey,' *Economist*, 11 March 2000, p. 12; *New York Times*, 1 February 2000, p. A12; *Economist*, 18 May 1996, p. 29.

9 Summary of Mexican report in David Simcox, *Backgrounder: Another 50 Years of Mass Mexican Immigration* (Washington, D.C.: Center for Immigration Studies, March 2002).

10 Peter Skerry, *Mexican Americans* (Cambridge: Harvard University Press, 1993), p. 289, also pp. 21–22.

11 Terrence W. Haverluk, 'Hispanic Community Types and Assimilation in Mex-America,' *Professional Geographer*, 50 (November 1998), p. 467.

12 Stephen Steinberg, *The Ethnic Myth* (New York: Atheneum, 1981), pp. 45–46.

13 Tech Paper 29, Table 5, *Language Spoken at Home for the Foreign-Born Population 5 Years and Over*, U.S. Bureau of the Census, 9 March 1999; *We the American Foreign Born*, U.S. Bureau of the Census, September 1993, p. 6; reported in *Miami Herald*, 6 August 2002, p. 4A.

14 Census Bureau, *We the American Foreign-Born*, p. 6.

15 Steinberg, *The Ethnic Myth*, pp. 272–273.

16 *Economist*, 8 April 200, pp. 29–29; Joan Didion, 'Miami,' *New York Review*, 28 May 1987, p. 44; Boston Globe, 21 May 2000, p. A7.

17 U.S. Census Bureau, 2000 Census of Population and Housing, *Summary Social, Economic and Housing Characteristics*, PHC-2-1 (2003), pp. 27–29; *Summary Population and Housing Characteristics*, PHC-1-1 (2001), pp. 32, 34, 36.

18 Fix and Zimmerman, pp. 256–258; *New York Times*, 1 April 2000, p. 1A, *Economist*, 8 April 2000, p. 27.

19 Cathy Booth, 'The Capital of Latin America: Miami,' *Time* (Fall 1993), p. 82.

20 Booth, p. 84; Mimi Swartz, 'The Herald's Cuban Revolution,' *New Yorker*, 7 June 1999, p. 39.
21 Swartz, p. 37; Booth, p. 84.
22 Swartz, p. 37, citing Alejandro Portes and Alex Stepick, *City on the Edge* (Berkeley: University of California Press, 1993); Booth, p. 85; Didion, p. 48.
23 Swartz, 'The Herald's Cuban Revolution.'

RETHINKING ASSIMILATION THEORY

RICHARD ALBA & VICTOR NEE

The Racial Distinctiveness of Many New Immigrant Groups

A common argument holds that the descendants of earlier European immigrations, even those composed of peasants from economically backward parts of Europe, could eventually assimilate because their European origins made them culturally and racially similar to American ethnic core groups – those from the British Isles and some northern and western European countries. The option of assimilation will be less available to the second and later generations of most new immigrant groups because their non-European origins mean that they are more distinctive, with their distinctiveness of skin colour especially fateful.

While we wish to avoid at all cost a Panglossian optimism about American racism, we find this argument less compelling than many do because we think that it treats perceptions of racial difference as more rigid than they have proven themselves historically. We grant that American treatment of non-Europeans has generally been characterized by racist discrimination of a more extreme cast than anything experienced by even the most disparaged of the European groups, as the well-known examples of the Chinese Exclusion Act of the late nineteenth century and the internment of Japanese Americans during World War II testify. Nevertheless, the view that the pathway to assimilation was smoothed for the descendants of European immigrants by their racial identification is an anachronism, inappropriately imposing contemporary racial perceptions on the past. There is ample evidence that native-born whites perceived some of the major European immigrant groups, such as the Irish, Jews, and Italians, as racially distinct from themselves and that such perceptions flowered into full-blown racist theorizing during the high-water period of mass immigration in the early decades of this century (Higham, 1970). This is not just a matter of a language usage in which 'race' was treated as a synonym for 'nation' or 'ethnic group.' Many Americans believed that they could identify the members of some groups by their characteristic appearance (e.g., 'Jewish' facial features), and nineteenth-century caricatures of the Irish frequently gave them a distinctly simian cast.

Over time, racial perceptions of the most disparaged European groups shifted. The Irish, and perhaps other groups, initially struggled to put some racial and social distance between themselves and African Americans (Ignatiev 1995;

Roediger 1991). But as these groups climbed the socioeconomic ladder and mixed residentially with other whites, their perceived distinctiveness from the majority faded. (World War II, a watershed in many ways for ethnic relations among whites, also had a powerful impact on attitudes towards European ethnics.) Intermarriage both marked this shift and accelerated it. We see no *a priori* reason why a similar shift could not take place for some contemporary immigrant groups and some segments of other groups. We think here particularly of Asians and light-skinned Latinos. In the case of some Asian groups, the relatively high inter-marriage rates of their US-born members suggest their acceptability to many whites, the most frequent partners in intermarriage, and the absence of a deep racial divide (Lee and Yamanaka 1990; Qian 1997). Loewen's (1971) study of Chinese immigrants who migrated from the Western states to the South in the 1870's documents a transformation of racial attitudes that parallels that for the Irish. When Chinese labourers first arrived in the Mississippi Delta they joined free blacks as part of the 'coloured' agricultural labour force in a race-segregated society. Chinese immigrants and their descendants gradually 'crossed-over' to gain acceptance in the white community by distancing themselves socially from blacks and acculturating to southern white culture. The post-1965 immigration of Asians to the United States takes place in a substantially different historical context of the post-Civil Rights Movement and a new era of mass immigration. Although Loewen's case study of the Mississippi Chinese may not be applicable to the current immigration, it nonetheless shows that ethnic identity and bound-aries are socially constructed and malleable.

The most intractable racial boundary remains that separating those deemed phenotypically black from whites. This boundary is likely to exert a powerful influence on the adaptation possibilities of immigrant groups, depending on where they are situated with respect to it. The evidence of this influence is already apparent; it is registered in the research observations about the identificational dilemmas confronted by the children of black Caribbean parentage (Waters 1994; Woldemikael 1989) and recognized in the concept of 'segmented assimilation' (Portes and Zhou 1993). But despite such evidence, there is also the countervail-ing experience of South Asian immigrants. Although South Asians have dark skin colour, they are the highest income group in the United States and are predomi-nantly suburban in their residence (Portes and Rumbaut, 1996). Their experience suggests that not dark skin colour *per se,* but the appearance of connection to the African-American group raises the most impassable racist barriers in the United States.

The Impact of Economic Restructuring on Immigrant Opportunity

The assimilation of European-ancestry Americans is linked to opportunities for social mobility that, within a brief historical period, brought about a rough parity of life chances across many ethnic groups (though not within them, as life chances remained structured by social class origins) (Greeley 1976; Lieberson 1980). These opportunities were in turn linked to historically contingent, broad avenues of intergenerational movement that allowed immigrants of peasant origins with few work skills of relevance in an urban industrial economy nevertheless to gain a foothold through steady employment, often beginning in manufacturing sectors (Bodnar 1985). According to a common view, similar openings are not to be found with the same frequency in the contemporary economy because of economic restructuring, which has led to the elimination of many manufacturing jobs and the degradation of others and to their replacement in the spectrum of jobs open to immigrant workers with low-level service jobs that do not offer comparable wages, stability of employment, or mobility ladders (Sassen 1988). This result of economic restructuring is described by Portes and Zhou (1993) as an 'hourglass economy', with a narrowed band of middle-level jobs and bulging strata at the bottom and the top. The presumption is that it will be more difficult for the descendants of contemporary immigrants, many of whom enter the labour force at or near the bottom, to make the gradual intergenerational transition upwards, because footholds in the middle of the occupational structure are relatively scarce (Portes and Zhou 1993). Movement into the top strata requires substantial human capital, particularly higher educational credentials, that is not likely to be within reach of all members of the second generation. A conclusion drawn by a number of scholars is that, to a degree not true of European ethnics, the current second generation is at risk of experiencing no, or even downward, mobility, unless the American economy becomes more dynamic than it has been since the early 1970s (Gans 1992).

Without question, economic opportunities are critical to the assimilation prospects of new immigrant groups. But the restructuring of the economy does not have an equally negative impact on the opportunities of all groups, because of the enormous variety among groups in the forms of capital – economic, cultural and social – they bring with them and in degree of support provided by the community contexts they enter (Light 1984; Portes and Rumbaut 1996; Waldinger 1986/87, 1996). Some groups, like the Cubans of Miami, have distinguished themselves by the development of ethnic sub-economies that are likely to afford the second generation better-than-average chances to succeed in the educational system and enter professional occupations. Others – several Asian groups spring readily to mind – enjoy, whether because of the professional occupations of their immigrant parents or the cultural capital they possess, high levels of educational attainment in the United States (Gibson 1988; Hirschman and Wong 1986; Model 1988; Nee and Sanders 1985; Light and Bonacich 1988). Moreover, the 1980s economic restructuring has stimulated economic growth in the 1990s, and this has brought about a sharp reduction of unemployment. As a result of tighter labour markets, even low-skilled manual labourers have experienced increases in hourly earnings.

The significance of economic restructuring for the second and subsequent generations would appear to be greatest for those groups described by Portes and Rumbaut (1996) as 'labour migrant' groups, like the Mexicans. Even here, we caution that the distinction from the experiences of comparable European groups (e.g., southern Italians) can be overdrawn, for they too did not enter an economy that was continuously generating a bountiful supply of opportunities for secure employment and upward mobility. A large portion of the second generation of the southern and eastern European groups came of age in the teeth of the Depression. Like the children of some contemporary immigrants, many in the earlier second generation responded to their perceived lack of opportunity and to their rejection at the hands of nativist whites by constructing what are now called 'reactive identities,' identities premised upon value schemes that invert those of the mainstream in important ways. We know for instance that, during the 1930s and perhaps afterwards, the children of southern Italian immigrants were widely perceived as posing problems in the educational system – they had high rates of dropout, truancy, and delinquency (Covello 1972), all signs that they were rejecting the conventions and values of a system that they perceived as rejecting them.

Yet the analyses of Lieberson (1980) demonstrate that the US-born members of these groups experienced a fairly steady upgrading of educational and occupational attainment, even in the cohorts whose life chances would have been most affected by the Depression. This suggests to us that the emphasis on economic restructuring in the discussion of assimilation chances for contemporary immigrant groups may produce a too pessimistic reading of their prospects. Our additional remarks can only be suggestive at this point. But, since there is as yet no fully satisfactory explanation for the assimilation of the once disparaged southern and eastern European groups, it seems premature to judge the assimilation chances of contemporary immigrant groups as diminished because the socioeconomic structure of the United States has changed in the interim. As Perlmann and Waldinger (1997) note, to insist that assimilation is likely only if the situation of contemporary groups parallels that of earlier ones in precise ways seems to require something that history almost never does – repeat itself exactly. With respect to mobility, such an insistence loses sight of the ability of individuals and groups to adjust their strategies to the economic structures they find. We note in particular that the focus of the economic restructuring argument as applied to immigrants has been almost entirely on the labour market, and it has therefore ignored the educational system. However, not only has the association between social origins and educational attainment weakened over time (Hout et al., 1993), but postsecondary education is more available in some of the states where immigrants have concentrated (California and New York, especially) than elsewhere in the nation. Perhaps the pathways followed by earlier groups have been narrowed over time, but other pathways are likely to have opened up.

We are not denying that there are differences, and important ones, between the immigrations of the past and present and in the circumstances facing immigrant groups after arrival, nor are we claiming that the parallels between the situations faced by the descendants of contemporary immigrants and those of earlier ones are so strong that patterns of assimilation among European Americans can be inferred as a likely outcome for new immigrant groups. But the distinctions between these situations are not as clear-cut as they are usually made out to be. None of them is, in our judgement, sufficiently compelling to rule out *a priori* the possibility of assimilation as a widespread outcome for some, or even most, contemporary immigrant groups. It is therefore imperative to examine with an open mind the cultural, residential, educational and other patterns established by the new immigrants and their children for clues about the potential importance of assimilation.

Immigrants in the Open Labour Market

In the analysis of economic assimilation of immigrant workers, labour economists have contributed important findings. Chiswick's (1977, 1978) pioneering studies of the earnings of immigrants indicated that after an initial period of income decline – which he interpreted as stemming from the 'cost of immigration' – the earnings of immigrants gradually achieved parity within a 10–to–15 year time-line and then surpassed the earnings of native-born workers of the same ethnic background. However, this finding was subsequently challenged by Borjas (1985, 1987) as inconclusive because Chiswick relied on a cross-sectional research design, which conflated aging and immigration-cohort effects. By examining cohort changes, Borjas's analysis suggested that in the past five decades there was a major decline in the skills of immigrants. He pooled the 1970 and 1980 census data and found that the earnings growth of recent cohorts did not exceed the earnings levels of the native born and was lower than the growth experienced by early cohorts of immigrants. He concluded that the third-world origin of many immigrants accounted for the decline in immigrant 'quality', or human capital, compared with the earlier immigration from Europe. Like Chiswick's, Borjas's conclusions are vulnerable because of the use of census cross-sectional data. Even though he pooled data from two decennial censuses to examine cohort effects, he was nonetheless unable to study changes in earnings for the same workers while they acquired work experience and human capital in the United States (his data were not longitudinal, in other words). Moreover, the effect of the deep economic recession in the 1980s could not be taken into account in his analysis.

The debate stimulated by Borjas's criticism of Chiswick's optimistic forecast has been largely inconclusive, according to the assessment of Tienda and Liang (1994). To be sure, considerable variation exists in the quality of cohorts by national origin in the post-1965 immigration. The lower average skill of immigrants overall stems from the large relative size of the immigration from Mexico and some less-developed regions of Asia and Latin America. Other contingents of immigrants, such as those from India and Korea, bring levels of education considerably higher than that of the average American. Moreover, the effect of lower skill on economic mobility depends on the comparison group, as LaLonde and Topel (1991) have shown. If the comparison group consists of the US-born members of the same ethnic group, then Chiswick's results are confirmed: even recent cohorts of immigrants quickly achieve economic parity. This is not the case when native-born Americans in general make up the comparison group. But immigrants who came to the United States as children do achieve economic parity with the latter group of workers (Borjas and Freeman, 1992). This finding is, of course, consistent with assimilation theory. Further, Kossoudji (1988) has argued that if English is learned promptly after arrival in the United States, 'then language assimilation, as it is translated into a job-usable skill, may represent one vehicle of upward mobility'.

A different order of problem with respect to economic assimilation is posed, however, by the large-scale migration of poorly educated and illegal aliens (Borjas 1994). One facet of the problem is that illegal immigrants concentrate in particular geographical locations (e.g., California) and then in enclaves within these.

Spatial concentration of undocumented immigrants probably leads to substantial differences from other immigrants in the extent of economic disadvantage, which in turn is translated into a lower rate of economic assimilation for the children of illegal immigrants. Farley (1996), in examining the low educational background of Hispanic immigrants – legal and illegal – conjectures that the children of Hispanic immigrants in general may continue to suffer the consequences of their parents' low stock of human capital.

Overall, the economic literature on earnings assimilation suggests that post-1965 immigrants are handicapped not so much by race as by a lack of usable human capital (Borjas 1994). If earnings growth is slow, this is accounted for by the low stocks of human capital of recent cohorts of immigrants from developing economies. Their slower pace of economic assimilation can be attributed to the transformation of the American economy, i.e., the general erosion of labour market demand for unskilled labour and the increasing demand for highly skilled workers (Katz 1994), though this affects natives and immigrants alike. By contrast, the sociological literature has highlighted the adverse labour market experience of racial minorities, with sociological analysts often conflating the cost of immigration with the cost of race. When the former is controlled for, however, the earnings gap between non-Hispanic whites and native-born children of immigrants narrows, so that Asian ethnics – mostly Chinese and Japanese among the US born old enough to be in the labour market – achieve substantive parity with whites in earnings growth (Nee and Sanders 1985; Farley 1996).

The relative openness of the American labour market stems from the regulatory environment facing large firms and bureaucracies. In the post-civil rights era, Title VII and other civil rights legislation make it more costly for firms (except possibly small businesses, due to difficulty of monitoring and enforcement) to discriminate by gender and race. As a result, the workplace is more regulated today than it was at the time of the earlier immigrant waves to the United States. The principle of equality under the law has been definitively extended to legal immigrants and naturalized citizens. Even illegal immigrants are entitled to due process and have legal rights. As Liebman (1992) observed in a review of key court cases defining immigrant rights,

> The net effect...would seem to be that aliens are a protected class for purposes of constitutional adjudication, that state rules barring aliens from particular occupations will be scrutinized carefully by courts to see whether it is appropriate that a particular job be restricted to persons...even federal restrictions are constitutionally dubious unless enacted by Congress and justified by significant needs. (p. 372)

However, equality under the law does not extend to illegal immigrants, even though they are entitled to due process and possess limited rights of access to public services. This class of immigrants, estimated to be about 2.6 million at the time of the 1990 census (Fix and Passel 1994), is likely to concentrate in the underground informal ethnic and open labour markets in order to avoid deportation. Undocumented status restricts their labour market mobility since it effectively closes off opportunities to find jobs in the regulated portion of the urban labour market – large firms and government bureaucracies, where monitoring and enforcement of immigration laws are routine. The penalty for illegal status to human-capital immigrants is high, which in part explains why there are so few highly educated workers among the undocumented. Most illegal aliens have no more than an elementary school education, and a sizable number have no formal schooling. Tienda and Singer's (1994) analysis shows that the pattern of earning growth of undocumented immigrants reflects 'economy-wide shifts in the structure of wages as well as changing returns to different levels of schooling'. In their view, the fact that 'wages of undocumented immigrants increased at all is remarkable', given the general performance of the US economy in the 1980s and the restrictions on labour mobility faced by illegal aliens.

The jobs that immigrants find in US labour markets closely correspond to their level of education (Bean and Tienda 1987; Farley 1996). Human-capital immigrant streams – from India, China, Africa, Western Europe, and Canada – have a higher proportion of professionals and managers than the native-born American population. By contrast, immigrant groups with large numbers of workers who come with little formal education – from Cuba and other Caribbean nations, El Salvador, Mexico, and other Central American countries – are disproportionately represented in low-wage blue-collar and service jobs. Consequently, there is a bimodal attainment pattern evident in the occupations and earnings of human-capital immigrants and labour migrants, roughly corresponding to the differences between Asian and Hispanic immigrants. Farley (1996) has compared the earnings of immigrants as reported in the 1990 census with the earnings of native-born workers in fourteen immigrant metropolises, including New York, Los Angeles, Miami, Washington, DC and Houston. He confirms the pattern, first discovered by Chiswick (1977), that the cost of immigration is most clearly felt in the years immediately following arrival to the United States, but that considerable economic mobility occurs over time. After 25 years of residence in the United States, immigrants reported earnings that are 93 per cent of those of native-born non-Hispanic whites. The earnings gap between immigrants and the native born was smaller for women than for men.

However, taking the national origins of immigrants into account unveils a mixed picture of economic assimilation for non-European immigrants in the nation as a whole. Hispanic men – foreign and native born – earn substantially less than Anglos, while Asian men – including the foreign born – earn as much as men from the majority group. For women, the wage gap between Hispanic and Anglo workers is nearly as large as among men, but Asian women report higher wages than do Anglos. When Farley controlled for social and demographic characteristics – place of residence, education, reported English-speaking ability, work disability and marital status – he found that Hispanic men earn 84 per cent and foreign-born Asian men 87 per cent as much as their Anglo counterparts. But native-born Asian men have achieved earnings parity with comparable Anglo males, and accordingly their position has improved since the 1980 census. The wage gap is less for women, with both native- and foreign-born Asian women and native-born Hispanic women earning more than comparable Anglo women. In sum, the early analyses of the 1990 census report results that are in line with expectations of assimilation theory. If anything, the economic assimilation of immigrants has progressed more rapidly for many post-1965 immigrants than it did for the earlier waves of immigrants from Europe due to the technological transformation of the American economy, which results in increased demand for high-skilled workers.

References

Bean, F. and M. Tienda, *The Hispanic Population of the United States* (New York: Russell Sage Foundation, 1987)

Bodnar, J., *The Transplanted: The History of Immigrants in Urban America* (Bloomington: Indiana University Press, 1985)

Borjas, G., 'The Economics of Immigrations,' *Journal of Economic Literature*, 32: 1667–1717 (1994)

—— 'The Self-Employment Experience of Immigrants,' *American Economic Review*, 21: 485-506 (1986)

—— 'Assimilation, Changes in Cohort Quality, and the Earnings of Immigrants,' *Journal of Labor Economics*, 3: 463–489 (1985)

Borjas, G. and R. Freeman, 'Introduction and Summary.' In *Economic Consequences for the U.S. and Source Areas*. Ed. G. Borjas and R. Freeman (Chicago: University of Chicago, 1992)

Chiswick, B., 'The Effect of Americanization on the Earnings of Foreign-Born Men,' *Journal of Political Economy*, 86: 897–921 (1978)

—— 'Sons of Immigrants: Are They at an Earnings Disadvantage?' *American Economic Review*, 67: 376–380 (1977)

Covello, L., *The Social Background of the Italo-American School Child*, (Totowa, NJ: Rowman and Littlefield, 1972)

Farley, R., *The New American Reality: Who We Are, How We Got Here, Where We Are Going* (New York: Russell Sage, 1996)

Farley, R. and W. Frey, 'Changes in the Segregation of Whites from Blacks during the 1980s: Small Steps towards a More Integrated Society,' *American Sociological Review*, 59: 23–45 (1994)

Fix, M. and J. Passel, *Immigration and Immigrants: Setting the Record Straight* (Washington: The Urban Institute, 1994)

Gans, H., 'Second Generation Decline: Scenarios for the Economic and Ethnic Futures of Post-1965 American Immigrants,' *Ethnic and Racial Studies*, 15: 173–192 (1992)

Gibson, M., *Accommodation without Assimilation: Sikh Immigrants in an American High School* (Ithaca: Cornell University Press, 1988)

Greeley, A., *Ethnicity, Denomination, and Inequality* (Beverly Hill: Sage, 1976)

Higham, J., *Strangers in the Land: Patterns of American Nativism, 1860–1925* (New York: Atheneum, 1970)

Hirschman, C. and M. Wong, 'The Extraordinary Educational Attainment of Asian Americans: A Search for Historical Evidence and Explanations,' *Social Forces*, 65: 1–27 (1986)

Hout, M., A. Raftery and E. Bell, 'Making the Grade: Educational Stratification in the United States, 1925–1989.' In *Persistent Inequality: Changing Education Attainment in Thirteen Countries*. Ed. Y. Shavit and H. P. Blossfeld (Boulder: Westview, 1993)

Ignatiev, N., *How the Irish Became White* (New York: Routledge, 1995)

Katz, L., 'Labor's Past and Future,' *Challenge*, 24: 18–25 (1994)

Kossoudji, S., 'English Language Ability and the Labor Market Opportunities of Hispanic and East Asian Immigrant Men,' *Journal of Labor Economics*, 6: 205–228 (1988)

LaLonde, R. and R. Topel, 'Labor Market Adjustments to Increased Immigration.' In *Immigration, Trade and the Labor Market*. Ed. J. Abowd and R. Freeman (Chicago: University of Chicago Press, 1991)

Lee, S. and K. Yamanaka, 'Patterns of Asian American Intermarriage and Marital Assimilation,' *Journal of Comparative Family Studies*, 21: 287–305 (1990)

Lieberson, S., *A Piece of the Pie: Black and White Immigrants since 1880* (Berkeley: University of California Press, 1980)

Liebman, L., 'Immigration Status and American Law: The Several Versions of Antidiscrimination Doctrine.' In *Immigrants in Two Democracies: French and American Experience*. Ed. D. L. Horowitz and G. Noiriel (New York: New York University Press, 1992)

Light, I., 'Immigrant and Ethnic Enterprise in North America,' *Ethnic and Racial Studies*, 7: 195–216 (1984)

Light, I. and E. Bonacich, *Immigrant Entrepreneurs: Koreans in Los Angeles, 1965–1982* (Berkeley: University of California, 1988)

Loewen, J., *The Mississippi Chinese: Between Black and White* (Cambridge, MA: Harvard University, 1971)

Model, S., 'The Economic Progress of European and East Asian Americans,' *Annual Review of Sociology*, 14: 363–380 (1988)

Nee, V. and J. Sanders, 'The Road to Parity: Determinants of the Socioeconomic Attainments of Asian Americans,' *Ethnic and Racial Studies*, 8: 75–93 (1985)

Perlmann, J. and R. Waldinger, 'Second Generation Decline? Children of Immigrants, Past and Present – A Reconsideration,' *International Migration Review*, 31 (1997)

Portes, A. and R. Rumbaut, *Immigrant America: A Portrait* 2nd ed. (Berkeley: University of California Press, 1996)

Portes, A. and M. Zhou, 'The New Second Generation: Segmented Assimilation and Its Variants,' *The Annals of the American Academy of Political and Social Sciences*, 530: 74–96 (1993)

Qian, Z., 'Breaking the Racial Barriers: Variations in Interracial Marriages between 1980 and 1990,' *Demography*, 34: 263–276 (1997)

Roediger, D., *The Wages of Whiteness: Race and the Making of the American Working Class* (New York: Verso, 1991)

Sassen, S., *The Mobility of Capital and Labor* (Cambridge: Cambridge University Press, 1988)

Tienda, M. and Z. Liang, 'Poverty and Immigration in Policy Perspective.' In *Confronting Poverty: Prescriptions for Change* ed. S. H. Danzinger, G. D. Sandefur, and D. H. Weinberg (New York: Russell Sage Foundation, 1994)

Tienda, M. and A. Singer, 'Wage Mobility of Undocumented Workers in the United States,' *International Migration Review*, 29: 112–138 (1994)

Waldinger, R., *Still the Promised City? African-Americans and New Immigrants in Post-Industrial New York* (Cambridge: Harvard University, 1996)

—— 'Changing Ladders and Musical Chairs: Ethnicity and Opportunity in Post-industrial New York', *Politics and Society*, 15 (1986/87)

Waters, M., 'Ethnic and Racial Identities of Second-generation Black Immigrants in New York City,' *International Migration Review*, 28: 795–820 (1994)

Woldemikael, T. *Becoming Black American: Haitians and American Institutions in Evanston, Illinois* (New York: AMS Press, 1989)

MULTICULTURALISM IN WELFARE STATES: THE CASE OF GERMANY

FRANK-OLAF RADTKE

The process of ethnic formation of migrant workers and their families in Germany must be discussed in the framework of the concept of political pluralism on the one hand and, on the other, the specific condition of the social democratic type of welfare state both of which seem to reflect conflicting principles. [This essay sets out to discuss]: (1) that migrants did not arrive in Germany as 'ethnic minorities' but were created as such as a result of the historic condition of the German nation state; (2) that there is in Germany unlike in other immigration countries no ethnic mobilization in terms of an ethnic bottom up movement which could efficiently claim group interests; (3) that multiculturalism has an unintended effect by transforming social conflicts into ethnic ones and has made them irreconcilable.

A precondition of the functioning of the liberal model of political pluralism is the chance for individuals to articulate and give voice to certain kinds of interest by forming interest-groups. The ability and power to organize one's interest depends, in the market model, on the equality of individual opportunities and rights. Only those interests which can be organized and confronted efficiently with conflicting interests will have the chance to become part of the social compromise in which the distribution of the social wealth is regulated. Common interest in the pluralistic concept cannot in advance be defined in political programmes but appears *a posteriori* as a result of the free game of social powers.

Within the normative model of liberal democracy the task of the state is endowed with the monopoly of force, to make sure a minimum of rules and norms which form the constitution are voluntarily maintained. Liberalism is based on the idea of a division of powers which is more exactly a division of social spheres: the public sphere and the private sphere. Both spheres are composed of different systems, each of them dominated by different principles.

In the public sphere is situated the political system where political participation is organized and state decisions are made and administered within bureaucratic organizations. The governing principle is the equality of universal human and political rights summed up as citizenship, symbolized in the right to vote and to be elected. The system of science, arts and the media also belongs to the public sphere but is strictly separated from the political system. It is governed by the freedom of opinion and the privilege of error. The core of the public sphere is formed by the economic system of the markets of goods, labour and services; this most dynamic system is ruled by the maxim of competition, rivalry and advantage. The youngest but nowadays one of the biggest systems in modern societies has become the educational system which has made socialization and education a public task. It is ruled by the principles of achievement and meritocracy and by the principle of homogeneity which strives to build a national identity by means of language and culture.

The religious community of ethics is situated in the private sphere. During the modernization process in the nineteenth and twentieth centuries in Europe it has more or less been expelled from the public sphere and is now based on the individual freedom of faith. The core of the private sphere is formed around the family which is historically the oldest part of society and one organized on the archaic principles of kinship and descent. Around the family there is the wider community of friendship and neighbourhood which is held together by the principle of exclusiveness (Rex 1986; Walzer 1992).

Political pluralism will work only if the different spheres are separated and their ruling maxims are not confused. But there is no pure realization of the concept of strictly separated spheres anywhere in the world. All existing societies that devote themselves to political pluralism have difficulties in keeping principles, institutions and practices distinct. Conflicts arise especially at those lines where institutions have only recently differentiated themselves or have (been) moved from one sphere to the other. That is the case, for example, with religion which was only recently moved to the private sphere but which frequently intervenes with moral standards into the political ('abortion') or educational system ('school prayer'). Other examples are when the private community claims particular ('cultural') rights ('mother tongue') in public education; when market principles undermine or political restrictions repress science, art, religion or education; when the state intervenes with regard to the principle of equality ('gender') into the labour market or into the privacy of the family etc.

Conflicts of this type are constitutive in plural societies and are part of the process of social change and modernization. The way they are solved gives every society a specific historic appearance. The decision over, for example, whether there should be more morality in the economic system or more commercialization in the science and art systems or more equality in the labour market or more cultural particularity in the education system is subject to political debate and is the outcome of conflicting interests. The existing pluralist societies can be differentiated along these lines.

The programme of the social democratic type of welfare state intentionally crosses the distinctions between the spheres and systems under the title of prevention and intervention. In this concept the task of the state is not only to guarantee certain formal rules and equal rights in the political process of conflict solving but also to create social justice by balancing individual disadvantages. The idea is that the principle of equality (of rights and chances) should not only be valid in the political system but has to be extended to an equality (of outcomes) in the other systems, too. Not satisfied with the mechanisms of self-control and -regulation by non-regulation in the market system, the state establishes a superstructure to manage and control the social process and to define the common welfare in advance. Starting with interventions into the economic system, the state occupies more and more of those tasks which in the liberal model are related to the market, to non-governmental organizations and self-organized interest groups. The importance of the civil society of organized interests (unions, federations, companies, professions, parties, movements) is reduced and transformed if the state claims an overall competence of problem solving.

An outstanding characteristic of the social democratic type of welfare state is the legal regulation of all social relations and the emergence of a client system. This tends to overthrow the old class relations (as group conflicts in the economic system based on solidarity) as well as the functioning of civil society (based on self-organization of social and cultural interests). This also establishes a direct relation between the individual and the state by splitting up interest groups such that their members are isolated against each other and become competing receivers of benefits and substitute payments. The civil society vanishes or is ousted to the private sphere. Freedom is seen to be 'time free of work' and public affairs become the domain of professional politicians and party managers. The process of individualization opens up an empty space between the bureaucratic state and the individual. The necessity of self-organization is superseded inasmuch as the individual has contentions and claims to make which result from premiums or social rights. Social and political participation is reduced to periodical voting in general elections; political parties are changed from interest groups to 'people-parties' working as clearing organizations to transmit state interest.

A stepped clientelism may emerge if existing organizations of the civil society which organize interests or provide services or care for the socially disadvantaged become dependent upon state money to fulfil their tasks. This is the case where the state follows the subsidiarity principle delegating its duties to private institutions, e.g. private companies or the churches or church-run welfare organizations. The clientele of the state are organizations which have a clientele of individuals themselves. In both cases the dependency is reciprocal: the institutional or individual client will try to present himself as fitting into the programme of the patron; the patron will continue to exist only if he has the lasting support and trust of his clientele. To compensate its notorious deficit the welfare state may not withstand the temptation to use civil institutions as instruments of policy implementation. At this point, civil society is transformed into a corporatistic system where individual rights and claims are only recognized as group rights depending on membership to certain categories. The liberal model of competing interests ends up in patronage, lobbyism and paternalism.

The German model of the 'social market economy' follows the concept of the social democratic type of welfare state even if it was initiated after the Second World War by neo-conservative Christian Democrats. There is a high amount of state interventionism into the economic, the cultural and the educational systems, even into the religious and family spheres. A debate on the limits of the welfare state has only recently begun, and a policy of deregulation, i.e. withdrawal of the state from several fields of activity, is now taking place.

The condition of the German welfare state together with an ethnic nation state tradition has shaped and sustained the way the state acted towards migrant workers. Until recently [West] Germany never considered itself an immigrant country, although more than 20 million people from eastern and southern Europe immigrated into the territory of the [former] Federal Republic between 1945 and 1989, among them 5 million 'guestsworkers' and their families. West German capitalism, confronted with a second socialist German state, presented itself as a system of social security. Unlike other immigration countries such as the US, Canada, Australia, but also the UK and France, immigrants in Germany are granted most of the social benefits provided to citizens but enjoy no political rights which would enable them to assert their interests effectively. Nobody can legally enter [West Germany] without immediately being endowed with nearly the full range of social rights. From the beginning of the recruitment of guest-workers in the 1950s until 1973, when a recruitment-stop was declared, the migrant workers were formally granted working conditions and social benefits equal to the German workforce (which could not prevent them from getting the badly paid and dirty jobs). None of the trade unions was interested in having a situation of competition between a German workforce and the legally weakened immigrants who would have to accept any payment and any working conditions – a strategy that eventually brought about illegal work.

Immigrant workers are on the one hand integrated into the social security system but on the other hand not admitted to the political arena. This is due to the ruling interpretation of the German constitution of 1949 which is in essential partly built on the concept of the 'jus sanguinis', reserving citizenship to ethnic Germans based on blood. As non-citizens, foreigners do not have the right to political rights. They cannot themselves struggle for their interests in the political system and have to find deputizing majority speakers. These conditions have made them prototypical clients. Private welfare organizations offered their services.

In the [former] Federal Republic of Germany social welfare under the subsidiarity principle is partly the task of private social welfare organizations which are nearly completely subsidized by state money. They are linked to the churches and the trade unions and thus are ideologically fixed. The care for the 'Ausländer' opened a new field of social work but also new spheres of interest: there was a pastoral-missionary interest not to let the uprooted migrants fall into moral disorientation or the influence of communist propaganda but there was also an interest to get state money to run the organization. To that purpose welfare organizations first created a 'guestworker problem'. As there are competing welfare organizations the growing number of migrants in the 1960s was distributed among them. To split up the clientele between the organizations it became necessary to find criteria for the sharing out. The differences of language and religion were emphasized: (1) the Catholic CARITAS got the (Catholic) migrants from Italy, Spain, Portugal and Croatia; (2) the Protestant DIAKONIE got the non-Catholic but Christian migrants from Greece; and (3) the ARBEITERWOHLFAHRT, a non-denominational organization close to the trade unions, got the non-Christian (i.e. Muslim) immigrants from Turkey and the Maghreb.

From a professional point of view it was a pragmatic decision to homogenize the client groups along the lines of language to make communication easier by way of specializing the translating capacities. The decisive factor here – one especially important for the process of ethnicization – was the emphasis on religion – a marker migrants themselves would not have used. The combination of language and religion for professional and administrative purposes created 'cultures', and subsequently 'ethnic groups', whose special needs the welfare organizations had to meet through particular measures.

In Germany today the language of the 'guestworkers' and the denomination or non-denominational orientation of the welfare organizations, turns out to be the hidden scheme of what, since the 1980s, is also in Germany called the 'multicultural society'. Language differences were charged with religious ones and then reintroduced into the society, re-emphasizing a difference that during the process of modernization and secularization had already lost its social importance. Migrants were turned into representatives of their national culture.

The organizations had created the cultures which they were to look after in the coming years by the installation of a system of counselling centres, support systems, learning courses etc. Migrants were no longer dealt with in their social roles as workers or family members, workless and/or homeless, pregnant, school failures, alcoholics, drug addicts etc. but seen from an ethnological viewpoint as representatives of their national culture of descent. Regional studies were conducted to get an idea of the difficulties and conflicts of a life between cultures. This approach opened a new field of operation for social advisers, and often resulted in an endless stereotyping of, especially, Turkish youth and Turkish women (who became the preferred object of social research). Detailed reports of the way of living in a village in Anatolia, in comparison with the living conditions in the German inner city, were used to draw conclusions and make prognoses about the migrants' ability or competence for integration. The differentiation of cultural, instead of social, characteristics offered the chance to constitute groups whose members' behaviour is deterministic. In this way pre- and intervention strategies need not be individualized, but instead can be applied to whole national groups.

When a public discourse on the limits of the welfare system arose, the situation of divided social and political rights allowed the state, after 1975, to start a policy of chicanery and nasty administrative tricks to expel those migrants who were now seen as illegitimate freeloaders. In reaction to the politics of social cutbacks and the restriction of living conditions, migrants themselves had no political means to oppose discrimination; hence they were only to avoid it as best they could. Legal action was taken whereby a group was created within the population whose members were the object of discrimination and paternalization at the same time. Without any power or right to political action, migrants needed deputy speakers and therefore became a permanent topic of the discourse of the majority. In the media migrants were presented as being illegitimate participants in the social welfare system or as victims of discrimination. All participants in the debate following their own aims and interests established a discourse about the migrants and not a dialogue with them.

The terms of the debate among the majority population began to focus attention on the immigrants' abilities and willingness to integrate into the majority culture. In the course of this assimilationist debate, migrants were no longer dealt with in terms of their legal status ('Ausländer') but turned into 'strangers'. The difference of passport was changed into a difference of 'culture'. 'Ethnicity' as an important issue and a category to draw differences was once again in German history, wilfully introduced into the society to discriminate against a social group.

The response of the benevolent part of the society, especially that of the Protestant churches and the welfare organizations, was to adopt the concept of 'multiculturalism' imported from the US and the UK. Multiculturalism was the only way to keep on dealing with cultural and ethnic differences in a positive way. The welfare organizations which, for organizational and professional purposes had once described society in terms of religious and language differences, now tried to get rid of the ghosts they had called up by turning unwanted immigration into a programme of cultural enrichment.

Parallel to the discussion in the social welfare organizations, welfare and labour market politicians who saw themselves confronted with demographic problems in the indigenous population also changed their viewpoint. To stabilize the social security system and to release future labour markets, they welcomed immigration. Looking for a fitting ideology to reconcile those who were afraid of the strangers, they picked up the idea of multiculturalism and painted a colourful picture of a society of cultural plurality in an integrating Europe.

To find an explanation for extremely high quotas of school failures among migrant children, last but not least educationalists in school referred to cultural differences and cultural conflicts. They adopted multiculturalism and transformed it into a concept of intercultural education. It is very rarely implemented in the daily school life, but has the advantage of allowing teachers and headmasters to talk and conform with the benevolent part of the majority by way of offering excuses for the unacceptable outcomes of their schooling practices.

The ascription of ethnic distinctions included a revitalization of the notion of 'Germanness' which after the Second World War had been totally tabooed. If the minorities had a national identity, why should the indigenous people not – definitely after the 'reunification' – feel German? The ethnic formation of the minorities 'from above' opened the floor for a new nationalism in the majority – a defensive nationalism of resentment induced by the political parties in the course of election campaigns to legitimate social cuts and economic disturbances following the national euphoria.

Having no political rights and being the discriminated and/or paternalized object of the discourse of the majority, the minorities in Germany cannot take advantage of the programme of multiculturalism to organize and to struggle for their own affairs; instead they had to accept help – individually in the client role.

One small exception where migrants as group representatives have a chance to articulate their interests is found in the 'Committees of Foreigners'. Their task was to inform the decision-makers (at the municipal level) about migrants' interests and claims. Only half the seats were reserved for migrants while the rest were given to representatives of social welfare organizations who felt themselves in charge of migrants and again acted as deputy speakers. During the 1980s, however, the members of these committees in several cities were elected by the migrant communities themselves. Although migrants now have the right to be heard in some city parliaments, they are far from being part of the majority representation with equal participating rights (Boanmes 1991). The number of participants in these migrant 'elections' is very low not only because of the symbolic meaning of the vote but also because social and political differences within migrant populations can hardly be represented within a quota system.

The modus of these para-elections together with the discourse of multiculturalism for migrants made it advisable to present themselves as ethnics emphasizing their cultural heritage. Having no space in the public sphere except as the subject of exploitation, paternalism, advice and help, migrants in the German context were ousted to the private sphere and forced to follow the 'communal option' intensifying their ethnic links. They formed ethnic homogeneous communities around religious and traditional symbols not only to protect a cultural identity in an unfriendly and sometimes racist environment but also to present themselves in the way that the majority wanted to see them. There is a strong interaction between the policy of multiculturalism and the cultural acting out of minorities and their representatives. When the city of Frankfurt, for example, establishes an 'Office for Multi-Cultural Affairs', people who want to get help, advice or money from the office have to present their problems with reference to their ethnic origin. If there is, for example, a conflict between a tenant and a landlord, let's say about noise and smell in a fast-food shop, then the office will surely intervene if one of the conflicting parties plays the ethnic card. The noise and smell must be identified as ethnic noise and smell. The shopkeeper therefore has to be labelled as or to present himself as 'Turkish' to turn a social conflict which would be the responsibility of the 'Office of Public Order' into an ethnic conflict between representatives of two national cultures.

The effect of multiculturalism in connection with clientelism is not ethnic mobilization but self-ethnicization of the minorities. As long as they do not have any political rights and as long as there is no policy of equal opportunity or affirmative action – and this is an important difference from the situation in the USA and the UK – multiculturalism inevitably ends up in folklorism. Minorities in Germany are kept away from the public sphere and invited by the legal system to form apolitical communities ('Gemeinschaften') in the private sphere instead of interest groups. The communal option in the German context will not favour ethnic corporatism as a means to struggle for one's rights. It is regressive and of doubtful value for coping with the problems of a modern society which follows the social democratic type of welfare state. It is regressive in the psychoanalytic sense of going back to former states of the psychogenetic development where the basic triad of 'individual', 'patria' and 'mother tongue' is reconstructed. Here, 'fundamentalism' finds fertile soil. And it is regressive in a historic sense as it prolongs differentiation patterns once invented in the nineteenth century which have no solving capacity for the global problems of the twenty-first century. Ethnicization and self-ethnicization bring about the danger that the division of the public and the private spheres which is a condition of modern functional differentiated societies is replaced by secret undeclared segregation.

Societies which are subjected to clientelism are characterized by a process of dissocialization, individualization and singularization. Privatism, egocentrism and the decay of universalistic orientations enforce particularistic thinking and acting. Political philosophers and increasingly politicians recommend a recollection of the idea of 'community' (cf. Taylor 1989) for the majority, too. Multiculturalism appears as a form of 'communitarism' promising the solution for the post-modern decay of the society. This might be a serious fallacy. The functioning of pluralism depends on bargaining processes concerning conflicting interests with common rules and shared values. Organized interest groups, in the concept of pluralism, are thought of as 'pouvoir intermédiaire' (in the Montesquieu sense) which guarantee the rules of the game in their own interest. Particularistic communities based on ethnic self-definition or external labelling are not able to guarantee the minimum consensus that is essential for pluralism because the principle of their organization is exclusiveness. When it comes to the questions of cultural identity, religious norms etc. differences become irreconcilable and compromises are reduced.

Multiculturalism translates the concept of a plurality of interests into a concept of a plurality of descents. Thus it offers, in the empty space between state and the individual, not an autonomous group but the believed community of those who have in common certain quasi-natural characteristics as religion and language. Multiculturalism is only a reversal of ethnocentrism. When ever more theoretical arguments are turned upside down, the categories used to draw differences remain the same. As long as ethnic differentiation is exclusively an issue for minorities, the German society is not really affected. But if the pattern of ethnic differentiation overcomes the majority as a national backlash – for example in the case of refugees and asylum seekers or in relation to the former 'brothers and sisters' in the connected territories in East Germany – then the fundamental principles of the republic are touched. Multiculturalism encourages such a development where ethnic differences are reified, revitalized and scientifically subsidized instead of deconstructed, reduced and demystified.

References

Bommes, M. (1991), *Interessenvertretung durch Einfuss*, University of Osnabrück, Osnabrück.

Rex, J. (1986), *The Concept of a Multi-Cultural Society*, Centre for Research in Ethnic Relations, Occasional Papers, University of Warwick, Coventry.

Taylor, C. (1989), 'Cross-Purposes: The Liberal-Communitarian Debate', in N. Rosenblum, *Liberalism and the Moral Life*, Harvard University Press, Cambridge, Mass.

Walzer, M. (1992), *Zivile Gesellschaft und Amerikanische Demokratie*, Rotbuch Verlag, Berlin.

'CULTURALISM' AND 'NATIONALISM' IN MODERN CHINA

MA RONG

The Terms Used in Contemporary China Concerning 'Nation' and 'Ethnic Group'

In China, *minzu* 民族 has been one of the most frequently used terms. Another word *zuqun* 族群 has appeared in the scholarly literature in recent years. The term corresponding to *minzu* in English is 'nation', while the latter corresponds to the English 'ethnic group' (or ethnicity). When we speak of the *Zhonghua minzu* 中华民族, the Chinese nation, and the 56 *minzu* or 'nationalities' in Chinese official translation, we actually confuse their conceptual difference by using the same word for two different concepts.

Accordingly, some years ago I made the suggestion to keep the term 'Chinese nation', and change any reference to the 56 'nationalities' to 'ethnic groups' or 'ethnic minorities' when these groups are referred to as a whole (Ma 2001: 156). My proposal was based on three considerations. First, the social and cultural Uygurs and Hui in China approximate to 'racial and ethnic minorities' in other countries, such as the American Indians, African Americans and Hispanics in the US. Thus, the term 'ethnic groups' reflects the structure of ethnicity in China more accurately. Second, by differentiating between these terms, conceptual confusion resulting from two different meanings (the 'Chinese nation' and 'ethnic groups' making up the 'Chinese nation') for the same term in Chinese will be avoided.[1] Finally, if we translate China's 56 ethnic groups *(minzu)* as 56 'nationalities', and name their requests on behalf of economic and cultural interests as 'nationalism',[2] we seriously mislead English-speaking readers who might associate these groups with independent political entities who have the right to carry out 'national self-determination' and establish their own independent 'nation states'.

The reason we distinguish between 'nation' and 'ethnic group' in the Chinese language is because the different use of these terms may actually imply varied orientations for viewing, understanding and managing ethnic relations.

Two Types of Policies for Managing Ethnic Relations: Politicization and Culturalization

Government policy plays an important role in guiding group identity and adjusting the boundaries of a political entity. Throughout the history of social development, governments have generally adopted two contrasting policies for regulating ethnic relations: one views ethnic groups mainly as political entities and the other views them primarily as cultural groups. The former policy emphasizes integrity, political power and 'territorial' conservation of ethnic groups. The latter prefers to treat ethnic relations as cultural interactions, and to deal with the problems between people of different ethnic backgrounds as affairs among individuals rather than between groups as a whole, even though the common characteristics of the ethnic group membership are given recognition. By emphasizing the cultural characteristics of ethnic groups, their political interests are diluted. Furthermore, in processes of migration, the historical connection between ethnic groups and their traditional residence is gradually loosened.

The Traditional Culture-centred View of Ethnic Relations in Chinese History

Historically, the eastern Asian continent has been a motherland to many ethnic groups. Among these groups were more 'advanced' Han Chinese and relatively less advanced minority 'barbarians', including nomads in grasslands and people living in mountainous areas in the south. In the traditional Chinese cultural norms, ethnic identity rested on the distinction between barbarian minorities and civilized Han. This distinction, according to Confucianism, does not refer to apparent differences in physical features or language. Rather, it is mainly shown in cultural differences with values and norms of behaviour as the distinguishing characteristics.

Two contemporary scholars have written (Zhang & Kong 1999: 285):

> According to Confucianism, the distinction between *'hua (xia)'* (civilized Han) and *yi* (minority barbarians) was a cultural boundary rather than a racial and national boundary…The barbarian–civilized distinction did not indicate racial or national exclusiveness. Instead, it was a distinction involving differentiated levels of cultural achievement.

In other words, the 'barbarian–civilized' distinction did not indicate division and exclusivity between different 'civilizations' such as that between medieval Christianity and Islam. Instead, it referred to the distinction between highly developed and less developed 'civilizations' with similar roots but at different stages of advancement. The less developed minorities ('barbarians') accepted such a distinction, and actively sought knowledge from Chinese civilization. Therefore, although there were conflicts and wars between the dynasties in the 'core area' and minorities in the peripheries, what characterized the interaction between the 'more civilized' and 'less civilized' groups was not mainly hostility and mutual destruction but cultural diffusion and learning.

The ancient Chinese viewed Chinese culture as 'the most advanced civilization' of the world, which would sooner or later influence surrounding 'barbarians'. In this point of view, those who were acculturated by Chinese civilization became 'members' of this 'civilized' world with 'Han' as its 'core'. Those who were unacculturated remained 'barbarians' who needed to be 'educated'. Ambrose King (1997: 177) argues that, as a political entity, traditional China was unlike any other nation states, since 'it was a political–cultural entity, or what is called the civilized state, which was marked by cultural rather than ethnic differentiations, and consequently followed a unique civilized order'. In discussing 'the nature of

Chinese nationalism', the great American Sinologist John King Fairbank (1979: 98) emphasized that:

> Undoubtedly this universalism has meant that culture (the way of life) has been more fundamental in China than nationalism. Early Chinese emperors asserted that they ruled over all civilized mankind without distinction of race or language. Barbarian invaders who succeeded them found it expedient to continue and reinforce this tradition. To any Confucian ruler, Chinese or alien, the important thing was the loyalty of his administrators and their right conduct according to the Confucian code. Color and speech were of little account as long as a man understood the classics and could act accordingly.[3]

Since culture can be learned and taught, Chinese traditional ideology therefore held that the two sides of the 'civilized–barbarian distinction' were transferable. That is to say: 'evil Chinese retreat to being barbarians, and fine barbarians advance to becoming Chinese' (Zhang & Kong 1999: 285). 'Fine' refers to 'civilized' whereas 'evil' means 'uncivilized'. This ideology articulates dialectic reasoning and echoes a tolerant attitude on the part of Chinese culture towards other cultures.

Chinese emperors, elites and people considered ethnic minorities that had accepted Chinese culture as 'civilized' citizens and treated them fairly equally. Yet, they adopted a discriminating attitude toward the 'barbarian' groups. The foundation of such discrimination, however, was 'cultural superiority' rather than 'racial superiority'. Behind this superiority was a flexible and dialectic view that accepted 'barbarian' groups to be 'civilized' through acculturation. Following the principle of 'teaching without discrimination', it was the Chinese cultural tradition to transform the 'uncivilized' minorities into 'civilized' members of society through acculturation rather than military conquest.

In the Chinese cultural tradition, the 'civilized–barbarian distinction' was advocated along with a unified view of 'the world' (*tianxia* or 'all under heaven'), which emphasized that 'all lands belong to the emperor and all people are his subjects'. Both 'barbarians' and 'civilized' were under the same 'heaven', and thus 'barbarians' could be 'educated'. Based on these thoughts, in the Chinese cultural tradition, all ethnic groups were considered equal to each other. This idea was most explicitly expressed in the Confucian saying that 'all people around the four seas are brothers', which emphasized that all ethnic groups should be treated equally; that their differences in biological characteristics,[4] language, religion, and customs should not override their common traits in basic ethics and norms or peaceful coexistence among them; and that the main difference between ethnic groups is cultural, with the 'superior (more advanced) culture' being capable of integrating all other cultural groups.[5] It is a 'diffusion model' (Hechter 1975: 6), but one that only emphasizes the aspect of culture. In Chinese history, it is quite clear that, when acculturation occurred among the 'barbarians', a diffusion process followed in other respects.

American sociologist Milton Gordon classifies ideologies concerning ethnic issues into two categories. One view maintains ethnic inequalitarianism or racism, while the other view supports ethnic equalitarianism or non-racism. Gordon further divides the second view into three sub-categories, namely (1) assimilationist structure, (2) liberal pluralism, and (3) corporate pluralism (Gordon 1975: 105–106). The Chinese traditional view of ethnicity ('teaching without discrimination') and practice ('transforming barbarian into civilized') belongs to the ideological type of assimilationist structure.

Although there is always politics in issues concerning race, nationality and ethnic groups, ideas on 'majority–minority relations' or 'civilized–barbarian relations' were to a great extent 'culturalized' in the Chinese cultural tradition, in both theory and practice. This strategy enabled the civilized group in the core region to unify and embody the ethnic minorities in periphery areas. In addition, the Chinese tradition of treating ethnic differences as 'cultural differences' made it possible to implement the policy of 'transforming barbarian into civilized', which resulted in attracting ethnic minorities from the periphery areas and the ultimate formation of a unified pluralist Chinese nation with the Han group in the central plain as the core (Fei 1989: 19). But it should be noticed that the idea of 'cultural racism' also emerged among the ethnic groups and their elites throughout the historical interactions among the groups. Sometimes, when the central government was weak, while ethnic minorities became a fatal threat to the Han group, then 'barbarians' were viewed as the enemy who could not be 'civilized' and become a part of China. For instance, during the late Qing dynasty when the western and Japanese invasions became a fatal threat to China's independence and culture, racism among the Han elites became very strong.

'Culturalism' and 'Nationalism' in Modern China

The Indian/American historian Prasenjit Duara has proposed looking at Chinese history from what he terms a 'bifurcating linear way', which he believes was how the ideas and narratives of Chinese history were formulated in the past. He recognizes 'culturalism' as the core of Chinese traditional views of different groups, and that this was a 'mode of consciousness distinct from nationalism'. He states (Duara 1995: 56):

> Viewing 'culturalism' (or universalism) as a 'Chinese culturalism' is to see it not as a form of cultural consciousness per se, but rather to see culture – a specific culture of the imperial state and Confucian orthodoxy – as a criterion defining a community. Membership in this community was defined by participation in a ritual order that embodied allegiance to Chinese ideas and ethics.

But Duara also claims that there was another 'nationalist' route in Chinese history in viewing minorities. When 'barbarians' could no longer be educated in the Confucian manner but became so strong militarily as to threaten the existence of Chinese empire and culture, the Chinese elite would be forced to turn to the 'nationalist route'. For example, 'during the Jin invasion of the twelfth century, segments of the literati completely abandoned the concentric, radiant concept of universal empire for a circumscribed notion of the Han community and fatherland *(guo)* in which the barbarians had no place' (Duara 1995: 58). Then a defensive 'nationalism' emerged among the elite and people.

Towards the end of the Qing dynasty (late nineteenth to early twentieth centuries), nationalism emerged among the Han Chinese elite who had supported the Qing for over two centuries mainly because of the failures of the Qing in the wars against imperialist invasions. Sun Yatsen and his colleagues, who were influenced by this nationalist movement, issued a call to 'expel the barbarian Manchus and restore China'. By contrast, Kang Youwei, the leader of the ideologically 'royalist' defenders of the Qing dynasty,

> cited Confucius to argue that although Confucius has spoken of barbarians, barbarism was expressed as a lack of ritual and civilization. If indeed they possessed culture, then they must be regarded as Chinese...he was convinced that community was composed of people with shared culture and not restricted to a race or ethnic group. (Duara 1995: 74)

When the Qing dynasty was overthrown in 1911, China faced a very different situation, and among its many problems were independence movements by the ethnic minorities. As Duara writes (1995: 76),

> Sun Yat-sen and the leaders of the new Republic sought to supplement their racialist narrative with the culturalist narrative of the nation espoused by their enemies – the reformers and the Qing court itself. The Chinese nation was now to be made up of the 'five races' (Manchu, Mongol, Tibetan, Muslim, and Han).

Prasenjit Duara applied his 'bifurcating linear way' mainly in examining Chinese history in the late Qing dynasty. But this approach can be applied to the period after the 1911 revolution and even to that after the 1950s.

During the Republican period, Chiang Kaishek followed the 'culturalist' framework and denied Mongol, Tibetan, Hui, etc. status as 'nationalities/nations', considering these groups as tribes of the Chinese nation. He emphasized that China should be 'one nation and one leadership'. Meanwhile, the Chinese Communist Party followed the Soviet model and 'nationalist' narrative, claiming that these groups were 'nationalities'. They should have the right to 'self-determination' and to establish their own nations.[6]

Sun Yatsen learned 'culturalism' from the royalists, and passed it on to Chiang Kaishek; the Chinese Communist Party learned 'nationalism' first from revolutionists of the late Qing and then from the Russians. This is the unimaginable historical dialect in a nation's development process. It switches its positions continually along a bifurcating linear route (see Figure 1).

The Policies of the Chinese Government Since 1949

Although there were some tortuous periods in ethnic relations in the thousands of years of Chinese history, the mainstream in ethnic relations and integration among the groups has always been 'culturalism'. This process lasted until the 1950s. Under the international circumstances at that time, especially the Korean War of 1950–1953, the Chinese leaders, who were extremely inexperienced in administrative matters, had to seek support from the Soviet Union. They copied almost all the Soviet models in terms of administration, education, the economy

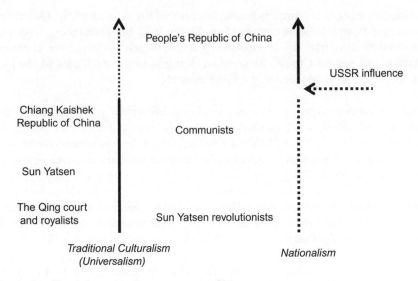

Figure 1. The bifurcating linear route in China

and military affairs. The government also followed the Soviet model by politicizing and institutionalizing the ethnic minorities in China.

First, the government organized the 'identification of nationalities' in the 1950s. Eventually 56 'nationalities' were identified, their population ranging from 718 (Hezhe)[7] to 547,283,057 (Han in the 1953 census). All Chinese citizens were registered by 'nationality status' in household registration and personal identification. This system is still in practice today.

Second, the system of autonomy was established for all ethnic minorities. There are five autonomous regions at the provincial level, 30 autonomous prefectures and 120 autonomous counties in today's China. The total areas of these autonomous places together make up 64 per cent of China's territory. The system assumes that the minority groups play a leading role and manage their own affairs in autonomous areas. The National People's Congress adopted the Autonomy Law of Minority Nationalities of the People's Republic of China in 1984. It contains detailed items regarding the administration, jurisdiction, education, religious and cultural affairs, and local regulations in the autonomous places and has become one of China's most important laws.

Third, the government has designed and practised a series of policies in favour of ethnic minorities in the administrative, educational, economic and cultural areas, and even in family planning programmes.[8] The central government provides large amounts of financial aid to these autonomous places each year. Aid accounted for 38–94 per cent of the total budget of the five autonomous regions in 2002 (Ma 2004: 525). These policies helped the minorities to speed up socioeconomic development and reduced the disparities between ethnic groups. But since these policies were targeted clearly at specific groups, they also strengthened ethnic consciousness, while the boundaries between ethnic groups became clearer and more stable than they had earlier been.

These policies link each ethnic minority to a certain geographic area, provide these groups with a political status, administrative power in their 'autonomous territory', and guarantee ethnic minorities the potential to develop at a higher speed. The process of establishing and implementing these policies and the institutions, with their emphasis on 'equality between ethnic groups' rather than 'equality among citizens', will inevitably politicize and institutionalize these groups and strengthen their group consciousness. This will have the effect of pushing them away from being 'cultural groups' and towards the direction of becoming 'political groups' in the 'ethnicity–nation' continuum.

One of the reasons why the governments of some nations, including China, pay attention to the political aspects of minorities has been the pressure from western countries to promote human rights and democracy. In response to critical comments from western countries, these governments have tried to enhance the political status and power of ethnic minorities in their countries. They have hoped that these measures would alleviate the criticism, but in fact this has not happened. The result is that minority groups ask for more powers, and their requests are always supported by the western nations. The political concessions of these governments towards minority affairs has done nothing to resolve the tension among their ethnic groups, but instead created a more solid base for future separatist movements.

Discussion

The successful strategy of 'culturalizing' ethnic minorities in the Chinese tradition has not been carried on in today's China, but plays a positive role in the US. In my opinion, the Chinese should carefully review this historical position. Although in general ethnic relations in today's China are smooth and cooperative, the differences among ethnic minorities in national identification still remain. The Chinese should learn from their ancestors and their experience for thousands of years in guiding ethnic relations. They also should look to other nations for both positive and negative lessons. China might in the future consider changing the direction of managing its ethnic relations from the 'politicizing' to 'culturalizing' route. The route of 'de-politicizing' ethnicity might lead China to a new direction, strengthening national identity among ethnic minorities while guaranteeing the prosperity of their cultural traditions. Of course, how to protect the rights and benefits of ethnic minorities in that process will still be a big task. But to guide ethnic relations according to a modern civic model (citizenship and diversity), instead of the traditional tribal model (group or regional autonomy–separatism) (Gross 1998), might be an alternative for China in the new century.

Notes

1 Some Western scholars used 'ethnic relations' to describe majority–minority relations, while using the term 'nationalities' in referring to Chinese official statements (e.g. Dreyer 1976).

2 'Regional nationalism' of minorities often appeared in Chinese documents. This term in Chinese interpretation only refers to the requests of economic benefits, cultural autonomy and limited political autonomy within the present system.

3 The fact that most groups in China belong to the Mongoloid also made the physical differences less significant in China.

4 In the Chinese tradition, there was no clear correspondence to the Western term 'race' (Stafford 1993: 609).

5 In his study, Frank Dikötter noticed the distinction between 'outside barbarians' and 'inside barbarians' and he also said that 'despite many disparaging comments on the supposedly bestial origins of the minorities, the Han perception of minority Chinese remained embedded in an ethnocentric framework that stressed sociocultural differences' (Dikötter 1992: x). Therefore, sociocultural differences, not biological differences, were major indicators of ethnic characteristics and boundaries in ancient China.

6 This attitude of the CCP changed after they assumed power in 1949 (Connor 1984: 87).

7 The Hezhe, a fishing group living along the Amur River, was officially recognized as a 'nationality' in the late 1950s and the registration records showed the group with only 718 persons in the 1964 census.

8 The members of the minority groups were usually allowed to have more children while the Han have been restricted to the policy of 'one couple, one child'. This was one of the most important reasons why many farmers tried to change their 'nationality status' from Han to a minority group. From 1982 to 1990, several minority groups doubled their population size mainly by re-registration (e.g. the Manchu population increased from 4.3 million to 9.8 million, and Tujia increased from 2.8 million to 5.7 million during these 8 years) (Ma, 2004, p. 662).

References

Connor, W. (1984) *The national question in Marxist–Leninist theory and strategy* (Princeton, NJ: Princeton University Press).

Dikötter, Frank (1992) *The discourse of race in modern China* (Stanford, CA: Stanford University Press).

Dreyer, J. T. (1976) *China's forty millions* (Cambridge, MA: Harvard University Press).

Duara, Prasenjit, (1995) *Rescuing history from the nation* (Chicago, IL: Chicago University Press).

Fairbank, John King, (1979) *The United States and China* (4th edn) (Cambridge, MA: Harvard University Press).

Fei Xiaotong (1989) Zhonghua minzu de duoyuan yiti geju [Pluralism–unity structure of the Chinese nation], *Beijing Daxue Xuebao [Journal of Peking University]*, 4, pp. 1–19.

Gordon, Milton M. (1975) Toward a general theory of racial and ethnic group relations, in N. Glazer and D. P. Moynihan (eds) *Ethnicity: theory and practice*, pp. 84–110 (Cambridge: Harvard University Press).

Gross, F. (1998) *The civic and tribal state* (Westport, CT: Greenwood Press).

Hechter, M. (1975) *Internal Colonialism* (Berkeley, CA: University of California Press).

King, Ambrose, (1997) *Zhongguo Zhengzhi yu Wenhua* [*Politics and culture in China*] (Hong Kong: Oxford University Press).

Ma Rong (2001) Minzu yu Shehui Fazhan [Ethnicity and social development] (Beijing: Minzu Press) (in Chinese).

Ma Rong (2004) *Minzu Shehuixue: Shehuixue de Zuqun Guanxi Yanjiu* [*Sociology of ethnicity: sociological study of ethnic relations*] (Beijing: Peking University Press) (in Chinese).

Stafford, C. (1993) The discourse of race in modern China, *Man: The Journal of the Royal Anthropological Institute*, 28(3), p. 609.

Zhang Lei and Kong Qingrong (1999) *Zhonghua Minzu Ningjulixue* [*Coherence of the Chinese Nation*] (Beijing: Chinese Social Sciences Press).

7

Migration in the Global Age

Modern migration includes people escaping religious and political persecution, fleeing war, famine and natural disasters. It also involves economic migrants. For our purposes here, it is crucial to differentiate between various types of immigrants according to their ethnic identity.[1]

First, immigrants who are culturally and socio-economically similar to the majority in the host society – for instance British in New Zealand and the USA, and Germans in Austria.

Second, immigrants who were initially discriminated against, such as the Irish in Britain or the Italians and the Poles in the USA, and who tend to form ethnic communities within which they maintain their cultural and linguistic heritage, but who have now fully integrated within the host society and attained citizenship. Finally, immigrants, who tend to share some phenotypical traits distinguishing them from the majority of the population, live within relatively closed ethnic communities, and are often the subject of racist discrimination and socio-economic disadvantage. Yet, while some countries, such as Britain, register high levels of naturalization for Asians, others such as the USA have comparatively low naturalization rates for Hispanics, by far the largest immigrant group in the USA. In Austria, large numbers of Turks have naturalized since the late 1990s, and in Germany many Turks have naturalized after Germany reformed its citizenship law in 1999.

Immigrants also vary according to the length of time they plan to spend away from their homeland, thus some are seasonal immigrants, others spend a considerable part of their lives in the host country and others decide to settle permanently in the new country.

The pieces included in this section consider the causes of migration, the specific nature and role of diasporas in the global age and a particular example of transnational migration, usually illegal, from China into different parts of the world.

Douglas S. Massey and his colleagues bring together theories from a number of disciplines and address the reasons for the initiation of migration as well as the structures through which it comes to be sustained. They argue that 'the conditions that initiate international movement may be quite different from those that perpetuate it across time and space. Although wage differentials, relative risks, recruitment efforts and market penetration may continue to cause people to move, new conditions that arise in the course of migration come to function as independent causes themselves'. They mention the spread of migrant networks, the creation of institutions supporting transnational movement and the social meaning of work in host societies as significant factors generally stimulating further movement of people.

This is followed by an essay entitled 'Diasporas'; its author, the anthropologist James Clifford, recognizes the value of the term but also acknowledges its limitations if used in a narrow sense. Clifford also clarifies the nature of other structures and groupings which differ from, even though they overlap with, true diasporas. According to him, diasporic populations do not come from elsewhere in the same way that 'immigrants' do. In his view, 'whether the national narrative is one of common origins or of gathered populations, it cannot assimilate groups that maintain important allegiances and practical connections to a homeland or a dispersed community located elsewhere. Peoples whose sense of identity is centrally defined by collective histories of displacement and violent loss cannot be "cured" by merging into a new national community'. This is especially true when they are the victims of ongoing, structural prejudice. He mentions the 'selective accommodation' of the Jewish diaspora with the political, cultural, commercial and everyday life forms of the host societies. He also refers to the effort of the black diaspora culture currently being articulated in post-colonial Britain to construct alternative ways of being 'British' without neglecting their relationship with Africa, the Americas, their experiences of enslavement, racist subordination, cultural survival, hybridization, resistance and political rebellion.

Li Minghuan offers a fascinating account of transnational labour brokerage in China since the seventeenth century. In so doing, she explores different perceptions and attitudes towards indentured labour not only on behalf of the Chinese authorities but also among the Chinese people. Her account of the nineteenth-century recruitment of Chinese coolies includes an assessment of the huge profits involved in the business of 'recruiting' male and, in particular, female labourers, reports of fraud and poor living and working conditions for Chinese workers abroad.

Li Minghuan moves on to study the position of the People's Republic of China towards migration abroad during the Cultural Revolution (1966–76) – when it was interrupted – up to the present day. She highlights the significance of transnational migration as an aspiration for those aiming to work and make money to return one day to their villages in China, where nobody will care about whether legal or illegal procedures were employed in searching for a better future. As she writes: 'Due to the contradictions between migration policies on the book and the practical labour needs in the relevant states, often the transnational activities of the average people are considered acceptable by participants but are illegal in a formal sense on the national level.'

CAUSES OF MIGRATION

DOUGLAS S, MASSEY, JOAQUIN ARANGO, GRAEME HUGO, ALI KOUAOUCI, ADELA PELLEGRINO AND J. EDWARD TAYLOR

[Since the 1960s], 30 years of immigration has emerged as a major force through-out the world. In traditional immigrant-receiving societies such as Australia, Canada and the United States, the volume of immigration has grown and its composition has shifted decisively away from Europe, the historically dominant source, towards Asia, Africa and Latin America. In Europe, meanwhile, countries that for centuries had been sending out migrants were suddenly transformed into immigrant-receiving societies. After 1945, virtually all countries in western Europe began to attract significant numbers of workers from abroad. Although the migrants were initially drawn mainly from southern Europe, by the late 1960s they mostly came from developing countries in Africa, Asia, the Caribbean and the Middle East.

By the 1980s even countries in southern Europe – Italy, Spain and Portugal – which only a decade before had been sending migrants to wealthier countries in the north, began to import workers from Africa, Asia and the Middle East. At the same time, Japan – with it slow and still declining birth rate, its ageing population and its high standard of living – found itself turning increasingly to migrants from poorer countries in Asia and even South America to satisfy its labour needs.

Most of the world's developed countries have become diverse, multi-ethnic societies, and those that have not reached this state are moving decisively in that direction. The emergence of international migration as a basic structural feature of nearly all industrialized countries testifies to the strength and coherence of the underlying forces. Yet the theoretical base for understanding these forces remains weak. The recent boom in immigration has therefore taken citizens, officials and demographers by surprise, and when it comes to international migration, popular thinking remains mired in nineteenth-century concepts, models and assumptions.

At present, there is no single, coherent theory of international migration, only a fragmented set of theories that have developed largely in isolation from one another, sometimes but not always segmented by disciplinary boundaries. Current patterns and trends in immigration, however, suggest that a full understanding of contemporary migratory processes will not be achieved by relying on the tools of one discipline alone, or by focusing on a single level of analysis. Rather, their complex, multi-faceted nature requires a sophisticated theory that incorporates a variety of viewpoints, levels and assumptions.

The Initiation of International Migration

A variety of theoretical models has been proposed to explain why international migration begins, and although each ultimately seeks to explain the same thing, they employ radically different concepts, assumptions and frames of reference. Neo-classical economics focuses on differentials in wages and employment conditions between countries, and on migration costs; it generally conceives of movement as an individual decision for income maximization. The 'new economics of migration', in contrast, considers conditions in a variety of markets, not just labour markets. It views migration as a household decision taken to minimize risks to family income or to overcome capital constraints on family production activities. Dual labour market theory and world systems theory generally ignore such micro-level decision processes, focusing instead on forces operating at much higher levels of aggregation. The former links immigration to the structural requirements of modern industrial economics, while the latter sees immigration as a natural consequence of economic globalization and market penetration across national boundaries.

Given the fact that theories conceptualize causal processes at such different levels of analysis – the individual, the household, the national and the international – they cannot be assumed, *a priori*, to be inherently incompatible. It is quite possible, for example, that individuals act to maximize income while families minimize risk, and that the context within which both decisions are made is shaped by structural forces operating at the national and international levels. Nonetheless, the various models reflect different research objectives, focuses, interests and ways of decomposing an enormously complex subject into analytically manageable parts; and a firm basis for judging their consistency requires that the inner logical propositions, assumptions and hypotheses of each theory be clearly specified and well understood.

Neo-classical economics: macro theory

[...]

The simple and compelling explanation of international migration offered by neo-classical macro-economics has strongly shaped public thinking and has provided the intellectual basis for much immigration policy. The view contains several implicit propositions and assumptions:

1 The international migration of workers is caused by differences in wage rates between countries.
2 The elimination of wage differentials will end the movement of labour, and migration will not occur in the absence of such differentials.
3 International flows of human capital – that is, highly skilled workers – respond to differences in the rate of return to human capital, which may be different from the overall wage rate, yielding a distinct pattern of migration that may be opposite to that of unskilled workers.
4 Labour markets are the primary mechanisms by which international flows of labour are induced; other kinds of market do not have important effects on international migration.
5 The way for governments to control migration flows is to regulate or influence labour markets in sending and/or receiving countries.

Neo-classical economics: micro theory

Corresponding to the macro-economic model is a micro-economic model of individual choice (Sjaastad 1962; Todaro 1969, 1976, 1989; Todaro and Maruszki 1987). [...] In theory, a potential migrant goes to where the expected net returns to migration are greatest, leading to several important conclusions that differ slightly from the earlier macro-economic formulations:

1 International movement stems from international differentials in both earnings and employment rates, whose product determines expected earnings (the prior model, in contrast, assumed full employment).
2 Individual human capital characteristics that increase the likely rate of remuneration or the probability of employment in the destination relative to the sending country (e.g. education, experience, training, language skills) will increase the likelihood of international movement, other things being equal.
3 Individual characteristics, social conditions, or technologies that lower migration costs increase the net returns to migration and, hence, raise the probability of international movement.
4 Because of 2 and 3, individuals within the same country can display very different proclivities to migration.
5 Aggregate migration flows between countries are simple sums of individual moves undertaken on the basis of individual cost-benefit calculations.
6 International movement does not occur in the absence of differences in earnings and/or employment rates between countries. Migration occurs until expected earnings (the product of earnings and employment rates) have been equalized internationally (net of the costs of movement), and movement does not stop until this product has been equalized.
7 The size of the differential in expected returns determines the size of the international flow of migrants between countries.
8 Migration decisions stem from disequilibria or discontinuities between labour markets: other markets do not directly influence the decision to migrate.
9 If conditions in receiving countries are psychologically attractive to prospective migrants, migration costs may be negative. In this case, a negative earnings differential may be necessary to halt migration between countries.
10 Governments control immigration primarily through policies that affect expected earnings in sending and/or receiving countries – for example, those that attempt to lower the likelihood of employment or raise the risk of under-employment in the destination area (through employer sanctions), those that seek to raise incomes at the origin (through long-term development programmes), or those that aim to increase the costs (both psychological and material) of migration.

The new economics of migration

In recent years, a 'new economics of migration' has arisen to challenge many of the assumptions and conclusions of neo-classical theory (Stark and Bloom 1985).

A key insight of this new approach is that migration decisions are not made by isolated individual actors, but by larger units of related people – typically families or households – in which people act collectively not only to maximize expected income, but also to minimize risks and to loosen constraints associated with a variety of market failures, apart from those in the labour market (Stark and Levhari 1982; Stark 1984; Katz and Stark 1986; Lauby and Stark 1988; Taylor 1986; Stark 1991).

[...]

The theoretical models growing out of the 'new economics' of migration yield a set of propositions and hypotheses that are quite different from those emanating from neo-classical theory, and they lead to a very different set of policy prescriptions:

1 Families, households or other culturally defined units of production and consumption are the appropriate units of analysis for migration research, not the autonomous individual.
2 A wage differential is not a necessary condition for international migration to occur; households may have strong incentives to diversify risks through transnational movement even in the absence of wage differentials.
3 International migration and local employment or local production are not mutually exclusive possibilities. Indeed, there are strong incentives for households to engage in both migration and local activities. In fact, an increase in the returns to local economic activities may heighten the attractiveness of migration as a means of overcoming capital and risk constraints on investing in those activities. Thus, economic development within sending regions needs to reduce the pressures for international migration.
4 International movement does not necessarily stop when wage differentials have been eliminated across national boundaries. Incentives for migration may continue to exist if other markets within sending countries are absent, imperfect or in disequilibria.
5 The same expected gain in income will not have the same effect on the probability of migration for households located at different points in the income distribution, or among those located in communities with different income distributions.
6 Governments can influence migration rates not only through policies that influence labour markets, but also through those that shape insurance markets, capital markets and future markets. Government insurance programmes, particularly unemployment insurance, can significantly affect the incentives for international movement.
7 Government policies and economic changes that shape income distributions will change the relative deprivation of some households and thus alter their incentives to migrate.
8 Government policies and economic changes that affect the distribution of income will influence international migration independent of their effects on mean income. In fact, government policies that produce a higher mean income in migrant-sending areas may *increase* migration if relatively poor households do not share in the income gain. Conversely, policies may reduce migration if relatively rich households do not share in the income gain.

Dual labour market theory

Although neo-classical human capital theory and the new economics of migration lead to divergent conclusions about the origins and nature of international migration, both are essentially micro-level decision models. Standing distinctly apart from these models of rational choice, however, is dual labour market theory, which sets its sights away from decisions made by individuals and argues that international migration stems from the intrinsic labour demands of modern industrial societies.

[...]

Although not in inherent conflict with neo-classical economics, dual labour market theory does carry implications and corollaries that are quite different from those emanating from micro-level decision models:

1 International labour migration is largely demand-based and is initiated by recruitment on the part of employers in developed societies, or by governments acting on their behalf.
2 Since the demand for immigrant workers grows out of the structural needs of the economy and is expressed through recruitment practices rather than wage offers, international wage differentials are neither a necessary nor a sufficient condition for labour migration to occur. Indeed, employers have incentives to recruit workers while holding wages constant.
3 Low-level wages in immigrant-receiving societies do not rise in response to a decrease in the supply of immigrant workers; they are held down by social and institutional mechanisms and are not free to respond to shifts in supply and demand.
4 Low-level wages may fall, however, as a result of an increase in the supply of immigrant workers, since the social and institutional checks that keep low-level wages from rising do not prevent them from falling.
5 Governments are unlikely to influence international migration through policies that produce small changes in wages or employment rates; immigrants fill a demand for labour that is structurally built into modern, postindustrial economies, and influencing this demand requires major changes in economic organization.

World systems theory

Building on the work of Wallerstein (1974), a variety of sociological theorists has linked the origins of international migration not to the bifurcation of the labour market within particular national economies, but to the structure of the world market that has developed and expanded since the sixteenth century (Fortes and Walton 1981; Petras 1981; Castells 1989; Sassen 1988, 1991; Morawska 1990). In this scheme, the penetration of capitalist economic relations into peripheral, non-capitalist societies creates a mobile population that is prone to migrate abroad.

[...]

World systems theory thus argues that international migration follows the political and economic organization of an expanding global market, a view that yields six distinct hypotheses:

1 International migration is a natural consequence of capitalist market formation in the developing world; the penetration of the global economy into peripheral regions is the catalyst for international movement.
2 The international flow of labour follows the international flow of goods and capital, but in the opposite direction. Capitalist investment foments changes that create an uprooted, mobile population in peripheral countries while simultaneously forging strong material and cultural links with core countries leading to transnational movement.
3 International migration is especially likely between past colonial powers and their former colonies, because cultural, linguistic, administrative, investment, transportation and communication links were established early and were allowed to develop free from outside competition during the colonial era, leading to the formation of specific transnational markets and cultural systems.
4 Since international migration stems from the globalization of the market economy, the way for governments to influence immigration rates is by regulating the overseas investment activities of corporations and controlling international flows of capital and goods. Such policies, however, are unlikely to be implemented because they are difficult to enforce, tend to incite international trade disputes, risk world economic recession, and antagonize multinational firms with substantial political resources that can be mobilized to block them.
5 Political and military interventions by governments of capitalist countries to protect investments abroad and to support foreign governments sympathetic to the expansion of the global market, when they fail, produce refugee movements directed to particular core countries, constituting another form of international migration.
6 International migration ultimately has little to do with wage rates or employment differentials between countries; it follows from the dynamics of market creation and the structure of the global economy.

The Perpetuation of International Movement

Immigration may begin for a variety of reasons – a desire for individual income gain, an attempt to diversify risks to household income, a programme of recruitment to satisfy employer demands for low-wage workers, an international displacement of peasants by market penetration within peripheral regions, or some combination thereof. But the conditions that initiate international movement may be quite different from those that perpetuate it across time and space. Although wage differentials, relative risks, recruitment efforts and market penetration may continue to cause people to move, new conditions that arise in the course of migration come to function as independent causes themselves: migrant networks spread, institutions supporting transnational movement develop, and the social meaning of work changes in receiving societies. The general thrust of these transformations is to make additional movement more likely, a process known as cumulative causation.

Network theory

Migrant networks are sets of interpersonal ties that connect migrants, former migrants, and non-migrants in origin and destination areas through ties of kinship, friendship and shared community origin. They increase the likelihood of international movement because they lower the costs and risks of movement and increase the expected net returns to migration. Network connections constitute a form of social capital that people can draw upon to gain access to foreign employment. Once the number of migrants reaches a critical threshold, the expansion of networks reduces the costs and risks of movement, which causes the probability of migration to rise, which causes additional movement, which further expands the networks, and so on. Over time migratory behaviour spreads outward to encompass broader segments of the sending society (Hugo 1981; Taylor 1986; Massey and Garcia España1987; Massey 1990a, 1990b; Gurak and Caces 1992).

[...]

This dynamic theory accepts the view of international migration as an individual or household decision process, but argues that acts of migration at one point in time systematically alter the context within which future migration decisions are made, greatly increasing the likelihood that later decision-makers will choose to migrate. The conceptualization of migration as a self-sustaining diffusion process has implications and corollaries that are quite different from those derived from the general equilibrium analyses typically employed to study migration:

1 Once begun, international migration tends to expand over time until network connections have diffused so widely in a sending region that all people who wish to migrate can do so without difficulty; then migration begins to decelerate.
2 The size of the migratory flow between two countries is not strongly correlated to wage differentials or employment rates, because whatever effects these variables have in promoting or inhibiting migration are progressively overshadowed by the falling costs and risks of movement stemming from the growth of migrant networks over time.
3 As international migration becomes institutionalized through the formation and elaboration of networks, it becomes progressively independent of the factors that originally caused it, be they structural or individual.
4 As networks expand and the costs and risks of migration fall, the flow becomes less selective in socio-economic terms and more representative of the sending community or society.

5 Governments can expect to have great difficulty controlling flows once they have begun, because the process of network formation lies largely outside their control and occurs no matter what policy regime is pursued.
6 Certain immigration policies, however, such as those intended to promote reunification between immigrants and their families abroad, work at cross-purposes with the control of immigration flows, since they reinforce migrant networks by giving members of kin networks special rights of entry.

Institutional theory

Once international migration has begun, private institutions and voluntary organizations arise to satisfy the demand created by an imbalance between the large number of people who seek entry into capital-rich countries and the limited number of immigrant visas these countries typically offer. This imbalance, and the barriers that core countries erect to keep people out, create a lucrative economic niche for entrepreneurs and institutions dedicated to promoting international movement for profit, yielding a black market in migration. As this underground market creates conditions conducive to exploitation and victimization, voluntary humanitarian organizations also arise in developed countries to enforce the rights and improve the treatment of legal and undocumented migrants.

For profit organizations and private entrepreneurs provide a range of services to migrants in exchange for fees set on the underground market: surreptitious smuggling across borders; clandestine transport to internal destinations; labour contracting between employers and migrants; counterfeit documents and visas; arranged marriages between migrants and legal residents or citizens of the destination country; and lodging, credit and other assistance in countries of destination. Humanitarian groups help migrants by providing counselling, social services, shelter, legal advice about how to obtain legitimate papers and even insulation from immigration law enforcement authorities. Over time, individuals, firms and organizations become well known to immigrants and institutionally stable, constituting another form of social capital that migrants can draw upon to gain access to foreign labour markets.

The recognition of a gradual build-up of institutions, organizations and entrepreneurs dedicated to arranging immigrant entry, legal or illegal, again yields hypotheses that are also quite distinct from those emanating from micro-level decision models:

1 As organizations develop to support, sustain and promote international movement, the international flow of migrants becomes more and more institutionalized and independent of the factors that originally caused it.
2 Governments have difficulty controlling migration flows once they have begun because the process of institutionalization is difficult to regulate. Given the profits to be made by meeting the demand for immigrant entry, police efforts only serve to create a black market in international movement, and stricter immigration policies are met with resistance from humanitarian groups.

Cumulative causation

In addition to the growth of networks and the development of migrant-supporting institutions, international migration sustains itself in other ways that make additional movement progressively more likely over time, a process Myrdal (1957) called cumulative causation (Massey 1990b). Causation is cumulative in that each act of migration alters the social context within which subsequent migration decisions are made, typically in ways that make additional movement more likely. So far, social scientists have discussed six socioeconomic factors that are potentially affected by migration in this cumulative fashion: the distribution of income, the distribution of land, the organization of agriculture, culture, the regional distribution of human capital and the social meaning of work. Feedbacks through other variables are also possible, but have not been systematically treated (Stark, Taylor and Yitzhaki 1986; Taylor 1992).

[...]

Viewing international migration in dynamic terms as a cumulative social process yields a set of propositions broadly consistent with those derived from network theory:

1 Social, economic and cultural changes brought about in sending and receiving countries by international migration give the movement of people a powerful internal momentum resistant to easy control or regulation, since the feedback mechanisms of cumulative causation largely lie outside the reach of government.
2 During times of domestic unemployment and joblessness, governments find it difficult to curtail labour migration and to recruit natives back into jobs formerly held by immigrants. A value shift has occurred among native workers, who refuse the 'immigrant' jobs, making it necessary to retain or recruit more immigrants.
3 The social labelling of a job as 'immigrant' follows from the concentration of immigrants within it; once immigrants have entered a job in significant numbers, whatever its characteristics, it will be difficult to recruit native workers back into that occupational category.

Migration systems theory

The various propositions of world systems theory, network theory, institutional theory and the theory of cumulative causation all suggest that migration flows acquire a measure of stability and structure over space and time, allowing for the identification of stable international migration systems. These systems are characterized by relatively intense exchanges of goods, capital and people between certain countries and less intense exchanges between others. An international migration system generally includes a core receiving region, which may be a country or group of countries, and a set of specific sending countries linked to it by unusually large flows of immigrants (Fawcett 1989; Zlotnik 1992).

Although not a separate theory so much as a generalization following from the foregoing theories, a migration systems perspective yields several interesting hypotheses and propositions:

1 Countries within a system need not be geographically close since flows reflect political and economic relationships rather than physical ones. Although proximity obviously facilitates the formation of exchange relationships, it does not guarantee them nor does distance preclude them.
2 Multi-polar systems are possible, whereby a set of dispersed core countries receive immigrants from a set of overlapping sending nations.
3 Nations may belong to more than one migration system, but multiple membership is more common among sending than receiving nations.
4 As political and economic conditions change, systems evolve, so that stability does not imply a fixed structure. Countries may join or drop out of a system in response to social change, economic fluctuations or political upheaval.

References

Castells, Manuel (1989) *The Informational City: Information Technology, Economic Restructuring and the Urban-Regional Process*. Oxford: Basil Blackwell.

Fawcett, James T. (1989) 'Networks, linkages, and migration systems', *International Migration Review* 23: 671–80.

Gurak, Douglas T. and Fe Caces (1992) 'Migration networks and the shaping of migration systems', in Mary Kritz, Lin Lean Lim and Hania Zlotnik (eds), *International Migration Systems: A Global Approach*. Oxford: Clarendon Press, pp. 150–76.

Hugo, Graeme J. (1981) 'Village-community ties, village norms, and ethnic and social networks: A review of evidence from the Third World', in Gordon F. Dejong and Robert W. Gardner (eds), *Migration Decision Making: Multidisciplinary Approaches to Microlevel Studies in Developed and Developing Countries*. New York: Pergamon Press, pp. 186–225.

Katz, E. and Oded Stark (1986) 'Labour migration and risk aversion in less developed countries', *Journal of Labour Economics* 4: 131–49.

Lauby, Jennifer and Oded Stark (1988) 'Individual migration as a family strategy: Young women in the Philippines', *Population Studies* 42: 473–86.

Massey, Douglas S. (1986) 'The settlement process among Mexican migrants to the United States', *American Sociological Review* 52: 670–85.

——(1989) 'International migration and economic development in comparative perspective', *Population and Development Review* 14: 383–414.

——(1990a) 'The social and economic origins of immigration', *Annals of the American Academy of Political and Social Science* 510: 60–72.

——(1990b) 'Social structure, household strategies, and the cumulative causation of migration', *Population Index* 56: 3–26.

——Rafael Alarcón, Humberto González and Jorge Durand (1987) *Return to Azilan. The Social Process of International Migration from Western Mexico.* Berkeley and Los Angeles: University of California Press.

——and Felipe Garcia España (1987) 'The social process of international migration', *Science* 237: 733–8.

——and Zai Liang (1989) 'The long-term consequences of a temporary worker program: The U. S. Bracero experience', *Population Research and Policy Review* 8: 199–226.

Morawska, Ewa (1990) 'The sociology and historiography of immigration', in Virginia Yans-McLaughlin (ed.), *Immigration Reconsidered: History, Sociology and Politics.* New York: Oxford University Press, pp. 187–240.

Myrdal, Gunnar (1957) *Rich Lands and Poor.* New York: Harper and Row.

Petras, Elizabeth M. (1981) 'The global labour market in the modern world-economy', in Mary M. Kritz, Charles B. Keely and Silvano M. Tomasi (eds) *Global Trends in Migration: Theory and Research on International Population Movements.* Staten Island, NY: Centre for Migration Studies, pp. 44–63.

Piore, Michael J. (1979) *Birds of Passage: Migrant Labour in Industrial Societies.* Cambridge: Cambridge University Press.

Portes, Alejandro and John Walton (1981) *Labour, Class and the International System.* New York: Academic Press.

Sassen, Saskia (1988) *The Mobility of Labour and Capital: A Study in International Investment and Labour Flow.* Cambridge: Cambridge University Press.

——(1991) *The Global City: New York, London, Tokyo.* Princeton: Princeton University Press.

Sjaastad, Larry A. (1962) 'The costs and returns of human migration', *Journal of Political Economy* 705: 80–93.

Stark, Oded (1984) 'Migration decision making: A review article', *Journal of Development Economics* 14: 251–9.

——(1991) *The Migration of Labour.* Oxford: Basil Blackwell.

——and D. Levhari (1982) 'On migration and risk in LDCs.' *Economic Development and Cultural Change* 91–31: 16.

——and David E. Bloom (1985) 'The new economics of labour migration', *American Economic Review* 75: 173–8.

——, J. Edward Taylor and Shlomo Yitzhaki (1986) 'Remittances and inequality', *The Economic journal* 96: 722–40.

——, J. Edward Taylor and Shlomo Yitzhaki (1988) 'Migration, remittances and inequality: A sensitivity analysis using the extended Gini Index', *Journal of Development Economics* 28: 309–22.

——and Shlomo Yitzhaki (1988) 'Labour migration as a response to relative deprivation', *Journal of Population Economics* 1: 57–70.

——and J. Edward Taylor (1989) 'Relative deprivation and international migration', *Demography* 26: 1–14.

——and J. Edward Taylor (1991) 'Migration incentives, migration types: The role of relative deprivation', *The Economic Journal* 101: 1163–78.

Taylor, J. Edward (1986) 'Differential migration, networks, information and risk', in Oded Stark (ed.), *Research in Human Capital and Development*, Vol.

4, *Migration, Human Capital and Development,* Greenwich, Conn.: JAI Press, pp. 147–71.

——(1987) 'Undocumented Mexico-U.S. migration and the returns to households in rural Mexico', *American Journal of Agricultural Economics* 69: 616–38.

——(1992) 'Remittances and inequality reconsidered: Direct, indirect and intertemporal effects', *Journal of Policy Modelling* 14: 187–208.

Todaro, Michael P. (1969) 'A model of labour migration and urban unemployment in less-developed countries', *The American Economic Review* 59: 138–48.

——(1976) *Internal Migration in Developing Countries, Geneva:* International Labour Office.

——(1980) 'Internal migration in developing countries: A survey', in Richard A. Easterlin (ed.), *Population and Economic Change in Developing Countries.* Chicago: University of Chicago Press, pp. 361–401.

——(1989) *Economic Development in the Third World.* New York: Longman.

——and Lydia Maruszko (1987) 'Illegal migration and US immigration reform: A conceptual framework', *Population and Development Review* 13: 101–14.

Wallerstein, Immanuel (1974) *The Modern World System, Capitalist Agriculture and the Origins of the European World Economy in the Sixteenth Century.* New York: Academic Press.

Zlotnik, Hania (1992) 'Empirical identification of international migration systems', in Mary Kritz, Lin Lean Lim and Hania Zlotnik (eds), *International Migration Systems: A Global Approach.* Oxford: Clarendon Press, pp. 19–40.

DIASPORAS

JAMES CLIFFORD

An unruly crowd of descriptive/interpretive terms now jostle and converse in an effort to characterize the contact zones of nations, cultures and regions: terms such as 'border', 'travel', 'creolization', 'transculturation', 'hybridity' and 'diasporas' (as well as the looser 'diasporic'). Important new journals, such as *Public Culture* and *Diaspora* (or the revived *Transition*), are devoted to the history and current production of transnational cultures. In his editorial preface to the first issue of *Diaspora,* Khachig Tölölian writes, 'Diasporas are the exemplary communities of the transnational moment.' But he adds that diaspora will not be privileged in the new *Journal of Transnational Studies* and that 'the term that once described Jewish, Greek, and Armenian dispersion now shares meanings with a larger semantic domain that includes words like immigrant, expatriate, refugee, guest-worker, exile community, overseas community, ethnic community' (Tölölian 1991: 4–5). This is the domain of shared and discrepant meanings, adjacent maps and histories, that we need to sort out and specify as we work our way into comparative, intercultural studies [...].

When I speak of the need to sort our paradigms and maintain historical specificity, I do not mean the imposition of strict meanings and authenticity tests. The quintessential borderland is El Paso/Juárez. Or is it Tijuana/San Diego? Can *la ligna* be displaced to Redwood City, or to Mexican American neighbourhoods of Chicago? William Safran's essay in the first issue of *Diaspora*, 'Diasporas in Modern Societies: Myths of Homeland and Return' (1991), seems, at times, to be engaged in such an operation. His undertaking and the problems it encounters may help us to see what is involved in identifying the range of phenomena we are prepared to call 'diasporic'.

Safran discusses a variety of collective experiences in terms of their similarity and difference from a defining model. He defines diasporas as follows: 'expatriate minority communities' (1) that are dispersed from an original 'centre' to at least two 'peripheral' places; (2) that maintain a 'memory, vision, or myth about their original homeland'; (3) that 'believe they are not – and perhaps cannot be – fully accepted by their host country'; (4) that see the ancestral home as a place of eventual return, when the time is right; (5) that are committed to the maintenance or restoration of this homeland; and (6) whose consciousness and solidarity as a group are 'importantly defined' by this continuing relationship with the homeland (Safran 1991: 83–4). These, then, are the main features of diaspora: a history of dispersal, myths/memories of the homeland, alienation in the host (bad host?) country, desire for eventual return, ongoing support of the homeland, and a collective identity importantly defined by this relationship.

'In terms of that definition,' Safran writes, 'we may legitimately speak of the Armenian, Maghrebi, Turkish, Palestinian, Cuban, Greek, and perhaps Chinese diasporas at present and of the Polish diaspora of the past, although none of them fully conforms to the "ideal type" of the Jewish diaspora' (Safran 1991: 84). Perhaps a hesitation is expressed by the quotes surrounding 'ideal type', a sense of the danger in constructing a definition, here at the outset of an important comparative project, that identifies the diasporic phenomenon too closely with one group. Indeed, large segments of Jewish historical experience do not meet the test of Safran's last three criteria: a strong attachment to and desire for literal return to a well-preserved homeland. Safran himself later notes that the notion of return for Jews is often an eschatological or utopian projection in response to a present dystopia. And there is little room in his definition for the principled *ambivalence* about physical return and attachment to land which has characterized much Jewish diasporic consciousness, from biblical times on. Jewish anti-Zionist critiques of teleologies of return are also excluded.

It is certainly debatable whether the cosmopolitan Jewish societies of the eleventh- to thirteenth-century Mediterranean (and Indian Ocean), the *geniza world* documented by the great historian of transnational cultures, S. D. Goitein, was oriented as a community or collection of communities, primarily through attachments to a lost homeland (Goitein 1967–93). This sprawling social world was linked through cultural forms, kinship relations, business circuits and travel trajectories as well as through loyalty to the religious centres of the diaspora (in Babylon, Palestine and Egypt). The attachment to specific cities (sometimes superseding ties of religion and ethnicity) characteristic of Goitein's medieval world casts doubt on any definition that would 'centre' the Jewish diaspora in a single land. Among Sephardim after 1492, the longing for 'home' could be focused on a city in Spain at the same time as on the Holy Land. Indeed, as

Jonathan Boyarin has pointed out, Jewish experience often entails 'multiple experiences of rediasporisation, which do not necessarily succeed each other in historical memory but echo back and forth' (Boyarin 1993).

As a multiply centred diaspora network, the medieval Jewish Mediterranean may be juxtaposed with the modern 'black Atlantic' described by Paul Gilroy (Gilroy 1993a). While the economic and political bases of the two networks may differ – the former commercially self-sustaining, the latter caught up in colonial/ neo-colonial forces – the cultural forms sustaining and connecting the two scattered 'peoples' are comparable within the range of diasporic phenomena. In Safran's prefiguration of a comparative field – especially in his 'centred' diaspora model, oriented by continuous cultural connections to a source and by a teleology of 'return' – African American/Caribbean/British cultures do not qualify. These histories of displacement fall into a category of quasidiasporas, showing only some diasporic features or moments. Similarly, the South Asian diaspora – which, as Amitav Ghosh has argued (1989), is not so much oriented to roots in a specific place and a desire for return as around an ability to re-create a culture in diverse locations – falls outside the strict definition.

Safran is right to focus attention on defining 'diaspora'. What is the range of experiences covered by the term? Where does it begin to lose definition? His comparative approach is certainly the best way to specify a complex discursive and historical field. Moreover his juxtapositions are often very enlightening, and he does not, in practice, strictly enforce his definitional checklist. But we should be wary of constructing our working definition of a term like diaspora by recourse to an 'ideal type', with the consequence that groups become identified as more or less diasporic, having only two, or three, or four of the basic six features. Even the 'pure' forms, I've suggested, are ambivalent, even embattled, over basic features. Moreover at different times in their history, societies may wax and wane in diasporism, depending on changing possibilities – obstacles, openings, antagonisms and connections – in their host countries and transnationally.

We should be able to recognize the strong entailment of Jewish history on the language of diaspora without making that history a definitive model. Jewish (and Greek and Armenian) diasporas can be taken as non-normative starting-points for a discourse that is travelling or hybridizing in new global conditions. For better or worse, diaspora discourse is being widely appropriated. It is loose in the world, for reasons having to do with decolonization, increased immigration, global communications and transport – a whole range of phenomena that encourage multi-locale attachments, dwelling and travelling within and across nations. A more polythetic definition (Needham 1975) than Safran's might retain his six features, along with others. I have already stressed, for example, that the transnational connections linking diasporas need not be articulated primarily through a real or symbolic homeland – at least not to the degree that Safran implies. Decentred, lateral connections may be as important as those formed around a teleology of origin/return. And a shared, ongoing history of displacement, suffering, adaptation or resistance may be as important as the projection of a specific origin.

Whatever the working list of diasporic features, no society can be expected to qualify on all counts, throughout its history. And the discourse of diaspora will necessarily be modified as it is translated and adopted. For example, the Chinese diaspora is now being explicitly discussed. How will this history, this articulation of travels, homes, memories and transnational connections, appropriate and shift diaspora discourse? Different diasporic maps of displacement and connection can be compared on the basis of family resemblance, of shared elements, no subset of which is defined as essential to the discourse. A polythetic field would seem most conducive to tracking (rather than policing) the contemporary range of diasporic forms.

Diaspora's Borders

The nation state, as common territory and time, is traversed and, to varying degrees, subverted by diasporic attachments. Diasporic populations do not come from elsewhere in the same way that 'immigrants' do. In assimilationist national ideologies such as those of the United States, immigrants may experience loss and nostalgia, but only *en route* to a whole new home in a new place. Such narratives are designed to integrate immigrants, not people in diasporas. Whether the national narrative is one of common origins or of gathered populations, it cannot assimilate groups that maintain important allegiances and practical connections to a homeland or a dispersed community located elsewhere. Peoples whose sense of identity is centrally defined by collective histories of displacement and violent loss cannot be 'cured' by merging into a new national community. This is especially true when they are the victims of ongoing, structural prejudice. Positive articulations of diaspora identity reach outside the normative territory and temporality (myth-history) of the nation state.

But are diaspora cultures consistently anti-nationalist? What about their own national aspirations? Resistance to assimilation can take the form of reclaiming another nation that has been lost, elsewhere in space and time, but powerful as a political formation here and now. There are, of course, anti-nationalist nationalisms, and I do not want to suggest that diasporic cultural politics are somehow innocent of nationalist aims or chauvinist agendas. Indeed, some of the most violent articulations of purity and racial exclusivism come from diaspora populations. But such discourses are usually weapons of the (relatively) weak. It is important to distinguish nationalist critical longing, and nostalgic or eschatological visions, from actual nation building – with the help of armies, schools, police and mass media. Nation and nation state are not identical. A certain prescriptive anti-nationalism, now intensely focused by the Bosnian horror, need not blind us to differences between dominant and subaltern claims. Diasporas have rarely founded nation states: Israel is the prime example. And such 'homecomings' are, by definition, the negation of diaspora.

Whatever their ideologies of purity, diasporic cultural forms can never, in practice, be exclusively nationalist. They are deployed in transnational networks built from multiple attachments and they encode practices of accommodation with, as well as resistance to, host countries and their norms. Diaspora is different from travel (though it works through travel practices) in that it is not temporary. It involves dwelling, maintaining communities, having collective homes away from home (and in this it is different from exile, with its frequently indi-vidualistic focus). Diaspora discourse articulates, or bends together, both roots *and* routes to construct what Gilroy describes as alternate public spheres (1987), forms of community consciousness and solidarity that maintain identifications outside the national time/space in order to live inside, with a dif-ference. Diaspora cultures are not separatist, though they may have separatist or irredentist moments. This history of Jewish diaspora communities shows selective accommodation with the political, cultural, commercial and everyday life forms of 'host' societies. And the black diaspora culture currently being articu-lated in post-colonial Britain is concerned to struggle for different ways to be 'British' – ways to stay and be different, to be British *and something else* com-plexly related to Africa and the Americas, to shared histories of enslavement, racist subordination, cultural survival, hybridization, resistance and political rebellion. Thus the term diaspora is a signifier, not simply of transnationality and movement, but of political struggles to define the local, as distinctive community, in historical contexts of displacement. The simultaneous strategies of community maintenance and interaction combine the discourses and skills of what Vijay Mishra has termed 'diasporas of exclusivism' and 'diasporas of the border' (1994).

The specific cosmopolitanisms articulated by diaspora discourses are in con-stitutive tension with nation-state/assimilationist ideologies. They are also in tension with indigenous, and especially autochthonous, claims. These challenge the hegemony of modern nation states in a different way. Tribal or 'Fourth World' assertions of sovereignty and 'first nationhood' do not feature histories of travel and settlement, though these may be part of the indigenous historical experience. They stress continuity of habitation, aboriginality, and often a 'natural' connection to the land. Diaspora cultures, constituted by displacement, may resist such appeals on political principle – as in anti-Zionist Jewish writing, or in black injunctions to 'stand' and 'chant down Babylon'. And they may be structured around a tension between return and deferral: 'religion of the land'/'religion of the book' in Jewish tradition; or 'roots'/'cut n' mix' aesthetics in black vernacular cultures.

Diaspora exists in practical, and at times principled, tension with nativist identity formations. The essay by Daniel and Jonathan Boyarin (1993) makes a diasporist critique of autochthonous ('natural') but not indigenous ('historical') formulations. When claims to 'natural' or 'original' identity with the land are joined to an irredentist project and the coercive power of an exclusivist state, the results can be profoundly ambivalent and violent, as in the Jewish state of Israel. Indeed, claims of a primary link with 'the homeland' usually must override con-flicting rights and the history of others in the land. Even ancient homelands have seldom been pure or discrete. Moreover, what are the historical and/or indige-nous rights of *relative* newcomers – fourth-generation Indians in Fiji, or even Mexicans in the south-western United States since the sixteenth century? How long does it take to become 'indigenous'? Lines too strictly drawn between 'origi-nal' inhabitants (who often themselves replaced prior populations) and subse-quent immigrants risk ahistoricism. With all these qualifications, however, it is clear that the claims to political legitimacy made by peoples who have inhabited a territory since before recorded history and those who arrived by steamboat or aeroplane will be founded on very different principles.

Diasporist and autochthonist histories, the aspirations of migrants and natives, do come into direct political antagonism: the clearest current example is Fiji. But when, as is often the case, both function as 'minority' claims against a hegemonic/ assimilationist state, the antagonism may be muted. Indeed there are significant areas of overlap. 'Tribal' predicaments, in certain historical circumstances, are diasporic. For example, inasmuch as diasporas are dispersed networks of peoples who share common historical experiences of dispossession, displacement, adaptation, and so forth, the kinds of transnational alliances currently being forged by Fourth World peoples contain diasporic elements. United by similar claims to 'firstness' on the land and by common histories of decimation and marginality, these alliances often deploy diasporist visions of return to an original place – a land commonly articulated in visions of nature, divinity, mother earth and the ancestors.

Dispersed tribal peoples, those who have been dispossessed of their lands or who must leave reduced reserves to find work, may claim diasporic identities. Inasmuch as their distinctive sense of themselves is oriented towards a lost or alienated home defined as aboriginal (and thus 'outside' the surrounding nation state), we can speak of a diasporic dimension of contemporary tribal life. Indeed, recognition of this dimension has been important in disputes about tribal membership. The category tribe, which was developed in US law to distinguish settled Indians from roving, dangerous 'bands', places a premium on localism and rootedness. Tribes with too many members living away from the homeland may have difficulty asserting their political/cultural status. This was the case for the Mashpee who, in 1978, failed to establish continuous 'tribal' identity in court (Clifford 1988: 277–346).

Thus, when it becomes important to assert the existence of a dispersed people, the language of diaspora comes into play, as a moment or dimension of tribal life. All communities, even the most locally rooted, maintain structured travel circuits, linking members 'at home' and 'away'. Under changing conditions of mass communication, globalization, post- and neo-colonialism, these circuits are selectively restructured and re-routed according to *internal and external* dynamics. Within the diverse array of contemporary diasporic cultural forms, tribal displacements and networks are distinctive. For in claiming both autochthony and a specific, transregional worldliness, new tribal forms bypass many visions of modernization seen as the inevitable destruction of autochthonous attachments by global forces. Tribal groups have, of course, never been simply 'local': they have always been rooted and routed in particular landscapes, regional and interregional networks. What may be distinctively *modern*, however, is the relentless assault on indigenous sovereignty by colonial powers, transnational capital and emerging nation states. If tribal groups survive, it is now frequently in artificially reduced and displaced conditions, with segments of their populations living in cities away from the land, temporarily or even permanently. In these conditions, the older forms of tribal cosmopolitanism (practices of travel, spiritual quest, trade, exploration, warfare, labour migrancy, visiting and political alliance) are supplemented by more properly diasporic forms (practices of long-term dwelling away from home). The permanence of this dwelling, the frequency of returns or visits to homelands, and the degree of estrangement between urban and landed populations vary considerably. But the specificity of tribal diasporas, increasingly crucial *dimensions* of collective life, lies in the relative proximity and frequency of connection with land-based communities claiming autochthonous status.

I have been using the term 'tribal' loosely to designate peoples who claim natural or 'first-nation' sovereignty. They occupy the autochthonous end of a spectrum of indigenous attachments: peoples who deeply 'belong' in a place by dint of continuous occupancy over an extended period. (Precisely how long it takes to *become* indigenous is always a political question.) Tribal cultures are not diasporas; their sense of rootedness in the land is precisely what diasporic peoples have lost. And yet, as we have seen, the tribal-diasporic opposition is not absolute. Like diaspora's other defining border with hegemonic nationalism, the opposition is a zone of relational contrast, including similarity and entangled difference. In the late twentieth century, all or most communities have diasporic dimensions (moments, tactics, practices, articulations). Some are more diasporic than others. I have suggested that it is not possible to define diaspora sharply, either by recourse to essential features or to privative oppositions. But it is possible to perceive a loosely coherent, adaptive constellation of responses to dwelling-in-displacement. The currency of these responses is inescapable.

References

Boyarin, Daniel and Jonathan Boyarin (1993) 'Diaspora: Generational Ground of Jewish Identity', *Critical Inquiry* 19(4): 693–725.

Clifford, James (1988) *The Predicament of Culture.* Cambridge: Harvard University Press.

Clifford, James (1992) 'Travelling Cultures', in *Cultural Studies*, ed. Lawrence Grossberg, Cary Nelson and Paula Treichler, New York: Routledge, pp. 96–116.

Ghosh, Amitav (1989) 'The Diaspora in Indian Culture', *Public Culture* 1(1): 73–8.

Gilroy, Paul (1987) *There Ain't No Black in the Union Jack: The Cultural Politics of Race and Nation.* London: Hutchinson.

Gilroy, Paul (1993a) *The Black Atlantic: Double Consciousness and Modernity.* Cambridge: Harvard University Press.

Goitein, Solomon Dob Fritz (1967–93) *A Mediterranean Society: The Jewish Communities of the Arab World as Portrayed in the Documents of the Cairo Ceniza.* Six volumes. Berkeley: University of California Press.

Mishra, Vijay (1994) ' "The Familiar Temporariness" (V. S. Naipaul): Theorizing the Literature of the Indian Diaspora', Paper presented at the Centre for Cultural Studies, University of California, Santa Cruz, 2 February.

Needham, Rodney (1975) 'Polythetic Classification', *Man* 10: 349–69.

Safran, William (1991) 'Diasporas in Modern Societies: Myths of Homeland and Return', *Diaspora* 1(1): 83–99.

Tölölian, Khachig (1991) 'The Nation State and its Others: In Lieu of a Preface', *Diaspora* 1(1): 3–7.

TRANSNATIONAL MIGRANT BROKERAGE IN CHINA

LI MINGHUAN

According to the global migration estimate provided by the IOM in 2005, there are between 185–192 million transnational migrants worldwide. Moreover, the stock of international migrants rose from 82 million in 1970 to 175 million in 2000, and again to 185–192 million in 2005 (IOM 2005). To put it differently, the total amount of transnational migrants has been more than doubled during the three decades. Cross-border movement is such an impressive phenomenon that no country can ignore its floating and multiple social consequences.

The explicit economic gap between the high income states and the developing ones is still the most influential factor of transnational migration. People are moving because of the pull of an imagined brighter future, of the push of danger, disappointed, demeaning or despairing lives in the original area, of the call of the human heart. Therefore, although the main destination states, most of which are high-income or more developed, have kept building up strict border controls and critical selective systems, thousands upon thousands of people that did not meet the immigration requirement have got into their destination state and even greater amounts of people are seeking the opportunities. When personal efforts cannot pave the way for the migration, the management of transnational migration has become a profitable market in itself. Often it is the private agents or agencies that have been actively involved. They are functioning between the state and the potential individual migrant, and acting between the legal and illegal approaches. Both the receiving and sending states are worried about such a situation, since it often results in unexpected consequences.

1. Emergence of the Transnational Labour Brokers: Byproduct of the Authorities' Migration Policy (from Late Qing to Early Republic Period)

Transnational labour brokers are nothing new in China. Although there were few direct records on the transnational labour brokers, many documents concerning migrant workers have more or less touched upon the subject. Its emergence was one byproduct of the institutional barriers of migration.

Chinese migration towards the South Sea, today's Southeast Asia, is a historical process that began long before the national border was set up. It was in the 17th century, however, that the historical records started to report how the Chinese people were shipped to work in groups abroad. After the first Opium War (the first Anglo-Chinese War, 1839–1842), the expansion of colonialists in China had involved bringing some harbour cities along the south coast of China like Xiamen (Amoy, an important harbour city of Fujian), Shantou (Swatow) and Guangzhou (Canton) into the early colonist globalization process. The exportation of Chinese coolies in considerable amounts to meet the demand for cheap labour in newly developing areas overseas was widespread by the beginning of the 19th century and reached its peak in the mid-19th century. At that time, the worldwide efforts to abolish slavery had resulted in the birth of the indentured labour system.

The regime that dominated China in the 19th century was the Qing authority. Since its establishment, the Qing authority maintained a negative policy towards emigration, not only to control the labour forces but because of the fear of military resistance from overseas. In the early decades of its establishment, the Qing authority carried out tough punishments towards any emigration activities. At the beginning of the 18th century, when Qing had consolidated its power, the relevant tough punishment was, step by step, maintained on paper rather than in practice. Then Western power became a new challenge and labour recruitment for working abroad emerged.

In 19th century, China was a country rich in human resources. Therefore it was one of the most important countries to send indentured labourers abroad. It is worth noting that one result of Western influences was a social evil in the form of the coolie trade, which directly pushed the materialization of the earliest labour market in south China; consequently, the first group of Chinese labour brokers emerged that was embedded in the 'coolie trade.' 'Coolie trade' is a negative name meaning to recruit indentured labourers for the plantations or mines abroad. Often the owners were Western colonists.

The first obvious record concerning the Chinese migrant labourers going to Malaya was in 1785, when dozens of Chinese workers were recruited by the British Indies Company in Guangzhou and sent to work in Malaya. Since then, more relevant records can be found, although the Qing authority still kept legal punishment for emigration officially. In 1805 and again 1820, a British company undisguisedly recruited Chinese labourers to work abroad. The recruitment escaped punishment simply by handing out bribes to the relevant Qing officials (Yuan 2002: 22–23). However, if looking at records abroad, it can be found that in the 1820s, at the time of the great famine in south China, each year thousands of Chinese people were transported to make their living in Singapore, Kalimantan, Penang and some other areas that were under colonial development (Barth 1964). Soon the cheap and rich Chinese labour resource had become an important 'commodity' that was traded and bargained between the Western and the Qing authorities.

In 1860, after its defeat in the Second Opium War (1856–1860), the Qing authority was forced to sign a new treaty with the British, in which the latter were given the freedom of recruiting labourers in China. Following this example, new similar treaties were signed between the Qing government and France (1860), Holland (1863) and the United States (1868). More precisely, by the late 1860s, all Western powers had got the right to recruit labourers in China. Then, initiated by Western traders, the earliest labour agencies were set up in Xiamen, Shantou, Guangzhou and some other south harbour cities one by one.

On the surface, the earliest labour brokerage for colonial industries abroad was carried out behind the tablet of some kind of Western foreign trading firm or their representative agencies that set up in China. Inasmuch as the majority of the potential coolie resource was in rural areas, Chinese brokers, who were familiar with the local situation and could speak the dialect, were indispensable to the running of foreign recruitment agencies. Going along with the materialization of the labour market in China, commercial labour brokers became an overt business. In Chinese, the earliest labour brokers were usually called by names such as *Ketou* (head of guests), *Shuike* (guest coming by water), *Baotou* (labour contractor), *Zhuzaitou* (head of piglet) or *Renkou fanzi* (trader of labourers). The last two names are very negative in particular. In the mid-19th century, Chinese labour brokers could be roughly divided into two groups.

One was formed by the earlier Chinese indentured coolies who had finished their contracts and settled down abroad. They were adopted and sent back with the assignment of recruiting new coolies and bringing them back for their employers, most of whom were Western planters or mine-owners. The brokers of this group were often called as '*Ketou*' or '*Shuike*.' The other group was formed by Chinese in China's provincial areas. They were directly or indirectly employed by the Western agencies that had been, illicitly or openly, set up in China. Walking around the countryside, these brokers attempted to induce either the parents to send their sons abroad, or the potential adults to sign a contract of working abroad. Some brokers gained high profits from recruiting labourers.

A study shows that, between 1840s and 1850s, the normal cost of recruiting a Chinese coolie was to give the coolie or his family member eight Chinese dollars as 'family allowance.' However, the broker could receive about 100 Chinese dollars when 'recruiting' one 'healthy coolie' to the relevant foreign agent (Chen 1999: 59). The profit of recruiting females was even higher. For instance, Xieyitang, a Chinese association in name but which functioned as a labour agency, had earned 200,000 Chinese dollars from recruiting 6,000 Chinese females in Guangzhou and selling them to San Francisco. It was reported that the cost of recruiting one female labourer in Guangzhou was about 50 dollars but the price of 'selling one Chinese female in San Francisco' was as high as 1,000 dollars (Liu 1981:123).

Most coolies however were deeply disappointed after arriving at their destinations. Their lives in either Western colonialists-owned plantations or mines were full of tears. Only a few could realize their dreams of returning home with some money. Moreover, 'it seems reasonable to assume that before the end of the nineteenth century one of every four coolies on Sumatra's east coast died before having served his or her contracted period' (Breman 1989:59). The situation of Chinese coolies based in other tropical jungles cannot be expected to be better.

Then, a striking contradiction came into sight. On the one hand, once the news of terrible conditions of indentured labour abroad spread in China, fewer labourers could be recruited of their own accord. On the other hand, the profits of commercial labour brokerage were huge, insomuch that the brokers wished to recruit more labourers, some even did it by any kind of means. The reports of fraud and kidnapping carried out by brokers appeared more and more.

Taking the early history of labour brokers in Xiamen city of Fujian as an example, in Xiamen, the earliest document on labour emigration was recorded in 1620 when 1,400 people were shipped from Xiamen harbour to the Netherlands Indies of the times, most of whom were economic emigrants (XMMYZ

1998: 261). The records concerning the coolie trade in Xiamen were in the 19th century, when Xiamen appeared to be an active transport harbour. For instance, according to an incomplete account, in the year of 1852, the amount of coolie exportation from Xiamen to America and Australia reached 5,691 in total; and again, in the first three months of 1853, 3,197 coolies were shipped to the two continents (Wu, 1988: 42–43). The amount of Chinese coolies who were shipped from Xiamen to Southeast Asia was even higher. A study showed that about 3.7 million labourers were shipped from Xiamen to Southeast Asia in the 19th century (XMMYZ 1998: 261–262), that is, more than one third of exported labourers left for Southeast Asia from Xiamen harbour.

The amount of service-fee charged by the package migration was rather high. For instance, in the 1930s, to arrange one person emigrating from China to Europe would cost about five hundred Chinese dollars. At that time, three dollars could buy one *dan* of rice (about 50 kg). Therefore, it can be seen clearly how expensive the fee was charged by the broker. Although the fee was high, some of my interviewees, who were still alive in the 1980s, gave reasonable comments on the brokers. According to them, 'we would not be able to be in Europe without their help'; or 'they were experienced persons and we completely relied on their support.'

Other references can be drawn from my recent research on the returned Chinese in Xiamen. Some interviewees also mentioned about how their parents were brought over by '*ketou*' to Southeast Asia in the early period of the 20th century. I noted that they were not critical of the brokerage; some also gave positive comments like the sayings quoted above. Also, some appreciated about their parents' lives after becoming a free labourer in Southeast Asia. One interviewee told me that he heard from his father that he had to work for five years to repay the debts to '*ketou*.' When asked what his father thought about such a big fee charged by the *ketou* who was his father's cousin, the interviewee told me that while his father was alive, he always paid his respect to the cousin. 'My father could not go to Indonesia without his cousin's help,' the interviewee said.

From a brief overview of the earlier history of the brokers in China, some points can be concluded. First, the corrupt late Qing authorities did not make serious attempts to protect the Chinese abroad, particularly those exported labourers. Second, the labourers moved in and out of China often through unofficial channels. Thousands of private labour brokers formed the nodes to interweave the transnational network. Then, in view of the private brokers, it is obvious that they had been pictured in two contrasting images: on the one side, they were fraudulent and criminal but on the other they were reliable and helpful.

2. Under the PRC Government's Comprehensive Umbrella: Working Abroad on the National-Project-Based Approach (1950s–1970s)

After the establishment of the People's Republic of China, the tradition of emigration abroad was interrupted and even condemned as a counterrevolutionary deed during the period of the so-called Cultural Revolution (1966–1976). At that time, apart from a few who were able to get permission to go abroad for family reunion, the only one official possibility of working abroad was national-project-based and often appeared as a comprehensive political task.

During the Mao period, China had carried out a series of projects in aid of friendly nations for free. The workers were selected, first on the basis of their political loyalty and second according to their skill and working attitude. Often they were sent to other developing countries that were friendly to China, such as Albania and Tanzania. The workers were normally named as honorary volunteers. The selection and transnational working process were highly institutionalized. During the whole period of working in the destination state, they not only worked in groups but also lived within a certain area under the full supervision of the Chinese diplomatic authority. Their income maintained the level of their peers in China, apart from having a little foreign currency as extra allowance. In general, to work abroad for China's project was a part of government's assignment. How long the workers would work abroad was also decided by the relevant authority. The workers usually worked abroad between one to three years, but some had worked longer than five years. Very few who rejected a return to China were condemned as detestable betrayers. They were migrant workers in a very particular way under the comprehensive umbrella of the Chinese government.

Since the end of the Cultural Revolution at the end of the 1970s, however, going along with the reform of foreign policies, China's assistance projects abroad were gradually replaced by a Foreign Economic Cooperation Programme based on mutual benefits. Then, the pursuit of commercial profits was no longer a taboo. Gradually, a few labour agencies with limited authority were organized under special permission.

Again, take Xiamen of Fujian Province as an example. It was in 1977 that the Xiamen Municipality set up the Foreign Aid Office. Literally, the major task of the office was to organize qualified technicians or skilled workers to work for China's aid foreign programmes. Although at the very beginning, the relevant 'volunteers' were selected among the existing employers rather than as an open recruitment, this step marked the beginning of a meaningful transition of the comprehensive job assignment system. Since the end of the 1970s, when commercial labour exportation projects between China and foreign companies had been developed, more workers were needed to work abroad. Then, under the reformed foreign policy, in June 1980, the Xiamen Foreign Construction Company was organized and took over the task of recruiting persons to work abroad. The Company was still affiliated with the Foreign Economic Cooperation Office of the Xiamen Municipality and had to deal with labour exportation under the special authorities issued by the latter. Nevertheless, the establishment of this company was a turning point in that a new institution, although a semi-government institution of the times, started to be in charge of the labour recruitment. Then, in 1984, the Xiamen Foreign Construction Company officially stopped its affiliation with the Xiamen Municipality and became an independent corporate body. It was renamed as Xiamen International Economic and Technical

Cooperation Company (XIETC Company). Its business was still mainly composed of recruiting labourers under foreign contracts.

In Xiamen, during the late 1970s and the early 1980s, the majority of recruited persons to work abroad were sailors. Most worked for international shipping companies that had their general offices set up in Hong Kong. Since its establishment and up until the end of the 1980s, XIETC Company was the only company authorized by the Xiamen Municipality to deal with labour recruitment for formal exportation. In the early 1990s, although more companies joined in the business, XIETC Company had kept its position of the number one recruitment institution until the mid-1990s. During that period, the XIETC Company had made huge profits from the labour recruitment business. According to its public reports, concerning the business of labour exportation, from 1981 and up until 1995, the total turnover was about 161 million USD and the net profit reached 30 million USD (XMMYZ 1998:272).

Fat profit came from the fact that the XIETC Company was holding the market. Since the early 1990s, however, the XIETC Company's recruitment business has been greatly challenged. When China started its transition from planned economy to market economy, more companies attempted to share the potential profits by involvement in the labour recruitment business. In the period between 1992 and 1995, at least five new companies had got the authorities to deal with labour recruitment in succession. They all functioned actively in the sphere of labour exportation. Or to put it differently, it is the business of labour exportation that resulted in the re-emergence of labour brokerage. Soon, the business was dominated by the private agencies rather than state-owned ones. The reasons will be explored from the following two case studies.

3. Functioning Beyond the State: Re-emergence of the Private Transnational Migration Brokerage

In the coastal area of Fujian, emigration abroad increased even before the open door policy had been fully put in practice.

In the early 1970s, before the Cultural Revolution ended, China's government enacted a policy for returned overseas Chinese and their family members; they were granted the right to go abroad as long as they could show the documents needed. The emigration permission was severely restricted but anyhow the possibility had more or less come into view. In Fujian area, some who had relatives settled in the United States quickly caught the opportunity to emigrate.

From the perspective of 'helping' the transnational migration, the brokers basically functioned in two avenues. One was to send the people in groups and the other individuals. The case of channelling people to work in Israel can represent the former; and the case of people travelling to North America the latter. Nowadays who acts as the migration broker? How do they function between the state and individual, when institutional barriers stop cross border migration? The following are cases based on my field research in Fujian.

A. Sending migrant workers to Israel

The PRC and Israel held contrary political standpoints during the Cold War period. From the Korean War and up till the mid-1980s, during a period of more than three decades, China had set itself strongly against Zionism and refused to have any direct contact with the state of Israel. However, since the mid-1980s, when China was carrying out an 'open door policy' and peace was progressing in the Middle East, PRC and Israel restarted their diplomatic contacts stealthily. Finally on January 24, 1992, China and Israel officially set up diplomatic relations.

In the late 1980s, a series of strikes, disruptions and terrorist attacks carried out by the Palestinians inside Israel had resulted in progressively eroding the recruitment of Palestinian workers. Finally the Israeli government decided to close Gaza and the West Bank in February 1993. The unavailability of Palestinian workers made Israeli employers search for alternative sources of inexpensive but reliable labour (Borowski & Yanay 1997; Amir 2002; Kemp & Raijman 2004). It is worth noting that just at this point on the state level, China and Israel had approached amicable settlement. One thing that is even more worth noting is that the first Chinese labour exportation contract between Israel and China was signed in 1992, before the official diplomatic relationship was established. On the state level, this is the start point of the Chinese labour exportation towards Israel.

Although Fujian has a long history of cross-border migration as described above, before the mid-1990s, no local community of Fujian had any contact with the Middle East. Therefore, it was due to the formal and informal brokerage that Israel has become one of the new destination states of Fujian migrant workers.

An interview with a local government official provided the information as follows. According to him, in the early 1990s, the Jian Long Company, one of the first companies that had been authorized to send contract labour abroad, came to TA County to recruit villagers to do plastering work in Israel. It was said that Jian Long first tried to recruit workers in the city of Xiamen but failed. No urban youth had interests in going to Israel, an enemy state with a bad reputation. One director of the Jian Long Company happened to be a native of TT village in TA County. He knew that his fellow villagers had a tradition in plastering. He went to recruit workers in his hometown area. Most natives were poorly educated and knew nothing about the outside world. What they were attracted to was the unbeliev-ablly high wage announced by the company. Soon many villagers went to sign up. This was how labour migration to Israel started in TA County.

For those wanting to work in Israel, however, recruitment is expensive. Different companies charge different recruitment fees. According to the local cadre mentioned above, officially, the recruitment fee to work in Israel cannot be more than 30,000 yuan including airfare. This is higher than Israel's Employment Service Law in 2004, which allows for direct expenses and a surcharge of 900 USD (Kruger 2005), equal to 7200 yuan. However, my field research data show that the migrant workers had to pay much higher fees. In the mid-1990s it was about 50,000 yuan and it increased to between 70,000 yuan and 90,000 yuan in 2004. Furthermore, after July 2005, when the minimum wage of a migrant construction worker in Israel increased from 2.9–3.5 USD to about 4.25 USD per hour, the recruitment fee reached 150,000 yuan too. According to information I have accumulated over the years, the recruitment fee floats with the wage level in the destination market. The underlying regulation here, or the tacit standard by usage, is that, on average, the migrant workers spend about the equivalent of a two year salary to cover the recruitment fee.

Although the recruitment fee is very high, migrants believe they can repay the debt within one or two years. Then the wages afterwards would be their 'real income.' In 2005, I saw an advertisement recruiting migrant workers in Israel on the street of TA County. It highlighted a monthly wage of 8,000 yuan as a construction worker in Israel with opportunities of overtime to earn even more. In Fujian, on average, the rural household annual income was about 2,048 yuan in 1995 and increased to 3,734 yuan in 2004 (NBS China). Although the economic situation in Fujian is improving, when comparing incomes in Fujian and Israel, the rising level has little effect on the potential profits of working in Israel.

Therefore, to a certain degree, the first group went to Israel almost by accident, although the income gap between a Fujian village and Israel is the most influential factor. Many were not supposed to go to Israel before they were recruited. A certain brokerage company happened to provide the opportunity to work in Israel and then the migration wave was initiated in an institutional way.

B. Channelling villagers to North America

The function of brokering potential migrants to North America shows a different picture. TJ village is one of my research fields as well. Located in the southeast coast area of China, Ti is at the outfall of the Min River. Nobody knows how long ago the local young men had started to enjoy a good name as sailors. After the establishment of the modern sea transportation business, many local youth were employed by foreign shipping companies. At that time, New York became an important international seaport and a paradise for adventurers. When the ships stopped at New York, often some seamen who got tired of the seafaring life would jump ship to make their living ashore. Some young sailors of TJ Region did it too. This is how people of TJ Region started to take root in the United States. It continued for decades in the first half of the 20th century.

In the mid 1970s, as mentioned above, returned overseas Chinese and their families received permission to travel abroad if they could provide the required documents. Permission was severely restricted but emigration had become possible again; TJ residents with relatives in the US seized the opportunity. Very soon brokerage became a well known professional group of the area.

In June of 2005, a series of reports that appeared in all Chinese media in the United States had attracted the close attention of the Chinese immigrants and their relatives in mainland China. It was about a woman on trial in New York. The woman is known as Ping Sister, who was accused as a big snakehead because she had made 40 million USD from smuggling Chinese into the States. Moreover, she was accused of being involved in several tragedies – dozens of stowaways died on their way. Who is this Ping Sister and how did she make such a huge amount of profit from smuggling people?

Ping Sister was born into a peasant's family in TJ Region. Her full name is Chen Chui Ping. All people who know her or who want to contact her, however, call her Ping Sister. She only received primary school education for a few years during her childhood. Together with her husband, she emigrated to Hong Kong in 1974. Then in 1981, she found the way to get into New York and settled in Chinatown as an undocumented worker. Nobody knows how she could get her 'green card' so smoothly so that she was authorized only one year after she had arrived in the States.

In view of the huge economic gap between the States and her home village, moreover, in view of the possibilities of making a living in the States without legal status, Ping, almost immediately after gaining legal status herself, started to 'help' her relatives and friends for emigration. At the very beginning, she only received kinds of 'rewards' for the arrangements. When it became an open secret that 'it needs money to buy every step of emigration,' the brokerage fee had a settled market price. In TJ Region, the first well-known price of channelling one person to the States was 18,000 USD. It was in the mid-1980s. During the coming years, however, the price rocketed. At the end of the 1990s, the price had amounted to between 60,000 and 70,000 USD for one person.

When Ping's business of transnational brokerage was at the initiative stage, an important policy issued in the States gave her business a strong positive encouragement, of which the latent influences cannot be overstated. That is the implement of the Immigration Reform and Control Act, which enabled 2.7 million irregular immigrants to get permanent status to live and work in the States. Among these 'lucky ones,' hundreds were the first 'customers' of Ping Sister. When the news spread in Ping's home area, she was highly admired as a local heroine.

Encouraged by the regularization news mentioned above, the potential emigrants could not wait but wanted to be channelled immediately. Although the exact time was not clear, it was around the late 1980s that Ping started to rent or buy a freighter for smuggling people in big groups. In order to get more stowaways to heighten the profits, each ship was planned to be boarded hundreds of persons. It was said the biggest group was composed of more than 500 people on board. Both costs and profits, moreover, the risk of transportation soared to a higher level. In June 1993 the world was shocked when about 300 Chinese on board a decrepit freighter Golden Venture made a forced landing on the American shore and eleven drowned. Although Ping was not the owner of the freighter, she was involved in the affair. Her name was listed at the top of the criminal Chinese smugglers. She did not stop her business, however, until she was arrested in Hong Kong airport in April 2000.

The emigration brokers, or snakeheads in the words of the official media, could be divided into three categories. On the top there is a small group like this Ping Sister. Most hold a legal right to stay abroad. Under their management, uncountable money was used to 'pave the way out,' that is, organizing and expanding the transnational networks of migration, getting necessary documents or facilities for the clients transnationally, and/or bribing the relevant officials both in China and in the relevant countries. In the middle, there are some active agents who often sit in an officially registered company in the sending area. Normally, these companies are authorized to deal with the business such as labour exportation, study abroad, transnational contracted projects and so on. These companies often provide types of training courses for their clients. The training courses can be very wide. It may include language used in the planned destination country, cooking, nursing, basic knowledge of computer, etc. It may also include subjects such as how to be interviewed, how to prepare the necessary documents and sometimes how to apply for legal status in the case of landing in a country illegally. The clients would expect to get the certificate they need in the name of the company or a certain school, so long as they had paid for it. These are the institutionalized brokers. Then, at the bottom of the brokerage networks, there are some locals who act individually. Normally they have connections with the middle group but some may have direct contacts with the big head such as the co-villagers of Ping Sister. Their mission is to find the potential customers and introduce them to the relevant companies or big snakeheads. For each intending migrant the local mediator recruits, the company or big head pays the mediator a certain commission, which can be between a few thousands to ten thousands of Chinese dollars.

Since the late 1990s, the relevant authorities in China have proclaimed repeatedly that any activities concerning human smuggling are illegal and have alerted the locals to give chase. After the Dover tragedy (2000) when 58 Chinese stowaways were found dead in a truck, according to the relevant reports, dozens of snakeheads were arrested and punished. Among them, most were actors at the bottom, because they had direct connections with the victims and could be identified easily. A few were big heads such as Ping Sister, who have been given chase internationally.

On the 30th of June, 2005, Ping's session was mistrial because the testimony had been judged as unacceptable. When the judgement was declared, it was said that many Chinese immigrants in New York were excited. According to the report, the popular saying is as follows: 'this 56-year old Ping Sister is a good migration broker because she helped a lot of her co-villagers realize their dreams of upward mobility. Only in the eyes of the American officials was what she did criminal.' When interviewed, a head of the Fujianese association in New York said: 'Ping Sister enjoys the best reputation among dozens of the snakeheads. She did offend the immigration law of America. But from the perspective of morals she is not criminal. She is innocent.'

In Ping's hometown, I interviewed dozens of locals, including local officials and average people. None of the interviewees regards Ping Sister as a criminal, although some kept silence on the question. One man told me that Ping gave him 'special discount' for channelling his son to the States, only because he was her former classmate. 'She is always kind in responding to the requests for help,' he said. 'My son could not get into the States without her help. I could not build this five-story house without my son's money.' When asked whether it is criminal that Ping charged a huge amount of money for emigration, most interviewees gave similar responses as follows: 'It is reasonable because she needed money to 'buy' the way for us. The money can be earned back so long as the person can get into the States.' 'All companies charge money for labour exportation. Only those who received money but did not send the payers to the destination state are criminal.'

The locals usually make comments on the transnational migration brokerage from three perspectives. First, whether the broker was competent to get the clients in the destination efficiently. Second, whether the travelling was safe. Third, whether what the broker had charged was reasonable or not. A local saying is as follows: it is more difficult to find the right broker than to borrow enough money to pay the brokerage fee. Taking these grass-roots principles into account, that Ping Sister got high compliments of her co-villagers is understandable. The immigration expert Prof. Kwong of Hunter College therefore made the following comments: we can only say that taking smuggling Chinese as her major business, Ping Sister is a good business woman. Then Kwong added the following comment as well: it is undoubtedly that high compliments of her compatriots cannot erase her criminal activities.

The most attractive point of working in developed countries – regardless of its validity – is that you can expect a high income if only you are a hardworking person. To the average people who are not qualified with the very selective system of the destination states, their expectation of upgrading their fate by emigration abroad cannot become accessible without the special 'help' provided by the brokers. If the brokers are competent to make the emigration become accessible, they are accepted; and if their brokerage business is highly successful, they would be admired. So much so that the brokers have formed an indispensable node to make transnational migration become prevalent among the average people.

4. Concluding Remarks: Channelling Migrants between the State and Individual

Some scholars have correctly pointed out: 'the [state's] ability to control migration has shrunk as the desire to do so has increased' (Bhagwati 2003) and 'undocumented migration keeps growing despite control efforts by states and supranational bodies' (Castle 2004). In China, after two decades of the development, a kind of 'transnational migration industry' has been institutionalized. Due to the contradictions between migration policies in the book and the practical labour needs in the relevant states, often the transnational activities of the average people are considered acceptable (licit) by participants but are illegal in a formal sense on the national level. Therefore the whole process of transnational migration brokerage has been played between legal and illegal approaches, both in China and in the destination states. None of the states, either sending or receiving ones, declare their support for any illegal practices, and yet the relevant states themselves have in practical terms, more or less, consciously or unconsciously, involved or pushed the activities.

From the perspective of the sending area, there is no doubt that the Chinese government has made great efforts to stop human smuggling. Severe penalties have been imposed specially on those snakeheads. In TJ Region, posters and

pamphlets can be seen everywhere publicizing the government's decision to crack down on human smuggling and educating the villagers not to join any illegal emigration activities. However, when the successful overseas Chinese return to their home area, moreover if they made investment or a kind of donation, they would be met with great honour. At this moment, no one would care about how the person realized the emigration processes. Such being the case, the latent information expressed by the end product is in itself significant.

From the perspective of receiving states, all of them have strengthened the official control on the immigrants. The government wishes to accept talented people, such as entrepreneurs and professionals; while the labour market and employers wish to obtain cheap labourers. However, often the relevant authorities let the irregular workers alone simply because they are the first group to take low paying 3D (difficult, dirty and dangerous) work, which would prevent the comprehensive social welfare system from corruption. Moreover, in some high income states the amnesty or legalized movement hold now and then. Although the government's purpose of regularization is to uphold the legal rights of employed irregular immigrants, the latent information of such an opportunity is to give the irregular immigrants a reasonable hope that their irregular status is temporary and may be changed overnight.

From the perspective of the brokers, often it is not easy to define the border between a smuggler (snakehead) and a legal agency that is dealing with the affairs of going abroad. Concerning the brokerage fee, paying the fee is a kind of investment for the intending emigrants; and the broker is to charge payment for the business. The deal is following some invisible market rules. First, it depends on the anticipatory income in the destination country. For instance, the brokerage fee for going to the States is always higher than going to Europe. Second, it depends on how difficult it is to pave the way for migration. The most expensive is to get an official immigration status. If the applicant agrees to go abroad as a contract worker to countries such as Israel or Kuwait, the charge will be lower. Third, it depends on the individual status of the applicant. If the applicant is more or less qualified with the selective requirement, the fee would be lower. If the applicant needs to be 'trained' to reach the standard, the price will be rising accordingly. On the approaches of migration, sometimes the legal agencies may channel their clients illegally but undocumented brokers may channel their clients legally.

Finally, in the eyes of the migrants and the people concerned, 'being channelled to another country' is not a criminal act but a worthwhile attempt chosen by the people who wish to make a fortune abroad but lack the legal entitlement. The most attractive point of working abroad – regardless of its validity – is that you can expect a high income if only you are a hardworking person. What they care for is the end product. So long as one day the migrant returns as a successful overseas Chinese, all processes, no matter how frustrated he or she had once been reduced to, no matter whether the migration process was legal or illegal, would be erased.

While information, capital and commodities are moving more actively than ever in the period of globalization, it will surely encourage a greater flow of people. No one can deny the fact nor can anybody stop it. Meanwhile, the function of brokerage at the transnational level will be indispensable. Although it is easy to declare the illegality of some transnational activities, more efforts are needed to explore its long-standing and wide acceptability.

Note

1 Castles, Stephen and Miller, Mark J., *The Age of Migration* (Macmillan Press Ltd: London, 1998 [1993]), p. 230.

References

Barth, Gunther, 1964. Bitter Strength: A History of the Chinese in the United States, 1850–1870. Cambridge: Harvard University Press.

Bhagwati, Jagdish N., 2003. Borders beyond control. *Foreign Affairs*, 82 (1): 98–104.

Bian, Yanjie, 1997. Bringing strong ties back in: indirect ties, networks bridges and job searches in China. In *American Sociological Review*, No. 62: 266–285.

Blecher, Marc, 1983. Peasant labour for urban industry: temporary contract labour, urban-rural balance and class relations in a Chinese county. In *World Development*, 8: 731–745.

Breman, Jan, 1989. *Taming the Coolie Beast*. Calcutta: Oxford University Press.

Cai, Fang, 2001. Institutional barriers in two processes of rural labour migration in China. Paper presented at the international workshop on Labour Migration and Socio-economic Change in Southeast Asia and East Asia, in Lund, Sweden, 14–16 May.

Cao, Ziwei, 2001. Ziye huode yu guanxi jiegou – guanyu nongmingong shehui-wang de jige wenti [Job attainment and the structure of relationships – some questions concerning social networking of peasant workers]. In Ke & Li eds, pp. 71–91.

Castles, Stephen, 2004. The factors that make and unmake migration policies. *International Migration Review*. 38 (3): 852–884.

Chan, Kam Wing & Li Zhang, 1999. The hukou system and rural-urban migration: processes and changes. In *The China Quarterly*. 160: 818–855.

Chen, Hansheng ed. 1984. *Huagong chuguo shiliao huibian* [Documents Collection on Chinese Coolies Abroad]. Beijing: Zhonghua shuju.

Chen, Kongli, 1999. Xiamen shihua [A history of Xiamen]. Xiamen: Lujiang chubanshe.

Chin, Ko-lin, 1999. *Smuggled Chinese: Clandestine Immigration to the United States*. Philadelphia: Temple University Press.

Ding, Jinhong & Norman Stockman, 1999. 'The floating population and the integration of the city community: a survey on the attitudes of Shanghai residents to recent migrants.' In Pieke et al. eds, 1999, pp. 119–133.

Granovetter, M., 1973. The strength of weak ties. In *American Journal of Sociology*, No. 78: 1360–80.

Hu, Angang & Yang Yuxin, 2001. Jiuye moshi zhuanbian: Gong zhengguihua dao fei zhengguihua [The model of employment in transition: from formal to informal]. In *Guanli shijie*, 2.

Huang, Ping ed. 1997. Xunqiu shengchu [In Search for Survival: a sociological study of rura-urban migration]. Kunming: Yunnan renmin chubanshe.

IOM, 2005. World Migration 2005: Costs and benefits of international migration. Volume 3, IOM World Migration Report Series.

Ke Lanjun & Li Hanlin eds, 2001. Dushi li de chunmin, Zhongguo dachengshi de liudong renkou [Villagers in the City, Rural Migrants in Chinese Metropolises]. Beijing: Zhongyang bianyi chubanshe.

Kwong, Peter, 1997. *Forbidden Workers: Illegal Chinese Immigrants and American Labor*. New York: New Press.

Kyle, David and Rey Koslowske, eds 2001. *Global Human Smuggling: Comparative Perspective*. Baltimore: Johns Hopkins University Press.

Li, Minghuan, 1999. *'We Need Two Worlds', Chinese Immigrant Associations in a Western Society*. Amsterdam: Amsterdam University Press.

Li, Qiang, 2000. Zhongguo chengshi zhong eryuan laodongli shichang yu dichenjingying wenti [Issues of the dual labour market and the underclass elite in urban China]. In *Tsinghua Sociological Review*. 1:151–167.

Liang, Zai & Hideki Morooka, 2004. Recent trends of emigration from China: 1982–2000. International Migration. 42 (3): 145–164.

Liu, Boji, 1981. Meiguo Huaqiao shi [Chinese in the United States]. Taiwan: Liming chuban gongsi.

Massey, Douglas S., Joaquin Arango, Graeme Hugo, Ali Kouaouci, Adela Pellegrino & J. Edward Taylor, 1998. *Worlds in Motion, Understanding International Migration at the End of the Millennium*. Oxford: Clarendon Press.

Nyiri, Pal and Igor R. Saveliev, eds 2002. *Globalising Chinese Migration*. Aldershot: Ashgate.

Peng, Jiali, 1980. Shijiu shiji kaifa xifang zhimindi de Huagong [Chinese coolies in developing the Western colonies in 19th-century]. In *Shijie lishi* [World history], 1: 1–7.

Pieke, Frank N. & Hein Mallee eds 1999. *Internal and International Migration, Chinese perspectives*. Curzon Press.

Pieke, Frank N., Pal Nyiri, Mette Thuno and Antonella Ceccagno, 2004. *Transnational Chinese: Fujianese Migrants in Europe*. Stanford: Stanford University Press.

Sharping, Thomas, 1999. 'Selectivity, migration reasons and backward linkages of rural-urban migrants: a sample survey of migrants to Foshan and Shenzhen in comparative perspective.' In Pieke et al. eds, 1999, pp. 73–102.

Skeldon, Ronald, 2000. *Myths and realities of Chinese irregular migration*, Geneva: International Organization for Migration.

Smith, Paul J., ed., 1997. *Human Smuggling: Chinese Migrant Trafficking and the Challenge to America's Immigration Tradition*. Washington, D.C.: The Center for Strategic and International Studies.

Solinger, Dorothy, 1997. 'The floating population in the cities: chances for assimilation?' in Deborah Davis et al. eds, *Urban Spaces: Autonomy and Com-*

munity in contemporary China. Cambridge: Woodrow Wilson Center Press and Cambridge University Press, pp. 113–139.

Tinker, Hugh, 1974. A New System of slavery, the Export of Indian Labour Overseas, 1830–1920. London: Oxford University Press.

White, Lynn T., 1994. 'Migration and politics on the Shanghai delta.' *Issues & Studies* 30, no. 9, pp. 63–94.

Wolf, Diane Lauren, 1992. Factory Daughters, Gender, Household Dynamics, and Rural Industrialization in Java. Berkeley: University of California Press.

Xiamen Daily (special issues), 1995–1999. Gongzhong diaocha [Public investigations]. (Editor. 1995. Ni zai taxiang hai hao ma? [How are you while making living in an alien city?]. Xiamen: Xiamen Daily, Nov. 27.)

Xiang, Biao, 2003. Emigration from China: a sending country perspective. *International Migration.* 41 (3): 21–48.

XMMYZ editing committee ed., 1998. *Xiamen duiwai jingji maoyi zhi* [History of foreign trade in Xiamen]. Beijing: Zhongguo tongji chubanshe.

XMNJ, 1998. Xiamen shehui fazhan nianjian [Almanac of the Social Development in Xiamen]. Xiamen: Xiamen University Press.

Yuan, Ding, 2002. *Jindia qiaozhengyanjiu* [*A* Study of Modem Overseas Chinese Policy]. Hong Kong: Tienma Press.

Yuan, Victor & Xin Wong, 1999. 'Migrant construction teams in Beijing.' In Pieke et al. eds, 1999, pp. 103–118.

8

Racism and Xenophobia

Racism involves a negative evaluation of the Other that requires an active censorship of any tendency to regard him or her as an equal. This process generates the emergence of boundaries that 'change over time in response to concrete economic, political or ideological conditions'.[1] Among the reasons given by those subscribing to racism are: cultural preservation, fear of the unknown and, above all, the maintenance of a political-economic *status quo*.

The key role of racism since its early manifestations in colonial times has been the denial of social, political and economic participation to certain collectivities and the legitimation of various forms of exploitation. Racism is embedded in power relations. It reflects the capacity of a certain group to formulate an ideology that not only legitimizes a particular power relation between ethnic communities but also represents a useful mechanism for the reproduction of such relation.

When considering racist attitudes, power fulfils a fundamental role in three different ways. First, power within the racist discourse is epistemologically exercised in the dual practices of naming and evaluating the other.[2]

Second, the socio-political consequences of racism depend on the power of the racists. Thus a group may consider their neighbours as endemically inferior, but if they do not possess power to implement their racist views, these would be limited and have no transcendence. What made possible the holocaust was the combination of a racist discourse with the political, social and economic power to make it effective.[3]

Third, when a group imposes a world-view that contains racist elements, the society in question becomes automatically divided between minority and majority groups. Minority groups, Spoonley argues, 'are not necessarily numerically smaller but are those groups who face prejudice and unequal treatment because they are seen as being inferior in some way'.[4] In this context 'minority' reflects relative lack of power. A 'majority group', by contrast, possesses political, economic and ideological power. The 'majority' assumes that its culture is the 'natural' culture of the whole society; its language dominates the private as well as the public sphere. From this perspective, the culture, language and ways of life of different ethnic communities – some of which could have an immigrant origin – are often considered as inferior.

Here we have included three essays on the various negative ways in which minorities can be viewed or even excluded, as in European and North American society. These reflect a number of different disciplines and theoretical and ideological trends.

Michel Wieviorka writes about racism and anti-racism in France from the viewpoint of the theory of social movements, developing some of the ideas of Alain Touraine. Racism is intrinsically linked with modernity, according to Wieviorka, and, in his view, it cannot be reduced to a single logic. He identifies four main lines of argument which cross the space of racism in its relation to modernity: these are related to the universalist nature of racism, its connection with processes of downward social mobility or exclusion, appeals to identity or to tradition which are opposed to modernity and, finally, its appropriation by anti- or non-modern positions, which are displayed not against groups incarnating modernity, but against groups defined themselves by an identity without any reference to modernity. To illustrate his point, Wieviorka offers an historical analysis of the recent evolution of racism in most of the major Western European countries.

Stephen Steinberg looks at the United States experience and argues that the movement to win civil rights for American blacks (now called African-Americans) reached its high point when the Johnson administration secured their legal and political rights. Subsequently, he claims, the perception gained ground that legal rights were not enough, but that this in turn led to two tendencies, one arguing that affirmative action must continue, the other that something had to be done to alter the nature of the African-American family and community. In his view much American sociology has wrongly supported the second position.

Étienne Balibar discusses how ideologies of nationalism and racism have come to compete with the ideology of Marxism based upon analysis of class. In his view, it is only retrospectively that the notion of race was 'ethnicized', so that it could be integrated into the nationalist complex. He compares 'aristocratic racism' and its imperialist legacy in the colonial context with the new racism of the bourgeois era targeting the proletariat as both an exploited and a politically threatening population. The emergence of class racism is affected by the both heterogeneous and fluctuating nature of its population in such a way that its 'boundaries' are by definition imprecise since they depend on the constant transformations of the labour process and movements of capital.

Notes

1 Anthias, Floya and Yuval-Davies, Nira, *Racialized Boundaries: Race, Nation, Gender, Colour and Class and the Anti-Racist Struggle* (Routledge: London, 1993), p. 4.
2 Golberg, D. T., *Racist Culture: Philosophy and the Politics of Meaning* (Blackwell: Oxford, 1993), p. 150.
3 Guibernau, M., *The Identity of Nations* (Polity: Cambridge, 2007), p. 148.
4 Spoonley, P., *Racism and Ethnicity* (Oxford University Press: Auckland, 1993), p. 4.

RACISM IN EUROPE: UNITY AND DIVERSITY

MICHEL WIEVIORKA

Observing growing racist tendencies that affect most European countries, an increasing number of scholars feel an urgent need for a comparative reflection that may bring answers to a central question: over and beyond the empirical evidence of differences, is there not a certain unity in contemporary racism in Europe? Is it not possible to elaborate a reasoned set of hypotheses that could account for most national racist experiences in Europe, while shedding sonic light on their specificities?

European unification, insofar as it exists, and the growth of racism are obviously distinct phenomena, and it would be artificial to try and connect them too directly. The most usual frame of reference for any research about racism and race relations remains national. And even the vocabulary or, more deeply, the analytical and cultural categories that we use when dealing with this issue *vary* so widely from one country to another that we meet considerable difficulties when trying to translate precise terms. There may be large differences in language, and words with negative connotations in one country will have positive ones in another. Nobody in France, for instance, would use the expression *relations de race*, which would be regarded as racist, although it is commonly employed in the United Kingdom.

The key preliminary task, therefore, is not to contribute direct empirical knowledge about the various expressions of racism in Europe, as can be found, for instance, in the important survey of 'Racism and xenophobia' published in 1989 by the European Community (CCE 1989). Nor is the initial task to compare elementary forms of racism, such as harassment, stereotypes, discrimination or political racism in a certain number of countries, in order to prove that they are more or less similar, or that they follow a similar evolution.

Rather the problem is primarily conceptual. If we want to test the idea of a certain unity of contemporary racism in Europe, we must elaborate sociological and historical hypotheses, and then apply them to the facts that we are able to collect. Thus the most difficult aspect of a comparative approach is not to find data, but to organize it with well-thought-out hypotheses.

My own hypotheses can be formulated in two different ways, one of which is relatively abstract and the other more concrete.

Racism and Modernity

An initial formulation of the problematic, in effect, consists in the construction of a global argument enabling us to demonstrate that racism is inseparable from modernity, as the latter developed from European origins, and from its present crisis (Wieviorka 1992a). Racism, both as a set of ideologies and specious scientific doctrines, and as a set of concrete manifestations of violence, humiliation and discrimination, really gathered momentum in the context of the immense changes of which Europe was the centre after the Renaissance. It developed further in modern times, with the huge migrations, the extension of trading relationships, the industrialization of Western society and colonization. But racism, in its links with modernity, cannot be reduced to a single logic, and even seems to correspond to processes which are sometimes so distinct that numerous demands are made for the discussion of racisms in the plural. This in fact gives rise to a debate the terms of which are badly posed. It is effectively possible to set up an integrated, global argument in which the various forms of racism, including anti-semitism, find their theoretical place, and which goes in the direction of a sociological, even anthro-pological, unity of racism. One can also consider each of these forms in its histori-cal specificity, which goes in the opposite direction. Both approaches are legitimate and complementary, but since we are thinking here about the unity of contempo-rary forms of racism in Europe, it is clear that we should privilege the former. This leads us to distinguish four main lines of argument which cross the space of racism in its relation to modernity.

In the first instance, as the companion of modernity triumphant, racism is universalist, denouncing, crushing and despising different identities – hence the apparition of inferior 'races' as an obstacle to the process of expansion, in par-ticular colonial expansion, or destined to be exploited in the name of their sup-posed inferiority.

Next, linked to processes of downward social mobility, or exclusion, racism is the expression, as well as the refusal of a situation in which the actor positively values modernity, but lives, or is afraid he/she will be exposed to a form of expul-sion which will marginalize him/her. The actor then assumes a reflex or an attitude of 'poor white', particularly common in contexts of economic crises or of retraction from the labour market. Racism here is a perversion of a demand to participate in modernity and an opposition to the effective modalities of its functioning.

A third line of argument corresponds not to a positive valorization of moder-nity, the rise of which must be ensured, or from which one refuses to be excluded, but to appeals to identity or to tradition which are opposed to modernity. The nation, religion and the community then act as markers of identity, thus giving rise to a racism which attacks those who are assumed to be the vectors of a detested modernity. The Jews are often the incarnation of these vectors, as are, in some circumstances, those Asian minorities who are perceived as being par-ticularly economically active. Finally, racism can correspond to anti- or non-modern positions, which are displayed not against groups incarnating modernity, but against groups defined themselves by an identity without any reference to modernity. It expresses, or is an extension of, intercultural, intercommunity, interethnic or similar tensions.

It is therefore possible to represent the space of racism around four cardinal points:

Modernity against identities
Identities against identities   Identities against modernity
Modernity against modernity

In a space of this type, the racist actors do not necessarily occupy one single position, and their speech and their behaviour are frequently syncretic and vary over time. There are even sometimes paradoxical mixtures of these various positions, when people, for instance, reproach a racialized group with symbolizing at the same time modernity and traditional values which they consider deny modernity: in the past, but also today, Jews, in many cases, fulfil this double function (Wieviorka 1992b). They are hated in the name of their supposed identification with political power, money, the mass media and a cosmopolitan internationalism, but also because of their difference, their visibility, their nationalism and support or belonging to the state of Israel, or because they flaunt their cultural traditions or their religion.

This theoretical construction of the space of racism may help us to answer our question. In effect, it enables us to read the European experience, and above all its recent evolution. The latter has long been dominated, on the one hand, by a racism of the universalist, colonial type and, on the other hand, by oppositions to modernity which have assumed the form of anti-semitism; today, much more than previously, it is directed by the fear or reality of exclusion and downward social mobility, and on the other by tensions around identity and vague fears of which the most decisive concern the question of belonging to the nation.

Formation and Restructuration of the European Model of National Societies

The argument outlined above can be completed by a much more concrete historical analysis of the recent evolution of most of the major western European countries. The latter, throughout this century, and up to the 1960s or 1970s, can be defined on the basis of a model which integrates three elements which are then weakened and destructured, reinvigorating the question of racism.

The era of integration

In most western European countries, racism, before the Second World War, was a spectacular and massive phenomenon, much more widespread than today. Colonial racism postulated the inferiority of colonized people of 'races', and modern anti-semitism gave a new and active dimension to former anti-Judaism. This is why we must introduce a sense of relativity into our perceptions of contemporary racism. This is why we must also think in terms of periods, with the idea of a certain unity in time for the phenomenon that we are discussing. This idea means not that there is no continuity in racist doctrines, ideologies, prejudice or more concrete expressions, but that a new era in the history of racism began with the retreat, as Elazar Barkan (1992) says, of scientific racism, the end of decolonization, and, above all, the 'economic crisis' that has in fact meant the beginning of the decline of industrial societies.

Until that time, i.e. the 1960s and 1970s, most European countries had succeeded, to a greater or a lesser extent, depending on the country, in integrating three basic components of their collective life: *an industrial society, an egalitarian state and a national identity.*

Most European countries have been industrial societies: that is, they have had a set of social relations rooted in industrial labour and organization. From this point of view, they have been characterized by a structural conflict, which opposed the working-class movement and the masters of industry, but which extended far beyond workshops and factories. This conflict gave the middle classes a possibility to define themselves by either a positive or negative relationship towards the working-class movement. It brought to unemployed people the hope and sometimes the reality of being helped by this movement. It was also the source of important political debates dealing with the 'social question'. Furthermore, it influenced intellectual and cultural life profoundly, and acted as a point of reference for many actors, in the city, in universities, in religious movements and elsewhere.

European countries, and this is the second basic component of our model of analysis, have also been able to create and develop institutions which aimed at ensuring that egalitarian treatment was imparted to all citizens as individuals. The state has generally taken over various aspects of social welfare and security. It has become a welfare state. The state also introduced or defended a distance between religion and politics. Although countries such as Spain, Portugal and Greece have recently experienced dictatorial regimes, states in Europe have generally behaved, since the Second World War, as warrants for democracy.

Lastly, most European countries have given a central importance to their national identity. This identity has usually included two different aspects, sometimes contradictory, sometimes complementary. On one hand, the idea of a nation has corresponded to the assertion of a culture, a language, a historical past and traditions, with some tendencies to emphasize primordial ties and call for a biological definition loaded with racism, xenophobia and anti-semitism. On the other hand, the nation has also been defined in a more positive way, as bound to the general progress of mankind and to universal values that could be defined in economic, political or ethical terms. In this last perspective, a nation is related to reason, progress, democracy and human rights.

Industrial society, state and *nation*: these three basic elements have never been consonant with their highest theoretical image. One can easily show the weakness of the working-class movement in some countries, or its constant subordination to political forces, the limits of the welfare state everywhere in the past, and the domination of the reactionary and xenophobic aspects of nationalism in many circumstances. Moreover, some European countries have defined themselves as bi- or pluri-national. But since we recognize these limits, and since we recognize many differences between countries, we can admit, without the danger of creating a myth, that our three basic elements are typical of European countries until the 1960s and 1970s. Not only have they characterized three countries, but they have also been relatively strongly articulated, so much so that various terms are used to express this articulation: for instance, integration, nation state and national society. We must be very cautious and avoid developing the artificial or mythical image of countries perfectly suited to the triple and integrated figure of an industrial society, a two-dimensional national and a modern and egalitarian state. But our representation of the past is useful in considering the evolution of the last twenty or thirty years, an evolution which is no doubt dominated by the growing weakness and dissociation of our three basic elements.

The era of destructuration

All European countries are experiencing today a huge transformation which affects the three components of our reflection, and defines what I have called, in the case of France, *'une grande mutation'* (Wieviorka 1992c).

Industrial societies are living their historical decline, and this phenomenon should not be reduced to the spectacular closing of workshops and factories. More important in our perspective is the decay of the working-class movement as a social movement. In the past, the working-class movement was, to various degrees, capable of incorporating in a single action collective behaviour corresponding to three major levels. There could be limited demands, struggles based on the professional defence of political demands, dealt with by the institutional system, and, at the highest level of its project, orientations challenging the control and the direction of progress and of industry. These orientations are quite out of place today: the working-class movement is breaking up, and this decomposition produces various effects (Touraine et al. 1987). Among workers, there is a strengthening of tendencies towards corporatism and selfishness – those workers who still have a certain capacity of action, because of their skill or their strategic position in their firm, develop struggles in the name of their own interests, and not in the name of more general or universal ones.

Sometimes workers' demands can no longer be taken up by the trade unions, which have been considerably weakened. This can result in violent forms of behaviour, or in spontaneous forms of organization, such as the recent 'co-ordinations' in France, which are easily infiltrated by extremist ideologies.

In such a context, the middle classes no longer have to define themselves by reference to class conflicts, and they tend to oscillate between, on the one hand, unrestrained individualism and, on the other, populism or national populism, the latter being particularly strong among those who experience downward mobility or social exclusion. These two distinct phenomena are closely related to social and economic dualization. In the past, most people could have a strong feeling of belonging to a society, 'down' as workers, or 'up' as elites or middle classes. Today, a good number of people are 'in', and constitute a large middle class, including those workers who have access to jobs, consumption, health or education for their children, while a growing proportion of people are 'out', excluded and marginalized.

Such an evolution may lead to renewed expressions of racism. Those who are 'out', or fear to be, have a feeling of injustice and loss of previous social identity. They think the government and the politicians are responsible for their situation, and may develop populist discourses and attitudes in which anti-migrant or ethnic minorities racism can take place. They then impute their misfortune to migrants, even if these migrants share the same experience. And those who are 'in' may develop more subtle forms of racism, trying to secure themselves with a colour bar or by individual or collective behaviours that create social and racial segregation and build symbolic but also real barriers. Furthermore, the logic of segregation, particularly at the political level, is always likely to become indistinguishable from a national and populist form of discourse which amalgamates the fears, anger and frustrations of the excluded and the social self-centredness of those who wish to defend their status and their way of life. This merging therefore gives a result which is only paradoxical in appearance, since it results in an identical form of racism in those people who have experienced living with, or close to, immigrants or similar categories of people, and in those who have not actually done so, but who have heard about it through the mass media or from rumours.

A second element of destructuration deals with the state and public institutions, which encounter increasing difficulties in trying to respect egalitarian principles, or in acting as welfare states. Everywhere in Europe, the number of unemployed people has grown, creating not only a great many personal dramas, but also a fiscal crisis of the state. The problems of financing old-age pensions, the health-care system, state education and unemployment benefits are becoming increasingly acute, while at the same time there is a rising feeling of insecurity which is attributed, once again, to immigrants. The latter are then perceived in racist terms, accused not only of taking advantage of social institutions and using them to *their own* ends, but also of benefiting from too much attention from the state. At the same time, the ruling classes have been tempted since the 1970s by liberal policies which in fact ratify and reinforce exclusion and marginalization.

The crisis of the state and the institutions is a phenomenon which must be analytically distinguished from the decline of industrial society and the dualization which results from its decline. But the two phenomena are linked. Just as the welfare state owes a great deal, in its formation, to the social and political discussions which are inseparable from the history of the working class, which is particularly clear in the countries endowed with strong social democracy, so too the crisis of the welfare state and the institutions owes a great deal to the destructuration not only of these discussions and conflicts, but also of the principal actor which informed them, the working-class movement.

A third aspect of the recent evolution concerns the national issue, which becomes nodal – all the more so as social issues are not politically treated as such. In most European countries, political debates about nation, nationality and citizenship are activated. In such a context, nationalism loses its open and progressive dimensions, and its relationship with universal values, and is less and less linked with ideas such as progress, reason or democracy. National identity is increasingly loaded with xenophobia and racism. This tendency gains impetus with the emergence or growth of other identities among groups that are defined, or that define themselves, as communities, whether religious, ethnic, national or regional. There is a kind of spiral, a dialectic of identities, in which each affirmation of a specific identity involves other communitarian affirmations among other groups. Nationalism and, more generally speaking, communal identities do not necessarily mean racism. But as Étienne Balibar explains, racism is always a virtuality (Balibar and Wallerstein 1988).

This virtuality is not nurtured uniquely by the presence, at times exaggerated and fantasized, of a more or less visible immigration. It also owes a considerable amount to phenomena which may even have nothing to do with it. Thus national identity is reinforced in its most alarming aspects when national culture appears to be threatened by the superficial and hypermodern character of an international culture which originates primarily in America, by the political construction of Europe or, again, by the globalization of the economy.

At the same time, it becomes more and more difficult to assert that society, state and nation form an integrated whole. Those who call for universal values, human rights and equality, who believe that each individual should have equal opportunities to work, make money and then participate fully in cultural and political life – in other words, those who identify themselves with modernity – are less and less able to meet and even to understand those who have the feeling of being excluded from modern life, who fear for their participation in economic, cultural and political life, and who retire within their national identity. In extreme cases, social and economic participation are no longer linked with the feeling of belonging to a nation, the latter being what remains when the former becomes impossible. Reason, progress and development become divorced from nation, identity and subjectivity, and in this split, racism may easily develop.

In the past, industrial society often offered workers disastrous conditions of work and existence. But the working-class movement, as well as the rulers of industry, believed in progress and reason, and while they were opposed in a structural conflict, this was precisely because they both valorized the idea of progress through industrial production, and both claimed that they should direct it. The nation, and its state, as Ernest Gellner explains (1983), were supposed to be the best frame for modernization, and sometimes the state not only brought favourable conditions, but also claimed to be the main agent of development. Nationalism could be the ideology linked to that viewpoint, and not only a reactionary or traditionalist force. Today, waters divide. Nationalism is mainly expressed by social and political groups frightened by the internationalization of the economy and culture. It is increasingly differentialist, and racism develops as social problems such as exclusion and downward mobility grow, and as anxiety develops in regard to national identity.

The Categories of the Sociological Analysis of Racism

The argument outlined above is historical and sociologial in nature, but a closer examination of the contemporary phenomenon of racism requires explicitness in the instruments and, therefore, the categories of analysis of racism properly speaking (Wieviorka 1991).

The two logics of racism

Contemporary sociological literature increasingly insists on the idea of changing forms of racism. Some scholars, relying on American studies, oppose the old 'flagrant' racism to the 'subtle' new versions (Pettigrew 1993). Others emphasize a crucial distinction, which could, in an extreme interpretation, lead to the idea of two distinct kinds of racism. Following authors such as Martin Barker or Pierre-André Taguieff, we should distinguish between a classical, inegalitarian racism and a new, differentialist one (Barker 1981; Taguieff 1988). The first kind considers the other as an inferior being, who may find a place in society, but the lowest one. There is room for inferior people in this outlook, as long as they can be exploited and relegated to unpleasant and badly paid tasks. The second kind considers the other as fundamentally different, which means that he/she has no place in society, that he/she is a danger, an invader, who should be kept at some distance, expelled or possibly destroyed. The point is that for many scholars the new racism, sometimes also referred to as cultural racism, is the main one in the contemporary world, while the inegalitarian one becomes secondary.

As long as this remark is intended as a statement of historical fact, based on the observation of empirical realities of present-day racism, it is acceptable. But it must not take the place of a general theory of racism. First, cultural or differentialist approaches to racism are not new. It is difficult to speak of Nazism, for instance, without introducing the idea that anti-semitism in the Third Reich was deeply informed by these approaches. Jews were said to corrupt Aryan culture and race, and the 'final solution' planned not to assign them to the lowest place in society, but to destroy them. Second, the opposition between the two main logics of racism should not conceal the main fact, which is that a purely cultural definition of the Other, as well as a purely social one, dissolves the idea of race. On one hand, Claude Lévi-Strauss is not a racist when he emphasizes cultural differentiation. One is a racist only when there is any reference to race in a cultural opposition, when beneath culture we can, explicitly or implicitly, find nature: that is, in an organicist or genetic representation of the Other as well as oneself. On the other hand, when the Other is defined only as socially inferior, exploited or marginalized, the reference to race may disappear or become, as William J. Wilson suggests (1978), less significant.

In fact, in most experiences of racism, the two logics co-exist, and racism appears as a combination of them both. There are not two racisms, but one, with various versions of the association of cultural differentialism and social inegalitarianism. The general analysis that has been presented for contemporary Europe helps us to refuse the idea of a pure, cultural racism, corresponding to a new paradigm that would have taken the place of an old one. The sources of European contemporary racism, as I have suggested, are in the crisis of national identities and in the dualization of societies, which favour a differentialist logic. But they are also connected with phenomena of downward social mobility and economic crisis, which lead to populism and exasperation and have an important dimension in appeals for an unequal treatment of migrants.

Two main levels

As I have indicated in my book *L'espace du racisme* (Wieviorka 1991), we may distinguish four levels in racism. The way that experiences of racism are articulated at the different levels where they act may change with their historical evolution. Our distinction is analytical, and should help us as a sociological tool.

A first level refers to weak and inarticulated forms of racism, whatever they may consist of: opinions and prejudice, which are more xenophobic and populist than, strictly speaking, racist; and diffuse violence, limited expression of institutional discrimination or diffusion of racial doctrines, etc. At this first level, racism is not a central issue and it is so limited, quantitatively and qualitatively, that I have chosen to use the term *infraracism* to characterize it.

We may speak of *political racism* at a second level, in reference to forms of racism which are still weak and inarticulate, but stronger and more obvious. At this stage, racism becomes a central issue, but does not give the image of a unified and integrated phenomenon, mainly because of the lack of a strong political expression.

We may speak of *political racism*, precisely, when political and intellectual debates and real political forces bring a dual principle of unity to the phenomenon. On one hand, they give it an ideological structure, so that all its expressions seem to converge and define a unique set of problems; on the other hand, they offer it practical forms of organization.

At the fourth level, we may call *total racism* those situations in which the state itself is based on racist principles. There is nowadays no real threat of total racism in our countries, and we may now simplify the distinction into four levels of racism by reducing them to two main ones, the *infrapolitical* level, including infra and split racisms, and the *political* one.

We can now come back to our general analysis of European contemporary racism and be more precise. This rise of the phenomenon, following what was previously said, is due to the evolution of three basic elements, and to their destructuration. We may add that it appears first at an infrapolitical level, and that it then ascends to the political level, with variations from one country to another.

In certain cases, a rather important political party appears and develops quickly, as in France with the *Front National*. In other cases, such a party appears but quickly declines, which means not that racism necessarily stays at the infrapolitical level, but that it informs political debates without being the flag of one precise strong organization – this could define the English experience. But above all, the analytical distinction into levels enables us to introduce a central question: is there not throughout Europe the same danger of seeing political actors capable of taking over and of directing infrapolitical racism?

On the one hand, we observe in several countries the growing influence of racist ideologies, but also of political organizations which are no longer small groups of activists and which may occupy an important space in political life. The French *Front National* appears as a leader in Europe, and sometimes as a model, but other parties or movements should be quoted too: the *Deutsche Volksunion* and the *Demokratische Partei Deutschlands* in Germany; the FPO (Freiheidlich Partei Osterreich) in Austria, which gained 22.6 per cent of the votes in the November 1991 elections in Vienna; the *Vlaams Blok* in Flanders, with twelve members of Parliament since November 1991; and the Italian Leagues.

One must he careful, however, not to exaggerate. The more extreme-right parties occupy an important place, the more they appear as populist rather than purely racist. Racism, strictly speaking, is only one element, and sometimes a minor one, along with strong nationalism or regionalism. Moreover, political and electoral successes force these parties to look respectable, and avoid overtly flagrant expressions of racism.

On the other hand, racism appears in non-political contexts, when prejudice and hostile attitudes to migrants develop, when social and racial segregation is increasingly visible (which is the case in France, where the issue of racism is constantly related to the so-called urban crisis and 'the suburban problem'), when violent actions develop, sometimes with a terrorist aspect, when various institutions including the police have a responsibility for its growth, when discrimination is obvious (for instance, in relation to housing or employment), and when the media contribute to the extension of prejudice. In such a context, all the European democracies have to face the same problem. There is a growing opportunity for extreme-right forces to capitalize on fears, frustrations, unsatisfied social demands and feelings of threat to national identity. Even worse, there is a danger that these forces will introduce new elements into infrapolitical racism. This is the case in France, for instance, where popular racism is strongly hostile to migrants, to black people and to gypsies, rather than to Jews, and where the *Front National* tries constantly to instil anti-semitisin.

More generally, there is still a real distance between infrapolitical and political racism, and this means that racism is not so much a widely extended ideology offering people a general framework in which to interpret their own lives and personal experiences, but rather a set of prejudices and practices that are rooted in these concrete lives and experiences, and which could possibly evolve.

In the present state of things, the development is dominated by a process of populist fusion in which popular affects and political discourse converge, but which, paradoxically, protects our societies from extreme and large-scale racist episodes. However, populism is never a stable phenomenon and is always potentially open to more frightening processes.

References

Balibar, Étienne, and Wallerstein, Immanuel (1988), *Race, classe, nation*, Paris: La Découverte.

Barkan, Elazar (1992), *The Retreat of Scientific Racism*, Cambridge: Cambridge University Press.

Barker, Martin (1981), *The New Racism*, London: Junction Books.

CCE (1989) *Eurobaromètre: L'opinion publique dans la Communauté Européenne*, Brussels: Commission des Communautés Européennes.

Gellner, Ernest (1983), *Nations and Nationalism*, Oxford: Blackwell.

Pettigrew, Thomas, and Meertens, R. F. (1993), 'Le racisme voilé: Composants et mesure', in *Racisme et modernité* (under the direction of M. Wieviorka), Paris: La Découverte.

Taguieff, Pierre-André (1988), *La fonce du préjugé*, Paris: La Découverte.

Touraine, Alain, Wieviorka, Michel, and Dubet, François (1987), *The Working Class Movement*, Cambridge: Cambridge University Press.

Wieviorka, Michel (1991), *L'espace du racisme*, Paris: Seuil.

Wieviorka, Michel (1992a), 'Racism and modernity', paper presented at the Congress of the American Sociological Association, Pittsburgh.

Wieviorka, Michel (1992b), 'Analyse sociologique et historique de l'antisémitisme en Pologne', *Cahiers internationaux de sociologie*, vol. 93, pp. 237–49.

Wieviorka, Michel (ed.) (1992c), *La France raciste*, Paris: Seuil.

Wilson, William J. (1978), *The Declining Significance of Race*, Chicago: University of Chicago Press.

THE LIBERAL RETREAT FROM RACE SINCE THE CIVIL RIGHTS ACT

STEPHEN STEINBERG

Racial backlash was not an affliction only of the political right [in the USA]. As early as 1963, the *Atlantic Monthly* published an article entitled 'The White Liberal's Retreat'. Its author, Murray Friedman, observed that 'the liberal white is increasingly uneasy about the nature and consequences of the Negro revolt'. According to Friedman, a number of factors contributed to the white liberal retreat. For one thing, after school desegregation came to Northern cities, white liberals realized that the Negro was not just an abstraction, and not just a Southern problem. Second, the rise of black nationalism exacerbated tensions with white liberals, especially when they were ejected from civil rights organizations. Third, escalating tensions and violence tested the limit of liberal support. As Friedman wrote: 'In the final analysis, a liberal, white, middle-class society wants to have change, but without trouble' (Friedman 1963).

The liberal retreat also manifested itself in a rift between white intellectuals and blacks. As an example, Friedman cited Nathan Glazer's laudatory review of Nathaniel Weyl's *The Negro in American Civilization*. Weyl cited the results of IQ tests to argue that 'a large part of the American Negro population is seriously deficient in mental ability', and warned against the dangers of 'random race mixing without regard to learning ability'. According to Friedman, Glazer was critical of Weyl's biological determinism, particularly his reliance on African brain-size data, but nevertheless declared that Weyl 'is clearly free of any prejudice and deserves credit for having raised for public discussion crucial aspects of the Negro question which receive little discussion in academic and liberal circles, and which are usually left in the hands of bigots and incompetents' (quoted in Friedman 1963). Then Glazer posed the rhetorical question that leaves the answer to the racialized imagination: 'What are we to make of the high rates of [Negro] crime and delinquency, illegitimacy, family break-up and school dropout?'

As Friedman observed, there was nothing new in the tendency for white liberals to withdraw support from the liberation movement – essentially the same thing had happened during Reconstruction. In both cases, liberals demonstrated a failure of nerve, and nudged blacks into curbing their demands. Friedman described the situation in 1963 in these epigrammatic terms: 'to the Negro demand for "now," to which the Deep South has replied "never," many liberal whites are increasingly responding "later"'(Friedman 1963).

It did not take long for the intensifying backlash and the liberal retreat to manifest themselves politically. The critical turning-point was 1965, the year the civil rights movement reached its triumphant finale. The 1964 Civil Rights Act – passed after a decade of black insurgency – ended segregation in public accommodations and, at least in theory, proscribed discrimination in employment. The last remaining piece of civil rights legislation – the 1965 Voting Rights Act – was wending its way through Congress and, in the wake of Johnson's landslide victory, was assured of eventual passage. In a joint session of Congress on voting rights in March 1965 – the first such session on a domestic issue since 1946 – President Johnson had electrified the nation by proclaiming, in his Southern drawl, 'And we *shall* overcome.' As a senator from Texas, Johnson had voted against anti-lynching legislation. Now, in the midst of a crisis engineered by a grassroots protest movement, Johnson embraced the battle cry of that movement as he proposed legislation that would eliminate the last and most important vestige of official segregation.

In retrospect, Johnson's speech represented not the triumph of the civil rights movement, but its last hurrah. Now that its major legislative objectives had been achieved, not only the future of the movement, but also the constancy of liberal support, were thrown into question. By 1965, leaders and commentators, both inside and outside the movement, were asking, 'What's next?' However, this question had an ominous innuendo when it came from white liberals. In *Why We Can't Wait*, published in 1963, Martin Luther King provides this account of his appearance with Roy Wilkins on *Meet the Press*:

> There were the usual questions about how much more the Negro wants, but there seemed to be a new undercurrent of implications related to the sturdy new strength of our movement. Without the courtly complexities, we were, in effect, being asked if we could be trusted to hold back the surging tides of discontent so that those on the shore would not be made too uncomfortable by the buffeting and onrushing waves. Some of the questions implied that our leadership would be judged in accordance with our capacity to 'keep the Negro from going too far.' The quotes are mine, but I think the phrase mirrors the thinking of the panelists as well as of many other white Americans (King 1963: 147).

By 1965 – even before Watts exploded – there was a growing awareness among black leaders that political rights did not go far enough to compensate for past wrongs. Whitney Young epitomized this when he wrote that 'there is little value in a Negro's obtaining the right to be admitted to hotels and restaurants if he has no cash in his pocket and no job' (Young 1963). As Rainwater and Yancey have suggested, 'The year 1965 may be known in history as the time when the civil rights movement discovered, in the sense of becoming explicitly aware, that abolishing legal racism would not produce Negro equality' (Rainwater and Yancey 1967: 77).

If laws alone would not produce equality, then the unavoidable conclusion was that some form of 'special effort' – to use Whitney Young's term – was necessary to compensate for the accumulated disadvantages of the past. By 1965 the words 'compensation', 'reparations' and 'preference' had already crept into the political discourse, and white liberals were beginning to display their disquiet with this troublesome turn of events. In *Why We Can't Wait* King observed: 'Whenever this issue of compensatory or preferential treatment for the Negro is raised, some of our friends recoil in horror. The Negro should be granted equality, they agree; but he should ask nothing more' (King 1963: 147).

[...]

In the spring of 1964 [there] was an early sign of the imminent breakup of the liberal coalition that had functioned as a bulwark of the civil rights movement. One faction would gravitate to the nascent neo-conservative movement. Another faction would remain in the liberal camp, committed in principle to both liberal reform and racial justice. This, however, was to prove a difficult balancing act, especially when confronted with an intensifying racial backlash. Even in the best of times, racial issues tended to exacerbate divisions in the liberal coalition on which Democratic electoral victories depended. As the polity swung to the right, liberals in the Democratic Party came under mounting pressure to downplay or sidestep racial issues.

Thus, the liberal retreat from race was rationalized in terms of *realpolitik*. The argument ran like this: America is too racist to support programmes targeted specifically for blacks, especially if these involve any form of preference which is anathema to most whites. Highlighting racial issues, therefore, only serves to drive a wedge in the liberal coalition, driving whites from the Democratic Party, and is ultimately self-defeating. That this reasoning amounted to a capitulation to the white backlash did not faze the political 'realists' since their motives were pure. Indeed, unlike the racial backlash on the right, the liberal backlash was *not* based on racial animus or retrograde politics. On the contrary, these dyed-in-the-wool liberals were convinced that the best or only way to help blacks was to help 'everybody'. Eliminate poverty, they said, and blacks, who count disproportionately among the poor, will be the winners. Achieve full employment, and black employment troubles will be resolved. The upshot, however, was that blacks were asked to subordinate their agenda to a larger movement for liberal reform. In practical terms, this meant forgoing the black protest movement and casting their lot with the Democratic Party.

Thus, after 1965 many white liberals who were erstwhile supporters of the civil rights movement placed a kiss of death on race-based politics and race-based public policy. They not only joined the general retreat from race in the society at large, but in fact cited the white backlash as reason for their own abandonment of race-based politics. In this sense, the liberal retreat from race can be said to represent the left wing of the backlash.

The Howard Address: a Case of 'Semantic Infiltration'

The ideological cleavage that would split the liberal camp was foreshadowed in a commencement address that President Johnson delivered at Howard University on 4 June 1965. The speech, written by Richard Goodwin and Daniel Patrick Moynihan, was riddled with contradiction, and for this very reason epitomizes the political limbo that existed in 1965, as well as the emerging lines of ideological and political division within the liberal camp (Moynihan 1986; Rainwater and Yancey 1967).

The speech, aptly entitled 'To Fulfill these Rights', began with the most radical vision on race that has ever been enunciated by a president of the United States. After reviewing the series of civil rights acts that secured full civil rights for African Americans, Johnson declared: 'But freedom is not enough.' He continued:

> You do not take a person who, for years, has been hobbled by chains and liberate him, bring him up to the starting line of a race and then say, 'you are free to compete with all the others,' and still justly believe that you have been completely fair. Thus it is not enough just to open the gates of opportunity. All our citizens must have the ability to walk through those gates.

Johnson's oratory went a critical step further:

> This is the next and more profound stage of the battle for civil rights. We seek not just freedom but opportunity – not just legal equity but human ability – *not just equality as a right and a theory but equality as a fact and as a result.*

With these last words, Johnson adopted the logic and the language of those arguing for compensatory programmes that would redress past wrongs. Equality, not liberty, would be the defining principle of 'the next and more profound stage' in the liberation struggle.

So far so good. Johnson's speech then took an abrupt detour away from politics to sociology, reflecting the unmistakable imprint of Daniel Patrick Moynihan, who only a month earlier had completed an internal report focusing on problems of the black family. Johnson said:

> ...equal opportunity *is* essential, but not enough. Men and women of all races are born with the same range of abilities. But ability is not just the product of birth. Ability is stretched or stunted by the family you live with, and the neighborhoods you live in, by the school you go to and the poverty or the richness of your surroundings. It is the product of a hundred unseen forces playing upon the infant, the child, and the man.

Compare the language and logic of this passage with the one that follows:

> Overt job discrimination is only one of the important hurdles which must be overcome before color can disappear as a determining factor in the lives and fortunes of

men.... The prevailing view among social scientists holds that there are no significant differences among groups as to the distribution of innate aptitudes or at most very slight differences. On the other hand, differences among individuals are very substantial. The extent to which an individual is able to develop his aptitudes will largely depend upon the circumstances present in the family within which he grows up and the opportunities which he encounters at school and in the larger community (Rainwater and Yancey 1967:125–32).

This latter passage comes from a 1956 book, *The Negro Potential,* by Eli Ginzberg, who was a leading liberal economist of that period. My point is not that Johnson's speechwriters were guilty of plagiarism. Rather it is to take note of their Machiavellian genius. With a rhetorical sleight of hand, Goodwin and Moynihan shifted the discourse away from the radical vision of 'equal results' that emanated from the black protest movement of the 1960s back to the standard liberal cant of the 1950s which held that the black child is stunted by 'circumstances present in the family within which he grows up'. The conceptual groundwork was being laid for a drastic policy reversal: the focus would no longer be on white racism, but rather on the deficiencies of blacks themselves.

[...]

The significance of the Howard address was that it drew a line in the political sands marking how far the Johnson administration would go in supporting the escalating demands of the protest movement. In throwing his support behind the Voting Rights Act, Johnson had gone further than any of his predecessors in jeopardizing the Solid South. The rhetoric of 'equal results' also threatened to antagonize blue-collar workers, Jews and other elements of the Democratic coalition. The covert message in the Howard speech was that, as far as the Democratic Party was concerned, the impending Voting Rights Act marked the end of the Civil Rights Revolution ('the end of the beginning', Johnson said disingenuously, quoting Churchill). If blacks were 'to fulfil these rights', they would have to get their own house in order. Literally!

Thus, behind the equivocal language in Johnson's address was a key policy issue concerning the role of the state in the era following the Civil Rights Act. Would future progress depend on an expansion of anti-racist policies – aimed not only at forms of intentional discrimination but also at the insidious forces of institutionalized racism that have excluded blacks categorically from whole job sectors and other opportunity structures? Or would future progress depend on programmes of social uplift that contemplate 'the gradual absorption of deserving Negroes one by one into white society'?

These alternative policy options were predicated on vastly different assumptions about the nature and sources of racism. The one located the problem within 'white' society and its major institutions, and called for policies to rapidly integrate blacks into jobs, schools and other institutional sectors from which they had historically been excluded. The other assumed that racism was waning, but that blacks generally lacked the requisite education and skills to avail themselves of expanding opportunities. This latter school included both traditional liberals who supported government programmes that 'help blacks to help themselves', and conservatives, including a new genre of black conservatives, who adamantly opposed government intervention, insisting that blacks had to summon the personal and group resources to overcome disabilities of race and class.

[...]

From Infiltration to Subversion: the Moynihan Report

The polarity between anti-racism and social uplift became even more sharply defined by the controversy surrounding the publication of the Moynihan Report three months after Johnson's address at Howard University. Officially titled: 'The Negro Family: The Case for National Action', the report presented a mound of statistics showing high rates of divorce, illegitimacy and female-headed households. Although Moynihan paid lip-service to the argument that unemployment and low wages contributed to family breakdown, he was practically obsessed with a single statistic showing that Aid to Families with Dependent Children (AFDC) continued to increase between 1962 and 1964, despite the fact that unemployment was decreasing. On this meagre empirical basis, Moynihan concluded that poverty was 'feeding upon itself', and that the 'disintegration of the Negro family' had assumed a dynamic all its own, independent of joblessness and poverty. In yet another leap of faith, he asserted that family breakdown was the *source* of most of the problems that afflict black America. In Moynihan's own words: '...at the center of the tangle of pathology is the weakness of the family structure. Once or twice removed, it will be found to be the principal source of most of the aberrant, inadequate, or antisocial behavior that did not establish, but now serves to perpetuate the cycle of poverty and deprivation' (Moynihan 1967a).

Moynihan's critics accused him of inverting cause and effect, and, in doing so, shifting the focus of blame away from societal institutions onto blacks themselves.

[...]

Notwithstanding the efforts of a number of writers, including Moynihan himself, to portray the controversy over the Moynihan Report as fruitless and even counterproductive, it proved to be one of the most formative debates in modern social science. The debate crystallized issues, exposed the conservative assumptions and racial biases that lurked behind mainstream social science, and prompted critics of the report to formulate other positions that challenged the prevailing wisdom about race in America. The principal counterposition – encapsulated in William Ryan's ingenious term 'blaming the victim' – blew the whistle on the tendency of social science to reduce social phenomena to an individual level of analysis, thereby shifting attention away from the structures of inequality and focusing on the behavioural responses of the individuals suffering the effects of these structures. The controversy also stimulated a large body of research – the most notable example is Herbert Gutman's now classic study of *The Black Family in Slavery and Freedom* (1976). This study demolished the myth that 'slavery destroyed the black family' – a liberal myth that allowed social scientists and policy-makers to blame 'history' for the problems in the black family, thus deflecting attention away from the factors in the here and now that tear families apart.

Yet leading liberals today contend that Moynihan was the victim of unfair ideological attack. Moynihan set the tone for this construction of history in an article that he published in *Commentary* under the title: 'The President and the Negro: The Moment Lost'. Again, Moynihan begins on the threshold of truth: 'For the second time in their history, the great task of liberation has been left only half-accomplished. It appears that the nation may be in the process of reproducing the tragic events of the Reconstruction: giving to Negroes the forms of legal equality, but withholding the economic and political resources which are the bases of social equality.' Moynihan goes on to argue, as I have here, that 1965 represented a moment of opportunity: 'The moment came when, as it were, the nation had the resources, and the leadership, and the will to make a *total* as against a partial commitment to the cause of Negro equality. It did not do so.'

Why was the opportunity missed? According to Moynihan, the blame lies not with the forces of racism and reaction, and certainly not with himself, but with 'the liberal Left' who opposed his initiative to address problems in the black family. Specifically, opposition emanated:

> ...from Negro leaders unable to comprehend their opportunity; from civil-rights militants, Negro and white, caught up in a frenzy of arrogance and nihilism; and from white liberals unwilling to expend a jot of prestige to do a difficult but danger-ous job that had to be done, and could have been done. But was not. (Moynihan 1967b:)

Thus, in Moynihan's recapitulation of events, it was his political enemies who, in 'a frenzy of arrogance and nihilism', had aborted the next stage in the Negro revolution that Moynihan had engineered as an influential adviser to the President.

[...]

In recent years there have been attempts to rehabilitate Moynihan, and to portray him as the hapless victim of the ideological excesses of the 1960s. For example, in *The Undeserving Poor* – a book that traces the poverty debates since that decade – Michael Katz asserts that 'because most critics distorted the report, the debate generated more passion than insight'. One result of the attack on Moynihan, he adds mournfully, 'was to accelerate the burial of the culture of poverty as an acceptable concept in liberal reform' (Katz 1989: 24). William Julius Wilson goes even further in suggesting that 'the controversy surrounding the Moynihan report had the effect of curtailing serious research on minority problems in the inner city for over a decade' (Wilson 1987: 4). Yet thanks to Wilson and others, Moynihan's theoretical and political positions would be given new life in the 1980s.

[...]

Wilson struck a number of themes that were at the heart of Moynihan's politi-cal analysis in 1965: that blacks had their political rights, thanks to landmark civil rights legislation; that there was 'a widening gulf' between the black middle class, which was reaping the benefits of an improved climate of tolerance, and the black lower class, which was as destitute and isolated as ever; that blacks were arriving in the nation's cities at a time when employment opportunities, especially in the manufacturing sector, were declining; and that future progress would depend less on tearing down racist barriers than on raising the level of education and skills among poor blacks. The underlying assumption in both cases was that the civil rights revolution was a watershed that more or less resolved the issue of 'race', but that left unaddressed the vexing problems of 'class'. By 'class', however, neither Moynihan nor Wilson was advancing a radical theory that challenged structures of inequality, or that envisioned a restructuring of major political and economic institutions. All they meant was that lower-class blacks needed to acquire the education and skills that are a prerequisite for mobility and that explain the success of the black middle class.

In *The Truly Disadvantaged*, published in 1987, Wilson spelled out the implications of his 'declining significance' thesis for politics and public policy. Again, he arrived at a position that Moynihan had articulated in 1965: that there was no political constituency for policies targeted specifically for blacks, and therefore 'we have to declare that we are doing it for everybody.' [...]

Originally Wilson intended to have 'The Hidden Agenda' as the title of *The Truly Disadvantaged*. Instead he used this as the title for chapter 7, in which he contended that, because there is no political constituency for policies targeted for blacks, it becomes necessary to 'hide' such programmes behind universal programmes 'to which the more advantaged groups of all races and class backgrounds can positively relate'. [...] The notion of a 'hidden agenda' also contradicts Wilson's claim that racism is of 'declining significance'. Indeed, it is *because* of racism that Wilson feels compelled to 'hide' his agenda in the first place. The underlying premise is that America is so racist – so utterly indifferent to the plight of black America, so implacably opposed to any indemnification for three centuries of racial oppression – that it becomes necessary to camouflage policies intended for blacks behind policies that offer benefits to the white majority.

At first blush it might appear odd to portray Wilson as a political clone of Moynihan. Wilson, after all, is an ivory-tower scholar and a political outsider who has described himself as a Social Democrat. Moynihan gave up any pretence of political chastity to become a major player within the Democratic Party. On closer scrutiny, however, Wilson is far from a detached intellectual. In two national elections he has gone on record, via op-ed pieces in the *New York Times*, to advocate race-neutral politics in order to enhance Democratic electoral prospects. And he has quietly served as President Clinton's exculpation for the administration's failure to develop policies to deal with the plight of the nation's ghettos. Whenever Clinton is confronted with this issue, his stock answer is to defend his do-nothing policy by invoking the name of 'the famous African-American sociologist William Julius Wilson', explaining how profoundly influenced he was by his book *The Truly Disadvantaged*, and ending with glowing projections about how blacks stand to benefit from his economic policies. [...]

Thus, whatever differences exist between Moynihan and Wilson, the factor of overriding importance is that both repudiated race-based politics and race-based public policy. Here we come to the delicate but unavoidable issue concerning the role that the race of a social theorist plays in determining what Alvin Gouldner

(1970) refers to as 'the *social* career of a theory'. Not only was Moynihan white, but he wrote at a time of heightened racial consciousness and mobilization, both inside and outside the university. As a white, he was susceptible to charges of racism and of resorting to stereotypes in his depiction of black families. Even the voluble Moynihan was reduced to silence when it came to parrying the charges levelled against him by black scholars and activists.

Wilson, too, has had his critics, but at least he has been immune to charges of 'racism'. Furthermore, Wilson appeared on the stage of history at a time when racial militancy was ebbing. The nation, including the academic establishment, had grown weary of racial conflict, and was eager, like the Democratic Party, to 'get beyond race'. Wilson, clearly, was the right person in the right place and the right time, and, as if this were not enough, his book *The Declining Significance of Race* had the right title – one that satisfied the nation's yearning to put race behind, to pretend that racism was no longer the problem it had been in times past.

[...]

Cornel West: the Left Wing of the Backlash

If books could be judged by their titles, one would think that a book entitled *Race Matters* (West 1993) would be the antithesis of a book entitled *The Declining Significance of Race*. But then again, one must beware of semantic infiltration, and the possibility that titles are subversive of meaning.

[...]

Two of West's essays serve as the basis of the following discussion: 'Nihilism in Black America' and 'Beyond Affirmative Action: Equality and Identity'.

The term 'nihilism' invites semantic confusion. Invoked by a professor of philosophy, the term conjures up hoary philosophical debates concerning the nature of existence and the possibility of objective knowledge. West surely is not claiming that the ghetto is an enactment of some dubious philosophical doctrine. Invoked by a political activist, 'nihilism' calls up associations with Russian revolutionaries who believed that the old order must be utterly eradicated to make way for the new. Again, it is doubtful that West, the political activist, is imputing these motives to ghetto youth. Nor does his use of 'nihilism' suggest the angst and denial of meaning that are often viewed as endemic to modernity. No doubt West could expound on all of these themes, but in describing the urban ghetto, he uses the word specifically to refer to destructive and self-destructive behaviour that is unconstrained by legal or moral norms. But this meaning comes dangerously close to the prevailing view of ghetto youth as driven by aberrant and anti-social tendencies. Alas, does 'nihilism' merely provide an intellectual gloss for ordinary assumptions and claims?

Any such doubts are seemingly dissipated by the book's opening sentence: 'What happened in Los Angeles in April of 1992 was neither a race riot nor a class rebellion. Rather, this monumental upheaval was a multiracial, trans-class, and largely male display of justified social rage.' With this manifesto, West establishes his credentials *as* a person on the left. By the end of the same paragraph, however, West says that 'race was the visible catalyst, not the underlying cause.' Already the reader is left to wonder: does race matter or doesn't it?

In the next paragraph West assumes the rhetorical stance that pervades his book: his is the voice of reason and moderation between liberals and conservatives, each of which is allegedly trapped in rigid orthodoxies that leave us 'intellectually debilitated, morally disempowered, and personally depressed'. Liberals, West avers, are burdened with a simplistic faith in the ability of government to solve our racial problems. Conservatives, on the other hand, blame the problems on blacks and ignore 'public responsibility for the immoral circumstances that haunt our fellow citizens.' Both treat blacks as 'a problem people'. West thus presents himself as mediator between ideological extremes. He is a leftist who does not resort to a crude economic determinism that denies human freedom and that relieves the poor of moral responsibility for their actions. And he is a theologian who does not use morality to evade public responsibility for social wrongs.

[...]

According to West, despite the tribulations going back to slavery, blacks have always been endowed with 'cultural armor to beat back the demons of hopelessness, meaningless, lovelessness'. He points out that until the 1970s the rate of suicide was comparatively *low* among blacks, but today young blacks have one of the highest rates of suicide. Thus for West the question becomes: what has happened to 'the cultural structures that once sustained black life in America' and 'are no longer able to fend off the nihilistic threat?' His answer focuses on two factors:

1 *The saturation of market forces and market moralities in black life.* By this West means that blacks have succumbed to the materialism and hedonism that pervade American culture and that 'edge out nonmarket values – love, care, service to others – handed down by preceding generations'. If blacks are more susceptible to these corrupting influences than others, it is because the poor have 'a limited capacity to ward off self-contempt and self-hatred'.
2 *The crisis in black leadership.* Here West bemoans the failure of black leaders to carry on a tradition of leadership that was at once aggressive and inspirational. One reason for this failure is the corruption of the new middle class by their immersion into mass culture.

But another reason that 'quality leadership is on the wane' has to do with 'the gross deterioration of personal, familial, and communal relations among African-Americans'. With families in decline and communities in shambles, the basis for effective leadership is lost.

Thus, West harks back to the halcyon days when there was 'a vital community bound by its ethical ideals'. Unfortunately, oppression does not always produce such pleasing outcomes, and the victims of oppression are not always ennobled by their experience and an inspiration to the rest of us.

West's problem, to repeat, is not that he discusses crime, violence, drugs and the other notorious ills of ghetto life. Rather the problem is that he presents social breakdown and cultural disintegration as a problem *sui generis*, with an existence and momentum independent of the forces that gave rise to it in the first place.

Moynihan, too, had held that centuries of injustice had 'brought about deep-seated structural distortions in the life of the Negro American'. But he added a remarkable addendum: 'At this point, the present pathology is capable of perpetuating itself without assistance from the white world' (Moynihan 1967b: 93). Similarly, West traces nihilism to centuries of injustice, but goes on to claim that nihilism is so embedded in the life of the ghetto that it assumes a life all its own. At least this is what West implies when he writes that 'culture is as much a structure as the economy or politics'. Indeed, the whole point of West's critique of 'liberal structuralism' is that nihilism is not reducible to political economy. It is precisely because nihilism is so deeply embedded that this 'cultural structure' must be addressed as a force in its own right.

It takes hairsplitting distinctions that do not bear close scrutiny to maintain that West's view of nihilism is different from the conservative view of ghetto culture as deeply pathological, and as the chief source of the problems that beset African Americans. Despite his frequent caveats, West has succeeded in shifting the focus of blame onto the black community. The affliction is *theirs* – something we shall call 'nihilism'.

It is also theirs to resolve. As with the Moynihan Report, the regressive implications of West's theory become clear when one examines his praxis. West asks: 'What is to be done about this nihilistic threat?' But his answer is sadly deficient. He calls for 'a politics of conversion' – a frail attempt to use radical vernacular as a cover for ideas that are anything but radical. 'Like alcoholism and drug addiction,' West explains, 'nihilism is a disease of the soul.' How does one cure a disease of the soul? West's prescription (to paraphrase Jencks) is to change the nihilist, not the system. To quote West again:

> Nihilism is not overcome by arguments or analysis; it is tamed by love and care. Any disease of the soul must be conquered by a turning of one's soul. This turning is done through one's own affirmation of one's worth – an affirmation fueled by the concern of others. A love ethic must be at the center of a politics of conversion (West 1993: 19).

Here, alas, is the reason for the acclaim that has been heaped on *Race Matters*. The cure for the nihilism that so frightens white America is not a resumption of the war on poverty. Nor is it a resumption of the movement against racism. West, of course, would endorse both, but he has also been explicit in saying that 'liberal structuralism' is not equipped to deal with 'the self-destructive and inhumane actions of black people'.

One can almost hear the national sigh of relief from those who feared that expensive new programmes of social reconstruction and a renewed commitment to affirmative action might become necessary to control the disorder emanating from the ghettos of America. Instead we have an inexpensive palliative: a crusade against nihilism to be waged from within the black community. So much the better that this proposal is advanced not by another black conservative whose politics might be suspect, but by a self-proclaimed Socialist. [...]

One cannot fault West for trying to bridge the chasm between religion and politics. However, he has not placed himself in the tradition of Martin Luther

King, who invoked religious symbols and appealed to spiritual values in order to mobilize popular support behind a political movement. King did not believe that a love ethic could ever serve as an antidote to spiritual breakdown. The only remedy was a political transformation that eliminated the conditions that eat away at the human spirit. West, on the other hand, offers no political framework for *his* so-called politics of conversion. Indeed, he explicitly divorces nihilism from political economy, thus implying that moral redemption is to be achieved through some mysterious 'turning of one's soul'.

West cannot escape the retrograde implications of his position with disclaimers that 'unlike conservative behaviorists, the politics of conversion situates these actions within inhuman circumstances.' He ignores his own admonition that 'to call on black people to be agents makes sense only if we also examine the dynamics of this victimization against which their agency will, in part, be exercised.' And while he is guided by 'a vision of moral regeneration and political insurgency for the purpose of fundamental social change for all who suffer from socially induced misery', he fails to translate this prophetic ideal into a political praxis. The practical implication of West's position is to substitute a vapid and utterly inconsequential 'politics of conversion' for a genuine political solution – one that would call upon the power and resources of the national government for what is at bottom a national problem and a national disgrace.

It should come as no surprise that the most prominent convert to West's politics of conversion is President Clinton. In a speech delivered to a Memphis church in 1993, Clinton practically echoed West in asserting that there is a crisis of the spirit. The ramifications for public policy should have been predictable: 'Sometimes, there are no answers from the outside in. Sometimes, all of the answers have to come from the values and the stirrings and the voices that speak to us from within' (*New York Times* 14 November 1993). Thus are legitimate spiritual concerns used as a subterfuge for political and moral abdication. The irony is made still more bitter by the fact that Clinton gave his speech in the same Memphis church where Martin Luther King delivered his last sermon the night before his assassination in 1968.

Not only does West shift the focus of analysis and of blame away from the structures of racial oppression, but in his chapter entitled 'Beyond Affirmative Action' he undercuts the single policy that has gone a decisive step beyond equal rights in the direction of equal results. West is *not* opposed to affirmative action, but he engages in a tortuous reasoning that subverts the whole logic behind it. Thus, he begins on the one hand by declaring that in principle he favours a class-based affirmative action (as does William Julius Wilson). On the other hand, he knows that such a policy is politically unrealistic. He also knows that if affirmative action in its present form were abolished, then 'racial and sexual discrimination would return with a vengeance.' Why, then, all this hairsplitting? Even if a class-based affirmative action could be enacted, few of the benefits would filter down to African Americans who are not only most in need, but also have unique claims for compensatory treatment. Nor would working-class whites who become lawyers and doctors on the basis of affirmative action provide the black community with the professional talent that it sorely needs.

In short, affirmative action is meant to counteract the evils of caste, not of class. It is predicated on a realization that blacks have been victims of a system of oppression that goes far beyond the disabilities associated with class disadvantage, and therefore warrants a special remedy. West's equivocation with respect to race-based affirmative action is the clearest indication of how little race matters in his theoretical framework and in his agenda for change.

Reminiscent of Moynihan and Wilson, West's approach for helping blacks is to help 'everybody'. Like them, he provides a respectable liberal cover for evading the issue of race, and still worse, backing off from race-targeted policies like affirmative action, all in the name of getting 'beyond race'. West prides himself on steering 'a course between the Scylla of environmental determinism and the Charybdis of a blaming-the-victims perspective'. Unfortunately, he ends up in a political never-never land where, as Du Bois once said in his critique of historiography, 'nobody seems to have done wrong and everybody was right' (Du Bois 1935: 714). And nothing changes.

This nation's ruling elites need to be told that there is no exit from the current morass until they confront the legacy of slavery and resume the unfinished racial agenda. It is *their* nihilism that deserves our condemnation – the crime, the immorality, the self-destructive folly of tolerating racial ghettos and excluding yet another generation of black youth from the American Dream.

Conclusion

Martin Luther King's 'Letter from a Birmingham Jail' has become a part of this nation's political folklore. However, its specific contents have been all but expunged from our collective memory. The letter was not a condemnation of racism. Nor was it, like his celebrated 'I Have a Dream' oration – whose contents *are* remembered – an evocation of American ideals or a prophetic vision of better times ahead. King was responding to a letter signed by eight priests, rabbis and ministers that appeared in the *Birmingham News* while he was imprisoned. The letter spoke sympathetically of 'rights consistently denied', but criticized King's tactics as 'unwise and untimely' and called for a 'constructive and realistic approach', one that would substitute negotiation for confrontation. In his response King acknowledged their sincerity in seeking 'a better path', but explained why confrontation and crisis were necessary in order to shake white society out of its apathy and intransigence. Mincing no words, King issued the following indictment of the so-called moderate:

> I have almost reached the regrettable conclusion that the Negroes' great stumbling block in the stride toward freedom is not the White Citizens' 'Councilor' or the Ku Klux Klanner, but the white moderate who is more devoted to 'order' than to justice; who prefers a negative peace which is the absence of tension to a positive peace which is the presence of justice; who constantly says 'I agree with you in the goal you seek, but *I* can't agree with your methods of direct action'; who lives by the myth of time and who constantly advises the Negro to wait until 'a more convenient season' (King 1992: 91).

Was there hyperbole in King's assertion that the great stumbling block in the stride for freedom was not the Council or the Klan but those who seek a middle ground and would settle for a negative peace? Perhaps. As is often argued, liberals are not *the* enemy. However, the enemy depends on the so-called liberal to put a kinder and gentler face on racism; to subdue the rage of the oppressed; to raise false hopes that change is imminent; to modulate the demands for complete liberation; to divert protest; and to shift the onus of responsibility for America's greatest crime away from powerful institutions that *could* make a difference onto individuals who have been rendered powerless by these very institutions.

The liberal retreat from race since the civil rights movement is full of political paradox. When forced to confront the issue, the liberal will argue that in a racist society, race-based politics are not viable precisely because blacks are an isolated and despised minority. As with much race-think, this is upside-down and inside-out. It is precisely because blacks were an isolated and despised minority that they were forced to seek redress outside the framework of electoral politics. The civil rights movement was triumphant in part because it tapped the lode of revolutionary potential within the black community, and in part because it galvanized the support of political allies outside the black community, including white liberals. Furthermore, this movement not only achieved its immediate objectives, but also was the major catalyst for progressive change in the twentieth century. As Aldon Morris writes at the conclusion of *The Origins of the Civil Rights Movement*:

> ...the civil rights movement served as a training ground for many of the activists who later organized movements within their own communities. Indeed, the modern women's movement, student movement, farm workers' movement, and others of the period were triggered by the unprecedented scale of nontraditional politics in the civil rights movement (Morris 1984: 288).

A common refrain from the right is that advocates of affirmative action are guilty of the very thing that they say they are against – namely, treating blacks as a separate class. Again, this reasoning is upside-down and inside-out. The truth is that it is the *refusal* to see race – the wilful colour blindness of the liberal camp - that acquiesces to the racial *status quo*, and does so by consigning blacks to a twilight zone where they are politically invisible. In this way elements of the left unwittingly join the right in evading any reckoning with America's greatest crime – slavery – and its legacy in the present.

References

Commentary (1964), 'Liberalism and the Negro: A Round-Table Discussion', *Commentary*, vol. 37, March.

Du Bois, W. E. B. (1935), *Black Reconstruction*, Harcourt Brace, New York.

Friedman, M. (1963), 'The White Liberal's Retreat', *Atlantic Monthly*, vol. 211, January.

Ginzberg, E. (1956), *The Negro Potential*, Columbia University Press, New York.

Gouldner, A. (1970), *The Coming Crisis of Western Sociology*, Basic Books, New York.

Gutman, H. G. (1976), *The Black Family in Slavery and Freedom, 1750–1925*, Pantheon Books, New York.

Katz, M. B. (1989), *The Undeserving Poor*, Pantheon, New York.

King, M. L. Jr. (1963), *Why We Can't Wait*, Harper & Row, New York.

King, M. L. Jr. (1992), 'Letter from a Birmingham Jail', in *I have a Dream and Speeches that Changed the World*, Harper San Francisco, San Francisco.

Morris, A. (1984), *The Origins of the Civil Rights Movement*, Free Press, New York.

Moynihan, D. P. (1967a), *The Negro Family: The Case for National Action*, reproduced in full in Rainwater and Yancey, op. cit.

Moynihan, D. P. (1967b), 'The President and the Negro: The Moment Lost', *Commentary*, vol. 43, February.

Moynihan, D. P. (1986), *Family and Nation*, Harcourt Brace Jovanovich, New York.

New York Times (1993), 'Excerpts from Clinton's Speech to Black Ministers', *New York Times*, 14 November.

Rainwater, L., and Yancey, W. L. (1967), eds, *The Moynihan Report and the Politics of Controversy*, MIT Press, Cambridge, Mass.

West, C. (1993), *Race Matters*, Beacon Press, Boston.

Weyl, N. (1960), *The Negro in American Civilization*, Washington DC, Public Affairs Press.

Wilson, W. J. (1978), *The Declining Significance of Race*, University of Chicago Press, Chicago.

Wilson, W. J. (1987), *The Truly Disadvantaged*, Chicago University Press, Chicago.

Young, W. M. Jr. (1963), *To Be Equal*, McGraw-Hill, New York.

'CLASS RACISM'

ÉTIENNE BALIBAR

Academic analyses of racism, though according chief importance to the study of racist theories, none the less argue that 'sociological' racism is a popular phenomenon. Given this supposition, the development of racism within the working class (which, to committed socialists and communists, seems counter to the natural order of things) comes to be seen as the effect of a tendency allegedly inherent in the masses. Institutional racism finds itself projected into the very construction of that psycho-sociological category that is 'the masses'. We must therefore attempt to analyse the process of displacement which, moving from classes to masses, presents these latter both as the privileged *subjects* of racism and its favoured *objects*.

Can one say that a social class, by its situation and its ideology (not to mention its identity), is predisposed to racist attitudes and behaviour? This question has mainly been debated in connection with the rise of Nazism, first speculatively and then later by taking various empirical indicators (Aycoberry 1981). The result is quite paradoxical since there *is* hardly a social class on which suspicion has not fallen, though a marked predilection has been shown for the 'petty bourgeoisie'. But this is a notoriously ambiguous concept, which is more an expression of the aporias of a class analysis conceived as a dividing up of the population into mutually exclusive slices. As with every question of origins in which a political charge is concealed, it makes sense to turn the question around: not to look for the foundations of the racism which invades everyday life (or the movement which provides the vehicle for it) in the nature of the petty bourgeoisie, but to attempt to understand how the development of racism causes a 'petty bourgeois' mass to emerge out of a diversity of material situations. For the misconceived question of the class bases of racism, we shall thus substitute a more crucial and complex question, which that former question is in part intended to mask: that of the relations between racism, as a supplement to nationalism, and the irreducibility of class conflict in society. We shall find it necessary to ask how the development of racism displaces class conflict or, rather, in what way class conflict is always already transformed by a social relation in which there is an inbuilt tendency to racism; and also, conversely, how the fact that the nationalist alternative to the class struggle specifically takes the form of racism may be considered as the index of the irreconcilable character of that struggle. This does not of course mean that it is not crucial to examine how, in a given conjuncture, the class conditions [*la condition de classe*] (made up of the material conditions of existence and labour, though also of ideological traditions and practical relationships to politics) determine the effects of racism in society: the frequency and forms of the 'acting out' of racism, the discourse which expresses it and the membership of organized racist movements.

The traces of a constant overdetermination of racism by the class struggle are as universally detectable in its history as the nationalist determination, and everywhere they are connected with the core of meaning of its fantasies and practices. This suffices to demonstrate that we are dealing here with a determination that is much more concrete and decisive than the generalities dear to the sociologists of 'modernity'. It is wholly inadequate to see racism (or the nationalism – racism dyad) either as one of the paradoxical expressions of the individualism or egalitarianism which are supposed to characterize modern societies (following the old dichotomy of 'closed', 'hierarchical' societies and 'open', 'mobile' societies) or a defensive reaction against that individualism, seen as expressing nostalgia for a social order based on the existence of a 'community' (Popper 1966; Dumont 1986). Individualism exists only in the concrete forms of market competition (including the competition between labour powers) in unstable equilibrium with association between individuals under the constraints of the class struggle. Egalitarianism only exists in the contradictory forms of political democracy (where that democracy exists), the 'welfare state' (where that exists), the polarization of conditions of existence, cultural segregation and reformist or revolutionary utopias. It is these determinations, and not mere anthropological figures, which confer an 'economic' dimension upon racism.

Nevertheless, the *heterogeneity of* the historical forms of the relationship between racism and the class struggle poses a problem. This ranges from the way in which anti-semitism developed into a bogus 'anti-capitalism' around the theme of 'Jewish money' to the way in which racial stigma and class hatred are combined today in the category of immigration. Each of these configurations is irreducible (as are the corresponding conjunctures), which make it impossible to define any simple relationship of 'expression' (or, equally, of substitution) between racism and class struggle.

In the manipulation of anti-semitism as an anti-capitalist delusion, which chiefly occurred between 1870 and 1945 (which is, we should note, the key period of confrontation between the European bourgeois states and organized proletarian internationalism), we find not only the designation of a scapegoat as an object of proletarian revolt, the exploitation of divisions within the proletariat and the projective representation of the ills of an abstract social system through the imaginary personification of those who control it (even though this mechanism is essential to the functioning of racism).[1] We also find the 'fusion' of the two historical narratives which are capable of acting as metaphors for each other: on the one hand, the narrative of the formation of nations at the expense of the lost unity of 'Christian Europe' and, on the other, that of the conflict between national independence and the internationalization of capitalist economic relations, which brought with it the attendant threat of an internationalization of the class struggle. This is why the Jew, as an internally excluded element common to all nations but also, negatively, by virtue of the theological hatred to which he is subject, as witness to the love that is supposed to unite the 'Christian peoples', may, in the imaginary, be identified with the 'cosmopolitanism of capital' which threatens the national independence of every country while at the same time reactivating the trace of the lost unity.[2]

The figure is quite different when anti-immigrant racism achieves a maximum of identification between class situation and ethnic origin (the real bases for which have always existed in the interregional, international or intercontinental mobility of the working class; this has at times been a mass phenomenon, at times residual, but it has never been eliminated and is one of the specifically proletarian characteristics of its condition). Racism combines this identification with a deliberate confusion of antagonistic social functions: thus the themes of the 'invasion' of French society by North Africans or of immigration being responsible for unemployment are connected with that of the money of the oil sheikhs who are buying up 'our' businesses, 'our' housing stock or 'our' seaside resorts. And this partly explains why the Algerians, Tunisians or Moroccans have to be referred to generically as 'Arab' (not to mention the fact that this signifier, which functions as a veritable 'switch word', also connects together these themes and those of terrorism, Islam and so on). Other configurations should not, however, be forgotten, including those which are the product of an inversion of terms: for example, the theme of the 'proletarian nation', which was perhaps invented in the 1920s by Japanese nationalism (Anderson 1983: 92–3) and was destined to play a crucial role in the crystallization of Nazism, which cannot be left out of consideration when one looks at the ways in which it has recently reappeared.

The complexity of these configurations also explains why it is impossible to hold purely and simply to the idea of racism *being used* against 'class conscious-ness' (as though this latter would necessarily emerge naturally from the class condition, *unless* it were blocked, misappropriated or de-natured by racism), whereas we accept as an indispensable working hypothesis that 'class' and 'race' constitute the two antinomic poles of a permanent dialectic, which is at the heart of modern representations of history. Moreover, we suspect that the instrumen-talist, conspiracy-theory visions of racism within the labour movement or among its theorists (we know what high price was to be paid for these: it is tremendously to the credit of Wilhelm Reich that he was one of the first to foresee this), along with the mechanistic visions which see in racism the 'reflection' of a particular class condition, have also largely the function of denying the presence of nation-alism in the working class and its organizations or, in other words, denying the internal conflict between nationalism and class ideology on which the mass struggle against racism (as well as the revolutionary struggle against capitalism) depends. It is the evolution of this internal conflict I should like to illustrate by discussing here some historical aspects of 'class racism'.

Several historians of racism (e.g. Poliakov 1974; Duchet and Rebérioux 1969; Guillaumin 1972; Williams 1944 on modern slavery) have laid emphasis upon the fact that the modern notion of race, insofar as it is invested in a discourse of contempt and discrimination and serves to split humanity up into a 'super-humanity' and a 'sub-humanity', did not initially have a national (or ethnic), but a class signification or rather (since the point is to represent the inequality of social classes as inequalities of nature) a caste signification. From this point of view, it has a twofold origin: first, in the aristocratic representation of the heredi-tary nobility as a superior 'race' (that is, in fact, the mythic narrative by which an aristocracy, whose domination is already coming under threat, assures itself of the legitimacy of its political privileges and idealizes the dubious continuity of its genealogy); and second, in the slave owners' representation of those popula-tions subject to the slave trade as inferior 'races', ever predestined for servitude and incapable of producing an autonomous civilization. Hence the discourse of blood, skin colour and cross-breeding. It is only retrospectively that the notion of race was 'ethnicized', so that it could be integrated into the nationalist complex, the jumping-off point for its successive subsequent metamorphoses. Thus it is clear that, from the very outset, racist representations of history stand in relation to the class struggle. But this fact takes on its full significance only if we examine the way in which the notion of race has evolved, and the impact of nationalism upon it from the earliest figures of 'class racism' onwards – in other words, if we examine its political determination.

The aristocracy did not initially conceive and present itself in terms of the category of 'race': this is discourse which developed at a late stage,[3] the function of which is clearly defensive (as can be seen from the example of France with the myth of 'blue blood' and the 'Frankish' or 'Germanic' origin of the hereditary nobility), and which developed when the absolute monarchy centralized the state at the expense of the feudal lords and began to 'create' within its bosom a new administrative and financial aristocracy which was bourgeois in origin, thus marking a decisive step in the formation of the nation state. Even more interesting is the case of Spain in the Classical Age, as analysed by Poliakov: the persecution of the Jews after the *Reconquista,* one of the indispensable mechanisms in the establishment of Catholicism as state religion, is also the trace of the 'multinational' culture against which Hispanization (or rather Castilianization) was carried out. It is therefore intimately linked to the formation of this prototype of European nationalism. Yet it took on an even more ambivalent meaning when it gave rise to the 'statutes of the purity of the blood' (*limpieza de sangre*) which the whole discourse of European and American racism was to inherit: a product of the disavowal of the original interbreeding with the Moors and the Jews, the hereditary definition of the *raza* (and the corresponding procedures for establishing who could be accorded a certificate of purity) serves in effect both to isolate an internal aristocracy and to confer upon the whole of the 'Spanish people' a fictive nobility, to make it a 'people of masters' at the point when, by terror, genocide, slavery and enforced Christianization, it was conquering and dominating the largest of the colonial empires. In this exemplary line of development, class racism was already transformed into nationalist racism, though it did not, in the process, disappear (Poliakov 1974, vol. 2: 222–32).

What is, however, much more decisive for the matter in hand is the overturning of values we see occurring from the first half of the nineteenth century onwards. Aristocratic racism (the prototype of what analysts today call 'self-referential racism', which begins by elevating the group, which controls the discourse to the status of a 'race' – hence the importance of its imperialist legacy in the colonial context: however lowly their origins and no matter how vulgar their interests or their manners, the British in India and the French in Africa would all see themselves as members of a modern nobility) is already indirectly related to the primitive accumulation of capital, if only by its function in the colonizing nations. The industrial revolution, at the same time as it creates specifically capitalist relations of production, gives rise, to the *new racism* of the bourgeois era (historically speaking, the first 'neo-racism'): the one which has as its target the *proletariat* in its dual status as exploited population (one might even say super-exploited, before the beginnings of the social state) and politically threatening population.

Louis Chevalier (1973) has described the relevant network of significations in detail. It is at this point, with regard to the 'race of labourers' that the notion of race becomes detached from its historico-theological connotations to enter the field of equivalences between sociology, psychology, imaginary biology and the pathology of the 'social body'. The reader will recognize here the obsessive themes of police/detective, medical and philanthropic literature, and hence of literature in general (of which it is one of the fundamental dramatic mechanisms and one of the political keys of social 'realism'). For the first time those aspects typical of every procedure of racialization of a social group right down to our own day are condensed in a single discourse: material and spiritual poverty, criminality, congenital vice (alcoholism, drugs), physical and moral defects, dirtiness, sexual promiscuity and the specific diseases which threaten humanity with 'degeneracy'. And there is a characteristic oscillation in the presentation of these themes: either the workers themselves constitute a degenerate race or it is their presence and contact with them or indeed their condition itself which constitute a crucible of degeneracy for the 'race' of citizens and nationals. Through these themes, there forms the phantasmatic equation of 'labouring classes' with 'dangerous classes', the fusion of a socioeconomic category with an anthropological and moral category, which will serve to underpin all the variants of socio-biological (and also psychiatric) determinism, by taking psuedo-scientific credentials from the Darwinian theory of evolution, comparative anatomy and crowd psychology, but particularly by becoming invested in a tightly knit network of institutions of social surveillance and control (Netchine 1978; Murard and Zylberman 1976).

Now this class racism is indissociable from fundamental historical processes which have developed unequally right down to the present day. I can mention these only briefly here. First, class racism is connected with a political problem that is crucial for the constitution of the nation state. The 'bourgeois revolutions' – and in particular the French Revolution, by its radical juridical egalitarianism – had raised the question of the political rights of the masses in an irreversible manner. This was to be the object of one and a half centuries of social struggles. The idea of a *difference in nature* between individuals had become juridically and morally contradictory, if not inconceivable. It was, however, politically indispensable, so long as the dangerous classes (who posed a threat to the established social order, property and the power of the 'elites') had to be excluded by force and by legal means from political 'competence' and confined to the margins of the polity – as long, that is, as it was important to *deny them citizenship* by showing, and by being oneself persuaded, that they constitutionally 'lacked' the qualities of fully fledged or normal humanity. Two anthropologies clashed here: that of equality of birth and that of a hereditary inequality which made it possible to re-naturalize social antagonisms.

Now, this operation was overdetermined from the start by national ideology. Disraeli (who showed himself, elsewhere, to be a surprising imperialist theorist of the 'superiority of the Jews' over the Anglo-Saxon 'superior race' itself; Arendt 1986: 68; Pourkov 1974, vol. 3: 328–37; Polanyi 1957: 290ff.) admirably summed this up when he explained that the problem of contemporary states was the tendency for a single social formation to split into 'two nations'. In so doing, he indicated the path which might be taken by the dominant classes when confronted with the progressive organization of the class struggle: first divide the mass of the 'poor' (in particular by according the qualities of national authenticity, sound health, morality and racial integrity, which were precisely the opposite of the industrial pathology, to the peasants and the 'traditional' artisans); then progressively displace the markers of dangerousness and heredity from the 'labouring classes' as a whole on to foreigners, and in particular immigrants and colonial subjects, at the same time as the introduction of universal suffrage is moving the boundary line between 'citizens' and 'subjects' to the frontiers of nationality. In this process, however, there was always a characteristic lag between what was supposed to happen and the actual situation (even in countries like France, where the national population was not institutionally segregated and was subject to no original apartheid, except if one extends one's purview to take in the whole of the imperial territory): class racism against the popular classes continued to exist (and, at the same time, these classes remained particularly susceptible to racial stigmatization, and remained extremely ambivalent in their attitude towards racism). Which brings us to another permanent aspect of class racism.

I am referring to what must properly be called the *institutional racialization of manual labour*. It would be easy to find distant origins for this, origins as old as class society itself. In this regard, there is no significant difference between the way contempt for work and the manual worker was expressed among the philosophical elites of slave-owning Greece and the way a man like Taylor could, in 1909, describe the natural predisposition of certain individuals for the exhausting, dirty, repetitive tasks which required physical strength, but no intelligence or initiative (the 'man of the type of the ox' of the *Principles of Scientific Management*: paradoxically, an inveterate propensity for 'systematic soldiering' is also attributed to this same man: this is why he needs a 'man to stand over him' before he can work in conformity with his nature; Linhart 1976; Coriat 1979; Balibar 1983). However, the industrial revolution and capitalist wage labour here effect a displacement. What is now the object of contempt – and in turn fuels fears – is no longer manual labour pure and simple (we shall, by contrast, see this theoretically idealized – in the context of paternalistic, archaizing ideologies – in the form of 'craft work'), but *mechanized* physical work, which has become 'the appendage of the machine' and therefore subject to a violence that is both physical and symbolic without immediate precedent (which we know, moreover, does not disappear with the new phases of the industrial revolution, but is rather perpetuated both in 'modernized' and 'intellectualized' forms – as well as in 'archaic' forms in a great many sectors of production).

This process modifies the status of the human body (the human status of the body): it creates *body-men*, men whose body is a machine-body, that is fragmented and dominated, and used to perform one isolable function or gesture, being both destroyed in its integrity and fetishized, atrophied and hypertrophied in its 'useful' organs. Like all violence, this is inseparable from a resistance and also from a sense of guilt. The quantity of 'normal' work can be recognized and extracted from the worker's body only retrospectively, once its limits have been fixed by struggle: the rule is overexploitation, the tendential destruction of the organism (which will be metaphorized as 'degeneracy') and, at the very least, excess in the repression of the intellectual functions involved in work. This is an unbearable process for the worker, but one which is no more 'acceptable', without ideological and phantasmatic elaboration, for the worker's masters: the fact that there are body-men means that there are *men without bodies*. That the body-men are men with fragmented and mutilated bodies (if only by their 'separation' from intelligence) means that the individuals of each of these types has to be equipped with *a superbody*, and that sport and ostentatious virility have to be developed, if the threat hanging over the human race if to be fended off...[4]

Only this historical situation, these specific social relations make it possible fully to understand the process of aestheticization (and therefore of sexualization, in fetishist mode) of the body which characterizes all the variants of modern racism, by giving rise either to the stigmatization of the 'physical marks' of racial inferiority or to the idealization of the 'human type' of the superior race. They cast light upon the true meaning of the recourse to biology in the history of racist theories, which has nothing whatever to do with the influence of scientific discoveries, but is, rather, a metaphor for – and an idealization of – the somatic phantasm. Academic biology, and many other theoretical discourses, can fulfil this function, provided they are articulated to the visibility of the body, its ways of being and behaving, its limbs and its emblematic organs. We should here, in accordance with the hypotheses formulated elsewhere regarding neo-racism and its link with the recent ways in which intellectual labour has been broken down into isolated operations, extend the investigation by describing the 'somatization' of intellectual capacities, and hence their racialization, a process visible everywhere – from the instrumentalization of IQ to the aestheticization of the executive as decision-maker, intellectual and athlete.

But there is yet another determining aspect in the constitution of class racism. The working class is a population that is both heterogeneous and fluctuating, its 'boundaries' being by definition imprecise, since they depend on ceaseless transformations of the labour process and movements of capital. Unlike aristocratic castes, or even the leading fractions of the bourgeoisie, it is not a social caste. What class racism (and, *a fortiori*, nationalist class racism, as in the case of immigrants) tends to produce is, however, the equivalent of a caste closure at least for one part of the working class. More precisely, it is maximum possible closure where social mobility is concerned, combined with maximum possible openness as regards the *flows* of proletarianization.

Let us put things another way. The logic of capitalist accumulation involves *two* contradictory aspects here: on the one hand, mobilizing or permanently destabilizing the conditions of life and work, in such a way as to ensure competition on the labour market, draw new labour power continually from the 'industrial reserve army' and maintain a relative overpopulation; on the other hand, stabilizing collectivities of workers over long periods (over several generations), to 'educate' them for work and 'bond' them to companies (and also to bring into play the mechanism of correspondence between a 'paternalist' political hegemony and a worker 'familialism'). On the one hand, class condition, which relates purely to the wage relation, has nothing to do with antecedents or descendants; ultimately, even the notion of 'class belonging' is devoid of any practical meaning; all that counts is class situation, *hic et nunc*. On the other hand, at least some of the workers have to be the sons of workers, *a social heredity* has to be created.[5] But with this, in practice, the capacities for resistance and organization also increase.

It was in response to these contradictory demands that the demographic and immigration policies and policies of urban segregation, which were set in place both by employers and the state from the middle of the nineteenth century onwards – policies which D. Bertaux (1977) has termed 'anthroponomic' practices – were born. These have two sides to them: a paternalistic aspect (itself closely connected to nationalist propaganda) and a disciplinary aspect, an aspect of 'social warfare' against the savage masses and an aspect of 'civilizing' (in all senses of the term) these same masses. This dual nature we can still see perfectly illustrated today in the combined social and police approach to the 'suburbs' and 'ghettos'. It is not by chance that the current racist complex grafts itself on to the 'population problem' (with its series of connotations: birth rate, depopulation and overpopulation, 'interbreeding', urbanization, social housing, public health, unemployment) and focuses preferentially on the question of the *second genera-tion* of what are here improperly called 'immigrants' with the object of finding out whether they will carry on as the previous generation (the 'immigrant workers' properly so-called) – the danger being that they will develop a much greater degree of social combativeness, combining class demands with cultural demands; or whether they will add to the number of 'declassed' individuals, occupying an unstable position between sub-proletarianization and 'exit' from the working class. This is the main issue for class racism, both for the dominant class and for the popular classes themselves: to mark with generic signs populations which are collectively destined for capitalist exploitation – or which have to be held in reserve for it – at the very moment when the economic process is tearing them away from the direct control of the system (or, quite simply, by mass unemploy-ment, is rendering the previous controls inoperative). The problem is to keep 'in their place', from generation to generation, those who have no fixed place; and for this, it is necessary that they have a genealogy. And also to unify in the imaginary the contradictory imperatives of nomadism and social heredity, the domestication of generations and the disqualification of resistances.

If these remarks are well founded, then they may throw some light on what are themselves the contradictory aspects of what I shall not hesitate to call the 'self-racialization' of the working class. There is here a whole spectrum of social experiences and ideological forms we might mention: from the organization of collectivities of workers around symbols of ethnic or national origin to the way in which a certain workerism, centred on criteria of class origins (and, conse-quently, on the institution of the working-class family, on the bond which only the family establishes between the 'individual' and 'his class') and the over-valorization of work (and, consequently, the virility which it alone confers), reproduces, within the ambit of 'class consciousness', some part of the set of representations of the 'race of workers' (Noiriel 1985; Duroux 1982; Fremontier 1980). Admittedly, the radical forms of workerism, at least in France, were pro-duced more by intellectuals and political apparatuses aiming to 'represent' the working class (from Proudhon down to the Communist Party) than by the workers themselves. The fact remains that they correspond to a tendency on the part of the working class to form itself into a closed 'body', to preserve gains that have been made and traditions of struggle and to turn back against bourgeois society, the signifiers of class racism. It is from this reactive origin that the ambivalence characterizing workerism derives: the desire to escape from the condition of exploitation and the rejection of the contempt to which it is subject. Absolutely nowhere is this ambivalence more evident than in its relation to nationalism and to xenophobia. To the extent that in practice they reject official nationalism (when they do reject it), the workers produce in outline a political alternative to the perversion of class struggles. To the extent, however, that they project onto foreigners their fears and resentment, despair and defiance, it is not only that they are *fighting competition*; in addition, and much more profoundly, they are trying to escape their own exploitation. It is a hatred of *themselves*, as proletarians – insofar as they are in danger of being drawn back into the mill of proletarianization – that they are showing.

To sum up, just as there is a constant relation of reciprocal determination between nationalism and racism, there is a relation of reciprocal determination between 'class racism' and 'ethnic racism' and *these two determinations are not independent*. Each produces its effects, to some extent, in the field of the other and under constraints imposed by the other. Have we, in retracing this over-determination in its broad outline (and in trying to show how it illuminates the concrete manifestations of racism and the constitution of its theoretical discourse), answered the questions we posed at the beginning of this essay? It would be more accurate to say that we have reformulated them. What has elsewhere been called the excess which, by comparison with nationalism, is constitutive of racism turns out at the same time to be a shortfall as far as the class struggle is concerned. But, though that *excess* is linked to the fact that nationalism is formed in opposition to the class struggle (even though it utilizes its dynamic), and that shortfall is linked to the fact that the class struggle finds itself repressed by nationalism, *the two do not compensate one another*; their effects tend, rather, to be combined. The important thing is not to decide whether nationalism is first and foremost a means of imagining and pursuing the unity of state and society, which then runs up against the contradictions of the class struggle, or whether it is primarily a reaction to the obstacles which the class struggle puts in the way of national unity. By contrast, it is crucially important to note that, in the historical field where *both* an unbridgeable gap between state and nation and endlessly re-emerging class antagonisms are to be found, nationalism necessarily takes the form of racism, at times in competition with other forms (linguistic nationalism, for example) and at times in combination with them, and that it thus becomes engaged in a perpetual headlong flight forward. Even when racism remains latent, or present only in a minority of individual consciousnesses, it is already that internal excess of nationalism which betrays, in both senses of the word, its articulation to the class struggle. Hence the ever-recurring paradox of nationalism: the regressive imagining of a nation state where the individuals would by their nature be 'at home', because they would be 'among their own' (their own kind), and the rendering of that state uninhabitable; the endeavour to produce a unified community in the face of 'external' enemies and the endless rediscovery that the enemy is 'within', identifiable by signs which are merely the phantasmatic elaboration of *its* divisions. Such a society is in a real sense a politically alienated society. But are not all contemporary societies, to some degree, grappling with their own political alienation?

Notes

1 The personification of capital, a social relation, begins with the very figure of the *capitalist*. But this is never sufficient in itself for arousing an emotional reaction. This is why, following the logic of 'excess' other real-imaginary traits accumulate: lifestyle, lineage (the '200 families'), foreign origins, secret strategies, racial plots (the Jewish plan for 'world domination'), etc. The fact that, specifically in the case of the Jews, this personification is worked up in combination with a process of fetishization of money is clearly not accidental.

2 Matters are further complicated by the fact that the lost unity of 'Christian Europe', a mythic figuration of the 'origins of its civilization', is thus represented in the register of race at the point when the same Europe is embarking on its mission of 'civilizing the world', i.e. submitting the world to its domination, by way of fierce competition between nations.

3 And one which substitutes itself, in the French case, for the 'ideology of the three orders' a basically theological and juridical ideology, which is, by contrast, expressive of the organic place occupied by the nobility in the building of the State ('feudalism' properly so-called).

4 Clearly, the 'bestiality' of the slave has been a continual problem, from Aristotle and his contemporaries down to the modern slave trade (the hypersexualization to which it is subject is a sufficient indication of this); but the industrial revolution brought about a new paradox: the 'bestial' body of the worker is increasingly *animal* and increasingly technicized and therefore humanized. It is the panic fear of *a super-humanization* of man (in his body and his intelligence which is 'objectivized' by cognitive sciences and the corresponding techniques of selection and training), rather than his *sub-humanization* – or, in any case, the reversibility of these two – which discharges itself in phantasies of animality, and these are projected for preference on to the worker whose status as an 'outsider' *[étranger]* confers upon him at the same time the attributes of an 'other male', a 'rival'.

5 Not only in the sense of individual filiation, but in the sense of a 'population' tending towards the practice of endogamy; not only in the sense of a transmission of skills (mediated by schooling, apprenticeship and industrial discipline) but in the sense of a 'collective ethic' constructed in institutions and through subjective identification.

References

Anderson, B. (1983), *Imagined Communities*, Verso, London.

Arendt, H. (1986), *The Origins of Totalitarianism*: Part One, 'Antisemitism', Andre Deutsch, London.

Aycoberry, P. (1981), *The Nazi Question: An Essay on the Interpretation of National Socialism*, translated by R. Hurley, Routledge and Kegan Paul, London.

Balibar, E. (1983), 'Sur le concept de la division du travail manuel et intellectuel', in J. Belkhir et al. *(ed.)*, *L'Intellectuel, l'intelligentsia et les manuels*, Anthropos, Paris.

Bertaux, D. (1977), *Destins personnels et structure de classe*, PUF, Paris.

Chevalier, L. (1973), *Labouring Classes and Dangerous Classes in Paris during the First Half of the Nineteenth Century*, translated by F. Jellinek, Routledge and Kegan Paul, London.

Coriat, B. (1979), *L'Atelier et le chronomètre*, Christian Bourgeois, Paris.

Duchet, M. and Rebérioux, M. (1969), 'Préhistoire et histoire du racisme', in P. de Commarond and C. Duchet (eds), *Racisme et société*, Maspero, Paris.

Dumont, L. (1986), *Essays on Individualism: Modern Ideology in Anthropological Perspective*, University of Chicago Press, Chicago.

Duroux, F. (1982), *La Famille des ouvriers: Mythe ou politique?*, unpublished thesis, University of Paris VII.

Fremontier, J. (1980), *La Vie en bleu: Voyage en culture ouvrière*, Fayard, Paris.

Guillaumin, C. (1972), *L'Idéologie raciste: Genèse et Langage actuel*, Mouton, Paris and The Hague.

Linhart, R. (1976), *Levine, les paysans, Taylor*, Seuil, Paris.

Murard, L. and Zylberman, P. (1976), *Le petit Travailleur infatigable ou le prolétaire régénéré: Villes-usines, habitat et intimités au XIXe siècle*, Éditions Recherches, Fontenay-sous-Bois.

Netchine, G. (1978), 'L'Individuel et le collectif dans les répresentations psychologiques de la diversité des êtres humaines au XIXe siècle', in L. Poliakov (ed.), *Ni juif ni grec. Entretiens sur le racisme (II)*, Mouton, Paris and The Hague.

Noiriel, C. (1985), *Longwy: Immigrés et prolétaires 1880–1980*, PUF, Paris.

Polanyi, K. (1957), 'Appendix II: Disraeli's "Two Nations" and the Problem of colored races' in *The Great Transformation*, Beacon Press, Boston, pp. 290–4.

Poliakov, L. (1974), *The History of Anti-Semitism*, translated by R. Howard, 4 volumes, Routledge and Kegan Paul, London.

Popper, K. (1966), *The Open Society and its Enemies*, 5th edn, 2 volumes, Routledge and Kegan Paul, London.

Taylor, F. Winslow ([1911], 1993), *Principles of Scientific Management*, Routledge, London.

Williams, E. (1944), *Capitalism and Slavery*, University of North Carolina Press, Chapel Hill, NC.

Index